Philip Ma

Philip Mansel is a historian o
East. His books include a stud
1789–1830 (1989), histories of *Constantinople: City of the World's Desire 1453–1924* (1995) and *Paris between Empires 1814–1852* (2001), and a life of the Prince de Ligne, *Prince of Europe* (2003). He has written for numerous publications, including the *Financial Times*, the *International Herald Tribune*, the *Times Literary Supplement* and *The Spectator*. He is a Fellow of the Royal Historical Society and the Institute of Historical Research, and editor of *The Court Historian*. His website can be consulted at www.philipmansel.com.

Also by Philip Mansel

Pillars of Monarchy
Sultans in Splendour: Monarchs of the Middle East 1869–1945
The Court of France 1789–1830
Constantinople: City of the World's Desire 1453–1924
The French Émigrés in Europe 1789–1814
(ed. with Kirsty Carpenter)
Paris between Empires: Monarchy and Revolution 1814–1852
Prince of Europe: The life of Charles Joseph de Ligne 1735–1814
Dressed to Rule: Royal and Court Costume from Louis XIV to
Elizabeth II

Louis XVIII

PHILIP MANSEL

JOHN MURRAY

© Philip Mansel 1981, 1999, 2005

First published in Great Britain in 1981

This revised paperback edition published in 2005 by John Murray (Publishers)
A division of Hodder Headline

The right of Philip Mansel to be identified as the Author
of the Work has been asserted by him in accordance with
the Copyright, Designs and Patents Act 1988.

1

A CIP catalogue record for this title
is available from the British Library

ISBN 0 7195 6709 2

Printed and bound in Great Britain by
Clays Ltd, St Ives plc

Hodder Headline policy is to use papers that are natural,
renewable and recyclable products and made from wood
grown in sustainable forests. The logging and manufacturing
processes are expected to conform to the environmental
regulations of the country of origin.

John Murray (Publishers)
338 Euston Road
London NW1 3BH

Contents

	Introduction	vi
I	A Bourbon and His World 1755–1774	3
II	A Prince and His Leisure 1774–1787	19
III	Monsieur and The Revolutions 1787–1791	40
IV	Coblentz 1791–1793	56
V	Louis in Exile 1793–1807	77
VI	Plans, Plots and Campaigns 1793–1807	110
VII	The King of France in the United Kingdom 1807–1814	137
VIII	Louis le Désiré? April–June 1814	170
IX	A New World June 1814–March 1815	189
X	The Blue and the Green March–May 1815	220
XI	The Return of the King May–September 1815	242
XII	A King and His Subjects 1814–1824	269
XIII	The King and The Ultra-Royalists September 1815–September 1816	320
XIV	The Liberal Years September 1816–February 1820	344
XV	The Triumph of Monarchy February 1820–September 1824	374
	Conclusion	409
	References	416
	Sources	459
	Bibliography	464
	Index	483
	List of Illustrations	498

INTRODUCTION

In Search of Louis XVIII

Published in 1981 in the age of the nation state, the first edition of this biography saw Louis XVIII as a '*Fils de France*', whose life and reign were dominated by the French monarchy, French revolutions and French nationalism. In 2005, the rise of the European Union demands an introduction from a new perspective. While extremely French, Louis XVIII was also, by history, geography, interest and birth, naturally European. Allied to Austria, Spain and Naples, related to most of the Catholic dynasties of Europe, the French monarchy led an even less isolated existence than others. It had, moreover, adopted a new view of France's place in Europe. At the Treaty of Aix-la-Chapelle in 1748, to the dismay of much French opinion, it had rejected expansion in the Austrian Netherlands. Despite the rise of Austria, Prussia and Russia, it believed that France had no need for further territory in Europe.[1] From the Treaty of Versailles in 1783, it also believed that peace and trade, rather than enmity, was the best policy for France to pursue towards Britain.

Continuing this tradition, during his twenty-three years as an exile between 1791 and 1814, in Germany, Italy, Russia, Poland, and for the last seven years England, Louis XVIII consciously Europeanized his cause. Promising not to profit from the 'conquests made by the pretended republic',[2] Louis XVIII presented himself to foreign governments as 'the future pacifier of Europe'.[3] As had been the case since the Hundred Years War, the state of the French monarchy depended on the state of Europe. Louis XVIII suspended his struggle for the throne only in 1802, when the French Republic was, exceptionally, at peace with all the powers of Europe including the United Kingdom. He considered retiring to Naples where, he wrote, he would deposit his claims to the throne in the heart of his friend and cousin the King of Naples, and live as a private person.[4] That was the reason why, in an uncharacteristic act of disobedience, his nephew and niece the Duc and Duchesse d'Angoulême refused to follow him to Italy (in any case the King of Naples would not receive him). That temporary hesitation may also be the reason why in 1803 Bonaparte made the mistake of offering 'great advantages' to Louis XVIII in return for the renunciation of his claim to the throne. He thereby gave the pretender the opportunity to make his famous Declaration: '*J'ignore les desseins de Dieu sur ma race et sur moi, mais je connais les obligations qu'il m'a imposées par le rang où il Lui a plu de me faire naître . . . Successeur de François Ier je veux au moins pouvoir dire avec lui "Nous avons tout perdu hors l'honneur".*' Since war had started again, British boats circulated the King's reply along the coast of France.' Alexander I of Russia, employing French royalists like Napoleon's earliest and most determined enemy Count Pozzo di Borgo among his advisers, also kept the restoration of Louis XVIII as one of his policy alternatives. He revealed his intentions in a letter to Louis XVIII in 1813. He promised that he would act once allied armies had crossed the Rhine and royalist movements had manifested themselves in France: 'patience, great circumspection and the most profound secrecy are essential. The moment is not yet propitious.'6

In March 1814 the monarchs of Europe finally abandoned hope of a lasting peace with Napoleon. Convinced of the reality of royalism in France by, among other demonstrations, a rising in Bordeaux on 12 March 1814 coordinated with the British army under Wellington, they came out openly in support of Louis XVIII. Their letters of congratulation on his restoration confirm that they were more interested in strategy than legitimacy. They refer not to his right to the throne of France but to his role as guarantor of 'the future tranquillity of Europe'7. As King of France, Louis XVIII renounced French conquests and followed a policy of 'union' with his fellow monarchs in what he called 'the great European family'.8 By their support in the Hundred Days, allied monarchs and statesmen showed that they, in their turn, believed that the cause of Louis XVIII was 'that of all Europe'.9

Thus if he was restored 'in the baggage train of the foreigners', neither he – nor, at the time, the thousands of Parisians who cheered Alexander I and Wellington as well as Louis XVIII himself – were ashamed by this Europeanization of French politics. The reign of Louis XVIII was an interlude in Europe's rush to nationalism. National interests, even nationality itself, were not always of paramount importance. Europe almost acquired an institutional framework. The most European of British foreign secretaries, Lord Castlereagh wanted to give what he called 'the European Commonwealth' 'the efficiency and almost the simplicity of a single state'. As Russian ambassador in Paris, Pozzo di Borgo felt that 'the union of Europe is a truth which is beginning to establish here all its empire' and hoped for the creation of 'a sort of permanent federal European diet'. Victor Cousin, the liberal philosopher, wrote that 'civilized Europe today forms no more than one family'.10

Louis XVIII's chief achievement in France was his reinvention of the French monarchy as a constitutional monarchy. The *Charte* which he helped to write in May 1814 guaranteed equality before the law, religious toleration, freedom of the press, of petition, irrevocability of judicial appointments, oblivion for all previous political acts, and sales of 'national lands'. Confiscation of private property was abolished. All government legislation, including the budget, had to be approved by the two Chambers, of Peers, and of Deputies. Whereas the constitution, like his frontiers and monarchies, disappeared with him, the *Charte* established an era of parliamentary government in France which lasted until 1848. Parliamentary power was no illusion. Three times, in September 1815, February 1820 and December 1821, Louis XVIII dismissed his ministers in favour of new ones who could secure a majority in the Chamber of Deputies.

Louis XVIII is often accused of looking backwards. Yet his principal monument looks to the future. He rebuilt the Château de Saint-Ouen at the gates of Paris, as a monument to the *Déclaration de Saint-Ouen*, the basis of the *Charte*, which he had issued in the previous building on that site. His adviser the Comte de Blacas called 2 May 1814, the day it was issued, 'one of the finest days of the monarchy'.[11] Given, magnificently furnished, to the King's last attachment Madame du Cayla, the new *château* was inaugurated on 3 May 1823, the anniversary of his entry into Paris in 1814. It contained a portrait by the *Premier Peintre du Roi* Baron Gérard, commissioned and 'composed' by the King himself, show-ing him in the Tuileries palace, sitting at the simple wooden desk ('*la table de Varsovie*') at which in 1803 he had written his rejection of Bonaparte's proposal to renounce his claim to the throne of France. The King is meditating on the institutions he will give his people. Opposite the portrait was a marble plaque inscribed with letters of gilded bronze: '*Ici le 2 mai 1814 a commencé une ère nouvelle*'.[12]

If Louis XVIII was the most European, he was also the most English of the kings of France. As an Englishwoman wrote soon after his arrival in England, he was 'extremely well informed about the country, its history and literature being perfectly familiar to him'.[13] In 1809 he told the Foreign Secretary Lord Wellesley that he considered 'the interests of his country as inseparable from those of France.'[14] The implication was that, if Britain supported a Bourbon restoration, the Bourbons would support a pro-British policy – as indeed, to the extent of alienating French opinion, they did.

For its part, since 1799 the British government had supported a restoration of the Bourbons, less out of a desire for their return to their former throne, than from a wish to see France return to its former fron-tiers. The restoration of the Bourbons, Pitt had declared in the House of Commons in 1800, provided 'the strongest and best security both to this country and to Europe' – although it was never a *sine qua non* of peace.[15] After Louis XVIII's arrival in England in 1807, thanks to the common struggle against the man he called 'the Beast of the Apocalypse',[16] he became a popular ally. In October 1808 the Prince of Wales visited Louis XVIII, went down on his knees and promised never to make peace until the King had been restored to the throne of his ancestors.[17] After the Prince of Wales assumed the regency in 1811, and news of Napoleon's first defeats in Russia arrived in 1812, Russian diplomats like Counts Lieven and Pozzo di Borgo and the Regent's trusted Hanoverian minister Count Münster came to see the King in his residence at Hartwell outside Aylesbury.[18] Louis XVIII became the British candidate for the throne of France. Castlereagh, in secret, advised Louis XVIII and Blacas on the terms of the Declaration of Hartwell of 1 February 1813, which endorsed most of the post-revolutionary settlement.[19] British officials and agents helped print and distribute it in Europe. As early as August 1813, to the horror of Austria, the British government suggested a restoration of the Bourbons.[20]

If Europe provides a new perspective on the monarch, recently opened archives provide new information about the man. His Bourbon façade hid an emotional, and occasionally unconventional, individual. Eager to show and receive tenderness, he compensated for a loveless, childless marriage by attachments to favourites of both sexes, and their children. His wife, Marie-Joséphine of Savoy, was neither beautiful nor, at first, clean. Madame du Barry urged the Sardinian ambassador to tell her to bathe and brush her teeth more – practices neglected at other courts but considered essential at Versailles.[21] Several pregnancies ended badly; thereafter their relations were based at best on mutual respect and interest.

Deprived of a family of his own, Provence adopted as a 'son' the Comte de Lévis who, as one of his two *Capitaines des Gardes*, was in attendance for six months every year. He loved Lévis, he wrote, at least as much as if he had taken the trouble to father him himself.[22] Provence's letters to Lévis between 1787 and 1791, first published in 1993, reveal a secret world of jokes, pseudonyms (Holy Nail for Saint-Cloud, Mr of Eyetown for M. de Villedeuil), literary references, love affairs and obscenity ('may you . . . awake drenched in as much sperm as your bawd had in her mouth', Provence wrote to him, in English).[23]

One letter to Lévis ends, in English, 'your Father blesses and embraces you with all his heart'.[24] Other letters show that he was obsessed with, and slightly intimidated by, Marie-Antoinette. At one time he denounced her 'bad heart', at others he proclaimed his love for 'my goddess', his desire to kiss her hand, or more; she only had to appear, he told her, to melt any ice in the world.[25] The letters also show that even before the opening of the States-General, Provence supported the abandonment of the nobility's financial privileges; he believed the King should have legislative and executive power, without the power to violate the properties or freedom of his subjects. He feared for the future of the monarchy and proposed the admission of himself and other princes into the council as a counter-balance to radical ministers.[26]

Provence's judgement that 'as for the King he is so changeable, because he is so apathetic that nothing can be done with him, he throws his confidence, as a man fishing for whales throws his harpoon' is harsh but, given the King's rapid changes of ministers and policy, justifiable.[27] In 1789 the King had let him act, during a hiatus between ministries from 14 to 17 July, as temporary head of the government. The papers of Louis XVI contain a draft in Provence's handwriting, dated 16 July 1789, of a letter from the King asking Necker, the popular minister who had been dismissed on 11 July, to give a proof of his attachment by returning as soon as possible to Versailles: 'the confidence which the Nation shows you obliges me to hasten the date of your return'.[28]

In early 1790 Lévis participated in unsuccessful manoeuvres with Provence, the Comte de La Marck and the revolutionary leader Mirabeau to make Provence head of the council. Thereafter their political views diverged. Lévis told his wife that Provence had become superstitious as well as weak.[29] On 20 June 1791, without consulting Lévis, Provence fled from Paris accompanied by a new, more trusted favourite – henceforth referred to as '*mon ami*' – the Comte d'Avaray.

In exile Louis's principal weapons, after the extremism of French governments and the Europeanization of the French monarchy, remained his personal qualities of calm, humour, tenacity, and optimism, much admired by his entourage.[30] His letters to the Comte de Blacas, a young royalist from Provence, who became the last and most important *Grand Maître de la Garde-Robe du Roi* in 1809, are as revealing as those to the Duc de Lévis. On 29 March 1803 he wrote to Blacas: 'Adversity is not very difficult to support when one has faithful subjects like you and one does not lose hope of employing their zeal in the service of the state'.[31] During a harsh English spring he wrote: 'fruit trees, vegetables are losses which can be repaired, but who will give me back my poor lilacs?'[32]

The King's optimism persisted even in crises like that of late June 1815, when he was returning to France after Waterloo. He had been forced to part with Blacas, the only minister who possessed his confidence;[33] Paris was threatened with pillage, both by the allies and by Parisians. Half of France was so belligerent and anti-royalist that in 1815, despite having just endured twenty-two years of war, it had begun a new war against Europe. Louis XVIII wrote to Blacas, who had left for London: 'the hope of a better future sustains me. I know that you do not share it but as for me I cannot stop myself feeling it.' Later, despite Prussian guns trained on the Tuileries palace and a ministry headed by Talleyrand, whom he loathed, he wrote: 'adieu dear Count *dum spiro spero*.'[34] He remained a European. When the great sculptor Canova came to reclaim works of art from the Louvre for the Pope, Louis XVIII complained about the forced restitution in French; he then switched to Italian to praise Canova's talent as a sculptor and to ask to be sculpted by him.[35]

More moderate than most of his court, he returned to France convinced, Blacas wrote to the Comte d'Artois on 15 April 1814, that 'the true force of the Government will be in public opinion and in the good principles of men who, having traversed the Revolution, best know how to end its agitations'.[36] In other words he would employ as ministers ex-revolutionaries like Talleyrand, Marshal Gouvion Saint-Cyr and Lainé, whom courtiers called a Jacobin and a republican respectively.[37] His letters to Blacas of 14 and 29 September 1816 explain his determination to dissolve the ultra-royalist *'chambre introuvable'* in part in terms of his horror of *'le gouvernement Salonocratique'*; he was particularly infuriated by his former protégé Chateaubriand, whose work attacking the dissolution was regarded by royalists as a fifth gospel, the author as 'one more Martyr. But what to do about it? Envelop oneself like Horace in one's virtue, say to oneself "Ai fait que du", whatever happens let us continue our work.'[38]

Letters to Blacas from Baron Hue, one of the King's four confidential *Premiers Valets de Chambre*, show some of the ways in which he tried to satisfy his sexual and emotional urges. Such insight into the private life of a monarch is due to the despatch of these letters by hand from Paris to Naples, where Blacas was ambassador. There was thus less danger of interception by the police; even so they are guarded. In September 1815 Madame de Narbonne, who had lived at Hartwell as *Dame du Palais* of

Marie-Joséphine, was received in secret by the King, who also corresponded with her about his choice of ministers.[40] A year later he was
receiving weekly visits from an attractive widow with 'a romantic face'
called Madame Princeteau, sister of his favourite minister Elie Decazes.
Every evening the King sent her a bouquet of roses, violets and
heliotropes in Decazes's ministerial portfolio. Every Sunday, wearing the
King's bouquet, she went to the Tuileries chapel, where she and the King
made eyes at each other. Although it was 'a fine but purely platonic
passion (trust me on this)', Baron Hue could hardly believe his eyes; it
compromised the King's dignity and did nothing but make him look
'ridiculous, indeed very ridiculous'.[41] Madame Princeteau's children, like
those of Madame du Cayla, were also showered with presents.

Blacas and Hue often sound like the elderly guardians of an uncon-
trollable young prince, rather than younger servants of a sixty-year-old
semi-invalid. The King's calm could yield to an emotionalism which
dismayed his courtiers. On his return to Paris on 8 July 1815, moved to
tears by the warmth of his welcome, 'in a state of great emotion' he had
mingled with the crowd in the Tuileries garden: an unusual step for any
monarch, let alone one who had just returned to a partly hostile capital.[42]
In 1817, if the guarded language of these letters is correctly interpreted,
the king was receiving secret visits from another, less respectable, young
woman: 'Can you remember the daughter of a certain gardener at
Wimbledon, who made visits there, to your great distress I have been
told, to a person whom I will avoid naming? All that has begun again
here and for my part I am now at my second introduction, you understand me . . . people who know the lady say that if she is young, she is no
novice. But what good is such a visit I have often asked myself, several
times, for . . . no I must stop and leave the rest to your imagination . . .
sometimes I am so angry I could be rude to the good Lord.'[43] The precise
meaning, in this letter, of the phrase 'All that' is unknown.

The search for Louis XVIII leaves many unsolved mysteries. Similarly
his reign has been obscured by the glamour of the Empire and the self-
destruction of his brother Charles X, whose bid for neo-absolutism led to
the revolution of 1830 and the installation of the Duc d'Orléans on the
throne. It is for readers to decide whether such oblivion is justified or
whether, moved by the King's success in giving a divided and devastated
country peace, prosperity and a workable constitution, and by the extent
of popular mourning for his death in 1824, his last *Président du Conseil*
the Comte de Villèle was right to call the reign of Louis XVIII 'among the
most glorious in the history of France'.[44]

References

1. Gaston Zeller, 'Les Frontières Naturelles: Histoire d'une Idée Fausse', in *Aspects de la
Politique Française sous l'Ancien Regime*, 1964, p. 107.
2. Baron de Barante (ed.), *Lettres et Instructions de Louis XVIII au Comte de Saint-
Priest*, 1845, p. 145: instructions du Roi, 26.5.1800.
3. West Yorkshire Archives, Leeds, Canning Papers HAR/GC/56 Comte d'Avaray to
Canning, 1.11.1807, Louis XVIII to Canning, 7.12.1807.
4. Benedetto Croce, 'Il Duca di Serra-Capriola e Giuseppe de Maistre', *Archivio Storico*

per le Provincie Napoletane, XLVII, 1922, pp. 338–339, Louis XVIII to Duca di Serra-Capriola, 25.1.1802.

5. Ernest Daudet, *Histoire de l'Émigration*, 3 vols 1904–1907, III, 255.

6. Archives Privées, Alexander I to Louis XVIII, 27.4.1813; cf. Daudet, III, pp. 511–515.

7. See e.g. Archives Privées, Francis I of Austria to Louis XVIII, 30.4.1814.

8. *Recueil de la Société Impériale Russe d'Histoire*, CIX, p. 710, Louis XVIII to Alexander I, letter of 4/16.5.1818.

9. Archives Privées, Prince of Orange to Louis XVIII, 22.3.1815.

10. Gregor Dallas, *1815: The Roads to Waterloo*, 1997, pp. 449–453; A. Polovtsov (ed.), *Correspondance Diplomatique des Ambassadeurs et Ministres de Russie en France et de France en Russie avec Leurs Gouvernements de 1814 à 1830*, 3 vols, St Petersburg, 1903–1907, III, 143, 187, Pozzo to Nesselrode, 14.7, 20.9.1819; André Monchoux, *L'Allemagne devant les Lettres Françaises de 1814 à 1835*, 1953, p. 148.

11. Archives Privées, Blacas to Comte de La Chatre, 2.5.1814.

12. Philip Mansel, *Paris between Empires 1814–1852*, 2001, pp. 191–193.

13. *Hary-O. The Letters of Lady Harriet Cavendish 1796–1809*, ed. Sir George Leveson-Gower and Iris Palmer, 1940, p. 277, to Lady Georgiana Morpeth, 29.12.1807, reporting the views of Lord Ossulston.

14. British Library Add. Mss. 37290 f. 1, Louis XVIII to Lord Wellesley, 9.5.1809; Daudet, III, p. 478, Louis XVIII to Comte de La Chatre, 1.3.1809.

15. Piers Mackesy, *Statesmen at War. The Strategy of Overthrow 1798–1799*, 1974, p. 69; Sir Charles Webster, *The Foreign Policy of Castlereagh*, 2 vols, 1925–1950, I, pp. 234, 238n.; cf. John Ehrman, *The Younger Pitt: The Consuming Struggle*, 1996, pp. 223, 230, 344n., 347.

16. Archives Privées, Louis XVIII to Blacas, 27.4.1813.

17. Dormer Papers, Diary of Elizabeth Duchess of Devonshire, 20.10.1808, 5.9.1818.

18. Marquis de La Maisonfort, *Mémoires d'un Agent Royaliste*, 1998, pp. 217–223.

19. Archives Privées, Comte de Blacas to Comte d'Artois, 8.1.1813 (draft).

20. Comte de La Ferronays, *En Emigration*, 1905, p. 338; Webster, *The Foreign Policy of Castlereagh*, I, p. 234.

21. Paul et Pierrette Girault de Coursac, *Provence et Artois les Deux Frères de Louis XVI*, 1999, pp. 35–36, quoting despatches of the Sardinian ambassador, 17.2.1772, 20.8.1773.

22. Undated letter, quoted in Duc de Lévis, *Souvenirs et Portraits, suivis de Lettres Intimes du Comte de Provence*, ed. Jacques Dupaquier, 1993, p. 380.

23. Ibid., p. 355, letter of April 1789,

24. Ibid., pp. 309, 318, letters of 30.11.1787, 12.8.1788.

25. Ibid., pp. 313, 333, 366, letters of 8.8, 12.12.1788, 28.4.1789.

26. Ibid., pp. 335, 361, letters of February–March 1789, 21.4.1789.

27. Archives Privées, anon. Note, *c*.1813, asking for a reward for returning this letter to Louis XVIII.

28. Archives Nationales, Papers of the Liste Civile C185 'Mr Necker'.

29. Lévis, *Souvenirs-Portraits*, p. 296, Lévis to Duchesse de Lévis, 14.3.1791.

30. Cf. Dečin State Archives, Czech Republic, Fonds Clary und Aldringen 103, Marquis de Bonnay to Prince de Ligne, 12.10.1803.

31. Archives Privées, Louis XVIII to Blacas, 29.3.1803, 13.3, 8.8.1809.

32. Ibid., Louis XVIII to Blacas, 27.4.1813.

33. Ibid., Wellington to Blacas, 28.6.1815.

34. Ibid., Louis XVIII to Blacas, 25.6, 30.7.1815.

35. Ibid., Duc de Duras to Blacas, 10.9.1815.

36. Ibid., Blacas to Artois, 15.4.1814.

37. Ibid., Duras to Blacas, 27.6.1815, La Chatre to Blacas, 1818.

38. Ibid., Louis XVIII to Blacas, 14.9, 29.9.1816.

39. Ibid., 20.7.1815.

40. Ibid., Hue to Blacas, 29.9.1815.

41. Ibid., 30.9.1816.

42. Viscount Castlereagh, *Correspondence, Despatches and Other Papers*, 12 vols 1848–1853, X, p. 420 Castlereagh to Lord Liverpool, 8.7.1815.

43. Archives Privées, Hue to Blacas, 10.8.1817.

44. National Library of Scotland, Stuart de Rothesay Mss., Lord Stuart de Rothesay to Canning, 9.9.1824.

CHAPTER I

A Bourbon and his World
1755–1787

The Court had never been more splendid. The old king's second grandson was getting married, and hundreds of people were expected to attend the explosion of balls, operas and fireworks traditionally arranged to celebrate such occasions. On the morning of the wedding, 14 May 1771, tickets giving access to the palace of Versailles were issued to 260 senior courtiers, 450 household officials, and 4,500 members of the public. But the guards on duty at the entrance to the state apartments ended up letting in so many people without tickets that it became difficult to line the processional route of the Royal Family to the palace chapel with suitably well-dressed and distinguished spectators. In the evening, although only 3,600 tickets were given out, and the palace was the largest in Europe, the apartments became blocked, since people refused to move on past the table at which the king, his mistress, the bride and bridegroom, and the rest of the Royal Family were playing cards.

The next evening the fireworks, including illuminations of the old king, Louis XV, the king's grandson and heir (his only son had died six years before) the Dauphin, and his wife Marie-Antoinette of Austria, and the bridegroom and his wife, the Comte de Provence and Marie-Joséphine of Savoy, were dazzling. In the gardens of Versailles, the public was particularly pleased with the illuminations of the Royal Family and burst into loyal applause.[1] But the most magnificent of all the celebrations was the ball given on 20 May in the recently finished theatre, which is still one of the wonders of Versailles. The pit was covered over with a sliding floor and this together with the stage created a vast oval gold and turquoise ballroom which seemed to the well-travelled Duc de Croÿ to be *'la plus belle salle qui eût jamais existé'* ('the finest room which has ever existed'). This sumptuous arena was packed with well-dressed people (1,719 tickets were given out, including an especially large number for the English ambassador and his party) watching members of the Royal Family and the highest aristocracy dance the slow, stately minuets traditional on such occasions. The Duc de Croÿ could not believe what he saw; the Duchesse d'Aiguillon wrote that it was *'le plus beau spectacle que j'ai vu de ma vie'* ('the finest spectacle I have ever seen').

Even the bride and bridegroom came up to expectations. The Comte de Provence, whom his grandfather had described a few years earlier as *joli à manger*, looked charming in the gold-embroidered robes of a *Chevalier du Saint Esprit*, the grandest of all French orders. *'Il avait bonne grâce, et l'air de la plus grande joie: aussi intéresse-t-il tout le monde'* ('He carried himself very well and seemed overjoyed: so everyone feels drawn to him'), wrote the Duc de Croÿ. The Comtesse de Provence was no beauty, being short and dusky with a long face, a huge nose and amazing bushy eyebrows which almost joined her hair. But at least she knew how to behave in a dignified way (she danced much better than her husband), and the old king, protesting a little too much, thought that she was *'très agréable . . . si j'avais quelques années de moins après l'avoir vue je l'aurais bien prise pour moi'* ('very agreeable . . . if I was a few years younger, after seeing her I really think I would have kept her for myself'). All in all, the celebrations went off very well; the public and the Court had been suitably entertained and it seemed to Louis XV, who had handed his grandson the nightshirt at the inevitable public royal bedding, that the Comte de Provence was *'très content de sa femme, et je le crois déjà plus avancé que son frère'* ('very happy with his wife, and I think he's already got further than his [elder] brother').[2]

However, this magnificent royal wedding had not taken place solely in order to marry the Comte de Provence. It was also meant to be an outward and visible demonstration of the power and prestige of the King of France, of the number of well-born and splendidly-dressed people who attended his Court, of the loyalty of his subjects and of the grandeur, fecundity and unity of his family. And on this symbolic and political level, the wedding was far from being a total success. Although, down in the garden, the public cheered loyally, considerably fewer of the elite of birth or success attended the celebrations up in the state apartments than had attended those held for the wedding of the Dauphin a year earlier. This was either because it was the wedding of the second grandson, so much less important than the heir to the throne, or because of the elite's resentment at Louis XV's dramatic reassertion of royal authority by the suppression of the *parlements* early in 1771. (These judicial bodies had provided the best institutional means of opposing the king's policies.) For example, only one of the king's distant but extremely prestigious cousins, the Princes du Sang (see Table 2), attended the Comte de Provence's wedding, since the others were forbidden to enter the king's presence '*à cause des affaires du Parlement*' ('on account of the affairs of the *Parlement*'). Moreover, as many people were aware, this magnificent wedding took place at a Court haunted, and almost halted, by bankruptcy: the crown was so far behind in its payments to its servants that the royal households themselves would soon cease to function, according to a letter written to Louis XV in 1772 by the *Contrôleur-Général*, France's chief financial official. Even the marriage itself was not the total success it had appeared to be. After a few months the Comtesse de Provence showed no sign of doing her duty and producing children, and gossip, which was to last all his life, soon began to blame her husband for her barrenness: he must be malformed, or impotent, or worse.[3]

Thus this glorious wedding, which marked Provence's first appearance in the eyes of the Court and the public as an individual prince rather than as simply another of the king's five grandchildren (the Dauphin, Provence, the Comte d'Artois, Madame Clotilde, also known as Gros Madame on account of her balloon-like proportions, and Madame Elizabeth), confronted him with profound problems which would last all his life: his family position as a childless second son; the effects of the crown's attempts to increase its power, authority and revenue; and the immense power of gossip, particularly at the Court of France, where so many people had so little to occupy their vast amounts of spare time.

To all appearances, however, to be born into the French Royal Family in the second half of the eighteenth century was to be guaranteed a very enviable existence. In an age dominated by respect for tradition, ancient lineage, the Church and military success, the status of Provence's grandfather, the King of France, was unique. He was head of a family which Provence's mother, the Dauphine Marie-Josèphe of Saxony, called '*la plus ancienne . . . la plus noble et . . . la plus illustre famille de l'Univers*' ('the most ancient . . . the most noble and . . . the most illustrious family in the Universe'). It had occupied the throne of France since the tenth century, at a time when the Habsburgs, the Hohenzollerns and the Savoys, by the eighteenth century rulers of Austria, Prussia and Piedmont, had been little better than robber barons (the Romanovs had not even been heard of). Moreover, the King of France, especially since the reign of Saint Louis, had a uniquely sacred character. After being crowned and anointed at

Reims he became a sub-deacon and, alone of all European monarchs, could touch for the King's Evil, or scrofula, a disease whose symptoms sometimes disappear unexpectedly. Not only was the king above the rest of humanity, but he was above other monarchs, and even had the power to suspend the laws of Nature.

In addition, the actual power as well as the prestige of the King of France was immense. Branches of his family, the Bourbons (so called because in 1589 they had inherited the throne of France, as descendants of the youngest son of Saint Louis, after being Ducs de Bourbon for three hundred years), had overflowed from their French base and occupied the throne of Spain since 1700, that of Naples since 1735 and were Dukes of Parma from 1748. Despite the disastrous war of 1756–1763, the King of France was still one of the most powerful monarchs in Europe, as well as the most prestigious.

Moreover, his power (unlike that of the Habsburgs or the Hohenzollerns) rested on the solid base of a definite national identity. This was fixed by well-defended national frontiers, and strengthened by a tradition of the French identifying themselves with the ruling dynasty and the dynasty identifying itself with the nation. Unlike almost every other dynasty, the Bourbons had not come to their throne from abroad: they were wholly French. The king's children and grandchildren were called 'Enfants de France' and years later, writing to his aunt Madame Adélaïde (see Table 1), Louis XVIII could find no higher praise for his niece, the Duchesse d'Angoulême, than to say that she was *'Française comme vous et moi'*.

This tradition of the nation and the dynasty identifying with each other was symbolized, and in theory strengthened, by the accessible and popular character of the French monarchy – as the public's presence and enthusiasm at Provence's wedding shows. Under Louis XV, the French Royal Family spent a large proportion of the day living in public. In a letter to her parents the Comtesse de Provence says she was amazed to find that *'pendant que nous dînons, on reçoit tout le monde'* ('while we are dining, we let everyone in'). One English visitor to Paris noted that even at the end of the reign of Louis XV, who was much less popular than Louis XVI, *'Roi* is a word which conveys to the minds of Frenchmen the ideas of benevolence, gratitude and love, as well as those of power, grandeur and happiness', and that Frenchmen were 'as vain of the palaces and all the paraphernalia belonging to the Court as an Englishman can be of his own house, garden and equipage'. Even Mercier, an irreverent Parisian writing several years later, thought the French throne *'de l'Europe le mieux af-*

fermi, le plus honoré, le plus tranquille' ('the firmest, the most respected, and the least threatened of Europe'). A symbol of the popularity of the French Monarchy was the national cult of that popular military monarch, Henri IV. The cult had begun with Voltaire's *Henriade*, published in 1724, and grew stronger throughout the century, and indeed throughout Europe: Gustavus III of Sweden paid tribute to it by translating the *Henriade* into Swedish in the 1770s.

As well as being the most popular and prestigious monarch in Europe, the King of France was surrounded by much the most splendid and amusing Court in the continent. He had the grandest and most beautiful palaces, and they were filled with the finest china, carpets and tapestries, Sèvres, Aubusson and Gobelins representing a peak of perfection and luxury which other monarchs could not hope to rival. For an example of the dazzling superiority of the Court of France over the other European Courts in the second half of the eighteenth century, one need only compare the two jewel-cabinets made for the Queen of England and for the Comtesse de Provence, both now in the English Royal Collection. The former is an admirably solid and practical piece of dark brown furniture which could, and no doubt did, double up nicely as a bedside table. The latter is an intoxicating golden vision, one of the finest and most elegant pieces of furniture ever made. The two are worlds apart.

Since the Court of France was the world in which Provence grew up, and one from which, in many ways, he never entirely escaped, it is necessary to understand what it was like, not only on a splendid occasion such as Provence's wedding, but also in its daily life. Although Versailles was the official residence of the King of France, perhaps it is best to think of it as the principal residence of a very grand landowner who adored living in the country, improving his estates and houses and hunting in the beautiful forests which surrounded them. For Versailles was devoted to pleasure as much as to power and profit. And the primacy of pleasure at the Court of France is symbolized by the relative informality of the palace's layout and routine, which were centred on the king's bedroom and *lever* and *coucher*, rather than on anything as stiff and formal as the throne-rooms and hand-kissing ceremonies so common at other Courts. As the Comtesse de Provence noted, there was no hand-kissing at Versailles.

In order to make life in his country house more agreeable, as well as to enhance the splendour and prestige of his Court, the king gave apartments at Versailles to all the members of his family, to the Princes du Sang, to 200 Court officials and ex-

Court officials, and to twenty other members of the Court nobility, as well as to the essential instruments of his authority, at least
ten senior guard officers, and ten ministers or senior government
officials. All these guests, except for the dukes and *grands officiers*
(the most senior Court officials), lived in an endless round of
squabbles and bickering about precedence. For Versailles was so
relaxed and informal that, as the future Louis XVI noted, there
was less of an ordered hierarchy and more confusion of ranks at
the Court of France than at any other Court in Europe – or,
indeed, than in the *Parlement* of Paris.[5]

The atmosphere of this beautiful hunting, shooting and ruling
Court is extremely hard to evoke. It was at the same time a
country house, an employment exchange, a riding-school (the best
in Europe), a bazaar, a casino, a government compound and a
military headquarters, all on an enormous scale. Simply considering the guard units stationed at Versailles, the *Gardes du Corps,
Cent-Suisses* and *Gardes de la Porte* guarded the interior of the
palace, and the five dazzling regiments of the *Maison Militaire*, or
Household Cavalry, whose men were of the same social status as
other regiments' officers, provided mounted escorts for the Royal
Family. The *Gardes-Françaises* and *Gardes-Suisses* guarded the
exterior of the palace (and were also the main repressive force in
Paris); and the *Prévôté* was responsible for maintaining law and
order at Court.

What kept these disparate and discordant worlds together was
not only love of the king and the desire to serve him, and oneself,
but also the easy, charming, self-assured Court manner – a compound of simplicity, politeness and flattery, which was the essential lubricant preventing the ambitions and discontentment of
courtiers' lives from flaring into something more dangerous. It
was the extension of this Court manner, and of the social life
which went with it, into a large part of the day and into many
official or private activities, which made life at the French Court
so different from life at other Courts. And it was probably her
lack of experience of such a social Court that made the young
Marie-Antoinette so ill at ease on her arrival at Versailles in 1770,
and led her brother-in-law Provence to contrast *manières de
Versailles* with *manières de Vienne*, at the same time homelier
and more formal.

Most forms of social life at Court were restricted to the 942
families who by 1789 had demonstrated sufficiently impressive
ancestry or, occasionally, connections, to have been formally presented at Court. In addition to certain privileges of dress (red
heels for the men, for example), these families had the right to

pay their respects to all the members of the Royal Family. They composed what was known as the *noblesse présentée*. Their social position was based not only on their noble birth but also on their wealth in land and investments, their marriage connections, their access to royal favour and the distinction of their services in war and diplomacy. Typical of the very grandest of such families were the Noailles, whom Saint-Simon, who loathed them, had called 'the most powerful family in France'. Enormously rich and well-connected and celebrated for the polish of their manners, they held the post of Governor of the Palace of Versailles, and provided two of the four captains of the *Gardes du Corps*.

However, beneath the smooth and splendid surface of Court life, and behind the outward signs of profound respect which surrounded the king and his family – guards standing to attention, courtiers always on their feet – there was discontent, as demonstrated by the absence of so many members of the elite from Provence's wedding. Despite the traditional feeling expressed in Montesquieu's remark, '*Sans roi, point de noblesse, sans noblesse, point de roi*' ('No king, no nobility, no nobility, no king'), and in the belief that one of the most glorious duties of the French nobility was to be the support of the throne, many nobles, and other members of the elite, were beginning to feel less than wholehearted in their devotion to the Bourbons.[6] France had suffered humiliating defeats in the Seven Years' War (1756–1763). The king's mistress, Madame du Barry, was a tart from the streets of Paris whose presence beside the king – she actually played cards at the same table as the Royal Family on the night of Provence's wedding – outraged almost every value of eighteenth-century French society. Moreover, the Court and the appearance and way of life of the king were beginning to seem absurd and outdated. The red-heeled shoes and the elaborate, embroidered silk *habit habillé* which the Bourbons and their courtiers usually wore (see illustration I), were going out of fashion in an age when almost every other monarch and Court were putting on uniform and jack-boots. The French Court was too relaxed, too social and too domestic for an age which wanted a more military image, and which found more to admire in Frederick II or Catherine II than in Louis XV.

The outdated image of the French Monarchy was particularly inappropriate at a time when it was trying to increase its power and modernize its power base. In 1770 the all-powerful minister Choiseul fell from power, and the *parlements* were in effect abolished. Even under Louis XVI, when the *parlements*, shorn of many of their powers, were restored, many of the Royal Government's reforms had the effect of increasing direct government intervention in French society, and it was in those years that Necker made his famous comment that '*Les bureaux de Versailles veulent gouverner la France du Béarn à la Flandre, de Strasbourg à Versailles*' ('the ministries of Versailles want to govern France from Béarn to Flanders, from Strasbourg to Versailles'). The French Crown was trying to increase its power without many of the advantages, such as military success and modishness, enjoyed by the less grand but more modern monarchies to the east. Above all, it lacked a large, prestigious bureaucracy at its service, with jobs available for nobles as well as non-nobles, which might have calmed nobles' antagonism to the Government as well as increasing its power. The royal bureaucracy had neither the numbers nor the prestige to compete with the *parlements* or even the provincial estates, as a suitable career for members of the elites. The royal army, which consisted of about 163,000 men in 1789, was too small to satisfy what one guards officer called the nobles' *fureur* to serve, and it was increasingly closed to non-nobles in the eighteenth century. By the time the future Louis XVIII was born, life for a prince was no longer likely to be the simple round of indulgence in pleasure and exercise of authority which it had been for so many of his recent ancestors. He was, in fact, born into a Court and a period which were witnessing what Madame de Boufflers called '*le choc de l'aristocratie avec la monarchie*' ('the clash of the aristocracy with the monarchy').

The future Louis XVIII was born on 17 November 1755 and christened Louis Stanislas Xavier six years later: in accordance with one of the Bourbons' many strange traditions, he remained nameless for the first years of his life. The name Louis befitted a French prince, Stanislas came from his great-grandfather, Stanislas Leczynski, the dethroned King of Poland, and Xavier from Saint Francis Xavier, for whom his mother's family, the Electors of Saxony, had a special devotion. Thus by birth Louis (as he will now be called) was not only a Bourbon, a member of the grandest family in Europe. He was also part of the exclusive world of Catholic European dynasties which by the late eighteenth century consisted essentially of five rival, power-hungry dynasties, the Bourbons, the Habsburgs, the Savoys, the Wittelsbachs (Bavaria) and the Wettins (Saxony) – each of which thought itself better than the rest. Although most of his ancestors came from other, rather less august, German and Polish families, Louis always remained part of this international dynastic world, much more so than most previous Bourbons. For by 1790 the chances of royal family life had made him first cousin of the Holy Roman Emperor, the kings of Spain and Naples, the electors of Saxony and Bavaria and the Duke of Parma, nephew of the Elector of Trier, and son-in-law of the King of Sardinia. Catholic European royalty was almost as closely related at the end of the eighteenth century as were the Protestant and Orthodox descendants of Queen Victoria at the end of the nineteenth.

Louis's early life was marked by death. His eldest brother, the Duc de Bourgogne, died after excruciating suffering in 1761. His father the Dauphin died in 1765. And his rather severe mother – she had exclaimed after her husband's death: '*Puisse mon âme être aussi nette de péché que mon visage le sera désormais de rouge*' ('May my soul be as free from sin as my face will now be from rouge') – died in 1767, after a heart-rending death-bed farewell to her children.[7] However, Louis could find real warmth and affection in his governess, the Comtesse de Marsan, a member of the highest Court nobility, whom he addressed all his life as *chère petite chère maman*, and whose favourite among his brothers and sisters he was.

At the age of seven, in keeping with tradition, he was transferred from the care of women to that of men – in this case the governor appointed to oversee the education of Louis and his brothers, a pious and traditionalist friend of their father, the Duc de La Vauguyon. In accordance with the French Court's passion for malicious gossip, every conceivable fault has been attributed to the education Louis and his brothers received. But in fact, as P. Girault de Coursac has shown in her brilliant and revolutionary book *L'Education d'un Roi: Louis XVI* (1972), they were given a perfectly adequate grounding in the essential subjects of the day, classics, divinity, mathematics and history. Moreover, Louis was an extremely intelligent child. His father, who took a personal interest in his sons' education (by no means predictable in a royal parent), was amazed at the extent of Louis's memory and comprehension, even at the age of six and a half: he wrote that he could not believe how many Latin words Louis had remembered in a month. Years later, Louis remembered that Berri (the future Louis XVI) was best at science and mathematics, that he was best at classics and literature, and that '*quant à d'Artois il était presque toujours le dernier*' ('as for d'Artois, he was almost always bottom'). Louis actually liked learning and at the age of eleven he horrified his mother by his eagerness to learn English, for which she insisted on substituting Italian – much less dangerous and immoral.[8]

An extremely important part of Louis's education was the rules and precepts laid down for his behaviour in the outside world. He was taught that firmness was an essential quality of kings: *'sans elle les peuples et le souverain sont toujours malheureux'* ('without it the people and the sovereign are always unhappy'). He was taught that the French always expect in their rulers *'de la bonté, de la douceur et de l'indulgence, de l'affabilité, de la politesse, et même une sorte de familiarité'* ('goodness, mildness and kindness, affability, politeness and even a sort of familiarity'). He was also taught that, as the Duc de La Vauguyon wrote, three qualities were essential for princes: *'savoir rentrer en eux-mêmes . . . aimer le travail . . . apprendre l'art de raisonner juste'* ('to know how to withdraw into themselves . . . to like work . . . to know how to reason correctly').

One aspect of Louis's education which should not be over-looked was that in contrast to a very irreligious Court, it was extremely Christian, which is understandable enough, since the authority of the King of France was partly Christian in nature. Louis's preceptor was a bishop, and four *abbés* were among his teachers. Divinity was an essential part of his education, and he would always be able to quote from the Bible at least as frequently as from the classics. All his life he remained a practising, and perhaps even a believing, Catholic.[9]

Finally, in April 1771, Louis's education was judged to be completed. At the age of fifteen and a half he was given his own household and a month later a wife. Both immediately plunged Louis into the dangerous and uncertain world of Court intrigue and of *le choc de l'aristocratie avec la monarchie.* Louis's household was partly formed by the Comtesse de Marsan and the Duc de La Vauguyon, influenced by the Duc d'Aiguillon who had replaced Choiseul as Minister of Foreign Affairs in January 1771 – in other words by the party opposed to Choiseul and associated with the attempts to increase the power of the Crown and with Madame du Barry. One of Louis's *Capitaines des Gardes*, for example, was the Comte de Lévis, a relation of the Maréchale de Mirepoix, one of Madame du Barry's few friends at Court; and one of his *Gentilshommes d'Honneur* was the Comte de La Chatre, a *protégé* of the Duc de La Vauguyon. In addition, Louis's wife, Marie-Joséphine of Savoy, was feared as a possible rival to Marie-Antoinette (and the sisters-in-law grew to detest each other) by the many supporters of the Austrian alliance, which had been the pride and joy of the Duc de Choiseul and was distrusted by the Duc d'Aiguillon. Thus Louis was the natural enemy and butt of what in the 1770s and 1780s was called the *parti Choiseul,* the group of ambitious and modish *grands seig-*

neurs and writers which was as popular at Court as it was in Paris. The effect of this influential and hostile body of opinion on Louis's existence and reputation can easily be imagined when we consider that malicious gossip about members of the Royal Family had become one of the favourite activities of the French Court, and that Court gossip was a more deliberate and luxuriant pheno-menon than any we are likely to know today: as his future con-fessor wrote, '*dans le monde elle est rarement charitable, à la Cour elle l'est encore moins*' ('in the world [conversation] is rarely charitable, at Court it is even less so').[10]

However, for the next few years, until the death of Louis XV on 10 May 1774, Louis's life seems to have consisted largely of an endless round of pleasure, of which his wife's laughing, slightly pitying letters to her parents in Turin give a remarkably vivid picture: plays and operas, both at Court and in Paris, almost every night; so many balls that she could not face any more; amateur theatricals put on by the young Royal Family in their own apart-ments, at which Louis and his younger brother, the Comte d'Artois, outshone everyone else; and when she had time to rest, she would spend the evening listening to her husband singing '*à casser la tête, et d'une fausseté admirable*' ('loud enough to split one's head open, and appallingly badly too').

As for the drama of the marriage bed, despite the apparently healthy start Louis was unlikely to be a father during the first few years of his marriage. There is a telling passage in a letter from the Sardinian ambassador where he passes on the complaints of Madame du Barry about the Comtesse de Provence's persistent reluctance to wash, to wear scent, or to have her eye-brows plucked; Louis's wife was ugly and she smelt. As late as 1773 her father had to write a special letter to tell her to try to please her husband and to pay some attention to her toilette. And for some time Marie-Joséphine seems to imply that they were not sleeping together.[11]

However, despite malicious Court gossip, Louis was perfectly virile. A doctor who helped perform his autopsy states that he had a very narrow opening in his foreskin, which is not necessarily an impediment to performance, although the man who could write to his mistress '*rien ne ressemble autant à une jouissance physique qu'une jouissance physique*' ('one physical pleasure is much like another') was clearly not obsessed with sex. In 1774, and again in 1781, Marie-Joséphine became pregnant, and Louis appointed governesses for the expected children – not a step undertaken without good reason at the Court of France. But the pregnancies ended in miscarriages, leaving Louis the only one of

his brothers not to have children, and this had incalculable consequences for his position in French politics and society. In a patriarchal age a prince without children was in a weak position
since he did not have the authority of a father over his heirs.
Without a family of his own, he was less likely to attract able and
ambitious men to serve or make use of him. Although she did not
have children, and so failed in the first duty of a royal wife, Marie-
Joséphine was not, however, a total disaster. She was at least
intelligent, and relatively loyal to her husband – qualities frequently absent from royal wives.

Louis's real feelings about the other members of his family are
difficult to discover. On the surface, Louis XV's French grandchildren got on extraordinarily well for an eighteenth-century
royal family. Their warm and loving behaviour toward each other
impressed an experienced courtier like the Duc de Croÿ as much
as it did a Paris bourgeois like Sebastien Hardy. After the accession of Louis XVI their relationship seemed to get even closer:
the young Royal Family began having supper together every evening in Marie-Joséphine's apartment, after the king had given the
password or *ordre* to the *Capitaine des Gardes de service*, at nine
o'clock. These were clearly relaxed and enjoyable occasions; servants were excluded, and one of them remembered the *grands
éclats de rire* ('great bursts of laughter') which used to come
from behind closed doors. The Royal Family still got immense
pleasure out of living at the heart of their critical and malicious
Court. They laughed at least as much as they were laughed at,
and indeed there was no question of them not all going on living
together in their luxurious and endlessly amusing family home.
After 1774 Louis and his wife occupied part of the ground floor
of the central block of Versailles, just below the king's apartments.
Only in February 1787 did they give it up to the Dauphin and
move to agreeable, south-facing apartments in the wing of the
palace near the Orangerie.[12]

Beneath this cosy façade, however, it seems clear that Louis's
relations with the rest of his family were neither particularly close
nor especially loving. He had little in common with his rowdy
and debauched younger brother, the Comte d'Artois, whose immense charm and two healthy sons, born in 1775 and 1777,
cannot have failed to be a little annoying. Louis never formed
part of the small, exclusive set which gravitated around Artois
and the queen. Indeed, there was even less in common between
Louis, who hated the *parti Choiseul* and *cette hydre* the House of
Habsburg, and his intensely Austrian sister-in-law (whose bedroom at Versailles is still decorated with double-headed eagles

and portraits of Joseph II and Maria-Theresa). In 1775 he tried
to establish some degree of *intimité* with her, but she was not
interested, and sneered at his *bassesse* and *fausseté* in a letter to
her mother, although she admitted that they continued to behave
'*sur le ton de l'amitié et de la cordialité*' ('in a warm and friendly
manner') toward each other. Although his opinions had probably
been affected by their disputes during the Revolution, Louis's
extraordinary *Réflexions Historiques sur Marie-Antoinette*, written in 1798, show how profound his dislike of his sister-in-law
was. He repeats all the accusations against her character, her
friends and even the legitimacy of her children, only of course to
deny them; but that he even mentioned the last accusation shows
how far his dislike could go.[13]

As for Louis's relation with his brother the king, it is probable
that they were cool to the point of dislike. They were two entirely
different characters: Louis XVI was tall, blonde and blue-eyed;
the future Louis XVIII was shorter, and much darker – physically
more of a Bourbon. The former was reserved and stubborn and
lacked the *vivacité d'esprit* and winning manners of his younger
brothers. Although both Louis and the king were equally well-
educated and intelligent, their tastes were completely different:
the former, a much simpler and more direct character, preferred
arithmetic and geography; the latter, one of the most complicated
and indirect characters in history, preferred classics and literature.
Even their tastes in wine were different, as the servants at the
family supper parties found out: wine that Louis liked very much
the king found *détestable*.

It must have been maddening for Louis, who had been at least
the equal of his elder brother in the schoolroom and in his parents'
affection, when this brother suddenly became that mysterious and
supernatural being *le Roi*, the centre of everything at Court, and
the object, for a time, of his subjects' passionate love. Louis XVI
was a far more forceful, intelligent and successful king than posterity has been led to believe, and it is probable that in accordance
with his confessor's advice he never ceased to behave as *le Roi*,
rather than as a brother, toward the members of his family.
Certainly, Louis complained later that his elder brother had lacked
'*ces formes sympathisantes qu'on cherche dans son ami*' ('that
understanding manner which one expects in one's friend'). But
then friendship was a new and alien concept in the traditional
world of superiors and inferiors, spouses and lovers, and Louis
himself would use and extend it extremely sparingly.[14]

After the king, the most important people at the Court of Louis
XVI, the people whom courtiers queued up to take coffee with,

who were flattered and envied and talked about and studied
without ceasing, were his ministers (as the diary of the Duc de
Croÿ, one of the best and least biased of observers of life at
Versailles, shows). In comparison, members of the Royal Family
were quite without influence except, in the case of Marie-Antoinette, over certain Court and military appointments. In 1774
Louis and his wife, who were now known as Monsieur and
Madame, the traditional French names for the king's younger
brother and his wife, had hoped that he would be made
a member of the Council of Ministers. However, the most
that happened was that in October and November of that year he
was given the opportunity of discussing the Government's reestablishment of the *parlements* with the king and the *Garde des
Sceaux*: it was an extremely important moment in the history of
the monarchy, and Louis, who was heir presumptive until 1781,
was assumed to have the right to be consulted. However, Louis,
naturally adopting the point of view of the d'Aiguillon party, saw
in this move a fatal retreat by the Crown, and after this disagreement, which became public knowledge, he experienced what he
called *'une lacune de douze ans dans ma vie politique'* ('a gap of
twelve years in my political life'). He was now left enshrined in
the grandeur and dignity of his rank, but quite without political
power or influence. He was simply a younger brother: even the
Captain of his own Swiss Guards, the Prince de Montbarey, had
more power and influence than his master when, from 1777 to
1781, he was Minister of War. Can Louis have quietly accepted
his gilded insignificance, which became even more total after the
birth in 1778 of a daughter, and in 1781 of a son and heir, to his
brother the king?

He was not expected to. One of the oldest traditions of the
French Monarchy was the importance and rebelliousness of the
junior male members of the Royal House, fired and justified by
the belief expressed by the Prince de Conti (one of the princes
who had not attended Louis's wedding) that, although the eldest
Bourbon wore the crown, it belonged to all of them. Such a belief,
which would seem to give Louis a certain right to power and
influence, might tempt him to play a part like that of Gaston
d'Orléans, an eternal conspirator against his brother Louis XIII
in the 1630s and 1640s. Louis was ambitious as well as intelligent
and he was deeply interested in politics. He had longed to enter
the Council in 1774 and in 1777, writing to his friend Gustavus
III of Sweden, who had visited Versailles in 1771, he complained,
with that terrible frankness with which he often judged his own
position, of being a *'ver de terre . . . inutile'* ('useless worm'), and

'*enrageant de tout mon coeur de l'inutilité dans laquelle on me laisse, mais prenant patience et vivant d'espoir*' ('only too peaceful from the political point of view, furious with all my heart at the state of idleness in which I am left, but waiting and hoping').[15] *Enrageant* is a strong word, and the same letter contains remarks on the state of the French army which, however true they might have been, are rather out of place in a letter to a foreign sovereign. How far did this rage go?

One way in which an ambitious prince was still expected to act was to try to alter the line of succession. In 1772 a pamphlet, whose instigator it would be extremely interesting to discover, had claimed that the crown traditionally went to the ablest, rather than the eldest, male in the Royal Family. In 1777, Maria-Theresa, who did not like the House of Savoy, pretended to be frightened that Monsieur and Madame might have Marie-Antoinette's children done away with.

But in fact although he was devoured with ambition, Louis's discontent with his position never sank to such depths and never got beyond the stage of grumbling and complaints. His reaction to the birth of his brother's daughter is put without pretence in a letter to Gustavus III: he had been '*bien aise*' ('very pleased') that it had been a girl but now '*à force de me raisonner j'avais fait mon sacrifice*' ('by dint of reasoning I have made my sacrifice') and he was prepared for a Dauphin '*avec assez de philosophie, pour ne pas dire d'indifférence*' ('with some philosophy, not to say indifference'). The letter trying to have his nephew the Dauphin declared a bastard, of which some historians have made so much, is one of a set of four crude forgeries which should never have been allowed outside the pages of the bad novel in which they were first published. Another story, that Louis leaked a *mémoire* attacking the *parlements* and the *intendants*, sent by Necker to the king, rests on the dubious authority of the Austrian ambassador, a natural enemy of Louis, who was outrageously mendacious and deceitful even by the standards of eighteenth-century ambassadors. Since Louis had been so firmly excluded from the Council, he was unlikely to have got hold of a confidential *mémoire*. The story's basis is probably the known ambition of Louis's *Surintendant*, Cromot, to replace Necker as *Contrôleur-Général*.[16]

However discontented Louis was, he knew he was part of the Bourbon family business, and he was prepared to play a relatively dutiful role in it. Thus he never went into open opposition to the king like the Prince de Conti or, in England, the brothers of George III – one of whom, the Duke of Gloucester, was the first person to sow ideas of liberty and opposition in the mind of the young La Fayette. Indeed the king used Louis in 1776 to present and register a financial edict in the *Chambre des Comptes*, and in 1777 to go on a provincial tour. He always behaved in an extremely respectful way toward the king – so respectfully, in fact, that the Abbé de Véry, unable to believe any good of a Bourbon, saw in it a proof of *fausseté*, when it is more likely to have been simple self-interest. At the delicious, informal suppers the king gave in his private apartments (the food had the réputation of being the best in France), which Louis attended frequently, he always called his brother *le Roi*, whereas the Comte d'Artois called him *mon frère*. Again, one gets the feeling of a distinct involvement in the family business from a passage in a letter to his *Capitaine des Gardes*, where he changes plans for a provincial tour because he does not want to leave *le Roi* alone (the Comte d'Artois was away), *'surtout au mois de juillet, où il n'y a jamais grand monde à Versailles'* ('especially in July, when there's never very many people at Versailles').

Indeed, a book published at Louis's printing press, dedicated to himself, contains an invocation to the king which is also, perhaps, a picture of the reign as it was seen from Versailles: *'O mon Roi! tout annonce la prospérité de votre Règne: excepté les ingrats, chacun vous bénit, chacun vous aime.'* ('O my King! Everything predicts a prosperous reign for you: except for the ungrateful, everyone blesses you, everyone loves you.')[17]

CHAPTER II

A Prince and his Leisure
1774–1787

To understand how Louis filled the endless stretch of empty days with which his princely but powerless state left him, it is important to recognize that his life consisted of five separate levels as different from each other as the tickets issued to courtiers, household officials and members of the public on the day of his marriage. There was the public level – dining in public, going to Mass on Sunday in public and attending reviews; there was the level of his relations with his Court officials and with those members of the *noblesse présentée* who were admitted into his society; there was the official or political level, which in Louis's case was so maddeningly unimportant; there was the mysterious area of his private life; and there was his family life. It was unusual for these different levels to coincide. Thus, in the case of the king's life, few members of his family or courtiers became ministers, while few ministers became intimate with their master (those from the *noblesse de robe*, or legal nobility, were not allowed to play any part in the Court's social life except at the *lever* and *coucher*). And Louis was well aware of these different levels: for example, he wrote of one person he knew, who had boldly asked what were his reactions to the queen's pregnancy, that they were '*en grande liaison de société mais non pas d'intimité de confiance*' ('great friends socially, but neither close nor intimate').

These separate levels of Louis's life were so different that they were lived out in different rooms and were the responsibility of different sets of officials. The public level was the responsibility of the *Capitaines des Gardes* who were in charge of Louis's safety once he had left his apartment. They never let him out of their sight, and received any petitions which were handed to him. The Court level of Louis's life was staged in the three rooms, *Antichambre, Salle des Nobles* and *Chambre*, which formed the centre of all the Royal Family's apartments, and to which only people who had been given the *entrée* were admitted. The officials who supervised these apartments, and the social life which went on in

19

them, were called the *Premiers Gentilshommes de la Chambre*. The official and private levels were lived out in the *Cabinet* immediately next to the *Chambre*, and in other *cabinets* nearby. Only in these rooms, which were the responsibility of the *Premiers Valets de Chambre*, could the members of the Royal Family occasionally be alone.

On the public level, Louis not only continued to participate in the public round of Versailles, but he also went on four provincial tours: he did not lead an exclusively Ile-de-France-based life. The members of his family of whom he was most fond were probably his aunts Madame Adélaïde and Madame Victoire and his sister, Madame Clotilde: twenty-five years later Madame Clotilde was still writing to him as '*mon bon cher et adorable frère*'. In 1775, he went to see her meet her future husband, his own brother-in-law the Prince of Piedmont, at Chambéry, and in the same year made a formal entry into Lyon. In 1785, he went to see his aunts at Vichy, which they were in the process of launching on its profitable medicinal career. Thus part of his exposure to the public was due to his family affections. But he also went on tours which were more in the line of duty. In 1777, he travelled to Bordeaux, Toulouse, Avignon and Marseille and during the tour, which lasted a month, he visited the inevitable series of schools, hospitals, and cathedrals. In 1783, he went to Metz where he reviewed his regiment of *Carabiniers*. However, these tours did not last long, and in all he spent only three months outside the Ile-de-France before 1791.

This was perhaps the centre of the civilized world. On 19 September 1783, for example, the first balloon went up from the courtyard of Versailles watched by the king and his Court. Surrounded by this atmosphere of greatness, the essential framework of his life was provided by his *maison* or household. This enormous institution, which numbered 390 in 1773 and 524 in 1791 (only the latter figure includes all the junior servants), had amazed contemporaries by its size and splendour, when it was set up in 1771. The red and blue of Louis's livery provided an unaccustomed rival at Court to the blue, silver and red *Maison du Roi*, from which it differed only in size, not in structure, nor in the social origins of its officials. Thus Louis had only two *Capitaines des Gardes*, the Comtes de Lévis and de Moreton-Chabrillant, and two *Premiers Gentilshommes de la Chambre*, the Marquis de Noailles (like his master, a younger son) and the Duc de Montmorency-Laval, whereas the king had four of each.

Like the king's, Louis's household comprised an *aumônerie* for his spiritual needs and charities (twenty-one people: all figures are for 1773), a *chambre* which looked after his personal and social life (ninety-three people), a *garde-robe* which looked after his jewels and clothes (twenty-two people), a *chambre aux deniers* which cooked and served his food (125 people), *écuries* or stables which provided him with transport (eighty people), a hunting staff of nine and a Council of thirty-seven officials which ran his household, finances and appanage. In addition, he had his own *Gardes du Corps, Cent-Suisses* and *Gardes de la Porte*, numbering 174 in 1773, although in other countries guards were usually reserved for the sovereign. This was in accordance with one of the strange traditions of the French Royal Family, which had always provided extraordinarily lavish establishments for its younger sons (no wonder so many had been so rebellious), in order to emphasize the power, prestige and wealth of the dynasty. Louis's household was directly modelled on those of the Ducs de Berri and d'Orléans, the younger grandson and brother, respectively, of Louis XIV, and his guards were admitted to have more to do with prestige than protection.[2]

One interesting difference between those households and Louis's, however, was the substitution in the latter of the position of *Gentilhomme d'Honneur* for that of *Gentilhomme de la Chambre*. The *Gentilshommes de la Chambre* were in effect underlings of the *Premiers Gentilshommes*, who had not been presented at Court and could not, therefore 'être admis à composer la Société du Prince' ('be admitted to compose the Society of the Prince'). They were supplanted by ten *Gentilshommes d'Honneur* mostly retired officers, 'personnes de qualité . . . pour l'accompagner partout' ('people of quality . . . to accompany him everywhere'). In this way Louis, like his younger brother, the Comte d'Artois, had almost as many members of the highest class of the nobility, the *noblesse présentée*, attached to his household as did the king – twenty-four compared to twenty-seven – and his household was in many ways better balanced. Instead of the traditional Bourbon household, whose outstanding idiosyncracy had been, as Stanislas Leczynski had complained, its *luxe de domesticité*, its hordes of servants, and the fact that all its officials, however grand, had definite domestic functions, Louis's household was more like other European royal households. It had a position which did not have to be bought, which was not domestic and which could be used to win over or reward members of the elite.

This household can be seen in operation on an occasion like Louis's *lever*, which was not only the moment when the finishing touches were put to his full Court dress but also, for him as for other grand or pretentious people of the time (see the picture *Le Lever du Petit Maître* in Restif de la Bretonne's *Tableaux de la Bonne Compagnie*, 1787), an occasion to see people, hear the latest news and arrange private audiences. According to the two surviving accounts, by a page and a *Valet de Garde-Robe*, both of whom disliked their master, it took place at half past nine in the morning, when Louis, already half-dressed, received his senior Court officials, and the people to whom he had given the *Entrée* (household officials and a few writers, as well as members of the *noblesse présentée*), who formed a circle round him. The *Maître de la Garde-Robe* or *Premier Gentilhomme* handed him his shirt, waistcoat and coat, the coiffeur powdered and dressed his hair, and the *Valet de Garde-Robe* put on his buckled shoes and sword. The whole process probably did not take more than about half an hour and, although it may seem undignified and ridiculous to us, it was really just an agreeable and useful way for Louis to get through the tiresome business of being dressed; the same process took place in reverse at his *coucher* at eleven o'clock at night. The *lever* and *coucher* were useful since people who wanted to see Louis could be sure of finding him there at a fixed time, and Louis could make pronouncements which he wanted to be known – as when he justified his *Surintendant*, Cromot, against the accusations of another financial official, de Limon, at a *lever* in 1776.[3]

Another traditional form of Court social life in which Louis played a part were the receptions for people who had been presented at Court and who had come to pay their respects, held by each member of the Royal Family in his or her apartment. In fact, this form of Court social life had been scaled down since the days of Louis XV and now only took place after Sunday Mass. Essentially it consisted of people bowing three times as they passed before the royal presence. *'cela s'appelle faire sa cour. Quelquefois ils vous disent un mot: cela s'appelle pour lors être bien traité; et quand ils ne vous disent rien et ne vous regardent pas, cela s'appelle perdre son temps. C'est ce qu'on fait le plus souvent à Versailles.'* ('That is called paying your court. Sometimes they say a word to you: that is called being well-treated; and when they say nothing to you and do not look at you, that is called wasting your time. Which is what one usually does at Versailles.') This form of Court life, which was so unsatisfying even to those admitted, was one of the few distinctions in the France of Louis XVI (another, after 1781, was officers' commissions) which was based almost exclusively on birth (see page 7), as Louis later recollected.

In contrast, because it was so much less exclusive, more people went to the Court of St. James's, where the king and queen actually talked to them, than to the Court of Versailles, which struck many observers in the 1770s and 1780s as deserted. Thus, just at the time when it was becoming more hostile, the most powerful class in the kingdom, the nobility, was also becoming increasingly isolated from the monarchy. At the same time it was losing its principal means of participating in the personal service of the monarch. In 1775, as an economy measure, three regiments of the *Maison Militaire* were disbanded, and the number of the *Gardes du Corps* were greatly reduced. In 1787 the *Gardes du Corps* was even further reduced, and the two remaining regiments of the *Maison Militaire* were disbanded.

However, no more than his public life, Louis's Court life of receptions, *levers* and *couchers* did not take up much of his time. It was an indispensable part of being royal, in the opinion of the Bourbons, to receive these regular and visible demonstrations that they were the heads of French aristocratic society, but it was not particularly important. So what did Louis do? According to the Austrian ambassador, he spent most of the day *'dans son cabinet; il s'y occupe à la lecture ou à l'arrangement de ses affaire'* ('in his study [where] he occupies himself with reading and business'). And as Louis himself recalled *'longtemps, j'ai vécu assez retiré* ('for a long time I led a rather retired life').[4]

The Court officials in charge of this private level of his life were the four *Premiers Valets de Chambre* one of whom always slept in his bedroom, and controlled his *cassette* or pocket-money. But the most important person whom he saw in his *Cabinet*, and one of the most important people in his life as a prince, was his *Surintendant des Finances, Bâtiments, Arts et Jardins*, M. Cromot du Bourg, who was succeeded in 1786 by his son, M. Cromot de Fougy. The father was a former *Premier Commis des Finances* or senior civil servant, and provides a perfect example of the complex power and social structure of late eighteenth-century France. Louis's *Premiers Gentilshommes* and *Capitaines des Gardes* came from the top of the social scale and enjoyed the appearances of intimacy with their master, and the right to participate in the traditional social life of the Court. But the people who had real power in Louis's household, and saw their master most frequently and privately, were the Cromots.

Cromot was not only, in effect, the head of Louis's household, but was also in charge of his private finances and of his appanage. The appanage was the estate or province traditionally given to the younger brothers of the kings of France, and their male descendants, to enable them to maintain a princely existence. In accordance with this medieval tradition in April 1771 Louis was made

Duc d'Anjou, and Comte du Maine, de Perche and de Senonches, the block of provinces in the west of France, south of Normandy and east of Brittany – although, confusingly, he remained known as the Comte de Provence, with which otherwise he had no connection. In December 1774 he was also given the Duché d'Alençon as a *Supplément d'Appanage*.

In fact, the appanage had declined since the late fourteenth century, when it had been used as the spring-board to colossal wealth and power by the ambitious brothers of Charles V. All Louis's appanage gave him was the vague right to appoint to certain minor offices and benefices and certain financial rights over royal forests and domains, which at first brought in only about 300,000 livres a year. Basically his appanage had been instituted in order to raise his status, and he enjoyed fewer feudal rights in his, and derived less income from it, than did the Premier Prince du Sang, the Duc d'Orléans, with whose appanage his own was constantly compared.[5]

In other respects, too, Louis's financial position was not as brilliant as he had expected. He received the immense sums of 2,272,982 livres from the Royal Treasury and 96,000 livres for his *cassette* every year, but the former sum was already wholly absorbed by the running costs of his enormous household. Yet almost every eighteenth-century *grand seigneur* regarded lavish expenditure on gambling, mistresses, building, works of art and conspicuous consumption in general as a necessity of life. The public too thought that princes had 'a hereditary right to every gratification and enjoyment that human nature is capable of receiving'.

Indeed, in the great green volumes of the *Décisions de Monsieur*, the very first decision Louis is recorded as having made in his Council was to raise his personal allowance from 72,000 to 96,000 livres a year. But this was not very much by royal standards, and at first the only really large sums he could raise came from what he saved on the money allotted for buying food for himself and his household. Since he normally ate at his wife's table or in private, he did not need the three fowls or roasts of veal, two hors d'oeuvre, one leg of lamb, two fat chickens, three partridges and three woodcock which had been allowed for his dinner table every evening; and so by making savings he was able to buy Brunoy, south-east of Paris, his first country estate in October 1774.[6]

In addition to a desire for a lavish way of life, and for a house like Brunoy which he could call his own, there was another reason why Louis wanted as much money as he could get. His financial position was basically dependent on the Royal Treasury (not the most reliable of paymasters) and hence on royal favour. Yet, in the nature of things, such financial generosity was unlikely to be extended on the same scale to Louis's descendants, who would be much further from the throne than the prince who was, until 1781, heir presumptive. Therefore it was essential for Louis to build up an independent financial position for himself as soon as possible, while he still had a certain claim on the Royal Treasury.

So, with the help and perhaps to a certain extent at the instigation of Cromot, who was naturally keen to improve his master's position, from the moment Louis had a household and appanage of his own, he began to try to make money with a passion and a thoroughness not yet seen in the Royal Family (although only too well known in the Princes du Sang). In 1772, pointing out that his income was barely able to cope with extraordinary and charitable expenditure, and that he had to save *'pour assurer un sort à mes descendants'* ('in order to ensure the situation of my descendants'), he wrote to ask for a rise of 50,000 livres a year. In the same year Cromot insisted that Louis ask for Touraine to be added to his appanage, for his children's sake as well as his own. Until 1789, Louis's agents tried to revive and exact every conceivable feudal right in his appanage, on trees, on legal transactions and on mineral wealth; and they succeeded in raising his income from this source from about 300,000 to 1,978,284 livres in 1788.[7] Louis even tried to make money out of exploiting or selling the estates of the Order of Saint Lazare, of which he had been made *Grand Maître* in 1772, and which had hitherto been regarded as an order of chivalry rather than a source of revenue.

Feudal in his appanage, Louis was wholeheartedly capitalist when it came to commercial and property speculation. For him, as for so many other people in France before 1789, there was nothing incompatible between the two forms of making money, and Louis's career shows how far from being exclusively 'feudal' the French ruling elite now was. Indeed he was the most capitalist Bourbon there had yet been – infinitely more involved in the realities and delusions of money-making than, for example, the Prince of Wales and his brothers. In 1774 he tried to obtain a monopoly on the clove and pepper trade in French Guiana, which was refused by Louis XVI. In 1775 he took a china-factory, henceforward known as the *Manufacture de Monsieur*, under his protection and supplied it with coal and cobalt from his own lands. He also backed, presumably in return for a share of the profits, one of the Farmers-General who managed tax-collection for the Royal Government.

Louis also tried to make money out of the spectacular Paris property boom of the 1770s and 1780s. In 1778, the year it became clear that the queen was capable of producing heirs to the throne, he was given the Palais du Luxembourg and its surrounding land in Paris, and he tried to launch a huge redevelopment of the whole area – partly in order to raise the money to make the palace habitable after years of being used as an art gallery. In fact Louis's main speculation was extremely unsuccessful. Only four building plots were sold in five years, and his plans made him unpopular with the local inhabitants. His only success was the sale of land north of the Luxembourg to other speculators for 1.5 million livres[8]; it became, and remains, one of the most beautiful areas of Paris, the five grey streets converging on the neoclassical façade of the Théâtre de l'Odéon.

It is not certain to what extent these speculations actually aided Louis's finances. They probably helped make possible his refurnishing and building programmes, and his purchases of works of art (see page 27). In the 1770s he was also able to spend 952,974 livres on diamonds alone and, by 1780, to have bought not only Brunoy, but also part of the Fôret de Brix and the nearby Château de Grosbois, for a total cost of 3,280,000 livres, and estates at Gray in the Franche-Comté and at L'Isle-Jourdain in Languedoc from the Comte du Barry for 950,000 livres. But to accumulate all this he started going into debt: in 1777 he borrowed three million livres in Geneva.

Inevitably the ownership of an appanage brought him into conflict with the Royal Government. In 1780, the Government's economy-drive began to affect his stables and kitchens. In the same year there was a violent row, which was probably the cause of the rumours about Cromot's hostility to Necker, over the edict reorganizing the *Receveurs-Généraux* of taxes, which deprived Louis of the right to appoint his own in his appanage. The king himself now personally distrusted Cromot, who at one time thought of resigning. In 1779, the Royal Government had failed to get Louis to pay the *capitation*, the income tax levied on all classes, although it was successful in 1787. One can only speculate on the degree of asperity there must have been in the conversation at the Royal Family's suppers.[9]

By 1783, Louis's debts, incurred on his household and guards, as well as on his personal expenses and those of his wife, came to 5,075,792 livres, although he had been given 2,477,529 livres since 1774 for extraordinary expenditure on his stables and guards. In 1783 an extremely complicated transaction took place between himself and his brother the king. The king generously gave him 7,650,000 livres and a 500,000-livre yearly allowance for his debts and increased household expenses, as well as 1,164,211 livres and 674,805 livres to be paid every year. In return Louis gave up his claims, amounting to 2,955,844 livres, on the estate of his grandparents and eldest sister, and bought the estate of the Prince de Conti at L'Isle Adam for his godson, the king's second son, the Duc de Normandie, reserving for himself the usufruct although not the rents (it cost 1,484,000 livres in addition to annual payments of 675,000 to Conti's creditors).[10] This transaction strongly suggests that Louis had by then given up all hope of an heir, and shows that, in the years before 1789, the Ile-de-France was becoming even more dominated by the Royal Family's vast and beautiful estates. In addition to the king's hallowed trinity of Versailles, Fontainebleau and Compiegne, Artois now had Maisons, Saint-Germain and Bagatelle, the queen had Saint-Cloud, Louis had Brunoy, Grosbois and L'Isle Adam, and Louis XVI had Rambouillet.

Louis's financial transactions must have taken up a lot of his time and energy; but they did at least enable him to indulge in the hereditary family passions of building and collecting. By 1781 he owned 180 pictures (all Dutch or Flemish, except for eleven Italian, seven French and four Spanish pictures) and 3,557 drawings (again all Dutch or Flemish, except for 612 Italian drawings). His architect, Chalgrin, added several rooms to the Petit Château at Brunoy and built a luxurious and intimate theatre there in 1780. Chalgrin also designed the enchanting *Folie de Madame* near the town of Versailles for Marie-Joséphine in 1784: a small, white *pavillon*, whose central room is a rotunda decorated by *trompe l'oeil* frescoes of wild flowers – harebells, hollyhocks and marguerites – which provide the perfect contrast to the oppressively gilded *boiseries* of the royal apartments at Versailles. Outside, thatched cottages and a dairy, practically obligatory for eighteenth-century princesses, were scattered round a huge park.

Louis also loved collecting furniture. He was the Jacob brothers' best, although ultimately fatal, client (his payments on his purchases stopped in 1791) and between 1781 and 1786 alone he bought 574 beds, 255 armchairs and 138 *tabourets* or stools. The little furniture of his which survives is quite enchanting. Like the architecture of the Petit Château at Brunoy (see the photograph in *Dubois-Corneau*, planche XXVII) and the floral decoration of the china made in his *Manufacture*, it is simple and light. His favourite colours seem to have been lilac and white, or blue and white, and the chair covers were decorated with urns and arabesques. What is particularly fascinating about Louis's furniture is that, as his *Dessinateur du Cabinet* and *Intendant des Bâtiments* Dugourc later claimed, it was utterly modern and up-to-date, and almost 1800 in its preference for the straight line, sphinx's heads and Pompeian motifs (not that these were unknown in other Louis XVI furniture). There is even at the Assemblée Nationale a marvellous flat-topped desk made for Louis in 1785 which is almost revolutionary in style: its legs are in the form of bundles of sticks with axe-heads sticking out – the old Republican fasces.[11]

Some of the finest furniture Louis ordered was for the *pavillon* or *folie* which Chalgrin built for him after 1781 near the Pièce d'Eau des Suisses at Versailles. As with almost all the buildings Louis ever inhabited, victims of the Germans, the property speculators, or Louis-Philippe, there is nothing left of it now (it was pulled down in the late 1790s). But from an exquisite extremely detailed plan of the house and park, showing every tree, almost every blade of grass, it must have been the most perfect even of that particularly perfect form of habitation, the French *pavillon* of the second half of the eighteenth century.

It was the only house in which Louis escaped the traditional Bourbon room pattern of guard-room/antechambers/*chambre*. Instead a hall lead into an octagonal dining room, to the left of which were a billiard room, an oval salon, a bedroom with a double-bed, a bathroom and an octagonal boudoir. To the right of the dining room a passage lined with pot plants (the house was centrally-heated, which was very advanced for those days) led to the magnificent library which was twice the size of any other room and was surrounded by a gallery supported by twenty-eight columns. The entire house was plunged in greenery, since all the rooms faced the undulating informal 'English' garden (the servants' rooms, however, faced a courtyard) with its lake shaded by weeping willows and crossed by 'Chinese' bridges leading to an island.

The garden is still there, behind the École Nationale d'Horticulture, and is a very private, rather mysterious place, well hidden from the outside world where Louis's brother was king. It contains an artificial hill of rocks, full of unlit caves and passages where it would be perfectly possible to get lost, or to hide. It may have been designed to contain an unseen, and unseeing, orchestra – one cave is easily big enough – playing magical music while Louis and his guests amused themselves in the garden. On the top of the hill hiding behind a draw-bridge is a tiny summer-house which would be just big enough for Louis and a friend to take tea in.

The *pavillon* and its garden were built for Louis's mistress,

Madame de Balbi, a sharp, witty, forceful member of the Court nobility who is as symbolic of this period of Louis's life as his later favourites were to be of other, busier periods. Born in 1758, she was a daughter of the Marquis de La Force, head of one of the oldest families in the French nobility (which boasted that the first La Force came to France with Hercules) and Louis's *Premier Gentilhomme de la Chambre* between 1771 and his death in 1773. In 1780, she became a *dame pour accompagner* (lady-in-waiting) of Marie-Joséphine, preferred to the Vicomtesse de Laval either because the latter was a coquette, or because she was the daughter of a financier, or because she was associated with the *parti Choiseul*. The variety of reasons put forward by the Court gossips, none of which of course is necessarily true, shows how hard it is to find out the real motives for what was going on at Versailles. The Vicomtesse's father-in-law, the Duc de Laval, resigned as Louis's *Premier Gentilhomme* in protest (he was replaced by the Comte de La Chatre), but a few months later Madame de Balbi became Marie-Joséphine's *Dame d'Atours*, Mistress of the Robes, a better-paid post which meant that she was almost permanently in waiting.[12]

Although at first she seems to have been more Marie-Joséphine's friend, Madame de Balbi and Louis soon began, in as much as his Court and public life allowed, to live together (her husband had gone mad and had been sent to a lunatic asylum). After 1781, as he later reminded her, hardly a week went by without them seeing or writing to each other. In Paris, they both lived in the Petit Luxembourg, Louis on the ground floor (now a Senators' restaurant), Madame de Balbi on the first, while Marie-Joséphine lived in the adjacent wing of the main Luxembourg palace. Madame de Balbi's apartment contained a dining room with five card-tables, a library with two *sièges tête-à-tête* and a bedroom with a double-bed: gambling, reading and love all catered for by her prince.

He was clearly absolutely devoted to her, and was proud to be something more than her *amant*, her *ami* – as he pointed out, a subtler and more permanent bond. A ponderous but amusing verbal portrait of Madame de Balbi written by Louis shows, at the same time as the terrible, but rather disarming, frankness displayed in his letters to Gustavus III, how fond of her he was. He admits that, badly marked by smallpox, she is far from pretty; that she is badly educated; that she is *farouche* in society (other people said rude); and that she is far too impatient with bores. But, clearly in love, he praises her natural wit and gaiety, and the enormous sympathy and generosity she showed to her friends:

'*A mon avis le bonheur d'être son ami surpasse tellement tous les autres qu'il n'y en a point sur la terre qui lui doive être comparé.*' ('In my opinion that the happiness of being her *ami* is so superior to all others that no happiness on earth can be compared to it.'[13])

The charm and liveliness of her company can be imagined from the extraordinarily amusing and outspoken letters she wrote to her family (unfortunately none to Louis has been found), and from the testimony of contemporaries. '*Je n'ai jamais trouvé de conversation plus animée que la sienne, ni plus intéressante*' ('I have never heard more animated or interesting conversation than her's'), wrote Dutems; while one of Louis's *Aides de Camp* in the 1790s called her '*vraiment extraordinaire pour son esprit naturel*' ('quite extraordinary for her natural cleverness and wit'). This emphasis on her natural wit was no doubt due to the contrast it provided with the artificial, premeditated and predictable conversation so common at Court, and in the salons. Since Louis's own conversation is recorded as being '*spirituelle, instructive et amusante*' ('witty, instructive and amusing'), and he had the awesome magic of his royal rank, they must have made a rather alarmingly sharp and sparkling pair.

Louis was clearly dependent on her. Even through the extraordinarily heavy and pompous tones of his letters to her between 1789 and 1794 (was he afraid of their interception?) one can detect his real misery at being away from her. And, like all Bourbons with their mistresses, he paid. In addition to her apartments at Versailles and the Petit Luxembourg, and her use of the *Pavillon de Monsieur*, she was given a *hôtel* of her own near the Luxembourg, built by Chalgrin (as is to be expected with a building connected with Louis, it contained a billiard room and an oval salon). And Louis gave large sums of money to her, and pensions or positions in his or his wife's households to many of her friends and relations.[14]

The relationship with Madame de Balbi inevitably affected Louis's marriage. In the late 1770s he and Marie-Joséphine were still quite devoted. She often went with him to Brunoy, where her apartment was next to his on the ground floor – their bedrooms were only separated by her boudoir and his library and *Cabinet*. But after 1780, their relationship probably sank to the level of fairly amiable mutual endurance, exacerbated by her hatred of Madame de Balbi. The lesbian legend which surrounds her may be unjustified. She did have a great friend, Madame de Gourbillon, by 1789 her *Lectrice de la Chambre et du Cabinet*, to whom she wrote loving, longing and submissive letters, which read to modern eyes very much like love-letters. For example in a letter of 12

April 1789, she wrote: '*Je vous vois partout, je ne pense qu'à vous, je ne rêve qu'à vous?*' ('I see you everywhere, I think only of you, I dream only of you.') But in fact Madame de Gourbillon may just have been one of those strong-willed, intelligent, ambitious servants who have at all times found it fairly easy to take over their employers' lives.[15]

The tragedy is that Marie-Joséphine, whom even the Austrian ambassador (naturally inclined to denigrate Marie-Antoinette's rivals) admitted to be a sensible and intelligent princess, turned to drink, no doubt because she had little else to do, a husband who was increasingly leading a life of his own, a Court in which she was neither smart nor influential and no children. Even in 1771, four days after her wedding, she had been asking the Piedmontese ambassador to send her some *vin de Piémont*. By 1789, her weakness was well-known at Court and to her family in Turin, while Madame de Gourbillon's exile in the same year can probably be attributed to the fact that she was held responsible for supplies of drink reaching her mistress. There was an obscure incident late one night in 1789 in a corridor at Versailles when the king and Louis found her taking Marie-Joséphine a bowl of '*bouillon*'. Drink can only have made Marie-Joséphine, who was naturally bossy and domineering at the best of times (she complained if her younger sister, the Comtesse d'Artois, did not do exactly what she had told her to), even more difficult to live with. But Louis seems to have supported it all with equanimity, and his wife's passionate letters to the exiled Madame de Gourbillon rather surprisingly contain little criticism of Louis and reveal his concern when Marie-Joséphine was ill. However, she does write to her *amie* that, although Louis was '*le metre chez moi, il n'est pas le maître de mon coeur, il ne la jamais eut*' ('the master in my house, he is not the master of my heart, he has never had it'). So Louis's marriage was loveless as well as childless.[16]

After 1778, Louis spent a large proportion of the year away from Versailles, although he continued to join the family's annual expeditions to Fontainebleau and Compiègne. Both at Brunoy and in the Petit Luxembourg he was able to enjoy not only private life with his wife and mistress, but also social life of a less exclusive sort than that provided by the Court. At Brunoy (which was run by Cromot, its governor) he often put on plays, especially during the occasional visits, two to four times a year, of the king during the hunting season. Louis loved the theatre – in 1781 a *Société de Gens de Lettres* dedicated an *Histoire universelle des Théâtres de toutes les Nations, depuis Thespis jusqu'à nos jours* to him – and it provided a link between him and the outside world. On 22

November 1780, with a large invited audience, Louis and the king watched *La Réduction de Paris*, a play by one of Louis's many literary *Secrétaires Ordinaires*, M. Desfontaines, which appealed to the national cult of Henri IV by celebrating his clemency and moderation when he reentered Paris in 1594. When the king was not there, the plays could be much more suggestive, and the audience contained many what were called *belies impures*.

In Paris, at the theatre, at his *lever* and *coucher*, perhaps in Madame de Balbi's apartment and at private parties – he was seen very much enjoying himself at one given by his *Premier Ecuyer* (Master of the Horse), the Marquis de Montesquiou, in 1781 – Louis was able to dip into the frenzied Paris world of the last decade of the personal reign of Louis XVI, a world which was different, although not cut off, from the world of the Court.[17] It was a world in which wealth and a common culture were beginning to replace birth or occupation as the distinguishing signs of the elite of power, influence and success. The old differences of accent, language and manners which had cut off the Court nobility from the rest of the Paris-based elite, and had distinguished members of different occupations, such as the law, finance and the army, from each other, were beginning to disappear. Mercier, for example, wrote in *Tableau de Paris*, a book which was in Louis's library, that *une noble familiarité* now united the judge, the bishop, the soldier, the financier and the courtier, that they all seemed to have taken on some of each other's characteristics, and that in Paris, six years before the Revolution, '*les hommes . . . sont plus égaux qu'ailleurs*' ('men . . . are more equal than elsewhere').

In this world nobility was relatively easy to obtain for the rich and successful. As M. Chaussinand-Nogaret has shown in his excellent book on the French nobility, after 1760 the monarchy was consciously using ennoblement to reward not only service in the army and at Court but also success in commerce or the arts. Thus there was little open conflict between the nobility and the Third Estate. A typical view, perhaps, was that put forward by the lawyers of Niorts in late 1788, who praised the nobility and its privileges 'because we are not excluded from them and because we can acquire them (through) great actions, gallantry, courage, personal merits, offices, fortune even'.

Louis and his household took to this Paris world with ease and eagerness. There was no cultural gap between them: the same ballet, *Les Caprices de Galathée*, could be as successful at Brunoy as it would later be in Paris, before the Court at Fontainebleau, and indeed under the Republic. Successful and fashionable writers such as Desfontaines, Ducis and Rulhière were among Louis's *Secrétaires Ordinaires* (posts which gave access to the prince but did not carry any functions), while Voltaire was delighted to compose a play for a fête Louis gave in honour of the queen at Brunoy in 1776: the aged courtier wrote to Cromot that it was '*la plus agréable commission dont on pût jamais m'honorer*' ('the most agreeable commission with which I could ever have been honoured').[18]

Another sign of the links between Louis, his household and the Paris world was the *Musée de Monsieur* founded in 1781 by Pilatre de Rozier, one of Louis's *Intendants*, which enjoyed the protection of Louis and his wife. It was essentially a lecture hall, one of the first in Paris, where such stars as Monge, Condocet, La Harpe and Marmontel, well-known scientists and writers, gave courses of lectures. In the list of founder-members there are ninety-six men and women with titles and eighty-eight without: it was a society which nobles and non-nobles united by the same cultural interests joined in equal numbers (and many of the people with titles had probably only assumed them on the purchase of an estate, or when they felt like it). As the prospectus stated, at the *Musée de Monsieur* '*les Citoyens de tous les rangs peuvent acquérir des lumières* ... [and enjoy] *cette égalité précieuse qui mêle les rangs sans les confondre*' ('where Citizens of all ranks can acquire knowledge ... [and enjoy] that precious equality which mixes the classes without confusing them').

Even the offices of Louis's household, which were open to purchase subject to his approval, further connected him with the Paris world. Boissy d'Anglas, at that time a struggling author, became his *Maître d'Hôtel Ordinaire* in 1785, while his *Premier Maréchal des Logis*, the Comte d'Orsay, and his *Premier Veneur*, the Marquis de Montholon, were among the first cases of a tax-farmer and a *Noble de Robe* being given senior Court office.

One of the most noticeable differences remaining inside the French elite was one of dress. On formal occasions the Court nobility and the Royal Family wore the brightly coloured *habit habillé* of silk or velvet such as Louis is depicted wearing in illustrations I and II, whereas the *Noblesse de Robe* and the Third Estate wore black suits. In 1782 there was a row over a place at the Comédie Française between the Comte de Moreton-Cha-brillant, son of one of Louis's *Capitaines des Gardes*, devastating in bright pink, and a legal official, in the black clothes of his estate. Although it was the Court noble who was punished, this might be seen as anticipating the Third Estate's humiliations over dress in 1789. However, during the 1780s most of the Paris elite,

even the Court on weekdays, and probably Louis when he was
relaxing in private, were increasingly united in wearing the *frac*
or tail-coat, which was to become the symbol and uniform of the
nineteenth-century ruling classes.[19]

When he was relaxing, Louis's favourite occupations were eating and reading. He adored food. When they were first married,
his wife had noticed that, if he wanted something to eat outside
meal times, he got hold of it *'aussi finement que piémont quand
il mangeait les châtaigners après dîner'* ('as cleverly as Piedmont
when he used to eat chestnuts after dinner'). By 1777, he was
recorded as being *replet* (stout) which, in the language of the
Court, became *gros comme un tonneau* (round as a barrel). By
1782, he was certaintly very fat and a gossip column claimed that
he had had an attack of apoplexy (heart attack?) due to his
embonpoint.

His increasing size emphasized and helped ensure that he was
one of the few Bourbons who did not spend half his life on a
horse. At first, however, he had quite enjoyed hunting and shooting: he would be accompanied by sixty-three horses, twenty
grooms, two *Ecuyers*, a *Gentilhomme d'Honneur*, a *Capitaine des
Gardes* and his *Premier Ecuyer* when he went hunting, and by
thirty-two horses and eighteen household officials and servants
when he went shooting – impressive testimony to the degree to
which his daily life was sheltered and surrounded by his household. And in the 1780s he was still going shooting once or twice
a month in the summer.[20]

However, the way Louis spent most of his leisure was neither
hunting nor eating, nor making money, nor playing billiards, nor
even in conversation with Madame de Balbi, but reading. A
catalogue of the library in his *pavillon* at Versailles shows that it
had 11,581 volumes – it was particularly strong in classic authors
such as Bossnet, Bordaloue, Horace and Cicero, and in medical
theses (owing to the method of cataloguing it has not been possible
to compare the library's categories). Although Louis owned a
copy of the *Encyclopédie* contemporary literature was not particularly well represented – nothing by Diderot; very little by
Voltaire; only the *Maximes, Lettres de la Montagne, Emile, Nouvelle Heloise,* and *Oeuvres* (1767) of Rousseau. The catalogue of
the library of his *Cabinet* shows that of 418 titles, 11 per cent
were theology, 2 per cent law, 27.5 per cent science and arts, 16.5
per cent literature, 5.5 per cent on classics, 29 per cent on history,
3.5 per cent on geography and 5 per cent on politics. Thus he
was most interested in history (including ancient history), and
surprisingly interested in science and arts, which includes his large

number of books on military subjects (the arts of fortification and manoeuvre, etc.), on medicine and on optics. In comparison the library of the Marquis de Boisgelin, who also lived at Versailles, since he was a *Maître de la Garde-Robe du Roi*, was 61 per cent literature, 20 per cent history, 6.5 per cent politics and 6 per cent science and geography. Perhaps as a result of his education, Louis's tastes were much more traditional, factual and serious – and religious – than those fashionable at Court.

Louis's love of books was well-known and we can perhaps detect a note of surprise in the comments of an official publicist writing in 1778: '*Monsieur mène une vie sédentaire, il protège et cultive les Lettres et les Sciences et passe regulièrement plusieurs heures de la matinée à étudier et à lire dans son cabinet.*' ('Monsieur leads a sedentary life, he protects and cultivates Literature and Science, and regularly spends several hours in the morning reading and studying in his *Cabinet*.') The same author claimed that Louis also wrote *vers charmans*. But according to Louis, frank as ever, they all had '*le sort qu'ils méritaient, c'est à dire qu'ils ont passé, avant même que l'encre en fût sèche, de ma table dans mon feu*' ('the lot they deserved, that is to say, even before the ink had dried on the page, they went straight from my table into my fire'). The only works of his which might survive, he says, are a few pages of memoirs which he wrote in 1772, and a translation of Horace Walpole's *Historic Doubts on Richard III*. He forgets, or prefers to overlook, that in 1789–90 he translated an English book on the revolution in Holland which had recently ended in the triumph of the pro-English, Orangist party – as odd a subject for a French prince to choose to translate as was a book on Richard III for a royal uncle. However, perhaps it was simply common sense, as he said, to want to know the enemy, and for a prince in the land of gossip to translate a book which contains a warning to historians to be as critical as possible of their sources.[21]

Here we come across one of the most fascinating aspects of Louis's character, the immense difficulty of discovering what were his real motives and attitudes. Moreau, his *Premier Conseiller*, complained that '*sa prudence ne lui permettait jamais de se déboutonner en entier*' ('his prudence never allowed him to open himself completely'), and anyone who studies Louis's life knows what Moreau meant. Already, in Louis's sex life and his attitude to his brother's ministers, and now in his translating habits, one gets the impression of layer after layer of reality sliding away underneath one's feet, and at the end what does one find? Perhaps only the sceptical, smiling face of a late eighteenth-century prince

at the heart of whose character were exceptionally large doses of
reason and realism. As his grandfather had written, when explain-
ing why he did not expect Louis to show too much emotion at
his wife being ill: '*c'est la raison même*' ('he is reason itself'). And
there was nothing more rational, even slightly chillingly rational,
than his exploitation of all his feudal rights, his capitalist speculations, or his reaction to being deprived of the prospect of the
throne.

He was a royal version of the rational and realistic man of the
world, someone who was capable of bending, of accepting second
best, and was rarely deceived by appearances. What, for example,
could be more realistic than his remark: '*Jamais je n'ai eu de
plaisir bien vif qu'il n'ait été accompagné de quelque amertume;
jamais aussi je n'a eu de douleur bien profonde sans quelque
consolation*' ('I have never had a really great pleasure which has
not been accompanied by some bitterness; I have never suffered
a great unhappiness without some consolation')? Or what could
be less deceived than his judgement of Joseph II as a dangerous
schemer '*poli jusqu'aux compliments avec les gens qu'il croit
devoir ménager, mais haut et même quelquefois brutal avec les
gens en-dessous*' ('polite and complimentary with the people he
thinks he should flatter, but haughty, and even brutal sometimes,
with the unimportant')?

Because he was a rational and realistic prince, he was well
aware of the dangers of life at Court and in the world, of the
hordes of people waiting to laugh or sneer, and of the extreme
rarity of disinterested service and loyalty. For private motives of
greed and ambition dominated public behaviour perhaps even
more in the second half of the eighteenth century than they do
now. As Soldini wrote, '*Personne n'est plus à plaindre que les
Rois . . . parce que le seul intérêt personnel guide presque tous
les hommes, et rarement l'amour de la gloire du Prince et du bien
public.*' ('No one is more to be pitied than Kings . . . because
personal interest alone guides almost all men, and rarely love of
the glory of the Monarch or of public interest.') Most courtiers
were only there for credit, power and consideration, in other
words for what they could get out of the Court, as the Maréchale
de Beauvau admitted; and she left out profit. Cromot, for example, already very well paid as *Surintendant* made Louis pay him
another salary for being Governor of Brunoy, all the time, of
course, protesting how little he wanted the money. Another
example of the dominance of private motives is that as the elite
grew increasingly detached from the monarchy, even the king's
ministers, as one of them admitted, wanted to '*ecarter le roi, de*

*s'attribuer le mérite de tout et surtout de vouloir être et d'être
effectivement (aux yeux du public) les distributeurs de toutes les
grâces'* ('leave the king out and attributing to themselves the
merit of every action, and above all of wanting to be, and really
being, in the eyes of the public, the distributors of all the favours')
– in other words jobs and pensions.[22]

In such circumstances, in a Court which was a minefield, with
members of the Royal Family the soldiers who had to get through
to the other side, Louis's best weapons were his realism and
rationality, and his manners. He could hardly fail to be respected
as an intelligent man in tune with his own times. Even his speculations were commonplace in a period swept by stock exchange
fever. And above all he knew how to behave like a prince, a vital
talent in an age which judged people, and especially royalty, by
their behaviour at least as much as by their actions.

In his manner and behaviour Louis was helped by his appearance. Although he put on so much weight, he remained good-
looking: his *belle figure* impressed a bourgeoise of Bordeaux in
1777 as much as it did his brother-in-law in Turin in 1793. Nor
was his the bland, expressionless face of the film star. He had
'fine black eyes' and 'a pleasing sensible countenance' according
to the Duchess of Northumberland, and he knew how to use them
to full effect. At the coronation of Louis XVI, for example, the
Duc d'Orléans thought that after himself Louis won the prize for
good looks and dignified behaviour. A few days later, at a conference of *Chevaliers du Saint Esprit*, over which Louis presided,
the Duc de Croÿ was equally impressed: '*Monsieur, avec une
grâce et un talent très marqués, récapitula tout, saisit
supérieurement le vrai, enfin parla à merveille . . . C'était réelle-
ment remarquable pour ses vingt ans . . . Grâce, force, justesse,
noblesse, enfin le ton et la chose, tout y est.*' ('Monsieur, with
marked grace and ability, recapitulated everything, intelligently
went straight to the point, really spoke very well . . . It was really
remarkable for a twenty-year-old . . . Grace, force, precision, nobility, both manner and matter, it is all there.') He at least was
quite won over, as no doubt he was meant to be, to the idea of
Louis entering the Council. Even on such a difficult occasion as
the birth of the Dauphin, the final shipwreck of his hopes of the
finest throne in the world, an onlooker thought that the behaviour
of Louis and his wife, who both had to witness the happy event,
was *parfaite*.[23]

Nor was Louis only capable of impressing aristocrats. On his
visit to Bordeaux in 1777, Madame Chazot-Duplessy, wife of a
lawyer, was greatly taken with his *démarche fort noble* and found

him '*plus modeste et moins gonflé que je ne l'aurais cru*' ('more modest and less puffed-up than I would have thought'). She admired the interest he showed in the merchant ships in the harbour – he was, after all, a commercial prince – and the trouble he took to ask questions, and thought that most people in Bordeaux had been '*très content de son air doux et affable*' ('very pleased with his mild and affable manner'). He had clearly taken to heart Moreau's lessons on the importance of politeness and affability in France. Most important of all, perhaps, he appeared, as she twice remarks, '*très gai et très content*'. – just as he had done at his wedding. He won people's hearts by looking as if he was enjoying himself, thereby fulfilling one of the most important and difficult parts of the royal performance, not only to look the part, but to be seen to be enjoying looking the part. It was this air of conviction and royalty, and his 'perfect' manner, which were to be Louis's best weapons in the troubled years to follow.

The main criticism of Louis's manner came from some of his courtiers, and from some of the people round the Court. In part this was due to his selfishness. He was not outstandingly kind to his servants – one page claims that Louis never spoke to him during his three years of service – nor was he nearly as charitable as, for example, his elder brother the king. The records of his *cassette* show that in July, a month taken at random, in the 1780s he would give to charity between 1.5 per cent and 7.5 per cent of his expenditure, although this only includes payments specifically recorded as charitable. He was prepared to try to force the locals at Brunoy to build a road to his Petit Château over their own land for nothing (the *corvée*), although eventually he backed down.

However, by the standards of eighteenth century royalty, his selfishness was not very surprising: it is difficult to think of others when everyone around you is boasting that they are only thinking of your royal self. A more legitimate complaint was his heaviness and pomposity. The Comtesse de La Marck thought he was *glorieux*, the Abbé de Véry uses the word *appesanti*.[24] One gets the impression that he never really relaxed with any of his courtiers or, perhaps, with anyone, as much as they wanted. Certainly his letters to Madame de Balbi are very heavy, while those to Gustavus III are over-involved in both style and structure. Louis must have seemed far too old for his age (he was only twenty in 1775): and his bookishness and seriousness, and the prudence which Moreau had noticed, must have seemed out of place at the determinedly frivolous Court of Marie-Antoinette.

But these were not dangerous failings for a prince. Certainly they were less dangerous than the simplicity and unpretentiousness of Louis XVI, who could be laughed at at his own *coucher*, or the open debauchery of Artois. Indeed his prudence, his bookishness, and his pomposity were almost virtues, which helped keep his courtiers in their place. This may also have helped ensure that Louis was the member of the Royal Family least attacked by the flood of hostile often pornographic pamphlets which came out in the 1770s and 1780s, some of which, such as *Anecdotes sur Madame la Comtesse du Barry* (1776), or *Les Contemporaines, ou Aventures des plus jolies femmes de l'age présent* (1780), he had in his library in the *Pavillon de Monsieur*. He even had a book called *Théorie du Libelle ou l'Art de Calomnier avec fruit* (1775).[25]

In his heaviness, in his preference for private life over Court or social life, in his capitalist speculations, even in such details as the centrally-heated comfort of his *pavillon*, the style of his furniture and his preference for billiards rather than hunting, can we not see something prophetically nineteenth-century in the future Louis XVIII?

CHAPTER III

Monsieur and the Revolutions 1787–1791

The War of American Independence (1778–1783) had been a rare and expensive triumph for France over England. By 1786 the Royal Treasury was in an even worse state than it had been at the time of Louis's marriage, and the *Contrôleur-Général*, Calonne, estimated the annual deficit at 112 million livres or 23.5 per cent of annual revenue. This deficit caused a crisis which enabled a series of revolutions to destroy the world in which Louis had been brought up. These revolutions, each of which had separate causes and aims, although they were often in alliance with each other, were staged by the Royal Government and the aristocrats, as well as by the democrats, the soldiers, the Parisians and the peasants.

At first, the crisis actually favoured Louis's political ambitions. It led to the opening on 22 February 1787 of an *Assemblée des Notables* which finally gave this rational, prudent and ambitious prince an opportunity to play an active political role. He presided over meetings of the joint Committee of the Notables and over sessions of the first Bureau. Since the other six bureaux were presided over by Artois and five Princes du Sang, this *assemblée* to a limited extent bore out the truth of the remark by a Prince du Sang (the Prince de Conti who died in 1776) which Louis and Artois were often to quote in the years to come: '*La Couronne nous appartient à tous; notre aîné la porte.*' ('The Crown belongs to us all; our senior member wears it.') Government had been shown to be the concern of all the male Bourbons.

With the other members of his Bureau – representatives of the Government, the *parlements*, the nobility, the clergy and the Third Estate – Louis at first confined himself to discussing the extremely radical proposals put forward by the *Contrôleur-Général* to raise a new land tax and to extend a system of elected *assemblées provinciales* throughout the kingdom. In these discussions, it is often hard to tell to what extent Louis influenced or reflected the views of the other members. But it is clear that, like almost

everyone else in 1787, including the king, Louis was in favour of
opening up the traditional edifice of royal power, stately, secretive
and authoritarian, to a degree of public participation. Documents
survive, in his own hand, which show that he supported the
assemblées provinciales having control over, rather than as
Calonne proposed just a say in, local taxes, roads and even the
militia, and that Louis was against the *Intendants*, the
Government's traditional executive agents in the provinces, having
trop d'autorité – an unexpected phrase from someone so closely
associated with the monarchy's attempts to increase its authority
in the 1770s. But these remarkably radical proposals are probably
as much a reflection of the views of Louis's Bureau as of his own,
since they appear in its *procès-verbal* two weeks before the date
of the notes in Louis's handwriting.[1]

However, Louis did take some personal initiatives. At the beginning of the *Assemblée* he made an admired and typically
realistic speech asking the *notables* not to be too indiscreet in
talking about their meetings, for fear of exciting public opinion.
He attacked the hated salt-tax, the *gabelle*, and suggested its
replacement by a different tax. Above all, he allowed discussion
of the nature of the Government's new tax, as opposed to the way
in which it should be raised, and himself asked for information
about the extent and origin of the financial deficit: he was clearly
not at all displeased to have this opportunity to show that the
king had been as unsuccessful a businessman as himself. Thus
Louis not only joined in the general opening up of royal authority,
but also, by implication, criticized the *Contrôleur-Général*,
Calonne, a remarkable but disreputable minister who was widely
blamed for the crash on the Bourse that was taking place at the
time, and who was eventually dismissed by the king in April.
Louis's distrust of Calonne was further shown at the meeting of
representatives of all the bureaux held, largely to answer criticisms
made by himself and leading archbishops, in his *Cabinet* on 2
March. Unlike Artois, Louis made no effort to defend Calonne,
and he made several acid comments on Calonne's figures.[2] Louis
must have been very ambitious indeed to have allowed himself,
for the only time in his life, to attack royal authority.

Thus he gained his first experience of assemblies and he was
able to find out for himself how extremely difficult they are to
control. He kept having to ask the *notables*, especially the bishops,
not to talk all at once and even this assembly of elderly nominated
members of the elite ended up discussing *droit naturel* – causing
Louis to observe, in his no-nonsense way, '*si l'on voudrait ramener
tout au droit naturel, il faudrait déranger bien des choses*' ('if we

want everything to return to natural law, rather a lot would have to be changed'). In the *Assemblée des Notables*, Louis also showed himself concerned for the position of the nobility. He never forgot, as the ritual of receptions and presentations at Court demonstrated, that he and his family were the heads of French aristocratic society. Louis was in favour of members of the clergy and the nobility keeping the presidency, and at least one third of the seats, in the *assemblées provinciales*, and he was prepared to call himself *le Premier des Gentilshommes*, and their *représentant*, in his final speech to the king.

But this concern for the nobility was more a recognition of where power and prestige really lay in France in the 1780s than an exclusive and antiquated bias – of which Louis had anyway shown few signs of in the composition of his household or of the *Musée de Monsieur*. Louis agreed that members of the Third Estate, however poor, should be given a vote and that the nobility should lose its tax exemptions – which, as he pointed out with his customary realism, were partly illusory anyway, since tenants simply took the cost of their taxes out of the rent they paid their landlords.[3] Thus Louis emerged as a partisan of moderate reform and a major but not exclusively dominant role for the nobility.

Thereafter he enjoyed a certain degree of popularity. His reputation in Paris and in his appanage as a prince who was too keen on money did not prove as important as his reputation as a prince who was not too keen on Calonne. In the next few months (May 1787 – August 1788) he witnessed the failure of the last efforts of the Royal Government, headed by the former leader of the opposition in the *Assemblée des Notables*, the Archbishop of Toulouse, to raise a new tax, replace the *parlements* and create *assemblées provinciales* throughout the country. Louis saw for himself that in reality the power of the King of France to transform his wishes into facts when faced with the massive opposition of the elite was extremely limited.

Many people had been alienated by the traditional style of the French Monarchy and by the prospect of only enjoying a political role by favour of the king and his ministers. The monarchy had made little effort to attract supporters and so did not really have a party of its own. Beyond the traditional obedience expected from the king's subjects, still powerful in the older generation, there was no force capable of drawing people to the Government's policies, which seemed to offer only increases in taxation and Government power. There was no system of Court favours or military or civil service, which could lure members of the elite to the service of the monarchy and away from the pursuit of their own interests. Half the Guards units had been disbanded, Court receptions had been reduced and the king's household had few positions for members of the elites.

Therefore discontent with the absolute powers of the King of France, which had previously shown itself in the extraordinarily malicious gossip and pamphlets circulating against the Bourbons, was now able to show itself in a refusal to have anything to do with his reforms. Although Louis dutifully played his role as an obedient prince registering and defending financial edicts in the summer of 1787 and May 1788, he was clearly dissociated in the public mind from the ministry's efforts. He was applauded at the *Cour des Comptes* in August 1787 (Artois was hissed at the *Cour des Aides*) and in 1788 he was so popular that a pamphlet appealed to him to stop the enterprises of the ministers.

In the end, faced with a tax strike by the clergy – a sure sign of the massive unpopularity of the Royal Government even in this traditionally respectful and Royalist body – and a cash-flow crisis in the Royal Treasury, the king and his ministers had to abandon their attempts at reform. The *parlements* were recalled, Necker returned to power, and the States-General were summoned for April 1789. In *le choc de l'aristocratie avec la monarchie*, the aristocracy had won. The king now lifted all censorship restrictions and called for advice on the mode of holding the States-General. Among the subsequent torrent of pamphlets, one, dedicated to Louis and printed at his *Imprimerie*, shows how confused and ill-defined the situation still was. Written by the Abbé de Lubersac, and called *Le Citoyen Conciliateur ... Idées Sommaires, Politiques et Morales, sur le Gouvernement Monarchique de la France* (3 vols. 1788), it is basically conservative, in favour of the *corps intermédiaires* and of maintaining distinctions of rank '*trop confondus dans la société générale*' ('too confused in general society'). But it calls all the Royal Family *citoyens*, attacks the ministry's *actes de despotisme*, asserts that the king should choose his ministers '*par la voie du peuple*', and that '*l'autorité du prince ne vient que du consentement de son peuple*' ('the authority of the prince only comes from the consent of his people'). It even attacks the king himself, saying that he rarely has '*une volonté ferme et assurée*' ('firm and assured will-power'). But this rambling, slightly mad work, which was on sale '*à Versailles, aux Galeries du Château*', should not be taken as the sole representative of Louis's attitudes. For a work by his old teacher, Moreau, *Exposition et Défense de Notre Constitution Monarchique Française* (2 vols. mars 1789), also dedicated to Louis, of which twenty-three copies – presumably intended for distribution

– were in Louis's library, is a passionate attack on the States-General, and a defence of royal power over troops, taxation and the king's subjects.[4]

In the last few months of 1788 and the first months of 1789, a new body of opinion appeared, opposed to the aristocrats' attempts to preserve the traditional mode of election for the States-General, and in favour of the relaxation of formal barriers between the leading members of the Third Estate and the nobility, which became known as the 'democrats' or the *parti populaire*. In many ways the appearance of this party, which was soon backed by a majority of educated opinion, especially among the debris of the *parti Choiseul*, was a blessing for royal authority, since it rescued it from the prospect of aristocratic tutelage like that under which Louis's friend, Gustavus III, had writhed until his *coup d'état* in 1772.

Certainly Louis still regarded the aristocracy as the main threat to royal authority. In the second *Assemblée des Notables*, called in November 1788 to debate the organization of the States-General, his was the only bureau which voted in favour of doubling the number of deputies of the Third Estate, so that they would equal the number of deputies of the nobility and the clergy combined. This celebrated vote, by which public opinion judged Louis for a long time, was largely due to Louis's personal intervention, appealing as befitted a rational prince, to the *notables' justice et raison*, and set him apart from all the other princes, except the Duc d'Orléans. However, he was no more in favour of relaxing all distinctions between the orders than he had been in 1787. He wanted a society which, like the Paris world into which he had dipped in the 1780s, gave a satisfactory role to each class, without destroying formal class distinctions.

Thereafter, having shown that he was not a blind supporter of aristocratic power and that he was in favour of moderate changes, Louis's political role was minimal. In his instructions to his representative at the electoral meeting of the nobility of Anjou, the Comte de Cossé (his *Premier Gentilhomme en survivance* and another younger son), Louis confined himself to advocating '*la modération en tout, le respect et l'amour du roi, les droits sacrés de la couronne, la sûreté de toutes les propriétés, le bonheur du peuple entier*' ('moderation in everything, respect and love of the king, the sacred rights of the crown, the security of all property, the happiness of the entire people'). There was no reason for thinking in March 1789 that these aims were in any way mutually exclusive. Louis also showed himself, in the spirit of the age, prepared to step down from some of the pretensions and pomposity of his princely status. Cossé spoke of Louis's *sensibilité* and *amitié* for the nobility of Anjou – words which before 1789 Louis had reserved for his tiny circle in the Ile-de-France (although not for the king and queen). And Cossé even spoke of Louis's feelings of *fraternité nationale*, a phrase totally unthinkable before the calling of the States-General. Louis also began to abandon his unpopular exactions as an *appanagiste*.

Louis sat beside the king at the opening of the States-General on 3 May, and was at Versailles throughout the long, hot summer of 1789, when the conflict between the 'democrats' and the 'aristocrats' degenerated into an irreconcilable power struggle, and all the Royal Government's attempts at reconciliation were unsuccessful. In this conflict it gradually began to appear that the 'democrats', who were now in an open and somewhat unexpected alliance with the Paris crowd (in other capitals, Amsterdam, Naples or Madrid, the crowd was monarchist and reactionary) were the greater threat to royal authority. They claimed to represent not their constituents but the entire nation, and to have the power to levy or suspend taxes. Moreover the crowd, which frequently invaded the spectators' seats at the Assembly, was now increasingly violent, driven on by the highest bread prices of the century. The Royal Government did not adopt a 'let them eat cake' attitude to the problem (according to Louis the original remark by the wife of Louis XIV had been '*qu'ils mangent de la croûte*' ['let them eat pastry'] – the pastry that in France often surrounds particularly good pâté. Indeed the Royal Family could not but be aware of the problem. By August 1789 the bread served at Marie-Joséphine's dinner-table was '*pourri et rempli de chaud*' ('rotten and full of chalk'). But the Government could not provide enough food to feed the enormous, expanding population of Paris after a bad harvest.

The struggle between the 'aristocrats' and 'democrats' was not a class struggle, although both sides tried to pretend that it was. The elite was by no means entirely 'aristocrat' in its attitudes. For example, almost the entire Noailles family (related to La Fayette) was 'democrat', and of Louis's Court officials who had been elected deputies, although La Chatre, Louis's *Premier Aumônier* and *Premier Maître d'Hôtel*, a *Maître de la Garde-Robe*, the Marquis d'Avaray, and a *Gentilhomme d'Honneur* were 'aristocrats', a *Capitaine des Gardes*, the Duc de Lévis, and the *Premier Ecuyer*, the forceful and influential Marquis de Montesquiou, were not. Even Marie-Joséphine seems, in the summer of 1789, to have been a 'democrat'. She certainly used the same language as the Paris mob about her detested sister-in-law –

l'autrichienne – whom she believed to be responsible for the exile of Madame de Gourbillon.

Thus there was nothing inevitable about Louis's turning against the 'democrats'. However, when on 22 June Louis was admitted to the Council, with Artois but not the queen, he came out against Necker's plan to unite the three orders, and in favour of maintaining certain distinctions between them, particularly in the organization of the States-General.[5] This decision shows not only that Louis's prime concern was with the maintenance of royal authority, within reasonable bounds, whether it was threatened by 'aristocrats' in 1788 or 'democrats' in 1789, but also that at this crucial stage in the history of the French monarchy he was thought to have a right to be consulted.

However, the king's *Séance Royale* was unsuccessful, the deputies of the Third Estate disobeyed his orders and, in the space of one month, the magnificent façade of royal authority fell apart. The *Gardes-Françaises* showed that they preferred to join the Paris crowd and attack the Bastille, rather than obey orders, and even the *Gardes du Corps*, who were meant to be the elite and epitome of loyalty, now preferred to defend the Revolution rather than the Royal Family. After the fall of the Bastille on 14 July 1789, the National Assembly cheerfully began work on the destruction of the old regime and of the Royal Government, and its committees soon had more power than the king's ministers. The Royal Family now found out what later generations find so hard to understand, that during a revolution almost no one is reliable. The servants of yesterday are the spies of today, and almost no one is willing to expose themselves for what looks like a losing cause. A sign of the sudden collapse of royal authority was that after July 1789 the Royal Family transferred their family suppers to the queen's apartment, rather than risk themselves in Marie-Joséphine's apartment, which was too isolated at one end of the palace.

On 5 October the fatal cycle of popular violence and royal retreat took a yet more sinister turn when a mob from Paris invaded the palace. Two *Gardes du Corps* were battered to death at the door to the queen's apartments; the king and queen were called to the palace balcony by the baying mob, and next day Louis and Marie-Joséphine travelled in the slow funereal procession of the Court to Paris, in the same carriage as the king and queen. The cortège was escorted not only by *Gardes du Corps*, equerries and footmen, but also by the bloodthirsty mob and by a new Revolutionary force, the *Garde Nationale de Paris*. Louis and his wife now lived in the Luxembourg and went every evening to have supper with the king and queen in their extremely uncomfortable palace of the Tuileries.

After October, the Court round of Sunday Mass, receptions and dining in public still went on. Louis still had his *lever* and *coucher*, at which conversation would still be about the latest Paris gossip and the latest successful plays (now sadly anti-monarchist). But there was one crucial difference The Royal Family were now guarded by, and in effect the prisoners of, the *Garde Nationale de Paris*, a Revolutionary force answerable to the Paris Commune: both Louis and the king use the word *captivité* to describe this period of their lives. This situation must have been particularly galling for Louis as the commander of the guards, the Marquis de La Fayette, had been a personal enemy since the days when they had quarrelled over investments in French Guiana, and La Fayette had refused (or had been refused?) a place in Louis's household.[6]

One of the most extraordinary aspects of this appalling, unprecedented and almost unbelievable situation was that Louis, like the rest of his family, remained calm and managed to view the tragic violence round him with the easy, detached manner of the Court – the best way, no doubt, to make it all bearable. Writing to Madame de Balbi, who had decided to take a holiday abroad, on 22 October, Louis simply calls the horrifying events which have brought him to Paris *'une scène au moins désagréable* ('a scene at best disagreeable'), and then, after referring to *'la fatale lanterne'* from which a baker has just been hanged, calmly discusses the exact differences between a crowd (*attroupement*) and a riot (*émeute*). Such poise, when faced with the collapse of his world, is a remarkable triumph of manner over reality and an impressive tribute to Louis's self-control.

However, Louis did not react to the change in his circumstance in the rather passive way of his brother the king, who signed the decrees the Assembly presented to him, as he admitted, *indistinctement*, in the hope that eventually public opinion, and the influence of the moderates in the Assembly, would bring France back to some degree of normality. Instead, since power now lay with the Assembly (busy with its reforms and with writing the most decentralized and least authoritarian constitution France has known), Louis, always realistic, got in touch with the man who was perhaps the Assembly's most popular speaker, the pockmarked, ambitious and boastful Comte de Mirabeau. As early as 13 October, Mirabeau was submitting a plan for escape to Louis through a great friend, Louis's *Capitaine des Gardes*, the Duc de Lévis.

It is probable that an extraordinary political contract in Louis's handwriting dates from this period. In return for the colossal sum of 50,000 livres a month, and the promise of an embassy, Mirabeau swears to '*aider le Roi de ses lumières, de ses forces, et de son éloquence dans ce que Monsieur jugera utile au bien de l'Etat et à l'intérêt du Roi, deux choses que les bons citoyens regardent sans contredit comme inséparables*' ('help the King with his advice, his powers and his eloquence in what Monsieur will judge useful for the good of the State and the interests of the King, two things which good citizens without doubt regard as inseparable'). With this document we slide into the unofficial world of political intrigue, deceit, plots, lies, forgeries, hopes and fears which Louis was to inhabit for the next twenty-five years. Indeed, this contract shows how completely Louis had adapted to this world. For a version Mirabeau showed La Fayette contains one crucial difference, namely that Mirabeau was to give advice on what *he* judged useful. Moreover it is extremely unlikely that the king knew anything about the contract although his signature is at the bottom. Would he have wanted *Louis's* choice of Mirabeau's advice?[7].

So what was Louis up to? It seems likely that his main aim in the period up to January 1790 was to realize the dream of his life and by using the force and fervour of Mirabeau, to enter the Council as the representative, at least in part, of the popular or democratic party. In other words, he had rallied to the winning side. Indeed, according to Gouverneur Morris, a friend of La Fayette and Talleyrand, in January 1790 Louis actually wrote to the king to ask for a place on the Council; and his desire to enter the Council at this time was common knowledge.

This ambition was, however, complicated by another, simultaneous intrigue in December 1789, when Louis told La Chatre, his *Premier Gentilhomme*, and Papillon, his *Trésorier-Général*, to try to raise a loan of two million livres with the help of a reckless and imaginative adventurer called the Marquis de Favras.[8] On the night of 23 December, a note distributed round Paris declared that there was a plot to kidnap the king and murder Necker, La Fayette and the Mayor of Paris, and that Louis was at its head. On 26 December 1789 Louis went to deny this charge before the Paris Commune and in a speech partly written by Mirabeau, calling himself a *citoyen* and his listeners *concitoyens*, and claiming that La Chatre had proposed the loan to *him*, he affirmed his solidarity with the Revolution: '*Je n'ai pas cessé de croire qu'une grande révolution etait prête; que le roi par ses intentions, ses virtus et son rang suprème devoit en être le chef, puis qu'elle ne pouvait pas être avantageuse à la nation sans l'être également au monarque. Enfin que l'autorité royale devait être le rempart de la liberté nationale et la liberté nationale la base de l'autorité royale.'* ('I have not ceased to think that a great change was imminent; that the king, by his intentions, his virtues and his supreme rank should be its head, since it could not benefit the nation without equally benefiting the king. Finally that royal authority should be the rampart of national liberty and national liberty the basis of royal authority'). On 19 February, Favras, on whom according to La Fayette and Sémonville, the supplest and subtlest politician of the age, a letter from Louis had been found, was executed. At his trial two witnesses had said that Favras had wanted to *enlever* (kidnap) the king to Péronne, where Favras hoped to have a band of loyal troops ready to receive him. Another witness, Tourcaty, said that Favras had been trying to persuade the infantry of the *Garde Nationale* (which had absorbed some of the former *Gardes Françaises*) to demand the recall of the *Gardes du Corps*, and to have Necker and La Fayette killed. Favras always said it was all a *'pure fable de leur imagination'* ('pure product of their imagination').

The exact connection between Louis's attempts to enter the Council and his relations with Favras is very difficult to establish. We are plunged into a labyrinth of intrigues even darker and more mysterious than the caves and passages in Louis's garden. They involve not only Louis, Favras, Mirabeau, and La Fayette, but also the king, the queen, Talleyrand, who now makes his first appearance in Louis's life, and a shame-faced chorus of bankers, intermediaries and Court officials (the king's as well as Louis's). It is the most mysterious episode in Louis's far from simple life. But if we begin with the loan of two million livres, it is unlikely that it was for his household and personal expenses, as Louis claimed at the Hôtel de Ville, nor can it all have been to pay Mirabeau's monthly retainer. However, Louis's extravagance, the decline in his income from the Royal Treasury (from 2,247,663 livres in 1788 to 1,564,207 livres in 1790) and the fact that he was now paying tax make it perfectly possible.[9]

A letter from Mirabeau provides one of the few direct links between the loan and Louis's political ambitions: he calls Louis *'au-dessous de tout ... Imaginez qu'on avait été jusqu' à lui donner de tels moyens d'argent que si votre valet de chambre avait à les offrir, il entrerait au Conseil, pour peu qu'il le voulût'* ('beneath contempt ... Imagine, people had gone to the lengths of giving him such financial resources that, if your *Valet de Chambre* had been able to provide them, he would have got into the Council if he had wanted to'). This is a rather mysterious comment since, even during the French Revolution, ministerial posts were not for sale. But it is possible that it refers to a project to bribe deputies in the Assembly to call for Louis's entry into the Council and, perhaps, to repeal the law forbidding deputies to become ministers, so that Mirabeau could enter it too.

Such a project would have gone against the interests of Necker, the most popular member of the Council but an enemy of Mirabeau, and La Fayette, a personal enemy of Louis, whom Favras wanted to have replaced as Commander of the *Garde Nationale de Paris*. Indeed the Favras Affair may have been encouraged by La Fayette, in order to keep out Louis and ditch Mirabeau's attempts to replace La Fayette as the most powerful man in the capital. Certainly, some of the witnesses against Favras were known to, and in favour of, La Fayette.[10]

Years later, Louis expressed regret at his role in the affair, and he never made any secret of the pension which, even in the darkest days of exile, he paid to Favras's widow. However, in his notes written in exile, he also refers to a plan to escape, which may be different from the one presented by Mirabeau in October. How this can be reconciled with the plans to enter the Council is hard to understand unless Louis was to enter the Council while the king and queen fled, or, more likely, Favras put forward several wild projects at the same time, some of which Louis vaguely encouraged.

Another mystery in the Favras Affair is the relations between the different members of the Royal Family, which now, for the first time, become really important. Clearly, Louis was not only prepared, like any good politician, to lie his way out of a difficult situation (his speech at the Hôtel de Ville, and his manner of delivering it, left a profound impression of *dignité* and *raison* on sympathetic hearers), but also was prepared to pursue a policy of his own, independently of the king, although not of the queen. Moreover, since the king did not know of the contract with Mirabeau, according to Mirabeau's close friend and adviser the Comte de La Marck, his signature at the bottom of the document was forged with Louis's knowledge.[11] It is probable that he uses the word king, in this and in many other documents, to mean his view of royal authority – '*Le Roi, idée complexe*', as he was later to put it – rather than to mean the elder brother whom he disliked and with whom he had even less in common following Louis XVI's adoption of a uniquely self-sacrificing attitude to the Revolution. This was a horrifyingly disloyal and sinister policy. But, at the time, it must have been difficult for Louis, intelligent, ambitious and self-assured, not to think that he knew best how to save the monarchy. The king himself had occasionally admitted that Louis had a right to be consulted about its destiny.

Louis's attempts to enter the Council and, perhaps, to escape from Paris are unlikely to have been simply a plot against the king, since they were later copied by the king himself. Louis's speech in the Hôtel de Ville was followed a month later by a speech from Louis XVI in the National Assembly also supporting the Revolution. His approach to Mirabeau was imitated by Louis XVI in June 1790, and the king gave Madame de Favras a pension of 4,000 livres a year in 1791 – which makes it unlikely, to say the least, that the Favras Affair was directed solely against his authority or his ministers' lives.

In fact the situation was so alarming and so critical that not only Louis, but also Artois and, incredible as it may seem, the queen, had their own policies, backed by an impressive array of advisers (ex-ministers, marshals, successful politicians) and pursued independently of the king – over whom the queen had no political influence. Indeed it seems that Marie-Antoinette eventually bought Mirabeau's services for herself; in September 1790 Marie-Joséphine referred sourly to the '*triomphe de Marie-Antoinette*' in a letter to Madame de Gourbillon.[12]

The Favras Affair not only showed Louis to be disloyal to the king but also laid himself open to the accusation of being weak and cowardly, as Mirabeau wrote, or '*un mannequin*', as a more left-wing deputy put it. This charge, which would be repeated throughout Louis's life, was certainly true, if by weak is meant someone who could be influenced by advice and could change his mind. For example, even in the 1770s and 1780s, Cromot, whom Montbarey praised as '*un ministre . . . qui savez . . . faire parler le prince avec la dignité qui lui convient*' ('an administrator . . . who knows how to *make the prince speak* [italics added] with the dignity that befits him'), certainly exercised a strong influence over Louis. Moreover, Louis changed his mind frequently in the early years of the Revolution. He was in favour of maintaining the nobility as a separate order in June 1789; in December, perhaps as a result of Lévis's influence, he was trying to use the democratic party and Mirabeau; and by September 1790 he was in favour of a counter-revolution and the destruction of the new constitution. Mirabeau at least decided that Louis was just not worth serving and happily transferred his allegiance to the cause of Marie-Antoinette.[13] It is likely that, if he had still been alive, Louis's governor, the Duc de La Vauguyon, would have been pleased with his pupil's ability to withdraw into himself and to reason correctly; but it is unlikely that he would have been greatly impressed by Louis's endowment of a third quality he thought essential for princes, namely firmness.

Yet the accusations of weakness and malleability could easily be transformed into commendations for discrimination and adaptability. Louis had no pretensions to being another Peter the Great, seemingly capable of forcing the outside world into the shape he wanted it to be. Louis was an intelligent, rational prince, who knew perfectly well that royal willpower and royal desires would not, and could not, go very far on their own in the late eighteenth century. He obviously had to take some people's advice and it is to his credit that he took the advice of intelligent and realistic contemporaries, such as Cromot, Lévis and Mirabeau, who had the advantage of working for his interests at the same time as they were working for their own (unlike some of the king's advisers). Louis adopted the policy of giving a lot and of adapting himself to differing viewpoints and circumstances so that he could exploit every situation.

Except in 1787, Louis's policies did have one thread running through them, namely his concern for royal authority – a cause which he mentioned in 1774, in his instructions of March 1789, and in his speech of December 1789 at the Hôtel de Ville. Royal authority strengthened by his own entry into the Council was the cause which he served during the Revolution, when he decided the king, whom he thought was 'a fool' (Louis used the English word), was abandoning his own cause for the sake of a popular constitution. The advantage of royal authority as a cause and phrase, of course, is that it leaves the actual extent of royal power undetermined. But what was important for Louis was not so much that the king should actually run the Government, like Peter the Great or Frederick II, but that he should have the possibility of doing so, and that everything should be done in his name.

After the Favras Affair, Louis had little to do but continue his routine of Court and public life, and watch what the king called *la destruction de la royauté* proceed unhindered. No doubt in his correspondence with Artois (who had left France in 1789) and his frequent private talks with the queen he complained of the fate of their family and the strangely sacrificial policy of its head. In 1790 he witnessed the denunciation and abolition of the appanages. Not one of his Court officials bothered to defend them.

But the chief event of the last year Louis spent in Paris until 1814 was a demonstration outside the Luxembourg, on 22 February 1791, by a crowd of Parisians. They were alarmed that Louis might follow the example of his aunts who had left on 19 February and decide to emigrate. As with most public occasions,

Louis managed to turn this 'visit', as it was called, into a sort of triumph. He came down to meet a deputation of women from the crowd and declared that he was equally attached to the constitution and the king, and that he would sooner lose his life than separate himself from the person of the king. Another version of his reply to their anxious questions is: '*En doutez vous? Jamais je ne quitterai le Roi*' ('Can you doubt it? I will never leave the King'). Afterwards, in one of the last demonstrations of the legendary popularity of the French Monarchy, the women insisted on kissing Louis; one can hardly imagine Habsburgs or Hohenzollerns letting themselves be kissed by some of their poorest subjects, even supposing any of their subjects had wanted to kiss them. Finally, escorted by the cheering, torch-bearing crowd, Louis drove off for his evening visit to the Tuileries.[14]

Of course what Louis told the women was a lie – the one thing the Revolution taught almost all its participants was the necessity of deception. According to his own account, Louis had been thinking of escape since November 1790, and only the orders of the king and queen stopped him leaving in April 1791. It is interesting that in November 1790, after some dreadful scenes, Louis, who now said '*il n'y avait pas de quoi fouetter un chat*' ('there was nothing in it'), allowed Marie-Joséphine to have her adored Madame de Gourbillon back again. No one could doubt Madame de Gourbillon's devotion and resourcefulness in an emergency.

In the organization of his escape, Louis received confirmation of what he knew only too well already, namely how utterly alone a member of a ruling family is in a time of Revolution. The first three people he turned to for help refused this dangerous commission and he had to make sure that his *Capitaine des Gardes*, Lévis, and his *Premier Valet de Chambre* knew nothing about it. He could not trust his own servants, who preferred to support the Revolution rather than the dynasty (the Court in general was far from being counter-revolutionary).[15]

In the end Louis chose the Comte d'Avaray, son of one of his *Maîtres de la Garde-Robe* and a friend of Madame de Balbi, to direct the operation. By 20 June all was ready, and the escape was timed to coincide with that of the king, the queen, their two children and Madame Elizabeth. Louis's description of their last evening together in his account of his flight (written in the next few months and dedicated to his *libérateur* d'Avaray) is extremely moving for its simplicity and understatement. We should remember that not only the lives of the Royal Family, but also the fate of millions, foreign as well as French, and perhaps even subsequent attitudes to violent revolution as a means of achieving political ends, depended on the success of that night's events. '*Nous soupâmes et nous restâmes tous les cinq ensemble, jusqu'à près de onze heures. Quand le moment de la séparation fut venu, le Roi, qui jusque-là ne m'avait pas fait part du lieu où il allait, m'appella, me déclara qu'il allait à Montmédy, et m'ordonna positivement de me rendre à Longwy, en passant par les Pays-Bas . . . Enfin nous nous embrassâmes bien tendrement, et nous nous séparâmes très – persuadés, au moins de ma part, qu'avant quatre jours nous nous reverrions en lieu de sûreté.*' ('We had supper and stayed together until about eleven. When the moment of separation came, the King, who until then had not told me where he was going, called me aside and declared that he was going to Montmédy, and expressly ordered me to go to Longwy, via the Netherlands. . . Finally we all kissed each other with great feeling, and we separated, firmly convinced, at least on my side, that in four days' time we would meet again in a safe place.')

After his *coucher*, which he made shorter than usual by pretending to feel ill, Louis and d'Avaray, heavily disguised as English merchants, slipped out of the Petit Luxembourg, taking care to avoid the patrols of soldiers of the *Garde Nationale*. Dutifully repeating a few phrases in English, like 'Come along with me' or 'I am ready', they then set off on the first stage of their journey to freedom – always trying to remember to speak French with an English accent when addressing the coachman.[16] There had been a time when Louis was accompanied by three relays of horses and a suitable number of courtiers and servants when he went out for a drive. Now he was alone with d'Avaray and an English servant, leaving his old world of colossal wealth and elegant luxury, his beautiful palaces and enormous household, for a new world of poverty and uncertainty. On this journey, for the first time, private life and its ordinary problems – the next meal, where to spend the night, dependence on friends – became almost as important as Louis's rank as a member of the oldest and grandest dynasty in Europe.

Apart from a broken wheel at Soissons, they had a relatively easy and rapid journey interrupted only by stops at inns while their horses were changed. D'Avaray would not let Louis get down for fear that his distinctive Bourbon waddle – the gait for slowly proceeding through a crowded palace – would betray him. Finally, on 23 June, they reached Mons in the Austrian Netherlands, where they found Madame de Balbi and an almost equally welcome supper of cold chicken and Bordeaux. That night, Louis wrote, '*Pour la première fois depuis vingt mois et demi, je me couchai, sûr de n'être pas réveillé par quelque scène d'horreur.'* ('For the first time in over twenty months, I went to bed certain not to be woken up by a scene of horror.')[17]

CHAPTER IV

COBLENTZ 1791–1793

When Louis left France, he did much more than simply cross a frontier. He left one world for another – the world of the Revolution, of speeches, mobs and the new constitution, for the world of the Counter-Revolution, of speeches, nobles and appeals to *l'ancienne constitution*. Both worlds were hysterical, violent, and more than a little mad. Neither really cared about royal authority in comparison to the realization of their own political programmes. At first, Louis remained in a limbo between the two, making his way towards Luxembourg and Longwy as the king had ordered, rather than going to join his younger brother, the Comte d'Artois, the hero and chief of the Counter-Revolution, in Coblentz. However, at Marche-en-Famenne near Luxembourg (which he was delighted to find did not deserve to be called Marche-en-Famine: the food was really quite good), Louis received the news that the king had been arrested, and so decided '*de me rejoindre au Comte d'Artois*' ('to join up with the Comte d'Artois'). They met on 27 June at Brussels, and Louis now found out for himself exactly what joining the Counter-Revolution involved. On 29 June, with Artois at his side, he received the leading *émigrés* in the palace at Brussels. According to the English minister, he made a 'very well worded address and very pathetically delivered', in which he praised Artois for having long expressed 'those sentiments which he himself always professed, but which his state of imprisonment in Paris had prevented him from sooner displaying'. In other words, before this large and influential audience, Louis solemnly retracted his speech of 23 December 1789 at the Hôtel de Ville. It was rather a humiliating experience for such a proud and dignified prince, and one which, hardly surprisingly, he chose not to record in his account of these days.[1]

By 7 July, after a journey which had taken in a stop at Aix-la-Chapelle to confer with his old friend, Gustavus III, now a paladin of the Counter-Revolution, Louis arrived at Coblentz. This beautiful city, situated only fifty miles from the French frontier at the confluence of the Rhine and the Moselle, was the residence of Louis's uncle the Elector of Trier, the only one of Louis's relations, in his twenty-three years of exile, who ever really did anything to help him. And for the next twelve months it became the head-quarters of Louis's and Artois's political, military and diplomatic activities.

The two short syllables of Coblentz have aroused so much loathing and contempt that the nature of the enterprise which was directed from that quiet German city has been obscured and confused with other forces. 'Coblentz' was not the same as 'the Emigration'. Most *émigrés* left France after 1792 and never went near Coblentz, while *les Princes*, as Louis and Artois were often known, preferred many of their supporters to remain in France. For example, they wrote to the Marquis de La Rouerie, head of a Breton conspiracy, to denounce emigration. Nor was Coblentz simply the Counter-Revolution in arms. Many extreme Counter-Revolutionaries, for example Peltier, or the Baron de Breteuil, stayed in France or the Austrian Netherlands, and had little contact with Coblentz. Nor was Coblentz the *Ancien Régime* in arms. Many of the officials, even the Court officials, of the *Ancien Régime* adapted surprisingly well to the Revolutions. For example Chérin, the genealogist who had been responsible for checking the ancestry of families who wanted to be presented at Court, became a general of the Republic. Silvestre, Louis's librarian and *Premier Valet de Garde-Robe*, became an official of the Minstry of the Interior. Of the fifty-one hereditary dukes, twenty emigrated and served the princes, but at least twenty-seven stayed in France. Even among Louis's own thirty-five senior Court officials only ten emigrated and served the princes.

Thus, in going to Coblentz, Louis had entered a new world, whose difference from the old Court was soon symbolized by changes in his household. He replaced his two *Capitaines des Gardes*, Lévis and the Comte de Moreton-Chabrillant, who both still supported the Revolution, by the faithful d'Avaray and Comte Charles de Damas, one of his *Gentilshommes d'Honneur*, loyal, charming, much-loved, but not particularly intelligent. That August the difference between Louis's old Court and Coblentz was again demonstrated by a remarkable incident when, much to Louis's and Madame de Balbi's disgust, his former *Capitaine des Suisses*, the son of the Prince de Montbarey, was forced to leave Coblentz because of his allegedly 'constitutional' views.

'Coblentz' was essentially a particular group of people, of varied social backgrounds who were reacting to the Revolution in a particular way – active, enterprising and, above all, military. And although a majority of them came from the old military nobility, in particular the provincial nobility, Coblentz did find considerable support from other groups such as the old *noblesse de robe* and the Third Estate, some of whose deputies (Guilhermy, Martin d'Auch) began to appear in the city in the autumn. In the summer of 1792, of the 24,004 troups in the princes' army, 1,414 were *Volontaires du Tiers*, 6,268 were *Troupes soldées*, almost all of whom would have been non-nobles, while few regiments were exclusively noble.[2]

The active and military nature of Coblentz fitted in with the extremely powerful trend, in late eighteenth-century Europe, towards an increasingly military society. This trend had already affected Louis's life. His education had had a military side, and this is reflected in the three drawings done by him at the age of eleven of Vauban's fortifications (now in the Bibliothèque Nationale) and in his libraries which contained many works on military subjects. Louis had also acknowledged the trend towards a more military society when he decided in 1778 that all knights of the Order of Saint Lazare, of which he was Grand Master, would have to be military or naval officers. However, he had not bothered to pay much attention to the three regiments of which he was honorary colonel, *Monsieur-Infanterie*, the *Dragons de Monsieur* and the *Carabiniers de Monsieur*, except for the smartest of them, the last. But at Coblentz almost everyone, even members of the *noblesse de robe* and Louis himself, now for the first time in their lives saw themselves as soldiers, and habitually wore uniform. Louis and Artois held Court on Sundays and Thursdays in the Elector's beautiful neoclassical palace (which is still there). But it was a Court of a different, more military and official sort to what they were used to. In accordance with what one *émigré* rather contemptuously called '*l'étiquette usitée en Allemagne*' ('the etiquette prevalent in the great military monarchies to the east'), they invited to their table or their gambling parties *officiers d'un grade supérieur*. '*Les épaulettes décident les convives*' ('Epaulettes decide who is invited'), noted one astonished arrival from France, and indeed there could be no greater contrast with Versailles.

In this new world where political loyalties and military rank were beginning to be more important than social status, it was almost embarrassingly clear that he was overshadowed by his younger, more popular brother, the Comte d'Artois. Although Artois often appeared frivolous, silly and irrational, he was an extremely forceful, self-confident, ambitious, charming and persuasive prince. Years later Artois would use an intermediary to deal with Louis, for fear that he would *s'impatienter* (lose his temper). It is doubtful if such considerations restrained him at Coblentz. Fersen's view of him in July 1791 would do equally well for any other month of the Emigration: '*D'Artois parle toujours, n'écoutant jamais, étant sûr de tout, ne parlant que de force et point de négociations.*' ('D'Artois is always talking, never listening, sure of everything, speaking only of force, not of negotiation.') Such a personality, coupled with his reputation for Counter-Revolutionary purity and his possession of two healthy sons, made Artois, rather than his silent, moderate, fat and childless elder brother, as a contemporary noted, '*le chef véritable*' at Coblentz.[3]

And when Artois went to Pillnitz in August 1791 to confer with the Holy Roman Emperor and the King of Prussia, the difference in the brothers' positions made itself all too apparent. '*Quoique Monsieur reçoive journellement tout le monde, on s'aperçoit bien cependant de l'absence de M. le Comte d'Artois. L'affluence n'est pas si grande ...*' ('Although Monsieur receives everyone daily, the absence of M. le Comte d'Artois makes itself felt. Those who come are not so many...') Not only in the outer life of Coblentz, but also in the inner workings of its government machine, that vast apparatus which Louis called '*une des plus grandes machines qui aient jamais existé*' ('one of the greatest machines which has ever existed'), and which already had its own Council of Ministers and its own agents at almost every European Court, there is much evidence to show that Louis was number two. Fersen thought he was '*entièrement subjugué*', while in May 1792 Louis himself told Lord Malmesbury that he was often 'overruled'. The chief minister of the Emigration was Calonne, Louis's old enemy from 1787, with whom he never got on. Calonne was devoted to Artois and had frequent rows with the one member of the princes' Council whom Louis may have chosen, a good friend of Madame de Balbi, the Marquis de Jaucourt.[4] When the Elector of Trier was worried about the threat to law and order that the *émigrés* might present, he wrote to Artois, not Louis. It was Artois, not Louis, who wrote the immense majority of their letters to their cousin the King of Spain; one of them even contains the words *nous* and *notre* – Louis's approval could just be assumed. An entry in the diary of the Prince de Condé, the formidable head of the most warlike and Counter-Revolutionary branch of the Bourbon dynasty (see Table 2) shows himself, Artois and Calonne holding a council while Louis holds an *assemblée*. If ever there was a period of Louis's life when he could be called a *mannequin*, it was surely when he was living at Coblentz.

One can only speculate on what Louis's reactions were. He must have resented his inferior position, although his own account of the first few days of his emigration speaks warmly of Artois as his *ami* (a word he never used for Louis XVI), and expresses deep gratitude to Artois for helping him to learn about the Counter-Revolution.[5] However, perhaps this remark only shows that Louis, like Talleyrand and many other contemporaries, felt that words should be used to hide rather than express his feelings. It is extremely unlikely that Louis approved of all the measures being taken at Coblentz. and he reacted by withdrawing into private life.

Madame de Balbi had joined him in Coblentz, and the Comte d'Espinchal, an *émigré* attached to the Prince de Condé, noted that '*Monsieur passe chez elle tout le temps qu'il n'est pas occupé d'affaires*' ('Monsieur devotes to her all the time that is not occupied with public affairs'). It is significant that in the house Louis and Artois shared in the country until they moved to the town of Coblentz for the winter, whereas Artois and Calonne lived on the second floor, Louis and Madame de Balbi had the first. They usually spent the evenings together playing word games and gambling (Madame de Balbi's favourite pastime) with a small circle of friends from nine o'clock until midnight. One of the most prominent of these friends was now d'Avaray: Louis says he ceased to behave as a prince with him after their escape together from Paris. These intimate supper parties, which could end up with them all going off to a country inn and gambling till dawn, were naturally not very popular with those *émigrés* who were not invited; and Madame de Balbi with her imperious tone made herself thoroughly unpopular. However, when Espinchal was invited he enjoyed it very much, admitting that Madame de Balbi could be an excellent hostess. He was also overjoyed to find that '*On y voit les princes tant qu'on veut, ainsi que tous les gens marquants passant à Coblentz*' ('one sees the princes there with absolute freedom, and one meets all the important people passing through Coblentz').

One person who was not invited was Marie-Joséphine, who had escaped from Paris at the same time as Louis with the aid of Madame de Gourbillon, always capable and resourceful. Marie-Joséphine remained at Coblentz, outspoken, sarcastic and neglected, until April 1792 when she went to Turin to stay with her father. Her journey was outrageously expensive and shows together with Madame de Balbi's supper parties that in the new political and military world of Coblentz, Louis had not lost all the habits and assumptions of his golden youth. However, she took Madame de Balbi, still her *Dame d'Atours* with her and so Louis was left with much more time to devote to politics. Espinchal wrote that his way of life '*a entièrement changé*' ('has changed completely').

Since Coblentz was primarily a particular way of reacting to the Revolution, its politics should be understood as essentially those of a party, with all that that involves in the way of party spirit, party intrigues and party government. Artois and Louis were at the head of this party, as they themselves realized and pointed out, not only because of their place in the order of succession, but also because of their party's overriding need for leadership. Because they were party leaders and princes at the same time, Coblentz, as well as being a reaction to the Revolution, saw the beginning of the long process by which a large proportion of the French elites retreated from their aggressive and hostile attitude to royal authority in the 1780s to one of cooperation and service. Moreover, the aristocrats now at Coblentz had been thoroughly frightened by the Revolutions, the abolition of the nobility, the burning of *châteaux* and the triumph of the democratic party. So they were now prepared to accept a much more subordinate position under royal authority than in the days when they had talked about *loi naturelle* and had wanted to dominate the Royal Government through aristocratic estates.[6]

But there was, of course, a quid pro quo. The programme adopted by the princes had to reflect many of the aristocrats' desires, to maintain the divisions of orders and reject what had taken place since the *Séance Royale* of 23 June 1789. A document which is particularly revealing of the continued although increasingly muted *choc de l'aristocratie avec la monarchie*, even at Coblentz, as well as of the restrictions their position as heads of a party imposed on the princes, is the notes hastily written down in November 1791 when it was thought that the king had escaped from Paris. The princes must not forget what they owe to their honour, '*l'engagement qu'ils ont contracté avec les Iers ordres de l'état, avec les braves chevaliers français qui sont venus se réunir sous leur bannière, avec la Nation entière . . .*' ('the *obligation* [italics added] they have contracted with the first orders of the state, with the brave French *chevaliers* who have hastened to range themselves under their banner, with the whole Nation. . .'). *Engagement* is not a word Bourbons had been used to hearing before 1789, and the notes go on to say that they must insist on suitable ministers, on the disarming of the *Garde Nationale*, and on the reestablishment of the non-constitutional priests, the old

taxes and heredity of office. Evidently the aristocrats of Coblentz
were far from sure their princes were 'aristocratic' enough.

In this frenetic, violent, over-confident, aristocratic, Counter-
Revolutionary world, what was Coblentz's attitude to the king
and queen? As so often in Louis's life, we come across layer after
layer of reality and deceit, in which the Royal Family's own loving
and respectful letters to each other (always, one gets the impression, written with posterity's and often contemporaries' reactions
in mind) are the least revealing of guides. What one needs are the
sincere and immediate comments of someone who knew all the
Royal Family well like, for example, the Baron de Vioménil. He
was constantly carrying messages between the queen and the
princes, attended the king's *lever* and *coucher* in July 1792 (it
took more than a revolution to alter this part of Court life), and
was mortally wounded in the defence of the Tuileries in August
1792. The extraordinary thing is that, until the appearance of M.
and Mme. Girault de Coursac's magazine *Découverte*, no one
had tried to find out what the different policies of the king and
the Royal Family were.

It seems clear that, as in 1789–91, each member of the Royal
Family had his or her own policy, which they pursued without
regard for each other's interests or, least of all, the orders of the
king. Towards the queen and her party Louis's policy was one of
secret, and occasionally open, hostility. He repeatedly wrote to
her chief adviser, formerly one of the king's most trusted ministers,
the Baron de Breteuil, to try to persuade him to stop acting as the
head of a separate, pro-Austrian party based on Brussels. On 20
February 1792, in what was probably his last communication, he
wrote to the queen ('*ma chère soeur*') saying that he alone was
the king's true representative and that he alone should be in
charge of the Royal Family's attempts to counter the Revolution.[7]
Thus, even before the departure of Madame de Balbi, he was
prepared to act as the head, at least on the surface, of the party
of Coblentz.

At the end of this letter, Louis says that, of course, the queen
can show it to the king. But it is extremely unlikely that she did.
As Louis and Artois were well aware, the king's policy was different from the queen's. Why else, for example, would one of
their closest advisers, the Marquis de Lambert, write that Breteuil,
who had the queen's confidence, '*est dans l'opinion le ministre
accrédité par le Roy, et, ... d'après cette opinion [cela ne fût-il
pas vrai] ...*' ('is the minister accredited by the king in the opinion
of the public and ... in accordance with this opinion [even if it
is not true]').

The king's policy did not, understandably enough, involve trusting his brothers or his wife. The *Pouvoirs* dated 7 July 1791, which Louis and Artois received that month, were probably forged, and in any case extremely limited. The private letters they claimed to have received, to the King of Prussia and others were probably non-existent. This flurry of lies and deceit was designed in the summer of 1791, when the king and queen were La Fayette's prisoners in the Tuileries, to try to help Louis become regent. Gustavus III even wanted him to have his own *Garde des Sceaux* and departmental ministers.[8] But the refusal of the King of Prussia and the Holy Roman Emperor, and the relaxation of the king's imprisonment in September, made this impossible.

The noblest course for Louis to follow would perhaps have been to return to France, as the king urged him. '*Votre véritable place est auprès de moi.*') ('Your true place is at my side.') Thereby he might have weakened the frenzy of Coblentz and he might have strengthened the king's hand in the king's desperate attempts to inspire confidence and rally public opinion. Barnave, one of the politicians with the most influence in the *Assemblée Législative*, even wrote secretly to the queen that if Monsieur returns, all is over.

But of course this was sheer self-deception, or deception. The situation was such that the odds were already heavily weighted against royal power. As Louis and Artois pointed out in the public letter they wrote to the king in September 1791, in which they made quite clear their differences with their elder brother, the new constitution excluded the king from any share in legislative power. They repeated the old arguments of the Princes du Sang in the early 1770s, claiming that, *dépositaire usufructier du trône*, the king had no right to destroy the old constitution. In a later letter, coldly refusing to obey his brother's order to return, Louis made the terrible accusation that '*vous dégradez le trône de votre propre main*' ('you are degrading the throne with your own hands').[9]

The constitution was indeed fundamentally anti-monarchical, extending the elective principle to some of the highest posts in the kingdom, even to judges and bishops. Many of the new deputies were from the beginning of the legislative session on 1 October 1791 openly hostile to the few remaining signs of royal authority, such as the continued existence of a shadow of a Court. They even denounced the constitutional ministers, and the officers of the new *Garde Constitutionelle du Roi*. The shape of things to come was soon shown with appalling clarity. On 18 November an ultra-Revolutionary, Pétion, was elected to the key position of Mayor of Paris; and the Assembly refused to punish those responsible for massacres in Avignon where sixty political prisoners had been killed in cold blood – two and a half years before the start of the Reign of Terror.

While Louis's decision not to return can be justified on a political level, on the personal level it does show an appalling indifference to the fate of the king and his family. Louis was far more concerned with the future of royal authority than with the present position of his brother the king. Indeed, he and Artois wrote to Louis XVI in September 1791 that '*nous irons droit notre chemin*' ('we will stick to our path') regardless of your orders. But their path was paved with acts headed *de par le Roi et par l'ordre des Princes*, and their party drew its strength, as one of their advisers wrote, from the opinion, which they encouraged, that '*si le Roi était libre, il approuverait toutes leurs démarches*' ('if the King were free he would approve all their acts').

Even more compromising than the vague phrase *de par le Roi* were Louis's and Artois's private assurances to French officers in February 1792 that '*celui de qui nous avons à coeur de suivre les intentions*' ('he whose intentions it is our heartfelt wish to follow'), i.e. the King, wanted Strasbourg to be handed over to the princes. Such assurances were not only untrue but were a real stab in the back to Louis XVI, whose policy was based on his efforts to win the confidence of the nation by the observance of the constitution. To pretend that he really wanted to hand over Strasbourg made him appear a traitor whose existence was of no use to anyone. Louis was indeed practising one lesson he had been taught as a child, namely that princes should see men in relation to their public utility, rather than for their private merits. It is to be feared that Louis no longer saw his brother as being very useful to the cause of the French Monarchy, and indeed, after their conference at Aix-la-Chapelle in July, Louis's great friend, Gustavus III, had written that it did not matter whether it was Louis XVI, Louis XVII or Charles who was restored so long as the monarchy was restored.[10]

However, Louis had also hoped that if the king wanted to accept the constitution he would do it in a frontier stronghold, surrounded by loyal *Gardes du Corps*. Thereby Louis showed himself both realistic and capable of thinking of the king's best interests. Many advocates of the constitution also thought that the king's adherence of it would only really be accepted by public opinion as sincere and voluntary if announced outside Paris, when he was in complete control of his guard.

Louis and Artois were also able to convince many *émigrés*

that they were acting not only in the long-term interests of the French Monarchy, but also in the king's own short-term interests. As Louis and Artois wrote to him, with disarming frankness, no one was likely to kill him if it was going to bring them closer to the throne. But this was to attribute to the Revolutionaries more rationality than they possessed. The princes' plan, after the king had accepted the constitution, was that while they carried on the glorious task of raising armies to fight the Revolution, the king should safely swim with the Revolutionary tide and go along with each new manifestation of public, or rather Parisian, opinion. Thus they were equally opposed to the efforts of the queen and her party, which would, as Louis wrote to her, be hopelessly compromising if they were found out (but no more so than his own), and to those of the moderate constitutionalists. In a letter to Catherine II they described the moderates as a party which '*quoiqu'un peu moins sanguinaire que l'autre n'en est peut-être que plus dangereuse*' ('although a little less bloodthirsty than the other [the Jacobins] is therefore perhaps even more dangerous').[11]

These are indeed immoderate sentiments which show that Louis had caught the infectious extremism of Coblentz. But it was in fact the king's and the moderates' attempts to keep the Jacobins out of the ministry, their denunciations of the Jacobin Club and veto of various Revolutionary measures, which led directly to the storming of the Tuileries on 10 August 1792. The mixture of callousness and royalism in Coblentz's attitude to the king, as well as its ridiculous optimism, is perhaps best expressed in a letter from Condé to Calonne, as the *émigrés* were beginning their invasion of France: '*Pourvu qu'on ne le tue pas, il se relevera bientôt de tout . . . je vous compte à Paris dans quinze jours, et nous chanterons le Te Déum.*' ('Provided they don't kill him, he will soon get over everything. . . See you in Paris in fifteen days, and we will sing the Te Deum together.')

If they wanted the restoration of *l'ancienne constitution*, Louis and Artois did not, however, despite their many protests to the contrary, intend to return to the state of powerlessness they had endured as young princes. Did Louis really expect the queen to believe him when, echoing his and Artois's proclamations, he wrote that all they wanted was to restore the king to his legitimate authority, and denied that they wanted part of his authority for themselves. In reality they wanted to dominate the king and his Council, in order to carry out the programme of their party – rather like the Whigs under George II, or George III's uncle, the Duke of Cumberland, in 1765. In November 1791, Calonne wrote that the princes should enter the Council (Louis's old ambition of

1774 and 1789) only when they had made sure that the ministers shared their views. In other words they wanted a ministry of their own party. In July 1792 Louis told Condé not to worry about what the king wanted, since he would only be freed sometime after the invasion '*et alors notre parti sera trop fort pour qu'il fût possible, à nous de dédire et à lui de nous contrarier*' ('and then our party will be too strong for us to back down or for him to thwart us').[12] It is revealing that Louis saw himself as distinct not only from the king, but also even as late as July 1792, from his own party. The situation was extremely fluid, everyone was after power and its rewards, everyone felt it was just within their grasp. No one foresaw what actually happened.

The day-to-day functioning of the party of Coblentz masterminded by Calonne and Artois was very disorganized, as the state and content of Calonne's hopelessly jumbled papers at the Public Record Office, leaping from fantasy to bankruptcy through endless zones of illusion, suggest. Essentially their activities had two aspects, first the raising of armed forces, and second the application of diplomatic pressure on the European powers to persude them to invade France. The two were linked, since to raise an army costs money and foreign powers were the princes' main source of income. Of the 6,884,460 livres they received in 1791, for example, two million came from Catherine II, and 1,888,874 from the King of Prussia. In May 1792 their cousin the King of Naples gave them 1,800,000 livres and the King of Prussia 500,000 livres. But such sums were simply not enough to pay for their army which they told Catherine II, cost 19.8 million to keep in the field in 1792 alone.

So they turned to forgery: it was the princes, not Pitt or Napoleon I, who were the first to use forgery of their enemy's currency (the Revolutionary *assignats*) as a political weapon. Their plan has all the trappings of a traditional cloak and dagger melodrama. The chief forger was a notorious crook with the splendid name of Harel la Vertu. *Émigré* priests wore themselves out in the holy work. Sacks of forged currency were carried off at dead of night from the factory at Neuwied on the Rhine. The whole process, which was transferred to Great Britain after 1793, shows how low party politics could drag the princes. The forgeries were not even entirely successful and were being recognized by the summer of 1792.[13]

However, with the help of these forgeries, which were planned in November 1791, and well underway in the following spring, the princes somehow managed to survive. But their financial situation was always desperate after 1791. In April 1792, Calonne could moan: '*La politique devient presque indifférente; c'est de l'argent qu'il nous faut.*' ('Politics is becoming almost unimportant; it is money that we need.') In June Condé wrote to him; '*Au nom de Dieu envoyez-moi au moins 24,000 livres.*' ('In the name of God send me at least 24,000 livres.') All this made Louis's continued habit of playing cards for money after supper rather inappropriate. However, now as when he was a prince, he was far less extravagant than Artois, whose personal expenses in early 1792 were over twice Louis's.

Most of the princes' money went on the army which in 1791 began to assemble in the Rhineland. In August 1791 Louis and Artois issued, *de part le Roi et par l'ordre des Princes*, regulations for the army's quarters. They also recreated all the regiments of the old *Maison Militaire du Roi*, the *Chevau-Légers* and *Gendarmes de la Garde*, and the *Mousquetaires Gris et Noirs*, which had been abolished by Louis XVI in 1775 and 1787. It was a clear sign of what their attitude to his authority would be if they ever assumed power. In addition, not only their own, but also the king's *Gardes du Corps* were recreated in Coblentz, to the fury of the king and the queen. By December 1791, there were 1,200 *Gardes du Corps*, of whom 400 were newcomers, and in all 7,838 troops.[14]

In January 1792, however, the king took steps to remove this armed threat to the constitution from the French frontiers and his diplomacy proved more effective than his brothers'. The Elector of Trier hastened to disperse units which might bring war to his peaceful Electorate; by 20 February he was able to write to the Holy Roman Emperor that only 420 *Gardes du Corps* were still there. Louis and Artois and the *émigrés*, many of whom found it extremely hard to find any German state to receive them (it was now that they tried to seize Strasbourg), were in despair. This was also the time when the king sanctioned the Assembly's decree confiscating the princes' property in France, so that their last link with their skeleton staffs and abandoned palaces in Paris was broken. In March some *émigrés* were so desperate that they wanted to *forcer les Princes* to invade France – anything seemed acceptable to get out of the impasse.

Ironically the princes were rescued from an impossible position in large part by the stupidity and aggressiveness of the Revolutionaries themselves, who created a situation where the king had to declare war on the King of Hungary (as the new Austrian Emperor was called until his coronation at Frankfurt) on 20 April. On 24 April, to his eternal shame, Louis wrote to Madame de Balbi '*j'en suis ravi*' ('I am delighted'). But like almost everyone else in France and Europe, he thought that the time had come for a showdown between the Revolution and its enemies, and he was convinced that his side would win.

The *émigré* army was soon reassembled. At the end of May, the princes estimated that they had 19,279 men, and by the end of July 24,004. This was a very impressive force considering the princes were in debt and in exile. And its size and fervour were due to the *émigrés*' feeling that they were fighting for their own personal interests – the traditional constitution in which they felt they had had such a prominent place their career prospects, which they thought were threatened by the competition of the democrats, and in general the cause of law and order – more than to any profound concern for royal authority. However, despite frequent complaints about the size of the princes' staff and the extravagance of their way of life (complaints which often came from people attached to the Condé family, or from the Prince de Condé himself who thought that he was the only serious warrior of the Bourbon family), service in this army did add a sense of personal loyalty to many of its officers' hitherto rather distant and tepid feelings for the Royal Family. Among the officers were many future ministers of Louis XVIII, for example Blacas, Chateaubriand, Richelieu, and de Serre.[15]

At Coblentz there was a tremendous sense of being in the same party together. This was heightened by a conviction that theirs was a just and noble cause and cemented by the material sacrifices everyone had had to make owing to the laws against *émigrés*' property enacted in February 1792. In the frenzied, partisan atmosphere of Coblentz the presence of the two royal brothers, whom, before 1789, most *émigrés* would have been lucky to glimpse through a carriage window or on the way to Sunday Mass at Versailles, had an immense effect. Louis and Artois invited *émigrés* to dinner. They talked to them. In some proclamations they even called them their *amis*, just as Louis had proclaimed his *amitié* for the nobility of Anjou in 1789. In his speech in January telling the *Gardes du Corps* that they had to disperse, Louis called them, '*nos braves compagnons d'armes, Français qui n'ont que l'honneur pour guide*' ('our brave brothers in arms, Frenchmen who have no guide but honour'). Especially after the departure of Madame de Balbi, he began to lose some of the reserve which had been such a mark of his character as a prince. He was *plus parlant* and was prepared to '*vous écouter avec attention lorsqu'on s'adresse à lui et de se montrer avec la dignité qui lui convient*' ('listen attentively when he is addressed and behaves with suitable dignity'). It is interesting, then, that despite all this emotional involvement, and all the commitment to a common cause, Louis crossed out the phrase *votre bon ami* from a speech he made to the *émigrés* in the summer of 1792.[16] Was he perhaps not entirely sure that their friendship was worth having?

The cause of Coblentz was a European cause as well as a French one; it had a particular appeal for the aristocrats of Europe who were delighted to help what they thought was the cause of their social order, and were flattered to be of use to such dignified and grateful members of the House of Bourbon. Throughout his exile, Louis was helped by aristocrats' continued respect and love for the French Monarchy. They had learned to love this from literature (Voltaire's *Henriade* and *Siècle de Louis XIV*, and the letters of Madame de Sévigné with their unforttgettable glimpses of the early days of Versailles, were as popular abroad as they were in France) as well as from their own visits to France. Moreover, Louis, calm, dignified, intelligent and extremely well-mannered, was very much the sort of prince they expected to see, perhaps rather more so than some of the members of their own royal families. Thus Lord Malmesbury, whom Pitt sent on a mission to Coblentz, found Louis 'the most steady and reasonable' of the *émigrés* and wrote of him and Artois that 'it is impossible to see them and the evenness of their temper and patience without being anxious and interested about them'. It was a reaction similar to that of the Duc de Croÿ at Louis's wedding twenty-one years earlier. By his outward behaviour and manner, Louis could draw people to his cause who might otherwise have been indifferent or hostile.

Edmund Burke saw the cause of Coblentz as the cause of civilization. Louis wrote him a suitably flattering letter, and his son became one of the princes' agents in England. The Prince of Hohenlohe raised a regiment for the princes' army and even lent his name as surety for a loan. The Prince of Neuwied was extremely helpful, Salm and Hesse-Darmstadt raised regiments, and three of the Irish regiments in the French army came over: descendants of the Jacobites provided some of the later Bourbons' most devoted adherents. Two of the eleven members of the princes' rather illusory Council, the Prince of Nassau-Siegen and Prince Xavier of Saxony, were foreigners. And the Elector of Trier refused to throw out his nephews, as well as their regiments, because '*je me déshonorerais devant toute l'Europe*' ('I would dishonour myself in the eyes of all Europe'). It was a feeling which was to be Louis's chief guarantee of shelter in other countries in the years to come.[17] Public opinion, both French and European,

played an enormous part in every stage of Louis's career. The eyes
of *toute l'Europe* followed him everywhere.

However, the monarchies of Europe were less enthusiastic and
less impressed than the aristocrats. Although some were prepared
to provide subsidies for the princes no monarchy, except perhaps
the Russian and the Spanish, had any interest in seeing the revival
of the strong Bourbon monarchy which before 1787 had been
altogether too grand, too powerful and too interfering (in Holland, in America, and in the Mediterranean) for comfort. It took
all the stupidity and violence of the Revolutionaries, as well as
the efforts of the queen and her party, to get Austria and Prussia
to invade France.

When the *émigrés* finally left Coblentz in early August, setting
off in a cloud of unpaid debts and unreliable promissory notes,
they were very much under the control of the Austro-Prussian
army of 80,000 commanded by the Duke of Brunswick: *'entièrement soumis aux puissances coalisées'* ('completely controlled by
the coalition'), as Artois complained in July; *'en seconde ligne'*,
as Louis complained in August. The foreigners went on ahead
and did the fighting; the *émigrés* ingloriously followed on behind.
However, they were wildly happy. They were on their way home
in triumph, and even Louis felt exalted. He wrote: *'Je me porte
bien, nous partons mercredi, et vogue la galère.'* ('I am in good
health, we are leaving on Wednesday, and devil take the
consequences.')

What were their aims when on 29 August 1792 they finally
reentered France? They did not want to restore the *Ancien Régime* in its entirety. All such accusations endlessly levied against
the princes and their adherents during the Emigration ignore two
facts. First, the reforms of Louis XVI meant that the France of
1774 and the France of 1787 or 1789 were so different from each
other that there was no single *Ancien Régime* to restore. Second,
France before 1789 had been so decentralized, had presented so
many barriers to royal authority and given so little institutional
power to the nobility that neither the princes nor their followers
were likely to want to return to the past.

Instead in the declaration they issued on 8 August, they denounced everything that had happened since 1789 and referred
to themselves as liberators come to fulfil the demands for reform
contained in the *Cahiers* of 1789. They disclaimed any desire for
private vengeance. *'Nous sommes pour vous plutôt que contre
vous'* ('We are for you rather than against you'), they claimed and
this strange, convincing and rather moving declaration ends with
a *cri de coeur* which may well come from Louis, the rational

prince, himself: '*Espérons . . . que l'empire des chimères va finir, que le bandeau tombera de tous les yeux, que la raison reprendra tous ses droits.*' ('Let us hope . . . that the reign of illusions will cease, that the band will fall from every eye, that *reason* [italics added] will recover all its rights.') The *émigrés* felt they were not just fighting for their party but for law and order, humanity and reason. In his rather childish message to the *Assemblée Legislative* in December 1791 refusing to return to France, Louis had again invoked *sens commun* and *raison* in contrast to the folly of the Revolutionary madmen in Paris. After all, there was nothing more irrational and counter-productive than a revolution, whose violence so often ensured the failure of its ends, and which had betrayed the hopes of 1789 by turning against royal authority. After 1790, Louis always remained one of those people for whom violent revolution is worse than a crime, it is a mistake: '*Je haïs toutes les révolutions parce que rien ne cause tant de maux aux peuples.*' ('I hate all revolutions because nothing brings greater unhappiness to the people.') Or, as he wrote to Madame de Balbi: '*Ah! La vilaine chose qu'une Revolution!*' In their attempt to defeat the French Revolution, Louis and Artois planned to disarm the bourgeois (i.e. the *Garde Nationale*), restore the municipal officials of 1 January 1789 and institute exceptional justice in the form of *jurisdiction prévôtale* and the *maréchaussée*.[18]

When they crossed the frontier, however, they left the dream-world of plans and declarations for the real world of a corner of north-eastern France (see Map 1) in the cold, wet autumn of 1792. The welcome they received there is extremely hard to assess since, of course, all the sources reflect the political views of their authors. But it is clear that it was by no means universally hostile. Although Thionville was opposed to them, Longwy was not – Louis was acclaimed with cries of '*Vive le Roi*', according to an English observer, and he wrote that he would never forget the welcome he had received there. Small towns like Dun, Briey and Etain were friendly, while Verdun, one of the strongest fortresses in the east of France, which surrendered amazingly easily on 3 September, was cool but not wholly opposed. In practice, faced with the reality of the new France, and above all with the difficulties of supplying their army, the princes were much less counter-revolutionary than they had promised. The old *curé* was restored in Longwy, the old bishop in Verdun, but the municipalities and taxes remained essentially unchanged. What were destroyed were the outward signs of revolution – the uniforms of the *Garde Nationale*, the tricolour cockades and the trees of liberty.[19]

However, the princes were unbending to their unrepentant political opponents. Claude, a former deputy of the *Assemblée Constituante*, was put in prison simply for refusing to sign an address of welcome to Louis, while a cold, cruel letter from Louis shows that he wanted to get hold of his old enemy La Fayette, whom he thought responsible for '*presque tous les crimes*' of the Revolution, until La Fayette could be judged '*suivant la rigueur des lois*'. Indeed, throughout the campaign, the princes kept begging their allies to practise and to threaten French towns with '*la plus grande sévérité*' or '*la plus extrème riguer*' if resistance continued. They believed that a revolution which had been ruined by violence had to be ended by violence, or at least the threat of violence. Indeed such threats had opened the gates of Verdun.

For Louis to use this violent language is a further sign not only of his personal hostility to La Fayette, but also of the degree to which he had accepted the comfortingly extreme mental world and illusions of the *émigrés* – that moderate revolutionaries like La Fayette were the most dangerous, that one man could be responsible for *presque tous les crimes* of the Revolution. One illusion which was being shattered, however, was that they were within grasping distance of the power for which they had waited so long.

Verdun had become the capital of the invaders, a new Coblentz as madly social and dedicated to political intrigue as the first. But at the long discussions on the composition of the government and on a regency that took place in the second week of September, the princes clearly emerged weaker than the queen's party headed by the Baron de Breteuil, who was soon surrounded by a court of admirers. His real strength was the support of the foreign powers who thought, like so many other people, that he represented the king. Calonne, on the other hand, was blamed for the appalling poverty and disorder in the *émigré* army. In consequence the King of Prussia and the Russian ambassador told Louis that he could only be regent if Calonne was dismissed, and Breteuil became chief minister. At a conference on 7 September, Louis declared that he should be regent, since his brother, the Revolutionaries' most precious hostage, was bound to be taken to the south (a belief that was at the root of the Girondins' association with Federalism). All Louis said he wanted was the *salut de la chose publique* and – a blatant lie – that '*il serait au désespoir de rien faire qui pût aggraver les malheurs et les chagrins du Roi son frère, en contrariant la moindre de ses volontés*' ('he would be in despair if he did anything which might increase the misfortunes and sufferings of the King his brother, by disobeying the least of his wishes'). But Breteuil was opposed to the regency of a prince whose confidence he felt he would never obtain, even when his deadly enemy, Calonne, left on 15 September.[20]

These discussions were inconclusive, but in any case the comfortable certainties on which they were based soon turned to doubt and despair. Although some of the towns and villages were relatively friendly to the *émigrés*, the peasants, the class which had benefited most from the Revolutions, were more hostile. Lévis, who like many other constitutional monarchists had now joined the *émigrés*, found the peasants extremely hostile. An English observer found 'in the great body of the people ... a general, I might almost say a universal, disinclination to *la bonne cause*'. As a result the *émigrés*' behaviour could be appalling when they did not get what they wanted. They burnt six villages for refusing supplies on their retreat.

The difference between the Revolution and the Counter-Revolution is shown by the fact that, at the same time, the Republican Government was paying people to carry out the barbaric September massacres of hundreds of prisoners in Paris: both sides were violent, but Revolutionary violence was crueller. Not only were the peasants hostile, but there was none of the mass desertions from the army which, from the evidence of his proclamations, Louis had been expecting. The garrisons of Longwy and Verdun remained resolutely hostile even after their surrender. No regiments abandoned the tricolour for the white flag of the Royalists. At the battle of Valmy, in which the *emigré* army as usual was not allowed to participate, the Republican army amazed Brunswick by its steadiness, and its artillery, which was the best in Europe, shattered his confidence in a military walkover. Indeed artillery, which was also crucial in the fall of the Tuileries on 10 August, destroyed Bourbon power for a generation. On 29 September 1792 Brunswick ordered a retreat.

The army and princes who had set off with such high hopes in August were now in a desperate state. Right from the beginning of the campaign they had had difficulty finding money for supplies and forage. Calonne was continually surrounded by a swarm of begging, cursing and insulting soldiers who blamed him for what was really a sign of the failure of their whole campaign. If they had conquered more territory, money would not have been such a problem. On 13 September, Calonne was writing to Artois '*dans trois jours on manquera de vivres*' ('in three days we will have run out of food'). The retreat, which was carried out in pouring rain and bitter cold, made things even worse. By 8 October,

Espinchal could write that the retreat has '*l'air d'être en pleine déroute, et la bataille la plus désastreuse ne produirait pas de plus facheux effets*' ('all the appearances of a complete rout, and the most disastrous battle could not have produced a worse result').[21] Louis's reaction to the total collapse of his hopes and world – a collapse which may have seemed even more final and frightening than that of the summer of 1789 – is not recorded. But even Espinchal, normally critical, praised his behaviour on the march. On 19 September, the night before they all thought they were finally going to see action, he said: '*Les princes passent tout ce temps au milieu de nous et donnent le meilleur exemple.*' ('The princes are with us the whole time and are an example to us all.')

The rout soon turned into a débâcle. Louis lost many of his papers and ciphers in his flight, which were seized by the Revolutionaries. Among the papers was a letter, implying that Louis XVI supported the *émigrés*, which was later produced at his trial. Louis, who was suffering from a bad attack of gout, now found out what all the feverish protestations of Coblentz really meant. At Arlon, near Liège, where Louis had to stay in an inn, his staff and Aides de Camp began to drift away; and with the rudeness of despair, they openly reproached and insulted Louis and Artois, '*dont la douleur est extrême et ne peut se cacher*' ('whose grief is extreme and more than they can conceal'). It would be interesting to know what form the insults took. Did the smooth façade of Court manners finally crack open? Were Louis and Artois actually treated as ordinary human beings, rather than as royalty?

All the time they were retreating further and faster from France. On 23 November, when they had got to Liège, Louis and Artois, on the urging of the King of Prussia, officially disbanded their troops in a proclamation in which they declared: '*Rien n'ébranlera notre fidélité aux principes sacrés dont nous avons entrepris la défense ... Notre unique ambition sera toujours de vivre pour vous ou de mourir pour vous.*' ('Nothing shall shake our fidelity to the sacred principles whose defence we have undertaken ... Our only ambition will always be to live for you or die for you.') Both phrases would sound less odd if they were addressed by subjects to royalty, rather than the other way round. They show that in 1792 Louis and Artois had to proclaim in public that the Counter-Revolution was a worthier cause than the restoration of royal authority, and that royalty existed to serve aristocrats and their interests, rather than the other way round. On 26 November they suffered another and worse humiliation.

Largely because Artois insisted on a few more hours with his mistress, Madame de Polastron, he and Louis were both imprisoned for debt for a morning in Aix-la-Chapelle. In every sense they had come a long way from Versailles.[22]

However, in comparison to Louis XVI and his family, imprisoned in the Tower of the Temple in Paris, Louis and Artois were lucky. They were at least still free and still served by a few faithful courtiers and servants. During the retreat Louis still saw Madame de Balbi, who was probably quite good at keeping his courage up. At Arlon, Espinchal noted that '*tout le monde voit Monsieur traverser à pied les boues . . . pour aller voir ces dames*' ('all the world may see Monsieur walking through the mud . . . to go and see these ladies').

Finally, on 28 December 1792, the King of Prussia gave Louis and Artois permission to move to Hamm in Westphalia. There they divided up 750,000 francs sent by Catherine II and Frederick William II: 150,000 francs for themselves, 80,000 francs for emergencies, 325,000 francs to the *émigrés*, 60,000 francs to the Prince de Condé, still battling on with a tiny army, and 140,000 francs to their creditors. In the Nassauer Hof in Hamm they led an existence quite unlike what they were used to. They had few courtiers and hardly any official business or public life. Artois wrote: '*Je ne connais rien qui ressemble davantage à la Trappe.*' ('I can think of nothing more like La Trappe.')

It was there on 26 January 1793 that they received the fatal news of their brother's execution, in what is now the Place de la Concorde, before a large, unprotesting crowd of Parisians. The execution seemed to emphasize the end of all possible connection between the Bourbon dynasty and the French nation. As Rivarol, an extremely intelligent Counter-Revolutionary journalist, wrote: '*L'échafaud et le silence du peuple seront toujours flétrissants pour la nation, pour le trône, pour l'imagination même.*' ('The scaffold and the silence of the people will always be damning for the nation, for the throne, for the imagination itself.') That day Louis wrote to Madame de Balbi: '*Je suis le plus malheureux des hommes.*' ('I am the unhappiest of men.') A few months later, down the Rhine at Haarlem, began the sales of the magnificent furniture of Versailles which have proved even more disastrous for the palace than the Revolution itself. It seemed as if Louis's world had been destroyed for ever.[23]

For this tragedy Louis himself bears a heavy responsibility. He had lent himself to an unscrupulous policy – the forgery of currency and the deception about the king's real intentions – of violent resistance to the Revolution which had both implicitly and explicitly compromised that sacred once adored figure the king. There is an undeniable, although small, element of truth in Napoleon I's judgement: 'It is Coblentz that killed him.' Furthermore, Louis had allied himself with foreign powers to invade France, his own country, the land to which his dynasty was meant to be so intimately connected.

It is extremely doubtful, however, if Louis felt many qualms about his behaviour and policies. In an unprecedented and violent situation, it was natural to have an unprecedented and violent reaction. If France was invaded by Austria, Prussia and the *émigrés*, it was only because France itself had declared war. Austria and Prussia were admittedly dangerous allies for Louis and Artois, but French patriotism and Russian pressure (the princes and Catherine II had extremely good relations) would probably ensure that they made no territorial gains on French soil. Even La Fayette, and other revolutionary politicians, had, it seems, begun negotiations with the Austrians in May and June 1792. Even to them the preservation of royal authority, and the destruction of the Jacobins, had become important enough to justify an appeal to foreign powers.

Louis had, indeed, felt *un petit mouvement de tristesse* at the news of the first insignificant French defeats in 1792. But he consoled himself with the feeling that his enemies were not real Frenchmen. They were dangerous, bloodthirsty lunatics, '*usurpateurs d'un si beau nom*' ('usurpers of such a fine name').[24] The real France was, as he told the Austrian Emperor, with him and his brother on the banks of the Rhine – just as General de Gaulle, who felt a revulsion for what was going on inside France between 1940 and 1944 comparable to that of the *émigrés* in the 1790s, declared that the real France was with him and his followers on the banks of the Thames. Time would tell if Louis, in the exile that now stretched before him on the Westphalian plain, would make as valuable a contribution to the history, honour and interests of France as General de Gaulle did in his exile.

CHAPTER V

Louis in Exile 1793 – 1807

During the next fourteen years, Louis was an exile. In 1800, when his old friend, Lady Malmesbury, asked him how he was, he simply wrote: *'Je suis à cinq cent lieues de ma patrie et ce mot dirait tout.'* ('I am 500 leagues from my country, and that tells you everything.') And Louis's existence between 1793 and 1807 was overshadowed by the two habitual adjuncts of exile, isolation and poverty. As Map 1 shows, he was almost always at least 200 miles from the French frontier – and, even more than at Coblentz, he was almost always short of money. Indeed, the isolation and poverty of exile so affected his character that he became nearly a different person: someone less prudent, less realistic and less rational, far more desperate and gullible, but never entirely sinking into the bitterness or hopelessness of most exiles.

To understand the shape of Louis's life and projects in exile, it is first necessary to know where he was living. This was largely dependent on foreign governments, as he was an exile, and needed their permission to reside somewhere. Since he also needed their money to survive financially, and their military help to restore the monarchy, one peril of his exile was that he would become their *mannequin*, as he had briefly been the *mannequin* of politicians of the Revolution and the Counter-Revolution.

Louis's first movements in 1793 directly confronted him with the problems of reliance on foreign powers. In August, Toulon, the great French naval base on the south coast, had, like half of France that year, revolted against the tyranny of the Revolutionary Government in Paris; and its revolt assumed an increasingly Royalist character, even going so far as to accept Spanish and English assistance and garrisons. Louis finally left Hamm on 19 November 1793, a month later than he had planned, having received Spanish permission to go to Toulon and an invitation from the *sections* of Toulon themselves. Louis's unpopularity as a leader of Coblentz was less real, at least some parts of France, than the unpopularity of the increasingly brutal and extremist Republic. However,

the English Government, which was, at this time, far more interested in territorial gains for itself than in a Royalist restoration,
did all it could, by indirect pressure through Madame de Balbi,
as well as by a direct refusal to let Louis arrive at Toulon, to
dissuade him from the venture. But Louis was not even eager to
reach Toulon; he was far keener to join the Spanish army in
Roussillon than to throw himself into a city under siege (Toulon
fell on 20 December) where the many constitutional Royalists
might well be extremely difficult to handle, and he himself might
fall into the hands of the Republicans under General Bonaparte.[1]

On 12 December Louis arrived at Verona to discuss with the
Comte d'Antraigues, a mysterious and powerful Royalist secret
agent with close links with the Spanish Government, *'si la Cour
d'Espagne insiste sur Toulon ou non'* ('if the Court of Spain insists
on Toulon or not'). Such a phrase, revealing that a foreign government was keener than Louis himself that he should return to
France is a damning indictment, a sign of political and perhaps
physical cowardice. On 28 December 1793 Louis arrived at his
father-in-law's Court in Turin – the only Court to which he would
be admitted for the next twenty years – without having made any
effort to go to France.

However, he was an unwelcome and compromising guest at
Turin, even though the English minister noted that Louis was 'in
a state of perfect Retirement and *Ennui. . . .* He appears much
dejected'. On 24 May he left for Verona, a town he may have
chosen in order to be near d'Antraigues and his almost totally
unreliable information network. Louis lived there in a small, ill-
furnished house just outside the town called the Casa Gazzola,
which Lord Macartney, who arrived fresh from his triumphs in
Peking on a mission from the English Government in August
1795, described as 'neither large, handsome nor convenient'.
Louis liked Italy, the climate, the antiquities and the language,
which he spoke and read quite well; and he often tried to return
there afterwards. But Verona was never more than a temporary
resting place: Louis wrote to George III, to Condé and to his
agent in London the Duc d'Harcourt that he wanted to go and
join the heroic Royalist risings in the Vendée. But this was a
desire which he had little intention of realizing, and the English
Government would have tried to stop him anyway. They wanted
him out of harm's way and safely under their control in Gibraltar
– a suggestion Louis naturally refused as being too far from
France. In the end he was expelled by the Venetian Government,
at the instigation of the French Republic, on 21 April 1796.[2]

Louis has left a full account of his journey over the Alps to join the *Armée de Condé* opposite Alsace on the Rhine. In it he relates, in a characteristic royal tone of amused amazement, the details of the journey, the people he met, the inns, the beds and the appalling meals. He was accompanied by his servant Guignet, the faithful d'Avaray and the Vicomte d'Agoult, an officer of the *Gardes du Corps*, and they had quite a jolly time. They celebrated their arrival at Zurich with Champagne, which they had not had for so long that, according to Louis, *'il nous arriva . . . ce qui devait nous arriver'* ('what was bound to happen . . . happened'). At Riegel, where he joined the *Armée de Condé*, he put on its grey uniform and spent the first three days reviewing the troops, still a force of 7,000 to 8,000 men. On 4 May 1796 he also 'showed himself' to what he and the *émigrés* called *les patriotes* camped on the other side of the Rhine. As in 1792, it is hard to find out exactly what their reaction was. But according to one Royalist agent they behaved *'assez bien . . . mais froidement cependant, de manière que . . . le roi [est] très embarrassé'* ('quite well . . . but coldly however, so that . . . the king [is] very embarrassed'). Reality had broken in for a moment, although Louis, and in particular d'Avaray, claimed that he had been well received.[3]

In July 1796, however, partly under Austrian pressure and partly for his own political reasons, Louis decided to leave. After a long and exhausting journey, he arrived at Blankenburg in the Duchy of Brunswick where the Duke grudgingly allowed him to stay – but not in the huge, empty Ducal Schloss. In April 1797, a Royalist envoy found *'le pauve Roy . . . dans une fort vilaine petite ville, dans un fort vilain logement, étroit, mal meublé ou presque point, un habit bleu fort sec, un veste et culotte noir rapée, mais l'air fort affable'* ('the poor King . . . in a nasty little town, in a nasty house, tiny, badly furnished, if at all, [in] a worn blue coat, shabby black waistcoat and trousers, but a very affable air'). At the beginning of 1798, he was thrown out, again as a result of French Government pressure. He wanted to go somewhere else in the Empire not too far from France, like Mecklenburg, but he had to accept Tsar Paul I's offer of hospitality at Mittau in what is now Latvia, over 1,000 miles from Paris.

He arrived there on 24 March 1798 after an appalling winter journey hampered by flooded rivers and broken wheels. He found the magnificent Baroque palace of the former dukes of Courland prepared to receive him in something like the style to which he was accustomed: deferential local authorities, a hundred *Gardes du Corps* equipped at the expense of the Tsar, and splendid apartments . . . to one of Louis's *Aumôniers* it seemed just like

Versailles.[4] However, on 22 January 1801, Louis was again expelled, this time as a result of a decision by the Russian Government. He and his court had another frightful journey in the depths of the Baltic winter. Their horses drowned trying to cross a river, their carriages overturned and they spent two hours with their feet stuck in the snow. The worst thing was that they had hardly any money and did not know where to go next. Louis hoped to go to Naples, residence of his cousin Ferdinand IV, but in the end he had to make do with Warsaw, at that time in Prussia. He spent the winters in the aristocratic quarter, first in the Hôtel Waliszewski, then in the Palais Kazanowski, and the summers in an annex of the royal palace of Lazienski, lent him by the King of Prussia.[5]

However, furious at a newspaper article by d'Avaray in September 1804 and at the endless nuisance this colony of unruly French *émigrés* made, the King of Prussia threw them out. After several weeks' hospitality from Count and Countess Königfeld at Blankenfeld in Courland, Louis was finally offered Mittau again by Alexander I of Russia, who would have preferred to pack him off to Kiev. '*Mittau Ier était Saint-Germain*', wrote Louis to Artois, thereby showing that he still judged palaces by the standards of the Ile-de-France of his youth, '*Mittau II ne sera plus qu'un lit à l'Hôtel-Dieu.*' ('Mittau II will be no more than a bed in the Hôtel-Dieu.') And for the next three years he was stuck in this cold Baltic palace, with its sweeping views of plains and sand-dunes, far from the eyes and thoughts of Europe.

This insecure, wandering existence was obviously extremely unpleasant and unnerving. In 1794, Louis wrote to the Maréchal de Castries, one of his chief advisers, that he really had no idea where he would be in six weeks. In 1798, he wrote to his niece that for six weeks he had been in an '*incertitude complète sur ce que j'allais devenir*' ('complete uncertainty as to what would become of me'). In 1801, after he had been thrown out of Mittau, and did not know whether the King of Prussia would allow him to go to Warsaw, he wrote to his wife, in his calm, realistic way, '*et puis nous irons chercher un autre gîte, et puis un autre, et puis, et puis, etc.*' ('and then we will look for another shelter, and then another, and then, and then, etc.').[6]

Moreover, despite the fact that Louis's residence moved steadily further away from the ever expanding territory controlled by the French Government (see Map I), he was never, as he well knew, completely safe. In Verona, according to Venetian police reports, there was an attempt by agents of the *Directoire* to have him poisoned. Just after he had left the *Armée de Condé* he was shot at by an unknown assassin: Burke wrote to congratulate him on his lucky escape from 'the Madness and Malice of Mankind'. However, this may have been a put-up job to arouse sympathy for a king who had just left – some said deserted – the army which was fighting for his cause. Louis went on at great length about the details of his wound to his soldier cousin, Condé's son, the Duc de Bourbon, and d'Avaray asked people to spread the news. But a doctor who attended his autopsy found no trace of a scar.

In late 1797, Talleyrand, who seems to have had a personal vendetta against the Bourbon dynasty in general, and Louis in particular, and who was just beginning his long and lucrative career as Foreign Minister, proposed to the French ambassador in Berlin that Louis should be abducted from Blankenburg, and taken via the sand-dunes of the north-west coast of Germany to France, where, no doubt, he would have suffered the same fate as another abducted Bourbon, the Duc d'Enghien, six and a half years later. In the summer of 1804 Louis was the subject of another poison attempt, to which d'Avaray gave a lot of publicity. However, it too may well have been an invention of the main witness, Coulon, who was either put up by d'Avaray in order to rouse sympathy for his unfortunate and increasingly forgotten master or, perhaps more likely, was trying to earn a reward for his revelations. Certainly the Prussian Courts repeatedly declared the case to be an invention. On the other hand at that time Prussia was as anxious to remain on good terms with the French Government, as it was to show that its guests could not be done away with. And there is something very sinister indeed in Bonaparte's remark to a spy he sent to Warsaw in the winter of 1803, that Louis was said to be *'atteint d'une maladie incurable'* ('suffering from an incurable disease') – a disease otherwise unknown to history. No modern spy, surely, could have any doubts as to what that meant.[7]

But two forces protected Louis in this period and ensured that he always eventually found shelter somewhere. First, the sentiment of aristocratic and monarchical solidarity and honour, which had been of such advantage to him at Coblentz, still existed, especially in such powerful monarchs as the King of Prussia and the Emperor of Russia. In 1797, the French ambassador in Berlin warned Talleyrand against his project partly because it would so alienate these two monarchs. In 1798, Paul I gave Louis shelter partly because it reflected well on his honour – and he wanted to repay the dazzling reception he had been given at Versailles in 1782. In 1801, the Queen of Prussia could write to Louis's niece *'désor-*

mais votre présence en Prusse nous honore' ('from this moment
your presence in Prussia is an honour to us'). In 1804, before
d'Avaray's article, the King of Prussia, like the Elector of Trier in
1792, at first resisted French pressure to throw Louis out because
it was so contrary to his *dignité* to be told how he should behave
to *cet infortuné Prince*.

Such sentiments were far stronger in these monarchs than in
the Catholic royal families related to Louis. Austria, continuing
the traditional Bourbon-Habsburg rivalry which had been so
strong even in the 1780s, was always personally hostile to Louis
(and vice versa), and hastened his departure from the *Armée de
Condé* in 1796. His other relations, because they were so weak,
were less able to stand up to French pressure. The King of Spain
refused Louis entry in 1793–94, the Elector of Saxony in 1796:
both were his first cousins. His father-in-law the King of Sardinia
tolerated him for a while at his Court but otherwise did nothing
for him, and refused to allow him to join the Piedmontese army
in May 1794. Louis was able to find out for himself that family
relationships counted for even less among the royal families of
Europe than inside the French Royal Family.

Louis was also protected, as at Coblentz, by the force of public
opinion. Europe was still so traditional and so monarchical, and
had become so hostile to the French Revolution, that it was
difficult to treat the head of the French Royal Family too harshly,
especially when he was accompanied, after 1799, by the daughter
of Louis XVI. The French Bourbons were so grand, so dignified
and so unfortunate that in 1796, according to the English ambassador, the people of Verona were horrified and ashamed at
Louis's expulsion, as were '*la noblesse courlandaise en général
et même le peuple*' ('the nobility of Courland in general and even
the people') in 1801, according to Louis. In Warsaw, one of
Bonaparte's spies wrote in 1803, '*tous les gens remarquables de
Varsovie*' ('all the important people of Warsaw') came to pay
Louis their respects on the great annual festival of the French
monarchy, the Fête de Saint Louis celebrated on 25 August.[8]
(Louis was related to many of them through his great-grandfather
Stanislas Leczynski.) Throughout his exile, he would be able to
use the sympathy and services of many members of the European
elite. At one time or another publicists like Grimm and Gentz,
and foreign diplomats like the Russian ambassador in Berlin, the
Spanish ambassadors in Rome and Venice and the Neapolitan
and Sardinian ambassadors in St Petersburg, all exerted themselves on his behalf.

Louis's daily life like his place of residence also depended on foreign governments, since they were almost his only source of income. What he called his *pauvres petites finances* despite the amounts being smaller were almost as complicated in exile as they had been when he was a prince. Thus the very detailed *État au Vrai des Recettes et Dépenses* in the *Archives Nationales* ($0^3 2667$) seems to refer to all royal expenses in Westphalia and England, including the salaries Louis paid there, but excluding his personal expenses after he left Hamm. It is not a reliable guide to his overall income and expenditure. Basically it seems that his two main sources of income were the two strongest powers in Europe, the two who could afford to be relentlessly anti-French and anti-Republican, namely England and Russia. England gave Louis £6,000 in November 1792 – probably in order to help him get out of the debtors' prison – and £12,000 in both 1794 and 1795. Thereafter most of the enormous sums the English Government lavished on anti-Republican activities went to Artois and the Government's many spies – some of whom, however, managed to send a lot of their money to Louis in Warsaw. But from 1801, thanks in part to the persuasion of Artois, Louis received £6,000 a year from the English Government.

The Russian Government was also very generous. In 1793, Catherine II sent 1,444,689 livres to Hamm, which gave Louis and Artois over eighty per cent of their income that year. After his arrival at Mittau, Louis received 200,000 roubles a year from Paul I (9 roubles were approximately £1). This was suspended in 1801, but was restored later that year, after the accession of Alexander I, to the level of 75,000 roubles a year. But even this modest sum had been reduced by 1807 to only 55,000 roubles a year.

In addition, Louis received 85,000 livres a year until 1807 from his cousin, the King of Spain, most of which seems to have stayed at Hamburg, a very important neutral banking and shipping centre in a period of almost constant war, in order to pay his many officials, agents and *pensionnaires*. As late as 1807, there were 109 people, including his household and Madame de Favras, on Louis's pay-roll. Louis also received small sums of money from Portugal (25,000 crusadas every year from 1799 to 1807) and Austria (50,000 florins a year); the latter was probably interest on the considerable fortune of the Duchesse d'Angoulême, orginating from the cash and diamonds wisely smuggled out by Marie-Antoinette in 1790–91.[9]

These sums of money were, however, never enough, given the cost of living in wartime, and of running an exiled royal government and a large household. Louis still had a colossal burden of debts left over from the days of Coblentz; his creditors tried to prevent him leaving Hamm in 1793 and Italy in 1796, and were still pestering him at Warsaw in 1802. So at the two low-points of Louis's fortunes in exile, 1793–95 and 1804–7, he was nearly desperate. In 1794, he was begging d'Antraigues to send him a few bottles of white wine to cheer him up. In December 1804, he was so poor that he wrote to Artois: *'En vérité il y a de quoi perdre la tête.'* ('Really, it's enough to make one lose one's head.')

Despite these trying problems, however, which must have been peculiarly exasperating to a prince who had been brought up in the lap of luxury, and who, before 1789, had so enjoyed making and spending money, Louis never allowed the horrors of his personal situation to take precedence over his royal duties as regent and, after the death of his nephew, Louis XVII, on 8 June 1795, king. In 1801–4 there were several attempts by the newly-established and extremely insecure government of the First Consul to buy Louis off with promises of material advantages, perhaps even a throne of sorts, in Germany, Italy, Poland or even Mexico. The First Consul had, after all, made Louis's cousin the Duke of Parma King of Etruria in 1801 and had carried out a massive programme of compensation for dispossessed German princes east of the Rhine. In 1802, Talleyrand, anti-Bourbon as ever, was saying that he expected Louis to take the money, so that *'l'avilissement des individus . . . sera complet de cette manière'* ('the degradation of the individuals . . . will thereby be complete').

But to his credit, and despite immense pressure from his Prussian host, Louis made his great refusal. Louis would never be as degraded as Talleyrand and so many other politicians of the period who, as Flaubert remarked of the next generation, would have paid for the pleasure of selling themselves. On 28 February 1803, he issued a stirring declaration of his rights which, despite Prussian pressure and threats he refused to modify or withdraw: *'J'ignore les desseins de Dieu sur ma race et moi, mais je connais les obligations qu'il m'a imposées par le rang où il lui a plu de me faire naître. Chrétien, je remplirai ces obligations jusqu'à mon dernier soupir. Fils de Saint-Louis, je saurai, à son exemple, me respecter jusque dans les fers. Successeur de François Ier, je veux du moins pouvoir dire avec lui: "Nous avons tout perdu fors l'honneur".'* ('I do not know God's plans for me and my race, but I do know the obligations which he has placed on me by the rank in which he chose to have me born. Christian, I will fulfill these obligations until my dying breath. Son of Saint Louis, I will know, like him, how to keep my self-respect even in a prison. Descendant of François Ier, I at least want to be able to say, with him: "All is lost save honour". ') That is the sort of firm, eloquent, royal language which Louis could produce for such occasions. Privately, he had put it less rhetorically, but no less sensibly: *'Timeo Danaos et dona ferentes.'* While to Cardinal Maury, his ambassador in Rome, he went into further explanations, pointing out that any thought of compensation in Lombardy or Poland was thoroughly impractical, and would only be seen by public opinion as a degrading bargain. As for his own uncertain and unpleasant existence, he wrote, *'Pour moi cet état est plus effrayant à voir que difficile à supporter.'* ('For me this state is more frightening to contemplate than hard to endure.') This was more than could be said for Cardinal Maury, who went over to Bonaparte a year later.[10]

However, nothing in the world, and least of all in the life of Louis XVIII, is entirely black and white. He refused Bonaparte's bribes. But he was not averse, in either 1801 or 1807, to receiving money from the French Government, provided it was part of a general European subsidy administered by a third power, probably Russia. This distinction seems rather trivial, since clearly the French Government could then threaten to withdraw or decrease its subsidy if Louis did something of which it disapproved. No doubt on the freezing shores of the Baltic the possession of money seemed the most important thing of all.

Louis was, therefore, encouraged to bear the rigours of exile by his firm conviction that the throne of France belonged to the descendants of Saint Louis and François Ier. Dynastic pride was the motor which kept him going through exile and middle age. This pride can only have been strengthened by the events of 1789–94, which proved (at least to the world of the Emigration) that the weakening and then destruction of the throne led directly to the collapse of the social order, property and religion, and to almost permanent war. The Bourbons were now shown to be not only legitimate but indispensable.

Moreover, after the death of his nephew Louis XVII, Louis was the head of the dynasty, and that mystical, semi-religious and eternal figure, *le Roi de France*. He was now not just a person but an institution – a distinction Louis frequently drew, especially in his correspondence with crowned heads. He was no longer a prince with the tastes and ambitions of a private individual or a politician but *le Roi* with, in theory, no other interests than those of his people. The distinction between these two roles was emphasized by the fact that after 1795 Louis was served not by his own household but, in accordance with tradition, by the *Maison du Roi*, an ancient, rather impersonal institution, many of whose

offices were almost as old as the House of France itself. For an
exile to realize that he is in fact an institution which is likely to
end the torments of his fellow countrymen must be extremely
encouraging to his self-confidence. And indeed Louis was now
convinced, as he wrote to his old friend La Chatre in 1804, just
before issuing another proclamation asserting his right to the
throne, that '*la Providence veille sur moi*' ('Providence is watching
over me').[11]

For Louis was helped to bear the rigours of exile not only by
his belief in his own royalty and his own dynastic rights, but also
by his fatalism, his superstitious conviction that God could not
desert the House of France, and also perhaps by his religious
beliefs. There is absolutely no proof that Louis, who attended
Mass every day, even in exile, was not a Christian, despite an
almost universal belief to the contrary among his contemporaries.
Louis looked so rational, sceptical and untrusting that he was
assumed to have the religious doubts of most of his onlookers.
But his upbringing had been extremely religious, his library had
been full of religious books, and he struck one of his *Aumôniers*,
Louis XVI's last confessor, the Abbé Edgeworth, as an extremely
religious man. Indeed Edgeworth went so far as to write that
Louis was 'endowed with every virtue that makes the saints' – a
tribute either to Edgeworth's naivety or to the extremely widespread use, in the eighteenth century, of letters as instruments of
propaganda rather as means of communication. Louis was certainly not a saint, but his charm, his unfailing politeness and self-
confidence had clearly worked on the Abbé Edgeworth.

One of the fascinating things about this essentially rational and
realistic prince was the strong superstitious side of his character.
He was constantly quoting books of prophecies like Nostradamus
with reference to his own position; and after his death a work
called *La Clé des Prophètes* was found in his desk. In his account
of his escape from Paris he shows a rather superstitious belief in
the efficacy of prayer and in the protection afforded him by a holy
image slipped to him by Madame Elizabeth. Throughout his exile,
despite his ceaseless efforts to bring about a restoration, one gets
a strong impression that in his heart of hearts he trusted even
more to luck, events, Providence, whatever one likes to call it, to
obtain this end. As he wrote to his old governess Madame de
Marsan in 1801, he would hardly have benefitted from her lessons
if he did not put his trust in Providence.[12]

Moreover he had an example ready at hand which could hardly
have failed to keep his spirits up. Like every educated eighteenth-
century Frenchman, Louis had read Hume's history of England

under the Stuarts, which was in his library at Brunoy – indeed, with his brothers, he had complimented the author when Hume visited Versailles in 1763. So he knew of another violent revolution, and another royal execution. And, like many of his contemporaries, he must have expected that the French Revolution, like the English, would also end in military dictatorship and, inevitably, in the restoration of the king.

Another factor which helped Louis put up with the horrors of exile was the fact that he remained in relatively good health. In 1795 Lord Macartney found him extremely fat and unwieldy, but he was still able to spend whole days in the saddle on his way from the *Armée de Condé* to Blankenburg in 1796. His regular attacks of gout were still fairly unimportant, and in 1803 a new Secretary, the Marquis de Bonnay, thought that he was in better health, and less fat, than he had been at Coblentz, Blankenburg or Verona.

Louis was also helped to endure his exile by the fact that, even then, he hardly ever left the comforting cocoon of royal life for the harshness of private life. Indeed much of the money Louis received from foreign governments went on the maintenance of the large, bickering and frustrated Court which continued to surround him. Other exiled monarchs have dragged out their days in miserable solitude, often caused at least as much by their own characters as by the hopelessness of their politics. However, because French royalism was so strong and hopeful, and because Louis himself was such a calm and dignified pretender, neither entirely senseless nor completely penniless, he was an exception. As he boasted to his sister Clotilde, Queen of Sardinia, who had had to ,lee Turin in 1798, he had never experienced '*cet abandon, ce délaissement universel qui ne sont que trop ordinaires en pareil cas*' ('that abandon, that universal neglect which are only too common in such cases'). As late as 1810 in England, the dethroned King of Sweden, Gustavus IV Adolphus sadly noted that in contrast to his own solitude, although '*voici bien des années . . . que Sa Majesté est hors de son pays . . . ses salons ne sont pas assez grands pour contenir tous ceux qui viennent lui rendre hommage*' ('it is now many years . . . that His Majesty is out of his country . . . his salons are not large enough to hold all those who come to pay homage to him').[13]

So at Verona in early 1795, even before he became king, Louis had an entourage of twenty-six servants, courtiers, ministers and army officers. Among them were the faithful d'Avaray, the Comte de Cossé, still, as he had been before 1791, Louis's *Capitaine des Suisses* and Peronnet, who had accompanied Louis on his escape from Paris and was his *Premier Valet de Chambre* from 1792 to 1824. Louis also had three personal servants, Coutent, Guignet and Dubreuil, who had been with him since before 1791, remained with him throughout his exile and survived to enjoy the good times when he was on the throne. They dressed him, shaved him, powdered his hair and looked after his clothes. They must have been the people who knew him most intimately, although not perhaps most completely, but alas their views of their master are not recorded. However, their spirit of devotion is shown in a touching note, not untinged with material self-interest, written by Coutent. He had been left behind in Königsberg during the uncertain months following the expulsion from Mittau and was now asking d'Avaray for back-payment for those months: '*Coutent saisit ... cette occasion de protester à Monsieur le Comte d'Avaray qu'il redoublera de zèle et d'assiduité, s'il est possible, dans son service auprès du Roi, bien persuadé que c'est le seul moyen de témoigner sa reconnaissance à Monsieur le Comte.*' ('Coutent seizes ... this opportunity to protest to M. le Comte d'Avaray that he will redouble his zeal and assiduity, if it is possible, in his service about the King, well knowing that that is the only way to show his gratitude to M. le Comte.') Louis's servants were devoted to their master, and he to them. They only complained if their duties were diminished or if they were sent away.

Louis's household was transformed when he became king in June 1795, and inherited the huge, venerable *Maison du Roi*. After 1795 therefore, in addition to d'Avaray, Cossé and his personal servants, Louis was served by many former Court officials of Louis XVI. The Duc de Duras, a *Premier Gentithomme* and the Marquis de Dreux-Brézé, the *Grand Maître des Cérémonies* whom Mirabeau had so rudely answered back in 1789, came to see Louis in Verona. The Duc de Villequier, and later his nephew the Duc de Piennes, acted as Louis's *Premiers Gentilshommes* at Verona, Blankenburg and Warsaw. The most interesting of these Court officials, the Duc de Gramont, who had been a *Capitaine des Gardes* of Louis XVI, hardly ever left the side of his exiled brother. The *Grand Aumônier de France*, the Cardinal de Montmorency, was in attendance until his death in 1808, when he was succeeded by the Archbishop of Reims, who had been a friend of Louis's father and was also Talleyrand's uncle. In all Louis had an entourage of 108 at Mittau in 1799–1801, and a hundred *Gardes du Corps*, fifty-three at Warsaw in 1801–4, forty-five at Mittau in 1805–7 and the same number in England in 1809. Since these figures exclude servants' servants and the ten to twenty courtiers and servants who always accompanied any other member of the Royal Family living with Louis, the real number of French people surrounding him was obviously much larger. In 1805, he wrote to his brother that he had to pay for the transport of 150 people from Warsaw to Mittau.[14]

Such a vast entourage in the poverty and isolation of exile seemed very out of place, especially to Louis's ministers. Moreover, the exiled Court of France was riddled with intrigues – even more, perhaps, than the Court of Versailles, since exile embittered the passions and left few other fields of action. Occasionally a dramatic event broke the customary monotony. On the dreadful journey from Mittau to Warsaw in 1801, one of Louis's secretaries, the Abbé Marie, committed suicide. According to another secretary, his dying words were *'faîtes renvoyer Mademoiselle de Choisy'* (the Duchesse d'Angoulême's *Dame d'Atours* until 1844). Alas, we can only speculate on the nature of the passions and tensions, embracing priests as well as spinsters, which these words uncover. In 1805, Hue, a former servant of Louis XVI who had become a *Premier Valet de Chambre* of Louis XVIII, left the Court, owing to what he called *tracasseries*: he had lost much of his royalist enthusiasm, and he did not like d'Avaray. Even the saintly Abbé Edgeworth got involved in what he called *'une vile et dégoûtante intrigue'* – unfortunately those words are all we know about it. Moreover, the exiled Court also kept up the endless extravagance of Versailles – Louis was always having to issue *règlements* to try to stop courtiers making money out of their right to free lighting, and to stop them getting the royal kitchens to send up special meals to their rooms.

That Louis should bother to maintain such an expensive and discordant Court seems extraordinary. But, no doubt, he felt that the King of France should not appear abandoned or neglected, and that having hordes of servants at his beck and call and being served by dignified, ducal representatives of families almost as old as his own, was part of being King of France. Moreover, it was just a Court. It hardly interfered with Louis's actual routine: up at eight, *déjeuner* at ten (in exile it was just bread and butter and tea), Mass, an afternoon drive or walk, dinner at four and perhaps a game of whist in the evening. The meals were distressingly simple – four *plats* or dishes for Louis and the nine people who regularly dined with him in 1801, three *plats* for Louis and the fifteen people who dined with him by 1806.[15]

Apart from meals and drives, Louis had little contact with his courtiers. They were agreeable, indispensable decoration, but little more. They were reassuringly honourable, loyal and devoted;

Louis called the Duc de Gramont '*au-dessus de toutes éloges*'. But they were not outstandingly intelligent as Louis always preferred his courtiers to be reliable rather than clever. Thus he was cut off from them by his intelligence, his rank – and by his silence. Words were a weapon which the King of France had to use with special care. Moreover Louis had always been *peu parlant* by nature like Louis XVI, and unlike their dangerously talkative younger brother.

But what cut Louis off most of all from his bickering court was his organization of his day. He did not spend it chatting or holding Court or enjoying social life. The only time he had an ordinary social life or left his royal world was on his journeys – although even these were considerably more royal in character than his flight from Paris had been. In 1801, he spent several nights in the frightful, stinking Prussian inns. In 1804, and again in 1807 on his way to England, he went to several parties while waiting for transport to his next destination. But otherwise he led an extremely restricted life, which he himself called monk-like, paying no visits and receiving only those to do with political business.[16] As usual people who met him came away extremely impressed. Even in exile he never lost his perfect manners, his self-control or his air of calm assurance. In 1793, Stein, the future regenerator of Prussia, found him 'a kindly and reasonable man with a clear judgement mellowed by experience'. In 1795, Lord Macartney praised his good understanding, good judgement and wit, and found him 'improved, not exasperated by adversity'. In 1797, La Thuillerie, a Royalist strongly prejudiced against Louis, had to admit that the king had been misrepresented, that he had '*de l'Esprit et des Connaissances*', and '*une patience et une douceur qui enchantent*'. Indeed Louis must have been patient to listen to this ambitious *émigré* attack his own agents every afternoon for three hours.[17]

But most of Louis's time was spent not in receiving visitors but in the organization, direction and formulation of policy of his Government in exile. For Louis, just as if he was a monarch actually on the throne, spent 'the greater part of the day . . . in his closet [or *Cabinet*] where he despatches his own business'. The degree to which, even on his journeys, he was surrounded by the atmosphere and structure of what he called *les affaires* (government business) is remarkable. When he stopped at an inn in Zurich on his way from Verona to the *Armée de Condé*, Wickham the English spymaster and director of secret operations in France and Duverne de Presle, a Royalist secret agent, were there to meet him. Even from Blankenfeld, the country house deep in

Courland where Louis spent a few weeks in 1804, he was correcting a political declaration and writing to England to assert his authority and keep up his agents' courage.

Since Louis was so far away from France, the main means by which he and his Government conducted business was by correspondence, of which they generated an incredible volume, usually in cipher or invisible ink. They had their own codes – in the one in use in the late 1790s, Louis was referred to as D4, although he signed his name 717. 1186. 1192. Hermann, a former official of the Ministry of Foreign Affairs, who would later serve both the Empire and the Restoration extremely well, was in charge of most of the ciphers. Louis's Government also had its own couriers. In February 1796 at Verona, Lord Macartney noted that 'ever since the death of Louis the 17th, the king's residence here has been assuming more and more the air of a Court', not from any outward show or splendour, 'but by the numerous correspondences, the arrival and departure of couriers from time to time'. In 1798 and 1799 Paul I issued repeated orders to try to intercept or stop the large number of couriers going to and from Mittau.[18]

To deal with this correspondence, Louis employed several secretaries, of whom the most important were the Abbé Fleuriel, a mysterious figure who remained at Louis's Court throughout his nominal and actual reign, and Courvoisier, a former member of the *Parlement* of Franche-Comté, and the secretary of the Council at Coblentz, who at times exerted considerable influence, but returned to France a disappointed man in 1801. Another secretary, who worked at Mittau from 1799 to 1801 before being sent on a mission to London, was Guilhermy, one of the Third Estate deputies who had been at Coblentz.

These people were far more important than Louis's Court officials, who were decorative and domestic rather than political figures. Thus Louis wrote of the Duc de Fleury, who periodically acted as his *Premier Gentilhomme*, that he did not mind receiving a message from the King of Prussia about Marie-Joséphine's arrival via Fleury, but that he would have minded for more important affairs. The Duc de Piennes, another *Premier Gentilhomme*, was not '*dans le secret de mes affaires politiques*'. Only exceptional gifts, such as d'Avaray's, enabled a Court official to cross the barrier Louis almost always maintained between the Court and the world of politics. The exception Louis made was when he simply needed an utterly loyal individual to transmit or receive a message. Thus the Duc de Fleury, who seems to have been quite a favourite (Louis paid his gambling debts in 1804 when he could ill afford to), was used in 1799 to find out if Barras was really interested in bringing about a Restoration.

Normally Louis kept politics and his Court so separate that, to their fury, his secretaries did not mix socially with their master or his Court officials. This separation produced great ill-feeling. In 1796, Courvoisier wrote: '*Qui n'est pas Grand Seigneur n'est rien*', although he had just boasted that he was completely in his master's confidence. Many of Louis's Court officials would have willingly exchanged a very large proportion of the hours they spent at his table or in his carriage for a share, however tiny, of the confidence Courvoisier enjoyed. But Louis, no more than any modern politician, probably did not want to spend all day surrounded by the same government officials. Moreover when he did lower the barrier between the two worlds there was only trouble. His invitation to Guilhermy, a former deputy of the Third Estate, to the wedding of his niece and the wedding dinner (so that Guilhermy sat at the same table as the King of France – an immense honour) caused a hurricane of protest in Royalist circles. What was the point of fighting the Revolution if the Court was to be conducted in such a revolutionary fashion? These were the sort of attitudes from which Louis found it so hard to escape.[19]

In addition to his secretaries, Louis also had his own ministers in exile – his proclamation of himself as regent on 28 January 1793 was counter-signed by two former ministers of Louis XVI, now ministers of the Royalist Government in exile, the maréchaux de Broglie and de Castries. Castries remained an extremely influential figure, in touch with both Louis and Artois. Although he was often in disagreement with Louis, he appeared at Verona in the summer of 1795 and at Blankenburg in 1796 and 1797. Indeed in one week at Blankenburg, Castries' secretary complained that he had to write 308 pages. Two ministers who were always with Louis from 1793 until their deaths in 1797 and 1800 respectively, were the Baron de Flaschlanden and the Marquis de Jaucourt. Flaschlanden was in charge of the bureaucracy of the *émigré* army: he and his successors kept the *Grand Livre*, with its *règlements* governing ranks, promotion and the award of medals – over 1,000 *Croix de Saint Louis* were awarded in the 1790s – which is still in the Archives Nationales. Indeed, Louis kept a paper army right up till 1814: in 1809, when he wanted to punish the Comte de Puisaye, he told Flaschlanden's successor, the Comte de La Chapelle, to cross off Puisaye from '*mon état militaire*'.

More important than either Jaucourt or Flaschlanden, who were both exhausted and pliable old men, were the Duc de la

Vauguyon and the Comte de Saint-Priest. They had both had experience of government business under Louis XVI, the former as an ambassador the latter as a minister, and they were at the head of Louis's affairs from February 1796 until March 1797, and from May 1797 until March 1800, respectively. Thereafter, Louis had no chief minister, although de Thauvenay was the *Secrétaire Intime*, in charge of his correspondence and the overall supervision of his household, from October 1801 to August 1803, and he was followed by the witty, worldly and moderate Marquis de Bonnay from September 1803 until August 1804.

In addition to a ministry, Louis maintained representatives in most of the larger European capitals. Their main function was to provide news – a particularly valuable commodity in the desolation of Blankenburg or Mittau, although Louis always received several French newspapers – and to procure or dispense funds. As late as 1807, Louis was still paying representatives at some of the last independent capitals in Europe – Rome, Vienna, Berlin, Palermo, London and St Petersburg.[20]

Louis also received information and news, albeit of dubious accuracy, from agents he maintained inside France. Between 1793 and February 1797, when an attempt to win over a Republican colonel led to the arrest of the colonel and the agents, Louis had a network of agents in France known as the *Agence de Paris*. Among them were the Abbé Brotier, perhaps the best of them all, Lemaître, a former pamphleteer against Calonne, Des Pomelles, a retired officer, Sourdat a former *Lieutenant de Police*, and Duverne de Presle, whom Louis met at the inn in Zurich in 1796, but who betrayed many secrets after his arrest on 31 January 1797.

The agents were at first controlled by their ringleader, the Comte d'Antraigues, who rewrote, edited or perhaps invented their reports before sending them to Louis and many foreign governments. But at least by April 1796 they were in direct contact and correspondence with Louis. The exact value of the information they conveyed has been the subject of ceaseless controversy. Before 1795 most of it seems to have been worthless: for example information they procured convinced both themselves and Louis that the Abbé Sieyès was the heart and soul of the Committee of Public Safety. However, they did provide Louis with a means of communication with the interior of France. Through them, for example, he was able to communicate with Charette, fighting in the Vendée, in June 1795. And the agents did have sources of information, or at least protectors, such as Tallien, in the Revolutionary Government itself. In addition to the *Agence de Paris*,

Louis also had independent agents in the French provinces, for example, Pourquery in Toulouse and Dupont-Constant in Bordeaux, from 1796 or earlier.[21]

After February 1797, Louis's main agent in France, who was at first more an agent of the English Government, was d'André, a former member of the *Parlement de Provence* who had been one of the three or four most influential Revolutionary politicians in the *Assemblée Nationale*. In 1797, with Des Pomelles, he was able to head a very effective electoral campaign in the interests of moderate Royalism. Between March 1798 and May 1801 he formed part of an agency known as the *Agence de Souabe*, although it was based on Bayreuth and Coburg which are in Franconia. It maintained a weekly correspondence with Louis and with agents in Paris. The other members were the Comte de Précy, a former officer of Louis XVI's *Garde Constitutionelle* who had led the heroic defence of Lyon against the Convention in 1793; the Président de Vezet, a former member of the *Parlement de Franche-Comté*; and the Abbé André, also known as Delamarre, who was their chief messenger between Paris and Mittau. In the winter of 1800, for example, carrying Louis's letters and instructions, he made the journey from Mittau to Paris in under two months.

In June 1801, however, the Prussian police, at the request of its ally the French Government, seized Précy (who was eventually released) and many of the papers of the *Agence de Souabe* were published. Louis's last agents in Paris, who corresponded with the *Agence de Souabe* before 1801, and with Louis until December 1803, were the Marquis de Clermont-Gallerande, a former agent of the queen, Royer-Collard, a *philosophe* and one of the leading French politicians of the first third of the nineteenth century, the Abbé de Montesquiou, a former member of the *Assemblée Nationale* whom Louis had known all his life (his cousin had been Louis's *Premier Ecuyer*), and the Abbé André, who all formed what was known as the *Conseil Royal*. They communicated with Louis through seemingly innocuous letters which were covered with invisible ink and addressed to German businessmen. They contained extremely realistic assessments of the situation in France, and often mentioned the popularity and extraordinary talents of Bonaparte.

Although their plans never came to very much, these various agents, all of whom had subordinate agents in the provinces, did at least ensure that Louis kept in touch with events in France. They provided him with a peaceful means of trying to influence people and events. Even as late as 1803, a French Government spy in Warsaw was impressed by the quantity of news Louis received from Paris, and the speed with which it reached him. So until 1804, he was never as isolated politically as he was geographically. Moreover some of Louis's agents, such as d'André or Royer-Collard, were intelligent, relatively youthful but experienced politicians to whom the new France created by the Revolutions was as much a familiar field of operation as was the old France to elderly ministers like Castries, Jaucourt and Saint-Priest. None of Louis's agents, except Montesquiou, had had any contact with the Court before 1789. Indeed, again with this exception, they had all been born outside the Ile-de-France. They showed that, even in the 1790s, the service of the king could attract people from extremely varied backgrounds, provincial, military, *parlementaire*, non-noble, as well as the dutiful courtiers of Verona and Mittau.[22]

One of the most important aspects of this scattered, long-suffering, but resilient apparatus was to decide who was in control. We have already seen that at Coblentz Louis could simply be a symbol rather than a chief for the *émigrés*' organization. Weakness, or *bonté* as it was often called in the smooth, courtly style in which an increasing number of Frenchmen were learning to express themselves, was the most frequent reproach levelled at the later Bourbons and as Louis's own *Secrétaire Intime*, the Marquis de Bonnay, wrote to him in 1803, '*celle de Sa Majesté elle-même n'a pas été à l'abri de cette reproche*' ('that of His Majesty himself has not been safe from this reproach').

One threat to Louis's authority could have been his own ministers and agents who, as happened to many eighteenth-century monarchs, might abuse his *bonté* and dominate his Councils, so as to make him little more than a *mannequin*. Louis certainly took their advice: a letter by d'Avaray shows that in 1795 both d'Antraigues and Flaschlanden worked on one of the most important documents of Louis's life, the Declaration of Verona. In 1796–97, Louis's policy was greatly influenced by Wickham and the Abbé Brotier, and in 1800 the Abbé André helped Louis write the instructions and letters dealing with his overtures to General Bonaparte. (He did not, as has been alleged, help with the 1803 Declaration, since he was not in Warsaw.)

Although Louis's ministers and agents did exert considerable influence, it was usually the sort of influence Louis wanted. He knew that, like every monarch there has ever been, he needed to take other people's advice. But he remained the master. In February 1797, the Duc de La Vauguyon, with whom d'Avaray had long been quarrelling, was exiled from Louis's Court for having tried to dominate Louis's Government, to counter his policies and to stop his agents and relations from corresponding directly with the king. In 1798, another over-ambitious minster, the Comte de Saint-Priest, wrote to La Fare, Louis's agent in Vienna, '*Vous etes le maître d'écrire au roy ou à moi. . . . Je pense que la dernière manière vous sera plus commode.*' ('It is up to you whether you write to the king or to me. . . . I think the last way will suit you best.')[23]

However, Louis was perfectly capable of conducting his own correspondence, as is shown by the existence of drafts of despatches in his own hand, and La Fare continued to correspond with him as well as with Saint-Priest and d'Avaray. Louis always insisted on consulting his advisers – and often other people as well – but the end result was often remarkably like his initial desires. Even a hint of despotism must be avoided, advice must be seen to be requested, but it need not necessarily be followed. Years later, in 1813, Joseph de Maistre, the famous Counter-Revolutionary minister, refused to advise Louis again about a proclamation since he knew that Louis's policy had a *motif*, a *pensée dirigeante*, which, unless one was admitted into its secret, made one's own advice useless. And indeed the proclamation came out before de Maistre's reply had even reached Louis.

But Bonnay, when referring to Louis's *bonté*, may well have been thinking not of Louis's ministers but of the constant presence at Louis's side throughout his years of exile of his strong-willed, self-confident and industrious deliverer the Comte d'Avaray. D'Avaray, was one of the few members of Louis's household as Comte de Provence, who occupied the same vital and prestigious position, that of *Capitaine des Gardes*, after Louis's accession, and he was Louis's closest friend. In late 1794, he was the only person who dared tell Louis what (apparently) everyone else knew, that Madame de Balbi (to whom Louis had bidden a very fond farewell before leaving Hamm) was openly having an affair with Talleyrand's brother, Archambaud de Périgord. She had had twins (*deux petites malheureuses*) as well. Louis was shattered. '*J'ai besoin d'être seul*' ('I need to be alone'), he moaned. Thereafter he had no further contact with Madame de Balbi, the constant companion of his happiest days. A sad, slightly desperate letter of 18 November 1794 exists telling the Comte d'Hautefort, a great friend of d'Avaray and Louis, to stop her coming to Verona at all costs. By 1795, therefore, d'Avaray was lovingly enthroned in the position of '*mon ami et le confident de toutes mes pensées*' ('my friend and the confidant of all my thoughts');

and every evening Louis and he spent an hour or two together to discuss the day's events and mail.[24]

Unfortunately, d'Avaray, who was in many ways the worst and certainly the silliest of Louis's intimates, was one of those friends from whom kings need more protection than from their enemies. He let his pen run away with him in a way unforgivable in any politician, let alone the friend and confidant of a royal pretender. In 1795, he used fatally violent language to express his loathing for Puisaye, a Royalist leader who had just helped turn the expedition to Quiberon into a disaster. His indiscreet expressions of contempt for Paul I of Russia – a ruler whose help his master desperately needed – helped lead to their expulsion from Mittau in 1801. In September 1804, another indiscretion, the publication of a note in a Hamburg newspaper suggesting that Louis's movements were decided *'de concert avec les puissances du Nord'* ('in concert with the northern powers') led to their expulsion from Prussia. D'Avaray was obsessed with his master's dignity in a rather puerile way. He wrote to one of the leading journalists of the Emigration not about policy or propaganda, but to point out that Louis had not been so undignified as to ask for a delay when expelled from Verona.

D'Avaray, however, did have a certain moderation and breadth of spirit, neither of which were particularly easy to find in the world of the Emigration. By 1796, he was preaching *'la sagesse, la modération, oublions nous-mêmes'* ('restraint, moderation, let us stop thinking about ourselves'), even in a private letter to a friend. Few other *émigrés* would have been capable of such broadmindedness as to write in 1797 that the *gloire* won by the Republicans' armies *'servira du moins de contrepoids à leurs crimes'* ('will at least serve as a counterweight to their crimes'). Perhaps a good judgement of his character is that of the Royalist agent de Vezet who wrote, after talking to him for the first time, that although not particularly impressive, *'sur l'aperçu et sur ce que m'en a dit Courvoisier ... M. d'Avaray a de la sagesse, du bon sens et de bonnes vues'* ('from what I have seen of him, and what Courvoisier has told me ... M. d'Avaray has *sagesse*, good sense and sound views').[25]

Inevitably this determined and self-confident character acquired a great deal of influence with Louis. He was with him every day and with him alone for part of every day. As Louis often explained, one of the reasons why he loved him so much was that he *'ne connaît jamais les déguisements ni les détours'* ('never tries to disguise or dress up the truth') – in other words he told Louis things he might not want to hear (and Castries agreed). He

presumably succeeded in influencing his master, since Louis re-
cognizes his remarks to be direct and truthful. He soon began to
assume an open, as opposed to a private, role in the running of
Louis's Government. By 1796, Courvoisier, one of Louis's secretaries, was with d'Avaray from half past eight in the morning
to three o'clock in the afternoon every day copying and writing,
ciphering and deciphering, and d'Avaray was a member of the
Council. By 1800, d'Avaray was having continued disagreements
over policy with Saint-Priest and, as he himself admitted, more or
less forced this respected and popular minister, who did at least
have the manners and discretion of a statesman, to leave. D'A-
varay even influenced the private side of Louis's life, helping him,
for example, to decide whether to invite the Abbé Edgeworth to
dinner, and even with his correspondence with his nephew and
niece, the companions of his daily life.[26]

But this influence was not really the domination that many of
d'Avaray's friends and enemies assumed. When d'Avaray, whose
health was very bad, wintered away from Louis in Italy in 1802
and 1803, Louis's policy and Government went on as before. In
1802, Courvoisier wrote to his old friend and fellow Franche-
Comtois, Vezet: '*Le roi est son premier ministre et fait tout.*' ('The
king is his prime minister and does everything'.) Louis insisted on
leaving d'Avaray behind before he went to meet Artois in Sweden
in September 1804 in order to issue a proclamation against the
creation of the Empire, although he consulted him on its text.
And in the following year Louis published the proclamation
against the advice not only of Artois, the Princes du Sang and
Alexander I, but also of d'Avaray, who had protested against it
'*avec cette franchise toujours récompensée par sa bienveillance*'
('with that frankness always rewarded by his benevolence'). At
least at this stage of his career no one was as persistently and
indomitably royalist as Louis himself.

Moreover, Louis's organization of his daily work ensured that
he retained his own personality, that he remained an individual
rather than a *mannequin*. In the day-time he remained alone in
his study and communicated with his ministers, his secretaries and
even d'Avaray via a *cassette* or box to which only he and they
had keys. Thus Louis could make his own decisions and write his
own comments on in-coming documents as is shown by the papers
of the Marquis de Bonnay, Louis's *Secrétaire Intime* from 1803
to 1804.

When he worked with an official in person Louis was also the
master – but in a very indirect, suggesting, restrained way – rather
than a *mannequin*. In 1794 Courvoisier described to his old friend

Vezet what it was like working with Louis. In the mildest and politest possible way the regent suggests changes of words and phrases in despatches, and reminds him of one of the basic principles of Louis's and Artois's policy, so often represented as one of bloodthirsty vengeance: *'intolérance pour les erreurs, tolérance pour les personnes'* ('intolerance for errors, tolerance for individuals'). Twenty years later the Comte de Blacas, at that time Louis's chief adviser, would give much the same description of working with the king.[27] Louis was not the master of every detail, still less the author of every despatch. Nor did he, as we shall find out, originate every change in his policy. But he was master of its overall direction; and it was not an entirely vain boast for him to write to Bonnay, quoting his favourite author, Horace: ' "Deunque sit quodvis simplex dantaxat et usum" – *il n'y a à la tête de mes affaires que moi.'*

The great extent of d'Avaray's influence was largely due to the fact that he said the sort of thing that fitted in with Louis's own views. Nothing surely was closer to Louis's heart, and to his view of his own interests, than the maintenance, in every conceivable circumstance, of his royal dignity. D'Avaray was wholeheartedly Louis's man, although he did occasionally long for a rest. He worshipped his master as a god, calling Louis's gout *'son tribut annuel à l'humanité'*. And his self-confidence and air of assurance, which so maddened the foreign statesmen he came into contact with, were effective in keeping up Louis's spirits. D'Avaray could even write that his profoundly unmartial master would have made a good general. Who could resist such a devoted and admiring friend?

D'Avaray's position has to be seen against the background of exile and the Emigration. Louis never lacked a Court or people coming to pay court to him. And most *émigrés*, like members of the elite who had remained in France, were gradually becoming reconciled to playing a relatively subordinate role under royal authority. However, a personal and whole-hearted devotion to Louis's cause such as that of d'Avaray was exceedingly rare. He was a bachelor who had given up family, friends and the prospect of 80,000 livres a year to follow Louis.[28] Few other people of his gifts showed the same devotion; for, as has been shown, in the world of violent royalism Louis was never wholly liked nor trusted, and throughout his exile he would find out how little he could rely in practice on the rather passive Royalism of his supporters. In early 1793, after his assumption of the regency, none of the eight political figures he wrote to for help – some of whom were inside France, thereby showing a desire to escape from the

attitudes of Coblentz – were prepared to come to his side. Later
that year, despite an outrageously flattering letter comparing him
to both Sully and Du Guesclin, Castries refused to follow Louis
to Italy, and perhaps Toulon. Two of Louis's agents, Guilhermy
and Vezet, only served him after considerable persuasion and
because they needed the money he could still afford to pay them.
One reason why Louis left the *Armée de Condé* in 1796 was
that it did not want him to stay. Condé wrote to ask him to leave
because of the danger he was in and because he might create
trouble for the army with the Austrians. Condé's grandson
Enghien, who did not get on with Louis at all, wrote to his father
that Louis was not much liked. It was a view confirmed by La
Vauguyon, among others, and of which Louis himself was well
aware.[29] He was too much of a failure to attract much support or
sympathy.

Many of Louis's agents were not just unenthusiastic about their
master, but actually became disloyal. D'Antraigues, whom Louis
and d'Avaray had already begun to suspect, betrayed the secret
of a royalist plot to General Bonaparte in 1797. In 1804, Cardinal
Maury, quite clearly motived by ambition, went over to the Empire (he received the doubtful honour of becoming *Premier Aumônier* of Prince Jérôme) while still Louis's agent in Rome.
Louis, showing an understanding of the personal and emotional
basis of political commitment which has escaped many historians,
commented that this defection can *'au moins servir à l'histoire
du coeur humain. Indépendamment de l'avarice, que ne peut
l'orgueil?'* ('at least serve for the history of the human heart.
Greed aside, of what is pride not capable?') By now faithful
Royalists, such as the extreme Counter-Revolutionary Comte Ferrand and the Comte d'Angivillier, who had known Louis since he
was a child, were showing total unwillingness to have anything
to do with his cause. Even Bonnay, Louis's *Secrétaire Intime*, was
suspected of treason (it seems unjustly, since he remained in his
service throughout his exile, and indeed after 1814). The Abbé
André, Louis's most effective secret agent, resigned in 1805, fed
up with both d'Avaray and Louis himself. Against this background of refusal and betrayal, Louis's reliance on d'Avaray,
utterly faithful and wholly devoted, seems understandable.[30]

In addition to control of his government machine, Louis remained at the head of his affairs in another more indirect but still
important way. He kept up an enormous private correspondence
with people of all nationalities, particularly those that might be
of use to him: he never seems to have had to worry about the
cost of couriers, postage, paper or ink. In these letters Louis was

prepared to lower the barriers of royalty and write as one man to another. However artificial and heavy-handed the distinction he so frequently made between Louis and *le Roi* might seem, one can imagine the effect a plea such as '*je ne vous l'ordonne pas comme votre roi, je vous en prie comme votre ami*' ('I do not order you as your king, I beg you as your friend') on a Royalist could be. And Thauvenay duly left Hamburg for Warsaw to be Louis's *Secrétaire Intime.*

Louis's many flattering letters at least ensured that he had a network of acquaintances and contacts who could not very well totally ignore his wishes or forget his existence. (In contrast Louis XVI had no such contacts and rarely wrote a personal letter after 1789.) A long, flattering, personal letter to a deputy who had been expelled from France after the *coup d'état* of Fructidor 1797 helped remind him and his companions of Louis's existence as an alternative to the Republic. A typical sentence is: '*Comme roi, comme père de mes sujets, je ne puis que gémir d'un événement qui retarde la fin des malheurs de ma patrie.*' ('As king, as father of my subjects, I cannot but lament an event which delays the end of my country's misfortunes.') A similar letter to Friedrich von Gentz in 1805 overwhelmed this experienced and important politician with delight. Louis also frequently used the words *ami* and *amitié* in his correspondence with his ministers and agents. These were words other monarchs used more cautiously but which Louis had learnt to wield as a prince. He used them not only with d'Avaray but also Castries, Saint-Priest and La Fare, etc., thereby forging another link, however fragile, with his service.[31]

In fact the greatest threat to Louis's control of his Government in exile, and of royalist policy, came not from overmighty ministers, ambitious Court officials, or his own favourites, but from within his family. In exile, as when he was on the throne or when he was a young prince, the greatest problem of Louis's life was his crippling family position. Not only was he childless, but he had a charming, ambitious and determined younger brother and heir, who could in many ways offer potential agents more than he could. From 1794 Artois lived in England, and soon established good relations with the English Government, from whom he was able to extract large sums of money for his projects and agents. He also offered better prospects, since his two sons, the Ducs d'Angoulême and de Berri, were likely to honour their father's debts and friendships. Guilhermy, who had the appallingly difficult task of being Louis's agent in London, a city swarming with Artois's devotees, wrote bitterly to d'Avaray in 1804 that he knew he was foolish to show *'un attachement exclusif à un roi qui n'a pas d'enfant'* ('an exclusive attachment to a childless king').

From the moment of their separation on 19 November 1793, there was a series of fundamental disagreements between the two brothers which the polite and affectionate language which they used in their enormous correspondence, the barrage of *mon cher frère, mon ami*, etc., only makes appear more bitter and more terrible. Basically, although Louis usually remained more moderate than Artois, it was a struggle over power, rather than principles: Artois wanted to control the Royalist Government machine and agencies. In 1794, Artois was still behaving as if they were both at Coblentz, telling Louis what to do and where to go and keeping nearly all the English subsidies for himself. After 1795 the tone of their correspondence changed, *tutoiement* disappeared and Artois (now, in his turn, called Monsieur, although he will continue to be referred to as Artois to avoid confusion) became outwardly more respectful to his king. But the power struggle went on.

Artois disliked the *Agence de Paris* and was always trying to give them orders contrary to Louis's. He was opposed to Hermann, the agent in charge of Louis's ciphers. In 1796–97, Artois and his agents, in particular Puisaye whom Louis disliked as an *intriguant de premier ordre*, were opposed to the increasingly moderate *Agence de Paris*, and openly rejoiced at its discovery and destruction.[32] In late 1797, Artois tried unsuccessfully to take over Louis's agent the Prince de La Trémoïlle. Louis, yet again using words to hide rather than to express his meaning, smoothly wrote to Artois *'je suis persuadé que vous serez fâché de l'ordre que vous avez donné'* ('I am sure you will regret the order you have given'). In 1799, to Louis's fury, Artois tried to get the Allies to send him to the east of France, a region which Louis had reserved for his own first appearance, and refused to tell Louis anything about his movements. A plan of campaign drawn up that year took over a year to reach Mittau, thanks to Artois's agent Dutheil. In June 1800, Artois, with the support of the English Government, tried to lure Louis's agent d'André to London to get him to reveal Louis's plans and the names of his agents, most of whom Louis kept secret from Artois.

In 1804–5, despite the fact that they had met in Sweden for two weeks in September 1804, relations between the two brothers reached their lowest point. Artois kept Cadoudal's plot to kill or kidnap Napoleon a secret from Louis. Bonnay, perhaps reflecting his master's opinion, called the plot *'une lâche atrocité'*. Later that year, having won over Louis's ambassador in London, the

Comte d'Escars, Artois prevented the Duc d'Orléans and the Prince de Condé from receiving the English Government's permission to go and pay their respects to Louis. According to Guilhermy, these struggles were so dreadful that no one dared write down the truth. In 1805, again according to Guilhermy, Artois tried to stop Louis's Declaration being distributed in France. Louis replaced d'Escars by La Chapelle, and thereafter showed considerably more trust in the Duc d'Orléans, an ex-Republican and the son of a Regicide, than in his own brother.[33]

The two could hardly agree on anything, not even on who should be their niece's ladies-in-waiting or which of their followers should receive medals. Artois thought he had a right, as Louis's brother, and *'un ami qui a tout fait pour lui'* ('a friend who has done everything for him'), to be consulted and influential, and he was prepared to invoke abstract principles – duty, friendship, *le service du Roi* – to justify his frequent acts of disobedience. Louis, who often had an example from the *Grand Siècle* to apply to his own, compared himself to the dying Louis XIII who replied *'pas encore mon enfant'* to the little boy who was proclaiming that he was now called Louis XIV. Artois really did want to be the Royalists' leader – but Louis had no right to complain since he had behaved no better to Louis XVI in 1791–92. Artois and his advisers, a wild indiscreet group headed by the Bishop of Arras, who occasionally lived at Louis's Court, were so eager for power that in 1795–96 they even tried to play the card of moderation and to spread in secret the view of Artois as more reasonable than Louis.

However, the relations between the two brothers never reached the point of an open rupture, although in 1796 this is what Louis's minister, the Duc de La Vauguyon, advocated. What good would it have done, since Artois was so strong and popular, and in such a good position to create as much trouble for Louis as Louis and Artois had done for Louis XVI in 1791–92? Louis realized that his younger brother was part of his life and that he just had to accept the fact. His attitude to his family is summed up in his remark to Gustavus III, who had had even worse problems as his mother had denounced his son and heir as a bastard. *'Que voulez-vous? Chacun a sa croix dans le monde qu'il faut porter.'*[34] ('What do you expect? We each have our cross that we have to bear in this world.')

So Louis tried as much as possible to associate Artois with his policy, to smooth over disagreements and to keep them out of the public eye. Indeed one of his main grievances against Artois was that he was not more active in the royalist cause and that he did not go to the Vendée and fight with the rebels. In 1795, Louis wrote to Artois via the *Agence de Paris* assuming that he had got to France. In 1800, he wrote that he kept hoping that Artois's next letter would say that he was on the way from England to France – a pointed reminder of that failure to risk his own person which even his best friends found impossible to forgive the Comte d'Artois. Louis himself, since he was the king, was not expected to involve himself in guerrilla warfare.

In January 1793, he made Artois Lieutenant-General of the Kingdom, with considerable powers over military and financial matters and over whom he should choose as advisers. These powers were extended when they separated in November 1793 and were renewed in January 1814. In 1793, he also allowed his agents abroad to report to Artois and execute Artois's orders, as well as his own, although if they had to ask for new orders – in other words if they received news which required action – they were only to write to Louis. Louis also gave Artois considerable control over Royalist efforts in Normandy, Brittany and the Vendée.[35] In 1800, to the horror of his agents in Paris, Louis seems to have been prepared to tell Artois of their existence (although not of all their names), to associate with them the Chevalier de Coigny, one of Artois's agents, and even for d'André to go to England, as Artois wanted. But by 1800, Artois had improved his position since he was now in touch with the English Government and in receipt of their funds. It was only the need for English money, Louis told Royer-Collard, which led him to approach the English Government. And Artois did get the English Government to send Louis £3,000 and to begin paying him an annual pension of £6,000 a year later, after his expulsion from Mittau, when he was desperate. Perhaps Artois was as frightened as some of his agents said they were that Louis would apply to Bonaparte for money. Artois's ambition never went quite as far against Louis as it had done against their elder brother. In 1804, again showing how much he believed Bourbon royalty to be a family business, Louis insisted on Artois's presence, and hoped for that of the other princes, when he was planning to issue a protest against Napoleon I's proclamation of the Empire.[36]

With the rest of his family, although they were of little help, Louis had fewer problems. His two nephews the ducs d'Angoulême and de Berri spent most of the 1790s fighting in the *Armée de Condé*. Berri was a short, hot-tempered and not particularly intelligent or sensible young man, whose reputation for debauchery ruined his chances of marrying a daughter of the King of Naples in 1802. His elder brother, although more sensible and restrained, was no more brilliant. But in 1795–97 he was a potential rival to Louis. Louis's standing had reached a nadir for personal as well as political reasons. He appeared violent, reactionary and negligible. Angoulême might well marry his first cousin, the daughter of Louis XVI, who left the prison of the Temple for Vienna in December 1795, and was young, beautiful and, as Louis well knew, considerably more popular than himself. They appealed as a potential king and queen to many Frenchmen on both left and right, to correspondents of the Prince de Condé as well as to Mallet du Pan and the Abbé de Montesquiou.[37]

Louis, however, was lucky in that neither his nephew nor his niece showed any sign of wanting to defy the traditional order of succession. He was also lucky that Madame Royale, as she was known until her marriage, did not inherit any of the profound hostility that had existed between her parents and her uncle in 1791–92 – although, like her father, she still believed that only by *douceur* would the Bourbons recover the throne, and she begged Louis to stop the war. What a relief it must have been for Louis to learn from her old governess, who visited her in prison, that she was *'au-dessus de tout espèce de ressentiment'* ('above any kind of resentment') and, from his agent in Vienna, where she lived with her Austrian relatives from 1796 until 1799, that she was everything she should be, *Française, sujette et Bourbon*. She showed no willingness to marry an archduke. She was prepared to love and obey her king and uncle – and indeed she showed much more eagerness to get to know her father's side of the family than, with the exception of Louis, they did to get to know her.

Finally on 10 June 1799 she was married to the Duc d'Angoulême at Mittau. Cossé, Louis's faithful *Capitaine des Cent-Suisses*, wrote that the marriage had made Louis look fifteen years younger. At first Louis found her quite delightful, cheerful, tender, attentive and dignified. Moreover she was, as Bonnay said, essentially *raisonnable*, and able to judge things with the *sang-froid* Louis himself possessed. She did not dwell on her past. In 1796 as in 1814, her view was always: *'Il ne faut plus songer au passé, il est trop affreux.'* ('We must not think of the past, it is too terrible.')[38] Although extremely pious, she did not scorn her royal rank or material possessions: one reason for the delay in her marriage had been her unwillingness to share Louis's insecure and poverty-stricken existence until either he was in a better position, or she had a regular income from the Austrian Emperor, the Tsar, or even the French Government. The tragedy of her life, which turned her into someone too often cold, sour and gloomy, was that she never had any children. And so in the dreary round of exile, never going to parties, never going to the theatre, this charming princess lost her looks, her youth and all her *joie de vivre*.

But even in his relations with his niece and nephew, who after 1799 were nearly always under his roof, sitting at his table and sharing in his conversation, Louis was crossed by his younger brother. For in a patriarchal society, Artois's authority over his son and daughter-in-law was as great as, and more personal than, the king's over his niece and nephew. And, as Louis wrote of Artois, in one of those sad, dry Bourbon phrases, which often reveal the key to his situation: *'Il connaît bien tous les droits d'un père.'* ('He is well aware of all the rights of a father.') This was made clear to him in January 1802 when he was again planning to go to Naples (in fact the king his cousin would not have him). He found out that because Artois, who was furious that Louis had not told him of his negotiations with Bonaparte in 1800–1, opposed the move, neither the Duc nor the Duchesse d'Angoulême would follow him. In moments of crisis, they obeyed Artois rather than Louis – a state of affairs which would have incalculable consequences in the future.[39]

One reason for the delay in Madame Royale's marriage had been her unwillingness to meet Marie-Joséphine who, as she well knew, had detested her mother. Since Louis had left Turin in 1794, he had not seen her either, although they kept up a correspondence: Louis's letters to her are considerably more relaxed, intimate and amusing than those to his brother. However, in 1799, out of a sense of duty rather than out of love, Louis summoned Marie-Joséphine to Mittau for his niece's wedding: the Queen of France could not be absent from such an occasion.

Immediately there were the most frightful scenes; as usual Marie-Joséphine was far from being *aimable et facile à vivre*, as Louis had dared write to his niece. She insisted on bringing Madame de Gourbillon, more violent and outrageously mercenary than ever, with her. Louis refused to have Madame de Gourbillon in his palace and when they turned up together, Madame de Gourbillon was immediately thrown out of Mittau. Marie-Joséphine threw fit after fit, crying, stamping her feet, threatening to leave, refusing to speak to Louis and d'Avaray, but it was all to no avail. Thereafter, sulky, less talkative than at Versailles, barely able to drag herself about and spending much of her time alone in her room writing passionately to her *amie*, Marie-Joséphine was an almost permanent and very sour presence at Louis's side. Madame de Gourbillon took her revenge by helping an adventuress show a minister of Paul I a letter from d'Avaray to another Royalist which sneered at the Tsar. This was shown to Paul I, with the result that Louis was thrown out of Mittau in January 1801, in the depths of winter.[40] No one could say that Louis and Marie-Joséphine were very wise in their choice of friends.

If Louis was unlucky in his wife and his younger brother, he was extremely fortunate with his other family imprisoned under conditions of barbaric cruelty in the tower of the Temple in Paris. Like the rest of the *émigrés*, he was lucky to get off with Louis XVI's mild condemnation in his will of their *faux zèle*, although Louis had hoped for a blessing, or some kind of acknowledgement or message. He was also lucky that the divisions and hostility of 1791–92 became less bitter in the face of the torments of imprisonment, exile and execution. By a miracle the queen and Madame Elizabeth smuggled out loving messages and Louis XVI's seal and wedding-ring to Louis and Artois, in May 1793. Louis was overwhelmed to receive such a *'gage de leur amitié, de leur confiance'* ('sign of their friendship, of their confidence'). And he showed real horror at the news of the trials and deaths of his sister and sister-in-law. *'Les cheveux ont dû vous dresser à la tête'* ('Your hair must have stood on end'), he wrote to Madame de Balbi about the latter. The old familiar family world was gone for ever, if he ever returned to France he felt it would only be *un exil prolongé*. And his horror and sorrow could hardly have failed to be increased if he had thought back to his own contribution to the tragedy.[41]

However, Louis tried to ensure that other people were not aware of this contribution, and that the divisions of 1791–92 would not continue to haunt him, or divide the Royalists. He spent a lot of time and energy in the 1790s putting the record straight, trying to prove that, in his heart of hearts, Louis XVI had favoured the *émigrés* and the invasion of 1792. Louis altered his niece's description of Louis XVI's reaction to the accusation that he was in league with the invading foreigners from *innocence* to *tranquillité*. He gathered round him, in addition to the Court officials, some of the most faithful servants of Louis XVI: the Abbé Edgeworth his last confessor, two *Gardes du Corps* who had accompanied the flight to Varennes, Hue and Cléry who had attended Louis XVI in the Temple. Louis also encouraged publications by the last two which had a tremendous effect in fixing in the minds and hearts of Europe the image of Louis XVI as the saintly, noble, martyred king, whose only fault was that he was too good for this world. (Louis even hoped that his brother would be canonized – another Saint Louis would be no bad thing for the Bourbons.) Indeed the sympathy which their books (published in 1797 and 1806 respectively) aroused would help Louis considerably in his later travels.

Only very occasionally did the conflicts of 1791–92 return to haunt Louis. When their memory was still fresh, foreign powers did occasionally reproach him with having willingly compromised Louis XVI's life. Louis blusteringly and untruthfully replied that Louis XVI had wanted him to be regent in September 1792. In 1801, the *Papiers Saisis à Bareuth*, published by the French Government, claimed that the *Affaire Favras* had been undertaken without the knowledge of the king and queen (which was untrue in her case). In 1809, d'Antraigues, lying as usual, claimed that he could embarrass Louis by producing a last minute denunciation by Louis XVI. But otherwise the memory of these divisions was smoothed away, leaving only in the minds of most people the sacred image of a devoted, united and extraordinarily unfortunate Royal Family.[42]

Louis was also lucky in that the death of his nephew in June 1795 gave him the throne. Only the Austrian Chancellor, Thugut, typically eager to embarrass the French Bourbons, was surprised that Louis took the title of king so rapidly, without checking on the details of his nephew's death. But, for the purposes of history and politics, Louis XVII was dead. Louis soon had a key witness, Madame Royale, who had already frequently expressed to Louis her conviction of her brother's death. And despite more research and books on Louis XVII than on almost any other King of France, no one has yet produced evidence to show that he did not die in the Temple. Only a brief remark in a letter to his niece in 1799 suggests that Louis was not quite so utterly convinced of his nephew's death as he pretended to be.[43]

Louis's relations with other branches of the family – his cousins the Ducs d'Orléans and the Princes de Condé – were, on the surface, fairly amicable. Louis-Philippe, Duc d'Orléans, whom Louis had long identified as '*à mon sens le plus dangereux de sa famille et de son parti*' ('in my opinion the most dangerous of his family and his party') and who, in 1795–96, had also been considered a possible king by many French politicians, in 1800 made his submission to Louis and returned to his station as a Prince du Sang: an encouraging sign for Louis of the beginnings of a return to normality. In 1804–7 in particular, Orléans was actually of some help to Louis in dealing with the English Government, and Bonnay contrasted his frank obedience with Artois's desire to keep Louis ill-informed and out of touch. However, a portent of things to come was Orléans's desire to be totally in charge of, rather than simply an agent for, Louis's affairs in Britain. He was an incorrigibly ambitious young prince who, in order to increase his own importance, was as willing to play the card of Ultra-Royalism as was Artois to play that of moderation.

The Condés, whose letters contain some fairly disrespectful allusions to Louis, were also extremely ambitious. They were prepared to disobey Louis quite happily: they all refused to go to the Vendée in 1796 when he commanded them to, and later that year they were relieved to see Louis leave their army. As d'Avaray said, they showed no concern for the glory of the reigning house. But no one did. The Republicans were their sworn enemies, annually repeating oaths of hatred to royalty. The Royalists had their own ambitions and policies, which were not always Louis's. Louis's foreign cousins had their own interests and subjects to think of. With the exception of a few of his servants and courtiers, his followers usually put their own private concerns before their duty to their king. In exile, even more than when he was a prince or on the throne, Louis was almost completely alone.

CHAPTER VI

Plans, Plots and Campaigns
1793–1807

One of the main functions of Louis's Government in exile was to produce a political programme to be applied on his return to France – an event which always, particularly between 1795 and 1800, appeared to be just round the corner. Here we descend into some of the most depressing episodes of Louis's career. Misled, exalted and transformed by the pressures of exile and of the maddened, violent world ot the Emigration, Louis issued declarations which are monuments of silliness and which helped delay the Restoration. On 28 January 1793, at the same time as declaring himself regent and Artois *Lieutenant-Général du Royaume*, Louis issued a manifesto from Hamm which was soon on sale in the Palais-Royal in Paris, declaring his intention to liberate the Royal Family, to restore the monarchy on the '*bases inaltérables de sa constitution*' (at the same time as reforming abuses), to reestablish the Church, the Magistrature and '*Français de tous les ordres sous l'exercice des droits légitimes*' ('Frenchmen of all orders in the exercise of their legitimate rights') and to carry out '*la punition sévère et exemplaire des crimes*' ('severe and exemplary punishment of crimes').

This manifesto, although probably deliberately vague (which *bases*? which *droits*? which *crimes*?), nevertheless firmly linked Louis's fate to that of the *Ancien Régime*, which had been moribund since at least 1787. It seemed deliberately intended to make enemies by the threats of punishment, rather than to try to rally support. The linking of the Royalist cause with that of the *bases inaltérables* of the old French constitution was particularly foolish since, as Louis well knew (at least this was what he had been taught as a child by Moreau), the old French 'constitution', in as much as it existed at all, far from being *inaltérable* was the result of frequent alterations or decisions by successive kings of France.

This declaration, like the next, was another sign of the degree to which Louis had absorbed the mental attitudes of the world of the violent Emigration. Because the Revolution had become so brutal, Republican and irrational, he had begun to subscribe to a bloc view of the Revolution, as a movement which had inevitably led to regicide and terror, which must therefore have been wrong right from the start, and so must be totally rejected. When that rejection had triumphed, then, of course, 'abuses' (he did not say which ones) could be 'reformed'. Louis and his advisers forgot that the Revolution was not a bloc but a series of quite separate and often opposed movements, many of which, such as the abolition of the provinces and the *parlements*, or the creation of a franchise based on property, could actually benefit royal authority or the power of the elite. But in the isolation of exile, when almost the only news from France was of chaos, terror and the triumph of atheism, Louis's loathing for the Revolution turned him against all reforms which were not absolutely necessary. '*Voilà ce qui nous coûte pour avoir voulu réformer*' ('Look how we are paying for having wanted to reform') he wrote to his nephew the Duc d'Angoulême in 1797, thereby showing that he believed that the reforms of the reign of Louis XVI had led directly to the horrors of the Revolution.[1]

On 7 July 1795, in one of his first acts as king, Louis issued the Declaration of Verona. In it, comparing the beginnings of his reign to the catastrophic and bloodthirsty start of that of Henri IV, he directly attacks the Revolution, blaming the French – *vous* – for having been misled by *hommes factieux et impies*, declaring his wish to reestablish the old government '*qui fut pendant quatorze siècles la gloire de la France et les délices des Français*' ('which for fourteen centuries was the glory of France and the delight of the French') and to possess royal authority in all its plenitude. The Declaration of Verona does, however, represent an advance on the declaration issued from Hamm. Despite advice to the contrary, Louis made no mention of the *parlements*; he specifically mentioned complete equality for all before the law and equal access to all positions; he made no specific mention of the *émigrés*' confiscated land; and he now threatened with punishment only those who had condemned the king, the queen and Madame Elizabeth to death.[2]

But this was very unwise, since many of these Regicides (who were by no means the most criminal of the revolutionaries) were still in positions of great power. The unforgivable thing about the Declaration of Verona, which delighted the more reactionary *émigrés*, was that Louis was at the time receiving advice that he must issue a declaration which would not *dégoûter* moderate opinion and the constitutional Royalists. Louis was to a certain extent a fish in a stream, caught up in the torrent of emotions, reactions and illusions of the violent Emigration – a world so violent and emotional that the French *émigrés* wrote more letters, articles, pamphlets, books and memoirs than any other group of that size in history; the trouble was they had too much free time and they were sure they were right. But, even at Verona in 1795, Louis could have chosen other streams to swim in.

On 1 June 1795 Castries, one of Louis's more sensible ministers, had written to him that he was feared for his vengefulness, his entourage and his '*tendances vers l'Ancien Régime*', which were only shared in France by Charette and the Chouans, and warning Louis of possible preferences for Orléans or a foreign prince as regent. The English Foreign Minister advocated holding out promises of forgiveness even to the Regicides.[3] Louis's own common sense and reason should have told him that the best course for an exiled pretender would be to promise as much as possible to as many different parties as possible, to threaten nobody, and then to sit back and wait for the idiocy, cruelty and unpopularity of the Republicans to drive everyone back into the arms of the king.

But Louis had now imprisoned himself in his bloc interpretation of the Revolution and perhaps in the exaltation of becoming king of France he felt impelled to return to the old, tried formulae of French royalty – the King, the three Orders and the *États-Généraux*, Henri IV. Castries, who came to Verona in August 1795, but left a few months later, complained that Louis wanted nothing less than the royal prerogative '*dans sa plénitude, telle que Louis XIV et Louis XV l'ont exercée.*'[4] ('in its fullness, as Louis XIV and Louis XV exercised it').

However, as with so many aspects of Louis's life, one has to look at the other side, in this case at his constant preoccupation with public opinion. He proscribed the Regicides because he did not want people to be able to say that he was so eager for the throne that he was prepared to forgive the murderers of his own family. Louis was indeed a king haunted by his past, by the fact that people knew that he had wanted to enter the Council and to come to power at the head of the party of Coblentz. And in reality, right from the moment the Declaration of Verona was issued, Louis was prepared to forgive the Regicides and allow them to go into exile, in the rather unlikely event of any of them helping him to recover the throne.[5]

Moreover, Louis's decision to issue the Declaration of Verona may have been due not only to an actual belief in its contents (although, as we have seen, he was prepared to suspend belief over punishment of the Regicides) but also, yet again, to his family position. Louis always had differences of opinion with Artois, although in these years the exact nature of these differences is hard to establish: in 1794 one document written by an adviser of Castries claims that, if they are separated, the two princes will never be able to agree on the *principes d'administration à établir*.[6] Artois's opinions would be followed by his sons and the powerful, pugnacious princes of the House of Condé. But Louis believed in the tradition which had been given visible form by his presence at the *Assemblées des Notables* and in the Council in June 1789, namely that French royalty was essentially a family business. He felt that if he changed the very nature of royal authority and did a deal with the Revolution *'ses successeurs seraient en droit de réclamer contre son consentement et qu'ainsi pour une paix passagère . . . il ouvrirait une source intarissable de discorde et de guerres civiles'* ('his successors would have the right to protest against his consent, and so for a transitory peace . . . he would open up an endless source of discord and civil war').[7] In other words, in this crucial letter, written at a particularly depressed moment of his fortunes, at Turin on 19 February 1794, Louis was saying that his heirs were prepared to fight him if he went too radically against their wishes. What a difference it might have made if he had had a son of his own!

Thus, in judging Louis's activities during the Emigration, we must always remember how concerned he was to prevent his heirs from behaving to him as he and Artois had behaved to Louis XVI in 1791–92. When we consider that an English diplomat not particularly well disposed toward Louis found him less 'confused and prejudiced' than his entourage, that one of Louis's agents offered to resign if Louis did not promise to restore the *parlements* the moment he recovered the throne, while as late as 1797 d'Avaray totally rejected the idea of advising Louis to put himself in the place of the Directory, one can launch a theory that Louis consciously decided to remain the King of the Emigration and of his Government in exile with a chance of recovering the throne of France, rather then risk doing a deal with the unreliable Republicans and so losing the support of his family and of the Emigration. He did not want, like Louis XVI in 1787–88 and 1791–92, or Joseph II in 1789–90, to find his policy sabotaged by a large section of the ruling elites in return for the chance of an unstable and unprestigious throne.[8]

On the other hand, Louis did commit himself personally to the Declaration of Verona over and over again. Lord Macartney found him extremely proud of his part in it, and regarding 'the French Constitution . . . with the same fondness as the Common Law was contemplated by My Lord Coke'.[9] Moreover, in 1795

Louis sacked as *Capitaines des Gardes* the Prince de Poix and the
Duc d'Ayen, two members of the Noailles family famous for their
moderate views. This measure, which left one of the four posts of
Capitaine des Gardes du Corps du Roi free for d'Avaray, had a
catastrophic effect on French opinion. Court office was usually
separate from political beliefs. (Louis XV had not sacked his
Capitaines des Gardes for their opposition to his abolition of the
parlements in 1770–71).[10] Was there, then, no hope for moderate
royalism?

It was in these years that moderate, aristocratic politicians with
considerable experience of the Revolution felt that it was all over
with the Bourbons. Talleyrand, who frequently failed to show
that perfect judgement with which posterity has credited him,
wrote to his old friend Madame de Staël, in the same month that
the *sections* of Toulon were asking for Louis: '*C'est une maison
finie . . . que la maison de Bourbon*' ('The House of Bourbon is
finished'); the *maison de Talleyrand*, by implication, was not.
Louis's ex-*Premier Ecuyer*, Montesquiou, now an exile from the
Republic he had served in 1792, was infuriated by the Declaration
of Verona, and wrote: '*Le sort a sans doute arrêté la fin de cette
race.*' ('Doubtless providence has decided the end of this family.')
While, in a famous phrase, which is all that most people know
about the later Bourbons, another *émigré* wrote that Louis would
never recover the throne, since '*personne n'a su rien oublier ni rien
apprendre*' ('they have learnt nothing and forgotten nothing').[11]

Fortunately, however, these prophecies were quite untrue. For
from 1796 Louis began the slow, blundering retreat from the
extremism of 1793–95 which ended in the *Charte* of 1814. Indeed
this retreat actually began the moment the Declaration of Verona
was issued. Louis was prepared to modify this disastrous document not on the representations of the English Government or of
French politicians, whom he had no reason to trust, but in order
to suit the needs of his representatives in the interior. On 8 July
1795, Flachslanden told Charette, the Vendéen general, that he
could leave out from the Declaration anything, except its basic
principles, which might have a dangerous effect, since '*ceux qui
sont dans l'intérieur peuvent mieux juger de la disposition des
esprits et de l'effet que la déclaration produira qu'on peut dans
l'éloignement*' ('those who are in the interior can judge public
opinion and the effect the declaration produces better than one
can from a distance'). It was a piece of common sense which
should have made Louis hesitate before issuing the Declaration at
all. A few months later Louis wrote much the same to another

Royalist leader.[12] He was always aware that exile was the dominating factor in his life in these years.

Moreover, Louis was soon told that his Declaration had had a
disastrous effect on public opinion, and that many French people
hated him because they feared he would bring back such detested
aspects of the *Ancien Régime* as the *Intendants*, the *gabelle* and
the *dîmes*: Louis rarely had to suffer from advisers who dressed
up the truth. In a remarkable sociological analysis of the situation,
he was told that the mass of French people, in particular the
bourgeois, '*cette classe véritablement règnante*', were attached
to the frequently illusory (new names for old practices) reforms
of the Revolution '*d'autant plus qu'ils les regardent comme le seul
dédommagement qui puisse compenser en quelque sorte tout ce
que la révolution leur a fait perdre et souffrir*' ('all the more
because they are regarded as the only way in which they can
somehow be compensated for all the Revolution has made them
lose and suffer').[13] The Revolution had to be accepted because it
had been so painful.

So in February 1796 Louis issued instructions to his agents,
which were still basically reactionary, but which disclaimed any
intention to restore the *Ancien Régime*, only a purified *Ancienne
Constitution*: and he stressed his promises of equality before the
law and equality of job opportunity. However, Louis also now
went into detail on the reestablishment of the *parlements* and the
organization of the States-General which were to be divided into
three orders, the *Tiers État* to be elected only by *roturiers propriétaires*, although in 1789 it had been elected by almost all
adult males. In March 1796, another Declaration stated that the
parlements were not to be restored immediately, *biens nationaux*
were to be returned to their original owners and new muncipal
authorities were to be elected by the *notables habitants*. This was
an early use of the word *notable* combining nobles and non-nobles
since there was no real conflict between the two, would be used
to describe the ruling class of nineteenth-century France.[14]

Biens nationaux were the confiscated lands of the Church and
the *émigrés*, which since 1790 had been sold off by the French
Government. Their sale was seen by many people as a profound
injustice (even Bonaparte handed back many unsold *biens nationaux* to their original owners after 1800). Most *émigrés* had left
France simply to escape danger, rather than for political reasons:
property, the foundation of all eighteenth-century society, should
not have been tampered with by governments for their own political purposes. Indeed such was the lack of confidence in the
Revolutionary settlement, that even as late as 1800 *biens nation-*

aux were being sold for only half to three quarters of their market
value. Louis, who regarded property as sacred and justice as the
first duty of a king, was particularly appalled at the injustice of
these confiscations, and for a long time could not bring himself
to sanction them, despite the political advantages he would have
gained in doing so.

In July 1796, Louis was still demonstrating his adherence to the
Ancienne Constitution by rejecting the advice of Wickham the
English spymaster, of Précy, of Boissy d'Anglas, his former
Maître d'Hôtel Ordinaire, and even of the Abbé Brotier of the
Agence de Paris, to negotiate with various 'constitutional'
Représentants of the *Conseils des Cinq-Cents* and *des Anciens*,
the two legislative chambers of the *Directoire*, the regime which
ruled France from 1795 to 1799. But Wickham, who was seeing
a lot of Louis at Riegel, 'obtained' that this refusal should be
concealed from the *Représentants*.[15] And thereafter, persuaded
also by La Vauguyon, d'André and above all the Abbé André,
who had returned to Blankenburg from Paris in late 1796, and
perhaps (but there is no proof) alarmed that moderate *Représentants* might consider the candidacy of the Duc d'Orléans or of a
Spanish Bourbon, Louis accepted the necessity of working within
the parliamentary system of the *Directoire*. In November 1796,
to the horror of d'Antraigues (now quite without influence) and
Artois, Louis issued instructions to his agents to work for good
elections.[16]

Such instructions did not necessarily mean that Louis was prepared to abandon his attachment to the *Ancienne Constitution*
but, as some contemporaries realized, the means of achieving
power often affects the nature of the power obtained, a regime
emerging from a republican assembly was likely to retain many
revolutionary characteristics, and institutions which were not restored immediately might well never be restored at all. Louis was
still profoundly attached to the *Ancienne Constitution*, as is
shown by the long treatise *Les Devoirs d'un Roi*, which he wrote
at Blankenburg in early 1797 for his nephew the Duc
d'Angoulême. Perhaps the last, but certainly not the most original, of such treatises, it states that a king should not rely solely
on the advice of his ministers, that he has an absolute duty to
enforce justice and ensure that religion is respected (Louis wrote
that it was better to encourage hypocrisy than to tolerate vice)
and that the king should wield the executive and administrative
power of the state. The king must also maintain a splendid Court,
since most people judge power by outward appearances, but he
must ensure that his favours go to those who deserve them. Louis

also stated that new laws and taxes needed the consent of the States-General, and reaffirmed his attachment to the *Ancienne Constitution*.[17]

This document was completely different in its assumptions and attitude from the advice he was receiving from his Paris agents and from his new minister, Saint-Priest. Saint-Priest was in favour of maintaining every really useful change since the Revolution and of accepting the existence of modern assemblies. Another plan which reached Louis in April 1797 was also essentially moderate and opposed to the division of Frenchmen into orders. It proposed a two-chamber legislature, and *parlements* which were simply law-courts, although, unlike Louis's plans, it was in favour of reviving *droits seigneuriaux*.[18]

Where the latter plan agreed with Louis's declarations was in basing recruitment of the army, whose role at Court and in the nation was to be increased enormously, on merit. Even in the Declaration of Verona, as well as praising the Vendée, Louis had praised the *courage* and *honneur* of the Republican army. By late 1796, he was sending out letters *en blanc* for use with Republican officers, promising them advancement if they helped bring about a Restoration.[19] The one thing Louis never had any difficulty in accepting about Revolutionary or Napoleonic France was its officers, whatever their background. Military success, had been one of the most admired qualities in France before 1789, indeed one of the bases of French society and of the power of the monarchy. The restriction of senior military positions to the nobility after 1781 had been to a certain extent theoretical and had gone against the traditions of the French army. It could be abandoned without any difficulty.

On 10 March 1797 Louis issued a more moderate proclamation from Blankenburg promising to protect religion and the *Ancienne Constitution*, but admitting that the latter could receive '*de nouveaux degrés de perfection*' as a result of consulting public opinion. He now disclaimed any idea of vengeance, even against the Regicides, and hoped that favourable elections and public opinion would bring about a success '*qu'elle seule peut rendre solide et durable*': at last moderation and common sense were beginning to appear, with more promises than threats. Louis's instructions to his agents in April, however, reflected the principles of *Les Devoirs d'un Roi*. He still wanted France to be organized into three orders, represented in the States-General, with laws administered by *parlements*. But he admitted that all new laws needed the consent of the States-General and renounced all arbitrary justice.[20] The length Louis had gone from the Declaration of

Verona can be measured by the horrified reaction of some Royalists: '*il paraît que l'on veut régner coûte que coûte*' ('it seems
he wants to reign whatever the price'), wrote the Marquis de La
Jaille to Puisaye.[21]

In 1799, when the successes of the Allied armies in the Empire
and in Italy made the Restoration appear simply a matter of
months away, he was still incorrigibly and irrationally attached
to the *Ancienne Constitution* – far more so than Saint-Priest. In
June he wrote a long self-congratulatory memoir praising his own
wisdom and foresight in having issued the Declaration of Verona
and having refused proposals of *accomodement*. If he had done
so, he wrote, he would have fared as badly as did Charles II with
the Scottish Presbyterians in 1651 – forgetting that support for
the Revolution was not as geographically limited in France as
Scottish Presbyterianism had been in Great Britain. However, he
did admit that '*autant qu'on peut en juger de loin, qu'il y a des
choses tellement détruites qu'on ne peut les rétablir, et que parmi
les nouvelles institutions il y a de bonnes à conserver*' ('as far as
one can judge from a distance [again the dominating fact of exile]
some things are so destroyed that one cannot reestablish them,
and among the new institutions some are good enough to be
preserved').[22]

His instructions to his agents of 29 April and 25 June 1799,
while still based on the desirability of the mythical *Ancienne
Constitution* and speaking of the summoning of the States-General, and the return of the *biens nationaux* to their original owners
(but not by force), did represent a further advance down the path
of common sense. He proposed to keep the administrative and
judicial structure of the Republic – at last no more *parlements*.
And in 1800 he finally abandoned his blind, mad, *émigré* attachment to the *Ancienne Constitution*, promised a total amnesty
and wrote to his agents that all he wanted was to avoid a permanent, unicameral legislature, to which ministers were responsible, and the confirmation of the sale of *biens nationaux*. He had
realized that post-Revolutionary France was a conservative, not
a revolutionary society, and so accepted its political and administrative structure and almost its social structure – the nobility
and the Church were just to be bodies without legal privileges.
Louis had finally realized that, as d'Avaray wrote, '*qui veut la fin
veut les moyens*' ('who wants the end wants the means'), and that
as Saint-Priest pointed out, the new France was an even more
favourable field for royal authority than the old.[23]

In 1805, Louis issued an even more moderate proclamation
(dated 2 December 1804) in order to protest against what he

called *l'horrible farce* of the coronation of Napoleon I. It reflects, in part, the influence of d'Avaray, by now boasting of his *esprit conciliant*, of the Archbishop of Reims and of an unknown adviser from France who came to meet Louis at Calmar.[24] In it Louis openly and explicitly renounced the Declaration of Verona and its *maximes antiques* since '*tant d'années et de bouleversements nous imposaient la loi de modifier nos idées sur les voies de la restauration*' ('so many years and changes compelled us to modify our ideas on the realization of the restoration'). It was quite an admission for such a proud prince. He stated that he wanted to keep the army and the administrative and judicial structure of France as they were, offered an amnesty to all who would not oppose a restoration and, in a new departure, promised to abolish conscription and political prisons, and to reduce taxes. Here is a precursor of the appeal of the Restoration in 1814, and the declaration, although it denounces Bonaparte's '*système de perfidie, de violence, d'ambitions sans limites*', lavishes praise on the army and on '*la profession guerrière, véritable origine de la noblesse*' ('the warrior's profession, the true origin of the nobility'). Only on the *biens nationaux*, despite the advice even of such a Counter-Revolutionary as Joseph de Maistre, was there still some hesitation. Louis could not bring himself to sanction their sale openly, and simply stated that he would adopt '*une direction conforme . . . au véritable voeu de la nation*' ('an attitude in accordance . . . with the real wishes of the nation').

These declarations were often the only thing French people knew about Louis, since they were widely distributed inside France, even, in 1797, being printed in the Government newspaper the *Moniteur*.[25] But they were not just the product of Louis's consultations with his ministers and agents in his *cabinet* at Verona, Blankenburg or Blankenfeld; nor were they simply a reflection of opinion inside the particular stream of the Emigration which Louis had chosen for himself. They were also the result of events in France, news of which always filtered through to Louis (he took three or four French newspapers). The first declaration, for example, was the result of the news of the execution of Louis XVI, which it promised to avenge.

Since then France had been in torment – civil war, terror, famine and inflation. To take only one example, Lyon, the second city in France, had revolted in 1793 against the tyranny of the Convention. Like the uprising at Toulon, the revolt began in the name of the Republic, but became increasingly Royalist in sympathy. After the fall of the city on 10 October 1793, its name was changed to *Ville Affranchie*. Fouché then instigated a reign of terror; special gutters had to be constructed under the guillotines, since the inhabitants complained of the stench caused by the congealed blood of the hundreds of decapitated bodies. A quicker way of killing suspects was soon found, however, by lining them up in chains and firing cannon at them. This particularly horrified contemporaries for its cruelty (not everyone died at once) and lack of dignity. Lyon is a particularly murderous example. But one American historian has estimated that during the Reign of Terror proper between 35,000 and 40,000 people were killed in France off the field of battle.[26]

A few months later Louis's old courtier Boissy d'Anglas, who was also a respected *Représentant*, could actually compare Robespierre to Orpheus, charming France by the magic of his voice. It is hard to know who was less realistic, Louis XVIII who wanted France to return to 1789, or the Revolutionary Government which wanted to create a new era even to the point of having a new calendar. The Revolutionary era was dated from the proclamation of the Republic, thus 22 September 1793 to 21 September 1794 was *An II de la République*. The Revolutionary Government was so irrational that it changed the names not only of towns like Lyon, but also of months and days, and substituted the *décade* of ten days for the week. No one can seriously call the Counter-Revolutionaries the only stupid side.

With the fall of Robespierre and the proclamation of the Constitution of the Year III, however, the Terror shuddered to a halt, although terror never wholly ceased to be used as an instrument of government until 1814. The new Constitution restricted the second round of the franchise to an incredibly small number of rich men, only 30,000 – probably even less than Louis's plans would have allowed.[27] This Constitution, which Louis called *purement aristocratique*, showed that there was an area of agreement between the Republic and the Counter-Revolution, since they both wanted a narrow, property-based franchise. And here the contradictions in the *Directoire*, and later the Empire, came to the fore. They were both regimes based on property. But a large proportion of property-owners, perhaps even a majority, were rediscovering their attachment to monarchy under the Republic. For the Terror and the Emigration had weakened, but by no means destroyed, the old ruling classes. Of the 16,500 victims of the Terror whose trials are properly recorded, only 6.5 per cent were from the clergy, 8.25 per cent from the nobility and 24.5 per cent from the middle class: the rest were peasants or urban labourers. Of the 129,099 recorded *émigrés*, 25 per cent were from the clergy, 17 per cent from the nobility and 33.25 per cent from the middle class: the rest were peasants or urban labourers. These figures underestimate the proportion of the *Tiers État*.[28]

Since there had been at least 200,000 nobles in France before 1789, this means many nobles remained on their estates during the Revolution or, like the future Marshals Davout, Marmont, Berthier and Pérignon, joined the army. Sometimes it seems that all it required was a minimum of discretion and a safe location to remain unaffected. A landowner could even increase his estates during the Revolution, since the market was flooded with so much extremely cheap land. The Duc de Luynes, for example, spent the entire Revolution at his beautiful *château* of Dampierre, ten miles south of Versailles, simply adding to his estates. Thus the nobility by no means disappeared from economic prominence in France after 1789.

There are no figures for changes in land-ownership for the whole of France. One historian estimates that the hypothetical average nobleman from the area round Toulouse lost only one fifth of his land, and one third of his income (owing to the increase in taxation and the loss of feudal dues), as a result of the Revolution, while another has estimated that in the Departément du Nord round Lille, the percentage of land held by the various sections of society in 1789 and 1804 were: the nobility, 21 and 13; the bourgeoisie, 16.5 and 28.5; the Church, 19.5 and 0; and the peasantry 30.5 and 42. The persistent wealth and power of the traditional elites in France is one reason why Louis was so grateful to the Court officials who shared his exile; he knew that, simply by following the torrent of events, they could have kept, or even increased, their fortunes.[24] It was the Church, not the elite, which was the greatest loser from the Revolution.

Land-ownership and government office or military position were indeed perhaps even more important after than before the Revolution, since they had become the most reliable sources of wealth. The great seaports of eighteenth-century France were now declining for lack of trade, for France was almost permanently at war. After his release from prison in 1794, the great eighteenth-century painter Hubert Robert had no need to go to Rome to paint ruins. There were enough in and round Paris. A report addressed to Louis's agent in Vienna in 1804 noted that commerce was languishing, bankruptcies were frequent and only agriculture was flourishing. The Revolutions, far from being 'capitalist' or 'bourgeois', had delayed France's industrial development by fifty years.[30]

Discontent with the disastrous, chaotic, barbaric, Parisian Republic did not at first, as the example of Lyon shows, take Royalist

form. Louis was feared even after 1795, and even in the Counter-
Revolutionary west, because he was considered too vengeful. It is
also probably true to say that in the 1790s 'monarchy by itself no
longer possessed the force to attract devotion from any significant
part of the population'.[31]

However, it was very easy for anti-Government movements to
become Royalist, since there were still so many devoted, military
and energetic Royalist leaders and members of the old elites
around. This is what happened in the Vendée. For example, two
nobles, Scépeaux and Donnissan, who had been among Louis's
Gentilshommes d'Honneur before 1791, were called from their
estates to head the revolt. A similar process took place in Toulon,
an example constantly cited by Louis after 1793.

To Louis's shame, when he was still afraid that Toulon was
'constitutional', the English commissioner was writing that 'the
white cockade is universal and Mon Roi in every mouth'. By the
end of the revolt almost everyone, except the *cannoniers* (always
revolutionary), was wearing the Royalist white cockade instead
of the Revolutionary tricolour, as a result of energetic Royalist
leadership from the *Comité Général des Sections*.[32]

After 1795 there were many signs of the continued strength of
French Royalism. Terrorist gangs led by diehard Counter-Revolutionary leaders killed thousands in the south of France – and an
even more impressive sign of the strength of Royalism – were not
punished by the authorities.[33] After September 1796, there was a
lull in their activities, which coincided with the change in Louis's
policy and in the elections of spring 1797 Royalists did extremely
well. Known Republicans were elected in only ten departments
and moderates like Montesquiou and Talleyrand, who had con-
fidently written off the Bourbons a few years before, were now
themselves rejected by the electors in favour of the Bourbons'
supporters.[34]

By 1799, as the Republic lurched from *coup d'état* to *coup
d'état*, demonstrating itself incapable of protecting its citizens
from chaos and war, France was even more Royalist. Portalis, a
sensible former *Représentant*, who had been expelled in 1797,
wrote: '*Il n'y a point de républicains. La lassitude qui termine
toutes les révolutions a ramené tous les esprits et tous les coeurs
à la monarchie.* ('There are no republicans. The exhaustion which
ends all revolutions has drawn all hearts and minds back to the
monarchy.') As Louis knew, not all hearts, particularly among the
rich and successful military and intellectual elites, had been won.
But even an aged *philosphe* such as Volney, according to a well-
known story of the time, told the First Consul Bonaparte, who

was talking about consulting the people: '*Mais citoyen consul, si vous écoutez le peuple, il vous demandera aussi un Bourbon.*' ('But Citizen Consul, if you consult the people it will ask you for a Bourbon.') This seems to be confirmed by reports from many parts of France in 1799. In November 1799, even in Belgium, which had had nothing to do with the Bourbons before 1789, rebel peasants were crying '*Vive Louis XVIII.*'[35]

Unfortunately, this anti-Republican and Royalist sentiment only helped consolidate the first years of the Consulate after November 1799, since it was seen as a government of order, possibly preparing a restoration of the monarchy. Building on foundations laid by the Republic and the Directory, Bonaparte (whom Louis called B.P.) was soon able to have a direct executive power such as no king, not even Louis XIV, had possessed. Restrictions to government power such as the *parlements* and the provinces had been swept away, as Saint-Priest delightedly noted. From 17 February 1800 the Government had its own network of permanent agents throughout the country, headed in each department by a prefect. There were now so many Government employees (at least 100,000) that France had finally, like the great military monarchies of the east, become a uniform, centralized and obedient bureaucratic state. And the French Government under the First Consul, soon to become Emperor, was now, as Louis noted, *monarchique dans le fait*[36] (which is, no doubt, why he was prepared to accept so many more aspects of post-Revolutionary France after 1800). All the anti-authoritarian and anti-monarchical sentiments and actions of the 1780s and 1790s had resulted in the strongest, most authoritarian monarchy France had ever known. The ministries whose ambitions Necker had noted in the 1780s (see page 10) had finally realized them.

This gradually more anti-Revolutionary and monarchical France clearly offered Louis considerable opportunity to apply the programmes outlined in his different declarations. The first method open to him was violence. France was constantly at war with a variety of powers between 1793 and 1801, always including England and except for a few months in 1797–98 Austria. Therefore Louis naturally turned to the different Allies for help. However, as has already been stated, the Allies (except perhaps England after 1795, and Russia in 1798–99) never committed themselves wholeheartedly to Louis's cause. They were prepared to give him shelter in Hamm, Blankenburg, Warsaw and Mittau. England and Russia were willing to give him money. But that was usually as far as they were prepared to go. Austria and Prussia in particular, after their experience of the campaign of 1792, and of the unenthusiastic reception the *émigrés* had received, regarded Louis as a loser. In 1793, when the Austrians occupied the slice of northern France round Valenciennes, they ruled it in the name of their emperor, to whom all authorities were forced to take an oath, rather than in the name of the King of France. In 1796, Austria insisted Louis leave the *Armée de Condé*. Even England probably hoped to annex Toulon in 1793, and governed Corsica in the name of George III between 1794 and 1798. In 1799, after a period of being quite pro-Louis, it withdrew financial support from his agents and prevented him from going to the eastern front. Spain even hoped to put a Spanish Bourbon, rather than Louis XVIII, on the throne of France.[37]

However, there was another possibility open to Louis, violence inside France. The first rising in the Vendée in early 1793 surprised Louis and Artois at Hamm as much as everyone else: they had had contact with the Marquis de La Rouerie in 1791–92, but his attempts to engineer a Royalist rising in Brittany had come to nothing. At first they thought the revolt was led by a mythical M. de Gaston, and they sent off anxious messages to find out '*si c'est le Roy de la constitution qu'il veut servir ou le roy de l'ancienne monarchie française*' ('if it is the King of the Constition or of the old French Monarchy whom he wants to serve') and to combat any '*préventions defavorables*' there might be against their entourage and the *émigrés* in general.[38]

Thus right from the beginning of the long saga of the Vendée we are plunged into the problems of the divisions in the Royalist movement. In fact Louis was relatively lucky with the *constitutionnels*, many of whom (Hervilly, Pontlabbé, d'André and Précy for example) would serve him very well, although Hervilly was worried about Louis's assumptions of the regency (which by French Royal tradition should have gone to the imprisoned queen). The main problem was that until 1797 Louis did not want the services of constitutional Royalists, unless they wholeheartedly subscribed to his Counter-Revolutionary views.

But the main Vendéen rising collapsed in December 1793, and the *émigrés*' attempted landing at Quiberon in 1795 was a disaster, largely because they and the Vendéens simply did not have enough men, although it was exacerbated by rivalry between Hervilly and Puisaye. And by 7 February 1796 Louis could write that he was opposed to *mouvements partiels*, which shed good Royalist blood pointlessly.[39] His opposition can only have been increased by the knowledge that any Vendéen movement was more likely to rebound to the credit of Artois, who always managed to keep Louis's nominees such as the Comtes de Chalus or de Béhague from having any influence in the area. Moreover, right from the beginning Louis was alarmed by the *prétensions* of any Vendéen army. Even Charette, with whom he had had good relations, disobeyed him. And even the Prince de La Trémoïlle, an agent of Louis on a mission to Mittau in 1798, was by his own admission more concerned to ensure a dominant role for the Vendée in a Restoration, than to bring about a Restoration with the help of the south and east of France. La Trémoïlle was one of the last examples of an independent great noble. Even in the middle of a revolution, he was still basically distrustful of royal authority, and annoyed by Saint-Priest's manners, bow and smiles, simply because he was a royal minister – a case of Louis's friends being almost as hostile to his cause as his enemies.[40]

They were certainly less effective. One of the reasons La Trémoïlle was at Mittau was to try to coordinate Royalist risings for the Austro-Russian 'final push' in 1799. But none of these risings went off at the right time to coincide with the invasion, which was, anyway, defeated. The *Agence de Souabe* could not control the Royalists on the ground in the south-west, although they did have contact through a Royalist organization, the *Institut Philanthropique*. In August 1799 near Toulouse, 10,000 men under an ex-Republican general, Rougé, rose two weeks early, but only 1,000 had guns, and the Royalists of Bordeaux did not join them.[41] The Vendée and Normandy only rose in October 1799 – on Artois's rather than Louis's orders. All these risings were defeated.

Thus Royalist violence was a failure. Moreover, even if one or two provinces had been conquered, would it really have helped bring about a Restoration? As in the Russian Civil War, the central Government's geographical advantages were likely to ensure its victory, if it only had to face piecemeal provincial insurrections. Only a really effective national organisation could have conquered France from within; and this never existed. But Louis also had peaceful means of bringing about a Restoration at his disposal: not only by spreading his declarations, which until 1797 were probably counterproductive, but also by using the resources of the Church. Louis, always extremely sensitive to public opinion, was trying as early as 1794, with some success, to use *curés* to uphold the cause of the king. He believed, as he wrote to the *émigré* bishops, that '*sans l'opinion publique, la monarchie ne sortira de ses ruines*' ('without public opinion, the monarchy will not emerge from its ruins'). In the election of 1797, some bishops helped to distribute royalist propaganda, although in October

1797 they refused to follow Louis's instructions to set up a network of royalist missionaries throughout France.[42] It is likely that
these efforts to use the Church for political purposes did have
something to do with the increasingly Royalist state of mind of
France.

But the most important example of Louis trying to use peaceful
means to recover his throne was in 1796–97. After he left the
Armée de Condé in July 1796, he proclaimed that he hoped to
rely on opinion rather than on force to regain his throne. He
hoped that, as a result of favourable elections, what had happened
at Toulon in 1793 would happen in Paris in 1797, and he would
be summoned back to his throne by his grateful subjects.[43] With
his new, relatively moderate declarations, the pardon of the
Regicides, the lull in Royalist violence in the south, and the arrest
of most of the *Agents de Paris* on 31 January 1797, most of
Louis's hopes were placed on the electoral activities of d'André,
basically working for Wickham, and Des Pomelles, a member of
the *Agence de Paris* and head of the *Institut Philanthropique*. This
covered large areas of France, but its exact degree of efficacy has
yet to be established, although Louis was in direct communication
with it through agents like Dubourg de Pourquerie. In April 1797,
Louis told a representative of Puisaye (who, with the backing of
Artois, was still advocating a policy of violence) that he did not
want to shed blood, that he was relying on elections, that each
new set of deputies would be better and that they only had a
year to wait. Indeed, the elections were extremely successful and
this success was helped by the fact that much of the press including
the Bertin brothers at the *Eclair*, Michaud at the *Quotidienne* and
the Abbé Royou at the *Véridique* was Royalist.[44]

The trouble with the plan for a Restoration by parliamentary
majority was that it ignored the key to political success in the
Revolution, physical control of the capital. Strangely enough, the
Directoire was unlikely to allow itself simply to be voted out of
existence. Here, Louis and his agents (some of whom had been
arrested in January because they had been trying to win over the
colonel of a regiment stationed in Paris) showed considerably
more realism than d'André and Wickham. Louis at least sent La
Trémoïlle to Paris in July to try to organize the defence of the
Conseils with other Vendéen leaders and d'André who only
gradually condescended to trust him. Louis also rather late in the
day suggested that Royalists should infiltrate the *Garde
Nationale*.[45]

But by September 1797 d'André and La Trémoïlle had raised
at most 1,500 men; the guard of the *Conseils* proved as weak and

unreliable as the king's guards in 1789 and 1792; and the Republican army was able, at the request of the *Directoire*, to carry out a purge of 140 Royalist and moderate members of the *Conseils*. How wrong Louis had been in 1796 to say that the Vendée was more useful than the squabbling and unreliable sections of Paris who had risen in Vendemiaire in 1795 against the Convention, and had only been suppressed by the brutal determination of General Bonaparte. At least the latter were in Paris.[46]

By late 1799, elections, invasions and provincial risings had all failed. They were not, however, the only means by which Louis might recover his throne. Another possibility was to appeal to the top, to the leading generals and politicians whose influence on events was becoming more and more powerful as the Revolution moved away from its 'popular' phase of 1789–94. This means had a particular appeal for Louis who, before 1787, had lived in a world of individuals, dominated by private ambitions, greeds and intrigues, rather than a world of institutions and parties. Louis always took an extremely elitist view of the Revolutions, seeing the great majority of French people as a *masse inerte* which had been led on by a *'minorité unie, active, intelligente'*. It is typical that when there was the possibility of Marie-Joséphine meeting Republican troops in Turin, he wrote to her to try to make a favourable impression on them, *'surtout les chefs'*.[47] That was where, quite rightly, at least after 1794, he thought that power lay.

Louis's method was to appeal not only to the ambition of different individuals (offering them the *Grand Croix* of the Order of Saint Louis, a provincial governorship, a duchy, money, anything. . .) but also to their emotions, assuring people like Boissy d'Anglas or General Berthier that, in their heart of hearts, they were Royalists. In fact many Republican generals did go over to the Royalists in the 1790s. They included Pichegru, with whom Louis was in contact at Riegel in 1796, and who served on the *Agence de Souabe* after 1798; Willot, who helped bring about Royalist electoral victories in his military command at Marseille in 1797; and Rougé, who led the rising at Toulouse in August 1799. Since another Republican general, Marceau was probably about to go over before he died, these examples suggest that Louis was not entirely wrong, that many people, even among those who had fought most fiercely for the Republic, did have a basic attachment to royalty. However, none of those approached by Louis in 1798–99, neither Barras (who was appointed *Commissaire-Général 'à l'effet de préparer et exécuter le rétablissement pur et simple de la Monarchie Française'* on 10 May 1799), nor

General Berthier, nor General Moreau, nor General Bonaparte
responded in any way to Louis's appeals.[48]

In February 1800, Louis again wrote to General Bonaparte,
now the First Consul, by way of the Marquis de Clermont-Gallerande, who was to give the letter to a friend of Joséphine and
the Abbé de Montesquiou, who was to give the same letter to
the Third Consul, Lebrun. Louis wrote another letter in June,
sending it again via the Abbé de Montesquiou, flattering and
praising Bonaparte for his military glory and the success of his
administration, but stressing that his true *gloire* would come from
the restoration of the king. When they met in the salon of the
Duchesse de Luynes, Talleyrand, who was Foreign Minister again,
assured the Abbé de Montesquiou that Bonaparte had been
touched by the letter, and tried to get a blank authorization,
signed by Louis, to conduct a negotiation (what use Talleyrand
would have put it to if Montesquiou had been silly enough to
agree?). But in fact, in a famous letter, in the tough, military style
with which France was becoming increasingly familiar, Bonaparte
rejected Louis's propositions: '*Il vous faudrait marcher sur cent
mille cadavres. Sacrifiez votre intérêt au repos et au bonheur de
la France.*' ('You would have to walk over a hundred thousand
corpses. Sacrifice your interest to the peace and happiness of
France.') If only he had practised what he preached! As Louis
wrote at the time, it was the sacrifice, not the assertion, of his
rights which would cause bloodshed. And Bonaparte, far from
assuring the '*repos et bonheur de la France*', would soon number
not a hundred thousand corpses but tens of hundreds of thousands
among the victims of his endless wars. In February 1801, to
Artois's fury, Louis indefatigably returned to the charge, writing
notes disclaiming any intentions of vengeance, or any connection
with the attempted assassination of Bonaparte in December 1800
by agents of Artois. He said how willing he would be to employ
hommes nouveaux and warned Bonaparte of the insecurity of his
position. But it is doubtful if Clermont-Gallerande or Montesquiou dared show these notes to Bonaparte or any of his circle.[49]

So all Louis's efforts to bring about his restoration had failed.
After 1804, with the establishment of the Empire, the increasing
power of its police, and the ever-increasing extent of its territory,
he was also almost completely out of touch with France. Reports
from his agents in France dried up after December 1803. To
distribute the proclamation of 2 December 1804 Louis was forced
to rely on the few contacts of Guilhermy, and on the distribution
network of the Swiss publisher Fauche-Borel, whose outlets turned
it over to the police.[50] Louis now had neither the opportunity nor

the financial means, as d'Avaray frequently complained, to keep in touch with France. In early 1807, when Louis grandly proposed to Alexander I, who had stopped at Mittau on his way to the front, that a diversion in the west of France should be combined with the Russian war effort, he was very embarrassed when the Tsar asked him about the actual details of where troops could land or who would support them. He simply did not know.[51]

That he was in such a situation after years of effort and struggle, after covering vast amounts of paper with plans, declarations and instructions, and after so much Royalist blood had been shed, must to a certain degree be Louis's own fault. He had had a very good cause, and what had he done with it? His failure to go to Toulon and his departure from the *Armée de Condé* discouraged people who could not understand the international pressures which had provoked those moves. His declarations of policy between 1793 and 1797, or even 1799, had immeasurably harmed Royalist prospects.

Louis was now personally associated with failure, which is, no doubt, one reason why many Royalists refused to serve him. He had failed to recover the throne after 1795, just as before 1787 he had failed in his attempts to make a fortune, and just as in 1789 he had failed to achieve anything by his intrigues with Favras. Moreover, Louis's failures were of a rather dishonourable sort. He was associated with foreign invasions of his own country in 1792 and 1799. In his behaviour towards his brother the king, in his attempts to win the support of the French and the foreign powers and to raise money, he had been a liar, a forger and a cheat.

One can understand why for some people Louis was now a negligible factor, even lacking the glamour so often conferred by Royal misfortunes, and why, in a proclamation of 1800, Bonaparte could call Louis and Artois '*deux hommes qui n'ont su honorer ni leur rang par des vertus, ni leurs malheurs par des exploits*' ('two men who have known how to honour neither their rank by their virtues nor their misfortunes by their exploits').[52] Too often, in his exile Louis was vain, pompous, self-satisfied, cowardly, unrealistic, ineffective and silly. For examples one has an *embarras de choix*. In a letter to Pichegru in 1796, full of praise for his own attachment to the mythical *Ancienne Constitution*, Louis declares that he would sooner die than leave the *Armée de Condé*, which of course he left three months later. In 1807, he wrote to Alexander I to claim that his presence at the front would '*fixer le succès*', and would persuade French soldiers to follow the white flag, rather than the tricolour '*que la France*

abhorre'.[53] In fact, one knows exactly what the French soldiers
would have done: they would have obeyed their officers' orders
to shoot.

Moreover, Louis was capable not just of being pompous and
silly, but of being unintelligent as well. This was shown in the
political misjudgements of which, hitherto, his political career had
been so full, and which were usually caused by the fact that he
was too dominated by the needs of the moment – money, power,
influence in the Revolution or the Counter-Revolution – to think
of his actions' long-term implications. Louis could often miss the
point of letters or speeches – something of which Artois was
rarely capable. Louis admitted, in a self-portrait he wrote about
1800: '*Je ne manque pas d'esprit, mais je n'y ai pas une grande
prestance; je ne saisis guère, le premier, une idée...*' ('I am not
without intelligence, but it is not outstandingly quick; I find it
difficult to be the first to grasp an idea...') Cases of Louis's lack
of *prestesse* or mental quickness abound, in his ordinary letters,
as well as in matters of politics. For example, it was bad enough
for Louis to compare himself to Charles II in 1651, when Scottish
Presbyterianism and the French Revolution were so different in
scope and nature (see page 118). But for Louis to compare himself
to James II or the Old Pretender, which he often did when asking
for money or wondering where to go, was not very intelligent.
Was French Royalism a lost cause like Jacobitism, even in the
eyes of its king? As many contemporaries knew, Louis could not
be relied upon to do or say the intelligent thing at the right time.[54]

That Louis could be so unintelligent, and could seem to be such
a personal failure, that he could be denounced by Bonaparte for
his lack of *vertus* and *exploits*, was extremely important. Louis
knew very well that there is a level of politics below the activities
of politicians and generals, below declarations of principle, legislative elections and the chances of war. Every minute of his
reigning life, he was aware of the immense power of public
opinion and individual reputations to determine political events.
Indeed, he was so concerned with public opinion that he felt that
one of his main tasks in exile was to acquire personal consideration and respect – in other words a good public image. '*Si je
n'acquiers pas une gloire personnelle, si mon trône n'est pas
entouré de considération ... je n'aurai pu construire une édifice
solide*' ('If I do not acquire personal glory, if my throne is not
surrounded by consideration ... then I will not have been able to
construct a solid edifice'), he wrote in a much-publicized letter in
1795. In his strange account of her years in France he blamed
Marie-Antoinette for having helped, by the disorder of her private

life, to '*enlever au trône la considération qui était sa sauvegarde la plus assurée*' ('to take away from the throne the respect which was its surest foundation'). In 1806, he wrote to Lord Grenville that '*en tout temps, et surtout dans les premiers moments d'une restauration, la considération personnelle du roi est le plus ferme appui du trône*' ('at all times, and above all in the first moments of a restoration, the personal reputation of the king is the surest support of the throne').[55]

This belief shows what an interesting man Louis was, since he is in effect claiming that the personality and reputation of a monarch are more important than his actual power, or the constitution of his country, in determining the strength of his monarchy – in other words that people are more decisive than principles. This view was undeniably true for monarchs in the years 1780 to 1830, which was an extremely dangerous and difficult period of transition and revolutions. All over Europe they were having to exchange their traditional, carefree, Olympian existence either for the more disciplined, military and bureaucratic monarchy of a Joseph II or a Napoleon I, or for the liberal and constitutional role of a King of England.

Now, more than ever, monarchs needed the armour of an impressive reputation to protect themselves from the onslaught of aristocratic pretensions and popular discontent. Without such protection, in this age of transition, they could easily be deposed or dispensed with, as was shown by the assassinations of such powerful monarchs as Louis's old friend Gustavus III of Sweden in 1792 and Paul I of Russia in 1801, the depositions of Charles IV of Spain in 1808 and Gustavus IV Adolphus in 1809, and of course, worst of all, the execution of Louis XVI in 1793. A monarch's personal character and reputation really was '*le plus ferme appui du trône*' in the years 1780 to 1830. If Louis XVI had been personally respected, trusted, loved and obeyed, could the French monarchy have fallen so ignominiously in 1792?

So it was extremely important that Louis XVIII should have a good public image; his personal reputation and *considération* might help decide the chances of his restoration. Here Bonaparte's denunciation of 1800 was not only unfair but also not wholly representative of public opinion. First, much of Louis's extremism and refusal to face facts in the 1790s are common to almost all exiles of all periods. Home is so far away, one has suffered so much, most exiles seem to feel a need to stick rigidly to emotionally satisfying, but politically disastrous, positions. No Palestinian leader dares publicly and explicitly recognize the existence of Israel, despite its thirty-one years of ever stronger statehood, and

ever increasing suffering for the Palestinian people. In 1945, the
Social Democratic Prime Minister of Prussia, expelled from office
in 1932, assumed he would automatically become Prime Minister
again after the defeat of the Nazis. Compared to these monuments
of unreality, Louis's absorption of the attitudes of the violent
émigrés between 1791 and 1799 seems relatively mild and mer-
cifully brief.

Louis's extremism was increasingly forgotten by public opinion.
Coblentz and the Declaration of Verona had been submerged by
the subsequent tide of blood. In contrast Louis's reputation before
1791, as a rational and realistic prince – a reputation partly based
on his vote, alone of the princes of the Royal Family, in favour
of doubling the deputies of the *Tiers État* in 1788 – began to
seem more true to life. For, as people were aware at the time,
Louis had learnt a lot and forgotten a lot during his Emigration.
One of Louis's principal qualities was, as has been seen during
the Revolution, his ability to adapt, to take advice and to reflect
changing situations. And by 1799, he had abandoned the extremism and rigidity of the Declaration of Verona, which anyway
had been less extreme than the Declaration of 1793. He had learnt
to be more realistic. The silliness of his letter to Pichegru in 1796
contrasts with the sense, clarity and moderation (although still
tarred with grandiloquence) of his letters to Bonaparte in 1800.

Louis's realism was not just a matter of public declarations. His
private writings also gradually became more sensible. For example, they show that he realized that the exclusiveness, and perhaps
above all the frivolity of Versailles were gone for ever. '*Je ne veux
pas être le roi de Versailles*', he wrote to Artois in early 1797,
rejecting some of his brother's proposals for undeserved favours,
and a few years later he was careful to exclude Artois's choices,
drawn from the old, unpopular Polignac set, for his niece's ladies-
in-waiting. For a Bourbon, even in exile, to say that he does not
want to be the king of Versailles is a sign of some realism. Louis's
awareness that the image of the Court as a centre of frivolity,
extravagance and undue influence had been a threat to royal
authority is shown by his note '*La Cour, mauvaise expression*' on
the manuscript of his niece's account of the Revolution, and by
the fact that he was careful to cross out *la Cour* when his niece
used it to mean the Royal Family and its immediate attendants.

Indeed, one can extract a dose of worldly wisdom from Louis's
writings in exile, which is perhaps no less representative of his
real personality than his grandiloquent public pronouncements:
'*toutes vérités ne sont pas bonnes à dire*' ('all truths should not
be told') which was endlessly repeated, and was of course par-

ticularly applicable to his own career; '*les promesses faites d'avance ne valent rien en général*' ('promises made in advance are generally worthless') – if only he had used this not to bother to commit himself so frequently to the *Ancienne Constitution*; '*tout chiffre est déchiffrable*' ('every cipher can be deciphered'), after years of secret service work, intercepted couriers and betrayals.[56]

Louis had few illusions about human nature or the nature of French Royalism. He knew that the Counter-Revolution was just as much a career as the Revolution, and that, although outwardly more respectful, it could be just as disobedient to the king. It is doubtful if Louis believed in the possibility of disinterested service of royalty: one of his favourite sayings, the product of years of experience and disillusion, was '*un petit présent entretient l'amitié*' ('little gifts keep friendship alive').[57] The frequent grateful or flattering letters he wrote to French Royalists and foreign statesmen were, as he well knew, often regarded as promissory notes, to be cashed in the event of a Restoration.

Louis had become a realist – quite a rarity in royal pretenders. His realism was a matter of deeds as well as words. He was not in favour of Royalist risings after 1796 unless they covered most of France and were combined with a foreign invasion. He wrote to a Royalist leader: '*Avant de revenir aux armes, il faut avoir de grandes chances de succès.*' ('Before resorting to arms, one must have a good chance of success.') He realized that an electoral campaign needed to be backed by physical force in the capital. He was not in favour of attempts to assassinate Bonaparte (which were dishonourable and unlikely to succeed).

Another aspect of Louis's character which helped to give him *considération* was his behaviour to those round him. His manners were always impressively and convincingly royal (see pages 37 and 90). Within the limits of his royal self-centredness, which made him automatically assume that his own welfare was of supreme importance to all round him – as indeed it was, since he was their *raison d'être* – Louis was a kind and mild master to his courtiers and servants, certainly much more so than Bonaparte.

He was extremely affectionate with the small number of friends he trusted – Hautefort, Charles de Damas and La Chatre, as well as d'Avaray. He got on well with his servants and was more generous to Péronnet, for example, than his secretary had proposed. He was always concerned with their future, writing to other sovereigns to try to get them jobs, sending a complete list of his servants, Court officials and *pensionnaires* to Alexander I in 1807, and appealing to him to look after them if he died. Even

Marie-Joséphine, embittered, irascible and heart-broken at being deprived of the company of Madame de Gourbillon, wrote to her *amie* that Louis was kind, and praised his '*sang-froid ordinaire et son sérieux*'.[58]

An important aspect of Louis's character, to which Bonaparte had referred by his mention of lack of *exploits*, was that he was a pacific, not to say cowardly, man. His failure to throw himself into Toulon in 1793 is damning, and a member of his official entourage actually wrote that Louis found the prospect of military action repugnant because Artois would be so much better at it. He need not have worried, but certainly Louis was no militarist: his very size made it improbable and impractical.

Yet even this trait was really, in political terms, a *virtu* in disguise. As he realized by 1796, it was not very wise for a king to begin his reign by fighting his own subjects. Indeed, Louis's pacific nature would become precisely one of his most respected characteristics in the years after 1800, when the one thing which the French, outside the army, came to detest most of all was war.

It was also an advantage for Louis that he was a clever, witty man of the world. The two qualities people who met him, whether they were Royalist agents, foreign ambassadors, or his own officials, always attributed to him were *connaissances* and *esprit* – *esprit* meaning much more than wit: alertness, sense and intelligence. D'Avaray, when he thought he was dying, begged the Abbé Edgeworth to tell Louis that he had '*trop de connaissances de tous les genres, et trop de justesse dans ses vues, pour avoir jamais besoin d'un premier ministre*' ('too much knowledge of all kinds, and too good a judgement, ever to need a prime minister'). A sign of what sort of wit and mind Louis had was his passion for Horace, a witty, worldly poet, as dedicated to common sense as to the avoidance of violent emotion. Louis could not stop quoting him, writing to Bonnay '*Il faut toujours en revenir à Horace*' ('One must always return to Horace').[59] His *esprit* was another useful quality; the French are prepared to forgive a great deal if they are ruled by *un homme d'esprit*.

Louis was also, like so many of his family, extraordinarily cool and calm. Even in the nightmare of exile, with all the problems of lack of money and living abroad, he remained poised and unruffled, speaking of the Revolution 'with a degree of calmness and dispassion that one could scarcely expect', and able to listen to a Vendéen's tirade against his agents for hours on end without displaying any reaction at all. Marie-Joséphine could not believe how calm and patient he was, despite some appalling problems. Again, this calm would be a positive advantage in years to come,

when France would be equally weary of the passions of the Revolutionaries and of the Ultra-Royalists.[60]

Louis's most unpleasant trait was his hypocrisy. His hostess at
Blankenfeld, Madame de Königfeld, a woman who can have had
few preconceptions, noted that in his behaviour *'ce qui manquait
le plus c'était le naturel'* ('what was most missing was
naturalness'). There was always a contrast between the frequently
effusive or grandiose words coming from Louis's mouth and the
cold, judicious, penetrating look in his eyes. Perhaps the worst
examples of his hypocrisy are his frequent assertions of his love
and affection for Louis XVI and Marie-Antoinette (in 1797 he
even compared Louis XVI, his despised brother, to Jesus Christ)
and for Artois. But this was almost a political virtue, certainly a
political necessity. He was not going to help his family's enemies
by advertising family disagreements.

Thus by 1799 Louis's character, as an intelligent, realistic,
pacific, mild, calm and increasingly moderate prince gave him a
sort of *considération*, at least in the political world, and made
his restoration less unlikely. Malouet, a famous moderate Royalist, could now praise him publicly, as a prince of a *caractère
sage et doux*, with incontestable *lumières*. The great question was
whether his *douceur*, and the evolution of his policy since 1795,
were really weakness, a sign of that lack of *fermeté* without
which, he had been taught, all Royal virtues were worthless. Only
the throne would tell.

Yet exile had already provided some indication. If Louis had
been really weak, he would not have stuck to the *Ancienne Constitution*, or d'Avaray, despite so much pressure, for so long. Nor
would he have refused to obey foreign pressure to go to Gibraltar,
to sign away parts of France, or to give up his throne in return
for a quiet life. He was tenacious rather than tough, or as he put
it, in an extraordinarily honest self-portrait: *'Je n'ai pas beaucoup
de caractère mais je crois etre plutôt timide et facile que vraiment
faible.'* ('I do not have a forceful character, but I think I am timid
and easy-going rather than really weak.') An impressive sign of
his tenacity is the way people who began serving other masters,
such as the *Agents de Paris* and d'André (who began serving
d'Antraigues and Wickham, respectively) ended up serving the
king. Louis simply by sticking to his policies and by being himself,
was in a strong position and was usually able, by tenacity and his
own personal qualities, to out-distance his rivals. This had already
happened in 1792–93, when he had gradually assumed a more
important role in the party of Coblentz, despite Artois's initial
advantages.

Above all Louis was the King of France, able to rely on the automatic reaction of love, honour and respect which those three words could still inspire. He had come through the dark tunnel of exile and emerged as a moderate, pacific king, willing to abandon his *maximes antiques*, and prepared to keep all the sensible gains of the Revolutions. At a time when Europe, and especially France, were charging into a period of unparalleled tyranny and carnage, it was impressive that one voice speaking of peace and liberty, and denouncing the French Empire as '*un système de perfidie, de violence, d'ambitions sans limites*' was that of the King of France. Eventually, he was convinced, his subjects would agree with him that although he might not be capable of starting or ending a Revolution, he was not '*incapable d'en faire oublier les maux*' ('incapable of causing its evils to be forgotten').[61]

CHAPTER VII

The King of France in the United Kingdom 1807–1814

What exactly made Louis, in the isolation and oblivion of Mittau in 1807, decide to leave Russia for England is uncertain: as with so many of the events of his life there are several equally convincing explanations. First and probably most important of all, there is a political reason, reflecting the state of Royalist plans in 1807. For a long time Louis and his agents in London had been bombarding the English Government with projects for a Royalist rising in the west of France, to be combined with an invasion from England – a prospect which seemed particularly attractive in 1806–7, when most of the Napoleonic army was fighting on the borders of the Russian Empire.[1]

As early as January 1806, Louis was using Orléans to try to persuade the English Government to allow him to land in England, since Mittau was so far from the centre of political action. Even in 1800, when he was being very well treated, Louis had wanted to leave for that reason. He also wanted to control the innumerable rival and disobedient Royalist agents operating from London. England was now, more than ever, the centre of anti-Napoleonic activity in Europe, its Government the only one which remained steadfast in its opposition to the endless expansion of the French Empire. It made sense for Louis to move there in order to try to concert measures with the English Government, particularly since his brother tended to arrogate this role to himself. In a letter to the English Foreign Minister, Louis states, with that characteristic calm which does not entirely hide the strength of his feelings, that he loves and respects Artois, but 'aimer son frère . . . ne signifie pas abandonner le timon de ses affaires. . . La providence a voulu le placer au premier rang; là il doit vivre et mourir' ('to love one's brother . . . does not mean abandoning the helm of one's ship. . . Fate has placed him [Louis] in the first rank; there he should live and die').[2]

The political and Royalist reasons for moving to England can only have been strengthened by the personal danger Louis and his

137

Court had undergone in the winter of 1806–7, when Napoleon I's armies were only 200 miles away in East Prussia. By June 1807, as the fighting drew nearer, Louis and his Court were actually preparing to leave Mittau.[3] In July, when the French and Russian Empires signed a treaty of alliance at Tilsit, the arguments for leaving must have seemed overwhelming, although Alexander I, who perhaps preferred to keep Louis as a pawn in his extremely complicated chess game with Napoleon I, wanted Louis to stay. It was extremely convenient that on 31 May Gustavus IV Adolphus, the ferociously anti-Napoleonic son of Louis's old friend Gustavus III, should have invited him to Sweden to help raise an army of *émigrés*, or French deserters, to fight Napoleon I.[4]

A third reason for Louis to leave Mittau, in addition to questions of politics and physical safety, was money. As has already been shown, although Louis was living in Russia, an increasing proportion of his income was coming from England. But it was not enough. While Artois was living in luxury in Mayfair, Louis and his Court and servants could not even afford new clothes: a few months later Orléans was struck by how shabbily dressed they all were. Louis's physical presence might be far more effective than any number of begging letters in untying English purse-strings. A Swedish noble who had known Louis at Versailles assured Gustavus IV Adolphus that he knew, '*de science certaine*', that Louis's main motive in going to England was to get access to the English money that Artois and his entourage were keeping for themselves.[5]

The actual circumstances of Louis's journey to England are typical of his career: appalling obstacles, many errors of tact and tactics, but a final semi-success. With Angoulême, d'Avaray, Gramont and some servants, he left Liebau on the west coast of Courland on 3 September 1807, on board a Swedish ship the *Troya*. They headed for Stralsund in Pomerania where they thought they would find the King of Sweden, but were struck by the worst storms in the Baltic for twenty-five years, and only just missed being swept onto the Pomeranian coast, now in the hands of Napoleon I. Everyone was sea-sick except Louis and Gramont. On 16 September they landed at Carlscrona for consultations with Gustavus IV Adolphus and then moved to Gothenburg, where more terrible storms kept them from setting out for three weeks. On 29 October they finally appeared off the harbour at Yarmouth.[6]

Well aware that he would not be entirely welcome, Louis had not asked the English Government for permission to arrive in England. Although there had been rumours that he was coming for some time, the first the Government knew of it officially was the arrival of a letter from Louis to George III, dated 16 October, assuring him that he was coming to offer the Government the aid of a powerful ally, *le Roi de France*. This was the last thing the Government wanted, especially since it had not yet given up all hope of signing peace with the French Empire, (a peace proposition actually arrived in late 1807). Canning, the Foreign Secretary, with George III's approval, sent officials to every port he could think of on the east coast – Chatham, Sheerness, Hull, Scarborough, Harwich, Whitby and Yarmouth – with orders to stop Louis landing. For five uncomfortable days Louis and his entourage of forty-four rocked and bobbed in frightful weather, three and a half miles off Yarmouth – royal boat-people whom nobody wanted.[7]

George III and his ministers were 'determined' that Louis should sail straight to Leith, where he would be allowed to live in the conveniently distant palace of Holyrood. Louis, who had hoped to be allowed to live in London (La Chatre had actually hired Grillon's Hotel in Albemarle Street), was furious, and ordered the ship's captain to return to Sweden rather than sail to Scotland. Yarmouth became a scene of endless conferences and rows, as Condé, Orléans and Artois (who assured the English ministers he supported their projects) arrived on board the *Troya*.[8]

Eventually, owing to Louis's firmness, a compromise was arranged. The Government was quite rightly frightened of the reaction of the public and of their political rivals to its treatment of Louis, as Canning admitted, 'like a scrub'. And Louis was allowed to land provided that he adopted the style of Comte de l'Isle (the name Louis took from one of his Languedoc estates, when he wished not to embarrass his hosts during the Emigration) not King of France, and stayed at least fifty miles away from London. A little late in the day two Foreign Office officials were sent to assist him to disembark, and like Canning they vied with each other in calling him Most Christian Majesty and Louis XVIII, though not King of France.[9]

The disembarkation, on 2 November, was a splendid scene. When Louis came on shore, the commanding officer, Admiral Douglas, knelt weeping in the dust to kiss his hand, and then entertained everyone to a sumptuous breakfast. According to Louis, the people of Yarmouth blessed him, saying, 'It is the King of France, it is Louis XVIII, it is the brother of Louis XVI'. He was cheered at Yarmouth and at Colchester, where he stopped for an enormous tea, he soon found himself surrounded by a curious and emotional crowd, on whom a few words '*dans mon mauvais anglais qui me servait si bien autrefois pour me tirer de prison'* ('in my bad English which was so useful, on another occasion, in getting me out of prison') had a gratifying effect. They cheered him as he left, and he thought to himself, as he later wrote to d'Avaray, *'Bon peuple . . . puisses-tu rester toujours le même!'* ('Good people . . . may you always stay the same!')[10]

But Louis was not just a *popular* success in England. From Colchester he went to Gosfield, a large country house in north Essex with a magnificent hall, ballroom and library, which had been offered to him, even before he received the Government's permission to disembark, by the Marquess of Buckingham, head of the extremely powerful Grenville family. Buckingham had many motives for his hospitality. Like Admiral Douglas, he probably saw Louis as an unfortunate king whom it was dishonourable not to help. Moreover, the French Revolution had had an immense impact on English politics. Many Whigs, particularly the Grenville faction, had broken with their leader Fox over the issue of his conciliatory policy towards the French Revolution in the 1790s; and their experience of the Empire after 1804 had done nothing to make them more enthusiastic about the Revolution and its results. In addition, the books of Hue and Cléry on Louis XVI (the latter of which had been subscribed to by the entire Royal Family, and almost the entire aristocracy, of Great Britain) had had an almost as immense an effect as the excesses of the Revolution and the Empire in predisposing people in favour of the French Royal Family. So Louis was cheered by the people of Yarmouth and Colchester and treated as an honoured guest by the Marquess of Buckingham. He was in the situation for which he had always been aiming whereby, if the English Government were to make peace with the French, it would be very difficult for them to expel their royal guest.[11]

However, the Government was absolutely firm in its refusal to allow him to live in London and have consultations with the ministers. In the second half of December 1807, Louis began to edge his way nearer the capital by moving to Wanstead, where he stayed with his cousin the Prince de Condé. The Government was furious, as were Artois, Angoulême and Orléans, whom Louis crossly called *'tout à fait anglais'*, and who now lost the royal favour which had been so marked in 1804–7. Even Gramont criticized his king to Orléans. No one wanted their comfortable English asylum endangered. But in fact Louis, though he denied an intention to live at Wanstead, won this round too. In 1808, and later, he spent several weeks there, and far from the Government being able to send him off to Edinburgh, which was still their ultimate intention, by March 1808 he could declare that he was now able to live more or less where he liked in England.[12] Not only his ultimate success in establishing himself in England, but also the mere fact that the Government was afraid of his presence, was a tribute to a certain strength in his position. He was not just another exiled royalty like the Prince of Orange or Gustavus IV Adolphus, he was still Louis XVIII, the King of France, a living institution and cause, whose political significance no one could deny.

One reason Louis had been staying at Wanstead was that he was on his way to Stowe, the huge, immensely impressive country house of the Marquess of Buckingham, who had invited his royal *protégé* to stay. In January 1808, the whole ordeal of a very grand nineteenth-century English country house visit – dinner parties for forty; revolting food, cold by the time it got to the table; a shoot, a ball, a ceremonial tree-planting, performances by the local band – was rolled out for the benefit of the Bourbons: not just Louis, his brother and his nephews, but also the Orléans, the Condés and their courtiers.

Louis coped very well. After Italy, England was the foreign country least alien to him. As a boy he had been eager to learn English; as a prince he had had English works in his library, had read English newspapers and had translated two English books. He was the most English King of France there has ever been, and indeed he was so familiar with English that at Warsaw in 1803–4 English phrases kept slipping in to his notes to Bonnay. In contrast, in all his years at Coblentz, Hamm and Blankenburg, he never bothered to learn German: at Stowe he amused one of Buckingham's nephews by asking him if he knew Welsh, since he wanted to know what the Prince of Wales' motto of *Ich Dien* meant. But Louis was able to show that he could speak as well as read and write English perfectly well. He answered Buckingham's after dinner toast of 'The Royal and Illustrious House of Bourbon and God Bless Them' with 'God bless the King and Old England for Ever', and gave another toast to 'Our Noble Landlord to whom our gratefulness is as rooted as the oldest Oak'.[13]

As so often in Louis's life there was a personal as well as a political and social reason for Buckingham's kindness and hospitality. Buckingham had an unmarried daughter of twenty-one, Lady Mary Grenville. Louis's nephew Berri was unmarried. For once in his life his family was of some use to him, since Buckingham was so proud and so grand that he saw nothing odd in a marriage between his daughter and the nephew and heir of the King of France. The result was rather comic, especially in the eyes of the hordes of observant relations staying at Stowe. Lady Mary was the life and soul of the party, walking, hunting, dancing, singing and 'setting everything in motion'. Berri, a lusty royal dwarf of thirty, appeared *'épris'* and *'se tuait pour la suivre'*, according to Orléans. At the ball everyone got rather out of control. Even Artois danced to please Lady Mary; Lord Carysfort had a nasty fall, while Miss Mary Oliver collapsed on top of Condé, who had fallen asleep in an armchair, and had to be pulled to her feet by Louis himself.[14] When 'the French party' finally left, Lady Mary wept and shrieked to show her despair, to the amusement of her cousins, but no more is heard of the planned Bourbon-Grenville alliance; and in 1810 she married the Catholic Lord Arundell of Wardour. (However, she may have kept a soft spot for the Bourbons, for she rushed to France to see Louis's entry into Paris in 1814.)

The Buckinghams and the Bourbons evidently got on quite well. Louis went to stay again at Stowe in 1810, and Lady Buckingham and Lady Mary went to stay with him. He erected a stone altar at Gosfield, expressing his gratitude for Buckingham's hospitality, which is now in the Bourbon Tower at Stowe, and he also gave Buckingham a tenth-century manuscript of the Gospels. But the most magnificent testimonial to this episode in aristocratic English enthusiasm for the Bourbons is a huge, superbly-bound blue and gold volume, containing portraits and locks of hair of all the members of the French Royal Family, and ending in a panegyric of Louis, which one of Artois's courtiers commissioned to be presented to Buckingham and which is now in the British Museum.[15]

In England, for the first time, one gets the impression that Louis was beginning to lead the life of a private individual as well as that of a Bourbon. He now had time to go on trips, to visit a rural dean and to see Oxford, Cambridge, Warwick Castle (which impressed him very much) and the factories of Birmingham: he was always as interested in economic reality as in historic monuments. The best picture we have of his daily life comes from the pens of the English visitors he would often invite down for dinner and the night, presumably for his own amusement: he had nothing much else to do.

English guests would usually arrive in the afternoon, having 'dressed', that is changed into the elaborate Court costume of brightly coloured silk and velvet which was still worn at the English Court, although not by Louis and his courtiers, who just wore plain frock-coats. Then they would be presented to the Royal Family as they were going through to dinner, which took place at five o'clock. On 14 March 1809, Edward Jerningham, an influential English Catholic who had been invited to dine at Wanstead, where the Court was staying on the way from Gosfield to Louis's next house, Hartwell, was presented to Louis as he was going through the salons on his way to dinner 'just as I remember him going through the galleries at Versailles'. He found him 'most gracious', just as a few years later Greville found him 'very civil and agreeable'. English enthusiasm for Bourbon manners – among the poor as well as the upper classes – must in part have been a reaction to the notorious manners of the Hanoverians, too often drunken or stand-offish in the case of the regent and his brothers, and absurdly direct and clumsy in that of George III.

After dinner, between six o'clock and seven-thirty or eight, people drank coffee and played cards or billiards. Louis would play whist, a game for which the *émigrés* had a passion, or would read out the English papers in French 'as if it had been in the latter language'. At eight o'clock everyone retired to their apartments, coming down again at nine for more cards and conversation until nearly midnight.

It is an extraordinary tribute to the lavishness of Regency England that one visitor (another Catholic called Thomas Clifford, whom Louis subsequently persuaded the regent to make a baronet) was actually impressed by the 'economy' and 'simplicity' of the dinner, although twenty-two people sat down to a first course of soup, *bouilli*, stew, veal, mutton and a meat pie, a second course of six fowl, two partridges (which Louis divided among the ladies), spinach and 'an immense tart', and a third course of pears and biscuits. But then the only drink served was a bottle of port, with a little malaga afterwards (perhaps so that Marie-Joséphine could not disgrace herself), which would indeed have appeared distressingly simple to the red-faced, ten-bottle English gentlemen of the time.[16]

In October 1808, Louis had been joined by Marie-Joséphine and their niece whom Angoulême, heart-broken at being parted from his wife, had gone to fetch from Mittau. Even Marie-Joséphine, by now a tiny, crooked old woman who had gone quite black with age, was cheered and blessed by the crowd at Harwich when she landed – probably more than Queen Charlotte had ever been.[17] The English loved the Bourbons with all the hatred they felt for Bonaparte.

Gosfield was far too small to cope with a total entourage, after her arrival, of 130 to 140 people: the servants had to sleep in the library, and Louis complained to Condé *'Tout cela est bien vilain, bien incommode'* ('It is all very sordid, very uncomfortable'). So

in April 1809 they moved to Hartwell House just outside Aylesbury, which had better communications with London, and more
bedrooms for the servants, and which Buckingham had arranged
for them to rent from Sir George Lee for £500 a year. It was a
curious house, slightly damp and gloomy, like Gosfield a mixture
of Tudor and Georgian. It has several large and sumptuously
decorated rooms, such as few French *châteaux* could provide,
and a beautiful park, dotted with temples and statues of Hanoverian royalty. It is not at all bad for a royal family in exile.

Louis and his Court soon settled into the routine of English
country life. Louis, who loved flowers, enjoyed strolling in the
garden watching the progress of his roses and camellias. Indeed,
he grew so fond of the English style of garden that one of the few
tangible remains of his reign in France today is the *Jardin du Roi*
in the park of Versailles (to the left, before the *Bassin d'Apollon*),
an 'English' garden of herbaceous borders and flowering shrubs
created to please Louis XVIII in the stronghold of the formal
French parterre.

Gonet, a personal servant of Marie-Joséphine who later became
one of Louis's *Garçons de Toilette*, married a Miss Eliza Turner.
Someone else passed the time painting the inside of one of the
garden temples with frescoes (now gone) of the adventures of Don
Quixote, who bore a strange resemblance to Napoleon Bonaparte.
Louis's entourage, in their practical French way, put every corner
of Hartwell to use: shops sprang up in the outhouses, the bedrooms and attics were subdivided to make tiny individual apartments, even the roof was used for growing plants and keeping
animals.[18]

However, they also had to endure the unacceptable side of
English country life: rain in August, a roof that leaked, a late frost
that killed off all the flowers, an east wind that froze Louis to the
marrow of his bones. . . He thought that poor Gustavus IV Adolphus, who came to England after losing his throne, in 1810,
would prefer even his climate to the '*variations, il faut l'avouer,
un peu fréquentes de ce pays-ci*' ('one must admit, rather frequent
variations of this country').

The ghastly weather and leaking roof cannot have done Marie-
Joséphine much good. By now she was really very ill and spent
most of the day in her bedroom, the best in the house (Louis
preferred two tiny rooms in an entresol), writing loving letters to
Madame de Gourbillon. She found it increasingly difficult to drag
herself down the strange, carved staircase for dinner. Her death,
in great pain from hydropsy, on 12 November 1810 was one of
those extraordinary Bourbon family occasions, like the will of

Louis XVI or the last smuggled messages of Marie-Antoinette and Madame Elizabeth, when years of rows and hostility appear to fade away, to provide a touching, and politically extremely useful, show of family unity. Indeed a reminder of the existence of a secret Bourbon family world of family jokes and traditions and assumptions, into which outsiders have never been admitted, was Marie-Joséphine's remark, as she was dying, that the weather was so awful that they would never again say *'le temps de la mort de Motte'* ('Motte's death weather') – a reference to the appalling storms which had marked the death of an old servant of the future Louis XVI in 1769, and had been used as a standard description of bad weather by the Bourbons ever since.

The whole family, including the Condés (the Orléans had gone abroad in 1808), rushed down for Marie-Joséphine's death, and her room was soon bursting with relations, courtiers and servants. She begged forgiveness of all the family, including Louis, for any *chagrins* she might have caused them, and assured him that she had nothing against him. She gave her blessing to the Duchesse d'Angoulême, whom she disliked, and to her nephews, and told Berri, who was living with a mistress in London, that he should reform his ways. Finally, just at the moment when Louis, who had been extremely attentive, smoothing down her ruffled sheets, trying to keep her spirits up, had gone out for a breath of fresh air, she died. Her funeral was a magnificent occasion. The ageing leaders of the Emigration, their names carefully recorded by the Napoleonic police for the attention of the emperor, packed into the French Chapel in Marylebone to hear the funeral oration. The funeral procession was followed by the carriages of the English Royal Family and the Buckinghams, and Marie-Joséphine was buried with due pomp and ceremony in Westminster Abbey (her body was removed a year later, on Louis's orders, to her brother's Kingdom of Sardinia, and is now in Cagliari Cathedral).

In his letters to d'Avaray, Louis admitted that he was surprised how much he missed her. She had been the person with whom he had shared news, memories, funny stories – far more than she had wanted. He had planted roses just for the pleasure of offering them to her, and now there was a gap in his life. He even compared himself to the Children of Israel by the waters of Babylon, weeping for the loss of Jerusalem.[20]

The chief woman in his life, and his official hostess, was now the Duchesse d'Angoulême, large-nosed, pious, inquisitive and not particularly clever. Indeed it cannot be denied that by 1810 she was rather a liability: not only was she abrupt and ungracious in manner, but she also now had the unfortunate and very noticeable feature of a 'redness about the eyes', which was no doubt physical in origin, but which everyone she met immediately assumed to be due to excessive weeping – thereby arousing feelings of pity, guilt and embarrassment which did not make her appearance in public or at Court particularly successful. In 1811, at the first party she had been to since her arrival at Mittau in 1799, it was noted that she appeared gauche and 'much depressed'. And even if many people may have assumed that she was gloomier than she really was, she certainly never exactly radiated *joie de vivre*.

One doubts if there was ever much real intimacy between this dry, fearless but rather rigid princess and her intelligent, erudite, adaptable uncle. Visitors to Gosfield and Hartwell were much impressed by the fact that the Duchesse d'Angoulême always curtsied to Louis when she entered the room, and that he always kissed her hands. But there are hints in Marie-Joséphine's spiteful letters that Louis found her a bit trying at times, although he was probably too polite, or hypocritical, to show it.[21]

Louis's life at Gosfield and Hartwell was based on the extremely generous financial help of the English Government. As early as 30 October 1807, although he had not received permission to land, he had been given £1,000 by Canning – money was the least of the English Government's problems. From 1808, Louis was given the huge yearly sum of £16,000 (out of which he had to support Marie-Joséphine). It was an extremely generous figure when compared with Artois's £6,000, and when one remembers that even sons of the King of England, like the Duke of Kent, had great difficulty in extracting £18,000 a year out of a reluctant Government. Louis had certainly succeeded in one of his aims in coming to England. Moreover, he was still getting the equivalent of £4,000 a year from Russia, although the catastrophic fall of the rouble after 1810 greatly reduced this sum in value; and after 1810, thanks to English influence, the Portuguese Government, now in Rio de Janeiro, gave him £1,600 a year.

However, to Louis, who estimated his minimum annual financial needs at £26,000, it was never enough: he was living in the most expensive country in Europe, at a time when the war had sent up all prices. He also had extraordinary expenses to pay, such as the installation of the Court at Hartwell (which Blacas estimated at £15,000) and the cost of Marie-Joséphine's funeral, which Louis tried to shift to the English Government. By 1809, he was having to pawn some diamonds he had recently inherited from an aunt. And most of his communications with the English Government in 1811–12 dealt with his attempt to obtain possession of the former private property of Louis XVI in French Guiana – the old dream of a secure and independent financial position based on America.[22]

In three ways his stay in England left more of a mark on Louis than all his years in the other countries he had lived in since 1791. First, it was in England that Louis finally assumed that huge size which, if nothing else, was to make him such a remarkable king. Greville found him so large that when he moved it was like 'the heavings of a ship'; when the Comte de La Ferronays stood up after kneeling down to kiss the king's hand (a habit unusual at Versailles, whose adoption was one sign of the increasing submissiveness of the French elites), his head rammed into the king's immense, jutting protuberance of a stomach. A few years later an Englishman wrote that even if Louis had not been the centre of all the ceremony and etiquette of the Court of the Tuileries, he would still, by his 'amazing corpulence', have been 'the principal figure' present.[23] He really must have been very large, judging by his pictures (see illustrations 7–13), since they were done by artists anxious to please and flatter him, yet show a very fat king indeed.

Of course Louis followed a *régime*, or said he did, but it does not seem to have done any good. His Saxon and Polish ancestors had been huge, his sister Madame Clotilde had been known from an early age as Gros Madame, since she was round as a ball, and Louis himself, whatever he may have said about a *régime*, ate a huge amount: food was one of the main pleasures of his increasingly restricted life. So Louis XVIII was destined to be not only the most English, but also the fattest, King of France there has ever been.

It was also in England that Louis's health for the first time became really bad. He had had yearly attacks of gout (a disease known to the medical dictionary as 'the disease of kings and the king of diseases' because of its traditional association with intelligence and high social status – even Louis's ill-health was effortlessly royal) since 1800, and a really bad attack in 1807. And it got steadily worse. In the winter of 1810, he became completely helpless, unable to do anything for himself, relying on a wheelchair to be pushed from his bedroom to his salon: a special chapel was now fitted up at Hartwell in the breakfast room for him to hear Mass in comfort, rather than having to go to the chapel at the other end of the house. Attacks of gout could now so cripple his legs and knees and hands as to make them quite useless – a particular hardship for a king whose preferred form of communication was the written word. In October 1813 he went to Bath, where he lived at 70–71 Pulteney Street, in the hope that

the waters would do him some good, but there was little change.
He was now a permanent invalid, resigned to his gout as *'un
ennemi avec lequel il faut vivre et mourir'* ('an enemy with which
I must live and die'), the illest, as well as the fattest and most
English, King of France there has been.

It was also in England that Louis's inner Court assumed its
final shape. His most trusted Court officials were Gramont, his
Capitaine des Gardes, the Archbishop of Reims, *Grand Aumônier
de France*, and the Duc d'Havré, an elderly member of the Croÿ
family who had been Marie-Joséphine's long-suffering *Chevalier
d'Honneur*, and in 1812 was made a *Capitaine des Gardes*. In
addition, La Chatre, *Premier Gentilhomme* when Louis was
Comte de Provence, was still in his service as his agent in London.
These four extremely elderly aristocrats – in 1810 their average
age was sixty-eight, thirteen years older than their king – were
Louis's intimate friends and courtiers, people he had talked to
every day for years on end. But it is probable that even with them
he always remained on his guard, only having a certain sort of
conversation, the royal sort, about the weather, literature, history,
their shared memories – anything but the immediate political
prospect. This was even more the case with his personal servants,
who in 1810 were rejoined by Hue, who became a *Premier Valet
de Chambre* and *Trésorier-Général de la Maison*.[24]

Therefore, even in England, Louis did not lead an entirely
private life. No doubt there were many long days when he had
nothing to do but waddle round the garden in his 'plain blue
frock [-coat] with gilt buttons', or read: he liked the novels of
Fanny Burney, or so he told her. When he was on the throne he
remembered his years at Hartwell as the time *'où il cultivait son
jardin'* ('when he was cultivating his garden') – in other words
leading a private life. But he was still surrounded by a large Court,
and Hartwell was used as a palace, not a private house: Artois,
Berri and Condé had their own apartments there, which they
used on their occasional, obligatory visits to their king, just as if
Hartwell was Versailles or Compiègne. Moreover, Louis was in
the European country with the largest number of *émigrés*, many
of whom would come down to pay their court to him. In 1809,
when he was staying with Condé at Wanstead, he held a reception
for all the women who had been presented before 1790 (how did
people remember who had been?) and for all men *indistinctement*
– quite a change from the rules for presentation before 1790.
Even in exile the Court of France, as a form of social life as well
as a domestic household, was a constantly changing institution.[25]

Louis was also still involved enough in politics to get mixed up in two affairs which show what cunning enemies he had and how gullible he could be, and which finally brought to an end his sorties from his royal world, bounded by his official agents and ministers and by the structure of his household, into the secret, treacherous world of conspiracy and espionage. During the wars of the 1790s and the 1800s there was a constant struggle between the secret service of the French Government and those of the Allies, Louis and Artois, which is curiously reminiscent of that which has been going on, since 1917, between the Soviet Union and the Western Powers. As in that conflict, agents frequently changed sides, it is often difficult to discover who they were really working for, and there were many independent master spies (d'Antraigues, Puisaye, Fouché) who were prepared to work for almost anyone with a lot of money and the ability to flatter their sense of self-importance.

In this nightmare world, Louis's Government in exile had not been particularly successful. D'Antraigues, des Pommelles and François had betrayed many of its secrets to the French Government; Bayard, formerly Louis's liaison man with Wickham, had gone over to the other side. On the other hand, the French Government also had its failures, although they were never quite as serious. The Swiss publisher Fauche-Borel, who was sent from Paris on a mission in 1804, promptly began to work for Louis, printing his declaration in Berlin and trying to get it distributed in France (see page 128). A Ministry of Police official wrote that of the six permanent agents sent by Napoleon I to spy on the Royalists before 1814, one, *Tripier dit Labruère dit Brière*, who had been sent to Mittau, *'avait fait connaître sa mission aux personnes qu'il était chargé d'observer'* ('had revealed his mission to the people he was told to observe'), while another *'n'avait voulu que gagner de l'argent'* ('only wanted to earn some money').[26]

However, one former Royalist agent turned Government spy, called Perlet, played the best joke of all on Fauche-Borel and Louis. He created, entirely out of his own imagination, a Royalist secret committee in Paris composed of leading figures of the regime, which from 1806 sent bulletins to Fauche-Borel, assuring him and Louis of its devotion to the good cause, relaying absurd or obvious pieces of news (the Archduke Charles was about to become King of Bulgaria, Napoleon I was very angry at his army's defeats in Spain), and above all trying to get something tangible and compromising out of Louis and his agents: a letter, a *plein pouvoir*, an emissary, perhaps even a prince. . .

At first Louis was pathetically excited about the *Comité de*

Paris. Perhaps it would serve him as well as Royer-Collard and his friends, whom he had also never met, had done. He gave Fauche-Borel instructions as to how to conduct the correspondence, and one of his motives for leaving Mittau was to be nearer this source of information – a ray of light in a particularly sombre period of his life. In June 1808, Perlet actually came to England (Morlaix, on the coast of Brittany, was the more or less obligatory 'dropping-point' for agents leaving or entering France) to try to convince Louis of the reality of the *Comité de Paris*. There were dramatic moments when Perlet was almost unmasked by a genuine Royalist secret agent in London, and d'Antraigues and Puisaye, the two equivocal master spies, refused to be taken in. But Perlet was actually given the honour of an audience with Louis at Gosfield on 22 June 1808 – even now an audience with the king was the summit of many people's ambitions (to his chagrin, Fauche-Borel never obtained one). Louis assured Perlet that he had every confidence in the *Comité de Paris*. But obviously he was finally becoming suspicious about what was happening. He said that he was disappointed at the absence of documentary proof or convincing names (the only ones Perlet produced were Senator Lenoir-Laroche and General Lecourbe), and that what he really wanted were generals like Berthier and Macdonald. Apart from the audience itself Perlet got nothing out of Louis. A disappointed police bulletin sent to Napoleon I concluded that his mission had had no success at all.[27]

Thereafter, at least until 1812, Louis remained in touch with Fauche-Borel through the Duc d'Havré, an honest old man whom he often used for such tasks. In 1809, Louis even wanted to send Bruslart, a prominent ex-Vendéen, and three others, to France, possibly in search of the elusive *Comité de Paris*. But the English Government refused them passports, because their mission had been publicized by one of Louis's Royalist enemies, Puisaye, the moving spirit behind the second, even less dignified affair in which Louis was involved in England.[28]

Since at least 1797, Louis had disliked and distrusted Puisaye intensely (see page 102). The distrust can only have increased, when Puisaye and his new friend d'Antraigues, now in England on a mission from the Tsar, wrote articles in the *émigré* papers in London opposing Louis's arrival in England. Thereafter a situation of perplexing complexity emerged. Louis and La Chatre were opposed to Puisaye and his agent Pringent, and wanted to stop them from being used by Artois (but in 1806 they had tried to use Puisaye and Pringent themselves to land agents in France). Puisaye wanted to keep all communications between the Royalists and France under his control although, according to the French Government, he himself had no contacts in France. When his agent Pringent did go to France he was quickly captured and shot.[29]

But a far more serious result of the hatred of Puisaye and d'Antraigues for Louis was the public scandal which began with the publication, in January 1809, of the sixth volume of Puisaye's memoirs, in which he accused d'Avaray of trying to have him murdered, of dominating the king, sending Louis's best advisers away, and intriguing against the English Government. The result was a shattering row. An enquiry was clearly necessary, and Louis actually stooped to agreeing that it should be conducted by three people – the Duc de Lorges and the Comtes de La Bourdonnaye and du Bourblanc – whom he chose from nine names given him by Puisaye. The King of France did not normally have his legal officials chosen for him by others (although, in fact, they had also been on Louis's list of possible judges), but he and d'Avaray were ready to do anything to force Puisaye, who had been hedging and teasing and delaying, to show his proof.[30] D'Avaray was so desperate that he even went down to try to see Puisaye in his house in Surrey, and got himself imprisoned for two days for using threatening language.

Finally, the *Examen Raisonné et Rapport* of 15 April 1809 showed that one letter of 13 March 1797 from d'Avaray to d'Antraigues (who was beginning to regret that he had supplied Puisaye with so many documents), where d'Avaray was apparently ordering Puisaye's assassination, was partly fake, and it criticized Puisaye's methods of getting hold of other documents. But d'Avaray did admit to the enquiry – how crestfallen he must have been – that he had written to d'Antraigues in 1795 that '*Le Comte Joseph de Puisaye est un drôle à qui il faut casser le cou*' ('Count Joseph de Puisaye is a fool whose neck needs breaking'). This was not an order to murder, but rather the rage of a Royalist whose hopes had been dashed, and who had just lost a brother, in part because of Puisaye's incompetence during the Quiberon expedition. Nevertheless, it was a catastrophically unwise phrase, out of which it is hardly surprising that the adventurers of the Emigration made a lot of mileage. And Puisaye's witty, mocking memoirs publicized issues, such as the rivalry between Louis and Artois, Louis and d'Avaray's dislike, in the 1790s, of the English Government and of *le gouvernement représentatif*, and the fall of Saint-Priest from favour, which were extremely embarrassing in England in 1809.[31]

Thus Puisaye and d'Antraigues, although discredited by their resort to forgery, did succeed in embarrassing Louis and d'Avaray. A sinister epilogue to this incident, which set the whole of *émigré* London (known as *le quartier de Manchester*, because they all lived round Manchester Square) abuzz, was d'Antraigues' murder, by an Italian servant called Lorenzo, who then shot himself. It seems very suspicious that the five pages dealing with this period in the diary of Broval, an agent of Orléans who knew d'Antraigues very well, have been torn out. Broval believed that Louis might have wanted a 'correspondence' between Louis XVI's lawyer and d'Antraigues denouncing him, but this is unlikely to have existed. D'Antraigues did have papers to worry a great many people, but Canning, who had a good look, wrote to a close friend that there was 'nothing suspicious nor anything very important' among them, although, naturally, he burned those papers to do with himself. Most of the papers which d'Antraigues had not given Puisaye seem to have been given by the English authorites to Louis, since they are now among his archives in the Quai d'Orsay. Perhaps the explanation for the murder is simply, as a friend of d'Antraigues wrote to Puisaye, that Madame d'Antraigues (formerly la Saint-Huberty, the star of the Paris Opera before the Revolution) was so foul to her servants, whom she starved and bullied, that one of them decided he had had enough.[32]

It will always be a mystery how d'Antraigues, mad, bad and dangerous to know, whom many people realized to be utterly untrustworthy, nevertheless managed to be employed, not only by Louis, but also by the English, Spanish, Austrian and Russian governments – all of whom could easily have found more reliable sources of information. Even in the last years of his life he was still part of a small, ambitious and cosmopolitan world, including Canning, Orléans, Dumouriez (who wanted Orléans to be *Lieutenant-Général du Royaume*), Guilhermy and the Duke of Kent who, when they were not plotting against each other, were always having dinner together. Perhaps d'Antraigues' career is simply yet another sign of how far boundless self-confidence and an air of conviction can take you in politics.

At first Louis reacted to the Puisaye Affair by giving d'Avaray every sign of favour. Even before the enquiry met on 24 March, he made d'Avaray a duke (the only title he created in exile), and held a *Conseil de famille* where he disgraced Puisaye with as much formality as possible. But afterwards, when Louis learnt details which he may not have known before, such as the rashness and indiscretion of many of d'Avaray's letters, his attitude may have changed. In August 1809, a *protégé* of d'Avaray, the Comte de

Blacas, was made *Grand Maître de la Garde-Robe du Roi*, a Court office which Louis had not filled before, and was put in charge of the entire *Maison du Roi* and of political affairs. Even more significant was the fact that d'Avaray began to spend more time in Chelsea than at Hartwell.

Of course this change may have been due to his frightful health, which had already caused him to leave Louis in the winters of 1802 and 1803, and to ask to resign in late 1807, before the Puisaye Affair. Louis's and Blacas's letters to d'Avaray after he left England for a rest-cure in Madeira on 23 August 1810 are extremely friendly. But it is probable that when d'Avaray died on 4 June 1811, alone except for one servant and a secretary, the Comte de Pradel, he knew that he had compromised the dignity of the king and master whom he adored. As he lay dying, he begged Pradel to read him out once more the last letter he had received from his king.[33]

Blacas was a noble from Provence, who was not only much younger than any of Louis's previous ministers or intimate courtiers (he was thirty-eight in 1809), but was also totally unconnected with the world of Court and Government before 1789; he was one of the many provincial nobles who had spent the 1790s fighting in the *Armée de Condé*. However, he was by no means a typical *émigré*. Like Louis, he adored the world of classical antiquity, and when he died he left one of the finest collections of antiquities ever assembled by a private individual (part is now in the British Museum); he was also a patron of Champollion, and helped to found the Louvre's collection of Egyptian antiquities. He was a cold, dry, authoritative and fairly sensible individual who would take to the world of ministers and ambassadors and sovereigns as if he had been in it all his life. Unfortunately, one gift he had not received was one of the most important of all for the favourite of the King of France, namely charm, winning manners and the ability to get on with people.

Typically, the first person to complain about him was Artois, whom many, including Marie-Joséphine, thought would succeed in having Blacas sent away. Indeed, Artois once made such a frightful scene that Blacas did try to resign. But Louis assured Blacas of his *amitié* for him personally as well as of his need for him as a minister. He also assured Blacas that it had only been a *premier mouvement* of Artois's bad temper: '*Il n'était pas de sang-froid. Il y sera lorsque je lui parlerai, et je prends d'avance du plaisir à panser la plaie qu'il vous a fait.*' ('He was not thinking. He will do when I speak to him, and I am enjoying in advance the pleasure of healing the wound he has given you.') If Artois persisted, then the king would give Blacas '*de nouvelles marques d'estime*.'[34] And thereafter we hear of no more scenes from Artois, although he never liked Blacas.

Indeed, after 1807 there appears to be a considerable difference in Louis's relations with his younger brother. Artois no longer seems to expect to be on a footing of equality with the king. And there are not quite so many acts of insubordination. Thus another of Louis's aims in coming to England had been realized. Henceforth they seem to decide on policy in consultation and perhaps in discussion Louis was able to assert his natural authority as the king; he was quite, but not wholly, convinced that Artois would regret his attack on Blacas '*lorsque je lui parlerai*'. At least in this period of their lives, Louis and Artois appear to have been (we will never really know their intimate feelings) in agreement on the basic questions of policy, sometimes taking decisions without consulting Blacas.[35] Furthermore, Artois had subscribed to the very moderate declaration of 2 December 1804, accepting most aspects of post-Revolutionary France. Louis now had no cause to fear the open disagreements with his heir, perhaps leading to rebellion, which made his life before 1807 and after 1814 so difficult.

The years 1808–11 were probably some of the gloomiest of Louis's life. He was involved in two wretched and depressing intrigues. He was stuck in the English countryside with very little to do and his health was getting worse. By 1811, his wife and his best friend were dead. On the continent, audacity and tyranny were bringing B.P., or *le Corse*, as Louis called him, fresh triumphs. Napoleon's Empire was now a vast, swollen monster, stretching to Hamburg, Barcelona and Rome. Not content with such an enormous slice of the present, he was also trying to take over the past, removing to France, in addition to the Pope and the King of Spain, the Archives of Simancas and the Vatican. He even entered Louis's own family world of Catholic European royalty, marrying the Archduchess Marie-Louise of Austria on 1 April 1810. Everyone at Hartwell was appalled, particularly the Duchesse d'Angoulême, who had been so proud of her Habsburg blood. Louis still hoped that Providence had not condemned the world to years of tyranny and suffering. But even in 1808, he had wanted to rent Hartwell for 'at least five years', which shows that he was resigned to a long stay in England. It is in these years, for the first time in his life, that we hear of him having fits of apopleptic rage, and of being '*dans une tristesse qui fait peine*'.[36]

However, two unexpected events come to console the lonely exile of Hartwell. First, he got to know the English Royal Family.

The Prince of Wales had promised to pay Louis a visit when he arrived in 1807 but was prevented from doing so by 'a spasm': he did not make the visit until October 1808. Thereafter they had had little contact, although the Bourbons kept an attentive and apprehensive eye on the political manoeuvres of the time, particularly in relation to their effect on the chances of peace with the French Empire. In February 1811, Louis wrote to the recently proclaimed regent to congratulate him on his *sagesse* in keeping on his father's ministers[37] – hitherto the prince's political opponents, but now, partly at least because they were so dedicated to the prosecution of the war against Bonaparte, his friends. One of the most remarkable and important political *volte-faces* in English history was inspired in part by hostility to the French Empire.

In June 1811 when the regent sent out invitations for the splendid fête held to mark the beginning of his regency, Louis wrote to d'Avaray, with delight and surprise, like an insecure poor relation (as indeed he was), '*sans me vanter, moi et tous les miens sommes invités*' ('I do not like to boast, but we have all been invited'). One longs to know what his feelings were on that beautiful June night when, for the first time since Turin in 1794, he stepped back into the gilded, scented, luxurious palace world of his youth, to be received, in rooms carpeted with fleurs de lys and lined with pictures of Louis XV and Madame de Pompadour (and the terrifying Reynolds of Philippe Egalité), by a fat, gracious, smiling, powerful prince who welcomed him with the magic words, '*Ici Votre Majesté est Roi de France*'. What was it like, for the first time in years, to wander through rooms even more sumptuous than those of Versailles, packed with 2,000 deafening, glittering members of the most self-confident aristocracy in Europe? Did Louis meet some of the statesmen who played such a large part in his life and had, hitherto, only been names to him? Did he admire the fashionable smartness of the military uniforms worn by half the male guests (including the regent and his brothers), or did he prefer the traditional splendour of the *habit habillé* still worn, at the English Court, by those without military or official rank? Did he feel part again of the international world of power, privilege, and royalty, from which he had been excluded for so long? Alas, all we know is that the Bourbons, like the rest of the guests, found the long wait before supper was served at two o'clock in the morning rather painful.[38]

Thereafter fairly regular contact was maintained between the two families. The regent loved the Bourbons not only because he hated Bonaparte and, like the Marquess of Buckingham, felt it was dignified and honourable to succour royalty in distress, but also because he saw them as living representatives of that eighteenth-century French paradise which, in his furniture and china and palaces, he tried so hard to recreate. The Hanoverians were the only other Royal Family Louis ever really got to know, apart from his wife's Piedmontese relations and Gustavus III and IV of Sweden. In August 1812, at the same time as the hordes of the *Grande Armée* were streaming into Russia, the Bourbons dined with the Duke of York and the entire English Royal Family at Oatlands, meeting Queen Charlotte and the princesses for the first time. Both parties felt that the occasion had gone off 'to perfection'; even the weather had been good.

The effect Louis had on the English Royal Family, and the immense importance attached in the early nineteenth century to manners and behaviour, can be seen in a letter by Princess Augusta describing her impressions of Louis. 'He has a very fine manner, and is very gracious. He is a well-informed man, speaks English very well, and understands it perfectly. He is very large, as large as Stephen Kemble. He converses in a Most agreeable manner and generally walks up and down the Room in the hope of its keeping down His fat. His countenance is very good, and he makes a very fine Bow without any affectation. My Brothers were delighted with him.' Unfortunately neither from this nor any other letter can we find out what the French and English Royal Families actually talked about. Did Louis and the regent discuss the advantages of constitutional monarchy and of dropping political supporters who were no longer useful, of both of which they were firmly convinced? They really had a lot in common in addition to a love of splendour and good food. One of the greatest links between these two fat, ageing, royal semi-invalids was that they had the same doctor: Père Elisée, a strange debauched old creature, who had been Chirurgien-Major of the *Armée des Princes*, and had the distinction of being the person who, on 21 May 1810, closed the eyes, and finally ascertained the sex (male), of the legendary transvestite spy, the Chevalier d'Eon.

Whatever he and Louis discussed, the regent had become a firm friend of the Bourbons. At another magnificent fête the last toast he gave was 'Henry IV and the House of Bourbon'. Such sentiments cannot have left his ministers totally unaffected, and as early as September 1812, after other meetings at the Prince de Condé's at Wimbledon, Blacas could write that his master felt that the ministers were now becoming a little more favourable to the Royalist cause.[39]

Another event even more promising for Louis than his friendship with the English Royal Family was the revolt of the Spanish

people against Napoleon I after the forced abdications of the
Spanish Bourbons in 1808. Even though Ferdinand VII of Spain
was in many ways the nadir of monarchy (if we overlook the
Bonapartes), without even the courage to stick to his own rank,
this revolt was as Royalist and Catholic as it was national. There
was, as it was Louis's lifework to show was the case in France,
no incompatibility between the three. In accordance with his desire always to be seen opposing revolutionary tyranny in all its
manifestations, Louis immediately tried to be sent to Spain: he
addressed a ridiculous proclamation to the Spanish people and,
with considerable foresight, showed concern that Spanish America
should remain loyal to the Bourbons, proposing that a special
regent be sent there. But the English Government was opposed to
any interference by a French Bourbon in the affairs of the Spanish
Monarchy, and stopped Angoulême from setting out for Spain in
1810.[40] The only Bourbon who got there, to the rage of his French
cousins, was Orléans; but he only lasted a few weeks.

The war in Spain, which gradually brought an English army
under Lord Wellington nearer and nearer the French frontier, and
Louis's growing friendship with the English Royal Family, were
not the only filips to Louis's spirits after 1811. In the summer of
1812, he received the visit of Comte Alexis de Noailles, a young
member of a Royalist secret society called the *Chevaliers de la Foi*
who was able to assure him that there were still Royalists in
France.

We now enter one of the most exciting periods of Louis's life,
the first time since 1787–88 that events – a much more powerful
force in the early nineteenth century than ideas or economic trends
– were moving in his favour. For, as the *Grande Armée* suffered
defeat after defeat, slowly, sporadically and timidly, in *châteaux*
and cottages and counting-houses, French Royalism began to reassert itself. One of the great myths of French historiography, still
enshrined in many text books, is that in 1814 the Bourbons were
completely forgotten, and that Chateaubriand's brilliant and moving pamphlet *De Buonaparte et des Bourbons* was, as its author
boasted in his memoirs, '*un certificat de vie*' for Louis XVIII. At
first this view seems convincing, since it was even held by some
of Louis's most loyal servants: in 1807, Havré wrote that most
French people did not know there was a King of France; in his
memoirs one of Louis's ministers claimed that in 1814 ninety-nine
per cent of the country did not even know that Louis XVIII
existed.[41]

But these views are completely untrue, and reflect either their
authors' own obsessive love for the Royal Family, beside which

every other attitude seemed indifference, or their desire to assert the unique distinction of their own Royalism. Indeed one only has to turn to *De Buonaparte et des Bourbons* itself, rather than Chateaubriand's very unreliable memoirs (as José Cabanis has said, the best novel he ever wrote), to read that Louis was *'un prince légitime . . . dont nos enfants savent le nom comme celui d'un de leurs voisins'* ('a legitimate prince . . . whose name our children know as well as if he was a neighbour'). This may be an exaggeration, but what is certain is that a very large proportion of supporters of the Empire, and of ex-Republicans, were well aware of the existence of a Royalist alternative to the Empire, and that there were still many Royalists in France. People may not have known the names and relationships of all the Bourbons (did they of the Bonapartes?), but they did know that a brother of Louis XVI, called Louis, was living in exile and had not renounced his claim to the throne. Not even the Revolution and the Empire could obliterate 1,000 years of French royalty.

The new strength of French Royalism came from three principal sources. First, even within the magnificent government structure of the Empire, Royalism was by no means dead. The regime had encouraged a revival of interest in the *Siècle de Louis XIV*, hoping that it would rebound to the benefit of the monarchy of Napoleon I. During the Empire editions of the works of Louis XIV and the letters of Madame de Maintenon, and pictures dealing with the life of Henri IV, reminded people of Bourbon glories; a life of *le grand Condé* by his descendant the hero of the Counter-Revolution was even on sale in Paris. Moreover, the regime, particularly after 1810, began to prefer servants from backgrounds with Royalist traditions: Baron Pasquier, of a family which had served in the *Parlement de Paris* and had suffered from the Revolution, replaced Perlet's master, Dubois, as Prefet de Police of Paris in 1810. Before 1814, the Prefet of the Vendée, the Baron de Barante, spent his spare time helping Madame de La Rochejaquelein write memoirs extolling the heroism of the Vendéens – and he turned a blind eye to the Royalist intrigues of her brother-in-law. Throughout France, in every walk of life, the old nobles were reoccupying the best positions in Government service and in the localities.

And as the regime began to suffer its first defeats in 1812, its fragility and lack of a firm, devoted power-base became apparent. On 23 October 1812, General Malet, a former soldier in the *Maison Militaire du Roi* who had served the Republic, seized power in Paris for half a day and proclaimed a Provisional Government which, despite his Republican antecedents, included

Alexis de Noailles and the head of the *Chevaliers de la Foi*, Mathieu de Montmorency – a sign that people were turning to Royalism as a source of strength. On 14 May 1813, when some of Louis's mail was intercepted, Caulaincourt wrote to Narbonne, in a phrase which shows how frightened he was: *'Quant aux Bourbons, vous ne devez jamais en parler.'* ('As for the Bourbons, you should never speak of them.')

But people were beginning to talk about them more and more. On 1 January 1814, according to Lainé, a deputy from Bordeaux who had denounced the emperor's policies in a sensational speech in the *Corps Législatif*, the emperor himself publicly admitted the possibility of his replacement by the Bourbons. In February, Napoleon's *Archichancelier*, Cambacérès, wrote to him that all over France local officials were insinuating that *'l'ennemi vient pour le bonheur commun'* ('the enemy is coming for the common good'). When Bourbon princes appeared on the continent in February 1814, servants of the regime like Maréchal Soult and Colonel de Castellane showed no signs of surprise or of not knowing who they were. Indeed the *Commissaire-Général de Police* at Boulogne was so frightened by what he called *'les partisans des bourbons en France'* that he decided to refer to the princes, in his despatches to the Minister of Police, as parcels. By March 1814, Talleyrand and his many followers were probably in favour of a restoration: and a cryptic phrase in a letter from La Chatre to Blacas suggests that Talleyrand was in touch with Louis's agents.[42] No regime has been more obviously about to collapse, or served by more disloyal officials, than the French Empire in 1813–14.

Outside the regime Louis XVIII was also beginning to receive support from an unexpected quarter, namely from ex-Revolutionaries who had stayed aloof from the flagrantly reactionary and illiberal regime of Napoleon I. In 1813, an almost forgotten conspiracy in Marseille linked Royalists, ex-Republicans and Barras in an attempt to raise the Midi in conjunction with the Royal Navy. General Moreau, in whom Louis had long had hope, returned from his exile in America in 1813 to fight under Alexander I against his old rival Bonaparte; and he spoke for many former Republicans and liberals when he is reported to have said that *'depuis que les républicains se font esclaves, c'est auprès des rois sages qu'il faut chercher la liberté'* ('since republicans have become slaves, one must hope for liberty from the wisdom of monarchs'). That Louis had become *sage* and that he was far more likely to create a liberal regime than Napoleon I, formed part of many people's political assumptions in 1812–14. And by early 1814, even an ex-Regicide like Merlin de Thionville seems to have been as much in favour of a restoration of Louis XVIII as his local Prefect, the Baron de La Tour du Pin (husband of the memoir-writer), one of the many ex-Royalist nobles appointed by Napoleon I. It was the only reasonable solution.[43]

The third factor was Royalism itself. Even in the age of the opinion poll, it is notoriously difficult to assess public opinion, and in Napoleonic France, which was a police state at war, it is almost impossible. Probably most people were prepared to support any regime that would give them peace, a reduction in taxation and the abolition of conscription. But there were also a large number of Royalists, or rather people with Royalist sympathies, in all classes. If we just take the best-recorded people, a large proportion of the French elite refused to serve the Empire, although there were some remarkable defections (particularly among the remnants of the old *parti Choiseul*). In the Noailles family, for example, not only Alexis de Noailles but also the heads of the two branches of the family, the Duc d'Ayen and the Prince de Poix, were opposed to the regime, although Louis's former *Premier Gentilhomme*, the Marquis de Noailles, and two other members of the family, were not. Another example of how widespread Royalism was is that simply among the most famous French writers of the early nineteenth century, Lamartine, de Vigny, Custine, Thiers, Victor Hugo, and of course Chateaubriand, all came from families which in 1812–14 were at heart Royalist. Their Royalism was of a rather passive sort, living on hopes and regrets, and waiting on events. However, as in the 1790s, there was a minority of active and dedicated Royalists from all classes, at a time when we are supposed to believe that the Bourbons were completely forgotten, who helped give popular discontent with the Empire a Royalist form. If we go around France clockwise, in the west Royalist agitation had never entirely died down, and from 1813 there was a Royalist band led by La Frégéoliere in Maine. From August to October 1813 there was what is known (or rather forgotten) as *la conspiration des Gardes d'Honneur* in Tours, when a few young recruits from Vendéen families drank Louis's health on the Fête de Saint Louis, and tried to murder their colonel. In the north of France near Lille, from November 1813 there was a peasants' revolt against conscription, led by Louis Fruchart, whose hat was decorated with the inscription *Je combats pour Louis XVII* (a sign, not of the peasants' belief in the survival of Louis XVII, but of their failure to remember that he had reigned before Louis XVIII). In the east, in Franche-Comté, there was a revolt with Royalist overtones in the

Haute-Saône in November 1813. When the Austrians took Dijon on 31 January 1814, a lot of people began to wear white cockades and fleurs de lys in the streets, despite the Allied commander's disapproval. In Provence there were not only Royalist conspiracies but also widespread dissatisfaction with a Government which was openly persecuting the Pope: four hundred people were found drinking Louis's health in a tavern near Marseille in the summer of 1813.

Except for sections of opinion among the poor in the Faubourgs, Paris had never really liked the Empire. In March 1814, it was not a cryptic message from a friend of Talleyrand, nor the arrival of an emissary of the Royalist secret society of the *Chevaliers de la Foi*, but the interception of a despatch from the Minister of Police to the emperor, informing him of widespread discontent in Paris and of the possibility of a rising against him, which made the Allies take their crucial decision to march on Paris. On 1 April, only one day after they took the city, and four days before the publication of *De Buonaparte et des Bourbons*, both the *Conseil Général de la Seine* (the nominated town council) and the *Chambre des Avoués* published declarations in favour of a restoration of Louis XVIII, even though there was no certainty that the Empire had been destroyed.[44]

In addition to these local outbursts of Royalism, there was the national secret society called the *Chevaliers de la Foi*. Founded in 1810, when some of its members had been interned in a nursing-home by the Government (the use of mental hospitals for the treatment of dissidents had not yet been invented), it was led by Mathieu de Montmorency, and included two Polignac brothers, Alexis de Noailles, the Duc de Fitzjames, the Marquis de La Rochejaquelein, Comte Ferdinand de Bertier, and many other nobles. The exact role of this essentially aristocratic group in the Royalist conspiracies of 1812–14 is hard to assess, since basically we only have their word for it, and conspirators are notoriously eager to exaggerate the effectiveness of their conspiracies. However, they certainly helped distribute Royalist proclamations and news all over France, in particular in the south, and in February 1814 they almost launched a rising in the Massif Central near Rodez.

But far the most significant area of Royalist dissatisfaction was in the south-west round Bordeaux. Bordeaux had been an important centre of Royalist activity in 1797–99, and like many great ports detested the Empire which had ruined its trade. The price of a *tonneau* of red wine had fallen from 2,850 francs in 1801 to 850 in 1813 – no more need be said. And in 1810, at the

height of the emperor's power, the year of the Austrian marriage
which so depressed the Court of Hartwell, a *négociant* from
Bordeaux came to England to remind Louis and Blacas of the
existence of a *noyau* of Royalists left over from the *Institut
Philanthropique* – of which they were well aware.[45] Thereafter
contacts multiplied: Louis had two agents of his own who were
frequently able to make the dangerous journey between England
Bordeaux: Perrin, whom Villèle, his future minister, remembered
having met near Toulouse in the summer of 1813, and Péfaut de
La Tour, who went to Bordeaux in early 1813. The chief agent
resident in Bordeaux was Taffart de Saint-Germain, who was busy
trying to recruit people to serve in a Royalist force. By December
1813, Napoleon I's officials were very worried about the spread
of Royalist propaganda from Bordeaux, as well as from Toulouse
and Montauban.[46]

The difficulty was to combine all these different manifestations
of Royalist feeling, and the widespread detestation of the Empire,
with the movements of the Royal Family and the progress of the
Allies, to bring about a restoration of the king. The first thing was
to produce a good proclamation. And on 1 February 1813 Louis
issued a declaration from Hartwell which promised *union, repos,
paix* and *bonheur*, the maintenance of all administrative and judicial authorities, and guaranteed no vengeance and no conscription. Except over the *biens nationaux* (whose purchasers Louis
still encouraged to make *transactions* with the old proprietors),
Louis now appeared as the chief guarantee of a status quo which
the emperor was wrecking by his mania for conquest. Louis included in the declaration a flattering appeal to the Senate (in
which he had had hopes since December 1812) *'ou siègent des
hommes que leurs talents distinguent à si juste titre'* ('to which
belong men so justly distinguished by their talents'), to contribute
to the Restoration. The whole declaration was a calculated appeal
not only to ordinary Frenchmen's desire for *repos et bonheur* –
desperate needs, whose power even Bonaparte had acknowledged
in his message to Louis in 1800 – but also to the ruling class of
Napoleonic France. It was a further advance down the path of
moderation and conciliation from the declaration of 1804, and it
may have been influenced by the English Government, which
certainly helped to spread it on the continent.[47]

But, faithful to his policy of always trying to oppose the Revolution and the Empire in as personal a way as possible, Louis
was not simply going to rely on declarations and Royalist zeal
inside France to bring about a restoration. As the English army
crossed the Pyrenees, and the armies of Austria, Prussia, Russia

and Sweden (led by Bernadotte) crossed the Rhine, it became imperative to try to commit them to a restoration by sending Bourbon princes to join them. But none of the Allies wanted to compromise their chances of making peace with Napoleon I, who had a habit of winning even the most unequal battles. Although Louis sent Alexis de Noailles to Alexander I in December 1812, the Comte de La Ferronays to Bernadotte and Alexander I in March 1813, the Comte de Bruges to Alexander I and Frederick William III in April 1813 and the Comte de Bouillé to Bernadotte in October 1813, none of these envoys managed to elicit any signs of support or recognition. Indeed, in July 1813 Artois and Angoulême, who had got to Colberg in Pomerania, were refused permission to join the Allied headquarters and had to return to England. Alexander I, in particular, no doubt remembering the constant demands for money from Mittau, was extremely unenthusiastic about the cause of Louis XVIII, whom he thought of as 'personally incapable'.[48]

But the one country whose Government was not wholly indifferent to the Bourbons, and whose Royal Family had relations of friendship and confidence with them, was England: and the one Allied general who, even as early as August 1813, was not opposed to the presence of a Bourbon in his army, was Lord Wellington. Wellington was one of the many members of the European elites for whom the magic of French royalty never failed. He could remember the *Ancien Régime*, he had been at a military school in Angers under Louis XVI and he had had friends among the *émigrés*. As a very old man at dinner, pointing to the pictures of Louis XVIII and Charles X, Alexander I, Frederick William III and George IV hanging in his dining room, he said with a smile, 'How much better after all . . . these two look with their fleurs de lys and Saint-Esprits, than the two corporals behind, or the fancy-dress in between!' As his latest biographer points out, for Wellington French royalty was always the real thing, the Bourbons a wonderfully genuine dynasty whom it was an honour to serve in a world of upstarts, usurpers and fakes.[49]

The subsequent course of events shows, at last, what Louis could accomplish with a favourable political and military situation, devoted secret agents, a friendly Allied commander and an obedient member of his own family. In March 1813 and again in December, La Chatre, Louis's agent in London, wrote to Taffard de Saint-Germain that he should not only organize the Royalists of Bordeaux, but also send deputies to Wellington to convince him of the strength of the Royalist party. And on 20 December 1813 Wellington was writing a 'most secret' despatch to the Prime

Minister, Lord Liverpool, informing him that he had received a
Monsieur Mailhos (a Royalist agent since the 1790s) from Bordeaux, who had told him that the people wanted the Bourbons
– which Wellington thought very probable, although he had seen
'no public demonstration' as yet. On the same day he wrote to
the Comte de Gramont, son of Louis's faithful *Capitaine des
Gardes* and an officer in the British army, telling him to go and
tell Louis of this visit, and encouraging the arrival of a Bourbon
prince in his army (while at the same time pointing out the dangers).[50] By this letter Wellington, on his own initiative rather than
that of his Government, did his best to help the Bourbons. It was
a letter which could be shown, which could be used to convince
the Government of the strength of the Royalists and of the advantages to be gained in helping the Bourbons. It is difficult not
to assume that Mailhos was sent by Taffard de Saint-Germain to
provide Wellington with a justification for demanding a Bourbon
prince, and that the whole negotiation was a long-term plan by
Louis and his agents, a remarkable tribute to the thoughtfulness
and effectiveness of this episode in Royalist intrigues.

    After Gramont's arrival in England, Louis, Artois and his sons
(all in agreement, for once) met at Hartwell, and Louis wrote a
letter to the English Government, presented by Artois at a meeting
with Liverpool's private secretary on 4 January 1814. In it Louis
claimed that '*la nation toute entière*' now wanted the Bourbons,
who had an obligation to '*les droits de leur naissance* and *la gloire
de leurs Ayeux*' to respond to the call, and demanded boats,
passports and money to help Artois and his sons to get to France.
Louis was now, as he would throughout his reign, basing his
dynastic aims on public opinion, and in conversation Artois
threatened to appeal to English public opinion – that old ally of
the exiled Bourbons – if the English Government tried to stop
their departure. But it is unlikely that the Government had any
such intention. It had been subsidizing the Bourbons since 1792;
it had allowed Artois to leave in 1813; and Liverpool himself was
personally in favour of a restoration. Moreover, the regent, whose
good-will always meant a lot to his ministers, was also in favour
of a restoration of his friend the King of France – as he said, in
one of his very rare direct interventions in policy, to the Russian
ambassador (another supporter of the Bourbons) on 25 January
1814.

    The English Government was, however, desperately keen to
protect itself from any accusations by its allies or the opposition
in Parliament that it had destroyed the chances of peace for the
sake of a restoration of the Bourbons. Thus it pretended not to

know anything of the princes' projects – which was a lie – and Liverpool wrote Artois a cold and hostile letter, refusing all material help, but not actually forbidding the departure of the princes. So, equipped with full powers to act in the king's name until his arrival in France, the princes left England in late January, under assumed names and in great secrecy, Artois for the east of France, Berri for Normandy via the Channel Islands and Angoulême for the south-west, where he arrived on 3 February.[51]

It is interesting that it was Angoulême who was sent to the south-west, since on 4 January Artois had told Liverpool's secretary that *he* wanted to go there. Was the change due to Artois's belief that his title of *Colonel-Général des Suisses* would help him recruit Swiss troops? Or was it due to the insistence of Louis? One of the most noticeable things about the whole Bordeaux negotiation is that it remained, at the English end, entirely in the hands of Louis's most trusted agents, Blacas and La Chatre. The notoriously indiscreet Artois is never mentioned. It is unlikely that Louis wanted to spoil one of his best negotiations by letting in his younger brother, so he probably insisted that Angoulême be sent there.

On their arrival on the continent the princes were greeted with disappointingly little enthusiasm. Only the *gendarmes* were ready to welcome Berri in Normandy, and no more is heard of him until his arrival in Paris four months later. Artois was very well received in Vesoul and Lure in eastern France in February 1814, but thereafter spent most of his time in rather embarrassing inactivity behind the Allied lines. Angoulême had the same fate behind Wellington's lines, his movements decided, and his attempts to inspire Royalist demonstrations criticized, by the great general. None of the conquered towns, neither Pau, Mont-de-Marsan nor Saint Jean de Luz, declared themselves for the king.[52]

In part this lack of enthusiasm can be attributed to the miraculous improvement in Napoleon's military situation in February 1814, and to the peace negotiations going on between him and the Allies (which Blacas called 'les désastreuses conférences de Châtillon') from 3 February to 20 March 1814. What was the point of committing yourself to the king, if at any moment the emperor might be free to turn all his attention to dealing with Royalist rebels? The fate in store for them was made quite clear by the execution, on 27 February, on the emperor's orders, of two Royalists from Troyes who had dared wear white cockades and the *Croix de Saint Louis*. Terrified, uncertain and apprehensive, however, Royalism was still alive. Both Stein in the east and Wellington in the south, men who, although sympathetic to the

Bourbons, were unlikely to have misrepresented totally the feelings of the areas they were passing through, reported to their governments that, if only the Allies would declare for the Bourbons, France would too. The *Commissaire-Général de Police* at Boulogne, exactly reflecting the views of Louis and the Royalists, reported that nothing helped the emperor more *'que d'affermir partout que les Alliés n'ont pas dit dans leurs déclarations un seul mot relatif à la restauration des Bourbons'* ('than to spread the news that the Allies have not put a single reference to the restoration of the Bourbons in their declarations'). A desire to rally to the winning side was more evident in most parts of France than nationalistic hatred of the foreigners.

But Louis's bold assertion that it was *'la nation toute entière'* that wanted the Bourbons was clearly not wholly true. Most French people were probably fairly indifferent to the form of regime that ruled over them as long as it was not too bad. And they could forget how bad the Empire was when faced with the exactions of the Allied armies which, in the east and north, became so terrible that both Artois and an agent of Louis's, the Marquis de Chabannes, began to fear that the enraged peasants would begin a guerrilla war against the invaders.[53]

However, in the south-west there were many extremely brave Royalists, a moderate prince who also had the prestige of being the husband of the daughter of Louis XVI and an occupying army which paid for its requisitions, and did not pillage or slaughter. The Mayor of Saint Jean de Luz declared himself for the king on 12 February 1814; and in early March, as the English army moved slowly northwards, Angoulême was joined by two Royalist agents from Bordeaux, Bontemps-Dubarry and La Rochejaquelein (a key figure, who was also in Tours in August 1813), who told him that all was ready for a Royalist takeover: even the Mayor, Comte Lynch, had promised La Rochejaquelein and Taffard de Saint-Germain he would take the white cockade. It was on their persuasion that on 7 March Wellington ordered Marshal Beresford and his Anglo-Portuguese forces to march on Bordeaux, which was abandoned without resistance by the extremely depleted Napoleonic forces on 12 March.

Lynch came out to meet Beresford, escorted by the *Garde Urbaine à Cheval*, composed of the Royalists whom Taffard de Saint-Germain had been recruiting for the last few months on Louis's orders. Lynch made a speech, frequently interrupted by cries of *'A bas les aigles! Vivent les Bourbons!'* ('Down with the eagles! Long live the Bourbons!'), and then, in one moment, everyone ripped off the colours and insignia of the Empire, and put on the white cockade. A few hours later, Angoulême, who had already been acclaimed on 11 March by the small town of Bazas, was given a triumphant, emotional reception by almost the entire population of Bordeaux – whose Royalism he raised to fever-pitch by his well-chosen exclamations of '*Plus de guerres! Plus de conscription! Plus d'impôts vexatoires!*' ('No more wars! No more conscription! No more oppressive taxes!')

After the frenzy of 12 March, reality reasserted itself. The Allies had not yet broken off peace talks with Napoleon I, and Wellington refused to countenance any measure or proclamation which might imply that England was committed to protecting the Royalists. Many officers and officials resigned rather than choose who to support. Many others remained faithful to the Empire and decided to leave Bordeaux.[54]

But 12 March in Bordeaux changed everything. It was the undeniable Royalist sign for which the Bourbons' friends had been waiting so long. Only when news of the rising reached headquarters at Dijon did the Allies finally adopt the cause of Louis XVIII: and on 28 March, when Metternich and Castlereagh drank the health of Louis XVIII, they also drank that of the Mayor of Bordeaux.

Bordeaux was the one success which made all Louis's years of plots and intrigues and conspiracies worthwhile. What can have been his thoughts, on the morning of 25 March, when he was hearing Mass in the breakfast room at Hartwell, and saw a carriage covered with white cockades, which he knew was bringing good news, sweep up the drive? The dream of twenty-three dreary years of exile had become reality, his faithful subjects were calling him to the throne, and when he received the two deputies come to offer him the homage of the city of Bordeaux (the courtiers had rushed out in the middle of Mass; the king and his niece had waited calmly inside), tears of joy were pouring down his cheeks.

Events now moved so fast that there was not time for Louis, who had 'a violent attack of the gout', to follow his original plan and go to Bordeaux.[55] On 31 March the Allies entered Paris. A Provisional Government headed by Talleyrand, but including Louis's old agent the Abbé de Montesquiou, was set up and persuaded the Senate to pronounce the *déchéance* of Napoleon I on 2 April. On 7 April the Senate proclaimed 'Louis-Stanislas-Xavier' *Roi des Français* if he accepted their constitution. All over France, quite independently of events in Paris, towns were now declaring for Louis XVIII – Lyon on 2 April, Dunkirk on 8 April, Toulouse on 12 April. Soon the road to Hartwell, empty for so long, was crammed with people wanting to see the king;

messengers from Talleyrand, from the regent, from Artois, from
Angoulême, from Dunkirk, from Cherbourg, from Montesquiou,
from the Tsar. . .

But Louis was still detained by his gout. It was only on 20 April
that he was able to set out from Hartwell (leaving behind piles of
unused proclamations and £100 for the poor of the parish) to
meet in a foreign capital a reception such as few monarchs have
obtained in their own. Just outside London, at Stanmore, the
crowd was so enthusiastic that it unhorsed his carriage and pulled
him to the local inn, where the regent was waiting. The two royal
friends embraced 'in the French fashion' (i.e. kissed) and then,
with Condé and the Duchesse d'Angoulême, got into the regent's
state carriage to make a triumphal entry into London escorted by
guards and by 'an immense concourse of English gentlemen on
horseback wearing white cockades'.

The entire route along Edgware Road, Park Lane and Piccadilly
was jammed with ecstatic spectators, cheering, weeping, waving
white handkerchiefs. . . Louis XVIII is probably the last monarch
to have received such a welcome from all classes in England (the
only rival, Queen Caroline, was not popular with the elite). His
entry was also one of the last occasions when monarchy, not yet
just a spectacle, was in close, natural contact both with the public
who volunteered to pull Louis's carriage, and the elite who volunteered to escort it.

The next three days passed in a whirl of celebrations. At a
reception the same evening at Grillon's Hotel in Albemarle Street
(where Louis was finally allowed to stay), Louis made the regent
a *Chevalier du Saint Esprit*, and declared, 'It is to your Royal
Highness's Councils, to this great country, and to the constancy
of its people that I shall always ascribe, under Providence, the
restoration of our House to the Throne of our Ancestors. . . '
Before an evening party at Carlton House on 21 April, the regent
made Louis a Knight of the Garter. And at another reception
given by Louis on 22 April, which lasted all day long, although
extremely tired, he outshone himself in flattering and kindly remarks in both English and French to the crowds of people, including the Corporation of the City of London, who had come to
offer their congratulations. 'The grace and dignity of his manners',
perfect as usual, moved spectators to tears.[56]

Finally, on 23 April, with a loan from the English Government
of £100,000 to pay for the journey, he set off at eight o'clock for
Dover, 'repeatedly bowing' to the cheering crowds, who cried out
'God bless your Majesty! A happy return to your native country!'
The Morning Post noticed that he 'appeared in the highest spirits',

as well he might. He was a man whose dreams had come true. The next day he set sail for France.[57]

CHAPTER VIII

Louis le Désiré? April–June 1814

The year 1814 was one of the most extraordinary years in the history of France. It witnessed the restoration of Versailles and the abolition of the political prisons; the foundation of parliamentary monarchy and the creation of more nobles than in any other year of French history; and the transformation of some of Louis's life-long enemies into apparently obedient servants, and of some of his most faithful friends into dangerous enemies. A few months were enough to establish the particular flavour of monarchism, liberalism and deceptive façades which was to be so characteristic of Louis's reign, and which owed so much to Louis himself.

To understand how the silent military despotism of the French Empire could be transformed so rapidly, it is first necessary to know what sort of country France was. The kingdom which was waiting for Louis XVIII as he sailed from Dover was a land of 29,340,000 people. Most of the population lived in rural areas, a situation that remained unchanged for the next fifty years: under a fifth lived in towns of more than 2,000 people. The Revolutions had had a disastrous effect on the French economy and some historians have written of the 'de-industrialization' of certain areas of the country after 1789. Great trading ports like Bordeaux and Marseille had declined, and even Paris, now more than ever the pivot of the bureaucratic French state, had decreased in population, from 650,000 in 1789 to a little over 600,000. Only a few towns, such as Lyon and Strasbourg, had done well during the Empire, owing to their geographical position and the Continental System.[1]

That France was still – perhaps even more than in the late eighteenth century – a primarily agricultural country is confirmed by a survey of the 670 richest *notables* in the country carried out in July 1821. It shows that there were very few fortunes which could compare with those derived from land: only 23 per cent of these *notables* were not landowners. However, the survey is incomplete for three departments, including the Seine (Paris) and the Nord (Lille) where many of the richest bankers and industrialists were established. It also confirms the persistent importance of large aristocratic fortunes after the Revolution: 75 per cent of these *notables* were nobles (20 per cent of these being *Noblesse d'Empire* who owed their titles to Napoleon I). Some of the nobles, for example the de Wendel iron-founders, derived their fortune from industry, although most of them, the Noailles, the Luynes and the Montmorency for example, were still primarily landowners.[2] Thus when the subjects of Louis XVIII bemoaned the absence of aristocracy or the disappearance of aristocratic wealth in France, they were indulging in the pleasures of ritual lamentation, or were envying the colossal wealth of a few English peers. They were not reflecting reality.

What makes early nineteenth-century France unique, however, is not that it was a rural society with a wealthy aristocracy, but that it was a profoundly, passionately and *logically* monarchical country. There were almost no Republicans: the First Republic had seen to that. It took all the disappointments of the early years of the reign of Louis-Philippe I to make the Republic popular and intellectually respectable again. Louis's old enemy from 1789 and 1792, La Fayette, wrote despondently to Jefferson in August 1814: '*Bonaparte ou les Bourbons, telle a été, et telle est encore, la seule alternative possible, dans un pays où l'idée d'un pouvoir executif républicain est regardé comme le synonyme des excès commis sous ce nom.*' ('Bonaparte or the Bourbons, such have been, and such still are, the only possible alternatives, in a land where the idea of a republican executive is regarded as synonymous with the excesses committed under that name.')

Indeed, Napoleon I had accustomed the French to all the necessary features of a monarchy: a vast army; an obedient and prestigious bureaucracy; a magnificent Court, established in 1804, to which many more people were admitted than before 1789; and an enormous aristocracy, founded in 1808. As Talleyrand pointed out to Louis XVIII in 1815, what remained of the *anciennes factions revolutionnaires* were now tied to the monarchical system by the titles and property they had acquired.[3] This was the period when Fouché, the monster of Lyon, was a duke; Sieyès, author of the sensational egalitarian pamphlet of 1788, *Qu'est-ce que le Tiers État?*, a count; and the great Carnot, the organizer of the armies of the Republic in the Year II and the Regicide grandfather of a President of the Third Republic, became a count, wore the cross of a *Chevalier de Saint Louis* and longed to be well received at Court.

It was not just self-interest, however, but also genuine conviction which made former Revolutionaries defend principles in
1814–15, which they had attacked with such ferocity in 1789.
People like Garat, Cambon, Manuel and Benjamin Constant, on
the far left of the political spectrum, now genuinely believed that
a hereditary peerage was one of the checks and balances necessary
for a good liberal constitution (Louis XVIII was much less convinced) and that a strong monarchical executive was essential in
France. From the point of view of the Frenchmen of 1814, the
anti-authoritarianism of 1787–92 and the 'democratic' Republi-
canism of 1792–1800 had been absurd aberrations – or as Maréchal Macdonald told Artois at Louis XVIII's lunch-table, a
means to advance their careers.[4]

The utter contrast in attitudes and assumptions between the
two periods seems inexplicable but is no doubt the result of their
different pasts. After more than a century of internal peace and
absolute monarchy, Frenchmen had wanted to attack authority as
eagerly as, after a decade of chaos and revolution, they longed
for firm government. By 1814 the transformation was complete
enough for those among Louis's ministers who had served the
Revolution or the Empire to be at least as monarchical and authoritarian as those who had served the *Ancien Régime* or the
Counter-Revolution. For example, in June 1814, the ministers
who had served the Revolution or the Empire would be much
more in favour of press censorship than the Abbé de Montesquiou, who had not. And the ministers of Louis XVIII, unlike
those of Louis XV or Louis XVI, would not try to build personal
empires of patronage and policy, or to lessen royal authority by
attributing Government measures solely to their own brilliance.
Except for Talleyrand – in many ways a child of the *Ancien
Régime* – the ministers of Louis XVIII would be so monarchical
that they would be eager to associate the king as closely as possible
with the process and decisions of government. Apart from a few
months in 1815, there was no equivalent in France to English
ministers' desire to exclude their monarch from cabinet meetings
or Government business.

If the attitude of the elite made life easier for the French monarchy in the early nineteenth century, so too did the attitude of
that indispensible motor of French Revolutions, the Paris crowd.
For reasons which have never been satisfactorily explained, but
which no doubt have a lot to do with full employment, the price
of bread and the absence of leadership, between 1795 and 1827
the Paris crowd was almost completely quiescent – except for a
few days in 1815 and 1820. '*Le peuple a donné sa démission*'

('The people has handed in its notice') was, understandably enough, a favourite catch-phrase of the French elites during the reign of Louis XVIII.[5] For it was this *démission* which enabled the monarchy and the elites to pursue their ends without too much interference from the people in the street.

It is very hard to recapture the flavour of this unique period, since not only its assumptions and attitudes, but also almost all its physical monuments, have sunk without trace. The *Ancien Régime* is at least reflected in a hundred *châteaux*, cathedrals and *hôtels*, and of course at Versailles. The period 1800–1830, on the other hand, did not see much building and, thanks to the Prussians and the Communards, has lost its two revered and adored power-centres, buildings which, for contemporaries, combined the hypnotic fascination of both Buckingham Palace and the White House: the palaces of Saint-Cloud and the Tuileries. Only in a few rooms of Fontainebleau and Compiègne, and in some public buildings of Paris like the Bourse, can one grasp some of the majestic grandeur of one of the most monarchical and elitist periods in French history.

One outward sign of this period which still remains, however, is the uniforms of the *Académiciens* and the *Polytechniciens*. For the French state was now so powerful and so prestigious that all its officials, for the first time, were proud to wear the uniform of its service. Every official, the sovereign himself, a *Conseiller de Préfecture*, a *Polytechnicien*, and even a *Député* now wore a uniform. When they were off duty, however, or if they did not have an official post, every member of the elites wore the dark (usually black) frock-coat, which had been coming into fashion even before 1789. No longer were there any of the differences of dress between *noblesse présentée, noblesse non-présentée, noblesse de robe* and *bourgeoisie* which had existed right up to 1789, to divide the ranks of those committed to the defence of the social order.

Another sign of the increasing deference and monarchism of the French elites, in addition to the prevalence of uniform, was the transformation in their manners. The easy, gracious, relaxed manners of the 1780s had been replaced by the colder, more pompous and more formal manners of the nineteenth century, as can be appreciated by comparison of almost any portraits of the two periods. For example, Calonne and Decazes, Louis's favourite minister between 1815 and 1820, were, as Louis was well aware, two ministers with rather similar personalities. But Madame Vigée-Lebrun's *Calonne* (1784) – alert and smiling in the costume of a *noble de robe*, quite at ease with his cluttered desk and

comfortable arm-chair – is completely different from Gérard's
Decazes (1816, see illustration 16), who, in his simple *frac* against
an ostentatiously stark background, looks the epitome of the
ambitious young man contemplating his next move. And the contrast would be even greater if Gérard's *Decazes*, like almost every
other male portrait of the early nineteenth century, were standing.
Madame Vigée-Lebrun's *Calonne*, like most male portraits in the
1770s and 1780s, is sitting comfortably.

The novels of the two periods present the same contrast. There
is a world of difference between Laclos's *Les Liaisons Dangereuses* and Balzac's *Les Illusions Perdues* and *Splendeurs et Misères des Courtisanes*, and it is not just the decreasing availability
of married women. In the latter the hero is dominated by ambition, in the former by sex; Valmont, the hero of *Les Liaisons
Dangereuses*, hardly thinks of money or his career. In *Les Liaisons
Dangereuses* people meet at the relaxed, lascivious *soupers* so
adored by eighteenth-century Parisians; in *Splendeurs et Misères
des Courtisanes*, the hero longs to be invited to a formal *dîner*.
It is typical of the new world of the nineteenth century that, in
the greatest love story of the period, Benjamin Constant's
Adolphe, the hero leaves his mistress not because she is so demanding and emotional, but because she might harm his career.

The elite had become colder and more single-mindedly ambitious and this surely is what Talleyrand meant by his celebrated
remark that only those who had lived before 1789 had known
'*la vraie douceur de vivre*'. The Abbé de Montesquiou, Louis's
old friend and secret agent, who became a minister in 1814, could
not get over the change in social life. '*Plus de gaieté*', he wrote,
conversation was now devoted to *les affaires*, rather than *les arts:
'l'avidité domine tout*'. Many other members of the elite, for
example the Vicomtesse de Noailles, whose family had recovered
much of its pre-1789 wealth and social prominence, also noticed
and lamented '*le refroidissement général*'.[6]

This cold, ambitious, greedy world clearly presented a favourable basis on which to found a monarchy, a form of government
which has never lacked the means to satisfy greed and ambition.
Morcover Louis would fit into this world very easily. He himself
was cold and ambitious. At Court in the 1770s and 1780s the
commonest complaint about him was he was too pompous and
formal. No one would find cause to complain about that now. So
in 1814, a monarchy was the natural regime for France. The
power base was there, the men were ready, the time was right and
the monarch was on his way from England. But what sort of
monarchy should it be?

One answer was provided by the Napoleonic Senate which, under the aegis of the Provisional Government headed by Talleyrand, had published a constitution on 7 April 1814. Many of its clauses were devoted, with a selfishness and greed typical of early nineteenth-century France, to perpetuating the Senators' own titles and pensions. But it was also a fundamentally un-Royalist constitution. It not only called for an annual two-chamber Parliament and a responsible ministry, but it also stated that Louis-Stanislas-Xavier, *Frère du Dernier Roi* (not uncle of Louis XVII) should only be proclaimed king when he had sworn to observe the constitution. The Senatorial Constitution, by not acknowledging the existence of Louis XVII, asked Louis to recognize the Republic and the Empire. It was based on the idea of a contractual monarchy, like the constitutional monarchy of 1791–92, when Louis XVI had only recovered his freedom and his monarchical powers so that he could sign the constitution, or the July Monarchy of 1830, when the Duc d'Orléans was only elected king on certain conditions. Indeed, like those two regimes, the Provisional Government at first wanted to keep the Revolutionary Tricolour flag.

Both Talleyrand, in the name of the Provisional Government, and the Tsar in the name of the Allies, urged Louis to agree to this constitution, which would have made him, like Louis XVI in 1791, or Louis-Philippe I in 1830, a king who owed his throne to a set of revolutionaries. And it has been said that Louis was so desperate to recover the throne that he did sign this constitution.[7]

However, in his papers at the Quai d'Orsay are Louis's *Observations* on the Senatorial Constitution which show how deeply he rejected it and how silly he could be. He points out that the Senate '*ne la faite que pour lui*' ('only made it for itself') which is fair enough. But he also, even now, wanted to encourage *transactions* between *acquéreurs* and ex-proprietors of *biens nationaux* although, at the same time, agreeing to maintain the validity of the present distribution of property. He did not want the state to pay Protestant priests, and as for crimes committed during the Revolution, '*que le criminel tremble. Mais tout français peut compter sur la clémence du Roi*' ('let the criminal tremble. But every Frenchman can count on the King's mercy'). These *Observations* (which are incomplete) show the worst side of Louis's character, blustering, self-satisfied, and self-contradictory: if criminals are forgiven, why should they need to tremble?

However, when he wrote that he did not want to be *Louis-Stanislas-Xavier* but instead '*Louis XVIII par la grâce de Dieu Roi de France et de Navarre*', and that he '*casse le présent Sénat comme complice de tous les crimes de Bonaparte et en appelle au peuple français'* ('disbands the present Senate as partner in all the crimes of Bonaparte and appeals to the French people'), he showed that he knew where his own strength and real interests lay.[8] The trouble with a contractual monarchy is that, as in many contracts, each side has a tendency to want to change the terms – or suspects the other side of wanting to. This is particularly true with absolute monarchs who are compelled to sign constitutions. Despite all the proofs of sincerity he gave, many of his subjects never believed that Louis XVI meant to observe the constitution which he signed in 1791. Who would have believed that Louis XVIII meant to observe a constitution written by Napoleonic Senators and backed by Talleyrand? Above all, a monarchy based on a contract destroys the aura of mystery and respect – what Louis called *considération* – which is the firmest foundation of a monarch's authority.

There was no sign, however, that the *peuple français*, as opposed to a few elderly Senators, really wanted a contractual monarchy – as Louis well knew. Dunkirk and Bordeaux had already hailed him as Louis XVIII, and at Bordeaux the Senatorial Constitution was actually burnt on the stage of the local theatre. On 24 April the *Conseil Municipal* of Lyon voted an address to Artois, who had entered Paris in triumph as *Lieutenant-Général du Royaume* on 12 April, attacking the Senatorial Constitution and the presence of Regicides in the Senate. Even the *Moniteur*, which was formally forbidden by Talleyrand to refer to Louis as Louis XVIII rather than Louis-Stanislas-Xavier, printed accounts of crowds in Angers and Toulouse cheering Louis XVIII. The difference between the natural feelings of most French people and the attempt of the Provisional Government to force its contractual monarchy on them can be seen in addresses in the Archives Nationales, on which Louis XVIII has been crossed out and Louis-Stanislas-Xavier written in by an alien hand.[9]

From the moment Louis arrived at Calais on 24 April, after a three hour crossing during which, typically the Duchesse d'Angoulême, but not her uncle, was sea-sick, he could see for himself how Royalist the French now were. An English friend who was at Calais wrote: 'the shouts, the exultation, the enthusiasm of the people on the pier at first overcame them and tears flowed from their cheeks.' After they landed and received the inevitable official deputations, including a group of virgins in white, Louis and the Duchesse d'Angoulême got into a carriage which was unhorsed and drawn through the streets of Calais to the cathedral. They were followed by a screaming crowd including Havré who, hardly knowing what he was doing, ran beside their carriage weeping with joy. In the evening, in accordance with one of the oldest traditions of French royalty, they dined in public, and a song was sung hailing Louis as *Louis le Désiré* – surely one of the most charming and flattering epithets a monarch has ever received.[10]

As he moved slowly and triumphantly through Boulogne, Abbeville and Amiens, cheered by cries of *Vive le Roi*, he was honoured by endless respectful deputations – among whom there was always a group of virgins in white. Huge crowds watched him dine in public every day after first being pulled by his loyal subjects to the church or cathedral (the fattest King of France was the one whose carriage was most frequently unhorsed and pulled). It really seemed as if Louis was *le Désiré*.

The elite were no less eager to show their Royalism than the crowds in the streets. At Calais the Marquis de La Rochejaquelein, who had come with despatches from Bordeaux, 'imprinted a thousand kisses on his hand' (the fashion for kissing the monarch's hand was an outward sign of the monarchism of the early nineteenth-century French elite). At Boulogne, Maréchal Moncey, the first Napoleonic marshal Louis ever met, also knelt, covered in white cockades, to kiss his hand. But Louis raised and embraced him, saying: '*Monsieur le Maréchal, vous portez une cocarde qui met le comble à vos lauriers.*' ('Monsieur le Maréchal, you are wearing a cocade which crowns your laurels.')

The white flag of legitimacy, not the tricolour of the Revolution (including the constitutional monarchy of 1789–92) and the Empire, was to be the flag of Louis's reign. The first mistakes had already begun. Nevertheless the emotional release which Louis had hoped to provoke, in 1798–99, by his appeals to the hearts of generals Berthier and Bonaparte now appeared to be taking place in the hearts of almost all his crying, cheering and carriage-pulling subjects. The Restoration was not just a dynastic event, it was also an outburst of emotions.

Finally, on 29 April, a day perhaps even more special for him than the day he returned to France, Louis arrived at Compiègne, the most attractive of all the royal palaces of the Ile-de-France. Slowly and painfully (he was still very weak from his attack of gout) he climbed the great staircase and found himself, as an account written for the regent put it, home at last. He had finally returned to the world of his youth, the sights and smells and atmosphere in which he had grown up. But it was a world transformed. Compiègne was covered with Ns and bees and eagles – even the wine-glasses had Ns on them. In the joyful noisy crowd, Louis found not only old friends like the Duchesse de Duras and

Lévis waiting to greet him, but also Marshals Ney, Berthier, Marmont, Jourdan, Mortier, Oudinot and Victor. Lurking in the antechambers were two of the most dangerous and ambitious politicians of the day, the Prince de Talleyrand (or de Bénévent, as he was then called) and the Vicomte de Chateaubriand.

Louis entertained all the marshals to dinner, said a *mot flatteur* to each about their victories and at the end drank their health: '*C'est sur vous, Messieurs les Maréchaux, que je veux toujours m'appuyer; approchez et entourez-moi. Vous avez toujours été bons français; j'espère que la France n'aura plus besoin de vos épées. Si jamais, à ce que Dieu ne veuille, on nous forçait à la tirer, je marcherais avec vous, si cela était nécessaire.*' ('It is on you, Messieurs les Maréchaux, that I want always to rely; come near and surround me. You have always been good Frenchmen; I hope that France will have no more need of your swords. If ever, which God forbid, we were forced to draw them, I would march with you, if that was necessary.') Thus Louis converted the rather awkward moment of meeting these vain and ambitious men, who had spent the best years of their lives fighting against his cause and his allies, into a dignified royal reception. And the marshals assured their king, with tears in their eyes, that they would be the '*colonnes de votre trône*'.[11]

However, there were more important things to do than to flatter the marshals' colossal vanity. The nature of the Restoration had to be decided. And the choices facing Louis, who had obviously been determined not to commit himself throughout the celebrations of the last three weeks, were symbolized by the fact that three men had rushed to Compiègne to do the honours as governor of the palace: General Delaborde, the Napoleonic governor; Mathieu de Montmorency, head of the *Chevaliers de la Foi*, and son of the governor under Louis XVI; and General Curial, sent by the Provisional Government.[12] Was Louis to reign as the successor of Napoleon I, as the heir of Louis XVI, or as the *protégé* of the Provisional Government?

Louis was totally opposed to the Senatorial Constitution. But a few people at the time, such as Metternich (who admired the Empire which bore so many resemblances to the Habsburg Monarchy) and Maréchal Marmont, thought that he should continue the tough authoritarian style of monarchy of Napoleon I, the most absolute monarch in French history. Napoleon I himself, as he was about to leave Fontainebleau for Elba nine days before Louis arrived at Compiègne, said that all the king had to do was to change the sheets on his bed.[13]

But this would have been impossible. First, Louis simply did not have either the industry or the desire to be an all-powerful, all-controlling bureaucratic monarch like Napoleon I. Second, it was not a style of monarchy suited to early nineteenth-century France. Napoleon I had only kept it going by the prestige of his innumerable victories and by the *dotations* (grants of land or Government bonds) he could offer so many people in the territories he had conquered (just as the Israeli Government offers its citizens property in its conquered territories). And the essential fragility of his regime had been demonstrated by the Malet conspiracy and by the dissolution of an angry *Corps Législatif* – even though its members were hand-picked by the regime – in January 1814.

Other people, more than is often realized, still thought that Louis should restore a modified form of the *Ancien Régime*. Several pamphlets came out to this effect in April 1814; and a petition in favour of the monarchy of Henri IV was signed by 2,000 Dijonnais. Ferrand, one of the most famous writers of the Counter-Revolution, whom Louis saw at Compiègne, preferred this solution, as did many provincial nobles and, according to his memoirs, the Baron de Vitrolles, a Royalist secret agent who had become *Secrétaire d'État provisoire*.[14] Even now some French Royalists have not forgiven Louis XVIII his failure to restore the *Ancien Régime* in 1814.

But this was a dream which Louis had already explicitly renounced in his declaration of 1804. Most Frenchmen utterly distrusted the *Ancien Régime*, and there was no way in which nineteenth-century France could escape a constitution, as Louis realized. His attitude to constitutions in 1814 is summed up in a remark destined for his Bourbon cousin, Ferdinand IV of Naples: he said that he had not wanted to be '*Roi par la grâce du Sénat, mais qu'il avait donné une constitution à ses peuples parce que c'était l'Esprit de notre siècle et qu'il valait toujours mieux la donner que la recevoir*' ('King by the grace of the Senate, but he had given a constitution to his peoples, because it was the spirit of the age, and it was always better to give one than to have one imposed on you').

Louis certainly regretted the *Ancien Régime*. But the *Ancien Régime* he regretted, by 1814, was not the world of privileges, *parlements* and Estates with all that phrase evokes. What he regretted was an institution which has been almost completely neglected by historians – the strong, silent and effective monarchy of the *Ancien Régime*, when for example, the laws protecting royalty and condemning treacherous politicians were much stronger, and the king could choose and keep any minister he wanted. But Louis knew that France had been *monarchique dans le fait* since 1800; and perhaps he realized that in 1814 neither a constitution nor the '*Esprit de notre siècle*' were necessarily incompatible with a powerful and prestigious monarchy.[15]

Louis's remark to the King of Naples shows that the form as much as the content of the new constitution interested him. What really mattered was that it should be granted by a free act of royal authority and that it should be seen to be a product of the traditions of French royalty. And the Declaration of Saint-Ouen, of 2 May 1814, which was written by Vitrolles, La Maisonfort (an agent of Artois) and Montesquiou, on a basis provided by Louis and Blacas, was a very liberal document indeed.[16] It guaranteed liberty of the press, a two-chamber legislature with powers over taxation (the one subject on which Louis's declarations of 1804 and 1813 had been silent), and the maintenance of all titles, decorations and jobs, and of the sale of *biens nationaux*. The next day Louis entered Paris, where he was greeted by crowds rather less enthusiastic than those which had greeted Artois on 12 April.

During the next few weeks Louis spent most of his time receiving innumerable loyal deputations in the palace of the Tuileries, and listening to their addresses of congratulation. Obviously these addresses, prepared by official bodies eager to please, are not wholly reliable as a guide to public opinion. Nevertheless no one forced these representatives of towns, departments and *Gardes Nationales* – there were very few addresses or deputations from regiments – to make the journey to the Tuileries from all parts of France. As far as one can judge from their addresses, which poured in from May to at least October at the rate of twenty or more a day, it was a monarchy in the royal tradition, not a revolutionary monarchy, that the deputations wanted. Every town seemed to take pleasure in recalling a stay by Henri IV, a visit from Louis XIV, or any ancient connection with the kings of France. The *Cour Royale* of Grenoble, the capital of Dauphiné, begged Louis to revive the tradition of calling the king's eldest son the Dauphine. A deputation from Varennes begged for words of consolation from Louis XVIII to wipe out the stain of having been the scene of the arrest of Louis XVI (Louis replied, quite correctly, that his brother had known that most of the inhabitants were opposed to the arrest).

It genuinely seemed as if the Revolution and the Empire had failed to break the immemorial connection between the Royal Family and the French people and perhaps even made it closer.[17] Indeed one of the oddest things about the return of the king in 1814 is that it did not seem odd at the time. Despite twenty-five

years of Revolutions and Empire, most French people seem to
have been able to revert to talking about *le Roi* and *les ministres
du Roi*, to moan *si le Roi le savait* and to celebrate *la bonté des
Bourbons*, as if it was the most natural thing in the world. No
one seemed to feel ill at ease with the Restoration, or to think of
it as an alien or artificial regime, as they did at the beginning of
the Republic, the Empire and the July Monarchy.

But Louis did not spend all his time receiving homage. In the
evenings of May 1814, he was reported to by the man he had
recently appointed Chancellor and the three *commissaires* he had
chosen to be his representatives in a commission of eighteen members of the Senate and the *Corps Législatif*, who were charged
with drawing up a constitution. The chancellor was an inoffensive
son-in-law of Louis XVI's *Garde des Sceaux* in 1789 called Dambray who, like so many nobles, had passed the Revolution and
the Empire quietly on his estates. The *commissaires* were Montesquiou, the most important of them all and the man who eventually countersigned the *Charte*, Ferrand, a reactionary to whose
advice Louis had appealed in 1804, and Beugnot, a former Napoleonic official prominent in the Provisional Government, who
would be as insistent as Dambray on maintaining the power and
authority of the monarch. Talleyrand and the other members of
the Provisional Government were, on Louis's express instructions,
totally excluded: so much for their hopes of a contractual
monarchy.

As with the Restoration itself, the extraordinary thing about
the *Charte*, as the new constitution was called, is that there was
very little controversy about most of its provisions, which in
themselves were not very different from those in the Senatorial
Constitution. All agreed on those clauses of the *Charte* which
made everyone liable to taxation, and guaranteed equality before
the law and of career opportunity, freedom from arbitrary arrest
and a reasonable liberty of the press. Everyone was now so much
in favour of strong monarchical government that they agreed that
the king should appoint all senior officials and officers (a complete
contrast as Louis noted to the constitution of 1791). There was
some controversy about making Catholicism the *Religion d'État*.
But it was agreed to in the end, in return for Louis agreeing to
pay Protestant ministers' salaries.

The most important matter to decide was the exact nature of
the national representation. In the end it was agreed there should
be a Chamber of Peers (who could be either hereditary or life
peers) and a Chamber of Deputies composed of 268 members
who had to pay more than 1,000 francs in taxes. A fifth of this

chamber was to be elected every year by everyone who paid more than 300 francs a year in taxes. The two chambers were to meet each year and also had to meet within three months of a dissolution. They could accuse and judge the ministers, who could be admitted to any of their debates.

Louis had wanted the crown to have the power (attributed by the Senate to itself) to choose deputies from a double list elected by the *Collèges Electoraux*. Indeed all Louis's comments on Montesquiou's first project and all his interventions in May were designed to increase the power and authority of the crown. Thus he insisted on the crown alone being able to initiate legislation – although the chambers were allowed to beg (*supplier*) the crown to take a matter into consideration. Louis also insisted that the crown alone should have the right to make war and peace, a provision which was not in Montesquiou's first project, claiming (quite rightly, as any ally of the United States knows) that if it did not have the right to make peace treaties '*les étrangers ne peuvent plus avoir de confiance dans le Gouvernement*' ('foreigners can no longer have confidence in the Government'). Louis frequently backed up this, and many other suggestions with references to the power of the English Crown. Typically, it was this power, rather than the benefits of parliamentary government (which he was prepared to concede at least by 1804), which was the main political lesson Louis had learnt while staying in England.[19]

However, on some matters Louis was prepared to back down: indeed his notes to Montesquiou in May were usually in the conditional tense – he was the mildest and most conciliatory of monarchs. He allowed more liberty for the press than he originally wanted; in April he had asked for the same censorship as before 1789. He allowed the deputies to be elected directly by the *Collèges Electoraux*. He had the *Charte* sent to the two chambers for their approval, a fact often forgotten by those who claim that it was simply contemptuously *octroyée* or granted.[20]

It is very difficult to assess the precise contribution Louis made to the *Charte*, especially since neither he, Montesquiou, nor Dambray have left detailed accounts of this period. The *Charte* was certainly not his work to the degree to which *Les Devoirs d'un Roi*, written in 1797 on the basis of very different principles, had been. He would have preferred some of its clauses to be different: as has been shown, in April he had been opposed to paying Protestant ministers, and in May he would have liked the crown to choose the deputies from a double list. He did not write the *Charte*, nor did he sit in on the debates that preceded its final form. According to Beugnot, he did not even read Beugnot's preamble, stating that the *Charte* was *octroyée* by Louis, in his name and in the name of his successors, for ever.[21]

On the other hand, he had chosen Dambray, Montesquiou, Ferrand and Beugnot, and he took a personal interest in everything debated during the meetings of the commission. He made his own contributions, with his suggestions about the crown's initiative in legislation and the crown's right to declare war and to make peace. He also insisted that the order of succession be left out of the *Charte* – the king granted the *Charte*, the *Charte* could not define who the king was. By existing, by rejecting the Senatorial Constitution, he made the *Charte* possible and throughout 1814, indeed throughout his reign, he was very insistent that his ministers should observe its provisions. It has almost as much right to be called the work of Louis XVIII, as has the Code Civil to be called the work of Napoleon.

And Louis XVIII tied himself to the *Charte* as closely and as personally as possible at a splendid ceremony on 4 June when, surrounded by all the pomp of royalty – *Gardes du Corps, Aides des Cérémonies*, trumpets, silence and then cheers as he entered the Palais Bourbon – he read out a speech to the Senate and the *Corps Législatif* which showed how well he knew that the Restoration of his dynasty could not simply be a dynastic and emotional event. It had to bring concrete constitutional and economic benefits as well. In this speech he praised '*la gloire des armées françaises*', and, at much greater length, the benefits of peace, such as the restoration of France's commerce and manufactures, and the preservation of the plundered works of art. At the end he referred to the past, to his dead nephew and brother, the principles of whose will, as well as his own experience and the advice of his councillors had, he said, helped him compose the *Charte*. Thus Louis XVIII did not fear the past. He regarded the fall of the monarchy and the experience of the Republic as justifications and reasons for his own reign.

After Louis's speech, Ferrand read out the *Charte*. And on 5 June a deputation from the Chamber of Deputies came to the Tuileries to thank Louis for the new constitution, and gave final official consecration to the title by which he had been called so often in the last few weeks, gratefully hailing him as *Louis le Désiré*.

The strangest thing about the *Charte*, to us is what seemed least controversial to contemporaries namely that, as Ferrand wrote: '*Chacun partait du principe que c'est dans la propriété que doit se trouver la garantie du citoyen à qui on confie les intérêts de l'État.*' ('Everyone started from the principle that it is property

that provides the guarantee of the citizen to whom is entrusted
the interests of the State.') The property-based franchise of 1814
gave the vote to only about 100,000 people. In a nation of twenty-
nine million this was an extraordinary limitation of political life,
particularly when one considers the many exciting opportunities
for participation in politics provided since 1789.[22] Yet a progres-
sive limitation of the franchise had been going on since 1789, and
its extreme limitation in 1814 seemed odd or reprehensible to
remarkably few contemporaries. Even as late as 1830, workmen
would fight in the streets of Paris for the preservation of the
Charte which deprived them of elementary political rights. The
early nineteenth century was as naturally elitist as it was essentially monarchical.

The *Charte*, Louis's speech on 4 June and his replies to the
loyal deputations he received in the Tuilieries throughout the
summer, show the way in which he thought of his reign and
kingship. His royal rank was the reason for his being in the
Tuileries palace, and one reason, as he had said in 1803 to the
envoy of the King of Prussia and in January 1814 to Lord Liverpool (see pages 84 and 164), for him wanting to be there. He
also had personal reasons for wanting to be on the throne (see
Chapter XII). But he was far too intelligent to believe that royalty
is enough on its own and that his reign needed no justification
beyond his dynastic rights. He knew, and experience of
Revolutionaries' and Counter-Revolutionaries' ability to disobey
or ignore the king must have drilled it into him, that a throne is
only strong if it brings something with it, if it contributes something to the life of the nation.

So throughout 1814, Louis spoke not of the rights of his dynasty
but of the benefits of peace and the virtues of his *Charte*. He did
not refer to himself all the time as the king, the legitimate ruler
with an inalienable right to the French throne. He kept such
sentiments to himself or for other monarchs. He was no Wilhelm
II, lavishing praise on his own dynasty and the loftiness of his
royal rank. On the contrary Louis usually referred to himself as
the father of his people, and above all – and this is typical of a
semi-invalid who even as a young prince had had an enormous
number of medical books in his library – as their doctor.

One of the words he used most frequently to describe his relations with his subjects was *soins*, the French word to describe
what a doctor provides for a patient. '*Comptez à jamais sur mes
soins*' ('You can always rely on my care'), he said to the *Garde
Nationale* of the Eure, for example, and he declared, '. . . *tout
mon peuple a un droit egal à mes soins*' ('. . . all my people have

an equal right to my care') to the *Bureau de Bienfaisance* of Paris. And his cure for his rather difficult patient was the classic one of peace, rest and forgetfulness.[23]

The tone of Louis's speeches and the *Charte* itself also showed the nature of his reign. It was not a reaction or a Counter-Revolution such as these launched in 1814 by Louis's cousin Ferdinand VII of Spain, who immediately revived the Inquisition and abolished the *Cortes*, and by his brother-in-law Victor Emmanuel I of Piedmont, who at once cancelled all laws passed since his flight in 1798 (except those increasing taxation). Under Louis XVIII, France was more like the Netherlands of William I or the Naples of Ferdinand IV, determined to retain anything of real value which had been accomplished during the long Revolutionary and Napoleonic nightmare. The Restoration was intended to be, as the Chancellor said, an *'oubli généreux du passé'* and the moment of *'réconciliation générale'*: it was not the triumph of the Counter-Revolutionaries. And it is hardly surprising that the people who were most appalled by the *Charte* were not former Revolutionaries but paladins and philosophers of the Counter-Revolution, men such as the Prince de Condé, the Vicomte de Bonald and, perhaps, the Comte d'Artois.[24]

Despite, or perhaps because of its extremely limited franchise, the France of Louis XVIII and the *Charte* was a genuinely liberal state – more so than the England of Liverpool and Castlereagh. What are the best, most foolproof tests of a liberal state? The treatment of minorities? The number of political prisoners? Censorship? In the France of Louis XVIII, religious minorities such as the Protestants and the Jews were equal before the law. The last remaining legal disabilities on the Jews which Napoleon, always reactionary when he dared, had reimposed in 1808, were removed in 1818, and Protestants could have as successful careers in government service as Catholics. Guizot was a high Government official in 1814–16, and Portal, another Protestant, was *Ministre de la Marine* from 1818 to 1821, at a time when all non-Anglicans were excluded from office in England. The Lutheran, Calvinist and Jewish *Consistoires* went to pay their respects to Louis XVIII in the Tuileries as often as did the Archbishop of Paris and his clergy. As Canning noted when visiting France, the English talked a lot about religious toleration; the French (at least in most parts of France) practised it.

The France of Louis XVIII was not a police state, as it had been from 1792 to 1814. One of Artois's first acts as *Lieutenant-Général du Royaume* had been to liberate the 640 *prisonniers d'État* (of whom 320 had been genuinely political) kept by Na-

poleon I in seven *Prisons d'État*. There were neither political
prisoners nor political exiles (a favourite weapon of Napoleon I
had been exile from Paris) in the first year of Louis's reign, for
the first time since 1789. Although some laws were suspended
during the reaction of 1815–17, and some Protestants suffered
horribly at the hands of provincial mobs, France reverted to the
rule of law by 1818. The chief remaining sign of the old police
state was the interception of letters, a habit which was, however,
almost universal in nineteenth-century Europe, including England.

The area where the France of 1814 was least liberal in theory
was censorship, since the Press Law of November 1814, in accordance with Louis's personal inclinations, allowed censors to
go through every newspaper before it came out, and gave them
the power to veto articles (censorship on books and periodicals
was far less severe). But this censorship was 'mild enough in
practice' in 1814 and certainly incomparably more liberal than
under the Empire. Newspapers were restored to many Royalist
ex-proprietors – the *Journal des Débats* to the Bertin brothers
and the *Quotidienne* to Michaud – and many new ones were
founded, as they were now worth publishing and reading.

Thus right from the beginning, in both intention and practice,
the restoration of Louis XVIII was more than just a royal event.
It brought to France, as well as the Bourbons, peace and a liberal,
tolerant regime which preached reconciliation and forgetfulness
of the past. Louis even told a deputation from the Vendée that
he would try to make them forget the past, which since they have
still not forgotten, was rather optimistic. The monarchy of Louis
XVIII far from being as so many people assume with ninteenth-
century monarchies, of little significance outside its own power
or impotence, affected the lives of millions of Frenchmen, trans-
forming their hopes, fears and assumptions. And that the mild,
liberal, conciliatory nature of his own monarchy was due in part
to Louis himself is suggested by the alternatives offered to him
before he entered Paris, by his role in the composition of the
Charte and, above all, by comparing his acts in 1814 with the
acts of Ferdinand VII, and with the plans of the Comte d'Artois
(see page 402).

The moderate nature of the Restoration was again shown by
Louis's choice of ministers on 13 May, after a delay on ten days
to enable him to get to know the candidates. Montesquiou became
Minister of the Interior, Malouet of the Marine, Dupont of War,
Talleyrand of Foreign Affairs, Baron Louis of Finance, Dambray
of Justice, and Blacas of the *Maison du Roi*[25]: that is one representative of moderate Royalism who had worked for Louis's Gov-

ernment in exile but also knew how to handle representative assemblies, having three times been President of the *Assemblée Nationale*; four representatives of the Napoleonic elite who had served the Provisional Government; one representative of the *Ancien Régime* chosen because his father-in-law had been *Garde des Sceaux* in 1789; and one of the Emigration. As *Ministres d'État* he inherited Dalberg, Jaucourt, Beurnonville, Dessolles and Marshals Moncey and Oudinot from the Provisional Government, and added Ferrand. Thus Louis accepted, rather than selected, most of his ministers, just as he accepted, rather than introduced most clauses of the *Charte*. Once he had accepted them, however, he treated them as his own.

Louis's choice of ministers showed that he was perfectly willing to use the men of the Revolution and the Empire. Twelve of the sixteen ministers of the first Restoration had served the Republic or the Empire: the proportion for Louis's entire reign is thirty-two out of forty-five (counting *Ministres d'État* who sat in the Council, but excluding *Ministres par intérim*) or 71 per cent. Almost without exception only the soldiers among them, and Talleyrand, had served the Republic, which shows the degree to which it had owed its existence to war. The proportion of *émigrés* among Louis's ministers was fifteen out of forty-five, or 33 per cent. Thus Louis XVIII was no more the king of the Counter-Revolution or *le roi des émigrés* than General de Gaulle was the leader of the Resistance after 1944. As Louis had written as early as 1795, he was more interested in people's present usefulness than in their political antecedents.

On the other hand his choice of Dambray, Ferrand and Blacas, the only ministers whom he did not inherit from the Provisional Government, shows his desire to associate with his policy of moderation and liberalism representatives of the *Ancien Régime*, the Counter-Revolution and the Emigration. He wanted every section of the political spectrum associated with the 'final' settlement of 1814, and Blacas was his indispensable favourite, right-hand man and secretary. With the exception of these three ministers, however, most of Louis's former supporters from the world of the Emigration found themselves sadly ill-rewarded in 1814. For example, de Vezet, who had been so loyal and had tried so hard in Louis's Government in exile, simply continued to draw his pension of 3,000 livres. When he went to court, Louis greeted him with the words, '*Comment se porte Madame de Vezet?*' ('How is Madame de Vezet?')[26]

This polite, royal enquiry, the reference to his old servant's *wife*, has rather heart-breaking implications. A whole world of

hopes and struggles and fears, the world of Louis's Government
in exile, was over and finished. Like Balzac's hero Rastignac, and
most politicians – a celebrated example being Louis's friend the
regent, who soon dropped his Whig cronies after his change of
politics in 1811 – Louis used people like post-horses, changing
them when they were worn out and useless. As a child, he had
been taught to see people '*dans le grand, c'est à dire par rapport
à l'utilite publique*' ('in their context, that is to say with regard
to their public usefulness') and he never found it difficult to put
this precept into practice. He realized that his old friends were,
with a few exceptions, simply no longer useful in the France of
1814. As de Vezet admitted, they found it '*impossible de prendre
l'esprit du jour*' ('impossible to adapt to the spirit of the day'): it
is, perhaps, the greatest eulogy of Louis that, at the age of fifty-
nine, he did not. So people like de Vezet were lucky to get the
very small pensions they did. Important jobs, not only at ministerial level, went to the *hommes nouveaux* whom Louis had been
planning to employ since at least 1803.[27] For example, Chabrol
remained *Prefet de la Seine*, General Maison who had rushed to
greet Louis at Calais was made Commander of the Military Division of Paris, and Baron Denniée became *Intendant-Général
de l'Armée*. The reign of Louis XVIII was clearly going to be a
new world, different from anything France had experienced
before.

CHAPTER IX

A New World
June 1814–March 1815

Once the ministry was named, and the *Charte* proclaimed, Louis had to decide what part he would play in the day to day business of government. In exile he had been at the head of his own affairs, seeing most despatches, frequently writing to his ministers and agents, and thinking of them as subordinates whose task was simply to spare him the minor details of government. But in exile he had been opposed to the doctrine of ministerial responsibility which, he felt, annihilated royal authority and respect for the king, and d'Avaray had wanted him to be his own Prime Minister. Now he was an older, wiser, tireder and much iller man, and the doctrine of ministerial responsibility was enshrined in the *Charte*[1]: each minister was responsible to the chambers for each law or *Ordonnance* countersigned with his signature underneath the king's.

However, Louis still regularly saw each minister alone in his *Cabinet* in the Tuileries. The Minister of War, for example, came to see him every evening between ten and eleven o'clock. But in this *travail*, to the surprise and dismay of his essentially monarchical ministers, he took almost no decisions himself. Beugnot found out that he could come with an *ordonnance* ready to sign, rather than a *rapport* to be criticized and altered, and that the king would sign it without even requiring an explanation of its contents. Dupont wrote: '*Le règlement, l'ordonnance avaient tout empire sur lui; il ne m'a jamais refusé une signature.*' ('The regulation, the *ordonnance*, were all powerful for him; he never refused me a signature.')[2] Many ministers, especially Talleyrand, who did not get on at all well with Louis, got the king to sign their *Ordonnances* at the end of the *Conseil des Ministres* without any discussion in private. Soon this method of government leaked out to the Parisian public; '*Le Roi signe tout ce qu'on lui présente*' ('The King signs everything put before him') grumbled an ex-officer of the *Grande Armée* in October. This was an exaggeration. But the most control that Louis exercised over his ministers' activity was to refuse to agree to a pension or to ask a minister to *représenter* a decision before the Council, in effect to delay approval.

The reason for this refusal of initiative, which was quite different from Napoleon I's manner of conducting business, lay in Louis's character as well as in his realization that, in a representative Government, ministers had to be allowed the initiative as well as the responsibility for decisions. He found most ministerial business very boring indeed. For France was now so monarchical, so eager to depend upon the monarch's will, that decisions about a *sous-prefet's* pension, commercial regulations, hospitals and subsidies for local roads, were all expected to be taken during the king's *travail* with his ministers.[3]

However, in the *Conseil des Ministres*, which met once or twice a week, Louis's influence was more considerable. He was extremely well-informed, since he saw all ministers *tête-à-tête*. He was the king, the man who had chosen them and whose favour was essential to their existence. In November 1814, when Beugnot was hoping to be made Minister of the Marine, Dambray wrote to him that he must go and have a *travail* with the king at the Tuileries, in order to give the king an opportunity to make *'quelque ouverture qui déciderait la chose'* ('an opening which would clinch the matter'). Although in December 1814, Artois was partly responsible for the choice of Soult as Minister of War, it was Louis and Blacas who chose Ferrand as *Directeur-Général des Postes* and d'Andre, his chief agent in 1797–1801, as *Directeur-Général de Police*.[4] And in the *Conseil des Ministres* whose minutes and *Procès-Verbaux* survive, it is clear that Louis played an important role, telling a minister to change his instructions to agents about Saint-Domingue, or taking the initiative on policy by stating that he was unwilling to abolish the slave trade to please England without getting something in return.[5]

Another area where Louis exercised personal influence was finance. Far from having learnt nothing and forgotten nothing, the later Bourbons were obsessed with one lesson of 1787–89, namely that a budgetary deficit can be fatal to royal authority. From the first meeting of the Council on 5 May Louis stated his determination to reduce expenditure, in particular that on the army, which in 1814 accounted for almost 55 per cent of the total. On 17 June, possibly on the prompting of his forceful Finance Minister, Baron Louis, he said that the expenditure of the Ministry of War should be reduced to 200 million francs, and on 11 July he allotted the expenditure for each ministry, again presumably after consulting the Minister of Finance. The Budget of

1815 roughly followed his indications. Out of a planned expenditure of 548 million francs, the *Liste Civile* took 7.5 per cent, Justice 3.7 per cent, Foreign Affairs 1.7 per cent, the Interior 15.8 per cent, War only 38 per cent, the Marine 9.5 per cent and Finance 2.5 per cent, while the National Debt and allied expenses took 21.5 per cent.

It is a sad indictment of Louis's character that, although very eager for cuts in the army and the bureaucracy, he did not consent to cuts in his own income, the *Liste Civile*: hypocritically, he said he would have liked to, but that '*la seule dépense qu'on ne peut diminuer, c'est la liste civile* ... *il faut du faste, de la représentation*' ('the only expense which cannot be reduced is the Civil List. . . We must have splendour, outward show'). Although in 1814 he did not spend all he received, and only 5,636,850 of the 12,346,245 francs he did spend went on the Court, it might have occurred to him to take a cut in income in order to help the thousands of soldiers and officials who were retired on half-pay as a result of the Government's economy-drive.[6]

One result of Louis's and Baron Louis's desire for economy was the crucial decision not to abolish the *Droits Réunis*, the extremely unpopular indirect tax on wine, tobacco and salt, which was one of the most easily collected sources of Government revenue. Thereby, Louis disavowed the promises made by Artois and Angoulême when they were trying to win support in March and April, and firmly aligned himself with the traditions of the French state (indirect taxes still form a far higher proportion of the revenue of the French than of other European states). He ignored the possibility of creating a new popular Royalism by abolishing indirect taxes, which weigh most heavily on the poor: he was more interested in balancing the budget. Louis's attitude on 10 May when Bordeaux, the first city which had proclaimed him king, rioted against the continued imposition of the *Droits Réunis*, was '*Bordeaux est la première ville qui a arboré la cocarde blanche, mais* ... *l'Obéissance doit etre égale pour tous*' ('Bordeaux is the first city which took the white cockade, but ... everyone has an equal duty to obey').

This is what Louis was interested in: obedience, authority, control, a law-enforcing but also law-abiding Government which did not upset the balance of the modern French state. Thus at meetings of the Council he said that the *Gendarmerie* should be increased in order to control possible *rassemblements* by the unemployed, but he resisted Artois's attempt to get its name changed back to the *Maréchaussée*, as it had been called under the *Ancien Régime*. He was very strongly in favour of a law to suppress the

licence of the press, but he was opposed to treating General
Exelmans, who had written a violent letter to Murat, too harshly.
He was so happy with the French state as he found it, and so
concerned with its needs – which he put higher than the need of
his regime to make itself popular – that he did not abolish the
Droits Réunis, especially as the only alternative would have been
to raise one of those huge loans which had been so fatal to the
French Monarchy before 1789.[7]

Louis and Artois were able to disagree about the *Maréchaussée*
and the *Droits Réunis* since one of the things which makes 1814
one of the strangest years in French history is that, for the first
time since 1700, princes of the Royal Family, Artois, Angoulême
and Berri, were members of the Council. It is extraordinary that
Louis, who had had to suffer so much from Artois's ambition,
extremism and threats since 1791, should choose to associate him
and his sons with the business of government. To a certain extent
it may have been a result of the particular situation of April 1814.
While Louis was immobilized at Hartwell, Artois was already
presiding over the Council of the Provisional Government in Paris;
and Angoulême had won considerable prestige as the prince who
had entered Bordeaux.

Moreover, in accordance with the curious Bourbon tradition,
all the princes, and particularly Artois, had enormous independent
households, which they filled with ambitious and reactionary politicians, such as Jules de Polignac, the Comte de Bruges and the
Duc de Fitzjames, a leading member of the Royalist secret society
of the *Chevaliers de la Foi*; their head, Mathieu de Montmorency,
Chevalier d'Honneur of the Duchesse d'Angoulême, was also an
honorary Aide de Camp of Artois, whom he adored. Another
circumstance which helps make the Restoration a unique period
of history is that, owing to the childlessness of Louis and the
Angoulêmes (although they did not wholly give up hope until
1821), all the princes of the Royal Family in this period were
heirs to the throne. This explains some of the extraordinary importance attached to their attitudes and approval; they were all
future kings, to whose fortunes many important politicians were
only too happy to attach themselves.

Therefore, Louis may have felt that these frighteningly powerful
and prestigious princes were less dangerous if they were in rather
than outside the Government, and so were committed to supporting its policies. And indeed one of the features of the First
Restoration is that, although there was considerable Ultra-Royalist feeling, there was no organized Ultra-Royalist party possess-
ing the incalculable advantage of the backing of the heir to the

throne, as there would be after 1815. The First Restoration was a particularly fluid and ill-defined period, when everyone accepted the regime and no one had yet established those stern partisan positions which were to make government so difficult after 1815.

Indeed there is a mystery about Artois's exact political position in 1814–15. He had been a moderate and conciliatory *Lieutenant-Général du Royaume* in April. His interventions in the Council were not outrageously reactionary and he had friendly relations with many Napoleonic officers. But one minister, Beugnot, was convinced, as he wrote to Louis, that Artois and his sons were in favour of restoring *les anciennes institutions*. On 4 June 1814 Artois stayed at Saint-Cloud, allegedly prevented by illness from appearing at the grand ceremony proclaiming the *Charte* – an absence which was widely commented on. When one considers that Dambray discussed the *Charte* with him on 3 June at the Tuileries, it seems clear that he was trying to make known his opposition to his brother's modern and liberal constitution. Certainly this is what informed Paris opinion came to believe.[8]

What Artois really wanted was power, which is probably why he remained in the Council of a government of whose policies he disapproved. The story of Louis's reign is written in the picture on the cover. The look in Artois's face, his pose with one commanding foot on the steps of the throne, make it quite clear that he had no doubts that, although his invalid brother might be king, he knew what was best for his family and his country. Consequently, in April he tried to get the ministers of the Provisional Government to 'correspond with', in effect receive the orders of, two of his agents, the Marquis de la Maisonfort and Terrier de Monciel, whom he had installed in the *Pavillon de Marsan* in the Tuileries, where he lived throughout his brother's reign. In May and June, Terrier de Monciel put forward an extraordinary scheme, which is a terrifying revelation of the sort of ideas discussed in Artois's entourage, whereby Artois would dominate the Council with the help of Malouet, Oudinot, Moncey and his sons, and with the armed support of the *Gardes Suisses* and the *Gardes Nationales* – he was Colonel-in-Chief of both. Terrier de Monciel also wanted to commission experts to write opinions for Artois on every subject coming up before the Council so that, quite peacefully, and without too much mental effort on his part, Artois's *sagesse* would dominate his brother's Council.

Terrier de Monciel, however, left Paris in disgust at the failure of his schemes on 4 July. Either Artois had refused to play or Louis and his ministers were too strong for him.[9] In fact the princes' influence in the Council seems to have been relatively

limited. Nearly all the appointments Angoulême had made in
Bordeaux and the Midi, and most of his recommendations after
May 1814, were quashed, to the dismay of the Bordelais. The
Droits Réunis were maintained despite his and Artois's ardent
opposition. No '*anciennes institutions*' were restored. In many
ways Berri was the most troublesome prince. He was always
losing his temper in the Council, especially with Talleyrand, and
frequently made idiotic suggestions, for example, that veterans of
the Vendée should join the veterans of the wars of the Revolution
and the Empire in the Invalides. But Louis was quite good at
controlling Berri. He rejected the suggestion about the Invalides,
pointing out, in his dry way, that it would lead to disputes. When
Berri wanted General Exelmans, who had been corresponding
with Murat, punished immediately, Louis said, '*Mon neveu,
n'allons pas plus vite que la justice.*' ('My nephew let us not go
faster than justice.')[10]

However, Artois was far more intelligent than his sons, and a
more persuasive speaker. From the succinct records kept by the
Secrétaire d'État, Vitrolles, it is not clear what degree of influence
Artois acquired over the Council meetings. He talked an awful
lot, but Louis always, having made sure that he had heard every
viewpoint, talked last. Louis did, weakly, agree to some of the
recommendations of the younger brother of whose possible open
disobedience he was always frightened. He chose Artois's candidate, Maréchal Soult, as Minister of War in December 1814, and
appointed Artois's Aide de Camp, the Comte de Bruges, as *Grand
Chancelier de la Légion d'Honneur* in February 1815 – an appointment only slightly less ridiculous than Talleyrand's appointment of the Abbé de Pradt to the same position in April 1814.
Probably Artois, balked of achieving power through the means
suggested by Terrier de Monciel, was now trying, with a degree
of success, to recapture it through personal pressure on his
brother. As at Coblentz in 1791–92, so in the Tuileries in 1814–
15, Artois was sometimes able to persuade his brother, in conversation, to agree with his views – especially if the ministers were
not present. It is difficult to judge which of the royal brothers had
the stronger character: their view of each other will always be a
mystery. But it is certain that in 1814–15 they were a lot closer
than in 1797–1807 or in 1816–1821.

That Artois's physical access to, and ability to talk with, Louis
was important is also suggested by the fact that, when the Duchesse d'Angoulême went to Versailles to see how restoration was
getting on, she refused the ground-floor apartment communicating
directly with the king's, and said that Artois would take it. Was

the family trying to ensure that Artois, so powerful and persuasive, would always be able to rush upstairs and exert his influence? Or was it simply that the Duchesse d'Angoulême wanted a more agreeable apartment facing south?[11]

Artois was also consulted by his brother on foreign affairs. To a degree sadly difficult for us to understand today, Louis and his subjects lived in an international and cosmopolitan world. Both the Emigration and the Empire had thoroughly shaken up the traditional patriotisms of the eighteenth century, and had made Frenchmen, and other Europeans, even more cosmopolitan than before. Many foreigners, among them two future ministers of Louis XVIII, Dalberg and Corvetto, had entered the service of the French Government. Thousands of *émigrés* had entered the services of Austria, Russia and Portugal, just as thousands of their political opponents had entered the services of Spain, Holland, Naples and Westphalia, when they were ruled by Bonaparte's relations. One Frenchman, Bernadotte, even became King of Sweden. The idea of national origin restricting people to the service of their own country was completely alien to early nineteenth-century Europe. Indeed the whole concept of a national state had not yet overshadowed the idea of a state simply being the service of a particular dynasty or institution, such as the King of France in exile, or the House of Habsburg.

In this fluid, international world Louis felt himself to be utterly French. His family was the *Maison de France*. He represented the real interests of the country far better than the Corsican ruler he had replaced. On 23 May he congratulated a deputation from Bordeaux, the town which had welcomed Angoulême and the English army, for coming from the first town which had declared itself *'d'une manière tout à fait française'* ('in a completely French way'). The fact that he had only come to his throne with the cooperation of an English general and as a result of a foreign invasion of France seemed to the king and to most of his subjects, although not to the army, irrelevant. The Restoration was a patriotic, national event, thanks to which France had left the artificial, cosmopolitan tyranny of Napoleon I, and was becoming French again.

This does not mean that Louis ever ceased to be passionately concerned with foreign affairs. They were his life, his world and his daily bread, the equivalent to him of office gossip to a bureaucrat: he was closely related to half the sovereigns of Europe and he knew many of the other rulers, the regent and the Tsar for example, very well. In 1814–15 in particular, Louis was completely immersed in foreign affairs: in January – March 1815, for

example, relations with Spain were discussed in the Council almost as much as the internal affairs of France. It was another sign
of the moderation and liberalism of Louis's Government that the
subject under discussion was whether to withdraw the French
ambassador from Madrid in protest at Ferdinand VII's refusal to
forgive the former supporters of Joseph Bonaparte. An outward
sign of Louis's immersion in foreign affairs and of his links with
the international world of European royalty was that on his *frac*
he now wore the Garter and the Russian Order of Saint Andrew,
as well as the French Orders of the Saint Esprit, Saint Lazare,
Saint Louis and the Lys (a Royalist Order founded in 1814). His
predecessors as kings of France had only worn the Saint Esprit,
the *Croix de Saint Louis* and the Golden Fleece (the Order of the
Bourbon King of Spain which Louis had returned when it was
given to Bonaparte, but which he is occasionally shown wearing
in portraits of the Restoration).

Since Louis had come to the throne partly as a result of the
defeat of the French army, one of his first acts as king had to be
to sign a peace treaty. The Treaty of Paris of 30 Mary 1814
reduced the swollen French Empire of 1814 to approximately the
size of present-day France and – an even more dramatic loss for
some people – it returned to the liberated countries almost all the
dotations Napoleon I had lavished on his officers and officials.
Before the treaty was signed – indeed, as a note in his writing
testifies, during the Emigration – Louis had hoped to be able to
keep Belgium, or at least a strip of land ten miles in from the
traditional French frontier. However, all he could keep of the
conquests of the Republic (there was never any question of the
absurd land-grabs of the Empire) was a slice of Belgium round
Philippeville and the Province of Savoy, giving France an increase
of territory containing 650,000 people over its 1792 frontiers:
France was not, as is often stated, reduced to the frontiers of 1792
in 1814. Nevertheless the disappearance of most of the conquests
of the last twenty years appalled the army and was its bitterest
grievance in 1814–15. As Jaucourt wrote in December 1814, '*La
France veut la paix et l'armée la Belgique.*' ('France wants peace
and the army Belgium.')[12]

After May 1814, Louis's main aim in foreign affairs, as he had
written to Gustavus III in 1778, was to obtain *considération* –
just as his main aim in internal affairs was to increase the *considération* belonging to the throne. And despite their almost complete indifference to his plight while he had been in exile, he seems
to have thought that one of the best means for France to gain
considération was to revive the traditional structure of Bourbon

rulers in Parma and Naples, which gave *considération* to the head of the Bourbon family, the King of France, and reduced Habsburg dominance in Italy. Even in exile in 1800, he had written in instructions to Saint-Priest that Austria must agree to restore Parma to the Bourbons. Moreover, in 1814 he had a particular reason for wanting to restore the Bourbons to Naples and Parma, one which was probably even more powerful than Bourbon family feeling. In 1814, Parma was promised to the Empress Marie-Louise and her son, and Naples was ruled by Murat. For the sake of the internal stability of France Louis did not want these two countries to be perpetual reminders of the empire of *l'autre*, or refuges for his supporters.

Another country where the restoration of the legitimate ruler also served the practical political interests of the King of France was Saxony. Since he had been an ally of Napoleon I longer than the rest, the King of Saxony had been dispossessed of his country, which the Tsar hoped would go to Prussia so that Russia could annex all of Poland. This horrified Louis not only because the king, whose family had ruled Saxony for centuries, was his first cousin, but because, even then, France was alarmed at the long-term ambitions of Prussia; and the annexation of the large Protestant state of Saxony, so conveniently close to Berlin, had been the dearest ambition of the Hohenzollerns since Frederick II.

Consequently, the instructions to Talleyrand, who went as French representative to the Congress of Vienna in September 1814, dealt largely with the questions of Naples, Parma, Poland and Saxony.[13] During the Congress Louis kept up an extremely interesting correspondence with Talleyrand which, together with the notes Louis wrote to Jaucourt, the interim Minister of Foreign Affairs left behind in Paris, show the degree to which he supervised the conduct of foreign affairs. However, from November Louis and Blacas also began to conduct a secret diplomacy of their own with Metternich behind Talleyrand's back, just as Louis's grandfather, Louis XV, had conducted a secret diplomacy behind the back of his foreign ministers in the 1750s and 1760s. The trouble with Talleyrand was that not only Louis but also foreign statesmen like Metternich did not really trust him; and, as ultra-legitimist under Louis XVIII as he had been ultra-Bonapartist under Napoleon I, he was trying to get the removal of Murat discussed by the Congress, although two of its most powerful members, England and Austria, were still officially Murat's allies. Talleyrand the patriotic, moderate Foreign Minister is as much a myth as Napoleon I the liberal, revolutionary emperor.

At first Louis threatened to send a French army to dethrone

Murat, but Austria refused to give access through northern Italy. At the end of February, Louis had to accept Metternich's promise that Austria would remove Murat within six months of the end of the Congress and he agreed to subsidise the Austrian expedition to the extent of 25 million francs. In return, although Marie-Louise was to rule Parma, the Bourbons of Parma were to be compensated with Lucca and they, not the son of Napoleon I, who had briefly been called the Prince of Parma, were to inherit Parma after Marie-Louise's death. This arrangement was finally confirmed in 1817. Thus if Bourbons reigned in Naples after 1815 and in Parma after 1847, it was partly due to the personal diplomacy of Louis XVIII: Louis kept Talleyrand informed of, but excluded from, these negotiations. There now only remained for Louis to revert to one of the most shameful of his habits, and to get the Abbé Fleuriel, one of his secretaries in exile, and now Blacas's secretary in the Tuileries, to forge the dates on a correspondence between Napoleon I and Murat to prove Murat had broken his treaties with England and Austria.

The other aim of French diplomacy in 1814–15, the restoration of the King of Saxony, was also accomplished, although his kingdom lost a million inhabitants. This restoration was largely due to the diplomacy of Talleyrand who signed a treaty with England and Austria on 3 January directed against the pretensions of Russia and Prussia. This policy has been attacked on the grounds that it resulted in Prussia being compensated with most of the Rhineland, thereby increasing its power and giving it a base from which it could attack France. But it was the strength of Prussia in Germany, not Prussia's ability to invade France, which was the main worry to Louis, Blacas and Talleyrand in 1814, and which was the ultimate cause of the German victory in 1870–71. To most contemporaries, especially to the Prussians, the survival of Saxony as an independent, pro-Austrian state seemed most likely to diminish Prussian strength in Germany.[14]

One of the main faults of Louis XVIII was his self-satisfaction, his tendency to congratulate himself on the slightest excuse. But by late 1814, he had a lot to be satisfied about. The invading armies had withdrawn and had left France with reasonable boundaries. A start had been made on restoring the finances, and a reasonable, liberal constitution had been granted. Furthermore, after June 1814, the actions of Louis's Government, like the *Charte* itself, were on the whole moderate and conciliatory. Nothing could be more untrue than to say, as did Orléans in one of the strange, treacherous letters he scattered far and wide during the Hundred Days: '*Le système du Roi était incontestablement*

*de ramener autant qu'il pouvait les institutions politiques et pub-
liques, les opinions, les usages et surtout les étiquettes à ce
qu'elles étaient avant la révolution.'* ('The King's system was
undoubtedly to return political and public institutions, opinion,
customs and above all etiquette, as much as he could, to what
they were before the revolution.') Orléans was blinded by the
fact that at Court receptions, although almost everything else had
changed, his position as a Prince du Sang had not. There were no
proscriptions. Public and political institutions functioned normally. The two chambers met in the autumn and vied with each other
in following the ministry's lead. The ministry's conciliatory intentions had been shown by the choice as peers of forty-seven dukes
of the *Ancien Régime*, ninety-six Napoleonic senators and marshals, and twelve individuals chosen by royal favour, six of whom
had served the Revolution and six the Counter-Revolution.
Thoughts of the Counter-Revolution were so far from Louis's and
his ministers' minds that in January 1815 Blacas wrote to Louis's
former agent, Prince Louis de La Trémoïlle, who was preparing
a list of deserving Vendéens in need of reward, that he must
follow the *règlements* of the Ministry of War, and that the Government wanted to *'effacer de plus en plus toute distinction entre
les différens défenseurs du Trône'* ('ever increasingly to efface
all distinctions among the different defenders of the Throne').

The ministry maintained the state of all property deals, although
in November a law was passed allowing it to hand back any *biens
nationaux* in its possession which were claimed by former owners.
In the winter of 1814–15 the ministry began selling unclaimed
biens nationaux at good prices as part of Baron Louis's attempts
to raise revenue. The ministry was so liberal that it outflanked the
Empire on the left in its choice of servants as well as in its
principles. General Lecourbe, long a Republican enemy of Napoleon I, became an *Inspecteur-Général de Cavalerie*; another
former Republican general, in disgrace since 1804, General Dessolles, was a Ministre d'État and *Major-Général de la Garde
Nationale de Paris*; and Maréchal Jourdan, a former Republican
die-hard, was made a count, a favour Napoleon I had always
refused him.

On the other hand, Orléans was quite right to go on to say in
the same letter that the *forme* often detracted from the *fonds* of
the Government's actions. It was bad enough that the white flag
had been chosen instead of the tricolour. But the Government of
Louis XVIII also seemed to take pleasure in using a mass of
antiquated phrases, procedures and formulae which were quite
unimportant in themselves but which were extremely irritating to

sections of public opinion: indeed during the Hundred Days these phrases were one of the main grievances advanced against the First Restoration. For example, Louis XVIII and his ministers insisted on putting on some of his acts, including the *Charte*, that they were done in the year of Grace 1814, '*et de notre règne le 19e*', although Talleyrand had persuaded Louis to leave this formula out of the Declaration of Saint-Ouen (another example, like his willingness to listen to Artois, of Louis's adaptability or *faiblesse*). This was a perfectly pointless phrase, since the theoretical foundation of Louis's reign was already established by his title Louis XVIII, which assumed that he had succeeded Louis XVII. Yet this tiny pin-prick was felt as an insult by many of the people who had served other regimes during the last nineteen years, and it would be constantly harped on in the anti-Royalist literature of 1815. Indeed as early as June 1814 a caricature was being sold in the streets of Paris of someone reading a book with blank pages and the title *Histoire des dix-neuf glorieuses années du règne de Louis XVIII* (History of the nineteen glorious years of the reign of Louis XVIII).

More seriously, in November a speech by Ferrand, one of the ministers chosen by Louis himself in May, condemning those who had deviated from the *ligne directe* of Royalism and had served Revolutionary regimes, infuriated the deputies and alarmed the *acquéreurs* of *biens nationaux*. Never was Louis's own favourite saying '*Toutes vérités ne sont pas bonnes à dire*' more applicable than to France in 1814. Yet Ferrand was introducing a law, returning *émigrés*' land still in the possession of the Government, which reflected Louis's personal ideas, as he told the Council.[15]

But the most dangerous of all *formes* was the form of the ministry itself. The *Conseil des Ministres*, consisting of the king, the princes, the Chancellor, Talleyrand, Blacas, Montesquiou and the *Ministres d'État* (Jaucourt, Dalberg, Beurnonville, Moncey, Oudinot, Dessolles and Ferrand) excluded three of the ministers (Louis, Malouet and Dupont), who were only summoned to the Council when they had something special to propose, or a *Rapport* to discuss. Moreover, the ministers were often opposed to each other over policy, although they all subscribed to the moderate, conciliatory framework of the *Charte*. Dambray and Beugnot were more authoritarian than Montesquiou or Talleyrand: Maréchal Soult, when he was Minister of War, was the most authoritarian and illiberal minister of all. All the ministers feared and distrusted Blacas, tall, blond and aloof, who had the exclusive confidence of the king, although his and Louis's views did not always coincide, for example, over the liberty of the press. Montesquiou, who had long been a friend and agent of Louis, was so jealous of Blacas that he told the king that the French *'passaient plutôt à leurs Rois dix maîtresses qu'un favori'* ('would rather put up with ten royal mistresses than one favourite').

The disorganization and disunity of the ministry alarmed all contemporaries, especially the ministers themselves. It formed a complete contrast to the unified Cabinet of England or the silent, subservient ministers of Napoleon I. Some attempt was made, perhaps on Louis's initiative, to give more unity to the ministry. The ministers with portfolios dined together every Thursday and met every Sunday in Blacas's apartment in the Tuileries, which infuriated Montesquiou. In February, the Chancellor, the minister most in Louis's confidence after Blacas, drew up a formal *règlement* stating that the ministers with portfolios should meet twice a week in secret to discuss issues before they were brought up in the Council.

But this did not alter the weak and disunited character of the ministry, which, with his weakness toward his brother and his occasional tactlessness, is the gravest indictment one can make against Louis's conduct during the First Restoration. In a very uncertain, fluid year what people wanted above all was to be reassured, and the most effective vehicle of reassurance would have been a firmly united ministry. Yet at some Council meetings Louis simply spent the time making conversation instead of getting on with government business or giving a lead.

Louis's refusal to form a solidly united ministry seems extraordinary, especially since he was constantly advised to do so, even by Blacas. Jaucourt was probably correct in saying that Louis's main motive was that he actually wanted to have a ministry which was not too united, and ministers who presented different points of view, in order to preserve his freedom of initiative and decision – a habit of the *Ancien Régime*, since the Council of Louis XVI had also included ministers of conflicting views (Breteuil and Calonne in the 1780s), and *Ministres d'État* without portfolios. By having a diverse and disunited ministry, not only would the king escape being, as in England, the passive instrument of his ministers, but also most of the viewpoints of his very disunited subjects could be reflected inside the Council rather than being left to fester outside.[16]

After the disunity of the ministry and the question of the *biens nationaux*, the main cause of discontent in France in 1814 was the organization of the king's service. In contrast to Louis's youth, which had been so troubled by *'le choc de l'aristocratie avec la monarchie'*, the reigns of Louis XVIII and Charles X witnessed

the apogee of aristocratic desire to serve the French crown. This
was yet another sign of the monarchism of early nineteenth-century France. Already in the 1790's there had been signs that
sections of the elite were prepared to accept a much more subordinate position in relation to monarchical authority than they
had hoped for in 1787–92. After 1800 the expansion, and rise in
prestige, of the bureaucracy and the army was the synthesis needed
to end the conflict between monarchy and aristocracy – which
had partly developed because neither the courtiers of Versailles
nor the members of the Parisian and provincial elites had had
enough opportunities to *serve* the monarchy in the 1770s and
1780s.

All the energies which, before 1789, had gone not into the
service of the monarchy but into the *parlements*, the provincial
estates, the tax-farms and, above all, the Church, or simply into
pleasure, were now devoted to obtaining a post in the adminstra-
tion or the army. (An indication of the former appeal of the
Church as a career is that three of Louis's ministers in 1814,
Montesquiou, Talleyrand and Baron Louis, had been *abbés* before 1789 – cf page 367). The wars and confiscations and block-
ades inflicted on France since 1789 had impoverished a great
many people, businessmen as well as *émigrés*. What better way
could there be of repairing this injustice than by entering government service? In addition, the thousands of officials and officers
of the French territories lost at the peace treaty, the thousands of
émigrés and Royalists who had spent the Empire deprived of the
joys of office and the many ex-Republicans or friends of
Napoleon's rival General Moreau, who had also been excluded
by the Empire, all wanted official positions in 1814.

It was now that Madame de Staël made her celebrated state-
ment: '*Le premier article des droits de l'homme en France, c'est
la nécessité pour tout Français d'occuper un emploi public.*'
('The first article of the rights of man in France is the necessity
for every Frenchman to occupy a public office.') Wellington wrote:
'The number of persons obliged to look for support from Publick
Employment is far greater even in proportion to the size and
population of France than in any other country.' And these general
comments are borne out by looking at individual biographies. For
example, Stendhal, formerly a bureaucrat of the Empire, and
Chateaubriand, formerly an *émigré*, both felt they deserved jobs
in the king's service in 1814. Benjamin Constant's diary for 1814–
15, one of the most disillusioning accounts of the male heart ever
written, reveals that beneath the sentimental superstructure of
têtes-à-têtes with Madame Récamier, rows with Madame de

Staël and worries about his wife, what really interested him was to obtain office, money, a Russian decoration, anything which meant that he had arrived. A typical entry reads: *'Dîné chez Beugnot, soirée chez Talleyrand. Mon article a fait bon effet, arriverai-je enfin?'* ('Dinner at Beugnot's, soiree at Talleyrand's. My article has had some success, will I make it last?')[17] Ambition, insecurity and a determined social life, this is what the First Restoration was all about: this is what the return of Louis XVIII meant to the French elite, once it had wiped away its tears of joy.

To satisfy all these burning ambitions was obviously going to be extremely difficult for a Government which had inherited a debt of 759,175,000 francs, and which had to reduce the army from a war to a peace footing. From the start the Council was appalled at the difficulty of reconciling so many conflicting pretensions.[18] The solution which it adopted was to leave the structure and personnel of the army and the administration basically as they were. There was no *épuration* or purge in 1814 as there would be after most changes of regime in nineteenth-century France, although there were fairly substantial changes among senior personnel. The number of prefects who were nobles, for example, rose from thirty to fifty-eight (of eighty-seven), although most of the new prefects were also former Napoleonic officials. The *Conseil d'État*, the *Cour de Comptes* and the *Cour de Cassation* were reorganized in June and January, a few people from the *Ancien Régime* were appointed and a few Napoleonic officials were excluded, although Napoleonic officials again continued to be in a majority, with 60 per cent, 100 per cent and 95 per cent of the members respectively. The army remained essentially Napoleonic in composition, although it was reduced from 531,675 men in April to about 220,000 by December 1814. The Minister of War said that of the 6,500 ex-officers of the armies of the Emigration who wanted to serve, he would only place 500.

However, Louis XVIII had long wanted, as he told the Council, *'l'amalgame, pour qu'il n'y ait pas deux espèces de français'* ('an amalgam so there are not two sorts of Frenchmen'). So the great files of his army in exile were sent to a commission of three Napoleonic and three *émigré* officers, presided over by Maréchal Perignon, with orders to regulate its officers' rank and pay. By 3 December, sixty of the 320 *Généraux de Division* and eighty of the 585 *Maréchaux de Camp* in the French army had been appointed since the Restoration, and the overwhelming majority of them were *émigrés*. But they were usually given honorary ranks rather than actual commands, and pensions rather than full salaries. As the events of the Hundred Days would show with dreadful clarity, the French army remained basically Napoleonic, under the command of Napoleonic officers, during the First Restoration.[19]

The great exception to the continuity in the organization of the army and the administration in 1814 was the revival and expansion of the *Maison Militaire du Roi*, which Louis announced at the first Council he held, on 5 May 1814. It was one of the *idées reçues* of the Counter-Revolution that the Revolution might have been averted if the king had had a reliable guard. Most people have poured scorn on his theory, but it does contain a degree of truth. The behaviour of the *Gardes-Françaises* in 1789 (and of the *Garde des Conseils* in 1797) was crucial, and in this and many other periods guards could sway the fate of nations, as was seen in Turkey in 1807, in Spain in 1820 and in Russia in 1825. Louis was also interested in using his *Maison Militaire* to satisfy the ambitions of the Royalists, who found almost all other jobs reserved for those who had served the Empire. Père Elysée wrote to the regent in an extraorinarily disabused letter, which probably reflected the feelings of his other Royal patient, that *'en laissant jouir ses ennemis de tout ce qu'ils avaient reçu de l'usurpateur, il fallait bien qu'il donnât quelquechose à ceux qui se disent ses amis'* ('while letting his enemies enjoy all they had received from the usurper, he really had to give something to those who call themselves his friends').[20]

So the internal palace guard of *Gardes du Corps*, *Cent-Suisses* and *Gardes de la Porte* and the external cavalry guard (abolished by 1787, even before the Revolution) of *Mousquetaires Gris et Noirs*, *Chevau-Légers*, *Gendarmes de la Garde* and *Grenadiers à Cheval* were revived, numbering 6,024 soldiers who all enjoyed the traditional privileges of pay and rank. But even in these units, although *Ancien Régime* connections were respected, there were a lot of Napoleonic soldiers. There was no incompatibility between service in the *Ancien Régime* and service of the regimes which replaced it. For example, the captains of the *Cent-Suisses*, the *Mousquetaires Noirs* and the *Gardes de la Porte* were all officers who inherited these titles from their families but had served the Empire, while the Captain of the *Mousquetaires Gris*, the Comte de Nansouty, and two of the six Captains of the *Gardes du Corps*, Marshals Berthier and Marmont, were appointed by Louis because they were distinguished soldiers of the Empire. All the *Grenadiers à Cheval*, 41 of the 176 *Mousquetaires Gris* and 84 of the 207 *Mousquetaires Noirs* had served in the Napoleonic army, as had many of the *Gardes du Corps*.[21]

However, the creation of these traditional elite units was basically to satisfy the Royalists. And the sight of people like Gramont, Havré and Charles de Damas, faithful old friends of Louis XVIII who had not seen much military action, as captains of the guard must have seemed strange, to say the least, to the soldiers of the Empire. Moreover, many of the soldiers of the *Maison Militaire* were veterans neither of the Napoleonic army nor of the *Armée de Condé* nor of the Vendée. They were rich, well-connected young men, as often non-noble as noble, who in 1814, given the opportunity of belonging to a smart regiment which gave them dazzling red and gold uniforms and contact with the Royal Family and the Court, suddenly discovered an unexpected enthusiasm for military life. The household troops of Louis XVIII in 1814–15 must have been very interesting to serve with – among them were Lamartine, de Vigny, Géricault and Salvandy – but the unforgivable thing is that they were not even a serious military body. There were in all only 6,000 troops and the foot guard of 5,000 and the special artillery corps were never even formed. This is rather a mystery. Was it over-confidence, economy, dilatoriness or perhaps a reluctance to form the *Gardes Suisses* of whom Artois would have had command, as he had before 1792?

The French elite's lust for jobs in the service of the king, and the Royal Government's solution to the problem, were made particularly obvious at Court. In contrast to the 1780s, when it had been smart to complain about the tedium of having to go to Versailles, in the early nineteenth century there was a universal passion for going to Court. In 1814 one journalist could write, not entirely ironically, that *'un gentilhomme qui ne se montre pas à la cour n'existe pas'* ('a gentleman who does not show himself at Court does not exist'), and Chateaubriand admitted that his generation was far more eager to go to Court than their parents – no doubt because it was so different. For just as the Government was reorganized as a synthesis of the Empire, the Revolution and the *Ancien Régime*, so the social life of the Court under the Restoration was different to what it had been before 1814 and before 1792. Basically, in accordance with the plans of the Emigration and the practice of the Empire, Court receptions, which took place after Mass on Sunday, were reorganized on the basis of official position, with certain officials and officers having right of access to certain rooms of the state apartments of the Tuileries. There was none of the confusion of ranks at the Restoration Court which Louis XVI had noted, when heir to the throne, as being so characteristic of the Court of Versailles (see page 7).

No longer, as at Versailles, was the hour of entry to the king's bedroom all-important: in accordance with the practice of Napoleon I and almost all other European monarchs, and probably in keeping with Louis's personal tastes the bedroom receded into the private apartments. The Court's social life now centred on the *Salle du Trône* and the *Grand Cabinet* of the Tuileries, and on the three rooms which preceded them, the *Salle des Maréchaux*, the *Salon Bleu* and the *Salle de la Paix*. The well-dressed public was allowed into the *Salle des Maréchaux*, a huge room lined with enormous portraits of Napoleon's marshals, where the *Gardes du Corps* were on duty night and day. The other rooms were reserved for officials and officers. Thus the Entrée to the *Salle de la Paix* was given to *Maréchaux de Camp*, peers, deputies, prefects and *Conseillers d'État*, and the Entrée to the *Salle du Trône* to ministers, cardinals, dukes and duchesses, *Grands d'Espagne*, ambassadors, marshals, five other senior generals, *Grands Officiers* of the *Maisons Civile* and *Militaire* and the Presidents of the Chambers of Peers and Deputies.[22]

Thus, although there were less prestigious receptions for men without official position and for women on Mondays, to show that you had arrived at the Court of Louis XVIII, you needed military rank or official position rather than, as at the Court of Versailles, social status or ancient lineage. And since in 1814 all marshals, most ministers, peers, deputies and generals, and even a fairly large proportion of dukes (particularly the Napoleonic dukes with their extraordinary foreign titles, Duc de Montebello, Duc de Gaëte, Duc de Plaisance . . .) owed their rank to the parts they had played during and since the Revolution, the Court of Louis XVIII was really, as many Royalists realized in horror, the social consecration of the new France. It was not a return to the *Ancien Régime*.

Another difference between the Court of Louis XVIII and that of the *Ancien Régime* was that almost everyone now wore uniform. The colourful, frivolous and extremely expensive *habit habillé* of Louis's youth was out of the question in the France of 1814, although in England many people had been prepared to wear it at the regent's fête in 1811. In France it was completely out of fashion and so agonizingly embarrassing that a young man without official position who did have to wear it, like Michelet, could still remember the ordeal years later when he wrote his memoirs. The *frac* was too simple and undignified to be allowed at Court, although Louis's own costume, combining simplicity and army spirit, was, as in England, a dark-blue *frac* with gold epaulettes. Therefore the frenzy to obtain official position in 1814 was not only because it gave a salary or a pension but also because it gave status at Court and the right thing to wear. It was partly for this reason that in 1814 so many generals were named *pour tenir rang*.[23]

The Restoration Court was in many ways a more satisfying place than Versailles. Simply being in the *Salle de la Paix* or the *Salle du Trône* was proof that you had arrived, and was far more satisfying to your vanity than languishing in the *Oeil de Boeuf* for a royal look which might never come. The receptions and the huge guard also meant that the monarchy was now much less remote from the elite than before 1789. On the other hand, going to Court in 1814 and seeing rivals sweep past into the *Salle de la Paix* or the *Salle du Trône* or the *Grand Cabinet*, where they could have useful conversations which could advance their careers and those of their friends, must have been fairly traumatic. For in 1814–15 the Court was the main meeting place both for Napoleonic generals and for recently returned *émigrés*. Davout was the only marshal who did not go to Court in 1814, while La Fare, formerly Louis's agent in Vienna, wrote: '*C'est là que je retrouve tout mon monde.*' ('It is there I meet everyone I know.')[24]

Inevitably, given the immense ambition and vanity of most early nineteenth-century Frenchmen, the Court became rather tense. Indeed this was probably the most explosive year in the history of the French Court since 1572, when the marriage of Marguerite de Valois and the future Henri IV had brought Huguenots and Catholics together at Court for the first time in ten years – a confrontation which ended in the Massacre of St. Bartholomew's Eve. In 1814, courtiers' feelings were no less powerful, although they were expressed in slightly less violent ways. It does not require much effort to imagine the comments of ladies who had known Versailles and had suffered since 1789 as they watched Napoleonic duchesses, many of whom, like Ney's wife the Duchesse d'Elchingen, were young, fashionable and attractive, glide gracefully past into the *Salle du Trône* (reserved for duchesses). The loud aside, and direct rudeness, were inevitable compensations. Even Madame de Chastenay, by no means a Royalist diehard, wrote in her diary that perhaps Maréchale Soult, Duchesse de Dalmatie, was learning to be *bien* a little late in life.

The smooth façade of Court manners broke down even more often between men. There was a violent quarrel at Court in May between the Napoleonic General Bondignon and the *émigré* General Vioménil, decided by Louis in favour of the former. By November soldiers who had fought in the Vendée and soldiers who had fought for the Republic '*forment des groupes différents jusques dans les salons des Tuileries*' ('form different groups even in the salons of the Tuileries'), while some Napoleonic generals

were complaining loudly, in the same salons, about their lost
dotations. These three salons, through which Louis waddled smiling on his way to and from Mass, must have contained more hard
feelings, and more hurt feelings, than any other rooms in Europe.
(The Bourbon waddle gave rise to a famous cartoon in 1814
showing Napoleonic eagles flying out of the Tuileries as a flock
of Bourbon geese waddled in – but this is unfair to Napoleon I
who, by 1814, had learnt to waddle like a king).

It was not just at Court that discontent was growing. In many
areas of France, and especially in Paris, public opinion was
alarmed by and hostile to the Government. Even before the arrival
of Louis XVIII, the regime had a lot of enemies, as the Bonapartist
loyalties of many officers and officials at Bordeaux in March 1814
showed. In May Louis was informed that there was a *masse
d'opinion bonapartiste* in the army and among the *acquéreurs*;
and probably nothing his Government could have done would
have altered this. How could *acquéreurs* relax so long as the
people whose property they had bought at such low prices had
not received compensation? How could an army which had
marched to a thousand victories under its emperor become attached to the rule of a fat, elderly, peaceful king?

Moreover the Government's policy over the *Maison Militaire*
and the *Droits Réunis* was actively unpopular. The *Garde Nationale de Paris* was furious at the insulting way in which the
Gardes du Corps took over the guard of the *Château* in June.
The Tuileries was always referred to as the *Château* during the
Restoration – Napoleon I lived in the *palais*; Louis XVIII, less
pretentious and more of a gentleman, lived in the *Château des
Tuileries*. At the subsequent banquet – the Restoration was a very
social regime – although *Gardes du Corps* and *Gardes Nationaux*
were seated together at dinner, they drifted into separate groups
over coffee.[25]

The reimposition of the *Droits Réunis* was particularly unpopular with the *cabaretiers*, whose wine thereby became more
expensive. There were 249,000 *cabaretiers* in France, with every
opportunity for influencing their many customers. Moreover a
law introduced enforcing Sunday closing-time in towns under
5,000 in population was also extremely unpopular. By the autumn
diplomats were reporting on 'the constant uneasiness' in the capital, the appalling discontent of the *émigrés* who had not found
jobs, and of the officials and soldiers who had been retired on
half-pay, and on the *position terrible* of Louis XVIII. Police reports were telling him that, although there was very little hatred,
and the bourgeoisie and the *premier étage* (the floor the rich live

on) throughout Paris liked him more than they had Louis XVI, distrust and fear were almost universal. By February, Maréchal Moncey, head of the *Gendarmerie*, was telling Louis that the Restoration had made much progress generally, but that there were Bonapartists in the Ardennes and Dauphiné, and that discontent was widespread in the countryside. Indeed, in the same month there was a very serious riot in Rennes in protest at the arrival of a commission to investigate the claims of soldiers of the Vendée to receive compensation.[26]

This almost universal discontent was not only the result of the mistakes of the Government. It was also the effect of the dissatisfaction expressed by the army and the Ultra-Royalists in 1814–15, as well as by the *acquéreurs*. The army remained outwardly, contemptuously obedient, but their real feelings often came out in the *cabarets*, where they would sing songs in praise of their emperor, or on parades where they would make rude gestures at the Duc de Berri. Even on 3 May, the day of Louis's entry into Paris, some soldiers lining the route cried *'Vive l'Empereur'*. In June a poster was put up by soldiers at Strasbourg complaining that *'L'Angleterre a vendu à la France un gros cochon de dix-huit louis pour un Napoléon'* ('England has sold France a fat pig at eighteen louis for one Napoleon'). The disaffection of most of the army was well known, and increased people's fears and uncertainties. Wellington pointed out that 'the King of France without an army is no king' – as Louis XVI had found out in 1789.[27] Without an army, how could the regime last?

But the greatest single source of weakness to the Government of Louis XVIII in 1814–15 were what Père Elisée called *'ceux qui se disent ses amis'*, the Ultra-Royalists and the members of his own family. For if the reign of Louis XVIII has a moral, it is the danger of having the wrong friends. And if it needed to be summed up in a phrase, it would be in the saying: 'I can take care of my enemies. But God protect me from my friends.' Already, during the Emigration, the verbal violence of the *émigrés* and the activities of Artois, Puisaye and d'Antraigues had done Louis's cause considerable damage. And it is clear from the many excellent local studies of France during the Restoration that, even before Louis XVIII had landed, the Ultra-Royalists were out for revenge, violence and blood. The last thing they wanted was for the Restoration to be as mild, rational and conciliatory as Louis XVIII intended. That was not what they had been praying and plotting and fighting for all these years – although, with the predictable attraction of extremes for each other, many Ultra-Royalists had in fact been ferocious Republicans. Consequently in April 1814, *chouans* physically threatened *acquéreurs* in the Eure, and Royalists were furious that 'all are received equally' by Angoulême in Bordeaux. The *Commissaires Extraordinaires* sent out by the Provisional Government in late April reported that the demands and pretensions of the Ultras (as they were soon known) were the factor most likely to destroy the credibility of the new regime. Froment, for example, who had worked for Louis in the 1790s and had been to see him at Verona, in 1814 wanted a violent Counter-Revolution and the command of a force which would *surveiller* all the king's enemies: all he got was the sinecure of *Secrétaire du Cabinet du Roi*. A few priests, as shamelessly reluctant to abandon their Church's material possessions after the Revolution as the Papacy would be after the Risorgimento, refused to give the last sacrament to *acquéreurs*, or preached sermons against them.[28]

It was simply too much for the Ultras and the Vendéens to sit back and accept that the Restoration was not their restoration, but was intended to be the restoration of all Frenchmen to peace, liberty and the pursuit of prosperity. (After 1815, however, when they had the reaction they wanted, their threats to *acquéreurs* diminshed considerably). And in addition to threatening *acquéreurs* and ex-Revolutionaries, the Ultras also reacted to the First Restoration by claiming in the provinces, in Paris and in the Tuileries itself that Louis did not really believe in the *Charte*, that it was just a temporary measure and that soon, like his cousin Ferdinand VII of Spain, he would revert to the absolutism of his ancestors. Gossip and rumour, so powerful in discrediting the Royal Family in the 1780s, were among the most dangerous enemies of Louis's Government in 1814. And the doubts spread about the sincerity of Louis's commitment to the *Charte* in 1814 may have been encouraged by his reputation for hypocrisy, and by public knowledge of his role in the Favras Affair – his speech to the Commune in 1789 was reprinted in 1814 – and of his past political variations.

The fear inspired by the Ultras in 1814 was a powerful political force, as real and decisive as the fear inspired by Communists in Germany before 1933 or in France since the 1920s. This fear was blown up and made more aggressive by the princes' tours in the provinces in the autumn of 1814, which made even more enemies for the Government. The most moderate of the princes, Angoulême and Berri, were thoroughly unimpressive to meet. Angoulême was short, ugly and gauche. Berri, as well as being short and ugly, had a *ton dur* and a violent temper which made him widely detested. Their father, who was extremely gracious and

charming, was, however, unbending on some things: on his tour
he refused to receive people who had revolutionary pasts such as
the Archbishop of Besançon. Moreover, he was suspected by the
public of not supporting the *Charte*. It was well known that he
had not been at the ceremony of its promulgation. And Lainé,
one of the most devoted, sensible and well-informed of Royalists,
when he referred in March 1815 to *inquiétudes* over '*la liberté
et les droits reconnus*' as coming from *la Cour*, was probably
thinking of the attitude of Artois and the Royal Family.[29]

What was the reaction of Louis, one of the most public-relations
conscious kings there has ever been, to this increasingly tense state
of affairs? He was aware of almost everything that was going on,
since he received police reports from the *Directeur-Général de
Police* which were frank enough, although always written in a
bland and courtly style, from other police officials, from Maréchal Moncey and – through the Archbishop of Reims – even from
Fouché himself. This shows again what an extraordinary year
1814 was: the king was getting police reports from a defrocked
Regicide via an elderly archbishop. Thus Louis knew that '*les
défiances se sèment jusques sur les intentions du Roi*', and that
'*les passions politiques commencent à fermenter, surtout à Paris*'
('distrust is growing even about the King's intentions . . . political
passions are starting to ferment, above all in Paris'). To the horror
of his family, he even read the most disrespectful opposition
newspapers, such as *Le Nain Jaune*.[30]

One of Louis's reactions to this situation was, quite consciously,
to try to calm people's fears by the welcome he gave them and to
rule through good manners, to use them as a soothing lotion
which, like a good doctor, he applied to his countrymen's wounds.
Thus, from the moment he stepped onto French soil he was as
charming and flattering as possible to the people he met. His
behaviour was appreciated all the more for the contrast it presented to the insults and tantrums of Napoleon I. The *Directeur
des Postes* of Amiens could not get over that '*dans presque toutes
ses audiences le Roi dit des choses qui surprennent, il les trouve
sans avoir l'air d'y penser. Tout le monde est enchanté de l'acceuil
gracieux qu'on reçoit de S.M.*' ('at almost all his audiences, the
King says amazing things; he finds them without it seeming deliberate. Everyone is delighted with the gracious welcome they
receive from His Majesty.') At Court he was always extremely
polite and did his best to win over the most difficult Bonapartists,
with some success. Tough Napoleonic marshals like Soult, Macdonald and Marmont were charmed by his manners. Prince Eugène and Queen Hortense, whom, to please the Tsar, he had

made Duchesse de Saint-Leu, were delighted by the way in which he received them when, like almost everyone else in the French elite in 1814, they went to the Tuileries. (It was probably the only time Bonapartes and French Bourbons ever met). She wrote that Louis was *'fort bien'*, although *'un peu embarrassé'*. In June, Louis singled out General Rapp to congratulate him on his defence of Danzig and in September he signed the marriage contract of General Reille with Mlle. Victorine Masséna.[31]

At the new year's receptions in 1815, Louis continued his soothing and healing mission. He had kind remarks for each legion of the *Garde Nationale de Paris*, to whom, with many flattering speeches, he had already given the privilege of guarding him every 3 May, the anniversary of his entry into Paris. He told the Tenth Legion: *'Elle est si belle que ... je suis tenté de dire comme César: voilà ma 10e légion.'* ('It is so fine that ... I am tempted to say like Caesar: here is my 10th legion.') Having reaffirmed, yet again, his commitment to the *Charte*, he told the deputies that they were *'les représentants d'enfants auprès de leur père'* ('representatives of children round their father') and, with a typical mixture of realism and optimism, said: *'Les opinions ne peuvent toutes s'accorder dans une grande assemblée, mais je suis sûr de l'unanimité de vos sentiments.'* ('Opinions cannot all be the same in a large assembly, but I am sure of the unanimity of your sentiments.') The philosopher Maine de Biran was delighted.[32]

Louis did not just try to soothe the elite in the state apartments on the first floor of the *Château*; he also paid attention to the ordinary people down in the *Jardin des Tuileries*. This was one of the main meeting places of middle class and even poor Parisians. It was open to anyone not in working clothes or wooden shoes: clothes were as vital an indicator of status in the garden as in the palace of the Tuileries. Throughout 1814, whenever Louis appeared on the palace balcony, or in the *Salle des Maréchaux*, he was cheered 'as loud as heart could wish', with men waving their hats and women their handkerchiefs. It is hard for us to realize how much significance used to be attached to every nuance of royal behaviour and gesture. Orléans, for example, bothered to record in a private letter to his old friend Madame de Saint-Laurent, mistress of the Duke of Kent, that the king regularly takes his hat off and 'salutes' the people. This sign of respect and of acknowledgement delighted the Parisians: a *femme du peuple* was reported to have said, *'Ah, on voit bien que celui-là est français, il est poli; en quinze ans l'autre ne nous a pas fait une seule révérence'* ('Ah! You can tell that that one is French, he is polite; in fifteen years the other did not make us a single bow').[33]

Napoleon I, unlike Louis XVIII, had been an extremely aloof, arrogant and inaccessible monarch.

In November 1814, in order to reply to a violent pamphlet denouncing the First Restoration by Carnot, Louis commissioned, proof-read and pointedly recommended to a group of deputies a pamphlet by Chateaubriand called *Réflexions Politiques*. This is a superbly rational and moderate document, which should be read by all those who think that the Bourbons had learnt nothing and forgotten nothing, or that the Restoration was a reaction. It tries to point out the advantages of the Restoration to everyone, even to those who might entertain the *chimère* of the Republic: it attacks people's fears, preaches restraint and reconciliation, and affirms, as if his actions did not speak loud enough, that the king '*ne sépare point ceux qui ont servi le roi de ceux qui ont servi la patrie*' ('does not differentiate between those who have served the king and those who have served the country'). And this pamphlet did greatly reassure public opinion.

However, for a king so very conscious of the force of public opinion, Louis could also be remarkably tactless. He always retained some of the self-satisfied, blustering pomposity which made it difficult for him to criticize his own inclinations. For example, he refused to wear the *Légion d'Honneur*, although it meant an enormous amount to the 28,000 French people who had it: in *Le Rouge et Le Noir* a Napoleonic veteran is even prouder of his *Légion d'Honneur* than is the Marquis de la Mole of his aristocratic birth. The *Légionnaires* could not be convinced that their order would last so long as the king did not wear its insignia. Moreover, they were further humiliated by the fact that the income attached to senior ranks in the Légion was abolished as part of the Government's economy drive. Louis with his rather cold common sense said: '*La Légion d'Honneur par son nom ne devrait pas etre payée.*' ('The *Légion d'Honneur* by its name should not be paid.') In addition, the *Maisons d'Education* for top *Légionnaires'* daughters were closed down, although later they were started up again as Louis and Blacas had not realized how unpopular the move would be.[34]

Another example of Louis's ability to wound the feelings of the Napoleonic elite occurred when only five *maréchales* and *générales* were among the thirty-six women he invited to dine with him at the Hôtel de Ville on 28 August to celebrate the Fête de Saintlouis. All the rest were women from the worlds of Versailles or the Emigration. More *maréchales* may have been invited and, like Maréchale Ney, been unable to go because they were in the country. But some of the Napoleonic elite did feel the guest list was an insult. And one of the first things Napoleon and Maréchal Ney talked about at the beginning of the Hundred Days – two hardened war-chiefs meeting on one of the most dramatic occasions in history – was who Louis XVIII had invited to dinner. Early nineteenth-century France was an extraordinarily vain and monarchical society.

Louis also wounded the feelings of many French people by his open attempt to heal the ancient rivalry with England and to make the two countries friends again. It does credit to his heart and sense of gratitude, but it was not very wise to proclaim that he owed his restoration 'after providence' to the regent. It was not even true. Furthermore, it was unwise of Louis to invite the regent to Paris for the peace celebrations and to be so obviously fond of the tactlessly chosen new English ambassador, Wellington, who had spent the last six years defeating the French army. Louis even allowed incorrectly dressed English visitors access to the Tuileries chapel while many well dressed French people were turned away.

In 1814 Paris was reeling from a tidal wave of English tourists, who had been cooped up in their island for eleven years. With their booming voices, red faces, frightful clothes – the ladies' bonnets were thought particularly dreadful – and confident wealth, they cannot have been very lovable. But Louis loved them enough to blow kisses to them when he saw them in the street: that they could be picked out by Louis from his carriage shows just how extraordinary their clothes must have been. By the autumn many people were reporting on the extraordinary unpopularity of the English, and of Wellington in particular. He was, quite rightly, suspected of trying to interfere in French politics: he told Louis to change the *Directeur-Général de Police*; he kept presenting dozens of English visitors at Court; and he did not even pay farmers in the Ile-de-France for the damage he did to their crops while hunting (Louis got Blacas to tell him to stop). It was '*la gloire de Wellington*', as well as the loss of his *dotations* outside France, which annoyed Maréchal Ney more than anything, according to a police report sent to Louis. Ney was now in debt, and a potential malcontent.[35]

Another way in which Louis alienated sections of public opinion, especially the Napoleonic elite, was that, in accordance with his personal preferences, his household was revived on basically the same lines as the traditional pre-1792 *Maison Civile du Roi*. Like his predecessors, Louis XVIII had an army of *Gentilshommes Servant* and *Valets de Garde-Robe*, etc, but no equivalent of the *Gentilshommes d'Honneur* he had had as a prince or of the Aides de Camp he had had at Coblentz. The only difference between Louis's household and that of Louis XVI in 1792 was that, in accordance with the general desire for economy, Louis's household was considerably reduced in comparison to his brother's (which itself had been greatly reduced in 1787 and 1789). So it was the only institution in France which had not been transformed since 1789. Although many of its officials owed their position to their role in the Counter-Revolution, at the Court of Napoleon I or in Louis's household in exile, most of them (twenty-one of the thirty-eight senior officials) held their offices because their family had held them before 1792: thus it was Mathieu de Montmorency who won the struggle to be Governor of Compiegne, although General Delaborde was given a large pension. This was particularly maddening for the Napoleonic elite, many of whom longed to be Court officials or *Aides de Camp du Roi*; and offering them such positions would have been a cheap way of satisfying them.

But what at first seems like Louis's most extraordinary defiance of public opinion was his decision to spend six months of every year at Versailles, the home of his childhood and the most glaring symbol of the *Ancien Régime*. In 1814–15 the whole palace underwent a massive restoration; it was then that the *Grands et Petits Apartements* were regilded and that the neoclassical pavilion on the left of the courtyard façade was begun. By August, the palace was so covered with scaffolding that it could not be illuminated for the Fête de Saint Louis, as Louis could see for himself when he went down for the first time on 12 August. In the autumn courtiers kept rushing down from Paris to report back to Louis on how the work was getting on. For the first time in the whole extravagant history of Versailles money was no problem, since Louis was paying for it out of the six million francs left in Napoleon's *Domaine Extraordinaire*. The war-chief's loot was being used to restore the Bourbons' family home.

Yet in the police reports, diplomatic despatches and private letters written in 1814–15, and in the many diatribes against the Restoration produced during the Hundred Days, all of which went out of their way to note causes of discontent, mentions of the restoration of Versailles are brief, infrequent and not particularly hostile. People were at most alarmed that, because it was to the west of Paris, it symbolized that the king was turning towards the Vendée – reasoning so absurd that it seems to indicate that people could think of no other comment to make. When one considers that one of the first things Napoleon I said to the *Conseil Municipal* of Paris in March 1815 was that he intended to con-

tinue the restoration at Versailles, one is forced to conclude that
early nineteenth-century France was so monarchical that people
really did not mind their monarch living in the most splendid of
all his palaces; Napoleon I had already had the idea in 1809.
Moreover contemporaries, especially among the poor, were delighted that employment should thereby be provided for nearly
2,500 people.

Louis's tactlessness about Versailles, the *Légion d'Honneur*,
the English, his own household and the *Fête de l'Hôtel de Ville*
cannot be entirely due to a lack of imagination, since he went out
of his way to calm people's fears about the intentions of his
Government and to make his receptions agreeable to the new
elite. Perhaps it is a sign of the degree to which he felt at ease in
the France of 1814, and found it a country in which he wanted
to indulge his own inner feelings and personal preferences, that
he showed himself still, to a certain extent, a product of Versailles
and the world of his youth.

In 1794, after receiving the news of the execution of Madame
Elizabeth, he had written that it would be impossible for him ever
to enjoy returning to France, that it would only be an *exil prolongé*.[36] But in 1814 he found a country which not only provided
a very favourable field for the exercise of royal authority, but one
which was also to his liking. The new worldliness, the taste for
pomp and pomposity, even the style of furniture and architecture,
appealed to him. This is hardly surprising since it was a development of, rather than a break with, the style which he had been
patronizing in the 1780s: for example, his architect Chalgrin, who
had built *Folies* for Madame de Balbi and Marie-Joséphine, had
gone on in the grim military world of the early nineteenth century
to be the architect of the *Arc de Triomphe*. In other fields too,
living in the new France cannot have seemed like an *exil prolongé*
to Louis XVIII. *La Partie de Chasse de Henri IV*, played in the
old days in the open air at Brunoy, was endlessly performed before
Louis when he went to the theatre in 1814. There was no barrier
of taste – the most insurmountable barrier of all – between him
and the Frenchmen of 1814, as there had been between Louis
XVI and a large proportion of his subjects, or between Charles I
and many of the Englishmen of his day.

In 1814 Louis felt that he was at home again. He *enjoyed* being
King of France. He saw no reason why he should not make
himself completely at home, use Versailles as a summer residence,
entertain the ladies of his world to dinner, go on being served by
his traditional household and wear the orders he wanted to rather
than the order founded by *l'autre*. These little *manies* were not

very important. What did it matter who he had to dinner, what he wore or where he spent the summer, so long as the constitution was in tune with *l'Esprit de notre Siècle*, the ministry was reasonable and peace, liberty and *repos*, as well as the Bourbons, had been restored to France?

This does seem to have been the opinion of most of his subjects, since 1814 saw the beginning of the extraordinary process by which Louis acquired at least some of the *considération* which he had felt would be necessary for his monarchy to become *un édifice solide*. Before he returned to France, except in the small world of the political elite, he was not known personally, as is shown by the absence of references to his personality in the proclamations of the Mayor of Bordeaux on 12 March 1814 and of the *Corps Municipal* of Paris on 1 April. When Louis returned to France it would have been easy for this fat, gouty and elderly gentleman, who had spent the last twenty-three years abroad, to become simply a figure of fun, as he did for most of the army, and as he has been regarded by posterity. Among some of his subjects, however, he became extraordinarily popular.

Contemporary accounts, with no particular reason for bias, state that when he went to the theatre he was *idôlatré* by the audience (see illustration 9) just as he was cheered by the less wealthy people in the gardens of the Tuileries. In October the Prefect of Loire Inférieure wrote to his wife privately: '*Personnellement on a pour le roi de la vénération; pour la cour c'est toute autre chose*.' ('The king personally is venerated; as for the Court, that is another matter.') In December, the Sardinian ambassador wrote that the king '*plaît infiniment*', and Jaucourt claimed that he was loved and trusted even by some of the most discontented Napoleonic generals. Louis's popularity was helped by his age and appearance: someone so old and fat and calm was really extremely reassuring in the tense, insecure atmosphere of 1814–15.[37] Indeed, Louis was more popular than he deserved. Even though he refused to order the *curé* to bury Mlle. Raucourt, who as an actress was thought unfit for Christian burial by the Catholic Church, the angry, violent crowd assumed that he had and, after forcing its way into the church with the coffin, dispersed crying '*Vive le Roi!*'[38] It is now that many sensible, observant people, Madame de Flahault, mother of one of the most Bonapartist generals, Talleyrand, Jaucourt, Beugnot and even the author of a Bonapartist pamphlet wrote that if only the princes behaved like the king everything would be all right. What a tragedy for France and Europe it was that Louis XVIII had no sons![39]

Yet perhaps everything would still have been all right. There is something extremely impressive about the violence of ex-Revolutionaries' complaints about the *biens nationaux*, the *Maison Militaire* and the attitude of the Court and the princes, and the bitterness of Counter-Revolutionaries' complaints about the *Charte*, the *biens nationaux* and the attitude of the king. Yet these were only complaints, words, to some extent simply the sheer joy of recovering freedom of speech, and of being able to indulge in everyone's favourite activity of complaining about the Government, after the terrified whisperings of the Empire. The Restoration was an outburst of conversation as well as a release of emotions: and while there were many complaints, there were few acts of opposition. The *Garde Nationale* came to accept the *Gardes du Corps*, and perhaps the army would have too. The Government got on remarkably well with the *Chambre des Députés*, which in January 1814 Napoleon I had had to dissolve after less than a month. Louis's enormous *Liste Civile* of thirty-three million francs a year for the whole of his reign (twenty-five million francs for himself, eight million francs for his family) was voted without incident. Thereby, he had a firm financial basis from which he could indulge every whim and fancy, and which he would be able to use for political purposes. Another sign of the strength of the regime is that Marie-Louise, who only five months before had been Empress of the French, visited the waters at Aix in August without exciting more than *'une sorte d'intérêt'*. Louis was quite right, when pressed by his worried ministers, to say that all that was necessary was *'une police sévère'*.

What is so fascinating about the First Restoration is that, for the first time in French history, people were learning the arts of parliamentary government (in 1789–92 and 1795-97 significant sections of the legislature and the electorate, respectively, were excluded for political reasons, and the threat of violence, from the crowd or the Government was always, often visibly, present). It was bound to take a long time for a set of rules or standards to emerge. The whole concept of party was completely alien, and indeed there were no well-defined parties in 1814: one reason why there was no united ministry was that there was no organized opposition.

Consequently, 1814 was an exceptional year – without parties, without an organized opposition, without a united ministry or a united Royal Family, and without political prisoners and exiles. In a way this was what Louis wanted, to allow everyone of every political opinion to board the ship of state, even though it became rather difficult to navigate. He was confident that time was on his side. In the extraordinary letter he wrote to the regent in November, Père Elisée claimed that the discontent of the army and the *acquéreurs* had actually grown less. He even claimed that, among the general public, *'un peu d'humeur'* was better than *'les folles espérances'* of May 1814 since it was so much easier to work with. In late 1814, Louis wrote to Talleyrand that all he needed was a little time *'pour panser . . . les plaies de l'état'* ('to heal . . . the wounds of the state') and the clouds of discontent, which he had foreseen, would disappear.[40] Perhaps there was some truth in this. The Restoration was a very social regime, which was only natural, since it was an outburst of both emotions and conversation. The carnival season of 1815 was particularly brilliant – there were far more private balls than under the Empire – and there was no sign of discontent on the dance floors. The most magnificent ball of all was that given by the Prince de Wagram, the same person whom, when he was still only General Berthier, Louis had tried to win over in 1798. A typical figure of the First Restoration, Wagram was both the richest and most important of the Napoleonic marshals, and a *Capitaine des Gardes* and finally a friend of Louis himself. Berri gave two balls in the Tuileries, at one of which Louis (it was the last informal party he ever attended) learnt a lot of names and got to know a lot of faces that he had not seen before. He even made the Duchesse d'Angoulême put on rouge, prompting Jaucourt to say that if the king had renounced conquests for himself he had not renounced them for his niece. In Beauvais, the Noailles company of the *Gardes du Corps* (which included Lamartine) seems to have spent the entire winter giving balls in honour of the Duchesse de Massa, daughter of a Napoleonic marshal and wife of a Napoleonic duke and prefect. Such occasions, like most French parties in 1815, even the Orléans's soirees in the Palais-Royal, always ended with recitals of songs or poems in honour of the king. But there was little time for dancing on the island of Elba.[41]

CHAPTER X

The Blue and the Green
March–May 1815

On 12 April 1814 Napoleon I had abdicated unconditionally and, largely due to the influence of the Tsar, was given the sovereignty of Elba, a yearly pension of two million livres for himself and other pensions for his family. Then, as Louis proceeded in state from Hartwell to Paris, wearing his blue tail-coat and breeches, in a carriage driven and escorted by footmen in the blue, silver and red livery of the kings of France, blessed and cheered wherever he went, Napoleon journeyed through France as a private individual (having, however, taken 3,966,915 francs with him from Fontainebleau), meeting with the indifference or execration of his former subjects. At Aix-en-Provence he even had to put on an Austrian uniform instead of his usual green and red uniform of the *Chasseurs à Cheval de la Garde Impériale* in order to escape being lynched. It had been a long time since he had travelled without the splendour of footmen in the familiar Bonaparte livery of green and gold.

What exactly made Napoleon I decide to leave Elba on 26 February 1815 and try his luck on the mainland again is hard to say. It may have been his understandable annoyance that the terms of the treaty were not being observed, and that the Royal Government was not paying him or his family anything. (But Napoleon I had also broken the treaty by having an army of 1,600 soldiers instead of 400 with him on Elba, and to please the Allies, at the end of February Blacas said that the Government would start paying the pension.) It may have been that, as Napoleon I well knew, Louis and his ministers were hoping, both by means of a secret mission to Italian governments at the end of 1814, and by means of diplomatic pressure at the Congress of Vienna, to have him removed to America, the Azores or even Saint-Helena.

It may also have been that, as some historians have considered, there was a plot by discontented Bonapartists in Paris to bring back their emperor. There is a strangely prophetic letter to Talleyrand from a senior foreign ministry official, dated 14 February, which records the conviction of leading Bonapartists like Savary, Maret and Daru that, owing to the faults of the Bourbons, Bonaparte would soon be back. And on Saint-Helena Bonaparte said that Flahault, one of the most discontented and Bonapartist generals in the French army, had told him that Colonel La Bédoyère, who took up command of a regiment at Chambéry on 25 February, was favourable to his cause.[1]

But although Napoleon I did have influential supporters in Paris, who also included General Sébastiani and Fouché, it is unlikely that his decision to leave was simply the result of a plot, or even of his knowledge of the hostile intentions of the Royal Government. Elba was temptingly near to France as Fouché, Castlereagh and Metternich had warned as early as April 1814. Napoleon I only needed to read the newspapers, or the letters his soldiers received from their families, to realize that there was considerable discontent in France. Napoleon I liked being a monarch and liked living in splendid and luxurious palaces. He had been a gambler all his life. Why not try for the throne of France again? Furthermore, although they were stepped up in early 1815, the measures of the French navy to guard the island of Elba were fairly inadequate, so he was able to land without difficulty near Cannes on 1 March.

Provence did not welcome Bonaparte. The Mayor of Grasse declared to General Bertrand the *Grand Maréchal du Palais* who was doubling as Chief of Staff, '*Nous avons notre souverain Louis XVIII et nous l'aimons.*' ('We have our sovereign Louis XVIII and we love him.') A coachman, whose job had recently taken him all over France, told Bertrand, '*Certainement vous avez des amis. Mais nous commencions à être tranquilles . . . vous allez tout troubler.*' ('Of course you have some support. But we were beginning to calm down . . . you will upset everything.') Such language exactly reflects Louis's view that France longed for peace and quiet, and that his reign was the best guarantee of France's *tranquillité*. However, when Napoleon I advanced over the hills to Dauphiné, public reaction was completely different. Moncey had warned Louis that Dauphiné was Bonapartist in a report in February, and the emperor found a clique of devoted Bonapartists, including a cousin of Stendhal called Edouard Rey, who were prepared to risk their lives to help him, telling him which direction to advance in, assuring him that popular feeling was on his side and that the troops would not shoot. Rey and his companions were far more important than the Bonapartist grandees in Paris. On 6 March Napoleon entered Grenoble in triumph, escorted by the troops sent to oppose him, which La Bédoyère had led over to his side.[2]

At first Louis and his ministers, who had received reports of Bonaparte's bad reception in Provence, thought that the invasion would be a failure. He would be captured by the troops Soult, Minister of War (who was replaced by the Duc de Feltre, formerly Napoleon I's Minister of War, on 13 March), had ordered to concentrate in the south-east, under Artois, Orléans and Maréchal Macdonald. Louis, who had recently recovered from a very bad attack of gout, declared at a diplomatic reception, '*Je vous prie, Messieurs, d'annoncer à vos Cours que je me porte bien, à un peu de goutte près, et que je ne suis nullement inquiet sur cet évènement. J'espère qu'il ne troublera pas le repos de l'Europe ni le mien*' ('I beg you, Messieurs, to inform your Courts that, but for a little gout, I am in good health, and that I am not in the least bit worried by this event. I hope that it will trouble neither the peace of Europe nor my own.')[3]

However, this mood of cool, egotistical self-confidence soon changed. As Bonaparte's forces advanced northwards from Grenoble, streaming towards Paris like a lighted fuse, it became painfully clear that French soldiers would not fight their emperor and that, in certain areas, he had enthusiastic popular support. Not even Maréchal Macdonald, who like many ex-Napoleonic officers did all he could to serve Louis XVIII in March 1815, let alone Artois, could persuade the soldiers under their command in Lyon to cry '*Vive le Roi!*' The soldiers were longing for the emperor, who received a rapturous welcome at Lyon on 10 March: crowds stormed through the streets yelling '*A l'échafaud les Bourbons! A bas la calotte! A mort les royalistes!*' ('The Bourbons to the scaffold! Down with priests! Death to the royalists!')

Meanwhile, throughout France, prefects' reports to the Minister of the Interior showed that the soldiers in their barracks were preparing to join their emperor at the right moment: and in some areas, in addition to Lyon, Bonapartist, or anti-Royalist, feeling was even stronger in the fields and on the streets than in the barracks. Peasants marched through the Burgundian countryside chanting: '*Roule ta boule, Roi Cotillon, Rends ta couronne à Napoleon*' ('Petticoat king, off you go, give back your crown to Napoleon') On 14th March at Lons-le-Saulnier, near Dijon, where Maréchal Ney was in command of an army assembled to block Bonaparte's route to Paris, he found, and his story is confirmed by other people who were there, that he and his officers could just about control the troops until they made contact with the *menu peuple*. Then it was like trying to stop water with your hand.[4]

Back in Paris, against a background of Government panic, Royalist exaltation and univeral suspicion, Louis and his ministers tried every possible means to stop Bonaparte. An army was to be formed in front of Paris at Melun, commanded by Berri, assisted by Maréchal Macdonald and General Belliard. But the Government was well aware of the dangers of relying on French troops to fire on Bonaparte. So on 12 March Blacas, in Louis's name and perhaps at his suggestion, told the Minister of War to plan to add *Gardes nationales*, who were being summoned to Paris from all over France to defend the king and the *Charte*, to the regular troops. And on 13 March Louis decided to raise a *Corps of Volontaires Royaux*, under the command of one *émigré* and one Napoleonic general.[5]

The Government also took political measures. In their desperate situation they turned to Fouché, a man who was always credited, not only by the Royalists, with far more importance and influence than he in fact possessed: how amused and delighted the old monster must have been to find himself suddenly sought out by Blacas on 12 March, by Dambray on 13 March and by Artois himself on 15 March! It is possible that Fouché was offered a ministry, or that the composition of a new and more 'revolutionary' ministry was discussed. But Artois was probably acting independently of Louis, for as early as 13 March, a day after his visit to Fouché, Blacas was thinking in terms of the arrest of people who had corresponded with Elba (he named Lavallette and the Princesse de Vaudémont, the former of whom, Napoleon's *Directeur des Postes*, certainly had). And on 16 March an attempt was made to arrest Fouché – he got away by climbing over the garden wall – only four days after Blacas had met him. It was a pathetic end to a pointless intrigue.[6]

Other, more sensible political measures were also taken. The *Conseils-Généraux* of the departments was instructed by Montesquiou to meet *en permanence*, and to correspond with each other in the interests of the *salut public*: this was 'revolutionary' language from a royal minister, because the ministers were very conscious of defending the constitution as well as the king. Against the opposition of Blacas, Soult and Dambray, and in accordance with the views of the more liberal ministers, Baron Louis, Jaucourt, and Montesquiou, Louis decided to summon the two chambers, which were in recess. On 16 March, at last wearing the *Légion d'Honneur*, he made a moving and emotional speech in the Chamber of Deputies, in which he asserted that he stood for liberty, peace and the *patrie*, whereas Bonaparte brought with him foreign and civil war; '*Pourrais-je à 60 ans mieux terminer ma carrière qu'en mourant pour sa* [the *Charte's*] *défense?*') ('Could I, at the age of sixty, better end my days than by dying in its defence?') Then, in what was clearly one point of the whole exercise, Artois came forward to swear to the *Charte* – finally, and far too late, openly associating himself with his brother's constitution.[7]

The great question now was which side would win, the blue of the king or the green of the emperor. Although the emperor was drawing nearer and nearer to Paris, the king appeared to have certain advantages – indeed the bets at White's were still '2 to 1 on Louis XVIII'. There were his 6,000 household troops: there were the *Gardes Nationales* and the *Volontaires Royaux*. An attempt to lead the troops stationed in north-eastern France on Paris between 6 and 12 March, probably in favour of Napoleon I, failed ignominiously owing to the energy of a few loyal commanders. Moreover, an important section of Parisian opinion was vociferously on the side of the king. '*Le peuple ne quitte pas la cour du château et montre beaucoup de dévouement pour le Roi*' ('The people are always in front of the palace and display great devotion for the King') wrote the Russian *chargé d'affaires* on 12 March, and the Sardinian ambassador also thought public opinion '*excellent*'. Indeed the next day two people who cried '*Vive Bonaparte*' in the *Jardin des Tuileries* were trampled to death by the furious Royalist crowd: as later events would confirm, Royalists could be just as bloodthirsty as Revolutionaries.

But it is doubtful whether the crowds surrounding the Tuileries represented all the people of Paris. It seems more likely, remembering the rules about dress in the *Jardin des Tuileries*, that they were more representative of the prosperous middle classes. The poor, that is to say the great mass of Parisians, appear to have had few feelings of love for Louis XVIII and, above all, to have regretted the national glory and Tricolour flag of the past. So Louis could not rely on a united and devoted capital as, for example, Maria-Theresa had been able to do when her throne was threatened in 1740–42.

Moreover, despite considerable enthusiasm among the *Volontaires Royaux*, neither they nor the *Gardes Nationales* were really very effective fighting-forces, as both the acting Foreign Minister, Jaucourt, and police reports sent to Louis concluded as early as 14 March.[8] At the best of times few people are prepared to fight for their political beliefs; even fewer would be prepared to fight in volunteer units against hardened veterans of their own nationality. The members of the *Gardes Nationales* were mostly, as Louis knew, *pères de famille*, more concerned with their own private lives than with political causes; and many members of the Paris bourgeoisie could not even be bothered to join the *Garde Nationales* in the first place. Their own ordinary day-to-day existence, and the preservation of their property, was far more important to most Frenchmen than the fate of the king. It is revealing that, all along Napoleon's route, when Royalist commanders tried to block his advance by cutting the bridges, they were forcibly prevented from doing so by the local inhabitants. People were perfectly prepared to fight for their bridge but not for their king.

So, to oppose Bonaparte, and the dedicated, ever-increasing army marching triumphantly on Paris, Louis only had his household troops, a few thousand enthusiastic volunteers, and what he so rightly called an 'inert disposition' in his favour in Paris and in much of France. Some people, for example Chateaubriand, and Maréchal Marmont, write in their memoirs, and perhaps even said at the time, that Louis should have stayed in the Tuileries. The king in his throne-room, on his left the deputies, on his right the peers, with *Gardes du Corps* and household troops on the staircase and in the courtyard, would surely have embarrassed even Bonaparte. What would he have done with them all?[9]

But Louis refused this opportunity of defying his greatest enemy and, perhaps, entering into history and the hearts of his people are gloriously as Maria-Theresa had done in 1740. Louis had been through one revolution and he had no desire to take part in another. He did not believe in the power of the great virtues, duty, love, honour and loyalty, to resist overwhelming physical force: and he thought that there were traitors even among the *Gardes du Corps*, who included many ex-Napoleonic officers. He later said that the worst thing of all would have been for him to become a prisoner, an undignified pawn in negotiations over which he had no control, and even Maréchal Macdonald, who was in favour of almost any violent measures, agreed.

Louis also realized that the dominant emotion in France in 1815 was not love of the king or worship of the emperor but fear of civil war, which was much stronger than fear of an international war. Most Frenchmen loathed the idea of killing each other. French soldiers in particular were unwilling to fire on their comrades, which was one of the reasons for the success of Napoleon I and his small army in March 1815: no one in the royal army wanted to fire the first shot and be the first to kill an old comrade. It is clear from his diary that even a devoted Royalist like Maine de Biran was as glad to see Louis leave as any indifferent Parisian,

simply because it meant there would not be any fighting. And
Louis himself showed no desire to stay and fight. He was, like
most of his subjects, afraid.[10]

Probably Louis finally decided to leave Paris on 18 March,
although as early as 14 March his closest servants and courtiers,
Gonet, Guignet, Gramont and the Abbé Fleuriel, had been given
small amounts of money, no doubt in order to help them get
away. Much larger sums of money were distributed among the
troops on Louis's instructions, in a vain but revealing attempt to
buy their loyalty. Money was also distributed to politicians like
the Prince de La Trémoïlle and Vitrolles to help them on missions
to keep the west and the Midi loyal. On 18 March, Hue, one of
Louis's most trusted *Premiers Valets de Chambre*, was entrusted
with the crown jewels, unmounted (worth 13,864,046.70 francs)
and four million francs in gold from the funds of the *Liste Civile*,
he set off from Paris with instructions to take them either to Lille
or to England.

There was still some hesitation as to where Louis should go.
Some people thought he should head for the Vendée; other suggested Bordeaux or Toulouse, which were still in Royalist hands.
But Louis did not want to run the risk of falling into the hands
of hostile troops in the centre of France, who had already adopted
the tricolour. On 19 March he gave the order for the *Maison
Militaire* to be ready to escort him out of Paris for Saint-Denis
and Lille.

His departure was an extraordinary scene. All day long the
Tuileries had been crowded with people desperate for the latest
news: Maine de Biran was impressed to find Louis '*toujours calme
et sérein au milieu des orages. La consternation, la crainte, la
stupeur sont partout*' ('always serene and calm in the middle of
the tempest. Consternation, fear and shock are universal'). In the
evening the palace emptied as most people went home. At half-
past eight Louis told Maréchal Marmont, commander of the
household troops, and Maréchal Macdonald, commander of the
army raised at Melun which was now rapidly joining the other
side, that he would leave at midnight. A deep silence fell on the
palace, broken only by the drumming of the torrential rain outside. Finally, just after midnight, the door of Louis's private apartments swung open to reveal the old king, escorted by Blacas and
the Duc de Duras, *Premier Gentilhomme de la Chambre*. '*A son
aspect vénérable et comme par un mouvement spontané nous
tombâmes à genoux en pleurant*' ('struck by his venerable appearance, we fell weeping to our knees, as if in a spontaneous
movement'), wrote one of the *Gardes Nationaux* on duty, and his

testimony is confirmed by the great picture by Gros which was the sensation of the salon of 1817 (see illustration 10). Louis, in his self-absorbed way, replied to their tears – tears of relief that there was going to be no civil war, as well as tears of sorrow at losing their king – and their efforts to seize hold of his clothes and his hands: '*Mes enfants, épargnez-moi, j'ai besoin de forces. Je vous reverrai bientôt. Retournez dans vos familles. . .*' ('My children, spare me, I need strength. I will see you again soon. Return to your families. . .') Then he slowly descended the palace staircase, clambered into his carriage and rolled off into the night.

The next day the official Government newspaper, the *Moniteur*, made the immortal announcement '*Le roi et les princes sont partis dans la nuit. S.M.l'Empereur est arrivé ce soir à 8 heures dans son palais des Tuileries, à la tête des mêmes troupes qu'on avait fait sortir ce matin pour s'opposer à son passage*' ('The king and the princes left in the night. H. M. the Emperor arrived this evening at eight o'clock in his palace of the Tuileries at the head of the same troops which had been sent to block his route this morning'). On 21 March, a huge crowd acclaimed the return of the emperor and the tricolour.[11] Had Louis's reign simply been a deceptive façade, hiding his subjects' real feelings?

Louis's journey north was a nightmare of confusion, treachery and cowardice, which was made even more unpleasant by the continuous drenching rain. He had ordered his ministers and the *Corps Diplomatique* to go to Lille in the north of France. But he himself, accompanied by a tiny retinue of servants, courtiers and *Gardes du Corps*, in three or four carriages, used the fresh post-horses which postmasters kept available on all main roads for the use of travellers, to head at great speed for Abbeville on the Channel coast, where he arrived at five o'clock in the afternoon on 20 March. Abbeville was not on the direct route from Paris to Lille, but it was one of the most passionately Royalist towns in France, as its reception of Louis in April 1814, and a recent loyal address, had shown – and it was conveniently placed for a dash to England. Clearly, Louis was a very frightened king, and he wanted to be sure that he and the four million francs which Blacas had withdrawn from the funds of the *Liste Civile* and the *Maison Militaire*, in addition to the funds entrusted to Hue, should be safe from a surprise attack by rebellious troops.

Meanwhile, it never stopped raining, and the *Maison Militaire*, commanded by Artois and Berri, was getting bogged down in the mud and grime of northern France – and it had to move much more slowly, since it used its own horses, which constantly needed rest, rather than post-horses. So while Louis waited at Abbeville, until the evening of 22 March, for news of his *Maison Militaire*, it was resting exhausted fifty miles away at Beauvais (where Artois dismissed the last remaining regular troops). On 22 March, on the prompting of Maréchal Macdonald, who throughout this period was admirably loyal, resourceful and energetic, Louis decided to head for Lille after all, and sent orders to the *Maison Militaire* to go straight there, rather than rejoining him at Abbeville. Although according to Macdonald, Louis still wanted to go to Lille via the coastal route, he was persuaded by Macdonald to go the quickest way via Saint-Pol and Béthune.

Louis's journey north showed that his reign had not been entirely a deceptive façade. In 1791, Louis XVI had fled Paris in disguise, but was stopped by the hostile authorities and a partly hostile population. In 1814, on his way from Fontainebleau to Elba, Napoleon I had been shunned by the authorities and greeted with indifference or hostility by the people. But in 1815, during his flight from Paris, Louis XVIII was treated completely differently. France was now a thoroughly monarchical country, and the pacific, liberal, legitimate monarchy introduced by Louis XVIII was, in many areas, extremely popular. Everywhere along the route from Abbeville to Lille Louis was treated as the king by the authorities and received an ecstatic reception from his subjects despite the shame and humiliation of his flight. At Béthune, where he took a bowl of chocolate, most of the population got up at five o'clock in the morning to greet him. At Lille, where he arrived on 23 March, the population cheered him wildly as he drove to the Préfecture. But, despite the Royalism of the town, the troops remained grimly silent.[12]

The failure of Louis's policy in March 1815 now became fully apparent. Not only had he and his Government refused to stay and fight in Paris as they had promised, but they had not even made plans for a place of retreat for the king on French soil. Orléans and Maréchal Mortier, who were in command in Lille, were more interested in the defence of the frontier than in the cause of the king, and had ordered the troops back into their barracks in Lille. The presence of troops sympathetic to the emperor inside the city walls was as crucial at Lille as it would be at Bordeaux in ruining any effort to hold those cities for the king in 1815. And Louis had no loyal force of his own since the troops of the *Maison Militaire*, rapidly decreasing through desertion, were still plodding through the mud of Picardie. (Fanny Burney, De Vigny, Lamartine and Aragon in *La Semaine Sainte* have left marvellous descriptions of this panic-stricken retreat).

Louis could still have tried to go from Lille to Dunkirk, a

passionately Royalist town with good communications with England, and he was urged to do so by Blacas and Orléans. But he was much less keen to take risks than any of his entourage, and he was still without any loyal armed force of his own. Indeed at Lille he received a letter from Artois stating that the *Maison Militaire* might be going to Dieppe. Louis insisted on putting a frontier between himself and the rebellious army, although Blacas stopped him leaving Lille the night of his arrival. The next day, 24 March, still cheered by cries of '*Vive le Roi*' from the people of Lille, and escorted by a regiment of *Chasseurs* and by the loyal *Garde Nationale de Lille*, Louis crossed the frontier into Belgium at Menin. Maréchal Macdonald claims that on the way to the frontier he saw '*les populations à genoux dans la boue, levant les mains vers le ciel et suppliant le Roi de ne pas les abandonner*' ('people on their knees in the mud, raising their hands to heaven and begging the King not to abandon them').[13]

Once he crossed the frontier, Louis proceeded via Bruges to Ostend, hoping to meet the *Maison Militaire* in Dunkirk, whither he had ordered it to proceed: he simply had not had the courage to take the direct route on French soil from Lille to Dunkirk. But the orders to Artois did not get through, and the commander of Dunkirk refused to hand the town over to Louis. Alone and abandoned in the house of Madame de Bal in Ostend, Louis probably thought of going to England, whither at Abbeville, he had ordered Hue to take the crown jewels. Blacas wrote to Castlereagh asking for boats '*pour le transporter où sa presence sera jugée utile*' ('to take him where his presence will be judged useful') – possibly Bordeaux but more likely Dover – on 25 March. And the next day Jaucourt, the only minister apart from Blacas who was with Louis, wrote to Talleyrand: '*La philosophie du Roi va droit à Hartwell*'. ('The King's resignation takes him straight back to Hartwell.') It was a sad, dry and revealing phrase which shows that Louis had almost lost hope. Indeed most people now assumed he would go to England like Feltre, the Minister of War, Montesquiou, the Minister of the Interior, many other officials and even Orléans.[14]

But on 26 March, Blacas went off to see Artois and the remainder of the *Maison Militaire* (450 men in all) at Ypres, and their consultations, as well as a letter from the Prince of Orange, produced the advice that Louis should not cross the Channel. For once Louis was quite right to listen to his younger brother, who was perfectly capable of giving excellent advice. On 30 March, having been refused the palace of Laeken by the King of the Netherlands, Louis moved to Ghent, where he was lent the beauti-

ful and majestic eighteenth-century *hôtel* of the Comte d'Hane-
Steenhuyse. That evening, after shaking hands through the windows of the enormous entrance-hall of the Hôtel d'Hane with
the cheering crowds outside, he sat down to a huge Belgian dinner
at which – but even for Louis it seems incredible – he ate a
hundred oysters.[15]

That night his sleep, as well as his digestion, must have been
rather disturbed. Only a month ago he had been reigning happily
in the Tuileries. But the reception accorded to Napoleon I had
revealed the existence of violent hatred of Louis's regime not only
in the army but also in certain classes in the east of France. Two
weeks ago he had been proclaiming his desire to die in the defence
of his *Charte*. Yet he had turned and run, which was exactly what
Bonapartists like Fouché and Sébastiani, and renegades like Mortier and Orléans, had wanted. In contrast Louis's niece, the Duchesse d'Angoulême, had displayed immense courage in Bordeaux.
Not only had she inspired and commanded her own forces, but
she had dared to enter hostile barracks to try to rally Bonapartist
soldiers to her side. Napoleon I himself had shown less courage
when faced with a hostile crowd, and his comment on the Duchesse d'Angoulême, which was common currency by 15 April, and
which Louis almost certainly read, showed genuine admiration:
'*C'est le seul homme de cette famille.*' ('She is the only man in
that family.')

This damning remark shows that the return of Napoleon I had
exposed not only the weaknesses of Louis's regime, but also
Louis's personal weakness of fearfulness and an inability to stand
firm in the defence of his own cause. It was, in part, as a result
of this weakness that at Ghent in the first days of April 1815,
Louis was almost completely alone, with only a discredited reputation for company. He was only accompanied by a few courtiers
like Duras, Poix and Havré, by personal servants like Guignet
and Gonet and by Blacas and Jaucourt. On 19 March, Louis had
ordered all his ministers, after they had done what they could to
maintain *le bon ordre* – the king might flee, the emperor might be
advancing, but the social order must go on – to join him in Lille.
But they did not obey: why should they when Louis himself fled
to Abbeville rather than going straight to Lille? They either bolted
to England or went to the country. Even Berthier, who had followed Louis to Ostend, decided to go and watch the crisis in
comfort in his castle in Bavaria, rather than do his duty as a
Capitaine des Gardes. As Louis had found out during the Revolutions and the Emigration, there was almost no one he could
rely on, not even his own ministers. If he gave an inconvenient or

unpopular order, his subjects were perfectly prepared to disobey him.

Louis was also alone in an even more serious way. His allies, who had reaffirmed their support of him by a declaration on 13 March, began to have their doubts. Was Louis really the right monarch to back? The Tsar, in particular, was sceptical, for he had little reason to like Louis. In 1814, Louis had refused the offer of the Tsar's sister, the Grand-Duchess Anne, as a wife for the Duc de Berri, largely on the grounds of religion. The Tsar insisted on her arriving in France as an Orthodox princess with Orthodox priests in her household, which Louis, who regarded Catholicism as one of the distinguishing traits of his family, would not allow. But Louis also disliked the Tsar because he had openly supported a more liberal version of the *Charte* and, against all principles of *moralité publique*, had wanted Prussia to annex Saxony; Louis wrote that the Tsar had '*le ton et les principes qu'avec raison on reprochait à B.P.*' ('the tone and the principles for which, quite rightly, B.P. was blamed'). In addition, it is more than likely that for Louis the Romanovs (or rather Holsteins as they now were) were simply a jumped-up family with a history of lunacy.

It was bad enough to have his own sister turned down and his expansion thwarted by a monarch who only a few years ago had been begging for more roubles. But Alexander I had also been bitterly offended that he had not been given the *Saint Esprit*, and that Louis had refused to make his great friend Caulaincourt, who had assisted the kidnapping of the Duc d'Enghien in 1804, a peer: Pozzo di Borgo, the Russian ambassador, had actually spent two hours in audience with Louis trying to convince him to give in, but the king had refused, saying that if Caulaincourt became a peer, Condé and Bourbon, Enghien's grandfather and father, would refuse to come to Court. After all these pin-pricks it is hardly surprising that on 11 April Wellington, who had returned from Vienna to take up command in the Netherlands, wrote that the Tsar 'detests and is decidedly against the Bourbons', and was thinking of backing Orléans or even his own brother-in-law, the Prince Royal of Württemburg, as sovereign of France. And even Wellington had his doubts, until the end of April, about the wisdom of supporting such an obviously weak king, who had not known how to maintain himself on the throne of France.

Louis, who realized that this was what the Allies would say, and almost certainly knew of Napoleon's devastating comment about his lack of courage, had an answer ready, as he always did. On 26 March, when he was at Ostend wondering whether or not to go to England, he wrote to Talleyrand that '*la défection totale des troupes ne me laissait pas le choix du parti que j'avais à prendre*' ('the complete defection of the troops left me no choice as to what decision to take'). It was all a question of force, and force, that is to say the French army, was with a few exceptions on the side of Bonaparte. In such circumstances flight was the only solution. This is confirmed by what happened in Bordeaux. The Duchesse d'Angoulême, unlike her uncles, was heroic; the people, the *Volontaires Royaux* and the *Gardes Nationales* were even more Royalist than in Paris. But nothing they could do was of any importance in comparison with the attitude of the regular troops, who easily put the amateur Royalist forces to flight. Even the Duchesse d'Angoulême, not by nature inclined to favour moderate solutions, saw that to prolong a civil war would only cause needless bloodshed, and on 2 April, after only three days' active resistance, sailed for England. Thus the major mistake of the First Restoration was not political but military: the decision to maintain the existing French army. Nothing, not even Ney's suggestion in May 1814 to keep on the *Garde Impériale* as the king's guard, could have stopped the Napoleonic army from preferring to fight for rather than against the emperor (in 1815 even Dutch troops who had been in his army demonstrated in favour of Napoleon I). But how could Louis have dissolved the old army, raised a new one and, at the same time, have hoped to act as a great power at the Congress of Vienna? As with the question of the *Droits Réunis*, Louis put the needs of the French state first, although he knew that they went against the interests of French Royalism.

Events at Bordeaux also bore out, to a lesser extent, another vital point in Louis's letter to Talleyrand: '*Buonaparte a donc pour lui la force armée; tous les coeurs sont à moi. J'en ai vu des preuves non équivoques tout le long de la route. Les puissances ne peuvent donc douter cette année du voeu de la France. Voilà le texte, je m'en rapporte à vous pour la glose.*' ('So Bonaparte has force on his side; all hearts are for me. I have seen unequivocal proof of this all along my route. So the powers cannot doubt France's desires this year. That is your text, I leave the commentary to you.') Like his letter to Liverpool in January 1814, this letter shows that Louis was prepared to base his kingship on popular feeling as well as on dynastic right.[16]

Louis's claims were an exaggeration. But public opinion during the Hundred Days was in many parts of France passionately Royalist. All northern France was fundamentally Royalist, as many reports addressed to Napoleon I testify. The mayors of the small frontier towns of Armentières, Hazebrouck, Bailleul and Aire even came to Ghent to offer Louis 500,000 francs. Normandy and the north-west also remained Royalist. Priests prayed for the king, not the emperor, at Sunday Mass; the Mayor of Verneuil in Normandy, when asked why he was displaying the white flag of the Bourbons rather than the tricolour, replied that rats and crows must have eaten the blue and red in the tricolour. Bordeaux, Toulouse and the Midi were passionately Royalist, and helped the Angoulêmes in their brave efforts to resist Napoleon. Marseille, which owed its *franchise* to the personal efforts of Louis XVIII, was suitably grateful. An English visitor to the port found it, like Bordeaux and Toulouse, 'a very Bourbon place', and in May a *Lieutenant de Police* wrote to Fouché that there were so many white flags that it was impossible to find any white cloth to buy.[17] In Paris itself, although sections of *le peuple* supported the emperor, much of the bourgeoisie remained loyal to the king. The *Garde Nationale* was unenthusiastic about the emperor, and thirty of its members are said to have gone to Ghent to exercise their privilege of guarding Louis on 3 May, the anniversary of his entry into Paris. One member of the *Garde Nationale de Paris* claimed that even the '*forts de la halle*' ('porters in the market') were Royalist. So the cheers which had greeted Louis every Sunday morning in the *Salle des Maréchaux* and the *Jardin des Tuileries*, to which Royalists often referred during the Hundred Days, had not been an entirely deceptive façade.

The main reason why Royalism was so widespread in France in 1815 was that it was not just a dynastic cause. What differentiates the Royalism of the reign of Louis XVIII, and of 1815 in particular, from the Royalism of the 1790s and the legitimism of the period after 1830 was that it was urban and liberal as well as rural and reactionary. Many people who were Royalist in 1815, such as Guizot, Lainé, Maréchal Gouvion Saint-Cyr and the student volunteers from the *École de Droit* who came to Ghent, were dedicated liberals who supported Louis for the sake of the liberal constitution he had granted, rather than out of respect for his dynastic rights – an impressive testimony to the degree to which the *Charte* carried conviction in 1815. A large proportion of the educated, urban middle classes had similar views. Very few great towns, with the exception of Dijon, Paris, Lyon and Strasbourg, displayed much support for Napoleon I, as is shown by the tiny proportion of adult males – all of whom had the right to vote – who voted yes in the plebiscite Napoleon I held in May to approve his new constitution: Dijon 23 per cent, Lyon 15 per cent, Paris 12 per cent, Strasbourg 11 per cent, Toulouse 5 per cent, Lille 4 per cent, Bordeaux 3 per cent, Orléans 2 per cent, Nantes 2 per cent, Marseille 1 per cent.

The same historian who has studied this plebiscite has also produced a fascinating map of Royalist and Bonapartist France which is confirmed by all contemporary sources. Very roughly speaking, the area within two lines drawn from La Rochelle in the centre of the west coast of France, north-east through Paris to the frontier near Mons, and slightly south-east past Lyon to Grenoble and the Alps supported Napoleon I and gave him his enthusiastic reception in March, while the area outside those lines supported Louis XVIII and made his retreat a triumph. Which monarch had the support of the majority of his subjects is impossible to say. If they had areas almost equal in size, Louis had the towns and the women. Only 21 per cent of the male electorate of about 7.5 million voted yes in the plebiscite, an immense decrease over the figures for Bonaparte's plebiscites in *An X* and *An XIII*. However, many of the peasants and workers who cheered Napoleon I in the Dauphiné and Lyon did not bother to vote – another sign of the *démission* of *le peuple*, which was such an essential feature of this period.[18] Perhaps each monarch had the support of about half of France.

If it is difficult to assess the exact extent of support for Louis XVIII and Napoleon I in 1815, it is even more difficult to decide why some people, towns or provinces supported one monarch and not the other. What seems clear is that it was not fundamentally a conflict of principles or class. In many ways the two regimes, at least in 1815, were remarkably similar politically and socially. On the surface Napoleon I had been converted to liberalism, and, in imitation of Louis XVIII, now offered a Chamber of Peers as well as a Chamber of Representatives, and a liberal constitution: there was far more liberty in France during the Hundred Days than before the return of Louis XVIII. It is not true to say, as Beugnot had in one of his police reports to Louis, that '*la vieille haine est toujours là entre l'ancien régime et la révolution*' ('the old hatred between the revolution and the old regime is still there'). People or towns who had figured prominently in the Revolutions found it as easy to support the king as the emperor. Marseille, which had sent so many volunteers to attack the Tuileries in 1792, and Bordeaux, the home of the Girondins who condemned Louis XVI to death in 1793, were passionately pro-Louis XVIII in 1815, while Lyon, which had been relatively Royalist in the 1790s, was enthusiastically Bonapartist. Many politicians who owed their prominence to the Revolution, such as Baron Louis, Talleyrand and Beugnot himself, supported Louis XVIII in 1815, just as many supporters of Napoleon I came from *Ancien Régime* families which detested the Revolution (for example the Montesquiou, the La Bédoyère and the Molé) and no doubt saw in Napoleon I the best man to master revolutionary fervour. Even the bitter question of the *biens nationaux*, the Revolution's most poisonous legacy, was not a decisive factor in all regions, since there were Royalist purchasers of *biens nationaux* in the Royalist areas of the Midi and the north: the same problem could have completely different effects in different parts of France.

The conflict between the king and the emperor, the blue and the green, was no more a matter of class than it was of political principles. This is shown by the number of splits which took place within families like the La Bédoyère or the Montesquiou (the *abbé* de Montesquiou was Louis's Minister of the Interior, the *comte* de Montesquiou was Napoleon's Grand Chamberlain). There was considerable support for both monarchs in every class. Napoleon I even had devoted admirers among the clergy. The Archbishop of Besançon, whom Artois had treated so rudely, wrote to the emperor that he was '*semblable à la Divinité même*' ('like God himself') – Louis XIV himself had never received such ecstatic praise.

Both monarchs had support from the urban and rural masses as well as fronm the elites. Indeed so great was the distrust and even hatred of the elites for the poor in this period that both Royalists and Bonapartists tended to exaggerate each other's support in this class. On 16 March the *Moniteur* actually proclaimed that the populace of Maçon and Tournus had welcomed Bonaparte while a few weeks later the *Garde Nationale* of Valence denounced the supporters of the Duc d'Angoulême to the emperor as '*la lie du peuple*'. The people of towns in the east like Nancy, Metz and Belfort, as well as Lyon, were sufficiently Bonapartist to riot in the emperor's favour. But the people of Marseille and Bordeaux were Royalist enough to try to assault military commanders like Maréchal Masséna and General Decaen, not for being Bonapartists, but for not being more Royalist.

What really induced different provinces, towns and individuals to support either the king or the emperor was not so much their social origins or political principles as their own particular interests, tastes and ambitions: in other words, as with the people who prevented the royal troops destroying their bridges, daily life determined political attitudes. In some cases the origin of these attitudes is quite obvious. Thus the support of Lyon for the emperor was clearly connected with the fact that it was one of the few towns to have done well out of the Empire, while great ports like Bordeaux and Marseille supported Louis XVIII largely because his restoration meant the restoration of peace and overseas trade. Many bourgeois or members of the elite supported the king because they felt that, as Maine de Biran stated, all social bonds were connected with respect and love for the legitimate king. In other words the king was the guarantee of the social order which protected their daily lives.[19] Maine de Biran, like many people in 1815, even felt that France was unworthy of such a good king as Louis XVIII.

But in many cases political commitment seems to have been as emotional and instinctive as, for example, the reasons why some people prefer blue and some prefer green, or why some prefer violets – the Bonapartist flower – and some prefer lilies – the emblem of the Bourbons. Indeed these differences of emblems and colours, rather than differences over social and political issues, are the contrast most frequently drawn between Louis XVIII and Napoleon I in the countless political prints of the Hundred Days (although the presence of priests in Louis's entourage is often noticed very unfavourably). Since emotions were particularly powerful during the Restoration, and helped determine the character of the two regimes as well as their chances of survival, it is necessary to analyze them in some detail. Moreover, popular emotions and opinions, rather than political principles and parliamentary debates, were the area of politics which Louis himself always thought most important, (see page 130).

Perhaps the most powerful emotion on the side of Louis XVIII was most French people's longing for peace and quiet and *repos*. Already, in the late 1790s, *lassitude* had been one of the most powerful forces drawing people back to the monarchy (see page 122). In 1815, after endless wars and the death of hundreds of thousands of Frenchmen on the battle field, this feeling was even stronger; and, as we have seen, Louis had made it one of the main themes of his speeches in 1814. Many people, like the Mayor of Grasse, believed that Louis was the best guarantee of France's tranquillity, and so were natural supporters of his monarchy.

Another powerful emotion on the side of the king, connected to the widespread longing for *repos*, was the instinctive love and support of most Frenchwomen. All contemporaries, whether they were in Toulouse or the Tuileries, noticed the especially enthusiastic Royalism of women. '*Les femmes qui faisaient la force du parti royaliste*' ('women who were the real strength of the royalist party') wrote Queen Hortense, and there were good reasons for this. The return of peace and reduction of conscription (but not, as had been promised, abolition) meant that Frenchmen were now available to act as brothers, sons and husbands rather than to disappear into an exclusive, male world of battles, barracks and brothels.

Louis was very conscious of being the restorer not only of his dynasty, peace, liberty, *repos* and commerce, but also of the French family: his parting words on 19 March 1815 – '*Retournez dans vos familles*' – show his concern quite clearly. A picture painted in 1814 and bought by the Duc de Berri also shows how eager the Bourbons were to found their reign not only on dynastic right but also on more solid, popular feelings. Called '*Une des Croisées de Paris le jour de l'Arrivée de S.M. Louis XVIII*' ('One of the windows of Paris the day of the arrival of H.M. Louis XVIII') it shows a mother with her son and daughter. Poor enough to be living in an attic, they have been restored to life and hope, less danger of conscription for the son, more likelihood of a husband for the daughter – by the return of the king.[20]

The appeal to women even extended, in the gentlest possible way, to gallantry. One of the most popular wallpapers of the Restoration, designed in 1814 or 1815 by Louis Laffitte, *Dessinateur du Cabinet du Roi* was called '*Les Amours de Psyché*': under the Empire wallpapers had usually depicted military victories. A favourite song of the *Gardes du Corps* of Louis XVIII was

> *Le Roi, nos dames et l'honneur*
> *Partagent notre vie.*
> *Aimer est le plaisir du coeur,*
> *Aimons donc à l'envie*

'The King, our ladies and honour occupy our lives. To love is the heart's delight, so let us love with all our hearts.' One could never imagine such lines being sung by the soldiers of the *Garde Impériale*. In 1817 a print of the *Garde Royale*, headed '*Vive la Gloire et les Belles*' had as its captions, *Honneur, Courage, Amour* and *Amitié*. Again it is unlikely the last two emotions would have been proclaimed by the *Garde Impériale*. The Restoration was a much more emotional, and social, regime than the Empire.

This great wave of appeal to women had its effect not only in demonstrations in the streets or the theatre but also in the hearts and minds of individual women. The letters and diaries of women as different as Madame Champagne, the wife of a legal official in a small town in Burgundy called Semur, and the Duchesse d'Abrantès, a sophisticated Napoleonic duchess, burn with real, passionate love for Louis XVIII in 1815: the Duchesse d'Abrantès even hoped that her lover would be jealous. A famous beauty like Madame Récamier was so Royalist that love for her made Benjamin Constant, one of the most influential journalists in the country, write a passionately Royalist article in the *Journal des Débats* on 19 March, when Napoleon was only a few miles from Paris, saying '*Je n'irai pas, misérable transfuge, me trainer d'un pouvoir à l'autre, couvrir l'infamie par le sophisme et balbutier des mots profanes pour racheter une vie honteuse*' ('I will not be a miserable traitor and drag myself from one power to another, disguising infamy with sophisms, and muttering shameless phrases to make up for an existence without honour').

Honour, which had already done so much to protect Louis when he was an exile, was another emotion which made people support his cause in 1815, as the song of the *Gardes du Corps* and the print of the *Garde Royale* imply. All soldiers and officials had sworn an oath to Louis XVIII in 1814, and Napoleon I himself had told his last defenders at Fontainebleau to serve the king as well as they had served him. Many people felt tied to Louis XVIII by this oath, from which he had not released them – just as, in World War II, the soldiers and officers of the German army felt tied to Hitler by the oath they had all sworn to him. At Gap on 5 March, when the emperor was only a few miles away, Captain Fantin des Odoards wrote in his diary that honour and duty bound him to the king, although he longed to join the emperor. At the time, he remained loyal to his oath.[21] It was probably honour, the refusal to change allegiance yet again, as much as love for the regime of Louis XVIII, which made so many generals and marshals of the Empire refuse to serve their emperor in 1815. Of the twenty surviving marshals of France, thirteen served Napoleon I, but three (Berthier, Victor and Marmont) followed Louis XVIII abroad and four (Pérignon, Macdonald, Oudinot and Gouvion Saint-Cyr) refused to serve the emperor and passed the Hundred Days on their estates.

If love and honour were, in 1815, Royalist emotions, ambition, fear and nationalism were the feelings which drove people to rally to the emperor. Napoleon I, the most glamorous and for a time most successful ruler in modern history, clearly had more appeal for the ambitious than Louis XVIII, who preferred to rely on Frenchmen's love of *repos* and family life. It was not only the fact that he had lost the official position he had held under the Empire which made Stendhal, fairly representative of the younger generation of Bonapartists, revere Napoleon I and detest Louis XVIII. It was also that the qualities he most admired, heroism, audacity, vaulting ambition, were characteristic of the Empire, but had little place in the quiet, domestic reign of Louis XVIII.

Moreover, there were more specific reasons why the ambitious should prefer Napoleon I. Thousands of people had suffered checks in their careers by the restoration of Louis XVIII. And it was among these people that Napoleon I found some of his most violent supporters in 1815: even a former Royalist conspirator in the 1790s, called J. P. Didier, who felt disappointed in his ambitions in 1814, supported Napoleon I during the Hundred Days. In 1814, the *Conseil d'État* had been reorganized to include many Royalists, and had become much less important with the increased role given to the two chambers. Naturally it presented the emperor with a violently anti-Royalist address. Fouché had been deprived of political office during the First Restoration; he became Minister of Police on 21 March.

The most extraordinary case of blind ambition determining someone to rally to the side of the emperor was Benjamin Constant who, for the sake of immediate success, did all the things he had said he would not do in his diatribe of 19 March. His diary for 14 April reads: '*Entrevue avec l'Empereur, longue conversation, c'est un homme étonnant. Demain je lui porte un projet de Constitution. Arriverai-je enfin?*' ('Interview with the Emperor, long conversation, he is an astonishing man. Tomorrow I will take him a draft of a Constitution. Will I make it at last?') And indeed the old yearning passion to arrive was finally satisfied: *Conseiller d'État* with a yearly salary of 20,000 francs, attendance at the *levers* of the emperor and Prince Joseph, dinners with Napoleonic duchesses ... Unfortunately for Constant, he had backed the wrong monarchy. No one in the political world would ever forget the shameful, ludicrous contrast between his words and his actions in 1815. He would never again hold political office until the fall of the Bourbons – only a few months before his own death.

Fear as well as ambition, drove people into the emperor's camp. There was widespread fear, fanned by Napoleon I's early proclamation in March, among the peasants that the nobles and the clergy meant to recover their feudal dues and their tithes. This fear partly explains the welcome the emperor received in Dauphiné and Bourgogne. Again, one sees how dangerous Louis's friends were to his cause; this fear must have had its origins in the furious words and threats of the Ultra-Royalists because nothing of the sort actually happened. The *Journal de la Côte d'Or* published in Dijon revealed the strength of this fear when it claimed on 2 April that '*Les Bourbons paraissaient ne régner*

*que pour un petit nombre de familles dont les prétentions deven-
aient chaque jour plus insolentes*' ('The Bourbons seemed only to
reign for the benefit of a few families, whose pretentions were
growing daily more outrageous'). Fear also drove people to support the emperor because the one thing almost everyone in France
was terrified of was civil war (see page 225). Thus events during
the Hundred Days were largely conditioned by three great fears:
fear of the Ultra-Royalists, fear of civil war and Louis's fear of
being captured.[22]

By far the strongest emotion working for Napoleon I was
nationalism. That Louis should come to the throne as a result of
the defeat of the French armies, and that he should display such
fondness for the English, was too much for many French people
to accept. Hatred of foreigners was widespread in France in 1814–
15 and the *Nain Jaune* rated the feeling of national humiliation,
and the loss of the victorious tricolour, as the most important
cause of the fall of the Bourbons, before the tactlessly antique
formes of the Government, the fears of the *acquéreurs*, the creation of the *Maison Militaire* and the princes' tours. Under normal
circumstances a monarchy's greatest strength comes from its appeal to nationalism, and from the emotional identification of king
and country. But in 1814 the monarchy of Louis XVIII was
deprived of this strength, since nationalist feelings in France tended to be associated with the emperor and his defeated army.

Moreover, Napoleon I cleverly played on these nationalist feelings in his first proclamations in March 1815, referring to Louis's
tactless speech of thanks to the Prince Regent and to the *gloire*
that France would recover under its emperor. Nationalist feelings
were particularly strong in the east of France, always the best
recruiting area for the French army, even in the eighteenth century.
Moreover, the east had a particular reason for feeling violently
nationalistic in 1815. The behaviour of the Allies, in particular
the Russian and Prussian troops, in the east in 1814 had been so
beastly that already, in March 1814, a guerilla war had broken
out against them. The inhabitants of the east were longing to get
their own back in 1815, and this is the explanation for the widespread support for Bonaparte in eastern France put forward by
Louis himself, who was quite as eager to blame his Allies for
everything as General de Gaulle would be a hundred and forty
years later.[23]

On the other hand, not everyone in France in 1815 was dominated by feelings of vengeful nationalism, and many people realized that Napoleon I was far from being the best representative
of the national interests of France. Despite his early, deceitful

declarations that he had returned by agreement with the Allies, it soon became clear that his return meant yet another war between France and the whole of Europe: the Allies' hesitations about backing Louis were not known to the public, and died down after April. Thus it was evident that to support Napoleon I was to invite another war, probably leading to another catastrophic defeat. Perhaps, after all, it would be wiser to support the king.

CHAPTER XI

The Return of the King
May–September 1815

The realization that Louis's Allies were likely to win, as well as the feelings of love, duty and self-interest which drew people to the royal cause, meant that very soon, at least among the political elite, it became apparent that it was not to support the Empire. '*L'opinion est toujours mauvaise*', ('Opinion is still unfavourable',) admitted Constant on 27 April; and Castellane wrote on 1 May: '*Le gouvernement de l'Empereur Napoléon marche à grands pas vers la dégringolade.*' ('The government of the Emperor Napoleon is heading straight for collapse.') Whereas for many people in 1815 Louis remained *le Désiré*, for even more he was *l'Inévitable*, the monarch most likely to succeed. An enormous proportion of officers and officials who had served the Empire before 1814 remained aloof from the Hundred Days, and only 39 per cent of the electorate of about 100,000 voted in the legislative elections.[1]

Gradually the empty antechambers of the Hôtel d'Hane, through which Louis waddled every day to hear Mass just as he had at the Tuileries, began to fill up with floating notables bravely rallying to the winning side. The Duc de Feltre arrived on 1 April, and provided Louis with an utterly loyal Minister of War as well with a visible sign that much of the Napoleonic nobility now preferred Louis XVIII to Napoleon I. Chateaubriand arrived on 10 April, Beurnonville in late April, Dambray in early May, Baron Louis and Beugnot on 12 and 19 May, and Guizot and Mounier at the end of May. By then Louis had the full panoply of a Royal Government in exile: forty-eight Court officials and servants, eighty officers of the *Maison Militaire*, eighty-six officers and thirty-three Government officials, all living in accommodation allotted to them by the *Maréchaux des Logis du Roi*, the body which from time immemorial had arranged the lodgings of the Court of France when the king was on his travels.

In addition, in nearby Alost, under the command of the Duc de Berri a small army, consisting of the remainder of the *Maison*

Militaire, Volontaires Royaux (including fifty-seven volunteers from the *École de Droit*), and some regular soldiers, sprang up, despite the disapproval of Blacas, who was terrified that public opinion would see in it a new Coblentz: from about 400 to 500 in early April, it rose to 816 on 22 April and 2,100 by early June.[2]

Ghent also soon filled up with people not directly attached to the Royal Government, arriving out of curiosity, loyalty or ambition: actors and actresses, journalists like Bertin, Lacretelle and Bergasse, bankers like Greffuhle and Ternaux, Chateaubriand's friends the Duchesses de Duras and de Lévis and Lamartine's future muse, Madame Charles. Louis could soon say, like his ancestors the Dukes of Burgundy of the fifteenth century, that he held '*Tout Paris dans mon gand*' ('All Paris in my glove' – Gand is the French spelling of Ghent).

Indeed after the moment of resignation at Ostend, Louis struck all observers at Ghent as remarkably cheerful and optimistic, convinced that France could not do without him, that Bonaparte not himself was to blame for the Hundred Days, that the faults of his Government were as nothing compared to the Allies', and in particular the Tsar's, mistake in putting Bonaparte on Elba in the first place. Louis's cheerful conviction of his own indispensability is apparent in the splendid, contemptuous remarks he made to his followers when they straggled in to Ghent. To M. de Barentin, a former *Garde des Sceaux* and a living embodiment of the traditions of the magistrature of the *Ancien Régime*, who was trying to explain the fact that he had sworn an oath which acknowledged Bonaparte as emperor, Louis said '*J'entends . . . vous avez jurotté; à votre âge on ne fait plus les choses qu'à demi*' ('I see . . . you muttered it; at your age one can only do things by halves'). To an officer of the *Gardes du Corps* who appeared at Ghent particularly late, he said '*Ah! vous voilà, monsieur d'Albignac! . . . Déjà!*' ('Ah! there you are, monsieur d'Albignac! . . . Already!') When Baron Mounier, a typical representative of the moderate and influential politicians whose support was so necessary for running France, whose arrival at Ghent was a striking coup for the royal cause, appeared at the Hôtel d'Hane, Louis said in his cool royal way, '*Bonjour M. Mounier, je suis bien aise de vous revoir*' ('Good morning, M. Mounier, I am very happy to see you again').

But the greatest tribute to the strength of Louis's character and to his imperturbable optimism comes from the pen of Chateaubriand, who had many opportunities to observe the king as he was appointed Minister of the Interior *par intérim* in early April. Although Louis based his appeal to his subjects on peace, liberty and *repos*, he himself never doubted that he was king by dynastic right, and it was this aspect of his character which most impressed Chateaubriand in the trying circumstances of the Court of Ghent. '*Louis XVIII ne perdait jamais le souvenir de la préeminence de son berceau; il était roi partout comme dieu est dieu partout ... La foi inébranlable de Louis XVIII dans son rang est la puissance réelle qui lui rendit le sceptre ... Le banni sans soldats se trouvait au bout de toutes les batailles qu'il n'avait pas livrées. Louis XVIII était la légitimité incarnée; elle cessa d'être visible quand il a disparu.*' ('Louis XVIII never forgot the preeminence of his birth, he was the king everywhere, just as God is God everywhere ... Louis XVIII's unshakeable faith in his own rank is the real force which gave him back the throne ... The exile without soldiers benefitted from all the battles he did not fight. Louis XVIII was legitmacy incarnate; it ceased to be visible when he died.')

Beneath the splendid prose, there is a core of truth: if Louis had behaved like Napoleon I in April 1814 and June 1815, Louis-Philippe I in 1848 or Napoleon III in 1870, if he had assumed that he had lost his throne when he lost his capital, then his exile would have been as ignominious as theirs. But, as he had shown in 1803, Louis was not the abdicating sort of monarch. Furthermore, his monarchy was a much more resilient institution than the First or Second Empires, or the July Monarchy, and it had the vital strength of widespread and active support in the provinces. Thus, even in the Hôtel d'Hane in Ghent, Louis seemed so much the King of France that not only his own subjects, but also hardened diplomats like the Russian, Austrian and English ambassadors, went out of their way to serve him far more than their own Governments wanted. 'I cannot but like old Louis, I have known him for twenty years, and really believe he is the best king for all of us', wrote Sir Charles Stuart, who deserted his post at the Hague to be ambassador to the exiled Court in Ghent.[3]

Underneath the smooth royal façade he presented to the outside world, however, Louis was having to make some grave decisions in his *Cabinet*. There were people in his entourage, such as Artois, most of the Court officials and Ferrand (who sent Louis notes from France), to claim that the débâcle of the Hundred Days showed how unsuitable the *Charte* was for a country like France, and that at the very least there must be punitive measures against the traitors who had helped the usurper recover his throne. Even moderate figures like Lainé, the President of the Chamber of Deputies and Pozzo, the Russian ambassador, were in favour of death and the confiscation of their property for the principal

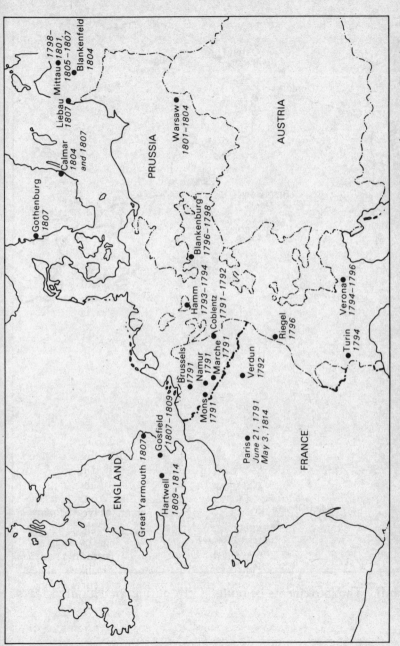

Map 1 Louis's travels in exile, 1791–1814. The frontiers shown are those of France, Prussia and Austria in 1795, except for the thick line, which represents the French frontier in 1789.

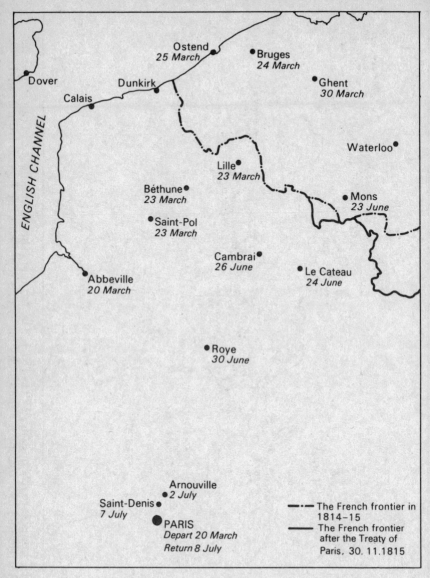

Map II   The movements of Louis XVIII during the Hundred Days.

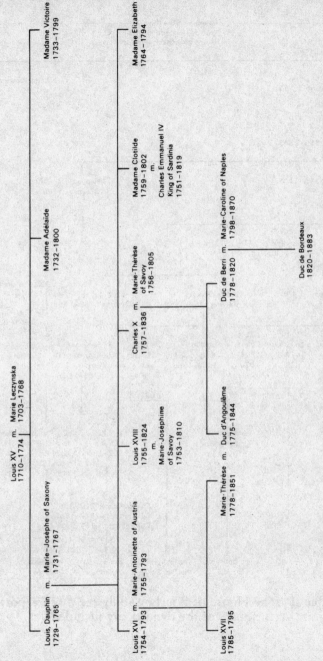

Table I The Royal Family of France (only people mentioned in the text are included).

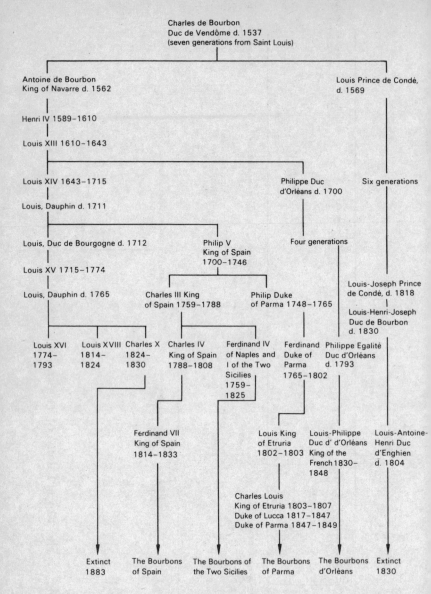

Table II   The House of Bourbon (only the most important members of the dynasty are included).

accomplices and officials of Napoleon I: those who were politically most moderate were often most extreme in their demands for vengeance. All round him people were telling Louis that a liberal constitution and a policy of forgiveness had been tried and found wanting. Would the adaptable king listen to these urgent, plausible voices?[4]

On the whole, with a few waverings, Louis stuck to the *Charte* and his policy of moderation. On 15 April a declaration was composed, countersigned by Feltre, promising rewards for the faithful but no vengeance on the guilty, and swearing to '*faire disparaître jusqu'à la trace des abus qui pourraient avoir eloigné de nous quelques français*' ('to eliminate every trace of abuses which could have alienated some Frenchmen from us') – a brave admission of mistakes, and a bold pledge of moderation. But this declaration was never published, probably because foreign powers, in particular Wellington and the Netherlands Government, were opposed to French declarations issued on foreign soil without their advice. From now on foreign advice, in particular that of Wellington, Stuart and Pozzo, carried a weight in Louis's Councils which it was not to lose for three years: Louis readily recognized the fact that the English and Russian armies were where power now really lay. The next manifesto, dated 24 April, but not published until 21 June, was also extremely mild, to the horror of Lally-Tollendal. He was a representative of liberal opinion whom with Chateaubriand, Louis had, on Artois's advice, called to the Council in early April, and who favoured a policy of severity. The manifesto of 24 April again promised forgiveness to the guilty and rewards for the loyal, acknowledged that the Royal Government had committed some faults, and swore to uphold the *Charte*.[5]

After this moderate beginning, however, Louis's Government became considerably more severe, and it is possible to see in this evolution the influence of Artois, constantly at Louis's side, whose letters are utterly direct, decisive, self-confident and self-satisfied, even in the middle of the most shattering crisis. On 21 April, Stuart wrote of Artois's 'ascendancy over the king's mind', and on 11 May, Jaucourt complained to Talleyrand that '*toutes les fois que le roi pense à loisir Monsieur pense avec lui*' ('Every time the king thinks at leisure, Monsieur thinks with him'). Certainly the year 1815 was the high point of Artois's influence over his brother until 1822. But the more severe policy probably also reflects the influence of foreign powers, who believed in force as the best solution for France's problems.

For the next declaration, published on 5 May, was drawn up,

at least in part, by Stuart and Pozzo as well as by Blacas (it was countersigned by Dambray). It insisted that the Allies would respect the territorial integrity of France, and stated that France and the Bourbon dynasty, representative of *la légitimité* (which now makes its appearance as a key theme in Royalist propaganda), had the same interests. But although it referred to *réconciliation générale*, this declaration was more threatening in tone, promising to punish '*chefs traîtres et parjures*' ('faithless and treacherous leaders'); and, although it emphasized Louis's desire to defend the constitution, it made no specific reference to the *Charte*. Although this is certainly simply a result of carelessness over words, it did alarm many people.[6] And the instructions sent to Louis's representatives in the provinces, including Angoulême who was waiting in Spain for a chance to recover the Midi, show that although the intention of Louis's Government was to stick to the *Charte*, its representatives were empowered to take emergency measures under Article 14, which gave the king the power to issue '*ordonnances nécessaires pour l'exécution des lois et la sûreté de l'État*' ('*ordonnances* necessary for the execution of the laws and the safety of the State').

From his hand-written corrections to another declaration it is clear that Louis himself was now in favour of a policy which used Article 14 to punish some of the Bonapartist leaders, although not the mass of Bonapartists, whom he wisely called '*hommes faibles et égarés*'. And an *ordonnance* of 20 May, drawn up by Dambray, Lainé and Chateaubriand in retaliation for the confiscations Napoleon I decreed but did not actually carry out, and for his Government's punitive measures against Royalists in the Vendée, threatened all ministers, judges and prefects who helped in the punishment of Royalists with confiscation of their property, and other penalties. This was an extreme measure which appalled Jaucourt, Baron Louis and Beugnot, who managed to stop its publication for a time. Thus in exile Louis had, to a certain extent, deserted the path of moderation by his invocation of Article 14 (the fatally tempting article which Charles X would use to justify the *ordonnances* of July 1830 which lost him his throne) and by his willingness to use harsh measures against some Bonapartists. But this was a mild enough reaction from a sovereign faced with an unprecedented avalanche of treason. And Louis had, as even the references to Article 14 prove, stuck to the *Charte*, the most useful document he ever signed.[7]

In addition to the differences over policy raging in Louis's Council, there were even fiercer rivalries over personalities. Louis was very worried about his cousin the Duc d'Orléans, perhaps even more than about Bonaparte. At Lille on 23 March, Orléans had expressly told the officers under his command to obey the dictates of their patriotism rather than of their military duty. This meant in effect that he relieved them of their oaths of loyalty to the king. Clearly Orléans was trying to dissociate himself from the cause of Louis XVIII, and throughout the Hundred Days he refused to obey Louis's orders to come and join him in Ghent. Instead he sent copies of their correspondence, in which he accused Louis of wanting to restore the *Ancien Régime*, to Talleyrand, Wellington, Castlereagh and the regent, obviously in order to discredit the king in their eyes.

He was almost openly proposing himself as a candidate for the throne of France. In May he received an emissary from Fouché, and during the Hundred Days many French officers and politicians came to think that Orléans was the best solution. The Tsar had expressed support for Orléans in April and the old nightmare of a *parti d'Orléans* seemed for the first time to be becoming reality. Even in Louis's Council Lally, Chateaubriand and perhaps even their patron Artois were in favour of putting Orléans at the head of the army – an extraordinary idea which could only have arisen in the panic atmosphere of exile. But Louis would have nothing to do with it.

Chateaubriand was also, like many others, in favour of putting at the head of the Council the second of the two dangerous monsters roaming outside the badly weakened stockade of French Royalism in 1815, the Prince de Talleyrand. One of the most remarkable examples of the rapid transformations so common in Court and political life is the deluge of devoted and servile letters which reached Talleyrand from Ghent, begging him to come and put himself at the head of political affairs. On 5 May Louis himself, aware of Talleyrand's immense prestige both at home and abroad, urged Talleyrand to come and give him the benefit of his *sages avis*.[8]

In concert with the plan to recall Talleyrand, who was still busy with the final act of the Congress of Vienna, was a campaign to get rid of Blacas. The First Restoration had ended in disaster and Blacas, who had few friends except the king, was the perfect scapegoat. Although he was not responsible for such mistakes of the First Restoration as the organization of the ministry, the formation of the *Maison Militaire*, Ferrand's speech and the behaviour of the princes and the Ultra-Royalists, Blacas was blamed for everything, not only at Ghent but also in Paris, where an English visitor found that Blacas was 'execrated'. From Ghent, Jaucourt wrote to tell Talleyrand to denounce Blacas to Louis not by letter, because Blacas saw Louis's letters, but by sending someone to speak with the king. (Jaucourt even said that Blacas wrote Louis's replies to Talleyrand, but this is untrue from the evidence of the original drafts in the Quai d'Orsay, all but one of which are in Louis's hand. Even assuming, for the sake of argument, that Louis wrote them at Blacas's dictation, would Blacas have thought of comparing Metternich and Caroline Murat to Antony and Cleopatra?). So Talleyrand sent Alexis de Noailles, the same person who had appeared in the summer of 1812 at Hartwell, to Ghent in May and when he was presented to Louis, Jaucourt was careful to draw Blacas aside to a window, so that Noailles and the king could have a private conversation. Louis's letter of 5 May to Talleyrand was probably a result of Noailles's mission.

Blacas was not only Louis's principal secretary, but also the official in charge of his Court, and as his *Grand Maître de la Garde-Robe*, a man who had the right to be constantly in attendance on him, except when he was giving private audiences; Noailles was given a private audience a few days later. A man with so much power who was responsible only to the king was bound to offend all those who, like Talleyrand, wanted a responsible, united ministry. Moreover, as his opposition to the summoning of the chambers in March had shown, Blacas was usually opposed to those measures which smacked of popularity – although he was by no means the mindless reactionary some of his colleagues tried to make out. Blacas's friend the Neapolitan ambassador showed that he knew what was going on when he wrote to Blacas to make sure that his colleagues wrote down their opinions on every important issue '*afin qu'ils ne puissent pas tout rejeter sur vous*' ('so that they cannot blame everything on you').[9] But this is exactly what they were succeeding in doing.

The problem of Blacas epitomized one of the greatest problems of Louis's reign. Louis divided people into the useful and the loyal. Because of the political events of the last twenty-five years he found that most loyal Royalists had no experience of political life inside France and were of very little use. So, as he complained to Lord Harrowby on 6 April, he was forced to employ people he could not trust because those whom he could trust were 'not fit to be employed'. And the instructions of early June to Angoulême, and to his representatives in Paris (Maréchal Macdonald, four representatives of the *Ancien Régime*, the Bailli de Crussol, the Président de Grosbois, the Vicomte du Bouchage and the Marquis d'Herbouville, and four representatives of the new France, Barthélemy, Sémonville, Chabrol-Crousol and Pasquier), show that Louis still made the distinction between the useful and the loyal.

They were enjoined to employ Royalists, but not those who were '*entièrement étrangères aux affaires*' or unpopular. Blacas had been utterly loyal, but he was neither experienced nor tactful. Above all, he was too unpopular to be kept on. Louis was probably resigned to letting him go by the beginning of June.

On the other hand, Talleyrand, the man the diplomats, the courtiers and the ministers now wanted at the head of affairs, was extremely capable. He had a past which was a guarantee to all those who had taken part in the Revolution and the Empire; but he was utterly untrustworthy. Louis could hardly forget that, as Foreign Minister of the Republic and the Empire, Talleyrand had ordered almost all the moves against him between 1797 and 1807, although it is doubtful if Louis knew of the suggested kidnapping of 1797 until after 1817, if then. And Talleyrand was as disloyal in the present as he had been hostile in the past.

For, as Napoleon I and the French army marched towards the Belgian frontier in June, Talleyrand began to wonder which side would win after all, the king or the emperor, the blue or the green. So like Louis's ministers after 19 March, and Orléans in April, he refused to obey Louis's appeals to come immediately to Lille or Ghent. He lingered as long as he could in Vienna, until 10 June, and then slowly made his way towards Belgium – or Wiesbaden, where he was said to have rented a house. Visibly, he was waiting to find out who was going to win the war, although his admiring biographers have been strangely reluctant to point this out. The great Allied victory at Waterloo on 18 June galvanized Talleyrand, and the entire French political world, into action.[10]

It had been a long day in the Hôtel d'Hane. Every coach was harnessed and ready to dash for Antwerp in case the French army won; and at ten o'clock a false alarm almost made Louis leave. But Berri reassured him and finally, early on the morning of 19 June, a letter from Pozzo brought the news of Wellington's splendid victory. At first Louis wanted to send the *Maison Militaire* – presumably escorting himself – south-west to Bailleul and Armentières, in the passionately Royalist area of French Flanders which had supported 'Louis XVII' in 1814. But Wellington, who on 16 May had refused to send troops to help a Royalist rising in this area on the grounds that it was more important to win the war than to help a side-show, did not want to let Louis out of his control. He wanted to use the prestige of the king's name to weaken French resistance and persuade French commanders to surrender the fortresses barring the route to Paris, thus ensuring a speedier end to the war and preserving the lives of his troops. For the French army had been defeated in battle but had by no means been wiped out, and as late as 2 July Wellington wrote to Blücher that he felt he could not take Paris by force. So Wellington instructed Feltre and Berri, on 20 June, to move south-east to Mons behind the victorious Allied army.[11]

Louis agreed to, or rather obeyed, this direction and so lent himself to the celebrated, never-forgotten accusation that he returned to his capital '*dans les fourgons de l'etranger*' ('in the baggage-train of the foreigners'). This is of course quite true for 1815 (although not for 1814). Moreover, not only did he return in the baggage-train of the foreigners, but he had done everything possible to bring about and associate himself with their victory over the French army. His devoted Minister of War, the Duc de Feltre, sent Wellington long and detailed reports on the numbers, position and morale of the French army in April and June, based on information brought to him from Paris by officials of the Ministry of War. On 19 June, Louis wrote a long and extremely pompous letter of congratulation to Wellington for winning the battle of Waterloo: '*je félicite de tout mon coeur le Premier Général du Monde*' ('I congratulate with all my heart the First General in the World'). Would not silence and neutrality really have been wiser?

The explanation of Louis's attitude – and that of almost all his followers, whether liberal or reactionary – in 1815 is that they felt that the enemy was Bonaparte and his army, not the French nation, which the Allies, or so Wellington proclaimed in a general order to his army, regarded as an ally. The twentieth century has known many examples of an army and its leaders acting in total opposition to the wishes of the people, and this was the Royalists' view of what was happening during the Hundred Days. So Louis felt that, in contrast to 1814, he could now drink to the success of the Allies against the Bonapartist army '*sans cesser d'être français*' ('without ceasing to be French') – and so he told Maréchal Victor, one of his many followers from the former French army, at dinner on 20 June. The best thing for all concerned in this terrible war would be to get it over as quickly as possible, and Louis was prepared to help in any way Wellington thought suitable.[12]

On 22 June Louis and his Court, escorted by the magnificent troops of the *Maison Militaire* and by the enthusiastic volunteers of the *Armée d'Alost*, set off for France. Louis was overjoyed to be leaving the dreariness of exile for the joys of Paris and said to Guizot that they were now '*du bon côté de la glissoire*' ('on top of the slide'). On 23 June, the Court reached Mons, the same town where, on exactly the same date twenty-six years earlier,

Louis had had his first dinner in freedom with d'Avaray and Madame de Balbi after his escape from France. Talleyrand also arrived on 23 June, and the conflicts over personalities and policies which had swirled round Louis at Ghent now reached hurricane force.

Talleyrand had come with well-prepared plans of his own. He wanted not only Blacas and the princes but also Louis himself out of the Council, and in this he was supported by political allies like Chateaubriand, Lally and Jaucourt. Thus he wanted to reduce Louis to the role and status of a King of England (Castlereagh was also enthusiastically in favour). He also wanted a revision of the *Charte* in a more liberal sense; and he agreed with Metternich, Foreign Minister of his favourite foreign country Austria, that Louis should not associate himself too blatantly with the foreign invasion, and should go somewhere not occupied by foreign troops like Lyon.[13]

The rage of the great diplomat, who felt called by public opinion and force of circumstance to command every aspect of the Royal Government, can easily be imagined when, on arriving in Mons, he found that Louis was holding a Council with Blacas, Artois, Berri and Feltre. After a deliberation of several hours, Louis decided, possibly against Blacas's advice, to follow Wellington's instructions and cross the French frontier behind the Allied army. Talleyrand was horrified, and he was supported by most of the politicians, Jaucourt, Baron Louis, Chateaubriand, Guizot, Mounier, Lally and Anglès. That night Louis said goodbye to Blacas, to whom he had already, on 22 June, written a cold, embarrassed, confused letter of farewell *'pour m'épargner la douleur de la prononcer'* ('to spare me the pain of saying it'). As with his words of farewell to the *Garde Nationale* on the night of 19 March, one notices the same desire on the part of an elderly king whom events were treating rather harshly to avoid anything as embarrassing as a scene.

As he set out for France at eight o'clock on the morning of 24 June, however, there was a very tense scene with Talleyrand. Only just out of bed, the treacherous prince, pale with anger, could not believe that his invaluable advice was being ignored. He threatened not to follow his master. The king, making a reference to the waters of Wiesbaden, where he suspected Talleyrand had been heading earlier that month, said in his cool, royal way, *'Prince, vous nous quittez? Les eaux vous feront du bien; vous nous donnerez de vos nouvelles'* ('Prince, you are leaving us? The waters will do you good; you will send us your news').[14]

Louis had stuck to the course he had intended to follow as

early as 6 April, and was making a quick dash for Paris. With
hindsight this decision seems extremely unwise, since it confirmed
his association with the foreign invasion. Perhaps Louis should
have gone to one of the many towns – Dunkirk, Amiens, Marseille
or Montpellier – which, all over France, were declaring themselves
for the king, without the help of a foreign invasion, at the end of
June.

But at the time there were very powerful reasons for pressing
on behind Wellington. Napoleon I had abdicated on 22 June in
favour of his son, but real power had fallen to the two chambers
and a Commission of Government headed by Fouché. The politicians in Paris, masters of the capital as it oscillated between two
(or three – Orléans had many advocates) monarchies, could not
fail to try to exploit their position. Louis would find it much
easier to keep them under control from the Tuileries than from
Amiens or Lyon: one of the first rules in politics, as C. P. Snow
has written, is 'never to be too proud to be present'. Moreover,
there were other dangers to parry. Blücher and the Prussian army
were marching on Paris and, as their conduct towards their own
allies in Belgium had shown, they were capable of anything. It
would clearly be best to get to Paris as quickly as possible. So
Louis pressed on.

At the frontier he was greeted by the local *curé* and his congregation in their Sunday best, and had the pleasure of listening
to the first loyal address he had heard for months. That evening
he arrived at Le Cateau where he was also 'very well received',
according to an English eye-witness. Meanwhile back at Mons a
storm of intrigues now raged round the livid Talleyrand. Finally,
but not until 26 June, he condescended to join Louis. Despite the
allegations of Beugnot and Chateaubriand in their memoirs, who
claim respectively that it was Talleyrand's uncle the *Grand Aumônier*, or Duras, a *Premier Gentilhomme*, who arranged the
reconciliation, it seems clear that, as both Talleyrand and the
Prussian ambassador wrote at the time, it was Wellington, the
commanding figure in the whole situation, who persuaded Talleyrand to swallow his immense pride and follow the king. He
must have been helped in his decision by the knowledge that
Blacas had finally left for England and that some perfectly moderate politicians, Laborie, Beurnonville, and Beugnot, as well as
Dambray, Feltre and the Court, had already left Mons to follow
the king.[15]

Meanwhile, Louis had been continuing the policy of relative
severity announced in the declaration of 5 May. On 23 June at
Mons, he had rejected a plan put forward by Vaublanc, an Ultra-

Royalist adviser of Artois, to govern France until further notice according to Article 14 of the *Charte* – a fatal proposal which might have advanced the Revolution of 1830 by fifteen years. But on 25 June, at Le Cateau, Louis did publish a proclamation, reflecting his own ideas and those of Dambray and Feltre which, although promising to govern according to the constitution he had given France, also promised to '*récompenser les bons, mettre en execution les lois existantes contre les coupables*' ('reward the worthy, put into execution the existing laws against the guilty') – a vague but, for many Frenchmen, extremely alarming phrase.

The next day Louis proceeded to Cambrai, where Talleyrand joined him on 27 June. Already what Wellington called 'the influence of His Majesty's name' was having an impressive effect, and the citadel of Cambrai, which had refused an Allied summons to surrender, and towns like Le Quesnay and Péronne, were opening their gates when called to do so in Louis's name. Louis was as useful to Wellington, as Wellington was to Louis, in clearing the route to Paris. On 27 and 28 June the Council furiously debated another proclamation; and there were some particularly violent scenes between Talleyrand and Berri. The final version of the Proclamation of Cambrai, probably on Louis's instructions, omitted many phrases in Talleyrand's and Beugnot's original drafts, such as '*devant faire des fautes et je ne sais si moi-même j'en ai toujours été exempt*' ('bound to make mistakes, and I am not sure if I myself have always been free of them'), which directly inculpated Louis and his family. Instead the Proclamation of Cambrai only admitted that Louis's Government may have made mistakes – a much more dignified solution.

But although Talleyrand had been eager to put the blame for the faults of the First Restoration on Louis or his family, he could be a wise as well as an unscrupulous politician. The Proclamation of Cambrai also contained promises of forgiveness for all who had served the usurper while Louis was on foreign soil between 23 March and 26 June 1815, except for the instigators and authors of the Hundred Days, and it contains a phrase which at once became very popular: '*je veux tout ce qui sauvera la France*' ('I desire everything which will save France'). The popularity of this merciful and sensible proclamation shows how unwise Louis had been to listen to the counsels of severity in May-June 1815. His old tendency to reflect the views and pressure of those round him – in particular of his younger brother – had made him seem weak and unreliable, the most dangerous qualities of all in a king.

Once the Proclamation of Cambrai was issued, the Court, now swollen by the magnificent troops of the *Cent-Suisses* as well as by emissaries from Fouché and from leading generals like Oudi-not and Lauriston, began to move, on Wellington's instructions, towards the capital again. It reached Roye, north of Compiègne, on 30 June. Even Talleyrand, persuaded by Louis, now admitted that he had been wrong about the Court's movements, and real-ized that most French garrisons off Louis's path would not sur-render 'until the fate of Paris shall be decided'.[16]

Meanwhile Wellington, whose headquarters was always further advanced than the Court of France, was listening to some prop-ositions which confirm that in 1815 Louis represented French national interests at least as well as his opponents. It has already been pointed out that the great strength of Napoleon I lay in his appeal to French nationalism and French hatred of the overbear-ing, plundering Allies. And the belief that Napoleon I was par-ticularly 'national' persists to this day. Yet in fact he and his supporters were just as keen as Louis and the Royalists for foreign intervention in French affairs, if it suited them, and they were even less French in their attitude to the throne. Before 1814 three of Napoleon I's four titles had been foreign (he was *Roi d'Italie*, *Protecteur de la Confédération du Rhin*, and *Médiateur de la Confédération Helvétique*, as well as *Empereur des Français*), and it could certainly not be said he was acting in French national interests after 1804. In March 1815, he returned boasting that he was acting in agreement with the Allies – a boast as treacherous and unpatriotic as Louis's and Artois's boast in 1792 that they were invading France on behalf of the king.

On 29 June and 1 July 1815 five deputies representing the two chambers asked Wellington to agree to 'any other Prince of a Royal House' becoming King of France instead of Louis (Queen Hortense, who may well have been aware of Alexander's mention of his brother-in-law, and Caulaincourt, in 1814, were more specific and mentioned a Romanov Grand Duke). That people who thought of themselves as patriotic Frenchmen should prefer 'any' foreign prince to Louis XVIII seems extraordinary, especially since Wellington told them and, according to Pozzo, they agreed, that the restoration of Louis XVIII would be *'le meilleur moyen ... de conserver l'intégrité de la France'* ('the best way ... to preserve the integrity of France'), since the Allies would trust him more than any other ruler.

But Bonapartist party spirit and fear of the Ultras were stronger than love of country. They wanted a monarch who would need them, rather than a king who had many devoted followers of his own, whatever the cost. Thus what really distinguished Napoleon I and what was sometimes called the *parti national* from Louis

XVIII and the Royalists was not in fact patriotism or love of France, but their competition for the same positions and their attitude to the Revolution. In July 1815 Benjamin Delessert, an important Paris banker who would become a leading figure of the July Monarchy, told Lady Shelley: 'We require a national King not a *roi des émigrés*. We resent any semblance of a reflection being made upon us for having served our country in the Revolution.' Thus the word 'national' had little to do with love of France. Nor did it mean love for the principles or gains or men of the Revolution, none of which could seriously be said to have been threatened by the Restoration. What really united the *parti national* was pride in the Revolution, which certainly was threatened by the Restoration, which could see in it nothing but a bloodthirsty and unnecessary waste. Private emotions such as pride and fear really were the most powerful forces of all in the public life of early nineteenth-century France.[17]

In fact Wellington sent the five deputies away with recommendations to rally to Louis XVIII, which they were all secretly preparing to do any way. Now escorted by detachments of the *Gardes Nationales* of the northern departments, as well as by *Volontaires Royaux* and the ever-swelling numbers of the *Maison Militaire*, Louis, on Wellington's instructions, moved from Roye to Arnouville, only six miles from Paris, on 2 July. Here he was greeted by 'all Paris', streaming out in their Sunday best to take advantage of the 'fine hot day' and have a picnic as well as display their loyalty to their king. With tears in his eyes, Louis greeted Vitrolles, the *Secrétaire d'État*, who had been briefly imprisoned by Fouché for his brave role in the Royalist resistance in the Midi, with the words '*Heureux ceux qui ont souffert, le royaume des cieux leur est réservé*' ('Happy are they who have suffered, for they shall enter the kingdom of heaven') – a remark which, as Vitrolles points out in his memoirs, did not promise much for them on earth. For now Louis faced one of the strongest intrigues of his reign, launched to get him to take as one of his ministers the defrocked Regicide who had spent the last four months as Bonaparte's Minister of Police, Fouché, Duc d'Otrante, President of the Commission of Government which was in control of Paris.

From before the beginning of the Hundred Days, Fouché had been in touch with the Royal Government and in May had started sending assurances of support to Ghent. Louis had said; '*Jusqu'ici je ne vois que des phrases, il faut pourtant que les services précèdent les récompenses.*' ('So far it is just a matter of words, but deeds really must come before rewards.') But Fouché had found the means to convince Artois and many Ultra-Royalists including

Vitrolles (who had already shown their weakness for violent ministers as well as violent policies by backing Soult as Minister of War in 1814), and above all the Duke of Wellington himself, that he was the indispensable fixer who would mastermind the dissolution of the Commission of Government and the two chambers, the entry of the king into Paris and the end of the war. Even Louis's own commissioners in Paris such as Maréchal Macdonald and Pasquier, who had entirely failed to form a government or take command of the situation, seem to have agreed.[18]

At Roye, when Talleyrand proposed taking Fouché as a minister, Louis had said '*Jamais! Jamais de vingt-quatre heures*', comments Chateaubriand. Louis was now paying the price of his haste to be back in Paris and his reliance on the Duke of Wellington. On 7 July, he arrived at Saint-Denis; according to Sergeant Mercer his face wore 'an expression calm, serious and unvarying in general, occasionally illuminated by a faint smile'. The smile must have faded at the prospect of seeing Fouché and receiving his oath as minister. One of the most celebrated passages of French prose has preserved the scene for ever. Chateaubriand was waiting in one of the rooms preceding Louis's study in the abbey of Saint-Denis. '*Tout à coup une porte s'ouvre et entre silencieusement le vice appuyé sur le bras du crime, M. de Talleyrand marchant soutenu par M. Fouché; la vision infernale passe lentement devant moi, pénètre dans le cabinet du Roi et disparaît. Fouché venait jurer foi et hommage à son seigneur; le féal régicide, à genoux, mit les mains qui firent tomber la tête de Louis XVI entre les mains du frère du roi martyr; l'évêque apostat fut caution du serment.*' ('Suddenly a door opens; silently there enters vice leaning on the arm of crime, M. de Talleyrand walking supported by Fouché; the infernal vision passes slowly in front of me, reaches the king's study and disappears. Fouché had come to swear allegiance to his lord; on bended knee the loyal regicide placed the hands which had caused the death of Louis XVI between the hands of the brother of the royal martyr; the apostate bishop stood surety for the oath.') Even though Louis had disliked his brother, had thought him a fool and had opposed his policies with violence and deceit in 1791–92, he had realized what a blow to the French monarchy Louis XVI's humiliating execution had been (see page 75). Now he was reduced to taking one of the people who had voted for his brother's death, the butcher of Lyon, as a minister. One royal official wrote that it was more startling and horrifying than the commander's statue coming to life at the end of *Don Juan*.[19]

Louis however, firmly rejected all attempts to persuade him to abandon the white flag for the tricolour, now more than ever a symbol of revolt. The tragedy was that, although convenient, it was not really necessary to take Fouché as a minister. Maréchal Davout, Commander-in-Chief of the defeated French army, was convinced of the inevitability of Louis's restoration as early as 27 June, and worked towards it throughout the crisis. From the evidence of the enthusiastic hordes at Arnouville and Saint-Denis Louis could have judged that he would be well received in Paris – not only out of Royalist fervour but for the very good reason that the Parisians, like Louis himself, saw him as the best protection from Prussian pillaging. At Saint-Denis one enthusiastic group of *École de Droit* students, crying '*Vive notre roi deux fois désiré*', went down on their knees weeping with joy at the sight of the calm, unruffled face of their *bon Père*.

His reception as he entered his capital on 8 July down the Rue Saint-Denis, underneath the Arc de Triomphe erected by Louis XIV, was much more enthusiastic than in 1814. Even Byron's friend Hobhouse, a fervent Whig Bonapartist who hated the Bourbons with all the contempt he felt for their ally the English Government, wrote that Louis was greeted by 'very long and loud' acclamations, at least from some quarters. Louis himself wrote to his old friend and courtier La Chatre: '*Dieu seul connaît le fond des coeurs; mais à juger par les apparences (qui ne trompent guère quand elles sont aussi générales) la journée du 8 juillet a été plus belle que celle du 3 mai.*' ('Only God can see into people's hearts; but to judge by appearances [which are usually reliable when they are so general] the 8 July was an even finer day than the 3 May.')[20] Throughout the day Louis, normally so cool and calm, was in one of his very rare states of 'great emotion and exultation' at the reception he had been given.

Louis now showed what an extraordinary man he was, and that an aged, infirm legitimate monarch, born and bred at Versailles, could on occasion display a desire for contact with the crowd which would not disgrace a twentieth-century politician. When he arrived at the Tuileries at the end of the morning he made the thousands of people who had crowded into the palace courtyard fall silent, and delivered a short speech which has not been recorded but in which he addressed them as his *amis* (the accolade he had refused the army of Coblentz in 1792) – perhaps the first informal speech a European monarch had ever made to his subjects. In the afternoon he went even further and, in an unparalleled act of condescension, went into the garden of the Tuileries to mingle with his subjects (see illustration 11). No other French monarch had ever *strolled* among his subjects in his own capital, except in disguise or under compulsion: just as he was less remote from the elite, Louis XVIII was less remote from the Parisians than Louis XV, Louis XVI or Napoleon I.

That evening, after telling Fouché to arrest Bonaparte, Louis gave Wellington and Castlereagh a long audience during which, Castlereagh wrote, 'it was almost impossible to converse so loud were the shouts of the people'. Finally, at the end of a long, tiring but exhilarating day, Louis had candles brought and showed himself at an open window with Wellington and Castlereagh to his fervent subjects. They ran from all corners of the garden to form 'a solid mass of immense extent, rending the air with acclamations'. Thereafter, throughout the summer, to the fury of Fouché, groups of people regularly assembled in the garden of the Tuileries, ecstatically singing '*Rendez-nous notre père de Gand (bis). Avec lui chacun était content*' ('Give us back our father of Gand [twice]. Under him everyone was happy'. *Père de Gand* is another pun, for *paire de gants*), crying '*Vive le Roi*' and even – and this is what most struck contemporaries – dancing in his honour (see illustrations 11 and 12). The Restoration was a social, as well as a political event, which inspired Royalists with the warmest feelings toward each other as well as toward their king: French nobles and foreign generals, surely for the only time in their lives, joined hands with perfectly ordinary people to dance in the *Jardin des Tuileries* in honour of the second return of Louis XVIII.[21]

How representative these crowds were of the mass of Parisian opinion is hard to say. Certainly the pro-tricolour, pro-Napoleon feeling of the end of March persisted in some of the poorer *Faubourgs*, where there had been disturbances between 4 and 6 July. The crowds in front of the Tuileries, on the other hand, look far too well-dressed to be representative of the poor (this is confirmed by a drawing of the Fête de Saint Louis in 1815, see illustration 12). One English observer thought that the dancers in the garden were above all the young, shopkeepers and their wives and farmers who had come in from the country. Every observer noticed the especially fervent Royalism of the women.

Thus enthusiastic Royalism was probably limited in Paris to the middle and upper classes. Louis was cheered by many fewer people, and sometimes by none at all, when he went out for his afternoon drive in his carriage. One Royalist from Bordeaux who often saw Louis in the streets, observed that he had '*l'air triste et préoccupé*', which was hardly surprising.[22]

For his palace was surrounded not only by enthusiastic crowds but also by English and Prussian troops, whose guns were trained

The meeting of Louis XV and Marie-Joséphine of Savoy in 1771.
The King is pointing Louis out to the bride.

Monsieur, Comte de Provence, by Duplessis. Duplessis was considered the most faithful portrait painter of the day.

Madame, Comtesse de Provence, pointing to a bust of Louis, in front of a portrait of her father. She was uglier than this portrait suggests.

Madame de Balbi. Madame de Balbi was Louis's closest friend from 1781 until 1794.

The Comte d'Avaray. D'Avaray, Louis's 'liberator' in 1791, was his devoted friend, courtier and adviser from 1791 to 1809.

Gosfield Hall, Essex. Louis is shown strolling in the grounds with three courtiers. He sent Melling to paint this scene of his exile in 1817.

Louis XVIII in 1814. This is one of the few pictures to be
frank about the extent of Louis's stomach.

Louis's arrival at Calais in 1814. The Duchesse d'Angoulême is on Louis's left.

Soirée at the Odéon, 1814. This shows Louis and the Royal Family being *idolâtré*, as they so often were in 1814. The women were especially enthusiastic.

The departure of Louis XVIII, 1815. He is saying goodbye to loyal Gardes Nationaux. Maréchal Macdonald is second from Louis's left, Blacas is looking over the King's left shoulder.

The return of the King, 1815. Some of his subjects were now so Royalist that they knelt at Louis's feet (cf. previous illustration). As always, Gardes du Corps are beside the King.

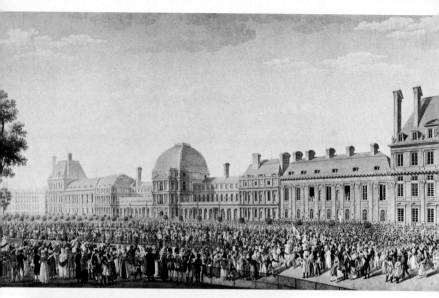

Above: The Fête de Saint Louis, 1815. Note the quality and variety of the crowd's clothes. Louis lived on the first floor, to the left of the right-hand pavilion.

Left: Louis XVIII in his Cabinet in the Tuileries. This portrait was held by those who knew him well to be the only one which really conveyed the look in Louis's eye.

The reception of the Duchesse de Berri, 1816. Artois and Angoulême are on Louis's right, Berri and the Duchesse d'Angoulême on his left. Talleyrand is standing behind him.

The Duc de Richelieu. He was a loyal and moderate *Président du Conseil* from 1815 to 1818, and 1820 to 1821.

The Duc Decazes. He was Louis's favourite, and a leading Minister, between 1815 and 1820.

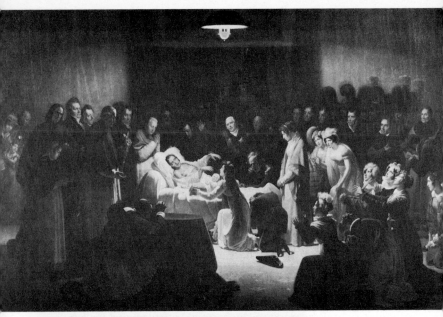

Above: The last moments of the Duc de Berri, 1820. Louis and the Royal Family are at the foot of the bed, Decazes and Chateaubriand to the right, Berri's illegitimate daughters on the far left.

Left: Madame du Cayla and her children. Madame du Cayla was Louis's last favourite, from 1821 to 1824.

on the Tuileries and whose soldiers guarded its approaches. Foreigners were everywhere in Paris, parading in the Place de la Concorde, camping in the Champs Elysées, behaving with all the insolence and swagger of conquerors. The Prussians distinguished themselves by their brutality and the English by their drunkenness: amazed Parisians could hear *les goddons* singing 'Louis dix-huit, Louis dix-huit, We have licked all your armies and sunk all your fleet', as they staggered down the boulevards. In the provinces the Prussians, in accordance with their traditions, had settled down to plunder without mercy a country which was officially their ally, and they even imprisoned four of Louis's prefects. They behaved so badly that Wellington suggested that they leave France.

Meanwhile, as Allied troops spread over most of France (by September 1815 1,226,000 occupied sixty-one departments – all but the south-western quarter of the country), Ultra gangs began to settle old scores in the Midi, killing hundreds of their enemies. Angoulême acted as his own master in Toulouse and Bordeaux, replacing the Royal officials appointed by his uncle, from 23 July to 14 August. It seemed as if France was falling apart, and to add to his difficulties Louis had a ministry he could not trust. In addition to Talleyrand who was *Président du Conseil*, and Fouché, it included two of Talleyrand's allies, Jaucourt and Baron Louis, as Minister of the Marine and Minister of Finance, and two Napoleonic figures who had been loyal Royalists during the Hundred Days, Baron Pasquier and Maréchal Gouvion Saint-Cyr as Minister of Justice and Minister of War. It was the most anti-monarchical ministry of Louis's reign, and was dedicated to measures such as the heredity of the peerage, the liberty of the press and the sharing of the crown's legislative initiative with the two chambers, to which Louis was personally opposed. Metternich wrote to his daughter that he would not be in Louis's place for anything in the world.[23]

One way in which Louis reacted to his terrifying situation was to withdraw even further from active political life. In 1814, his Council had included three princes and seven *Ministres d'Etat*, who were not responsible to the chambers, as well as three ministers with departments (Talleyrand, Dambray and Montesquiou), who were. Louis had not felt bound to take the advice of his responsible ministers, and he had occasionally taken initiatives over policy: for example over the creation of the *Maison Militaire* and the composition of the *Charte* (which had been drawn up independently of the Council), over Parma and the Two Sicilies and in financial matters.

After the Hundred Days, however, Louis accepted a completely different sort of Council, without princes or *Ministres d'État*. The ministers now thought of themselves as members of a united, responsible ministry, headed by the Prince de Talleyrand, Louis's first *Président du Conseil*, a post approximately the same as that of prime minister. Nearly all documents issued from Talleyrand's office in the summer of 1815 bear the ostentatiously collective signature of *le Ministère du Roi*. For the rest of his reign, Louis not only almost always accepted the proposals of his responsible ministers, but left almost all policy initiatives to them. Consequently Louis had become a fully constitutional monarch, far more prepared to leave the business of government to his ministers than, for example, his cousin Orléans would be after he ascended the throne as Louis-Philippe I in 1830.

Louis was helped to adopt this new role by his own experience and inclinations. When advised, a year later, to intervene with a senior politician in order to get a new law adopted, he refused, saying *'je n'aime pas à sonner souvent mes grosses cloches'* ('I do not like to bring up my heavy artillery too often'). And this phrase is very characteristic of Louis's attitude in government. He had been disobeyed so often – by his family, by his ministers and by his subjects – that he saw little point, and considerable humiliation, in trying to govern by use of his own authority. It was much better to leave almost all aspects of policy to his responsible ministers. So in the summer of 1815, he accepted the heredity of the peerage, although he thought it gave too much independence to the peers – one of the last manifestations of that monarchy/ aristocracy conflict which had been so strong in his youth. According to Talleyrand, Vitrolles (still *Sécretaire d'État*) and Ferrand, Louis allowed Talleyrand to name all the new peers, and he left it to Talleyrand to add on the names of Blacas and La Chatre. Pasquier, Minister of Justice, reorganized the *Conseil d'État*, removing most of the incompetent *Conseillers d'État* appointed in 1814, and appointed many new prefects, including six who had served in the Hundred Days – was treason to be rewarded with promotion? – without any interference from the king.[24]

Even during the Talleyrand ministry, however, the nadir of Louis's power and prestige during his reign, he was never as cut off from the actual day-to-day business of government as was, for example, his friend the Prince Regent. Although the organization of the Council of Ministers, and of ministerial business, can only be deduced from a few references in politicians' memoirs and letters, it seems clear that Talleyrand's plan to exclude the king from the Council (confirmed by an *ordonnance* of 8 July) was quietly dropped, as was his plan to share the crown's legislative initiative with the two chambers – a tribute to Louis's ability to defend his royal authority in a characteristically calm and unobtrusive way. Although the ministers now met every day in Talleyrand's *hôtel*, they also, as in 1814–15, met once or twice a week, on Wednesday and Sunday afternoons, in Louis's *Grand Cabinet* in the Tuileries. Louis also continued to *travailler* alone with each of his ministers (which, almost always, meant him signing what they put before him) at least once a week.

According to most of the evidence, and to the recollections of at least some of his ministers (for example Portal and Clermont–Tonnerre, ministers of the Marine from 1818 to 1821, and from 1821 to 1824), Louis showed considerable interest in the more important issues of politics, such as the progress of the elections, the state of the navy and the passage of a law through the chambers. Until the end of his reign he continued to see many, although not all, diplomatic despatches (it is not known what criteria were used for choosing which despatches to show him), and to be at the centre of the French Government's policy-making and information-receiving machinery. For example, in the autumn of 1818, when the *Président du Conseil* and Minister of Foreign Affairs was away at a congress, he kept Louis informed of its progress in frequent letters, sent Louis all relevant documents, and showed great curiosity about Louis's conversations with foreign sovereigns.[25]

Louis retained the opportunity of exerting influence over policy and, very occasionally, he used it. For example, at one Council meeting in 1815, against the wishes of Talleyrand but in accordance with the inclinations of Fouché, Louis was able to ensure that censorship of newspapers was continued: as he had shown in 1814, he was least liberal about the liberty of the press.

Another important matter in which Louis intervened in the summer of 1815 was in the organization of his guard. One of the most crucial tasks facing the Royal Government during this period was to reorganize the French army. An *ordonnance* had been issued at Ghent, allegedly dated from Lille on 23 March, which dissolved all rebellious army units. And, after the remains of the French army beyond the Loire had submitted to Louis on 14 July, this dissolution took place. For a time the French army practically ceased to exist, while Gouvion Saint-Cyr organized a new volunteer royal army, consisting of one legion per department, and composed of 'guaranteed' Royalists (the western and northern departments were, naturally, much quicker to raise their legions than the eastern departments). In addition, between October 1815

and March 1817 two commissions, one headed by General Beurnonville, the other by Maréchal Victor, both containing majori-
ties of ex-Napoleonic soldiers loyal to Louis XVIII, examined the
careers of the officers in the different Royalist forces of the last
twenty years and the officers in the former French army, and
decided whether they were sufficiently useful or sufficiently loyal
to serve in the new royal army. The process had begun which was
to give Louis XVIII a loyal and effective army.

The army which had fought at Waterloo was not the only
military force to be dissolved in the summer of 1815. The old,
splendid, but ineffective *Maison Militaire* of 6,000 officers was
dissolved (but the *Gardes du Corps* and *Cent-Suisses* were retained). It was replaced by a *Garde Royale* which enjoyed considerable privileges of pay and rank, but was composed of regular
officers and soldiers like the rest of the army. It was modelled, in
part, on the *Garde Impériale* of Napoleon I, and like the *Garde
Impériale* was commanded by four marshals in turn: Macdonald,
Oudinot, Victor and Marmont. Louis was *Colonel-Général*.

At first the ministry had wanted the *Garde Royale* to number
only 6,000, or at most 12,000, soldiers. But Louis's desire for a
strong guard can only have been confirmed by recent events.
Following the advice of the Tsar, who took a professional interest
in an allied monarch's guard, he managed to obtain from his
ministers that the *Garde Royale* should be 25,000 strong. It was
recruited, in order of preference, from former *Volontaires Royaux*
who had served in the regular army; from the sons of rich farmers
and artisans; and from soldiers in the pre-1814 Napoleonic army.
So, partly owing to Louis's intervention, the crown now had a
large, effective and loyal military force stationed in and around
the capital, and closely connected with the Royal Family and the
Court. No single measure did more to increase Louis's power and
authority.[26]

Therefore after the Hundred Days, in matters of Government
policy Louis had an intermediate role. He did not have the decisive
power of Louis-Philippe I, whose reign was dominated by politics,
who often succeeded in acting as the head of his own Government
machine and whose ministers often decided policy in his presence
and under his supervision. Louis spent much of his time doing
things which had no direct connection with politics (see Chapter
XII) and confined himself on most matters of policy to the expression of approval, encouragement or reserve.

But his approval was always necessary and never automatic —
as the Talleyrand ministry had found out over censorship and the
guard. As late as 1823, when Louis was very ill, the *Président du*

Conseil could write to Angoulême that '*Monseigneur ne pourra donner aucune suite à ce que je lui dits confidentiellement aujourd'hui que si le Roi m'autorise demain à le convertir en ordre définitif de sa part*' ('Monseigneur may only carry out what I am telling him today in confidence if tomorrow the King authorizes me to convert it into a formal order on his part').

In addition to his knowledge of his ministers' plans and policies, and the need for his approval, another factor which prevented Louis from being simply a political figurehead was his role in choosing his ministers. Although this was not very great in the formation of the Talleyrand ministry in July 1815, subsequently Louis did play a vital part in the choice – and even more in the exclusion – of some ministers. He could even influence the choice of ambassadors; he stopped Blacas going to Vienna in 1823, for example.

Nor was Louis's ability to impose his own likes and dislikes the only way in which he affected the choice of ministers. Louis's arguments were also used, quite often, as the final, very flattering weapon to convince reluctant, or allegedly reluctant, politicians to serve his Government – for example Lainé in 1816 and 1821, Ravez in 1817, Portal in 1819, Mounier in 1820 and Chateaubriand in 1822. It is not hard to decipher the pride and joy behind Chateaubriand's boast to Madame Récamier, after stating that he had refused the *Président du Conseil's* offer of a ministry: '*Le roi m'a envoyé chercher ... et m'a tenu une heure et demie à me prêcher, et moi résistant. Il m'a enfin donné l'ordre d'obéir. J'ai obéi.*' ('The king sent for me ... and kept me for an hour and a half, trying to persuade me, with me resisting. Finally he gave me the *order* [in italics in the original] to obey. I have obeyed.') So Louis's knowledge of his ministers' plans and policies, the need for his approval and his influence over the choice of ministers, ensured that the façade of royal authority which covered his ministers' acts – Government documents signed by the king, the ministry called the *Ministère du Roi*, the endless invocations of the king's commitments to his ministers as a reason for his subjects supporting their policies – was not entirely deceptive.[27]

Louis's intermediate role in Government business is symbolized by the composition of the speeches with which, every year, he opened the legislative session. Until 1818, he wrote them almost entirely himself, in consultation with his ministers. After 1818, he based them on his ministers' drafts, but even then he frequently made alterations of style, emphasis and wording. His ministers could never be entirely sure what he would include or exclude.[28]

Another factor which kept Louis directly involved in politics was the relations of his family with his Government. These were particularly important in the terrible summer of 1815, since Angoulême had set up a more or less independent 'kingdom' of his own in the Midi. Out of provincial sentiment, Royalist exaltation and general hatred for Talleyrand and Fouché, he might easily have built up a very serious threat indeed to his uncle's authority. As with so many crucial events within the Bourbon family circle, we do not know what made Angoulême change his mind when he returned to Paris in early August. Was it the commands of his father, the persuasion of his uncle, or his own fundamental, if intermittent, common sense? One clue is that when he and the Duchesse d'Angoulême returned to the Midi at the end of the month, a prefect noticed in the Duchesse, in addition to an inclination towards severity, and considerable common sense and force of character, '*un grand respect pour la volonté du Roi*' ('a great respect for the will of the King'). Whether this respect was genuine, and the reason for her husband's change of heart, or whether it was put on for the benefit of Louis XVIII's subjects, would be extremely important in the next few years.

Meanwhile the ministry's two great problems were the signature of a peace treaty and the election of a new Chamber of Deputies. At first, France's situation seemed desperate. The Allies were masters of the country and showed little disposition to make life easier for their ally, the King of France. Contrary to Royalist legend, it was not Louis but Wellington and, above all, the King of Prussia who prevented Blücher from blowing up the Pont d'Iéna in Paris, named after the most humiliating of their defeats, on 10 July. By 22 July the situation was so terrible that Louis wrote to Talleyrand denouncing the behaviour of the Allied armies and threatening to retire to Spain – a letter obviously intended to be used to persuade the Allies to behave better.

France was saved by a split within the Allies' camp. In contrast to the situation during the First Restoration, and despite his dislike of Louis and Talleyrand, the Tsar now emerged as a great friend of France. A weakened France would dangerously increase the power of Austria and Prussia. Moreover, the personal influence of Pozzo di Borgo was on the side of Louis XVIII – partly, no doubt, because the king gave him 1,500,000 francs, in circumstances which are not fully known. Louis's large *Liste Civile* was a very useful political weapon. As early as 28 July the Russian Government advocated great leniency in Allied demands on France, and even suggested that no peace treaty was necessary, since Louis XVIII was, in fact, the invaders' ally. However, this was a rather idealistic position; the Austrians and Prussians were eager to make France pay a vast indemnity and lose most of the fortresses on its eastern frontiers. In the end the Allies' demands, presented to Talleyrand on 20 September, were that France should lose two thirds of the territory it had gained in 1814; that it should pay an indemnity of 800 million francs; and that an Allied army of 150,000 should remain in occupation of north-eastern France for seven years.[29]

Talleyrand would not sign these appalling conditions and went to the Tuileries the same day to offer his resignation which he probably hoped would be refused. But the unwillingness of the ministry to sign the peace treaty made it appear to Louis as inadequate in its foreign policy as it was unreliable in internal affairs. For Talleyrand, the great advocate of a united, responsible ministry, had in Fouché a colleague who had acted independently of the other ministers, and utterly irresponsibly, by publishing in August two violent, defeatist *Rapports*, which not only prophesied civil war, another international war and the dissolution of the social order, but also proclaimed that only 20 per cent of the country were *franchement* in favour of the king.

Fouché was probably trying to weaken the Royal Government in order to make himself indispensable. For within the Government, despite his curious alliance with Vitrolles, who was still *Secrétaire d'État*, and although he received a sign of royal favour as impressive as Louis's signature on his marriage-contract with a Mademoiselle de Castellane on 1 August, Fouché felt that his position was getting weaker. Although he was Minister of Police, the Prefect of Police of Paris was an able, ambitious, charming and independent young man of thirty-five from Bordeaux called Elie Decazes, a former courtier of Napoleon's brother the King of Holland and a *protégé* of Baron Louis. Like many young liberals he had remained a loyal Royalist during the Hundred Days, and had received his office as a reward. On 10 July, Decazes had won the king's admiration by showing that a bottle of 'poison' found in the Tsar's bedroom was in fact a bottle of furniture-polish. To the horror of Vitrolles, Louis, always anxious to know the state of public opinion in his capital, soon gave Decazes permission to communicate with him directly through his *Premier Valet de Chambre*. On 12 August, Decazes could boast as he was going off to see Louis at ten o'clock *'que le roi était pour lui'* – not for Fouché, and increasingly less for his ministry.

Moreover, the ministry's attempt to produce a chamber reflecting what Pasquier called Louis's *'esprit d'ordre et de conciliation'* had failed. In the month of September violently Ultra-Royalist deputies, to whom not only Fouché but even Talleyrand were anathema, began to arrive in Paris, where they formed a chorus of furies increasingly eager to denounce the country's central political figures. On another level of politics, the mysterious level of Bourbon family relationships, whose exact importance we will never be able to measure, Artois and the Duchesse d'Angoulême, who returned to Paris on 12 September, seemed to many observers, such as Castlereagh, to be exerting a powerful influence on Louis to change his ministers.

So when, on 20 September, Talleyrand offered his ministry's resignation, the king, to his fury and amazement, accepted, saying (according to Decazes's *Souvenirs*), '*Eh bien* ... *je serai obligé de faire comme en Angleterre et de charger quelqu'un de composer un nouveau Cabinet*' ('Ah well ... I will have to follow the English custom and charge someone to form a new Cabinet'). The ministers had failed Louis's two tests, and had shown themselves to be neither loyal nor useful.

Louis's great new friend the Tsar, rather than Wellington and Castlereagh, who both inexplicably continued to believe in the indispensability of Fouché (perhaps they liked having such perfect justification for their contempt for all French politicians), now emerged as the decisive figure in the formation of the new ministry. It was to the Tsar that Louis, hoping to get better peace terms, wrote a letter threatening abdication on 23 September (although it is similar to the letter of 22 July, it may even have been drafted by a Russian official, Capodistria). The salons of Paris were now emerging, for the first time in their history, as real power-centres, and it was in the salon of the Tsar's new soulmate, the mystical Madame de Krüdener, that discussions went on far into the night as to who the new ministers should be.

Largely to please the Tsar, as well as the Royalists and his own family, Louis now turned to one of his four *Premiers Gentils-hommes*, a man who had been Governor of the Odessa since 1804, who had won a reputation for moderation and commonsense when he appeared in Paris in 1814–15, and whom Talleyrand had already been trying desperately to get to join his ministry, the Duc de Richelieu. Richelieu was understandably appalled at the prospect of taking power in France in September 1815. He was an utterly honourable, honest, independent *grand seigneur*, whose main fault was a tendency to look on the dark side of life. It took the orders of Louis and the Tsar, as well as the persuasion of Jules de Polignac (probably acting for Artois), to induce him to accept the offer.

During the next few days he formed a ministry with the help

of Louis and Decazes. Louis suggested Vaublanc, a politician close to Artois, as Minister of the Interior and Barbé-Marbois, *Premier Président de la Cour des Comptes* since the Consulate, as *Garde des Sceaux*; Baron Louis suggested Corvetto as Minister of Finance; Feltre and the Vicomte du Bouchage (one of Louis XVI's last ministers, and one of Louis's representatives in Paris during the Hundred Days) were chosen by Richelieu as Ministers of War and the Marine for their unequivocable Royalism. Decazes was now so high in Louis's favour that he automatically became Minister of Police. The names of the ministry were announced in the newspapers on 27 September.

Meanwhile, in the same week, Louis and the Parisians had been the horrified spectators of Allied soldiers taking down from the walls of the Louvre some of the works of art which had been looted from all over Europe in the last twenty years. Louis was furious and his relations with Wellington took some time to recover. He had the arrogant self-importance of a true Parisian, and could see absolutely no reason why the horses of San Marco should be taken down from the *Arc de Triomphe du Carrousel* opposite his palace, and returned to Venice. Was not Paris much the best place for everything?

For Louis it was only the last of the many humiliations he had had to suffer during 1815. In the last seven months he had witnessed the desertion of the entire army and the revolt of half his subjects, many of whom had shown real hatred for the Bourbons. He had been abandoned by some of his own ministers and guards. And his own Allies were now treating his kingdom as enemy territory.

It was not just Louis's throne which had suffered disastrously. He himself had emerged from the Hundred Days as a permanently diminished figure, who would never again be treated with quite the same awe and deference in the political world as in 1814–15. In March 1815, he had not only failed to make a stand in Paris, which was very understandable. He had also failed to prepare a safe retreat for himself in Abbeville, Lille or Dunkirk, and had insisted on leaving his kingdom with a very large amount of money. Popular prints emphasized the humiliating and egotistical aspects of his flight. For example, '*Le Départ Souhaité*' ('The Welcome Departure') shows Louis, wearing a blue coat, sitting in a carriage driven by blue-liveried coachmen, packed with bags marked *Pierres Presieuses* and *Diamants*. In June 1815, just as he had shown himself to be changeable and malleable in 1789, Louis had shown that his policies could be influenced by Artois, and that he could change his mind in the space of a few days about something as important as the degree of vengeance to be practised on the rebels. In July 1815, he had been willing to return to Paris in the baggage-train of the foreigners and had been weak enough not to resist the appointment of Fouché as Minister of Police.

Beneath the weakness and waverings so visible on the surface of his policies, there was, however, a fundamental strength in Louis's position, which was only partly due to the strength of monarchical feelings in France. Louis had avoided the worst mistakes and the most serious dangers in 1815. In accordance with the wishes of most Frenchmen he had avoided a civil war. By escaping in such an undignified way he had avoided becoming a prisoner, which could have been as disastrous for him as it had been for Louis XVI after 1789. He had, in the end, not gone to England. He had avoided infringing or suspending the *Charte*, and had resisted the temptations of government by Article 14. Although he had taken Fouché as his minister, he had kept the white flag, thereby maintaining at least the appearance that Fouché was serving the royal cause. By dashing back to Paris he had prevented any possibility of Orléans or a foreign prince being seriously considered for the French throne. He had avoided submitting to humiliating conditions, such as the revision of the *Charte* or the consent of *la nation* for the recovery of his throne, which had been proposed by the Tsar and by Talleyrand.[30]

Moreover, the very dangers and treasons which had beset him had strengthened and developed the passionate Royalism of a large proportion of his subjects. As illustrations 10 and 11 show, some of his subjects now treated Louis XVIII as almost a religious figure, going down on their knees before him, stretching out their hands to touch his clothes and hands with loving awe. In 1815, this Royalist sentiment had shown itself to be just as widespread and just as passionate as the feelings of hatred for the Bourbons. It was this sentiment which had sent the Ultra deputies to the new chamber which was assembling in Paris in September 1815. Consequently, having had to cope with so many enemies in the last few months, Louis XVIII was now faced with a new trial, that of dealing with a host of enthusiastic 'friends' who were longing to act in what they knew to be his best interests. It did not need much imagination to realize that they would be almost as difficult to deal with as declared enemies. One wonders what gave Louis XVIII the strength to go on.

CHAPTER XII

A King and His Subjects 1814–1824

What was it like to be King of France in the early nineteenth century? Or, as Byron put it in the *The Age of Bronze*,

'Good classic Louis is it, can'st thou say,
Desirable to be the Désiré?
Why wouldst thou leave calm Hartwell's green abode,
Apician table and Horatian ode,
To rule a people who will not be ruled,
And love much rather to be scourged than schooled?'

The answer is that it was very 'desirable' indeed to be on the throne even after the Revolution.

Like other candidates for the French throne in this period, such as the Duc d'Orléans, Louis had had long experience of life as a prince. He had had plenty of opportunity to experience private feelings and personal ambitions. Like most individuals he wanted to succeed, although it must be admitted his definition of success – the throne – was rather special. But the throne could satisfy perfectly ordinary human emotions – love of money, desire for a splendid and comfortable existence and longing to succeed in one's profession – as well as dynastic pride.

In Louis's case, one of the threads connecting the different periods of his very varied life was a thread of gold: he loved money. This passion for wealth, already very strong as a prince, could only have been strengthened by the hardships and insecurities of exile. Throughout his reign Louis was to show, in his dealings with his subjects and in his asides to his friends, how aware he was of the power of money and property. Like his contemporaries who, with almost no pressure from the throne, had restricted the franchise to the 100,000 richest men in France, Louis felt the power of what he called '*le démon de la propriété*'. He even thought that the main advantage of marriage was that it provided '*un bonheur en propriété*'. He admired wealth and economic activity so much that he stressed, at great length, how much they could benefit from his reign in his speech of 4 June 1814 promulgating the *Charte*. It is typical that one of the most distinctive decorative motifs of his reign, which often appeared in the carpets in the Tuileries, and beside the royal coat of arms, and which dominates the cradle executed for the heir to the throne, should be *cornes d'abondance* (horns of plenty). Louis meant his reign to offer abundance to himself as well as to his subjects.

An unmistakable sign of the importance of money and private ambition, is that during the Hundred Days, out of the money taken away from Paris, Louis deposited £211,004 and 300,000 francs in London banks. He had received a great shock from the Hundred Days, possibly even greater than from the Revolutions. Whereas in 1814–15, although well aware of the existence of serious discontent (see page 211), Louis had probably thought his troubles and travels were over, after 1815, until toward the end of his reign he could never be entirely sure. In 1816, he made the sad and disillusioned comment to the Duchesse de Berri, who had had to arrive in France via a quarantine hospital, '*C'est donc par un hôpital, par une espèce de prison, que vous faîtes votre entrée en France! mais il fallait bien payer un tribut au temps où nous vivons, et j'espère que ce sera le seul*' ('So you have made your entry into France by a hospital, by a sort of prison! But after all some tribute to the age we live in was inevitable and I hope it will be the only one'). Few royal brides can have received such a discouraging (or prophetic) welcome to their new country. And although Blacas was allowed to draw on the interest of the money deposited in London (hence the superb Blacas collection of antiquities now in the British Museum), and although 200,000 francs were withdrawn in 1820, the bulk of the money remained in London, an unequivocal tribute not only to the political uncertainty surrounding the throne of France in the nineteenth century, but also to the financial rewards it could confer. Louis had made sure that, if he had to experience another period of exile, it would be considerably more comfortable than the last.

For someone so keen on money, one of the most 'desirable' aspects of his kingship must have been the vote to him on 8 November 1814, by a loyal Chamber of Deputies, of a *Liste Civile* of twenty-five million francs a year, and of a royal domain containing all the traditional palaces of the King of France (Versailles, Fontainebleau, Compiègne and the Tuileries), the more recent acquisitions of Saint-Cloud and Rambouillet, the parks and forests surrounding the palaces and the great royal factories of Sèvres, Gobelins, Aubusson and Beauvais.

The *Liste Civile*, as it was meant to, put Louis in a very strong financial position. The same income had been voted to Louis XVI in 1790, but although prices had gone up enormously since 1790, Louis XVIII was in a much stronger position than his brother. Louis XVI had had to pay for his *Maison Militaire* and for the households of his children, sister, aunts and wife, as well as for his *Maison Civile*. But in 1814, the Ministry of War agreed to pay for Louis XVIII's *Maison Militaire*, while for once his family position was of some help to him. Because Angoulême, Berri and Artois were not his direct family and responsibility, but formed a cadet branch of their own, they were given (as had been planned, although on a lesser scale, for Louis and Artois in 1790) separate incomes amounting to eight million francs a year. These very large incomes dangerously added to their already alarming tendency to act as their own masters. They were now in the same independent financial position as a Prince of Wales, since they could only be deprived of their income by a law passed in parliament, rather than by the will of the king. But at least they were not a charge to the *Liste Civile*. Another strong point of Louis's financial position was that his *Liste Civile* was voted for his entire reign. So there was no opportunity for what he called *débats facheux*, which would inevitably have occurred if it had been voted annually.

The size of Louis's *Liste Civile* enabled him to maintain a suitably lavish Court. In 1820 there were 1,622 people in his *Maison Civile* alone, compared to 1,630 in the Court of Napoleon I in 1814 (some of whom had served the empress). The aspect of this Court which most affected Louis personally, and helped make his throne 'desirable', was his own daily life and routine, which took place in his private apartments: the *Cabinet de Toilette*, *Chambre à Coucher*, two *Cabinets Particuliers*, the *Salle à Manger* and *Salon de Famille*, looking out on to the *Jardin des Tuileries* from between the *Salle des Maréchaux* in the middle of the palace and the *Pavillon de Flore* next to the Seine (see illustration 12). In these rooms he enjoyed an enviably comfortable and luxurious existence. There is a story that, when asked by someone he had known at Hartwell, how he found life in France, he replied: 'Madam, I have always felt it my duty to make myself comfortable in every situation to which I am called.' He was helped in this agreeable task by the state in which he found his palaces, which alone would have made the throne of France worth aiming for. Louis told Metternich on 4 May 1814, that Bonaparte had been a good tenant, and indeed in 1814 Louis found his palaces sumptuously furnished and decorated in the glamorous neoclassical *Style Empire*, whose lavish use of gilding, bright colours and such symbols of power as military trophies or representations of Fame, History, Jupiter and Apollo made it seem particularly suitable for the decoration of palaces. All visitors to the Tuileries were impressed by its splendour. The Duchesse d'Orléans, who knew Schönbrunn and Caserta, wrote *'Rien n'est plus magnifique, plus digne d'un grand Souverain, que cet admirable Palais'* ('Nothing is more magnificent, more worthy of a powerful Sovereign, than this admirable Palace'). Her husband could not control his enthusiasm and envy: *'Quelle grandeur, quelle splendeur, quelle magnificence!'* A visitor to Saint-Cloud, Louis's main country palace, thought it 'perhaps one of the most magnificently furnished palaces in Europe'. Louis's bedroom in the Tuileries was 'entirely of purple velvet sumptuously embroidered with gold' (fleur de lys); his dressing room was radiant 'with the most delicate golden filigree'. Lady Blessington, who admired the whole palace, was particularly impressed by this bedroom. Louis had come a long way from Verona and Blankenburg.[1] He so liked the taste of Napoleon I that he made very few alterations to the furniture and decoration of his apartments. Even the Ns and eagles and bees remained on his throne, and walls and ceilings in 1814. Only after the Hundred Days were Bonaparte emblems, like Bonaparte's supporters, systematically purged and special techniques were developed for turning the Ns and bees in the carpets into harmless floral decoration.[2]

However, Louis did not just adopt the taste of Napoleon I. Instead, as Lamartine wrote, *'le Roi aimait à se rappeler le proscrit'* ('the King liked to remember the exile'). Louis installed in his *Cabinet Particulier* a hand-bell which he had had since the *Armée de Condé*; a *chiffonnier* or waste-paper basket which he had had since Mittau; and a little white wooden desk which he had been using since Warsaw, and which was there waiting for him in his *Cabinet Particulier* when he entered the Tuileries after the Te Deum on 3 May 1814 (it is now in the Archives Nationales). Nothing could be more different from the luxurious desks of Louis XV, Louis XVI and of Louis himself when young. Another sign of Louis's simplicity – or perhaps of a bad back – is that he did not sleep in the magnificent, rather heavy state bed of Napoleon (which can be seen, all its Bonaparte emblems transformed into lilies and Saint Esprits and horns of plenty, in the Louvre), but in a little iron bed with green curtains which was set up every evening at the foot of the state bed. Louis not only had simpler tastes than Napoleon, he was also fatter, and in 1817 two new *fauteuils de bureau* were installed in his study because the others were not *'assez solides pour le service du Roi'*.[3]

Not only his physical surroundings but also the servants who looked after him made Louis's life on the throne very 'desirable'. It was an age when personal comfort, as well as public respect, depended to a large extent on the number of servants one had. Louis had always liked having a lot of servants, and after 1814 to the two *Premiers Valets de Chambre* (Hue and Peronnet) and seven personal servants he brought back from Hartwell (including two, Gonet and Potin, he had kept on out of regard for their former masters, Marie-Joséphine and d'Avaray) were added two more *Premiers Valets de Chambre*, Thierry de Ville d'Avray and Lorimier de Chamilly, and nineteen *Valets de Chambre* and *Garçons de la Chambre*, almost all sons of heirs of people who had held the same offices under Louis XVI. The *Valets de Chambre* and *Garçons de la Chambre* looked after Louis's private apartments, two of them sleeping there each night. For more menial outdoor jobs, Louis had an enormous number of *Valets de Pied*, who wore the blue, silver and red livery of the King of France, and powdered wigs, two of whom can be seen descending the Tuileries staircase, in illustration 10. Two were on duty all day in the *Galerie de Diane* from seven o'clock in the morning until the *coucher*, ready to receive Louis's orders for his daily drive, and to run his messages and deliver his letters. They later had the task of carrying him up and down the stairs.

The most important of Louis's servants were his *Premiers Valets de Chambre*. The *Premier Valet de Chambre de service* (they changed every three months) slept in an apartment above Louis's rooms, which communicated directly with Louis's bedroom by an *escalier dérobé*. He controlled Louis's private funds or *cassette* and, because he was Louis's most trusted and confidential servant, it was through him that some politicians communicated their views or information to the king: for example, it was through Hue that in July 1815 Decazes first began to send reports directly to Louis.[4]

But Louis was physically closest to, and most dependent on, his private personal servants who, unlike almost all other people who surrounded him, even the *Valets de Chambre*, were not from the educated elite. They were slightly younger than him and he treated them all quite severely, complaining if there were not enough to dress and undress him, shouting with annoyance if they did not position his wheelchair in the right place. But, outside their duties, Louis generally treated them well. He was particularly friendly with Gonet, Marie-Joséphine's faithful servant, and the only person allowed to shave the king. Descoeurs, who had joined Louis's service in 1807, was kept on although he was often so drunk that

he was sick in the Tuileries corridors. When Coutent, who had
been with Louis since before 1791, retired in 1821, Louis insisted
that he continue to draw his full salary and that he receive the
title of *Valet de Chambre Ordinaire Honoraire*, which meant that
he could still go to the palace and see his old master, despite the
horrified opposition of the *Premier Gentilhomme*, who feared that
such rewards would raise everyone else's expectations.[5]

Louis not only lived in luxurious surroundings, waited on by
a very large number of well-trained servants, but he also enjoyed
to the full the advantage of being King of France during one of
the greatest ages of French gastronomy. One of the distinguishing
features of the Court of France had always been its *luxe de
domesticité* (see page 21). A sign of the Court's *domesticité* was
the enormous size of the *Bouche*, the department dealing with
Louis's food, which numbered 158 people in 1815, far more than
under Napoleon I. Many of these were purely ceremonial figures,
serving Louis at table only when he ate in public, two or three
times a year, at the *Grand Couvert*. But the others worked in the
Tuileries kitchens or served at table: the first time the Duchesse
d'Orléans dined with Louis she was amazed at the '*quantité
incroyable*' of servants waiting at table.

The food itself was delicious. The *Premier Maître d'Hôtel du
Roi*, the Duc d'Escars, was a gourmet of European reputation.
Under his supervision Louis's table was served with the best of
everything: fruit and vegetables from the crown gardens, such as
the *Potager du Roi* at Versailles (in one month, October 1818,
the *Maison du Roi* received 2,928 *livres de raisins* and 4,890 pears
from the crown gardens); game from the crown forests; truffles
from Piedmont (their safe arrival in Paris was the subject of
lengthy negotiations by the French ambassador in Turin); oysters
from the Channel; and wine from Greece and Cyprus. Louis ate
and drank them all with the seriousness and slowness of the true
gourmet: his *déjeuner* lasting from ten to ten-thirty, and his
dinner from six to seven, were in complete contrast to the hurried
snacks of Napoleon I and to the meagre repasts of Louis's exile.
Louis's dinners were clearly something to remember. In 1816,
after dining at the Tuileries, the Duke of Cambridge wrote to his
brother the regent, no stranger to the pleasures of food himself:
'It is impossible to live better than he (Louis) does'; and Cambridge passed on a message from Louis for his friend George that
'I shall be happy to see him here, and I think he will find my table
not inferior to his own'. One notes that food was the first subject
which came to Louis's mind when comparing his life and the
regent's.[6]

Another aspect of Louis's life as king which was extremely
'desirable' was his transport. He had the choice of 179 carriages
in the stables left him by the emperor, with hundreds of horses
and postilions and footmen to drive them: in 1815 the Hartwell
carriages, like the Hartwell linen, were sold off as being worn-out
and too old-fashioned. Five days a week, from two to six in the
afternoon, Louis went out for a drive escorted by *Valets de Pied*
and equerries and guards and followed by an empty carriage in
case his own broke down. It was during these afternoon drives
that Louis was able to enjoy the entrancing countryside of the Ile-
de-France, to revisit the haunts of his youth – Versailles, Brunoy,
Meudon and Saint-Germain – and to inspect newer pleasure-gar-
dens like Malmaison. He always insisted on going at a great speed,
to give himself the illusion of taking exercise; if he thought he had
gone really fast he would say, with a satisfied smile, '*j'ai obtenu*'.
   The guards surrounding his carriage were another extremely
'desirable' aspect of his daily life for Louis. He loved his *Gardes
du Corps*, and was proud to think that they were the same units
which had served his predecessors since Charles VII. Throughout
his reign he did his best to defend their status and privileges. And
to conceive of how his subjects saw their king, we have to remember that he was always surrounded by a hedge of *Gardes du
Corps*, in their blue, silver and red uniforms – two *Gardes du
Corps* can be seen, in their magnificent crested helmets, on the far
left of Gros's picture of Louis's departure from the Tuileries in
1815 (see illustration 10). Twenty-two *Gardes du Corps* were
always stationed in the *Salle des Gardes* which led into Louis's
private apartments; fifty-one, and sixteen more on Sundays and
Fêtes, were in the *Salle des Maréchaux*. They also escorted
Louis's food when it came up from the kitchens to his dining
room: a King of France was always threatened by poison.
   In addition, the *Garde Royale*, although always, at Louis's
insistence, in a less exaltedly intimate position than the *Gardes
du Corps*, escorted Louis's carriage and guarded the outside of
his palaces; the *Major-Général de la Garde Royale de service*
had his headquarters in a wing of the Tuileries running east from
the *Pavillon de Marsan*, now the only surviving part of the Tuileries of the nineteenth-century French monarchy. Louis was well
aware of the importance of the *Garde Royale*. He wrote in 1818,
quite rightly, '*c'est notre véritable force*', and he frequently intervened in the nominations of colonels; Clermont-Tonnerre in
1815, Castellane in 1822 and Chabannes and Talon in 1823, for
example, owed him their jobs. In 1823, Angoulême was told that
he could make any military appointments he liked except in the

Garde Royale, which Louis had reserved for himself. In all, including soldiers from the *Gardes du Corps de Monsieur*, the *Gardes à Pied Ordinaires* (as the *Cent-Suisses* were known after 1817) – one of whom can be seen presenting arms as Louis is leaving his private apartments in illustration 10, and the *Garde Nationale*, which helped guard the *Pavillon de Marsan*, residence of its *Colonel-Général*, there were about 500 soldiers guarding the Tuileries at any one time.[7]

Louis was thus surrounded by a comfortable, protective and well-oiled machine devoted to his physical well-being. On the throne he never had to think about such torments of his exile as food, heating, lighting or money. Everything was provided or done for him. He did not even have to shave himself. Even during the Hundred Days he was surrounded by a large Court at Ghent, while courtiers who stayed in Paris remained loyal to the king. Louis was also cushioned from the outside world in another sense, in that at the head of the Court's different departments or *services* as they were known, since their *raison d'être* was the service of the king, were a group of elderly Court officials, almost all dukes, who were his servants, his confidants, his companions and in some cases his friends. They consisted of the Cardinal de Périgord, his *Grand Aumônier*, Gramont and Havré, *Capitaines des Gardes*, and Blacas, *Grand Maître de la Garde-Robe* in 1814–15 and *Premier Gentilhomme* after 1820, who had all been appointed by Louis and had been with him at Hartwell. The Ducs d'Aumont and de Duras, *Premier Gentilshommes*, the Ducs de Mouchy (a Noailles) and de Luxembourg, *Capitaines des Gardes*, the Duc de Mortemart, *Capitaine des Gardes à Pied*, the Duc d'Escars, *Premier Maître d'Hôtel*, and the Marquis de Boisgelin, *Maître de la Garde-Robe*, were all heads of extremely grand Court families who had, with the exception of Mortemart, remained loyal to the Bourbons throughout the Empire. In 1814, they recovered their quasi-hereditary Court offices, held by their families since the reign of Louis XV, as if it was the most natural and inevitable thing in the world. In addition the Duc d'Avaray, father of Louis's great friend, became a *Maître de la Garde-Robe du Roi* in 1814. Louis's preferences in Court appointments also showed themselves clearly after the death in January 1815 of the Duc de Fleury, a *Premier Gentilhomme*, whom he replaced by the Duc de Rohan; Rohan was replaced in 1816 by the Duc de La Chatre, who had been Louis's *Premier Gentilhomme* before the Revolution. Evidently Louis preferred aristocratic and familiar faces round him.

To understand Louis's relationship with these dignified, polite and honourable, but not outstandingly brilliant, men one must remember that they were, as his Court officials always had been for him, primarily servants. The *Maître de la Garde-Robe* handed Louis his hat, Saint Esprit and sword in the morning, and received them back in the evening (this is, unfortunately, the only reliable contemporary information we have on Louis's *lever* and *coucher* during his reign) as if he was a valet. The *Premier Gentilhomme* was a mixture of secretary and footman, presenting Louis every morning with an analysis of the most interesting of the deluge of petitions, *placets* and demands which flooded into the Tuileries (there were 1,294 in the last five months of 1816 alone), and naming people to Louis at Court receptions. The *Premier Gentilhomme* also ushered into Louis's presence those people who had been granted audiences, and managed all aspects of the entertainments and receptions at Court. The *Capitaine des Gardes* was responsible for Louis's safety and always walked behind the king once he had left his private apartments, like the body-guard of a modern millionaire.

These Court officials, models for the Ducs de Lenoncourt and de Chaulieu in the *Comédie Humaine*, were perfectly competent servants. D'Escars provided Louis with delicious food. In the difficult circumstances of the Restoration Court, when people from different and hitherto hostile backgrounds were continually thrown together, the *Premiers Gentilshommes* managed to remain consistently polite and charming. For example, Madame de Gontaut wrote of the Duc de Rohan, '*J'ai rarement vu un homme aussi aimable et aussi attachant*', and d'Aumont was able to boast of how universally acknowledged his good manners were. The *Capitaines des Gardes* were utterly loyal. Louis wrote to Decazes in August 1817 that the Duc de Gramont, a great friend of Louis, and the only Court official to have his own personal apartment in the Tuileries as well as the apartment he occupied when *de service*, '*a été créé et mis au monde pour la place qu'il occupe; outre sa compagnie qu'il mène à merveille, il a encore de l'influence sur les autres*' ('has been created and brought into existence for the office he holds; as well as his company, of which he is an ideal commander, he has considerable influence over the others').[8]

On the other hand, these Court officials were not just servants. They were also people whom Louis knew socially. Louis saw his Court officials every day for three months, or longer in the case of Mortemart or d'Escars, who had no colleagues. They all came from the same social and cultural world as Louis himself. Most of them had shared Louis's experiences of the Court of Versailles, the Revolution, the Emigration and the Hundred Days. In such circumstances even the most aloof of masters would be tempted to relax a little with his servants. And there were two occasions which gave his Court officials an opportunity to be in the same room as their master outside their Court duties: the *déjeuner du Roi*, an innovation of Louis's which all his most senior Court officials could attend, and the *ordre*, the ceremony of giving the password in turn to the *Major-Général de la Garde Royale*, the *Capitaine des Gardes à Pied* and the *Capitaine des Gardes du Corps*, which took place as it had done at Versailles, every evening at nine o'clock in the *Grand Cabinet*. It could be attended by people with the *Entrées du Cabinet* (for example the Duc de Laval or Louis's first cousin the Duc d'Esclignac) as well as the most senior Court officials. In addition, the *Capitaine des Gardes*, the *Premier Gentilhomme* and the *Maître* or *Grand-Maître de la Garde-Robe de service* sat with Louis in his carriage when he went out on his afternoon drives. Duras and Blaças can be seen, on Louis's left and right respectively, in illustration 10, as they are about to accompany Louis down the Tuileries staircase into his carriage and away from Paris on the night of 19–20 March 1815.

Louis thought of some of his Court officials as friends as well as companions. He called the Cardinal de Périgord, who did not attend the *déjeuner* or the *ordre*, his *ami*; he wrote of Rohan '*je l'aimais véritablement*', and to La Chatre of '*notre vieille amitié*'. A letter he wrote to 'my dear Charles' (Charles de Damas, who came to the *déjeuner* and the *ordre* frequently after 1815, when he stopped being *Capitaine-Lieutenant des Chevau-Légers*) about the marriage of the Duc de Berri, is very familiar and affectionate, more familiar even than a letter he wrote about the same occasion to Decazes: Louis refers to the Duchesse de Berri as *la petite* and is sure that she and her husband, royal highnesses and heirs to his throne, will form a '*petit ménage du Bon Dieu*'. It is hard to think of any other monarch writing so familiarly about members of his own dynasty to a courtier. Louis liked Aumont, La Chatre, Duras and the Cardinal de Périgord enough to give them considerable sums of money (411,000, 173,837, 115,000 and 60,000 francs respectively), in addition to the large salaries, and generous army retirement pay, which all his secular Court officials received.[9]

But this friendship and companionship, real though they were, were of a rather special, royal sort. Louis probably saw in his courtiers not only the individuals who served him and were his friends, but also the offices they occupied, whose prestige and dignity he was determined to maintain in order to increase the prestige of the master they were serving. He also saw in his Court officials members of families famous for the antiquity of their services to his crown: in 1822, when agreeing to allow Duras to transmit his name to his son-in-law, Louis said, *'Je ne veux pas perdre le nom de Duras'*. For all these reasons, as well as his dislike of new and possibly inefficient faces, Louis did not replace his Court officials with each change of ministry, nor did he ban them from his palace or threaten not to give them the Saint Esprit when they voted against his ministers' policies in the *Chambre des Pairs* – all of which he could have done quite easily. The most he was prepared to do was to give them sermons after the *déjeuner* or the *ordre* on the advantages of his Government's measures and to praise his ministers, and the virtues of obedience, at the slightest provocation. He would prolong his afternoon drive in order to stop his three accompanying Court officials from voting against his Government.

The political disagreements between Louis and his Court officials were a sign of the intensity of political passions under the Restoration. Devoted Court officials were prepared to flout their king's wishes and even to stand up to him in conversation: as so often in Louis's life, his friends were prepared to act as his enemies. Louis's refusal to sack or discipline his Court officials after 1814 showed that, like many other monarchs – George IV, for example – he did not want politics to affect the dignity and efficiency of his Court. Except in November 1820 (see page 317), Louis succeeded in keeping Court offices, and the key position of *Ministre de la Maison*, the man actually in charge of the Court and its finances, outside the political manoeuvres of the day.

But Louis's refusal to force his Court officials to vote for his ministers – which shocked many of his subjects as well as his ministers – also showed what sort of a man he was. He was essentially moderate and conciliatory, or from the point of view of his ministers, weak. Even with people attached to him who were not Court officials, such as the Abbé de Montesquiou, the most he was prepared to do was to urge them to abstain from voting against his Government, which often, against their better judgement, they did.

Louis's determined defence of his Court and its officials did not, however, mean that they were profoundly important to him. They were simply the furniture of his life, agreeable, dignified and highly polished, but they did not form part of his real, inner life. This is confirmed by the sort of conversation they had, which was rather different from ordinary conversations. Since Louis was always surrounded by deferential silence, there was never a reassuring background of noise against which a conversation might

be started. Even when he visited Rambouillet in 1818 with his
Court, on the only hunting expedition of his reign, when conditions were presumably slightly more informal than in the Tuileries,
the *sous-prefet* noted that '*en présence du Roi tout est dans le
silence le plus respectueux. Tous les yeux sont fixés sur lui et si
les princes, et Madame elle-même, parlent, c'est très bas et la
tête tournée vers lui*' ('in the King's presence there is the most
respectful silence. All eyes are fixed on him and if the princes, and
Madame herself, talk, they do so very quietly and with their eyes
turned towards him'). In 1821, the Comte de Saint-Chamans
noted that at the *déjeuner*, '*le Roi n'a pas causé et en général
il parle peu à table (sans doute à cause des domestiques)*' ('the
King did not make conversation, and in general he talks little at
table [no doubt because of the servants]'). In 1820, when Gramont
and Charles de Damas showed sympathy to Louis at a particularly
tense moment of his reign, he wrote '*qu'il y avait d'expression
dans leurs regards*' ('how much expression they put into their
looks'): they did not use words, unless their master spoke to them
first. When Duras gave Louis a letter from Charles de Damas,
applying for the position of *Premier Gentilhomme*, Duras said
that it had been '*décachetée tout de suite et lue, sans qu'il eût
pu pénétrer son effet*' ('opened at once and read, without him
having been able to judge its effect'). The king so transcended
ordinary language that he was often referred to in the passive
sense, and anonymously, and Court officials still, as in the days
of Louis XIV, had to be prepared to read his expression rather
than to receive a direct reply. The Duchesse d'Escars judged a
demand hopeless '*par le premier regard qu'elle a reçue en entrant
dans la chambre*' ('by the first look she received on entering the
room').[10]

If there was conversation at the *déjeuner* or the *ordre* it was
started and dominated by Louis and usually revolved round travel,
literature, poetry, food or dirty stories – almost never round
politics. The Duc d'Escars could write to his wife '*ce soir à l'ordre
il n'ait été question pendant une forte demi-heure que de cette
horrible affaire de Rhodes et de Mde. – les opinions et les juge-
mens du Roi me paraissent devoir être ceux de tous les gens
sensés*' ('this evening at the *ordre* for a good half hour conversation was just about this horrible business of Rhodes and Mde.
– the opinions and judgements of the King seem to me those that
all sensible people should share'). Remembering Louis's conversation at the *déjeuner*, Saint-Chamans wrote '*j'ai vu peu
d'hommes aussi aimables, aussi gracieux et aussi spirituels, quand
il le voulait*' ('I have met few people so amiable, so gracious and

so witty, when he wanted to be'), and most other people agreed; even Talleyrand, an exacting judge, admitted that Louis's conversation was *piquante*. Louis talked of things that might interest the two Court officials on either side of him, he teased his *Premiers Gentilshommes*, and he told stories, some of which, particularly in the half hour after the *déjeuner* when the ladies had left the room, were extremely salacious. For example, after hearing that the Duchesse d'Orléans had born her husband yet another healthy son, Louis told the story of Madame de Beuvron who said to her husband, '*Mon petit, donne moi une prise de tabac, je l'ai bien gagnée, car je viens de te donner un garçon, je l'ai bien senti au passage*' ('My dear, give me a pinch of snuff, after all I deserve it, for I have just given you a boy, I could feel it as it came out'). On other days he told stories which were so funny that people laughed until they cried (but what royal jokes are not laughed at?) or, tantalizingly, stories so lewd and so full of *gros mots* that Saint-Chamans refused to write them down in his diary.

Conversation at Louis's Court could therefore be quite amusing, but it was rarely very sharp or interesting. The exception was when Talleyrand was present. As compensation for losing office in September 1815, he was made *Grand Chambellan* with a salary of 100,000 francs a year. This post in theory gave him the *Grandes Entrées* and the right to be present at the *lever, coucher, déjeuner* and *ordre*. Louis detested Talleyrand – and no doubt the feeling was reciprocated – and it is doubtful if Talleyrand made use of his *Entrées* very often. But some exchanges are recorded which probably took place in Louis's private apartments. When Louis suggested a Latin inscription for the *Arc de Triomphe*, Talleyrand was able to correct his Latin. When Louis asked how far Valençay was from Paris, Talleyrand replied as far as Ghent is from Paris.

Louis's life, run by a large and formal Court, was set apart from ordinary private life by Court etiquette, a web of manners and customs and traditions which were so deeply embedded in Court life that they were rarely recorded. Court etiquette is often regarded as synonymous with pointlessness and waste of time. But in fact, as Hugh Murray Baillie has shown, it is often the very formality of Court etiquette which gives a sovereign the time and space to lead his or her own life, protected from outside pressures. For example, all the doors in Louis's apartments, guarded by the *Huissiers* or *Valets de Chambre*, were always kept shut. Although this used up a lot of manpower, it meant that Louis could never be burst in on unprepared, and helped create the atmosphere of deferential silence which was so characteristic of his Court. In contrast Louis-Philippe I, who, as Queen Victoria noted with distress, had 'no Court', was surrounded by 'noise, confusion and bustle', and sometimes had to lock his doors himself in order to ensure that he could have a private conversation with an ambassador.

Louis's Court and its etiquette were, in fact, a necessity of royal life. They did not exist simply because he loved pomp and formality. Indeed he could have fairly simple personal tastes. At Hartwell he had chosen a tiny bedroom in an entresol, and he installed simple furniture in his *Cabinet Particulier* in the Tuileries. In 1821, he bought a clock which, according to the *Intendant du Garde-Meuble*, was *'si simple qu'il paraissait peu convenable de le placer dans les appartements du Roi'* ('so simple that it seemed hardly suitable to put it in the King's apartments'). He preferred to be served by servants rather than Court officials at table, and the blue *frac* he wore was simplicity itself compared to the glittering uniforms of other sovereigns. Even his prose style in his private letters to people like d'Avaray or Decazes is simple and direct.

But just as he sometimes, in proclamations and speeches, felt it more suitable to speak in grandiloquent language, so he felt that he must appear to the public surrounded by pomp and ceremony. He had always been deeply concerned with *considération* (see page 131). And in a passage of *Les Devoirs d'un Roi*, in praise of *éclat* and *magnificence*, which almost exactly reflects, although in a simpler style, the feelings expressed in a passage of the memoirs of Louis XIV, Louis wrote that *'Les hommes se gouvernent en grande partie par les yeux; il faut donc qu'un Roi captive ceux de ses sujets … s'il ne se montre pas en public avec un appareil imposant, on le respectera moins'* ('Men are governed in large part by their eyes; so a King has to dazzle those of his subjects … if he does not show himself in public with an impressive outward display, he will be less respected'). In the early nineteenth century, visual splendour or *éclat* was thought essential to a monarch just as in the late twentieth century a good television image is thought essential for a politician. Frederick II of Prussia alone had dispensed with a Court. But, Louis wrote, to be able to live as simply and privately as Frederick II, you first had to win as many battles.

The *appareil imposant* of Louis's large and splendid Court was normally on show in Paris since he only spent five to eight weeks a year at his country palace at Saint-Cloud, just over eight miles from Paris. Louis liked the country and being able to stroll alone in the private garden of Saint-Cloud, just as if he was back at Hartwell. He loved flowers. Every piece of china made in the

Manufacture de Monsieur before 1791 had been decorated with flowers, and one of the few things he changed in the book-lined *Cabinet Particulier* he inherited from Napoleon I was to install a bouquet of dried flowers on a table (see illustration 13; it is not known if he changed the books). One of the main differences in the decoration of the Tuileries under the Restoration and under the Empire is that after 1814 garlands of flowers, not only Bourbon lilies but also roses and acanthi, began to appear in the new carpets ordered for the palace. But to the horror and distaste of his courtiers Louis always, every year from 1817 to 1824 (except 1820 and 1823), insisted on leaving Saint-Cloud at the height of summer, in late July or early August, when most people who could afford to had fled the capital's unwholesome heat.

For Louis loved the Tuileries even more than the country. On one side was the *Jardin des Tuileries*, full of life and (often very strange indeed) activity, since it was the main meeting place and fashion parade for Parisians. On the other side was the *Cour du Carrousel*, the scene of constant parades, and of the arrival and departure of endless carriages. But its chief attraction for Louis was that the Tuileries was in the heart of the capital and at the centre of power. In 1814, Louis had wanted to spend half the year at Versailles. But he had learnt his lesson. After the Hundred Days, although some redecoration continued (there were going to be *dessus de portes* by Ingres in the *Grands Appartements* of Louis XIV), Louis abandoned all thought of Versailles, and made sure that he was never far from Paris for long.

So Paris under Louis XVIII was a royal city, more than at any time since the reign of Louis XIII. *Le Château* was one of the city's main centres of news. As in modern London, the changing of the guard in front of the palace was a regular daily event at eleven in the morning, and the royal coat of arms adorned hundreds of shop fronts. Not only was Paris a very royal city, but Louis was a very Parisian king, the most Parisian since Henri III. Instead of spending much of his time hunting in the crown forests, like his predecessors, he went on afternoon drives, and these drives connected him with the Parisians in two ways. First, he could judge public opinion, and his own popularity, from the way in which he was received. For example, in 1816 he drove through the formerly Revolutionary district of the Faubourg Saint-Antoine, in order to assess public opinion there. Thus Louis was a very visible and familiar figure to the Parisians. Indeed '*le gros Louis XVIII*' could be seen so frequently in the streets of Paris that Stendhal, a dedicated Bonapartist, decided to leave for Italy. The second way in which his afternoon drives connected Louis to the Parisians was that, in accordance with the ancient French royal tradition of showing the *Chambre du Roi* to the public, his bedroom and state apartments were shown to the crowds of people who obtained tickets to see them. So, since Louis, unlike his predecessors, had no formal state bedroom and slept in his private apartments, the magnificent setting of his daily life, as well as his face, were even more open to public scrutiny than his predecessors' had been.[12]

Louis was also visible to the public and the elite at the receptions after Mass on Sundays. Only people *vêtue négligemment* and men in boots and trousers, rather than breeches, were excluded from the *Salle des Maréchaux*; and this rule was relaxed for soldiers, and on the ground floor of the Tuileries chapel. When Louis reached the *Salle des Maréchaux*, surrounded by magnificently uniformed *Gardes du Corps* and *Gardes à Pied*, and by a glittering array of courtiers, *Valets de Pied, Aumôniers* and pages, preceded by the governor of the palace, the *Capitaine des Gardes à Pied*, and the *Major-Général de la Garde Royale*, flanked on his left by the *Premier Gentilhomme* and on his right by the *Grand Chambellan* and the *Maître de la Garde-Robe*, and followed by the *Capitaine* and the *Major des Gardes du Corps*, the *Gardes du Corps* on duty stood to attention, rapping their guns on the floor. The public, especially the women, cheered and cried '*Vive le Roi!*', even after 1815. They then began to thrust petitions at Louis, which he received 'very graciously, kindly addressing the people who presented them', and then passing them on to a Court official who would send them to the appropriate ministry.

When Louis reached the royal gallery on the first floor of the chapel, the *Gardes à Pied* beat their drums, the *Gardes du Corps* stood to attention with fixed bayonets, the folding doors were flung open, and two heralds announced '*Le Roi!*' to the expectant congregation. Every eye was fixed on the king, who to different English visitors appeared as 'very benevolent, very soft and very sorry'; 'grossly fat but of a pleasant enough countenance and a considerable dignity'; or (to a Protestant priest disgusted by the Catholic Mass) with 'an air of dejection in his countenance and a melancholy wildness in his eye'.[13] The service lasted about half an hour, from noon to twelve-thirty, and was remarkable for some of the finest singing every heard at the French Court, conducted by Cherubini, a dedicated enemy of Napoleon I, who in 1816 became joint *Surintendant de la Musique* with Lesueur, formerly the emperor's *Surintendant*.

After Mass, Louis, still surrounded by his glittering escort, and now accompanied by the Royal Family, returned through the *Salle des Maréchaux*, and then began a ponderous regal progress through his crowded state apartments, which was the climax of the Sunday reception. Louis was one of the last sovereigns in Europe to hold such frequent receptions. His friend the regent held at most six or seven levees a year. Other sovereigns, even the Austrian Emperor, lived very private lives: Mathieu de Montmorency thought the Austrian Court '*de la plus grande simplicité*'. For Louis needed the reassurance of such regular demonstrations of deference and loyalty from the French and, on Tuesdays, European elites. Even when he was dying he returned to the Tuileries to receive on the Fête de Saint Louis. Moreover, these receptions, which had been going on in different forms since the Directory, fitted in with the monarchical, palace-haunting mood of the French elite in the early nineteenth century. And, since they were attended by people not necessarily supporters of the ministry – Ultras in 1816 and a liberal like Royer-Collard in 1822, for example – they were an occasion to emphasize the political stability of the regime, and the breadth of support for the king from all parties, just as the receptions for ambassadors and foreigners on Tuesdays emphasized his friendly relations with the rest of Europe.

The state apartments in which the receptions were held were suitably splendid, enrolling painting, carpets and furniture in the effort to surround the king with *éclat*. The most splendid room of all was the *Salle du Trône*, dominated by a great crimson velvet, plume-crested canopy surrounding a blue throne, both of which were smothered in golden fleur de lys. It was redecorated in January 1822 with tapestries showing scenes from the lives of Saint Louis, François I and Henri IV, the holy, cultured and popular kings who were the predecessors Louis most cared to remember (the later Bourbons were a little ashamed of Louis XIV), and with a sumptuous new carpet designed by Dugourc, who had been Louis's decorator in the 1780s.[14]

When Louis went through his state apartments, crammed with officials and officers wearing the uniform of his service (after his health got worse in 1819 he heard Mass in his bedroom and went through in the other direction in his wheelchair), an awed silence surrounded him, and his every word was awaited with anxious attention. Narcisse de Salvandy, an ambitious young writer and politician who went to a reception in 1817, although he found the king's entourage rather old, was impressed with the king: '*Son front Louis XVI semble porter la couronne depuis huit cent ans. Sa bouche prête à sourire, son demi-salut inconscient de la tête branlante et altière, semblent un discours royal non interrompu*

et non achevé avec ses sujets qui l'entourent.' ('His Louis XVI
brow seems to have been wearing the crown for eight hundred
years. His perpetual half-smile, the barely perceptible nod of his
shaking and imperious head, seem an uninterrupted and unfin-
ished speech from the throne to his subjects around him.') A
deputy like Maine de Biran, or a general like Roger de Damas,
waited eagerly for a sign of royal recognition, and felt genuinely
alarmed, not if Louis did not talk to them, but if he did not look
at them in a friendly way. A revolution had exploded, Bonaparte
had twice usurped the throne, but the face of the king on his way
back from Mass was still scrutinized for signs of favour by
hundreds of dedicated courtiers.

In the *Grand Cabinet*, reserved only for the most senior Court
officials, marshals, *Ministres d'État* (a title given to ex-ministers),
ministers and members of the Royal Family, Louis would address
each member of his family in turn, and then each minister, loud
enough to be heard. Then he spoke to the marshals and *Ministres
d'État* in turn, for example asking Maréchal Jourdan, every
Sunday, if he had come from his estate of Du Coudray. These
questions, and the similar questions he would address to people
in the other rooms about their wives or their health, were completely banal and predictable. They were not, however, totally
pointless. They were not so much a succession of words as a
highly valued sign of royal favour. If Louis talked slightly longer
than usual to Talleyrand, people thought Talleyrand might be
asked to form a ministry. If Louis was polite to an Ultra, the Ultra
thought he might as well ask for a peerage. If Louis did not
address someone he used to address, it was an unmistakable sign
of disgrace, which meant for Comte Molé after December 1818,
or for Blacas in November 1822 (see page 385) that their political
careers were almost certainly over.

At the Tuesday receptions for diplomats and foreigners Louis
also used almost exactly the same words to everyone: *'Le Roi se
porte t'il bien?'* went a long way in this monarchical age. But
diplomats noted the gestures accompanying the words – which
Louis could turn into marks of favour – and were very hurt if
Louis forgot to address them. The king's words and behaviour
were still of the utmost significance for foreigners as well as for
his subjects.[15]

Louis was not only head of state, he was also head of society.
His Monday receptions for men and women at twelve-thirty in
the afternoon and eight in the evening respectively (which, like
any hostess whose *jour* it happened to be, he called *mes lundis*)
were designed to fulfil this role. Each person had to make three

révérences, the first on entering the room (either the *Salle du Trône* or the *Salle de la Paix*, depending on one's rank), the second in the middle, and the third in front of the king, surrounded by his terrifying Court. The person then had to leave without turning his or her back on the king. There are no complete lists for who were presented at the Restoration Court. But the list for the period 1 January 1816 to 2 February 1822 shows that of the 421 French people presented (three quarters of whom were women), 38 per cent came from the old Court nobility, 45 per cent from the nobility which had never been presented at Versailles, and 18 per cent were non-noble. When compared to the practice of the Court of Versailles, where presentation had essentially depended on tracing one's family back to before 1400, this shows that the Restoration Court was far more open to the bourgeoisie, and the provincial or Parisian nobility. The only difference between it and the Napoleonic Court (for which a list of presentations from 1809 to 1815 has been preserved) is not the proportion of the old Court nobility which went to either – it was almost exactly the same – but the greater importance at the Restoration Court, as in Restoration politics, of the provincial nobility compared to the bourgeoisie (the figures for the Napoleonic Court are 38 per cent, 38 per cent and 24 per cent respectively).[16]

Thus the Court does, to a certain extent, reflect on the social as well as the political level Louis's desire to reconcile and absorb different classes and parties. His social world as king was no more exclusive than it had been, in Paris, as a prince. Throughout his reign he tried to do at his Court what his prefects were trying to do in the provinces, in Bordeaux, in Caen, in Lyon: to mix different political parties and the different classes of the *haut commerce* and the *noblesse* as well as officials and officers, and unite them in homage round his throne. He was far less snobbish and exclusive than the hostesses of the Faubourg Saint-Germain. In *Le Cabinet des Antiques* the Duchesse de Maufrigneuse admits that although she would not receive Madame Camusot, the king would receive that ambitious bourgeoise with pleasure. When one considers that sections of the Napoleonic elite and the old nobility still formed two or more separate societies in the 1880s, the presence at Louis's Court of so many people from each world – for example, at the Saint Louis of 1817, of the sixty-one women using tabourets in the *Salle du Trône*, fifteen were maréchales or duchesses of the Revolution and Empire – is remarkable. Louis always, after the Hundred Days, as well as in 1814, tried to make the Napoleonic elite feel at ease at his Court. For example, in 1821, he insisted that Gramont take to the coronation of George

IV a Champagny (nephew of the Duc de Cadore) and two sons of Napoleonic marshals, the Marquis Oudinot and de Perignon.[17]

The opposite of a Court is a salon – inevitably more select, more intimate, more likely to create a clique or a coterie. Louis, who was very interested in different forms of social life, disliked salons and their influence. He probably realized how easily they could exalt and exaggerate political passions, particularly during his reign, when political feeling and social life were both so intense. Although Louis was too determined to maintain his royal dignity – or too wary of the example of Marie-Antoinette (whose *société*, he felt, had been a disaster) – or simply too old to want to entertain informally himself, as his ministers occasionally suggested, he realized that his formal receptions were not enough. So, from 1814, almost certainly at his instigation, his *Premier Gentilhomme de service* and his *Premier Maître d'Hôtel* regularly gave huge soirées and dinners. They took place at least twice a month and meant that, contrary to a widespread belief, the Restoration Court was a great social centre, which tried to unite different groups and parties. In 1814–15, an English visitor noticed that the *Premier Gentilhomme's* salon was full of Napoleonic marshals and maréchales, while Madame de Chastenay met there Maréchales Soult, Moreau and Suchet. The Restoration Court also mixed people from the political world and distinguished foreign visitors. The Duc d'Escars's delicious dinners were above all for ministers and ambassadors; in 1816 Madame de Staël and Canning had a famous row about Allied policy towards France in the salon of the Duc de La Chatre.

The importance of the political and social role of his Court to Louis is shown by the eagerness with which he counted the number of women who came to Court one Monday in 1820: seventy-five in the *Salle du Trône*, 193 in the *Salle de la Paix*, 'total deux cent soixante-huit. Le compte est bon'. And indeed because the rules were stricter, and the sense of involvement with the regime was less, many fewer people had gone to the Court at Versailles. Another sign of the importance of the Court receptions in Louis's world is an extraordinary letter from Blacas to Artois on 8 March 1815 which seems to compare, no doubt for the benefit of the many people who were going to read it, the absurdity of Bonaparte's expedition in Provence with the reality and importance of Court life. '*Le succès dépendoit de la première journée. Sa Majesté recevra jeudi les personnes qui n'avaient pu depuis longtemps avoir l'honneur de lui faire la cour.*' ('Success depended on the first day. On Thursday his Majesty will receive the people who for a long time have been unable to pay him their court.')[18]

In his contacts with his Court officials and with those of his subjects who came to Court receptions, Louis was always figuratively, although not literally (it was too awkward), on his throne. He was always the king, directly or indirectly receiving the homage of his subjects, not completely different from a modern multimillionaire who expects, and often receives, the homage and deference of all around him. But just as the millionaire feels that his only real equals, the only people to whom he need not condescend, are the heirs to his fortune and other millionaires, so the centre of Louis's social world were his family, and the other European royal families. To Louis, as to almost all his contemporaries, European royalty was something quite apart from other forms of humanity. It was an unimaginably exalted social pantheon with which he was determined to maintain his connections. So the only people he ever had to dinner in France were members of his own family, European princes and a few extremely favoured foreigners. Louis's ties with European royalty were given visible form by the traditional practice of wearing Court mourning for foreign as well as French royalty, which meant that the Court could be in mourning for as many as 122 days in the year, although it was usually for between twenty and fifty days a year. The length of Court mourning depended on royal rank abroad, not on the closeness of relationship to Louis himself.

Another link between Louis and European royalty was that, of the seventy-three *Chevaliers du Saint Esprit* he appointed, twenty-two – almost a third, a far higher proportion than before 1789 – were from European royal families. They included members of the Spanish, Neapolitan, Portuguese, Austrian, Russian, English, Prussian and Danish Royal Families – the latter the first non-Catholics to receive the honour. In addition, Louis named Wellington, his hero; Prince Hohenlohe, who had fought devotedly in the *Armée de Condé*; and two *Ambassadeurs de Famille*, the Duc de San-Carlos and Prince Castelcicala.

Louis was extremely keen to keep up his own status among European monarchs. Indeed, one reason why Louis had such a lavish and aristocratic Court may have been a desire to impress his fellow monarchs, who certainly were impressed by the *Gardes du Corps* and the *Garde Royale*. In 1814 (but not in 1815), when the Allied monarchs were in Paris, Louis took precedence of them all and had himself served first at table, as if it was the most natural thing in the world, and as if their armies were not in occupation of his capital. In 1818, Richelieu had to ask Decazes to try to persuade Louis to go out of his *Cabinet Particulier* to greet the Tsar (on a short visit to Paris) in the next room, and to let him sit on an armchair in the *Cabinet Particulier* – a tribute not only to Louis's unwillingness to do these things, even for a fellow monarch and ally, but also to the great importance they still had in his world.

A much more constant presence and concern for Louis, however, was his own family. He had two main reasons for leading a close family life during his reign, neither of them particularly loving. Louis based his regime, in part, on his appeal to the family. He was also dedicated to strengthening the Catholic Church, one of whose main precepts is the sanctity of family life. He himself wrote to a niece that *'il faut que ceux qui sont élevés au-dessus des autres donnent l'exemple de la soumission aux règles'* ('those who are raised above others should give the example of obeying the rules'). And what more powerful rule is there than that to lead a Christian family life?

A second factor uniting Louis to his family was that in this period, as has already been explained (see page 192), all the princes of the Royal Family were particularly important. Even Orléans, by his ideas and intrigues and past, was more important than a Prince du Sang in the eighteenth century. Therefore, throughout his reign, Louis was dedicated to maintaining the appearance of a devoted and united Royal Family. All the Royal Family (except Berri after his marriage) lived together in the same palace – which they had not done before 1791, and which the Bonapartes had not cared to do. Chateaubriand's famous remark that, in 1814, *'Le Château des Tuileries, si propre et si militaire sous Napoléon, au lieu de l'odeur de la poudre, se remplissait de la fumée des déjeuners qui montait de toutes parts'* ('The palace of the Tuileries, so clean and military under Napoleon, instead of the stench of powder, was filled with the aroma of *déjeuners* from every corner'), reflects not only the importance of food in Louis's life, but also the fact that all his family, and some of their Court officials, had kitchens in the palace (although there are no complete lists, it seems that the Tuileries was inhabited by about 100 Court officials – half the number at Versailles – most of whom served the princes not the king). Under the Empire only the emperor did.

Louis not only lived with his family, but saw a lot of them each day. The Duchesse d'Angoulême attended Louis's *déjeuner* every morning, and her husband and Artois came to join in the conversation at ten-thirty. All the Royal Family (except the Berris) met almost every day for dinner at six in the evening – like the rest of Paris, the Royal Family had given up their pre-1789 habit of eating a late *souper* (see page 14). Dinner lasted until seven, when the Royal Family moved from the *Salle à Manger* to the *Salon de Famille* for an hour of cards, sewing and conversation. So they were together for two hours almost every evening. The Royal Family and the Princes du Sang also came to the receptions every Sunday, and this was seen as an important symbol of unity and deference. When they were particularly opposed politically, Louis agreed that Artois's threat to stop seeing him would endanger '*la marche du gouvernement*'.[19]

To show the unity of the entire dynasty Louis also invited the Orléans to dinner, three or four times a year. These occasions could be surprisingly jolly, especially when the Orléans's children were old enough to attend: they could then be questioned about their studies by Louis, and petted by the poor, childless Duchesse d'Angoulême. But Louis did not allow his concern for family life and for the prestige of his dynasty to run away with him. Although the Orléans and the Condés now enjoyed an inferior rank in relation to foreign dynasties (so many of which had risen in status since 1789), Louis, to their intense bitterness, refused to raise them from their traditional rank of *Altesse Sérénissime* to the full glory of *Altesse Royale*. Since Orléans's wife, daugher of the King of Naples, was an *Altesse Royale*, Orléans suffered constant mortification at Court. Two wings of each door were opened for his wife. He only went through after one had been shut in his face.

There were also embarrassing scenes in public, at the baptisms of Berri's children, and at the annual memorial services for Louis XVI and Marie-Antoinette when, by Louis's *volonté positive*, Orléans was refused such royal privileges as the right to kneel on two hassocks instead of one, or the right to be passed a pen by the *Grand Aumônier* rather than by an ordinary *Aumônier*. No doubt Louis felt that neither Orléans's Republican past, nor his ill-disguised ambition for the throne in 1815, nor his later treacheries, were reasons for a rise in status.

That Louis did not forget Orléans's ambitions is shown by a remark he made in January 1819. The old French custom of celebrating *la fête des Rois* (Twelfth Night) by eating a cake containing a bean or *fève* which gives the person it falls to the title *le roi de la fève*, was kept up by the Royal Family, as it still is in many French families and offices. Louis always invited the Orléans. Since Orléans knew his cousins knew about his royal ambitions, he must have rather dreaded these occasions, especially the chance of his being made 'king'. Indeed, when Orléans did draw the bean in January 1819, Louis was very amused by his sullen face, and wrote to Decazes '*peut-être . . . . il trouve que cette royauté est bien peu de chose'* ('perhaps . . . he finds that this royalty does not amount to much'). The emphasis is on the *cette*, rather than on the *royauté*.[20]

The contrast between a deceptive façade of friendliness and very different inner feelings was probably also the case within the Royal Family. Louis always proclaimed his love for his family, especially Artois, most emphatically. A *sous-prefet* who saw the entire Royal Family at dinner wrote in his diary, like the people who saw them in the 1770s, *'Il est impossible de trouver une famille plus unie et de moeurs plus simples que la famille royale . . . tous se donnant publiquement des témoignages d'attachement'* ('It is impossible to find a more united and simpler family than the Royal Family . . . all giving each other signs of attachment in public'). He was particularly impressed, as onlookers always were, by the respectful tenderness with which Louis kissed the Duchesse d'Angoulême's hand when she came in to, or he went out of, the room.

But in fact politics drove Louis and all his family, except Angoulême, apart. To Angoulême (as to many courtiers) the King of France was still *'le représentant de Dieu sur la terre'*. Moreover he was, usually, personally in favour of Louis's policies. So Louis often referred to him as *Sp.*, short for *Spes*, or hope, and was increasingly delighted by him, although Louis always remembered that Angoulême was apt to change his mind rather quickly.

With the other members of his family, however, Louis was often on bad terms, as a result of their constant political disagreements. Just as he called his old friend Havré *un séide* (a lackey) for opposing his policies, so he could compare the Duchesse d'Angoulême to Goneril and Regan, admittedly during a particularly dramatic political crisis. Just how explosive the tensions raging below the deceptive façade of royal good manners could be is shown by the fact that a *pétard* or bomb, which went off just outside Louis's bedroom on 18 January 1821, was probably put there by one of the Duchesse de Berri's servants or followers, perhaps in order to discredit Louis's moderate Government. Certainly Louis said in public the next day: *'Dites à ma nièce que ce n'est pas moi qui ait mis le feu au pétard.'* ('Tell my niece it was not I who put the light to the fuse.') As for Artois, Louis thought he was devoured by ambition to be king.[21]

Some people, Balzac for example, have seen in Louis's *haine intime* for his reactionary brother the main cause of his political moderation, and Balzac even claimed that Louis did not want Artois's reign to be long. But if Louis had really hated his brother he would not have made Artois a member of the Council in 1814—

15, nor would he have constantly tried to associate Artois with his Government. Even when Artois was in open opposition to Louis's Government, Louis continued to make such conciliatory gestures as sending Decazes to tell him of the arrest of people who had helped a political prisoner to escape, insisting on making some of Artois's friends and *protégés* peers in 1819 and making Soult appear to owe his restoration to the rank of Marshal of France in 1820 to his former patron Artois.

In the same way Artois was never as extreme in his opposition to Louis as some members of his entourage would have liked. He did not withdraw to Fontainebleau or Spain, even when Louis's Government most horrified him; nor did he make any gesture of retaliation when Louis deprived him of his powers as *Colonel-Général de la Garde Nationale*. Either there was a fundamental mutual respect between the two brothers which encouraged them to stick together, or they now realized that nothing weakens a family business like a split within the family.

Louis also showed his desire to conciliate his family by encouraging Decazes to go and see Berri and Angoulême, and to pay his respects to the Duchesse d'Angoulême on her birthday.[22] The French Bourbons were different from the Spanish Bourbons or the Braganzas, who so detested each other in this period that they ended up fighting. The French Bourbons not only observed a certain measure in their behaviour but may even, in a curious royal way, have quite liked each other. Why did Louis cry after his nephew's funeral – the first funeral attended by a King of France for centuries? (Louis, so often represented as a slave of etiquette, was in fact prepared to break many hallowed traditions, even the tradition that monarchs, living embodiments of sovereignty and the state, should not come into contact with death.) Why did Louis ennoble and give titles to Berri's two little illegitimate daughters, who became Comtesse d'Issoudun and Comtesse de Vierzon on 9 June 1820? Why did the family spend two hours together every evening? The French Bourbons were convinced they were the grandest family in Europe. Perhaps they quite enjoyed sitting together and laughing over the pretensions of their rivals and subjects.

As for Louis XVI and Marie-Antoinette, the royal martyrs, as they were called during Louis's reign, throughout France every 21 January anniversary services were held during which Louis XVI's extremely moving will was read out to the congregation. The services at Saint-Denis, the traditional royal burial-place, were attended by representatives of the Royal Family, the Government, the Court, the army and the law-courts. Louis himself encouraged this cult and maintained the façade of brotherly love even to his closest confidants. He wrote to Decazes, incredibly, that he felt for Marie-Antoinette *'une douleur que vingt-trois années n'ont point attenuées'* ('a sorrow which twenty-three years have not diminished'), and told his ministers in 1822 that one of the main reasons he wanted to help the King of Spain was gratitude for what Ferdinand VII's father had done for Louis XVI in 1793.

But he was still worried about the past. The Duchesse d'Angoulême's account of her imprisonment in the Temple, which laid great stress on her conviction of her brother's death, was published in 1817 and again, in a less bowdlerized version, in 1823 – no doubt partly in order to weaken doubts about the death of Louis XVII. And in 1815 and 1823 Louis asked to see some of Louis XVI's papers from the Revolutionary period – in 1823 he was shown the receipt, signed by Marie-Antoinette, which proves that it was she, not Louis XVI, who organized secret missions to Austria in 1792.[23] All these details were, however, hidden by the smoke-screen of family feeling which Louis created, and which, during his reign, provided another emotional base – pity, respect for Louis XVI's noble death, the cult of the royal martyrs – for his regime.

In his relationships with his family and with the members of other European dynasties who came to Paris, as in his relations with those of his subjects who were Court officials or who came to his Court, Louis was always the king, a figure whose royal life was quite different from other people's. Living in the lap of luxury, surrounded by awe-struck silence, he enjoyed the overwhelming magnetism of real power combined with elaborate pomp and ceremony. He was so magnetic that he transformed language itself. Not only was his conversation more often a mark of favour than a means of communication, but he himself was often referred to in the third person, anonymously (*on*), or in the passive sense. In his presence even his own family were not allowed to address each other as *tu*.

In keeping with his unique status as king, Louis became increasingly self-obsessed and oblivious of others. Like many elderly invalids he thought his own health of unique, overriding importance – which, indeed, in his case it was. His comment on 19 March 1815 – *'On aurait du m'épargner cette émotion'* – is a fairly clear indication of his order of priorities. Some of his greatest intimates were people devoted to his physical well-being, such as Père Elisée, his lascivious surgeon, and Alibert, his *Premier Médecin Ordinaire*, who had an apartment in the Tuileries and always went with Louis to Saint-Cloud. Richelieu, a minister who knew Louis well, was careful to insert concerned and detailed enquiries about Louis's health in letters which he thought the king might see. Nothing would be more likely to increase his favour.

As Louis grew older, his concern for himself increased. He was terrifyingly selfish in 1818 when his faithful *Premier Valet de Chambre* Baron Hue died: he was more interested in who would replace Hue than in expressing regret for the dead man, or consoling his widow. His speeches in public, which at the beginning of his reign were largely concerned with his subjects, toward the end began to revolve shamelessly round himself. In 1821, at the baptism of his great-nephew, he expressed the hope that Mary, Queen of Heaven, would conduct the Duc de Bordeaux *'par une route plus douce que la mienne au bonheur éternel'* ('by an easier route than my own to eternal salvation') – although he did hope that Bordeaux's life would be *'consacrée au bonheur de la France et à la gloire de notre sainte Religion'* ('dedicated to the happiness of France and the glory of our holy religion'). The same year Louis said that he had made the Pantheon a church again partly in order to attract *'les faveurs de Dieu sur moi et ma famille'* ('the favours of God on me and my family') – like many contemporaries, Louis thought of God as a monarch who might show favour to his subjects. But at least, right to his death, Louis did proclaim that he only wanted to go on living in order to contribute to the *'bonheur de mon peuple'*.[24]

For Louis was never wholly absorbed by his royal world and royal life. He loved being king, but he also found it involved *'un continuel exercice de devoirs pénibles et de grandeurs fatigantes'* ('a continuous exercise of arduous duties and exhausting grandeurs'), which implies the existence of other inclinations. And although he thought them a necessary aspect of royalty, Louis escaped the *grandeurs fatigantes* of his royal life in two ways: through his religion and his favourites.

Louis remained, as far as can be judged, a believing Catholic: Pasquier, a liberal minister, Sosthènes de La Rochefoucauld, an Ultra courtier, and Blacas all thought so. He heard Mass every day, usually in his bedroom, and communicated three or four times a year. On 24 December 1822, for example, a crucial Council meeting was postponed so that he could prepare himself for communicating on Christmas Day. Only his ill-health stopped him (except in 1818) from communicating in public at the Tuileries parish church of Saint Germain-l'Auxerrois on Easter day.

But it is doubtful if Louis's faith went very deep. It did not pervade his whole life, giving him the strength and courage to wear his earthly crown, as it did with Louis XVI. What really

filled Louis XVIII's inner life were his favourites. Louis has often
been represented as a monster of egoism, producing his favourites
to an astonished public, solely in order to convince himself and
his subjects that he was not completely selfish. But in fact his
attachments seem to have been genuine. He defended both Blacas
and Decazes longer than anyone else did. After they left his Court
and lived abroad as ambassadors he did not forget them. Blacas
received considerable financial benefits, and was given the position
of *Premier Gentilhomme* in 1820. To the Duchesse Decazes's
surprise, Louis remembered Decazes's wedding anniversary after
Decazes's fall from power, and continued to see him against his
ministers' wishes. Until his death, Louis kept a picture of Decazes
in his *Cabinet Particulier*: Louis really adored him and this adoration extended to his sister Madame Princeteau, to her children,
and after 1818 to Decazes's sixteen-year-old wife as well.

She came to see him once a week in his *Cabinet Particulier*. He
allowed her to sit down, played with her, asked her how she spent
her day and told her stories of his youth and amorous conquests.
One can see the sort of life and interest such relationships, far
more than his own family, gave him, by the amused but also
excited questions in a letter to Decazes while Decazes's marriage
negotiations were still going on: '*La demande officielle a-t-elle
été faite? La Dsse. a-t-elle consentie? Les conditions sont-elles
réglées?*' ('Has the official demand been made? Has the Duchess
consented? Are the conditions agreed on?') For a time, through
Decazes, Louis had a substitute family, whom he called by their
Christian names: Elie (Decazes), Egédie (his wife), Louis (his son),
Zélie (his sister) and Aurore (her daughter). Louis's courtiers
were torn between rage, contempt and envy.

Other people who entered Louis's personal life were Madame
de Narbonne, Marie-Joséphine's last *Dame du Palais*, who continued to see Louis in private in the first years of his reign and
whose husband he made a duke in 1816. Madame de Vennevelles,
daughter of one of his pre-1789 *Chevaliers de Saint Lazare*, received as much as 107,000 francs during his reign, but nothing
else is known about her (application to the family has been fruitless). Madame de Mirbel, born Mlle. Lyzinska Rue, daughter of
a *Commis de Marine* at Cherbourg, won the title *Peintre en
Miniature de la Chambre de Sa Majesté* on 21 August 1818 by
her charm and talent and perhaps by some mysterious connection
with the Royal Family: her name Lyzinska is only another form
of Louis's grandmother's family name of Leczynska. Her youth
– she was only born in 1798 – also clearly helped. Louis loved
the young, as his fondness for Decazes's family and for Lyzinska

Rue shows. He wanted to enjoy the high spirits and intimacy of which his childlessness had deprived him. In 1819, Lyzinska Rue was even given Gramont's apartment, next to Louis's, at Saint-Cloud. Louis was very generous to her, giving her 76,000 francs in the 1820s, after the rise of a rival, to help her marry Monsieur de Mirbel, a botanist and former adviser to Decazes – two sure paths to Louis's heart.

Louis's personal life was also enlivened by the visit of the Duchesse d'Angoulême's greatest friend, Princesse Esterhazy (French by birth) to Saint-Cloud in 1822. Louis found her charming and frequently invited her to dinner – which, as has been seen, was an almost unheard-of honour. The Duchesse de Duras wrote to Chateaubriand '*Toutes les dames en meurent de jalousie*' ('It makes all the ladies die of jealousy').

But Louis's greatest friend in the last years of his life was Madame du Cayla (see page 382). Here again the friendship seems to have been genuine, again showing itself in a great interest in the favourite's children and family, as well as in the favourite. Madame du Cayla wrote that he was occupied with her and her children's happiness until his dying day: and, in the financial sense, nothing could be truer. Louis received 250,000 francs in May 1822, 150,000 in April 1824, 100,000 in July 1824 and 804,309 in August and September 1824, most of which, probably, went to Madame du Cayla.

Nevertheless, Louis's favourites no more dominated his time or his day than did his Court officials, his receptions, or his family. His favourites, like everyone else, were only admitted into his presence at certain carefully regulated intervals: Decazes for an hour every evening from nine to ten; Madame du Cayla every Wednesday afternoon from three to six, the others much less frequently. Much of his time was probably spent seeing no one, alone in his *Cabinet Particulier*, reading. He had always loved books, and even as king he found time to read a lot of history and travel. In 1820, the *Bibliothèque Particulière du Roi* bought many illustrated travel books, for example Baron Taylor's *Voyages Pittoresques et Romantiques . . . dans l'Ancienne France*, the first Romantic travel book (by a former *Garde du Corps*), a lot of classics, and – rather advanced for the period – the works of Shakespeare, Schiller and Cervantes (but there is no proof that Louis actually read them). Louis was interested enough in Italian history and literature to have the reports of Galileo's trial taken from the Archives in 1814 for him to read and to give one of his doctors 6,000 francs in 1818 for a commentary on Dante.

As for Louis's attitude to the literature of his day, here we come across another of the deceptive façades so characteristic of the Restoration. Few monarchs, perhaps not even Louis XIV, have been so well served by the writers of their reign as Louis XVIII. The genius of Chateaubriand was always ready to defend French royalty. Indeed a book he wrote in 1820 contains one of the most eloquent sentences of dynastic panegyric ever written: '_Quand il n'y aurait dans la France que cette maison de France dont la majesté étonne, encore pourrions-nous, en fait de gloire, en remonter à toutes les nations et porter un défi à l'histoire._' ('If the House of France, with its startling grandeur, alone remained in France, we would still surpass every other nation in glory, and be able to present a challenge to history.')

That year two poets of genius showed that youth was still on the side of the Restoration, and that the new literary revolution of Romanticism was Royalist in origin. Lamartine's _Méditations_, the gospel of the Romantic movement, contained an eloquent _Ode sur la Naissance du Duc de Bordeaux_; Victor Hugo, who had already written poems on the Vendée and Louis XVII, in 1820 wrote poems on royal births and deaths. In addition to this trinity of Royalist genius, there was an army of equally Royalist journalists and _académiciens_, forgotten now but great names then: Charles Nodier, Alissan de Chazet, the Abbé de Feletz, Narcisse de Salvandy, Villemain, one of the most admired writers of the day and a great friend of Decazes, and the Vicomte d'Arlincourt (who changed his name from Victor to Vicomte in 1816), all of whom were very ready to turn a graceful phrase in honour of Louis XVIII.

Louis was naturally delighted by such loyal literature. He used Chateaubriand's pen for political purposes in 1814–15, although not later. In 1820, he frequently praised Lamartine's _Méditations_, which had been brought to his notice by the Duc d'Escars (just as Lucien de Rubempré's poems are shown to Louis by the Duc de Navarreins in _Les Illusions Perdues_): Louis's Court officials were more often links than barriers between him and his subjects. Louis gave Victor Hugo a _gratification_ of 500 francs on 9 March 1820 and in 1822 an annual pension of 1,000 francs – not enough, but still quite a lot for a struggling young poet. Lucien de Rubempré would have appreciated it.[26]

But much as he appreciated the Romantics' sentiments, it is doubtful if Louis really liked their verse. Since 1789, he had changed almost everything in his life: his political ideas, his friends, his daily habits and his style of dress. But he could not change the sort of books he liked. They remained, indelibly, those of his youth: Louis was, as Byron realized, 'classic' at heart. He loved the classics, knowing much of Horace by heart, and reading Racine every year. He probably read Shakespeare in the calm, classic translation of his old secretary Ducis, an enemy of Napoleon whom Louis called '*mon cher Ducis*'. He gave Ducis a pension of 6,000 francs a year and his life was written, no doubt on Louis's prompting, by a *Lecteur du Roi*, another forgotten Royalist academician called Campenon. Such a classic king cannot really have liked the Romantics' style. Indeed, Louis wrote how much he disliked Chateaubriand's *emphase* and *jargon ampoulé*. A characteristically indirect comment by Louis was to send Lamartine, the revolutionary Romantic, a collection of Greek and Latin poets: classics for a Romantic! No direct criticism could have been clearer.

If we want to read a book by an author whom Louis favoured, which also reflected Louis's own tastes and interests, there is *Physiologie des Passions* (first published in 1825) by J. A. Alibert, his favourite doctor. As has already been stated, the Restoration was a very emotional period, dominated by emotions such as fear, ambition, vanity and exhaustion as much as by political or social conflicts. And in *Physiologie des Passions* Alibert, as detailed in his analysis of emotions as a Marxist sociologist in analysis of class conflicts, tries to reduce all feelings to the four instincts of *conservation, imitation, relation* and *réproduction*.

Despite many rather obvious remarks, too many banal little moral tales and too much flattery of Louis XVIII, *Physiologie des Passions* contains some interesting passages. As could be expected with a Royalist book written to please Louis, it praises restraint, moderation, and social life, claiming that '*de tous les peuples, les Français sont ceux qui sont les plus aptes à la sociabilité*' ('of all peoples, the French are most made for social life'). It attacks the Bonapartist emotion of ambition – *la démence de l'âge* – and denounces, at great length, love of war. It observes that fear or distrust – the emotion which poisoned Louis's reign – increases with civilization. It totally omits the un-Royalist emotion of aggressive nationalism, even though Alibert must have known how widespread it was.

But it is most original in its analysis of vanity, which Alibert (and his master), like Stendhal and many others, saw as the dominating emotion of nineteenth-century France: '*Il y a eu des siècles pour la gloire; il y en a eu d'autres pour le fanatisme; mais le siècle où nous vivons est manifestement celui de la vanité.*' ('There have been ages of glory; there have been others of fanaticism; but the age we live in is demonstrably that of vanity.') Alibert writes that vanity, or desire for *considération*, is the real

origin of bravery, of the desire to serve in the army, of artistic
achievement, of young men's desire to get on, and even of good
works. He felt that in comparison, love of money was far less
important. And he wrote that vanity was '*le sentiment dont ceux
qui gouvernent savent tirer le meilleur parti*' ('the emotion which
those who rule can put to greatest use'). Clearly Louis's Court,
with its frequent receptions, its distinctions based on official position or success, and the many opportunities it provided for contact with the Royal Family, quite deliberately set out to satisfy
the national wave of vanity. Louis, whose own life was affected
by his search for *considération*, found his contemporaries easy to
understand.[27]

Louis not only passed many hours reading; but also found time
to look at pictures. His taste in the visual arts was as 'classic' as
in literature. Louis greatly admired Baron Gérard, one of the
most typical neoclassical painters of the age, and was delighted
with Gérard's *Entrée d'Henri IV à Paris* (1817) which he had
commissioned, and which depicts on canvas that reconciliation of
royalists, rebels and revolutionaries which Louis was trying to
bring about in real life. Louis hung the picture in the Tuileries,
and made Gérard *Premier Peintre du Roi*.

In 1816, Louis had commissioned another painter, Baron Gros,
to paint pictures of his departure from the Tuileries, and of the
Duchesse d'Angoulême's farewell to the Bordelais, in 1815. They
are quite unlike the majestic calm of most royal or imperial pictures, and vividly commemorate the emotionalism, unpretentiousness and popular appeal – Louis and his niece extending their
hands to weeping soldiers and *Gardes Nationaux* – of the royalism in 1815. In 1816, Louis also commissioned portraits of Generals Moreau and Pichegru, and of eight Vendéen leaders, which
were hung during his reign at Saint-Cloud: Royalist counterparts
to the marshals' portraits in the *Salle des Maréchaux* in the
Tuileries. But his interest in painting was not entirely political. As
a prince he had collected a very large number of pictures and
drawings (see page 27): and as a king, Louis often had pictures
brought for him to see, for example Girodet's *Atala* in October
1819. Louis went to the Salon most years, flattered the artists –
again the royal attempt to satisfy Frenchmen's vanity – and
stopped at length in front of their pictures. He also went round
the Louvre several times. In 1815, he was appalled at the Allies'
attempts to take back their art treasures, and actually wrote to
the Pope to denounce Canova for trying to recover treasures from
the Vatican. But realism broke through, and in 1817 when Louis

went round room after glorious room bursting with the treasures of antiquity, he commented, '*Allons, nous sommes encore riches*'.

However, much of Louis's interest in the arts was directed not toward painting, sculpture, or antiquities (although, probably at Blacas's suggestion, in 1824 Louis did give Champollion, a Bonapartist from Grenoble, a gold box and an audience as a reward for the decipherment of the Egyptian hieroglyphics), but toward the more complicated domains of china, miniatures, and mineralogy. Louis's interest in mineralogy probably dates from the scientific education he received in his youth. After 1814, at considerable expense, the *Cabinet de Minéralogie du Roi* was installed in the Louvre, under the Comte de Bourdon, a famous mineralogist who, like Ducis and Cherubini, had been a dedicated enemy of Napoleon I. Indeed Louis had probably got to know him in England, where Bourdon had stayed until 1814.

Louis's love of china, and miniatures, and miniatures painted on china or enamel – reality represented in particularly artificial forms, at even more removes than in painting and sculpture – is extremely revealing of his own character, also hidden under many layers of polished artifice. In art, as in literature, in conversation and in politics, he showed a consistent preference for what was small, manageable, intimate, and artificial over the grandiose or the uplifting. One of the objects most closely associated with Louis, the *Coffret de Louis XVIII*, now in the Louvre, is a box *en plaques de porcelaine montée en vermeil*, which he bought in 1820 to house a collection of miniatures by Madame Jacotot, his *Peintre sur Porcelaine*, of kings and queens (many foreign – Frederick II, Maria-Theresa, Charles XII – as well as French) and of famous French men and women: Richelieu, Turenne, Madame de Sévigné, Molière, Racine, Bossuet. . . No doubt Louis whiled away many an idle moment looking at these extremely fine and delicate, but rather bland, representations of the great.

Louis's *coffret* came from Sèvres, and not the least enjoyable aspect of his royalty must have been that he now controlled that unrivalled china factory instead of his former, slightly second-rate factory at Clignancourt (see page 25). He showed his interest in Sèvres by reviving the old royal custom of holding an exhibition of its products every New Year's Day in his palace – where the king, and courtiers inspired by his example, could buy their New Year presents. In 1816, the exhibition was moved from the Tuileries to the Louvre, in order to allow easier access on other days to the public, and from 1818 the exhibition also included products of the crown tapestry and carpet factories of Beauvais, Savonnerie and Gobelins.

Louis's purchases from Sèvres for himself were fairly modest (although lists for the First Restoration do not survive). In 1815, he bought thirty-six blue and gold plates showing *vues diverses* and a cup painted with views of Hartwell: he had sent Develly, one of the Sèvres artists, to paint the views in 1814, and would send Melling, his *Peintre Paysagiste* (more used to representing the domes and minarets of the Bosphorus), to paint Hartwell and Gosfield in 1817 (see illustration 6). Of all the countries he had lived in exile, England had left Louis with the happiest memories.

In 1816, he bought two blue and platinum vases decorated with cameos, one *déjeuner* or breakfast-service decorated with scenes from one of his favourite books, the *Fables* of La Fontaine, another *déjeuner* covered with scenes of harvesting, thirty-six more plates with *vues diverses*, a bust of Artois, and a plate with Raphael's *Belle Jardinière* painted on it by Madame Jacotot: it is noticeable that he usually preferred subjects with simple, peaceful scenes drawn from nature. In 1820, Louis bought a miniature of François I painted on porcelain and a cup with a portrait of Louise de la Vallière, in 1822 two busts of his great-niece and great-nephew, and in 1824, for his *Cabinet de Travail* at Saint-Cloud, four *vases à bouquets* and two vases showing the *Pavillons de Flore* and *de Marsan* – a visible reminder, in his country palace, of how much he loved the Tuileries.

But Louis spent far more on presents to others than to himself. The lists preserved at Sèvres show that every year he gave extremely generous presents to all members of the Royal Family. In January 1824, for example, Louis's present to Artois of a huge vase, now in the Louvre, showing Augustus closing the gates of Janus – a symbol of the end of civil war in ancient Rome and, perhaps, of strife in the French Royal Family – cost 27,000 francs. In addition, not counting the official presents Louis gave to foreign sovereigns and French ambassadors abroad, he gave the extraordinary *Table des Grands Capitaines* in 1817 to the regent (and the huge vase worth 20,000 francs sent from Sèvres to London in 1814 was probably a present for the regent also), and less valuable pieces of Sèvres, in 1816, to the Dukes of Kent and Cambridge. In 1817, the Duc de Richelieu received a cup decorated with a portrait of the Cardinal de Richelieu; in 1818 Signor Burlo of Trieste, who had helped arrange Louis's aunts' funerals, was sent a vase; and in 1816 Blacas, in 1821 Decazes, in 1823 Madame du Cayla, and in 1824 Baron Gérard – a sign of how much Louis liked his pictures – received sets of Sèvres.

Louis's patronage of the arts and literature, like his palaces, his Court, his receptions and even, to a certain extent, his friendships, was run on, and made possible by, money. Thanks to the *Liste Civile*, the king was still, as in the most carefree days of the *Ancien Régime*, a fount of gold, able and expected to spend lavishly on his own comfort, pleasures and friends. But not all the *Liste Civile* was spent on Louis's own wants. As has been pointed out, Louis was not completely selfish, or self-obsessed. And, as some deputies had hoped when voting such a large *Liste Civile* in 1814, one of the largest items in its expenditure was the money spent on rewards and compensations for former Royalists and *émigrés*.

Here, even more than usual in the Restoration, we come up against a conflict between reputation and reality. A well-established tradition has it that thousands of Royalists had selflessly devoted their lives, careers and property to the king – only to be spurned and forgotten after 1814. For many French people, particularly in the west of France, *l'ingratitude des Bourbons* after 1814 achieved and still maintains the status of a fact. In reality, Louis and his family did not owe the Royalists very much. As has been pointed out, most *émigrés* or Royalists were much more attached to other aspects of the *Ancien Régime* – their own property and status, or the Church – than to the Bourbon dynasty; and few had been unwilling to disobey or criticize Louis's Government in exile. Louis felt that he owed his Restoration to Providence, or events, rather than to one set of Frenchmen. Moreover, if the Vendéens and *émigrés* really had been as Royalist as they pretended, then the Restoration of the king was reward enough in itself. Surely their political activity had not been an investment, expected to provide tangible returns in the future.

But some people had ruined themselves fighting for the king, or helping Louis's Government in exile, and in 1814 a shower of rewards and compensations began to fall on some of the Royalists. In October 1814, *Commissions mixtes*, appointed by the Ministry of War, began to examine the claims of Royalists from the west of France. There were immense difficulties in judging these claims because the bloodthirsty nature of the Republican repression meant that Royalists had tended to destroy proof of their services. But by 1815, in the four departments of Ille-et-Vilaine, Mayenne, Morbihan and Finistère – by no means those where there had been most fighting – pensions worth 24,935 francs a year had been given to 231 soldiers, *gratifications* of 24,786 francs to 333 soldiers and widows' pensions worth 88,555 francs to 2,037 people. In January 1815, when it became clear that the Ministry of War could not pay any more, Louis and Blacas admitted, rather late, and a little unwillingly, that the *Liste Civile* would do so. Louis had already sent 200,000 francs to the *Commission des*

Émigrés and had made a few individual presents – for example, 10,000 francs to the Cadoudal family.

By 1819, 2,080,326 francs were being spent on pensions to 3,327 people '*ruinées par suite des évènements politiques*', and this was just money from Louis's *Liste Civile*. Many more pensions were being paid by the Ministries of the Interior and War, and by other members of the Royal Family. In the same year, 1,361,000 francs were being spent on pensions to 1,813 former servants of the Royal Family. These pensions ranged from the 25,000 francs a year given to Madame de Tourzel, former *Gouvernante des Enfants de France*, to 300 francs a year to the '*petitefille d'une femme de chambre de Madame Adélaïde*'. The Bourbons did take good care of their former servants.

Louis also looked after people to whom he was personally indebted. To take only a few examples, the Comte de Königfeld, from Blankenfeld, received the *Ordre du Lis* and, later, the title of Comte. He was particularly cross that he shared his order with a local saddler and blacksmith, which shows that, although Louis was far from generous with the Königfelds, he, or perhaps Gramont, had not forgotten much humbler people. Thomas Clifford, who had been very kind to Louis in England, was made a Baronet in 1815, at Louis's request. Edward Jerningham, who had been to see Louis and had written pro-Bourbon articles in the English press, received a magnificent gold box worth £1,000. Of Louis's French friends and servants, Madame de Balbi received a pension of 12,000 francs a year, which helped her continue gambling merrily into old age: she died in 1842 at the age of eighty-four. During the Restoration she never went to Court, but Louis always asked after her when her niece did. Favras's widow received 10,000 francs in 1814, and then a pension of 6,000 francs a year and another of 1,500 francs a year for her son, who served in the royal army throughout the Restoration. In 1822, he was given another pension of 1,200 francs a year. Madame de Gourbillon, Marie-Joséphine's rapacious friend, who had returned her mistress's love letters to Louis, received 3,600 francs a year. Perrin, the secret agent who had helped run messages between Bordeaux and Hartwell, received 3,000 francs in 1814, as did the Abbé de La Marre. Taffard de Saint-Germain, head of one of the Royalist organizations in Bordeaux, was made *Intendant* of the royal palace in Bordeaux.[29]

Other old servants of Louis were given positions in the army or the administration. The logical reward for dedicated Royalists, favoured by Louis himself, was to serve in the *Maison Militaire* or, later, the *Garde Royale* – elite units particularly satisfying for good Royalists since they were designed to surround the king with utterly loyal soldiers. And many Royalists, who had conspired before 1814, for example the Marquis de La Rochejaquelein, 'Louis XVII', or some of the people who had helped in the Bordeaux rising, did serve in these units.

People who had served Louis's Government in exile were also given places in the Royal Government after 1814. Guilhermy, for example, became *Intendant* of Guadeloupe in 1814. He was dismissed with a very large pension in 1816; but in 1820 it was partly due to Louis's pressure that he was given the place of *Conseiller-Maître à la Cour des Comptes*. D'André received the lucrative and prestigious sinecure of *Intendant-Général des Domaines et Forêts de la Couronne*, and all his sons did extremely well under the Restoration. Royer-Collard received the post of *Directeur-Général de l'Imprimerie* in 1814. Bonnay became minister to Copenhagen in 1814, then was posted to Berlin and finally ended up as Governor of Fontainebleau and Peer of France – positions he could hardly even have dreamed of before 1789: the Counter-Revolution was as much a means of social ascension for some as the Revolution.

Therefore, Louis did look after some of those who had been closely attached to him. Even the son of Cromot de Fougy, his chief official before 1791, became a prefect due to Louis's protection, and received 80,000 francs from the *Liste Civile*. The people Louis did not help tended to be those who, even older than himself, were of very little use in the new France. De Vezet, born in 1743, simply went on drawing his meagre pension; the Comte de Précy, born in 1742, who had been one of d'André's most important agents, was only given the *Grand Croix de l'Ordre de Saint Louis*. Vellecour, born in 1742, who had at one time been in charge of Louis's household, had to be content with a gracious royal question when he went to Court. Thauvenay, who had at one time been Louis's private secretary, remained forgotten at Potsdam: did he ever receive the portrait of Louis which he begged for in order to be able to wear it against his heart? Saint-Priest, born in 1744, remained equally forgotten on his estates near Lyon. Moreover, it is true that Louis and the *Liste Civile* did not rush to reward his former followers and helpers in 1814. Demands tended to be treated with great caution and to take a lot of time to be satisfied, despite some Royalists' often desperate circumstances. Many justified demands, particularly those from the poor and helpless, were not met.

In addition to rewards and compensations to former Royalists, over a tenth of the *Liste Civile* was spent on charities, particularly in and round Paris.[30] A large proportion of Louis's *Liste Civile* was also spent for reasons of state, to make his Government's task easier. In 1817, for example, 627,143 francs were spent on orders in the *Manufactures* of Lyon and elsewhere, the main purpose of which was to encourage industry rather than to redecorate the Tuileries. From 1822 to 1830 the Prefect of Lyon obtained 800,000 francs. He also received 40,000 a year for building works in Lyon. In 1816, the *Liste Civile* gave eight million francs, and in 1817, 2.8 million francs (the princes also gave large sums), to help pay the cost of the Allied occupation. In 1820, Louis was able to give Richelieu one million francs (mostly raised from Rothschilds) to be spent in secret on increasing the *Gendarmerie* of Paris, in order to meet the revolutionary crisis of that year. Louis did not leave the defence of his throne to chance, and the Rothschilds were always eager to help legitimate monarchy in the nineteenth century: James de Rothschild was known in the 1820s as *le roi des juifs et le juif des rois*. From 1818, the *Liste Civile* also contributed about 3,900,000 francs a year to the cost of the *Gardes du Corps* and *Gardes à Pied Ordinaires*. It also absorbed other extraordinary expenses, such as the cost of royal funerals and baptisms.[31]

Thus very approximately, after 1818, out of a total income of between twenty-eight million and thirty million francs, Louis spent six to seven million francs a year on his Court; six million on pensions; three million on charity; and 3,900,000 on the *Maison Militaire*. At least one million to two million a year went on buying houses round the Tuileries which were thought necessary for the use of the Court and on vital repairs to the palaces: 1,352,912 francs were spent on *Bâtiments: Dépenses Extraordinaires* in 1818 alone, for example. Between seven million and eight million a year went on the upkeep of the museums, *Manufactures* and other crown property, expenses which are still born by the Republic. Thus only a little more than a third of the *Liste Civile* was spent on the king and his Court.

Despite the impressive proportion of his income spent on pensions, charities and the needs of the state, Louis's charity and concern for others was kept within very restricted limits. In 1814, he stated: '*Si tout mon peuple a un droit égal à mes soins, je me dois cependant plus particulièrement à la classe indigente.*' ('Although all my people has a right to my care, I owe myself more especially to the indigent class.') But these were just words. There is a telling contrast between Louis XVI, with his boundless charity, or Charles X, who devoted an immense proportion of his *Liste Civile* to the poor, to victims of fires or storms and to churches which needed new bells, and Louis XVIII, who spent a large proportion of his *Liste Civile* not, as he had promised, on the *classe indigente*, but on an extraordinary mixture of individuals from his social, political and personal worlds. The sums given to Court officials and favourites have already been dealt with (see pages 278 and 297). In addition, a mysterious *abbé* called Louis Leduc, an illegitimate son of Louis XV who is said to have been connected with the Favras Affair, received over 400,000 francs from Louis, for his 'debts' after 1817; unfortunately nothing more is known about him.

The two people who received most from Louis XVIII were two foreigners. In 1815 Pozzo di Borgo, Russian ambassador to France, whom Louis called *'le pauvre homme!'*, received 500,000 francs in cash and one million francs in *rentes sur l'État* (which meant he drew the interest on one million francs and could withdraw the capital whenever he liked). Wellington received almost as much from Louis XVIII as Madame de Pompadour had done from Louis XV. In 1814, he was given two large Sèvres vases and a Sèvres *déjeuner*. On 20 March 1818, after he had received the rare honour of dining with the king, Louis gave him the Egyptian service now in the Victoria and Albert Museum. Louis had chosen it himself, in order to try to convince Wellington that modern china was just as good as china of the *Ancien Régime* – another sign of how much the new France was to Louis's taste. *'Je vous prie d'accepter quelques assiettes, my dear lord'* ('I beg you to accept a few plates my dear lord') is a very royal way of giving someone a 102-piece dinner service, one of the most original and entrancing services ever made at the Sèvres factory. It is hardly surprising that, a few months later, Louis found Wellington *'parfait sur tous les points'* over the end of the occupation and the liquidation of the French debt to the Allies.

That autumn Wellington was rewarded with the plaque of the Order of the Saint Esprit set in diamonds worth over 600,000 francs, some of which Louis had no right to give away, since they had belonged to the crown since the seventeenth century (it is now at Apsley House). The next year, Wellington was given one of six collections of the medals of Louis's reign in gold, silver, platinum and bronze; and in 1823, he received a service of forty-eight blue and gold Sèvres dessert plates, decorated with views of France, which Louis had specially ordered for him. It was three times as valuable as the service Louis gave three months later to Madame du Cayla.[32] Louis must have found Wellington very loyal and very useful.

Louis also spent a lot of money on his debts. The vast and

appetizing sum of thirty million francs was voted in 1814 to pay
the debts he and Artois had contracted in exile. Out of this came
huge repayments to the people they had lived off in the 1790s:
2,678,827 francs to the King of Prussia; 718,030 francs to the
heirs of Calonne; 2,947,418 francs to the d'Arlincourt family,
who had helped support Louis's aunts in exile; 169,878 francs to
the heirs of the Elector of Trier, who had entertained Louis and
Artois at Coblentz, and so on. Large sums were also spent on the
debts of Condé and even of Orléans, who was certainly rich
enough after 1814 to pay the debts he had run up when he was
a Republican prince in the 1790s.

There are two mysteries about these repayments. First, why
were so many made to people who claimed they were owed money
by Louis XVI, when it is almost certain that he died without
leaving any debts? One can understand the 1,975,308 francs paid
to Madame de Staël, as the heir of Necker, in late 1815; it
probably represents an attempt, rather naive it is true (nothing
could have stopped her from intriguing with Bonaparte and Orléans as well as writing passionate letters to Blacas declaring
France's love for Louis XVIII), to buy the support of this extremely influential liberal. But why give 355,000 francs to Bertrand de Molleville, a former minister of Louis XVI, and even
more to the heirs of the Duc du Châtelet, one of his most devoted
supporters? Perhaps blackmail was involved, by people who knew
that in 1791–92 Louis and Artois had been enemies of Louis
XVI.[33]

The second mystery is why it took Louis so long to repay the
money lent to him for his journey to Paris in 1814 by the English
Government and the Rothschilds, which he could have repaid out
of the funds voted in 1814. It was not until 1817 that 476,000
francs were repaid for a loan of 420,000 francs from Rothschilds
in April 1814; and not until 1818 that 2.2 million francs (of
which 509,000 came from the princes) were repaid for the English
loan of £100,000 in April 1814, and for the pension that Louis
had continued to draw until July 1814. The King of France drawing an English pension while he was on the throne of France!
Although it was probably spent on winding up Hartwell, Louis
was fortunate that Bonaparte did not find out about it during the
Hundred Days (Bonaparte did try to go through Louis's papers,
but was defeated by the archivists).[34]

The size of his *Liste Civile* enabled Louis to lead an extremely
comfortable and self-indulgent life, to maintain a magnificent
Court and guard, to patronize the arts and to reward his favourites
and followers. It must have been very satisfying to a man who

had always deeply respected the power of money that he now had enough to be able to appear to his subjects as a fount of gold and an embodiment of prosperity. But even without the *Liste Civile* he would have been associated with prosperity, and cash. His head appeared on all the coins minted very quickly by the *Monnaie Royale* after the Restoration, and this was the principal way by which most of his subjects outside Paris would have known what he looked like. In addition, in his speeches Louis frequently stressed the economic advantages of his peaceful reign (see page 183). He was also able to spread prosperity round him in a more personal way, because he gave money to almost all those with whom he came into contact. From 1821, he received 50,000 francs a month, and 60,000 francs a year in cash; presumably he received equally large but unrecorded sums before. Therefore he was able to ensure that every event with which he was personally connected should bring cash to those present. At the first Council meeting of his reign, on 5 May, he had insisted that the troops which escorted his *Entrée* into Paris should receive double pay. In March 1815, he tried to buy his troops' loyalty. In April 1815, he scolded Hue for not having given bigger tips in order to ease the passage of the crown jewels out of France. In 1816, the only time during his reign that he came into personal contact with a peasant, his instinctive reaction was to give the man gold. In *Servitude et Grandeur Militaires*, de Vigny describes Louis arriving at Vincennes to see a battalion of the *Garde Royale* which had suffered losses in an explosion, and distributing not *croix d'honneur* but *rouleaux d'or*.[35]

It might seem that, surrounded by this golden halo, and enshrined in the formal routine of his Court, Louis would never come into contact with real life, or with people who were not overwhelmed by love of money or by the reverential Court atmosphere. But in fact a chink of reality was let into Louis's royal life by the number of audiences he gave. If someone wanted to have a conversation with the king, they could apply for an audience. These were usually given by Louis in the morning, between his *déjeuner* and Mass. Their importance was that they took place in his *Cabinet Particulier*, with only Louis and the person to whom he was giving the audience present. Therefore, they were an immense favour, since for the duration of the audience all the normal constraints of Court life – silence, crowds, pomp and ceremony – were suspended. Only the fact that Louis was seated, and most of the people to whom he gave audiences, except women, remained standing, made the audiences different from most interviews.

To take a few months at random, Louis gave thirty-five audiences in November 1815, eleven in November 1816, eighteen in May 1817, and thirty in November 1817. This was a very large number, probably more than other kings of France had been in the habit of giving, and more than other early nineteenth-century monarchs gave. It shows how eager Louis was to keep in touch with the world outside his Court, and with countries beyond the French frontiers: a great number of audiences, particularly in 1815, were given to foreigners. Louis, always very aware of the force of public opinion and *considération*, wanted to have the opportunity provided by an audience to try to win people over to his side, to explain his policies in person to deputies like Maine de Biran and Camille Jordan (granted audiences in November 1816), and to have the chance to make a favourable impression on important members of the diplomatic world like Canning, Capodistria or Princess Lieven.

The number of audiences was restricted by two factors. First, although people who had not been presented at Court could be granted audiences, audiences were nearly always (but see page 333) granted to members of the social and political worlds who were already connected to the regime or known to Louis. If they were not important diplomats, politicians or generals, the people received in audience tended to be the socially prominent: the Duchess of Devonshire, Princesse Kourakine, Madame de Staël, etc. Thus in 1816 the reply to an application for an audience from the Baronne de Bonté was *'qu'elle écrive son affaire, le Roi ne la connaissant pas suffisament'* ('let her put her request in writing, the King not knowing her well enough') – although the audience was later granted – while in 1815, the Duchesse de Choiseul, whose husband, like many of the old *parti Choiseul*, had served Napoleon I in the Hundred Days, was refused an audience. Politics affected whom Louis received in audience as it affected so many aspects of his life. Louis and his *Premiers Gentilshommes* were careful not to grant audiences to people who had recently been traitors or who might cast doubt on his support for his ministry. A royal audience, like a royal letter, or a royal conversation, was not just a means of communication but was also a sign of favour which could create a political sensation. Thus in May 1820, a police report stated *'Depuis l'audience qu'a eue M. le Maréchal Soult, les Libéraux le portent au Ministère de la Guerre'* ('Since Marshal Soult's audience, the Liberals say he will be Minister of War'), while later that year a journalist wrote that *'Le grand événement du jour est l'audience que M. de Vitrolles a obtenue de Sa Majesté*' ('The great event of the day is the audience which M. de Vitrolles has obtained from His Majesty').[37]

What would it have been like to be received in audience by Louis XVIII? The first impression as you went up the staircase of the *Pavillon de Flore* and through the *Salle des Gardes* was one of profound, almost religious silence. Outside was the noise and bustle of Paris, the shrieks of children in the *Jardin des Tuileries*, the stamp and bark of the guards in the *Cour du Carrousel*. Inside all was silent, even in the *Salle des Gardes*. It is this silence surrounding the king, noticed by all his visitors, politicians as well as peasants, which must have made his words and gestures seem all the more significant and deliberate.

After being received by the *Premier Gentilhomme*, you were ushered in to the *Cabinet Particulier*. You were almost certainly in a terrible state of doubt, insecurity (had it really been wise to ask for an audience? What were you going to *say*?) and above all fear. What else could you have felt, alone with the head of the oldest reigning dynasty in Europe, the king acclaimed by his subjects as *le désiré, le regretté*, the king who could still make or break a minister or even a ministry, the king who could still have a decisive effect on your fortune or career? Guizot, who had his first audience of Louis XVIII on 1 June 1815 at Ghent, was honest enough to write that day: '*Qu'on est sot la première fois qu'on se trouve en tête-à-tête avec un roi*' ('How stupid one is the first time one is alone with a king'); and if Guizot felt like that in the relative informality of the Hôtel d'Hane, how would less self-confident people feel in the magnificent setting of the Tuileries? Maine de Biran, who had often been to Court and had often been greeted by Louis, was absolutely terrified the first time he had an audience: '*mon estomac était comprimé, et ma tête embarrassée ... j'ai éprouvé un battement de coeur extra-ordinaire*' ('my stomach was heaving and my head throbbed ... I felt a terrible beating of the heart'). Even the Duchesse d'Orléans, daughter of a king, granddaughter of an empress, who had often seen Louis at Court and at the family dinners, felt she needed God's help to give her the courage to face a private audience.

Inside the tranquil, book-lined *Cabinet Particulier*, once you had recovered your nerve and focussed on the fat, red, smiling, powdered head of the king, who sat behind his simple white desk cluttered with almanacs and calendars (see illustration 13), whether you were allowed to sit down or left to stand, what would most rivet your attention were the king's eyes. These ironic, severe, frightening brown eyes were unforgettable. They seemed to the

Duchesse de Gontaut, writing her memoirs many years later, to penetrate *'jusqu'à la conscience'* and to force you *'de dire nettement la vérité'*. They were so piercing that Maréchal Macdonald remembered Louis's look as *'son regard pénétrant de lynx'*, and one of Artois's Aides de Camp wrote of the king's *'magnifique regard . . . profondément scrutateur'*. Years later, in one of the most eloquent passages of his *Memoirs Inédits*, Lamartine called them *'les plus beaux yeux que j'eusse jamais vus'*. For, like an Arab woman enveloped in shawls and veils and social taboos, Louis, surrounded by the constraints of his royal life, aware that his words might commit or compromise him, often spoke with his eyes. But eyes can say as much as lips.

Under this penetrating royal gaze, you would try to begin a conversation. Many people went into the *Cabinet Particulier* determined to say or ask for something which they suspected Louis might not want to hear or give. But it seems that despite the intimidating surroundings and the fear Louis inspired, they were usually able to say what they wanted. Guizot did, according to the account he wrote that evening, tell Louis of the fears of the Protestants and the *acquéreurs*, and blame the success of the Hundred Days on the *'désunion et incapacité du ministère'*: disagreeable frankness could hardly go further. The Duchesse d'Orléans did tell Louis how much she feared foreign intervention to save her father's throne. People asking for favours did ask for favours.[38]

But from the surviving accounts of audiences it seems that, after the first moments when the person in front of Louis's desk stated what had made him apply for an audience, Louis usually dominated the conversation. To people asking for favours he always replied with Louis XIV's phrase, *'Je verrai'*. From Guizot's account, what Louis said, blaming the Hundred Days on Napoleon I and promising to observe all that he had sworn to in the *Charte*, probably took up as much time – although not, in Guizot's account, as much space – as what Guizot said to Louis. Maine de Biran's audience was spent in Louis telling the trembling, emotional deputy of *'la nécessité de la . . . fusion des deux nations dans la même'* ('the necessity of the . . . fusion of the two nations in one'). To Princess Lieven, Louis praised his own guard as finer – *plus belle* – than Bonaparte's, and asked her if she did not find him *rajeuni*: his health and his guard were two of the subjects closest to Louis's heart, and of which he was most anxious that foreigners should form a favourable opinion. So Louis dominated the conversation, and made sure it was about things he wanted to talk about – usually the excellence of his Government's policies and the strength and stability of his throne. Even Ferrand, who had an audience once a week, who was one of the few non-ministers with whom Louis talked politics, and who must have had time to get over his timidity, wrote that *'je reprenais une autre conversation dès qu'elle m'était indiquée par lui'* ('I took up another subject of conversation as soon as it was indicated to me by him').[39] Audiences often ended on a highly emotional note, with Louis holding out his hand to be kissed. On 6 March 1815, for example, at the end of an audience, Maréchal Ney kissed Louis's hand and promised to bring back Bonaparte in an iron cage.

If you had more than one audience, or were able to get over your timidity and observe, as well as listen to, the king, some of his real characteristics might become apparent. This king who could be so flattering to the people he met and so grandiloquent in his speeches, and who was himself lapped in deference and flattery, remained fundamentally realistic. His words came from his mouth, but his eyes saw what was going on. Madame de Staël's daughter (one of the many people whose personal lives were transformed by Louis: she had only become Duchesse de Broglie because she had been able to bring her Duc a dowry consisting of the money Louis had 'repaid' her mother) noted in 1821 that *'il n'y a pas d'accord entre sa bouche et ses yeux; son sourire est constant et son regard sévère jusqu'à la dureté'* ('there is no consistency between his mouth and his eyes; his smile is constant and his look severe, even harsh'). An English spectator in the Tuileries chapel in 1817 noted that the king 'looked around him as if uneasy and distressed – as if suspicious of some lurking danger'. How well he knew that not all the people attending his Court were as loyal as they appeared.

Often in his audiences or in conversation Louis appeared most inappropriately cheerful and self-satisfied, for example when he was at Ghent. But this was largely to instil confidence in others, or to convince people that his cause was far from hopeless. He himself was a great worrier, who was much too intelligent to overestimate the strength of his position. One can deduce a close acquaintance with worry from the familiarity to which he referred to his fears, in a letter to Decazes, as *'tout un régiment de dragons'*. His *'dragons'* afflicted Louis throughout his reign, but were often surprisingly different from what actually happened. Thus in 1815, he was extremely alarmed by Orléans's ambitions, but they came to nothing. In 1816 he was very worried about possible bread-riots, but they never became a real threat. He was always very concerned about the progress of the anti-Royalist left

in elections, but they never achieved a majority. After 1815, he
was often alarmed by the possibility of Talleyrand returning to
power, but Talleyrand never did.[40] It is only Louis's refusal to
share his worries with most of those round him which made him
sometimes seem absurdly self-congratulatory. Unlike many modern leaders, for example Mrs Gandhi, who in 1977 seriously
believed she was going to win the elections which annihilated her
party, Louis was rarely deceived about public opinion, or about
other people.

If you were lucky and found the king in a relaxed mood, you
could have found his conversation in private as amusing as it
often was at the courtiers' *déjeuner*. He could be quite funny and
perceptive, in a quiet, indirect way. For example, Louis wrote to
Decazes, to console him for marrying an ugly heiress, that it was
better for her to be known as Madame Decazes, than for him to
be known as '*le mari de Madame Decazes*'. His ways of teasing
the late arrivals at Ghent, or of referring to his Court receptions
or of flattering Chateaubriand (see pages 286 and 394), are quite
amusing. He liked dirty stories, particularly those which implied
their point rather than stating it bluntly. One of his ministers
wrote of Louis's *petits contes fort gais* that '*un coup d'oeil ex-
pressif suppléait à une réticence obligée ... aucun n'approchait
le talent de Louis XVIII pour conter sans embarras tout ce qu'il
voulait*' ('an expressive look made up for an obligatory suppression ... no one came near Louis XVIII in the talent of saying
everything he wanted to without embarrassment'). Louis particularly liked jokes which made his enemies seem ridiculous. He
compared Comte Molé's service of the Empire, which had been
praised as simply the result of Molé's desire to serve the monarchy, to the lust of the Grand Dauphin, who had been so eager
for sex one day that he grabbed the madam rather than the girl
she had brought. Louis could also write that his ministers returning to the Tuileries after shaking the hand of a Chateaubriand or
a Duc de Broglie reminded him of Messalina bringing back to the
imperial bed the odour of the low haunts she had been to.

Although some of his remarks and writings, particularly when
he was in exile, were clumsy and ill-expressed, Louis could have
great facility and grace of expression. He wrote to Decazes in
1817 that Decazes's birthday was as superior to his own '*autant
que le bonheur l'est à la vie*' ('as much as happiness is to life').
Louis's letter to a minister, consoling him for the death of his
father, is a masterpiece of sympathy, flattery and reassurance,
such as few sovereigns have been capable of writing. Some of
Louis's phrases have passed into common currency, for example,

'*L'exactitude est la politesse des Rois*' ('Punctuality is the politeness of Kings'), made to his ministers in the Tuileries. On 8 August
1819 it was Louis who made the famous remark to the pupils of
Saint-Cyr, that '*Chacun de vous porte dans sa giberne un bâton
de Maréchal de France*' ('Every one of you carries in his knapsack
a Marshal's baton'). Of course he may have appropriated it from
someone else. But no dictionary of quotations attributes it to
Napoleon I.

One of the charms of Louis's conversation and writings was
that he was not, by royal standards, very vain. Just as he could
usually see and observe correctly, so he normally saw through the
wall of praise and flattery with which his Court surrounded him.
In 1814, he refused to allow his head to be placed on the *Légion
d'Honneur* where Bonaparte's had been, and he never encouraged
official statues or monuments to himself during his reign – unlike
almost every other Bourbon king except Louis XVI. He refused
to allow a Paris school to be called Collège Louis XVIII. He was
very aware of the limits of his power and influence, referring with
scepticism to Richelieu's praise of the royal '*séduction à laquelle
rien ne résiste*', and with candour to the accusation of *faiblesse*
so often directed against him.[42]

Louis's reputation for *faiblesse* was indeed one of his most
dangerous enemies. Could the king be relied on? Were his moderation and liberalism just one of the endless deceptive façades
of the Restoration? Would he be able to stand up to the unrem-
itting pressure of his reactionary family? How intelligent was he
really?

People's doubts can only have been increased by the insincerity
so often detectable at his audiences, and in his public pronouncements. The effect of the flattering words was so often diluted by
the critical expression in his eyes. All the grandiose declarations
of concern for *la classe indigente*, of determination to stay and
resist Bonaparte in March 1815 and of undying love for his
family, were so frequently contradicted by the facts. There were
also the frequent gyrations of his policy during the Revolution
and the Emigration. Many people left their audience equally un-
convinced of Louis's sincerity as a person and of his reliability as
a monarch. But reliability and strength of character are as hard
to judge in the space of one meeting or audience as intelligence.
The character of a king, in particular, shrouded by his Court, his
routine and the magic of his rank, only becomes apparent in the
course of his reign, and by an even closer study of his actions than
of his words.

Louis's audiences no more dominated his life than did his re-

ceptions, his Court officials or his family. There were usually two
or three a day, lasting from ten minutes to eleven to eleven-thirty.
Thus if his daily routine is worked out from the rather inadequate
evidence at our disposal, it is: up at seven o'clock (the time when
a *Valet de Pied* had to be on duty at the Tuileries); *déjeuner* from
ten to ten-thirty, followed by conversation with his courtiers until
ten to eleven, then audiences until eleven-thirty. Mass followed
immediately, and then a long reception until two or three on
Sundays, and a shorter one until noon or twelve-thirty on Mondays and Tuesdays; a drive in his carriage from two to six, except
on Sundays and Wednesdays; dinner and conversation with his
family from six until eight; and the *ordre* in his *Grand Cabinet*
from nine to nine-fifteen or nine-twenty.

The gaps between seven and ten in the morning, between noon
and two in the middle of the day and between eight and nine and
after nine-fifteen in the evening were filled with politics. Politics
already affected almost everything he did or said. It was the need
for political reassurance which made Louis devote so much time
to holding receptions for the elite; it was the political needs of the
moment which largely determined what Louis said to whom at
the receptions. It was partly for political reasons that Louis spent
so much time with his family. Politics determined who was his
favourite of the moment, just as politics partly determined whom
he spent his money on, what sort of picture he commissioned,
which poet he praised, and what he read.

Thus in the morning Louis read intercepted letters (see page
365) and newspapers: he probably spent more time reading newspapers than books. He certainly read the *Courrier Anglais, Moniteur, Journal des Maires, Journal Général, Quotidienne, Journal
des Débats, Fidèle Ami du Roi,* and the *Constitutionnel,* which
were newspapers representing his Government, the Ultras and the
liberals – although he did tend to read articles which annoyed
him rather faster than the others.[43]

In the middle of the day and in the evening he saw his ministers,
and on Wednesday afternoon held a Council meeting. The middle
of the day was reserved for formal sessions of *travail* with his
ministers. But in the evening between dinner and the *ordre* and,
at the beginning of his reign, after the *ordre,* they could come and
find him in his *Cabinet Particulier* ready to sign their *ordonnances*
and talk business. Louis's last Minister of War said that the king
never made him wait, and other ministers' memoirs agree. Louis
talked completely freely, in a serious and interested way, about
political business. No other people, not even the most important

Court officials, had such automatic and intimate access to the king.

Louis also showed that, with him, his ministers came first in other ways. Few other people received so much money from the *Liste Civile*: of his post-1815 ministers, Lainé received 140,000 francs and a pension of 20,000 a year, the Comte de Serre 230,000 francs, Richelieu's nephew and heir 210,000 francs, Peyronnet and Decazes 100,000 francs each and Villèle's daughter 100,000 francs in 1824. Although eleven Court officials and five former Royalist activists also shared large sums from the *Liste Civile*, another category of people rewarded from the *Liste Civile* confirms the primacy of politics in Louis's life: thirteen marshals and generals who had proved their loyalty during the Hundred Days.[44]

The importance to Louis of his ministers, as well as the ability to keep his snobbery under control, was also shown by his nomination of *Chevaliers du Saint Esprit*. This extremely impressive and passionately desired order – in Louis's eyes the first in Europe – had been reserved almost exclusively, before 1789, for members of the old Court nobility. Under Louis XVIII, of the forty-seven French *Chevaliers* appointed, eight were non-noble and thirteen provincial or Parisian nobles. Three *Chevaliers* were or had been ambassadors, five archbishops, seven marshals, fifteen Court officials and fifteen ministers (only two fit into none of these categories). The proportion of *Chevaliers* who were or had been ministers is unique in the history of this, or perhaps any other, order.

The primacy of his ministers in Louis's life is also shown by the fact that in September 1815 Gouvion Saint-Cyr was allowed to reorganize the *Maison Militaire*, and in 1820–21 Richelieu was allowed to transform, rather less drastically, the *Maison Civile*. Even the guard and the Court bowed to ministerial power. In 1820–21, amid much streamlining, the abolition of old titles and the creation of new costumes, the main change for the king was the introduction into his household of 107 new Court officials (including 41 pages). This hardly affected his daily routine: it just meant that there were now two *Gentilshommes de la Chambre* at his *déjeuner*, and more officials escorting him on his way to Mass and during his afternoon drive.

But it did have the incalculable advantage of introducing new blood into the *Maison du Roi*. Sixty per cent of the new adult officials had served Napoleon I, often during the Hundred Days. Twenty-two per cent were non-nobles, often from extremely humble backgrounds. Colonels Druault, Mermet and Coutard, for example, of the *Garde Royale*, who became *Gentilshommes de la*

Chambre in 1820 were, respectively, sons of a *négociant*, a *maître-tailleur* and a peasant. For the Court of France, for any Court, this was a revolution. That Louis had not tried such a transformation in 1814, when it might have had a very useful effect on public opinion, and that he only accepted it in 1820 on Richelieu's prompting, suggests the limits to his character which were to become so apparent during his reign. He did not always use his imagination.

Compared to his other subjects, Louis's ministers had unique power, access, rewards and importance. Most of them came from quite different worlds than Louis's Court officials or relations: of the forty-five ministers of his reign, eighteen were non-noble and sixteen came from the nobility which had not been presented at Versailles before 1789. But it is they who were most important, and in some cases closest, to the king. And just as the ministers could transform his guard and Court, so the most important person at Court was not a Court official, however intimate, but a minister, the *Ministre de la Maison*. After Blacas's fall from power, the post went to the Comte de Pradel, the former secretary of d'Avaray, who was to last until 1820 as Louis's chief adviser over his palaces, his Court and his finances. He was replaced by the Marquis de Lauriston a descendant of John Law and a former Aide de Camp of Bonaparte, who became quite a favourite of Louis XVIII.

Another sign of the unique importance in Louis's life of his ministers is that they were almost the only political advisers he had. As he boasted in 1821, he had no *Cabinet Vert* – a reference to the horde of unofficial advisers and adventurers whom Marie-Antoinette had received in her *Cabinet Vert*. No other politicians saw Louis regularly in his *Cabinet Particulier*, or had any real contact with him, except for Chancellor Dambray, the *Directeur-Général des Postes* two mornings a week (see page 365), and Ferrand, to whom he gave an audience once a week (Louis's fondness for this rather reactionary, not very competent politician is a mystery). Otherwise even the most important politicians or the most senior civil servants were simply names or faces to the king if they were not ministers: he only saw the Comte d'Hauterive, the most senior official of the *Ministère des Affaires Etrangères*, when the minister was away at a Congress.[45]

The unique position of ministers in Louis's life is also shown by the fact that after 1814 the enormous network or private correspondence which he had maintained in exile seems to have dried up. This may have been due to natural causes, the people he had needed to write to either dying or now being available for audiences. But it meant that after 1814 his correspondence was, like so much of his life, nearly always official and political and conducted with or through his ministers. Thus to get a realistic image of Louis's life we should think of him not as he is represented in the pictures of his reign, surrounded by his family, his soldiers, or his Court, but as surrounded by his ministers. They formed a magic circle of magnificently uniformed, lavishly paid and rewarded, bitterly envied successes round the king.Symbolizing the degree to which politics dominated his life, they were the most important of his subjects.

CHAPTER XIII

The King and the Ultra-Royalists September 1815– September 1816

Politics, which so dominated Louis's life, were completely transformed by the Hundred Days. Before the return of Napoleon I, almost all Frenchmen, however discontented they had been had accepted the Government of Louis XVIII, and were prepared to work for their political ends within the framework of the Restoration: one sign of this acceptance is that in March 1815, although the emperor was advancing on Paris, even politicians as liberal as La Fayette and Benjamin Constant had reasserted their support of Louis XVIII.

After July 1815, the Restoration became as narrow and partisan in character as other nineteenth-century French regimes. From now on there would always be a hard core of Bonapartist opponents to the regime who, even when they were no longer suffering under the repression launched in the summer of 1815, showed their hostility by continuing to live in exile, by dabbling in conspiracies, or by abstaining from any act which implied acceptance of the Bourbons. Thus, after the Hundred Days, many Bonapartist generals stopped going to Court until 1819 or 1820, in the case of a few irreconcilables like Generals Mouton, Lamarque and Foy, until after the death of Louis XVIII. His state apartments would never again be as packed as they had been in 1814–15.

Moreover, this Bonapartist opposition was given greater importance, and powerful and articulate allies, by the backing of that fraction of liberal opinion which had been foolish enough to support Napoleon I or the Commission of Government during the Hundred Days. By doing so it had broken the bridges leading it to success and office under the Bourbons, since even a monarch as mild and conciliatory as Louis XVIII could hardly want to employ politicians who had unequivocally rejected his dynasty. Indeed of the thirty-five ministers who served him after 1815 only one, Comte Molé had served the Government of the Hundred

Days. So after 1815 liberals like La Fayette, Benjamin Constant and the famous journalist Etienne de Jouy, who had compromised themselves during the Hundred Days, were far more hostile to Louis XVIII's Government than they had been before 1815. It was not essentially a hostility based on principle, for Louis's Government remained faithful to the *Charte* of 1814, and would be more avowedly liberal in 1818-19 than in 1814-15. It was basically a struggle for power and office, which was now waged outside as well as within the framework of the Restoration, by plots and riots as well as by debates and intrigues. And many liberals, with the instinctive monarchism of early nineteenth-century France, now began to play with the idea of another dynasty: the Prince of Orange (who in 1816 married the Duc de Berri's reject, the Grand Duchess Anne, and might be imagined to have the backing of the Tsar) or the Duc d'Orléans, whose refusal to return to live in France after the Hundred Days emphasized, as it was meant to, his opposition to Louis XVIII or Prince Eugène.

However, although the popular base of the Restoration was now narrower than before the Hundred Days, it had not been entirely negative for Louis XVIII. It was now clear who his friends and enemies were, and the treachery of his enemies had given him an excuse for entrusting the main posts in the Government and in the army to people who had proved themselves his friends. The vague discontent of 1814–15 was now replaced not only by more active hostility in those parts of France which had supported Napoleon I, but also by frenzied Royalism in those areas which had remained loyal to the king. And this Royalism found expression in the extraordinary Royalist ceremonies which exploded all over France in the summer of 1815. In Toulouse on 21 July a magnificent procession of *Gardes Nationaux*, students of the *École de Droit* and women (three of the most stalwart pillars of French Royalism in 1815) escorted the bust of Louis XVIII, decorated with the Saint Esprit, to the Hôtel de Ville. In Marseille, the bust of Louis XVIII was paraded through the streets every day by members of popular confraternities, singing songs in *patois* especially composed in his honour. In Bordeaux and Toulouse in late August, the Duc and Duchesse d'Angoulême were given the most triumphal reception of their lives. Their carriage was un-horsed and pulled by the adoring population, they were pelted with flowers, and the duchesse, weeping with happiness, was barely able to stop her admirers from tearing her clothes to pieces in their rush to possess something she had worn. So great was the local adoration for the Angoulêmes that in Bordeaux the white flag of the Bourbons was now always edged with the green of the

Angoulêmes livery (which was also the colour of the Artois's livery). That August the Duc de Berri from Lille, the Duc de Lévis from Arras and Chateaubriand from Orléans reported to friends in Paris that people in the capital simply had no idea of the strength of Royalism in the provinces.[1]

In fact Royalism, so often thought of as most at home in palaces and salons, showed itself, in France in the reign of Louis XVIII, to be at least as much at home in the streets and the provinces. And throughout France endless ceremonies in the streets, celebrating the *Fête de Saint Louis*, the anniversary of the return of the king, or the installation of his bust in the Hôtel de Ville, continued to be attended with fervent enthusiasm into 1816.

These ceremonies did not rely on emotions and enthusiasm alone to create a Royalist atmosphere; they also offered bread and wine, paid for by the authorities or the local Royalists. On 13 January 1816 at Semur, for example, to celebrate the installation of the bust of Louis XVIII in the Hôtel de Ville, the townspeople were given white bread (coarse brown bread was what they normally ate), as well as the opportunity to sing Royalist songs '*où les femmes exprimaient encore plus vivement tout leur amour*', ('where the women expressed their love for the king even more passionately'), and to swear an oath of loyalty to the king. Then there was a banquet, probably restricted to the middle classes, where many toasts to *Louis le Désiré, le tant regretté* (Louis particularly liked the latter epithet, which had been coined during the Hundred Days, and thought it was even more flattering than the former) were drunk, followed by a ball given by the *Garde Nationale*, '*où tout ce qui est royaliste de toutes les classes a été invité*' ('where all the Royalists of all classes were invited'). Again, as with the scenes in the *Jardin des Tuileries* in July, the surprised phrase *de toutes les classes* shows that Royalism briefly broke down the fierce class barriers of early nineteenth-century France. Madame Champagne ends her entry for what was clearly one of the most memorable days of her life with an ecstatic expression of popular Royalism: '*Puissions-nous jusqu'à cent ans crier vive Louis XVIII le désiré, vive notre bon Roi, vive celui qui nous a sauvé tous, vive celui que nous chérissons et que nous n'aimerons jamais autant qu'il mérite l'étre*' ('May we live for a hundred years to cry long live Louis XVIII *le désiré*, long live our good King, long live he who has saved us all, long live he whom we adore and whom we will never love as much as he deserves.')[2] Few Kings have ever inspired such adoration.

It is against this background of enthusiastic Royalism, even in a town like Semur in the province of Burgundy not renowned for its Royalist fervour and in the presence of a widespread revulsion against the Bonapartists and liberals whose support of the emperor had led to a second foreign invasion, that elections to a new Chamber of Deputies took place in August 1815. There was a much larger turnout than in May – 68.5 per cent compared to 37 per cent of the tiny electorate of about 100,000 – and everywhere Royalist deputies were elected. Indeed 78 per cent of the new chamber were Ultra-Royalists devoted to the most extreme doctrines of the Right, and usually uncontaminated by service of any other cause than that of the Bourbons.

One of the most surprising aspects of the election is that it went completely against the wishes of the Government (see page 265) although, incredibly, Fouché was elected in two constituencies. But even those involved in the *Chevaliers de la Foi* which was still a very powerful Royalist secret society, did not think that their society had had more than a marginal effect on the Ultras' electoral success. It was, essentially, a reflection of the swing in public opinion against those held responsible for the Hundred Days. And the composition and attitude of the new chamber were so different from those of previous legislatures that Louis gave it the name by which it has been known ever since: the *Chambre Introuvable* ('the unbelievable Chamber').

The first issue which occupied the new Chamber was vengeance. For the fervent Royalism of 1815–16 was founded not only on love of Louis XVIII and the Royal Family, but also on hatred of all those thought to have aided Bonaparte, among whom, inevitably, the Royalists often included their own personal enemies. And Royalists, as they had shown in the *Jardin des Tuileries* on 12 March, could be almost as brutal towards their enemies as the Revolutionaries in the summer of 1815, quite independently of Louis's Government in Paris, Ultra-Royalist gangs in Marseille, Nîmes and Toulouse, sometimes known as *verdets*, after the colour of Angoulême's and Artois's livery, launched a reign of terror against all whom they thought to be their enemies. In Marseille in late June, at least fifty people were killed and hundreds fled. In Avignon, Maréchal Brune, who had commanded Provence for the emperor, was murdered on 2 August, and his lacerated corpse tossed into the Rhône. In Nîmes, many Protestants suspected of having supported the emperor were killed by their traditional enemies, the Catholic Royalists: in an orgy of hate, women were stripped and beaten with boards studded with nails in the shape of fleurs de lys if they were accused of not being good Royalists.

This terrible violence affected only certain parts of France and

was, although apparently Royalist, often more concerned with
other issues. In Nîmes, for example, it really reflected the hatred
between the town's Catholic and, much richer, Protestant com-
munities which was so strong that Meyerbeer's *Les Huguenots*
could not be performed there until after the World War II. Moreover, these Ultra partisans some of whom had strong connections
with the *Chevaliers de la Foi*, showed their contempt for royal
authority when they murdered two of Louis's commanders, General Ramel in Toulouse on August 15, and General Lagarde in
Nîmes (where he was trying to reopen a Protestant church) on
12 November simply because they did not conform with all the
Verdets' plans. The trials of their murderers, which could only
take place two years later, resulted, like those of modern Mafiosi,
in some scandalous acquittals, although two of the six accused of
murdering Ramel were sentenced to a few months' forced labour.[3]
It seemed possible that green, the colour of the emperor's livery
and uniform, was making a second appearance as a threat to
Louis's authority, this time as the symbol of rebellious Ultra
bands.

But after the fall of the Talleyrand ministry in September 1815,
conflict between the Government and the Ultras died down for a
time. The Government now introduced three laws, setting up
Cours Prévôtales, authorizing the imprisonment of political suspects without trial during the next year and inflicting rigorous
punishments for *cris, discours et écrits seditieux*, which provided
a legal basis for Royalist repression. Under these laws perhaps as
many as 6,000 people were convicted between 1815 and 1817.
At Lavaur in the Tarn, for example, two farmers and an iron-
worker were given sentences ranging from two months to a year
for crying '*Vive l'Empereur et merde pour le roi*'. In Lyon, the
most Bonapartist of cities, 210 people were tried for political
offences between July and December 1815; 45 were acquitted,
but 165 were imprisoned. A laundry-woman, for example, got
two years for what may have been simple clumsiness: 'tearing off'
someone's *fleurs de lys* buttons.[4]

This repression was not the result of Louis's personal intervention, although it again shows how much his reign affected the
lives of ordinary people. However, he was personally involved in
the punishment of the generals and politicians found guilty of
having favoured the success of the emperor, since one of the finest
prerogatives of his crown was the right of pardon. The Government had excepted fifty-six Bonapartists from its amnesty on 24
July (the number of exceptions gave rise to some acid jokes :
Fouché was said to have forgotten none of his friends). Whereas

most of the accused had the good sense to get out of France, three, Lavallette, La Bédoyère and Maréchal Ney, who had all helped Bonaparte before Louis left France on 23 March, stayed and were captured.

They were all condemned to death for treason, as they had to be if the régime was to show that it took itself seriously. But Louis showed himself inexorable in his refusal to pardon them. His palace was now guarded not only against possible attack by his enemies but also to prevent the entry of three desperate women, Madame de Lavallette, Madame de La Bédoyère and Maréchale Ney, to stop them begging for mercy as Louis went through the *Salle des Maréchaux* on his way to Mass. Louis refused all pleas for La Bédoyère, even those of one of his oldest friends, a relation by marriage of La Bédoyère, Charles de Damas. Louis said that he was the guiltiest of the Bonapartists, guiltier even than Bonaparte himself; La Bédoyère had led his regiment over to Bonaparte at a time when determined leadership, or a bullet in the right place, might still have turned the tide. Even so, Louis must have been cold-hearted not to accept the extremely moving, deeply Royalist plea not for forgiveness, La Bédoyère's crime was too atrocious, but for permission for the traitor to hide his shame in exile, which came from his mother-in-law, a former lady-in-waiting of Louis's aunt Madame Victoire.

Louis also refused the pleas of Madame de Lavallette, whom Marmont boldly escorted into the Tuileries, although Lavallette was only guilty of taking over his office slightly earlier than Napoleon I's other officials on 20 March. Lavallette in fact escaped in January 1816 disguised as his wife. Maréchal Ney was not so lucky, despite all the factors which might have pleaded in his favour. Unlike La Bédoyère, he had led his troops over to the emperor on an impulse swept along by the torrent of events and by the emperor's deceitful blandishments. But despite his legendary reputation as *le brave des braves*, Louis refused to forgive him. He was shot on 7 December.

The reason for Louis's heart of stone was that, as in the world of the Emigration, he was caught by the particularly vengeful mood, not only of the *Verdets* of the Midi, but also of the Royalist political world in Paris. Court officials' wives were wearing earrings in the shape of gallows. Old friends like Bonnay and La Chatre begged their master to show some firmness, and assured him that he would only reign in peace if he punished and executed enough. The deputies, in the *Chambre Introuvable* were furious at what they saw as the criminal weakness of the king in not punishing more. On 28 October for example, Piet whose salon was a principal meeting place for the large number of deputies who belonged to the *Chevaliers de la Foi* declared in the Chamber '*c'est à vous à garantir ce Roi qui ne s'appartient pas à lui-même*' ('it is for you to protect this King who does not belong to himself'), a clear sign of how easy these Ultras would find it to flout the king's will. For the Ultras Louis did not belong to himself, he was not the king, he was their king who should behave as they wished. And the Ultra majority in the chamber, some of its number being prepared to excuse the massacres in the Midi, was out for blood.[5]

Even Louis's niece, who in 1796 had begged her uncle to show more *douceur*, was now in favour of severity and what she called a *parti vigoureux*. In contrast to the Empress Joséphine who had successfully interceded with Napoleon for the lives of the Polignacs and other Royalist conspirators in 1804, the Duchesse d'Angoulême, to the amazement of many Government officials, remained adamant in her refusal to beg Louis for Bonapartists' lives. What good had mercy and forgiveness done her family in 1814? It is significant that people felt only she could save the Bonapartists. Her uncle was already suspected of being dangerously moderate.

Vengeance however, was not confined to Ney, La Bédoyère and Lavallette. Throughout 1816, trials of other generals, if they had begun before the promulgation of the Government's final amnesty on 12 January, continued and three were executed – these deaths were perhaps even more shocking than those of Ney and La Bédoyère. The final amnesty also banished all members of the Bonaparte family from France and forbade them to own property there, although their property had already been sequestrated in December 1814. The same law also banished those Regicides, including Fouché, who had shown support for the emperor during the Hundred Days. This was against the personal wishes of the king, formally expressed to the Chamber by his *Président du Conseil*, since it infringed the article of the Charter which guaranteed freedom from all pursuits relative to political behaviour before 1814. But the Chamber, angered by Lavallette's escape in January, which they blamed on Decazes, was reaching new heights of delirious blood-lust. Blondel d'Aubers, brother-in-law of Artois's chancellor, denounced the ministers and declared the deputies' duty '*de défendre le souverain contre sa propre clémence*' ('to defend the sovereign against his own mercy'); the Comte de Béthisy, an Aide de Camp of the Duc de Berri, ended a speech calling for more vengeance and denouncing the *faiblesse* of the Government with the famous cry '*Vive le Roi quand-même*'

('Long live the King despite everything').[6] And the Regicides were banished, providing yet again how ready Louis's subjects were to disobey the formally expressed wishes of the king.

The conflict between the chamber and the Government was scarcely less bitter over the second main demand of the Royalist reaction, for a purge or *épuration* of Bonapartists from political life, and in particular from Government service. No such purge had taken place in 1814, and this omission, it was felt with some justification, had helped Napoleon I's return in March 1815: many mayors and prefects had helped and welcomed him as he marched on Paris. So now, for the first time, the Government of Louis XVIII did what every other nineteenth-century French régime did on seizing power; it sacked its enemies and installed its friends in office, satisfying many more Royalist ambitions than in 1814, but creating a much larger pool of discontented and hostile former officials of the Empire.

The exact size of this purge has never been established. But in one department of Normandy, the Calvados, the Prefect, Ferdinand de Bertier, a founder member of the *Chevaliers de la Foi*, sacked two of the six *sous-prefets* and over 300 *maires* and *adjoints*, which shows something of the scale. It was now that prominent Bonapartist officials who had been maintained in 1814, such as Denon, the great Egyptologist and Director of the Louvre, lost their jobs. Probably, as Bertier's descendant and the best modern historian of the Restoration, Père de Bertier de Sauvigny estimates, as many as 50,000 to 80,000 people, a third to a quarter of all civil servants, were affected.

What is certain is that it was not enough for the chamber. For the *Chambre Introuvable* was now beginning to show itself as a dangerous parliamentary threat to Louis's authority and ministers, not just over their policy toward the Bonapartists, but also over the day-to-day running of the Government. The supporters and *protégés* of the *verdets* – Ultra deputies did defend the massacres in the Midi – really were almost as much of a menace to Louis's authority, in a verbal and political way, as Bonapartist soldiers and conspirators. They wanted the triumph of their party not only in the provincial administrations and the law-courts, but also at the national level, in the king's Council. And the means they used to attack the king's ministers, paradoxically for people so united in their detestation of the Revolution, was their parliamentary majority. From the beginning they wanted, according to Villèle, a deputy from Toulouse who in 1814 had advocated a return to the *Ancien Régime*, to '*nous emparer de cette Charte absurde ... le seul levier qu'on puisse en ce moment substituer au pouvoir royal*' ('seize hold of this ridiculous Charter ... the only lever we can substitute at this moment for royal power'). These enthusiastic Ultras, who were becoming increasingly distinct from those Royalists who supported the king and his ministers, showed as little regard for the wishes of the king as some modern 'democrats' do for the wishes of the people.

Throughout the session the Ultras attacked Louis's ministers with relentless and irrational verbal violence, more or less openly accusing them of not executing the repressive laws and *ordonnances* against the Bonapartists (31 October), and even of favouring the escape of Lavallette (4 January). They also attacked the budget itself, the lifeblood of the state, which was particularly dear to Louis's heart. On 8 April there was an appalling scene when Villèle, who had rapidly established a reputation as one of the most capable of the Ultras, accused Lainé, President of the Chamber, a brave moderate Royalist personally favoured by Louis, of being a liar. Some Ultra deputies also openly advocated a return to certain aspects of the *Ancien Régime*. Blondel d'Aubers wanted to abolish the penalties now in force against those who advocated the return of the *biens nationaux* and the reimposition of the tithe. Another deputy proposed that the *état civil* (registers of births, marriages and deaths) should be returned to the clergy. Villèle himself, on 19 March, denounced the Government's efforts to *calmer les inquiétudes* of the purchasers of *biens nationaux*; and he was meant to be one of the more moderate Ultras.

Faced with this mounting opposition, which was backed by most of his Court officials and relations, Louis continued to support his ministers – although, in their opinion, never forcefully enough. He took great interest in the operations of the chamber, as he did throughout his reign, discussing the order of speakers with Decazes, his favourite minister, and writing long comments, which were obeyed, on aspects of the law against *écrits séditieux*. Like his ministers, he was dismayed by the violence of the deputies' vengefulness telling Pozzo, with some truth, '*si ces Messieurs avaient pleine liberté, ils finiraient par l'éurer lui-même*' ('if these gentlemen were allowed their own way, they would end up by purging him'): few of the Ultra deputies would have been sorry to see Artois ascend the throne. Only over the question of religion did Louis share some of the extremism of the chamber, and hope (as in 1814) that the State would stop paying salaries to Protestant priests. However, Richelieu, wise and moderate, prevented him from carrying out this plan.

Louis's decision to support his ministers was just as much due to his satisfaction with their policies as to his growing love for Decazes. Richelieu had obtained better terms for France in the Second Treaty of Paris, signed on 20 November 1815, than Talleyrand had been able to hope for. France now only had to pay an indemnity of 700 million francs and to support an army of occupation of 150,000 for five years (instead of 800 million francs and an occupation of seven years). But it was finally reduced to the frontiers of 1790, losing Savoy and towns on the Belgian and German frontiers, in all about 300,000 people. The ministers were appalled, calling the treaty *'un des monuments les plus affligeants de notre histoire'* ('one of the greatest disasters in our history'). But to people who were not French it seemed that, largely due to the return of a king trusted by the Allies, the prestige of Richelieu and the moderation of the Tsar, France did very well by the treaty: in similar circumstances it had treated Austria and Prussia much more harshly. By the middle of December all foreign troops had left Paris, and by January 1816 they were restricted to the seven northern departments proscribed by the Treaty of Paris.

The Commander-in-Chief of the Army of Occupation was the Duke of Wellington, and in December 1815, to show that he had forgotten their quarrel over the Louvre, Louis proposed to offer him the magnificent estate of Grosbois, between Paris and Fontainebleau. This would also have been a subtle way of reassuring the owners of *biens nationaux*, since it would have meant Louis buying an estate he himself had owned as a prince from the heirs of Maréchal Berthier, but it was not very tactful to want to instal a general, who had frequently defeated the French army, at the gates of Paris. As with his proposal over the Protestant priests, however, his ministers prevented Louis from committing this blunder.

Among Louis's ministers, Richelieu, sensible, moderate and loyal, was the most important. Louis knew Richelieu commanded great respect by his honesty, his patent sincerity, his friendship with the Tsar and his name: in this elitist age, an aristocratic name carried much more weight in politics than it had done in the eighteenth-century, since ambassadors and deputies were more easily impressed by a Richelieu or a Montmorency than Louis XV and Louis XVI had been. But, much as Louis XVIII respected and valued Richelieu, he did not really like him. Richelieu was too upright and too independent – in the Emigration he had not hidden his preference for serving the Tsar rather than the king. He was extremely sensitive and enjoyed nothing better than complaining about the ordeal of being *Président du Conseil* – Louis's old friend Lady Malmesbury called him '*Jean qui pleure*' someone always gloomy and pessimistic.[8]

The minister whom Louis really loved was Decazes. For Decazes was not just a minister whose skill Louis deeply admired; he was more than a friend, a substitute for the son Louis had never had, and on whom the aged invalid lavished all the tenderness which found so little outlet within his own family circle. In an entirely un-sexual way, Decazes was the love of Louis's life, someone to whom, by 1816, he was closer than he had ever been to Madame de Balbi, d'Avaray or Blacas. Louis's daily letters to Decazes are far more natural, amusing and intimate than those he wrote to anyone else, and they reveal how close these two men from different worlds, different generations and different political backgrounds, had become.

On 18 April 1816 Louis wrote yearningly '*ne songez-vous jamais que vous avez un père? Je songe si souvent que j'ai un fils*' ('Do you never feel you have a father? I feel so often that I have a son'). Their intimacy deepened and by 11 July Louis was begging Decazes to let him be a friend and to share his problems for, as Louis put it, '*les peines qu'on garde pour soi rongent, minent, celles qu'on épanche dans le sein d'un ami se soulagent et s'atténuent*' ('the troubles we keep to ourselves eat us away and wear us down, those we share with a friend seem lighter and less oppressive'). Even a king can need a friend of the heart.

Louis, who was so fond of miniatures, also had a mania for initials, which was perhaps a sign of his desire to reduce words and the outside world to manageable proportions. He had referred to his greatest enemy as B.P., and he would often end his letters to Decazes with a whole series of initials, which the poor minister had to decipher. The letter of 11 July, for example, ended m.e.j.t.p.s.m.c.e.j.t.b.m.e.m.f. ('*mon élie, je te presse sur mon coeur et je te bénis, mon élie, mon fils*': (my elie, I press you to my heart and I bless you, my elie, my son'). Thus already, by the summer of 1816, Louis and Decazes were the most intimate of friends, so intimate that Decazes received an honour which none of Louis's other favourites had been given, which in all Louis's long life only Artois, in the early days of the Emigration and sometimes Angoulême enjoyed, and which was the most unequivocal mark of royal favour and intimacy of all. The king called him *tu*.

Whether Decazes was a worthy recipient of so much favour and intimacy has long been an object of controversy. He was a very Balzacian character. Like Rastignac and Lucien de Rubempré, he came from a small town in the Royalist south-west of

France, and he too was determined to rise to the top of the world of power and pleasure in Paris. It is even more Balzacian that Decazes owed his final triumph, his entry into the Council, not only to his good looks, charm and intelligence, but also to his position as *Prefet de Police*, which first gave him access to the king.

From 1815 to 1818 Decazes was Minister of Police at a time when the police was unbelievably complex and very important: Balzac's secret societies, *contre-polices*, and crooks turned policemen, are no exaggeration. Perhaps it was inevitable that Decazes should display some of the characteristics of politicians who rely too much on secret information, *agents provocateurs* and intercepted letters. Metternich's love letters to Princess Lieven, Metternich's letters from Talleyrand, offering to sell him French official documents, and the Prussian ambassador's despatches to Berlin, are only some of the correspondence intercepted by Decazes's agents and, at least in extracts, shown to Louis. He felt that he knew everything, had anticipated everything and had all the answers. He infuriated many officials, for example the Prefect of the Gironde, by claiming to know what was going on in their own departments, when in fact his information was often incorrect.[9] Moreover, he had other defects. He could give the appearance of being a rather light-weight person, vain, talkative, and eternally optimistic. Indeed he was '*Jean qui rit*' to Richelieu's '*Jean qui pleure*', and this was one reason for his success with Louis who, like most people, enjoyed having his spirits raised.

These were, however, minor defects in 1816 compared to the fact that Decazes was a moderate minister devoted to the king. It has often been said that Louis was influenced by Decazes to turn against the *Chambre Introuvable*. Influence is the least definable of qualities, and certainly Decazes was soon appalled by the chamber's violence and its attacks on himself. But everything in Louis's past, his moderation, his caution, his love of reason, his pride in the Charte and his devotion to royal authority, combined to disgust him with this passionate and extremist chamber which attacked all his ministers (not only Decazes), and threatened certain articles of the Charte it despised. As early as March Richelieu, the *Président du Conseil*, whom Louis so respected, wrote that he was '*au désespoir*' from all the Chamber's attacks on the Government.

What made these attacks particularly dangerous, he added, was that they were supported by the princes and the Court. And Louis was in turn attacked by many well-informed people, by Richelieu in letters to the Tsar, and by Wellington in a stern letter to Louis himself, for his fatal weakness in not forcing his family and entourage to follow his political line. But this was easier said than done. In France in 1815–16 political feelings ran so high that not even the persuasion of the king could have much effect on Court officials who knew that he disliked using Court office as a political weapon, and so felt secure in their offices. Only with courtiers such as La Chatre, who were friends as well as servants, did Louis have some success, not in persuading La Chatre to change his views, but in persuading him to vote for a law of which he disapproved.

If it was difficult to extract obedience from the Court: it was even more difficult to obtain it from the Royal Family. Richelieu wrote that he wished Louis had the courage to be the master of his own family. But Louis had no control over the independent and wholly determined minds of his niece and his brother, the most extreme members of his family. They had their own political ideas, bred of considerable worldly experience and much personal suffering, and the persuasion of the king was not going to alter them. Five years later, finally realizing what Louis had known all his life, Richelieu wrote of Artois: '*Dans toutes mes conversations avec lui, tel je le trouvai en entrant dans son cabinet, tel je le laissai en en sortant; toujours je l'ai vu chef de parti, jamais l'hériter présomptif du Royaume de France.* ('In all my conversations with him, I always left him in his *cabinet* exactly the same as when I entered it; I have always seen him behave as the leader of a party, never as the heir presumptive to the Kingdom of France.') Conversation had no effect on Artois. Conversation was almost the only weapon Louis and his ministers had. The princes' incomes had been fixed by a law in 1814 for the duration of the reign, money could not be used. Exile from Court would only make them even more magnetic centres of opposition to the king – as Louis and Artois had been at Coblentz in 1791–92. Louis could no more stop the opposition of his family than George II or George III could that of the Prince of Wales.

So, as in 1814, Louis tried to keep the princes as much as possible on his Government's side. In September 1815, Louis himself suggested Vaublanc, who admits in his memoirs that he was considered to be more devoted to Artois than to the king, as Minister of the Interior, and Artois probably began by supporting the Richelieu ministry. But very soon the course of events, and the extremism of the chamber – some of whose most *exalté* members were connected with Artois's household (see page 326) – drove the two brothers apart yet again. Artois and his courtiers did not control the Ultras in the chamber as Richelieu and Wellington alleged. The deputies were independent and dedicated provincial Ultras who, as Villèle's letters show, needed no encouragment from Bourbon princes and Parisian courtiers to be violently opposed to the king's Government. But Artois's publicly known – although never publicly expressed – attitude certainly encouraged them. It was not easy for such loyal Royalists to oppose their king. However, they could at least comfort themselves with the thought that the heir to the throne was on their side. And surely, given the contrast between his glowing good health and his brother's enormous bulk, their prince, their chief, would soon be king.

Some people could not bear to wait until that longed-for day of the realization of their policies. In 1816, Louis was in quite good health, which may have encouraged him in his independent political line. In July, Lady Malmesbury found him looking 'ten years younger than last year . . . and indeed [he] is quite brisk' His gout had eased to such an extent that he could even wear boots. So how could the king be persuaded to change his policies and his ministers? France was not yet a wholly parliamentary monarchy. The Richelieu ministry stayed in power because it pleased the king rather than because it had a majority in the Chamber of Deputies. Perhaps the time-honoured techniques of Court intrigue would be more effective in changing Louis's policy than opposition in the chambers – he had, after all, shown himself to be open to personal pressure at Ghent and Cambrai in 1815, and in Paris in 1789. So in early 1816 there was a plan to bring back Blacas, now ambassador in Naples, to act as Louis's right-hand man again. Originally Wellington supported it in the hope that Blacas would act as a buffer between Louis and his family. But by March the princes and Stuart, the English ambassador, were also in favour, probably in the hope that Blacas would persuade Louis to follow a less liberal and moderate course. However, Blacas, who was basically loyal to his master, refused to move without a written order from Louis. And the order never came.[10]

It cannot be entirely a coincidence that it was after the failure of the attempts to engineer Blacas's return that people began to talk about a peasant from Gallardon, near Chartres, who said that he had a message from heaven for the king. On 15 January 1816, Martin de Gallardon had seen an angel wearing a gleaming white robe and – since this was the nineteenth century – a top-hat, who told Martin to go and warn the king that he was in danger, that he was surrounded by traitors, that he must institute a *police générale de ses états*, that he must take measures to

strengthen the Church and that Lavallette's escape had been
planned by his own officials. This nineteenth-century Joan of Arc
– la Pucelle had also been visited by angels who told her to go
and see the king – like his predecessor impressed all who met him
by his honesty and patent sincerity. He was not out for money or
fame. Indeed to begin with, his visions brought him nothing but
trouble since, after being examined by Decazes, he was sent to
Charenton, the celebrated insane asylum, on 8 March. But the
doctors there did not think him in the least bit mad.

It is now that the key to the riddle begins to be clear. Evidently
Decazes thought that Martin should be seen by doctors rather
than by the king. But some very powerful people thought otherwise. On 29 March three people came to see Martin at Charenton
(how did they know he was there?) including an Aide de Camp
of Artois, Vicomte Sosthènes de La Rochefoucauld, and a priest
from the *Grand Aumônerie*. On 2 April, Martin was granted
what few other Frenchmen, and no other peasants, ever received,
an audience with the king. When one considers that Martin came
from Gallardon near Esclimont, one of the *châteaux* of the Duchesse de Luynes, who was mother-in-law of the Ultra leader Mathieu de Montmorency and grandmother-in-law of Sosthènes de
La Rochefoucauld; that Sosthènes de La Rochefoucauld says in
his memoirs that the Montmorency already knew Martin; and
that Martin's message denouncing Louis's *trop grande bonté*,
calling for more repression, more religion and the removal of
traitors about the king (i.e. Decazes), *exactly* reflected the immediate political preoccupations of the Ultras; then it seems impossible that this extraordinary chain of events could simply have
been a series of coincidences. It is tempting to suggest that Martin,
whose visions could have been inspired or suggested by the conversation of the guests at Esclimont, was launched at Louis by
Ultras who were Catholic enough to know about Joan of Arc in
order to further their political aims. Another connection between
Martin and the world of Catholic Ultra-Royalism was that after
he started having his visions, he saw his very ardent *curé* every
evening; the *curé* would have had little difficulty in contacting
Louis's revered *Grand Aumônier*, Mgr. de Périgord.

However, Martin was an honest man who clearly believed in
his visions. And the whole mysterious business would never have
taken place if Louis, like many extremely rational and sceptical
people, had not had a strong superstitious side to his nature (see
page 86). Two accounts of the audience survive, written down
from Martin's own words by a doctor at Charenton and by
Martin's *curé*. From both it is clear that the king and the peasant

got on very well, Louis pressing Martin's hand, allowing him to sit down and listening to his message with deep respect. At one point Louis even cried – were his tears perhaps caused by a growing realization of what Martin's message really meant? Martin also told Louis '*choses secrètes du temps de son exil*', which ten years later he announced to be that Louis had once thought of killing Louis XVI during a hunting expedition, and that Louis XVII was still alive.

This is, however, extremely unlikely. It agrees neither with the accounts written under his dictation in 1816, nor with his reverence for Louis XVIII, whom he frequently referred to as king and sire, and '*un brave homme*'. At the end of the audience, which lasted about half an hour, Louis, polite as ever, asked to be remembered in Martin's prayers and summed up the audience in the phrase, used by Louis XIV when he too was subjected to a visionary, '*voilà des choses qui ne doivent etre connues que de vous et de moi*' ('these are things which should only be known to you and me'). Martin left the palace singing the king's praises, and an extraordinary aspect of the whole affair, which naturally became the talking-point of France, was that there was no attempt to cover it up. Everyone knew of the angel's attacks on the king's policy, and an account was published the next year by the official *Imprimeur de S.A.R. Mgr. Duc d'Angoulême*. Martin himself returned to his village, where his new-found fame had not made him any more popular. By 1820, he was forging letters signed *Dieu* to increase his own importance, and in the 1830s he believed that Naundorff was Louis XVII.[11]

Whatever the truth behind this Royalist mystery (and one historian has suggested, extremely implausibly, that it was a treble bluff by Decazes to discredit the Ultras even further in Louis's mind), it shows that political feelings in the years 1815–16 were running very high. The Ultras were going mad with rage as it became clear that Louis was not giving in to the pressures to change his ministers. Madame de Montcalm, a sister of the Duc de Richelieu, found that she was being deserted by many of her oldest friends, including Chateaubriand, because they could not stand her brother's policies. For one of the most distinctive features of the Restoration was that politics dominated not only Louis's life, but also the lives of many of his subjects – as was to be expected in an age when people's careers and fortunes and physical safety could be so affected by political events. Members of the elite now chose their lovers, their friends, the salons they went to, the cafés they patronized, the *quartiers* they lived in (in Paris the Faubourg Saint-Germain was Ultra, the Faubourg Saint-

Honoré moderate Royalist and the Chausée d'Antin liberal), the flowers they wore in their button-holes (violets for Bonapartists, lilies for Royalists) and the lines they applauded in plays, according to their political beliefs. Politics so dominated people's lives that men and women who hitherto had talked about little else but hunting and dancing after 1814 suddenly began to hold forth with great earnestness on the budget, the circulation of wheat or the best mode of recruitment for the army. In Paris salons, where political feeling was even more *exaltée* than in the chamber, snobbery itself, as at the time of the Dreyfus Affair, proved weaker than party spirit; if he was extreme enough the most obscure Ultra deputy, for example M. Piet, could find himself more fêted than the Duc de Duras or the Prince de Poix.

This party spirit was now directed with increasing violence against the king and his ministers. The mother of the deputy who cried '*Vive le Roi quand-même*' had carriages queuing up outside her door for four days to congratulate her. The Ultras were so crazy they were prepared to believe anything, not only that Martin had received a message from heaven, but also that Decazes, whom they detested, was a Jacobin, spending all his evenings with Madame Joseph Bonaparte and '*toute la troupe du 20 mars*'. All this occurred at a time when the official repression and *épuration* were proceeding vigorously, when the *Cours Prévôtales* which would try 2,028 cases, of which more than 265 were political, were just beginning to function, and when the Didier Affair (a feeble revolt near Grenoble in May in favour of Napoleon II, possibly involving Stendhal, which won a certain amount of support from feelings of nationalism and the peasants' fear of the return of feudal dues and the tithe) was, on Decazes's orders, being very severely repressed.[12]

What made many of his subjects for a long time refuse to believe that Louis was opposed to the Ultras was that they were very much part of his world. It was Madame Charles de Damas, wife of one of his oldest friends, who thought that Decazes was a Jacobin. Most, though not all, of Louis's court officials (exceptions were Poix and Gramont) and most of his family, except Angoulême, were opposed to his ministers. The Duchesse d'Escars's salon in the Tuileries, instead of being, as Louis had intended, a centre of social reconciliation, was ablaze with Ultra-Royalism. Yet now Louis was pulling away from his world and his past, more decisively than ever before. In 1814, when he granted the *Charte*, most members of his world had seen the necessity of some sort of constitution, and had been only too delighted to accept one which seemed to promise peace and stability in France. The opponents of the *Charte* had been, on the whole, die-hard Counter-Revolutionaries in the provinces and the Royalists who had not been given jobs at Court or in the Government.

Now people round Louis, for example Mgr. de Périgord, his *Grand Aumônier*, and the last surviving friend of his father, were among the most extreme Ultras, and were prepared to use strange methods to advance their views. Yet Louis was impervious to their influence and, as the summer of 1816 wore on, the gulf between the king and the Ultras grew even wider. In May, Richelieu finally got Louis to replace Vaublanc, who was incompetent as well as Ultra, by the moderate Royalist Lainé as Minister of the Interior. But Louis, who was still trying to keep Artois on his Government's side, insisted (according to Madame de Montcalm) on consulting Artois first. And to balance this move Chancellor Dambray, right-wing although no friend of Artois, was made Minister of Justice instead of Barbé-Marbois, whom the Ultras detested.

Artois's chief power base was the *Garde Nationale*, of which he was *Colonel-Général*, and which was particularly important in these years since the new royal army could only be formed very slowly. Recruitment was proving rather more difficult than anticipated, and in April 1816 the Minister of War wrote that the army could only provide half the forces necessary for garrisoning French fortresses. From the autumn of 1815, the *Garde Nationale* was reorganized on a national scale, under three *Inspecteurs-Généraux*, the Comte de Bruges, Allent and Jules de Polignac, and it now incorporated many former *Volontaires Royaux* and *Verdets*. Soon it seemed even to a right-wing minister like the Duc de Feltre that the *Garde Nationale* might be posing a threat to royal authority. Feltre wrote to denounce the '*tendance marquée des nouveaux chefs de la garde nationale à sortir des limites de leurs attributions*' ('the marked tendency of the new chiefs of the *garde nationale* to overstep the bounds of their duties') – a tendency of which their *Colonel-Général* was guilty all Louis's reign. Was the *Garde Nationale*, well-organized, well-disciplined and devoted to its chief, going to be a threat to Louis's authority like the *Verdets* in the summer of 1815?

Relations between the two brothers degenerated. On 1 June, Gérard's portrait of Artois was ordered to be *promptement retiré* from Louis's apartments – surely after a furious royal row. On 17 July, against Artois's opposition, an *ordonnance* countersigned by Lainé placed the *Garde Nationale* more strictly under the control of those crucial agents of royal authority, the prefects, although Artois's national organization was not abolished. But this measure did not lessen Artois's political importance. He was, as Richelieu had finally realized, '*un mal sans rémède*', a hostile heir whom neither the king nor his ministers could control.[13]

Meanwhile a welcome break from the storms of political life was provided by the marriage of the Duc de Berri. Marie-Caroline, granddaughter of Ferdinand IV of Naples, had first been suggested in January 1815 by Talleyrand, who had been totally opposed to the Russian match. In his heart of hearts Louis probably agreed with Talleyrand that it was '*conforme à la grandeur de la Maison de Bourbon, surtout à l'époque où toutes ses branches, battues par une même tempête, ont été relevées en même temps, de ne chercher que dans son sein les moyens de se perpetuer*' ('in keeping with the grandeur of the House of Bourbon, especially when all its branches, battered by the same tempest, have been simultaneously restored, to seek to perpetuate itself only by marriages within the dynasty'). One of the ideas learnt at Versailles, which Louis never managed to shake off, was the unique grandeur and distinction of his own family. So family pride as well as religious sentiment let slip the chance of an alliance with the most powerful sovereign in Europe and compelled Berri, after a moment's hesitation over a Saxon or a Portuguese princess, to marry a Bourbon rather than a Romanov.

That Louis was still in many ways a child of Versailles is also shown by the fact that the wedding celebrations followed almost exactly the pattern of those held fifty years ago to celebrate his own wedding to Marie-Joséphine: the meeting in the forest of Fontainebleau (see illustration 14), *Festin Royal, Jeu, Bal Paré*, plays... However, there were also enormous differences. The setting was different: the Royal Family drove from Fontainebleau not to Versailles but through the Faubourg Saint-Antoine (briefly renamed, in this Royalist year, the Faubourg Royal) to the Tuileries. The marriage ceremony took place not in the chapel of the palace but in Notre Dame, the cathedral of the capital: a difference which probably reflected Louis's constant desire to bring his Court into contact with the public. And the guest list was different.

Of the 241 guests invited to the *Jeu*, for example, excluding Court officials and their wives who were automatically invited, 142 came from the old Court nobility, sixty-one from the nobility which had never been presented at Court before 1789 and thirty-eight from the bourgeoisie, including people like the banker, Comte Greffuhle, and Decazes's sister, Madame Princeteau, who could never have dreamt of going to a royal *Jeu* before 1789. One of the first ceremonial duties of the Duchesse de Berri, in the stern world of the nineteenth century, was to hand out flags to the newly formed regiments of the *Garde Royale*. They looked particularly splendid in the June sunlight, and Louis was delighted, as he told them, not only by their strength and appearance but also, above all, by the *bon esprit* they displayed. At last the king had a reliable military force in the capital.

As royal marriages go, the Berris' was a success, although communication cannot have been very easy at first since the Duchesse de Berri had been so badly educated that she still needed to take French lessons. She charmed everyone, including her husband, by her liveliness and naturalness – a welcome relief from the pompous, formal atmosphere surrounding the rest of the family. Louis was also delighted with her, and wrote to Decazes '*Yeux, nez, bouche, rien n'est joli, tout est charmant, faite à peindre . . . le duc de Berri est amoureux et tout le monde est son rival*' ('Eyes, nose, mouth, nothing is pretty, everything is charming, a pleasure to look at . . . the Duc de Berri is in love and we are all his rivals').[14]

Once the wedding festivities were over, however, Louis was faced with what he himself realized was one of the most important political decisions of his life. What should he do with the *Chambre Introuvable?* Richelieu and Decazes had an answer ready. Richelieu's exasperation with the chamber which made life so difficult for his administration had reached the point where, on 13 June, he wrote that if things went on as they had '*c'en est fait de la France et de la famille royale*' ('it is all over with France and the Royal Family'). He was convinced that a dissolution was the only solution, and he was fortified in his belief by the influence of Pozzo and the Tsar, both of whom, like most foreign statesmen, had long been in favour of a dissolution.

Decazes, who had been attacked so bitterly and in such an insulting and personal fashion by the Ultras, shared this view. Indeed it has been said that it was he who persuaded Richelieu of the necessity of a dissolution. While this cannot be verified, it is unlikely, since Richelieu's letters to the Marquis d'Osmond, French ambassador to England, and his correspondence with the Tsar, show that he was sufficiently exasperated to urge a dissolution on his own. Louis was also exasperated by the assembly which had made life so difficult for his Government: a letter he wrote to Decazes on 18 August shows that by then he thought of the majority of the chamber as an enemy to be confronted rather than a friend to be relied on.

However, he thought that the best means of confronting the chamber was to recall it as it was (there had been suggestions of renewing a fifth of the deputies or – Lainé's preference – of reducing them to the number prescribed by the *Charte*), and to dissolve it only if it displayed the same *opposition constante* as before. Then he would consult *la nation* on whether the king or the chamber was right about the king's ministers – admirable constitutional language which shows the degree to which Louis XVIII had absorbed the assumptions and learnt the practice of parliamentary government.

However, Decazes now launched a well-planned campaign to make Louis accept a dissolution. This campaign clearly shows that, although they were not divided about ends, Louis and Decazes did differ over means, and that Decazes's influence over the king could, as the Ultras feared, be decisive. For it was Decazes who, by the letters he wrote, and the notes and letters he showed, to Louis persuaded him to accept a dissolution.

Decazes knew his king very well by now, and the two main themes which emerge from these notes and letters were well calculated to appeal to Louis's deepest political instincts. The first theme was that the Ultras, who so loudly proclaimed their love of the king, were more interested in their own domination than in '*l'affermissement de l'autorité royale*'. And much as Louis liked to be loved, and to be called *le Désiré* or *le Regretté*, he liked to be obeyed even more. But the Ultras' speeches and actions showed that they were perfectly prepared to flout his wishes. For example, in June, Villéle, who had won a reputation for relative moderation and had rapidly risen to the position of being regarded as the 'general' of the Ultras, refused to form part of the Commission of the Budget: he was more interested in weakening the king's Government than in helping it to survive.

Decazes also pointed out that by their violence and instability, the Ultras were preventing France from freeing itself '*du joug de l'étranger et de la honte du tribut*' ('from the yoke of the foreigner and the shame of the tribute'). Louis was more nationalistic and hostile to foreign domination than has been thought. He very much looked forward to being master in his own house again, and to being the equal in power, as well as the superior in dignity, of the Austrian and Russian Emperors. The *Chambre Introuvable* was clearly delaying this process.

The second theme of the notes and letters Louis read in the second half of August 1816 was that the Ultra deputies were not only hostile to royal authority but were also so reactionary as to threaten the stability of the kingdom. They wanted not only power but also, Decazes claimed, the return of the *biens nationaux*, civil war and alterations to the *Charte*. And Decazes showed his knowledge of Louis's character by pointing out that many of these views were held by courtiers of Artois – which can only have added to Louis's distrust of the Ultras. The menace of the Ultras was also stressed in a letter which Maine de Biran, a rational, moderate and extremely intelligent Royalist deputy, who was devoted to Louis, wrote from the provinces to Decazes and which was shown, as he probably knew it would be, to the king. Maine de Biran wrote what many other people felt, that the Ultra deputies would return to Paris *'beaucoupe plus exaltés et plus fous'* ('a lot madder and more exalted') and that their behaviour was convincing people that Louis was *'le roi des anciens privilèges seulement'* ('king just of the old privileges') – that fatal belief which had been shown to be so widespread in parts of France by the Lyon crowd's denunciations of priests, nobles and the Bourbons, all in one breath, in March 1815.[15]

All this was true. Maine de Biran had been seeing the Marquis de Castelbajac, a leading Ultra deputy, and his violently Counter-Revolutionary views also horrified Comte Molé, the former minister of Napoleon I, and Louis's old friend the Abbé de Montesquiou. Indeed the arrogance of the Ultras and their violent opposition towards the king's Government horrified not only relative liberals, but also right-wing Royalists like Ferrand, Bonnay, the Marquis de Clermont-Tonnerre, a future minister and Haussez, a future prefect. Nothing could be done with them. They were the party of blind reaction and mad exaltation.

But the conflict between Louis's Government and the Ultras went deeper than the immediate political issues of 1816. It was also a conflict between two opposite views of how to run a modern state. The Ultras wanted to use Royalist enthusiasm, Royalist dominance in the chamber, the Government and the army, and the momentary eclipse of the Bonapartists and the *parti national*, to turn France into a party state. They believed that the Hundred Days had shown what happened if all Frenchmen were expected to rally peacefully to the Bourbon monarchy. The only solution was to use force and relentless partisanship to create a monarchy so strong that even those who had shown themselves its sworn enemies would have to accept it.

However, in early nineteenth-century France a party state was almost impossible, as had been shown by the collapse, amid general execration, of the Jacobin Republic of 1793–94. A French Government lacked most of the means of control – relentless propaganda, an elaborate party organization, state domination of economic activity and an orchestrated fear of the external enemy – which have made modern party states like Franco's Spain or

the Soviet Union so stable and secure. The main force of French
Royalism came from popular enthusiasm, that wave of feeling,
infinitely more spontaneous and more widespread than popular
enthusiasm in most modern party states, which had resulted in
the enormous Ultra majority in the Chamber of Deputies. But, as
Maine de Biran wrote in his diary on 2 August, political enthusiasm, by its very nature, cannot last. And after the crisis years of
1815 and 1816, Royalist enthusiasm did die down. The *Gardes
Nationales*, pillars of Royalism in 1815, became progressively less
willing to mount guard. After 1816, cheering crowds filled the
Tuileries gardens only on special occasions, rather than every
Sunday. Once the bust of Louis XVIII had been installed in Hôtels
de Ville all over the country, there were fewer great Royalist party
rallies. Bordeaux itself, the most Royalist city of them all, lost
some of its fervour as the *quais* filled up with ships, and the
Bordelais returned to the more characteristic business of making
a living. And, as Louis and his ministers never forgot, there was
another un-Royalist France, the France which had supported the
Hundred Days, which could not remain in eclipse for ever.

Even if Royalist enthusiasm and party spirit had been able to
provide royal authority with a secure power-base – which is
unlikely – it is doubtful if Louis and his Government would have
wanted to rely on it. It is, surely, in the nature of royal authority
to want to appeal to all its subjects, and to prefer to hold the
balance between different groups and parties rather than to rule
through – and face the danger of becoming the instrument of –
one party. George III, with whom Louis often compared himself,
had tried to reign above party after his accession in 1760. After
he recovered his throne in 1823 even Louis's illiberal and reactionary cousin Ferdinand VII of Spain turned against his Ultras
and his *Voluntarias Realistas* (who, like their French counterparts,
preferred the king's younger, more glamorous and more extreme
brother, Don Carlos) and adopted a middle policy. Even Ferdinand VII did not want to reign as the king of a party. Nor, as he
had shown by his words and actions in 1814, did Louis XVIII.

Another reason which turned Louis against the Ultras was not
only that they were a party, but that they were a particularly
violent and *exaltée* party. Louis's main desire for his kingdom,
as well as for himself, was *repos*, the reverse of party spirit; after
disloyalty what he disliked most in politics were enthusiasm, exaltation and exaggeration – all essential ingredients of the Ultras'
speeches and policies. In 1819 one of the two phrases he inserted
in his speech opening the chambers was an attack '*contre la
violence et l'astuce des passions*' ('against the violence and perfidy

of passions'). And in the notes submitted to him in late August 1816 the Ultras were presented to him, quite rightly, not only as disobedient subjects and dangerous reactionaries, but also as the party of agitation and passion, fatal to the *repos* of France. As Guizot wrote, in much the most brilliant and convincing of the notes Louis read, which explicitly dealt with the level of political life which Louis thought most important, it was the Ultras who now threatened '*la tranquillité des esprits et la sécuritié des existences*' ('peace of mind and security of livelihood'). If only the king abandoned the idea of ruling France through this party, the immense majority of all Frenchmen would rally round the king and the *Charte*. The fatal division of the kingdom into two sorts of Frenchmen, which Louis wanted to abolish so much (see pages 203 and 345), would cease, and he would reign as king of all his subjects.[16]

However, Louis still hesitated to take such a decisive step. Was it really wise to dissolve a chamber which, however dangerous it might be, was at least passionately and wholeheartedly loyal? It needed more letters from Decazes, lengthy conversations with Richelieu, who wrote that getting Louis's consent was like besieging a fortress, a long and difficult discussion in the Council of Ministers on 20 August, and Decazes's threat that he and his colleagues would resign (a threat made with the consent of only some of them) to convince Louis to take this great step. Finally he signed the famous *ordonnance* of 5 September 1816, dissolving the *Chambre Introuvable* and calling for new elections. That evening, when the news broke, Richelieu was cheered at the theatre. In the palace of the Tuileries, Artois, appalled, rushed to remonstrate with his brother. But he was too late. Louis had gone to bed, and had given orders that he was not to be disturbed.[17]

CHAPTER XIV

The Liberal Years September 1816 – February 1820

The news of the dissolution of the *Chambre Introuvable* was greeted by the country with relief and by the Bourse with delight: Government stocks went up three francs from fifty-seven francs to sixty. To many people's surprise, the subsequent elections were a great success. The Government's hopes for a chamber of '*hommes purs mais modérés . . . qui aiment le Roi avec amour et respectent la Charte avec franchise*' ('pure but moderate men . . . who love the King with passion and respect the Charte with sincerity') as a circular by Decazes stated, were largely realized. The new chamber of 238 deputies contained 146 supporters of the ministry (of whom about ten were ultra-liberals possibly hostile to the dynasty) and only ninety-two Ultras. Louis, whose doubts about the wisdom of a dissolution had vanished once he had taken the decision to dissolve, personally intervened, by a letter to his old friend Charles de Damas, to prevent the election at Dijon of a particularly dangerous Ultra, M. Brenet, whom he called a 'mad dog'.

For the next few months the Government, with its firm majority in the chamber (it was the last Government to have one until 1822), seemed as strong as it was moderate. It seemed so secure and so constitutional that on 16 April 1817 the Orléans family, rather shame-facedly, returned to the Palais-Royal from their disapproving exile in Twickenham. Louis, who gave Orléans an audience the next day, concluded from their conversation that his cousin was resolved to behave better now. And these hopes were fulfilled. For the rest of the reign Orléans, carefully watched by the police, was no longer a real problem. Indeed he was less of a problem than the Princes du Sang had been to Louis XV and Louis XVI before 1789, since after 1815 he was deprived of the right to express his views, in the *Chambre des Pairs*, which they had used to such effect in the *Parlement* of Paris. Another sign of the Government's strength was that Chateaubriand who, like many previously moderate politicians, had become a violent Ultra since September 1815, entered into negotiations with the Government in May 1817, hoping to return to office But talks were broken off when it became clear that he and Richelieu could not agree on whether his apologies, or their rewards, should come first.[1]

Chateaubriand's unforgiveable sin in Louis's eyes was that, in a pamphlet published in September 1816, he had suggested that Louis's real desire was to see the Ultra majority in the *Chambre Introuvable* returned. The suggestion that there was a contradiction between the king's official wishes and his real desires had been one of Coblentz's most powerful weapons against Louis XVI in 1791–92, used to great effect by Louis himself (see page 63). So he knew how dangerous it was. But Louis was careful to associate himself with his Government as much as possible. He was, as has already been stated, extremely interested in the political game, and spent much of his day working with his ministers.

He also intervened in politics outside the formal bounds of his *travail* with his ministers. He was prepared to lecture his Court officials at *déjeuner* or at the *ordre* in an attempt to get them to vote for his Government. He would write a letter to a minister, with the intention that it should be publicized, to try to persuade peers to vote for a Government press law. And he used the audiences he granted to presidents of electoral colleges on the eve of elections, to deputies and to a recently appointed mayor to assure them that his Government's policy was his own and that it was based on the maxim that '*Je ne suis pas le roi de deux peuples*'. This was so fundamental to his policy in these years that it appears in documents as different as the instructions of one Lyon police official to another, and Louis's magnificent and prophetic letter of 29 January 1818 to Artois. He had abjured the temptations of party government, and was trying to rally all Frenchmen, rather than just the Royalist half of France, round the *Charte*. He had adopted a policy of moderation, as he wrote to Decazes on 9 March 1817, '*pas par paresse, ni même par goût personnel, mais par raison, mais parce que je crois que seul il peut empêcher la France de se déchirer de ses propres mains et en faire à l'avenir un Etat florissant au-dedans et au-dehors*' ('not from laziness, nor even from personal inclination, but from reason, but because I believe that it is the only way to stop France from tearing itself to pieces and to make it in the future a flourishing state both at home and abroad'). Here we can recognize the familiar tones of a king who had always believed in the supremacy of reason, who had always claimed that his own policies were essentially rational, and the guiding light of whose life, in his opinion, was the cold light of reason.

Such an open and personal commitment to end the divisions among his subjects, and to follow what he called a *route moyenne*, was particularly admirable on the part of a king who had spent much of his adult life fighting the Republic and Empire, in other words one of the two peoples he was now trying to reconcile. He had certainly come a long way from the days of his Emigration, as the great Counter-Revolutionary philosopher Joseph de Maistre, Louis's adviser in 1804, found when he had audiences with his former admirer in 1817 and 1818. From the first moment, de Maistre wrote to Blacas, in the indirect but perfectly understandable language so often used to analyze royal reactions, he realized that '*le vent était contre moi*'. Next year Louis determinedly talked about Joseph's cousin *Xavier* de Maistre's lighthearted book *Voyage Autour de ma Chambre* – the clearest of indications that the king and the philosopher now had nothing in common politically.[2]

Whether Louis's *route moyenne* was as wise as it was admirable was another matter. At first, as the Government's majority in the chamber and the return of the Orléans showed, it seemed to have paid off. But one of the most disastrous single Government measures of Louis's reign, adopted on the advice of his sensible, moderate ministers, was the electoral law of 8 February 1817. This law decreed that elections should take place over a period of several days in the capital of each department, and that, in accordance with the letter of the *Charte*, although not with the practice of 1815 and 1816, there should be elections for one fifth of the seats every year. It also slightly extended the franchise. This law had two drawbacks. First, by making the elections (which lasted several days) take place only in the departmental capitals, it deliberately discouraged rural landowners, naturally among the most conservative of Frenchmen, from voting, since they had to spend a lot of time and money staying in the departmental capitals to do so. In his *Souvenirs*, Decazes, although he had been an enthusiastic advocate of the law, estimates that as many as a third of the voters were discouraged from voting by this law. The Government had chosen to rely on the urban *notables*, rather than on possibly Ultra landowners.

Second, by having elections every year, this law introduced a permanent element of instability into French political life – which is particularly odd from a Government and a king whose declared aim was to give France the *repos* it longed for. Moreover, the new electoral law not only introduced an element of instability into the life of the country, but also made it much more difficult for a Government to maintain a working majority in the chamber. Since one fifth of the chamber changed every year, the Government was likely to have to change its direction every year in order to keep a majority. By 1817, Louis's old adviser Ferrand, one of the few leading Ultras who remained in contact with the Government, was writing that the only cloud on the horizon was the prospect of elections. On 17 December 1818, Louis himself, at a meeting of the Council, could say that '*Tout l'embarras de notre situation . . . se réduit à un seul point, les élections*' ('All the difficulty of our situation . . . can be reduced to one point, the elections').

The people who deplored the law of 8 February 1817 most vociferously, and pressed for the complete renewal of the chamber every five or seven years, were the Ultras, who thereby, not for the only time, showed their good political sense. And the Ultras included not only deputies like Villèle and Piet, and the *Chevaliers de la Foi*, but also all the Royal Family except Angoulême and almost all the Court. Louis's family and courtiers could show more political sense than his constitutional ministers.[3]

It was this occasionally justified conviction of their own rightness, and the feeling that the Government's measures were ruining the monarchy, which gave the Ultras of the liberal years of Louis XVIII's reign their passionate intensity. And the drama of Louis's situation was that, because of the nearly unanimous opposition of his world and Court and family, he felt, as he wrote to Decazes in one of his daily letters, that he was almost completely alone. He knew that even Angoulême who, except over the electoral law, steadfastly supported Government measures in this period, was hardly '*une garantie bien solide*': in 1815, during the brief temptation of the '*royaume du Midi*', he had been '*plus exagéré que personne*'. So throughout this period Louis was very insistent that Decazes should see Angoulême as regularly as possible to keep him convinced of the rightness of the Government's policies – Louis himself hardly ever had a real conversation with members of his family – '*car l'ennemi ne s'endormit pas*'.

L'ennemi to whom Louis is referring is probably that able and determined political partnership, the Comte d'Artois and the Duchesse d' Angoulême (Berri, who was also an Ultra, was politically much less important). The Duchesse d'Angoulême in particular was such a relentless opponent of her uncle's *route moyenne* that in 1819 Louis felt he could not allow her to go on a visit to her favourite city of Bordeaux for fear of how she would behave. Thus one reason for the Bourbons' failure to keep alive the passionate provincial Royalism of 1814–15 was their political dissensions.[4]

Artois, although considerably more flexible than his niece, was far more of a danger. He frequently saw Ultra leaders like Ferdinand de Bertier and Villèle (Villèle every Wednesday by 1819) and it was from his household and entourage that many of the most determined blows at Louis's Government came. In 1816, 1817, and 1818 Vitrolles, now a violently Ultra servant of Artois, wrote *Notes Secrètes* for the Allies denouncing the Royal Government, asserting the strength of the Revolutionaries and quoting with approval a saying by Artois that the only way to govern France was to '*se placer au milieu des siens et tendre la main aux autres*', ('to surround oneself with one's own people and hold out one's hand to the rest'): in other words to govern first and foremost as the king of one people. By pointing out the weaknesses of the Royal Government, these notes in effect, though not directly, urged the Allies not to withdraw from France. This was incredible behaviour from any Frenchman, let alone a Royalist supposedly devoted to Louis XVIII. These notes, which were publicized by Decazes in 1818, only confirmed Louis's detestation of the Ultras, whom he now considered to be dangerous lunatics.

For the Ultras used even more treacherous methods to attack Louis's Government. It is, surely, not wholly a coincidence that only a few weeks after the dissolution of the *Chambre Introuvable*, in November 1816, Madame Simon, widow of Louis XVII's warden in the Temple, began claiming that Louis XVII had been smuggled out of prison, that he had visited her in hospital in 1805 in the company of a black man and said 'Aslikos Morlinghot', and that she had recently been visited by two ladies who, after hearing her story, gave her money. Although these seem to have been the incoherent ramblings of an old woman trying to show that her charge had been grateful to her – 'Aslikos Morlinghot' has no meaning – she was visited by the Duchesse de Berri (who had told her about Madame Simon?) and even by the Duchesse d'Angoulême. In 1817 and 1818, both liberal and Ultra opponents of Louis XVIII in the provinces made use of the gossip and rumours generated by Madame Simon's ramblings, and by the appearance of a false Louis XVII called Mathurin Bruneau who was tried at Rouen in 1818, to assert that Louis XVIII was not the rightful king.[5]

However, these rumours, so useful to Louis's enemies and so perturbing to his police, eventually died down. And in April 1817 the Ultras tried another method to shake Louis's unwavering support of his ministers and the *route moyenne*. On 23 April,

Blacas, who was now ambassador in Rome, arrived in Paris like a messiah, determined to save his king and his country. The motives, and perhaps the motive force, behind this visit were shown by the fact that the first person he saw was the Vicomte d'Agoult, *Premier Ecuyer* of the Duchesse d'Angoulême – a much bolder opponent of her uncle's policies than Artois. Blacas, who did not have Louis's permission to return, was going to try to change his policies. Richelieu, pretending not to see Blacas's arrival as a political challenge, took him to Louis's *déjeuner* saying *'Sire, c'est un voyageur en frac que je présente à Votre Majesté'* ('Sire, it is a traveller in a tail-coat whom I am presenting to Your Majesty') – probably the only person so dressed whom Louis ever received in his palace.

Louis greeted Blacas very warmly as, naturally, did the courtiers, and Blacas recovered both his place at Louis's lunch-table and his apartment in the Tuileries. But Richelieu and Decazes insisted that Blacas must go. Inexplicably, Louis was for a few days unwilling to give Blacas a formal order to leave. It was a display of real personal weakness, unless there are some hidden motives of which we are unaware. Blacas was able to show himself to the crowds at the salon of 1817. But the great picture by Gros (see illustration 10) showing Blacas escorting Louis out of the Tuileries on 19 March 1815, which was the centre of public attention, emphasized not the return but the transience of his favour. On 3 May, Blacas left for Rome on Louis's orders, having assured his friend Madame de Staël that he found things much better than he had hoped.

Blacas's departure demonstrated Louis's commitment to his ministers and the *route moyenne*. Perhaps the only solution was violence. In the summer of 1818, it is almost certain that some Ultra colonels of the *Garde Royale*, such as Colonel Canuel, one of the many former Republicans who had become an enthusiastic Ultra (he is alleged to have said that if he had waded up to his knees in blood for the Republic, he would wade up to his shoulders in blood for the king), discussed the possibility of kidnapping the ministers, perhaps even the king, on the way to Saint-Cloud. This affair, which Louis took quite seriously, was hushed up for fear of the august names – Decazes mentioned Artois's influential Aide de Camp, the Comte de Bruges – that might be compromised by a prosecution. But it was a sign that, like other guards, the *Garde Royale* might not be content just to guard the monarch.[6]

An instigating force, as well as a symptom, of these Ultra plots and intrigues was the violent hatred for Louis's ministers and policies expressed and encouraged in Ultra salons all over France, especially in Paris. Most aristocratic *hôtels*, and even most courtiers' apartments in the Tuileries, now echoed with fervent denunciations of the king and his ministers. The tone of the conversations in Balzac's *La Duchesse de Langeais*, the attacks on Louis as a '*jacobin fleurdelisé*', are no exaggeration: Balzac knew the Duc de Fitzjames, one of the most enflamed of Artois's courtiers, quite well. Some Ultras now openly longed for the death of Louis XVIII.

One reason for the Ultras' violence and desperation was that they felt they were missing the unique opportunity presented to them by the circumstances of 1815-16 to realize their political aims. For the annual elections held in accordance with the law of February 1817 gave ever increasing importance to the liberals: they composed 29 per cent of the new deputies in 1817 and 53 per cent in 1818. It was becoming clear that among the elite with the vote the Ultras were a minority, and that their triumph in 1815 had been a result of special circumstances rather than a sign of genuinely widespread support. Further proof is that their papers, the monthly *Conservateur* and the daily *Journal des Débats*, had fewer subscribers than the liberals' equivalents, the *Minerve* and the *Constitutionnel*: 8,500 and 12,000 compared with 10,000 and 20,000 in 1818.

The rising liberal tide in the country and the chamber did not, however, strengthen the ministry in its struggle with the Ultras. For many liberals were now just as much Louis's enemies as his so-called friends. Thirty-nine per cent of liberal deputies elected in 1817–19 had served in the Hundred Days, and they included such dedicated enemies of the Bourbons as the banker Laffitte, one of the richest men in France, in 1817, Manuel and La Fayette in 1818, and the Abbé Grégoire and Benjamin Constant in 1819. Guizot's assurance to Louis in August 1816 that, after the dissolution of the *Chambre Introuvable*, the great majority of Frenchmen would rally round the *Charte* and the king was being proved wrong.

These liberals adopted a hostile attitude to the Royal Government in part because they were separated by political issues such as the Concordat and the freedom of the press and of the individual. For although the *Cours Prévôtales* stopped operating in the summer of 1817, restrictions on individual liberty such as liability to arbitrary arrest remained in force until November 1818, and censorship of daily newspapers, although not of periodicals, until May 1819.[7]

But the real reason for the liberals' aggressive attitude to the

Government – even someone like Laffitte whose election in 1817 had been supported by the Government and who held office as a Gouverneur de la Banque de France – was their fear of the future, and of the Ultras. If many people were frightened of the Restoration in 1814–15, how much more likely they were to be after 1815, when the Ultra opposition had the backing of the heir to the throne, and many liberals knew that their involvement in the Hundred Days made them suspect to the Royal Government. Why should they rally to a regime which depended on the life of an elderly royal invalid?

The fact that the future, and an emotion such as fear, were just as important as the present, and actual events, as well as the unique character of the king, the regime and the age, helps to give the Restoration its extraordinary emotional and dramatic quality. For, now that he was no longer in the Council, it seemed clear that Artois (one of whose *Premiers Gentilshommes*, the Duc de Fitzjames, was directly descended from an illegitimate son of James II) was an obstinate and extremist prince, who was likely to do for his family what James II had done for the Stuarts. Wellington thought so, Madame de Staël said so to her friends, Laffitte hinted at it in his first speech in the chamber. Louis himself, who had been consoled by Hume in his exile, compared Artois to James II in a draft for a note about the policy the powers should adopt when he died, written on 9 December 1819. The comparison was omitted in the official note, but the same year a translation of Hume's *History of England under the Stuarts* by one of Louis's Lecteurs, de Campenon, came out: surely a warning, indirect but unmistakable, from the king to his younger brother. After all there was a French prince very willing to act the part of William III waiting in the Palais-Royal, in the person of the Duc d'Orléans. Fear of the Ultras and their chief explains why many liberals who had been devoted Royalists in 1814–15, such as the students of the *Écoles de Droit*, members of the Paris bourgeoisie like Baron Ternaux, and politicians like Guizot, Camille Jordan and Royer-Collard, also began to move to the left and to adopt an increasingly critical attitude not only to the Ultras, but to the Government itself – even though Guizot admitted, in an article published on 13 June 1817, that '*la Monarchie a accompli toutes les promesses raisonnables de la Révolution*' ('the Monarchy has fulfilled all the reasonable promises of the Revolution').

However, not all liberals were frightened of the Bourbons. For Angoulême was a loyal supporter of his uncle's Government, and between 1816 and 1820 he went on many provincial tours repeating his uncle's motto of *Union et Oubli* and trying, with considerable success, to calm people's fears and rally them to the régime.[8] Just as, at the end of the reign of Louis XIV, many courtiers had attached themselves to his grandson the Duc de Bourgogne rather than to the Grand Dauphin, so during the reign of Louis XVIII many Frenchmen were prepared to ignore Artois and to invest their hopes in Angoulême – whose reign might well, since there were only two years between Louis and Artois, follow Louis's quite quickly.

Although the elections were a built-in factor of instability, outside the election period and below the class of electors, France after 1816 was beginning to find that *repos* for which it and its king longed so ardently. Although crowds in towns like Lyon and Strasbourg still refused to cry '*Vive le Roi*', they had now grown to accept, or were resigned to, the Restoration. All of France, even the most Bonapartist areas, was entering the great calm of the Restoration, that brief return to tranquility before the revival of the Revolutionary tradition in 1830. Political passions on both sides, the blue as well as the green, were gradually dying down, outside the extremist minorities. The people of Paris continued to be as calm and obedient as before, delighted with any distraction, such as the free food and entertainments provided on the Fête de Saint Louis. Among the electors of Paris a Government survey of 1818 found few ultra-liberals and even fewer Ultra-Royalists. Most electors were indifferent or undecided about politics, torn between resentment of Government interference and influence in the elections and an eagerness for the jobs, scholarships, honours and invitations to dinner which Government officials could offer. A *marchand de vin* recorded as being '*opiniâtrement exalté contre toute espèce de distinctions sociales et, quoique d'une grande cupidité, inaccessible à la voix de la raison*' ('totally opposed to all forms of social distinctions and, although extremely greedy, deaf to the voice of reason') was definitely an exception. Indeed the naively worldly *quoique* confirms what an ambitious, worldly, money-making period the Restoration was.

The basic stability of French life and society in these years helped to rub away some of the more extreme demands of Ultras and liberals. It was very hard to preach drastic change in a country which was settling down to enjoy the status quo. Most Ultras gradually stopped talking about vengeance, restoring the *État Civil* to the Church, or the culpability of the *biens nationaux*. The Ultra leader Villèle was becoming so moderate that in 1819 he even supported a ministerial candidate in an election in Toulouse. In the same way, by 1818 the liberals' great rallying-cry was, as it would be until 1830, '*La Charte, toute la Charte, et rien autre que la Charte*' ('The *Charte*, the whole *Charte* and nothing but the *Charte*'). Perhaps partly because the attachment of Artois and the Ultras to the *Charte* was known to be rather unenthusiastic, this essentially monarchical, rational and workable constitution had become the idol even of those liberals who had been in favour of a revised and less monarchical constitution during the Hundred Days.[9]

The increasing acceptance of the Restoration, and the basic stability of its political structure, enabled Louis and his ministers to get on with the business of governing. They weathered the dreadful peril of the bad harvests of 1816 and the resulting bread shortage with relative ease. Louis, who had learned much from the French Revolution, was particularly concerned by the possibility of bread shortages in Paris, probably more so than his ministers. On 17 April 1816 he was urging Decazes either to start a programme of public works or to give out *secours* in the Faubourg Saint-Antoine, a traditional centre of popular revolt, and he always insisted that Paris should be fed first. On 16 May, he was appalled at the sight of that most sinister omen of all in any economy, rotten ears of wheat, when they were brought to his well-furnished lunch-table. But in fact, although there were some heart-rending scenes at market-places until the 1817 harvest came in, and although, as in the French Revolution, the *Gardes Nationales* often sympathized with the rioters, there was no serious trouble, except for those who went away with empty stomachs. The *Garde Royale* showed its mettle by remaining absolutely loyal, unlike the *Gardes-Françaises* in 1789, and the Government was able to take various necessary measures, such as importing Russian wheat, subsidizing bakers, and enabling grain to circulate freely throughout the country, without interference from the population. It was all very different from 1789.[10]

One of the most important Government measures in this period was the reorganization of the army after Maréchal Gouvion Saint-Cyr succeeded Feltre as Minister of War on 12 September 1817. By laws of 12 March and 10 August 1818 (partly prepared under Feltre), the volunteer army of 1815 was abandoned for lack of volunteers: it was still under 117,000 strong in 1817. Instead, conscription was introduced at the rate of 40,000 conscripts a year to bring the army up to a strength of 240,000. Although this infringed the *Charte*, since it brought back compulsory service (but only for a tiny minority: 300,000 reached the required age every year; 40,000 were selected and of them only 10,000 were fit enough to enter the army), it passed the chamber without trouble. The most controversial measures, bitterly opposed by the Ultras and by many moderate Royalists, were those which insisted that all officers must have served as *sous-officiers* (N.C.O.s) or in an *École Militaire*, that officers could only be promoted if they had served four years in the preceding rank, and that up to the rank of Lieutenant-Colonel two thirds of the places would be awarded according to seniority, and only a third according to the king's wishes. These measures in effect favoured former Napoleonic officers, since they were more likely to have served four years in their present rank, and a later measure guaranteed half of all new promotions to *officiers en demi-solde*. This infuriated not only Ultras who were convinced that the army was being packed with traitors but also people like Wellington who had previously supported all the ministry's measures. Richelieu and even Louis himself turned against laws they had agreed to in the Council: Louis felt that semi-automatic promotion would not make the promoted officers suitably grateful and attached to himself.

But in fact these measures, which also substituted non-territorial regiments for the *Légions Départementales*, did give France a large, and on the whole effective, modern army of over 150,000 (the theoretical size of 240,000 was never reached). The paranoid fears of the Ultras, many of whom convinced themselves that there was not a single loyal regiment left in the army, about the loyalty of the ex-Napoleonic officers were not justified. The Ministry of War's list of *officiers en demi-solde*, some of whom were now recalled to the army, shows how strong Royalism, or realism, now was. In the splendidly dry language of the Restoration bureaucracy, it lists 5,541 *Royalistes*, 2,891 *passables*, 2,064 *mauvais*, 1,707 *douteux* and 658 *très mauvais*. Moreover Gouvion Saint-Cyr, who had proven his loyalty in the Hundred Days, only altered a few of Feltre's extremely Royalist, but often doubtfully competent, appointments. For example, only 21 of 137 colonels of infantry and cavalry regiments – the men actually in command of the barracks and garrisons of France – were changed between 1817 and 1819.[11]

Another great achievement of the Richelieu ministry was that, by the end of 1818, it had raised the enormous sum of 1,905,950,000 francs necessary to pay off all the Allies' claims on France resulting from their occupation after the Hundred Days. Louis and the Royal Family more generous than in 1814, contributed twenty millions from the *Liste Civile*. When one considers that this figure does not include the direct cost of the war to France in terms of human lives, destruction of property, loss of territory and army expenses, the sheer waste of the Hundred Days becomes apparent. Bonapartes were, in every way, more expensive to run that Bourbons.

The prompt payment of the Allies' indemnity enabled Richelieu, at the Congress of Aix-la-Chapelle which met in October-November 1818, to obtain the final departure of Allied troops two years ahead of schedule and, much against the will of Metternich and Castlereagh, the end of all formal alliances and conferences uniting England, Prussia, Austria and Russia against France. Louis, who had been begging for Allied withdrawal since 1817, and had written to Wellington on 19 April that it '*occupe toutes mes pensées*', was delighted. At last he was master in his own house again. And he called the congratulatory visit the Tsar paid him on 28 October one of the happiest moments of his life. They even seem to have got on quite well this time. Louis said how grateful he was for the Tsar's share in Richelieu's success. The Tsar said he thought the *Garde Royale* '*superbe*', and assured Louis that Richelieu would not, as he had threatened, resign. To show his pride and gratitude Louis sent Richelieu the first French Saint Esprit of the reign, with the familiar phrase, '*Les petits présents entretiennent l'amitié*'.[12]

But when Richelieu returned to Paris from Aix on 28 November he was faced not with the applause of a grateful country, but with one of the tensest political situations of Louis's reign, which would only be solved by some of the most complicated and unfathomable political intrigues since Louis's return through Mons and Cambrai in June 1815.

As at Mons and Cambrai, Louis still occupied the centre of the political stage. For the king's 'will', although not decisive over individual matters of policy, was still at least as important as support in the chamber in determining the survival of a ministry, or a minister. Louis's support alone had enabled his ministers to withstand the attacks of the *Chambre Introuvable*, and his decision to call new elections and his openly-proclaimed desires for *hommes purs et modérés* had created the new moderate majority in the chamber. Louis had made Decazes, and it was only through Louis that Decazes was able to exert so much influence outside the sphere of the Ministry of Police.

In the autumn of 1818, Louis's ministers had to decide whether the Government should continue its *route moyenne*, turn to the left to prove the Government's enthusiasm for constitutional liberty, or return to the right. Equivalent effects, in a totally different political direction, could be achieved if Louis changed his mind or his favourite, and this is why some Ultras had been so eager for Blacas's return in 1817 or for a coup by the *Garde Royale* in 1818. Restoration politics were still very much those of the palace and the antechamber, as well as of the ministry and the chambers. So the King sitting at his little white desk in the Tuileries, 'working' at least once a week with each of his ministers, talking to Decazes every evening, going through the enormous number of despatched, intercepted letters and newspapers brought to him every day, occasionally emerging into his *Grand Cabinet* for a Council meeting or on his way to Sunday Mass, was still the crucial player in the political game. And his feelings about a minister, his attitude to candidates for a ministry, and the nuances of his behaviour (a nod, a phrase, a conversation) to politicians at Court receptions, could still determine the result of the political game.

What gives the political game of Louis's reign its distinctive flavour is not only the continued importance of the king, but also that, far more than the politicians of, for example, Whig England or the July Monarchy, the politicians of Louis's reign liked to claim that they were motivated solely by a disinterested desire to serve the king, or constitutional liberties. Because politicians had only had a few years to learn the rules of the game in the constitutional monarchy, and because the regime itself was not entirely secure, both were still controversial issues which could be invoked with impassioned, and often very advantageous, sincerity.

In the autumn of 1818, Louis's ministers had to decide whether the Government should continue its *route moyenne*, turn to the left to prove the Government's enthusiasm for constitutional liberty, or return to the right, in order to strengthen the regime. Hitherto, largely owing to Decazes's influence, the Government had been slowly drawing away from the Ultras, as their attacks grew more vehement. Moderate politicians such as Pasquier and Molé had replaced Dambray and Dubouchage, both of whom still sympathized with the Ultras, at the Ministries of Justice and the Navy in 1817. In August 1817 Decazes, who had already been instrumental in elevating Molé, persuaded Richelieu and Louis, against their original inclination, to replace Feltre by Gouvion Saint-Cyr at the Ministry of War. In a very convincing letter, Decazes told Louis that capacity was more important than fidelity, and that Gouvion Saint-Cyr would be more likely to increase the army and get the military budget through the chambers, thus increasing '*notre force dans l'intérieur et notre considération à l'extérieur*', than Feltre. Decazes knew his king well enough to appeal to his love of *considération*. As so often before, Louis chose to put usefulness before loyalty and the interests of the

French state before those of French Royalism; and as has been stated, Gouvion Saint-Cyr gave France a much larger and more effective army.

In September 1818, the Government made another attack on the Ultras by abolishing Artois's national organization for the *Gardes Nationales*, which were now placed firmly under the authority of the prefects. Much to Louis's relief, largely owing to pressure from the Austrian ambassador and Francis I – who knew what it was like to have to deal with ambitious and independent younger brothers – Artois made no public protest against this public humiliation. He confined himself to changing from the uniform of the *Gardes Nationales* to that of his regiment of *Carabiniers*.[13]

But Richelieu, who had supported all these anti-Ultra measures, now began to turn back. He was appalled by the elections of October 1818 which returned such relentless enemies of the regime as La Fayette and Manuel. He feared *l'invasion des principes democratiques*, thought that the Government's liberal moves had been a failure and wanted, as he wrote to Decazes, '*un rapprochement avec les Ultra*'. Decazes, who had been so frequently and so virulently attacked by the Ultras, felt that there was no hope for the Government, or for himself, from such a *rapprochement* – although when such a reconciliation had been discussed in January 1818 Richelieu had been most impressed by Decazes's moderation and restraint in dealing with men like Villèle and Corbière who were his personal enemies.

Another, even more personal reason which drove Decazes against an accommodation with the Ultras was that he wanted to leave the Ministry of Police, which could hardly survive the ending of the repressive laws in November 1818, and move to the Ministry of the Interior. But this post was held by the one minister still in touch with the Ultras and who still went to pay his respects to Artois, a minister with whom Decazes had already had many quarrels, the proud and touchy Royalist from Bordeaux, Lainé.[14]

Richelieu told Decazes of his desire for a *rapprochement* with the Ultras in November. But he did not tell Decazes that he and Molé, who having prostrated himself before Decazes when he wanted to get into the ministry, was now trying to push Decazes out, were already, by 2 November, thinking of replacing Decazes and Gouvion by Villèle and Pozzo. Once Decazes was out of the Council, Molé wrote with glee, his influence on Louis would cease to exist.

Decazes, however, was infinitely superior to Richelieu in the art of political intrigue, and much better at keeping his head. He would never have written, as Richelieu did on 13 November, that a *coup d'état* was the only solution. Probably deliberately, Decazes did not (at least according to Louis) tell him of Richelieu's plans for a reconciliation with the Ultras. Louis was left to learn them from a courtier and from Dambray, and was understandably annoyed at what he called, in the account he later wrote of the crisis, '*une marche qui ne pouvait guère qu'être opposée à celle que je suivais depuis deux ans*' ('a policy which could hardly but be opposed to that which I was following for the last two years').[15] Louis himself, although very worried by the results of the elections – far more worried than he admitted in conversation with the Tsar – and not very fond of Gouvion Saint-Cyr, wanted, as he told Richelieu in November and the Council in December, to continue the policy pursued since 5 September 1816: '*Tendons toujours la main à droite et à gauche, en disant avec César: celui qui n'est pas contre moi est avec moi.*' ('Let us hold out our hands to right and left, saying like Caesar: he who is not against me is for me.')

This attitude reflected Louis's view of government. Influenced by his years in England, after the Hundred Days he wanted French politics too to be a game between a united Government and a united opposition. '*Tout ce qui est contre le gouvernement est dans l'opposition*' ('All who are against the Government are with the opposition'), he wrote to the Abbé de Montesquiou when trying to persuade him not to vote against the 1817 electoral law. In 1818, Louis naturally wanted to keep in existence such a capable and moderate Government, which contained his beloved favourite, and was horrified that some of his ministers should be flirting with the Ultra opposition.

But as Louis often complained (he once actually wrote '*O torys! O whigs! où êtes-vous?*'), the nature of the political game was different in France. The opposition to the French Government was both right-wing (the Ultras) and left-wing (the extreme liberals); and each of these oppositions was sub-divided into different factions. In England, Louis pointed out, the Grenville faction had joined the Whig opposition after it left the Government in 1806. But in France political passions were too high to enable the two extremes to form a united opposition. For the same reason Louis's Government and its majority in the chamber were beginning to be torn apart by the magnetic attractions of the right, advocated by Richelieu, and the left, pushed by Decazes. There was no longer a firm political base for a Government of the centre, as was shown by the miserable figures for subscriptions to moderate Government newspapers. Readers much preferred the *Constitutionnel* or the *Journal des Débats* to *Le Publiciste* or the *Journal des Maires*. Louis's hopes that his Government could continue on its *route moyenne* were in vain.[16]

There was, however, one exception to the lack of contact between the right and the left oppositions: Talleyrand. After his fall from power in September 1815 he had found writing his memoirs as unsatisfying as sacked politicians generally do. No one was ever more conscious of the rewards of office, and in the autumn of 1816 he opened his magnificent *hôtel* in Paris, and began to entertain on a princely scale in the hope of rallying discontented politicians to his side and catering himself into the Council. At first he did not have much success, but by 1818 his parties were much better attended, particularly by the Ultras who, having loathed him all their lives, were now prepared to use him as a leader in their attacks on Louis's Government. Many Ultras, at that legendary dinner-table, enjoyed laughing at their host's digs at Louis XVIII, such as the lament that the king's health was so good '*qu'il enterrera la monarchie*' ('that he will see the monarchy into its grave'). After 1815, Talleyrand's role in French politics was rather like that of Lloyd-George in English politics after 1922: an able and ambitious statesman, far more respected abroad than at home, slightly outside (he would have said above) conventional politics, impatiently awaiting his inevitable return to power.

Louis detested Talleyrand, a minister who, as well as being disloyal and disrespectful, had tried to cut him out of political life. He feared and despised what he referred to as Talleyrand's '*vanité blessée*' and '*ambition aigrie*' and was particularly appalled at the emergence of a separate party, basically liberal but appealing to many Ultras, headed by Talleyrand, in addition to the two oppositions. Throughout what he called '*cet étonnant mois de decembre 1818*' his main consideration, even more than to keep Decazes, was to avoid a Talleyrand ministry, which he was only prepared to consider '*en désespoir de cause et avec la plus excessive repugnance*' ('as a last resort and with the most extreme repugnance').[17] The unusual directness of Louis's language is an indication of how strongly he felt.

The complicated intrigues of December 1818 need not be recounted in full here. It is clear, however, that Louis, so often represented as the slave of his favourites, was finally prepared to part with Decazes in order to keep Richelieu, the senior and more respected minister, as his *Président du Conseil*. On 23 December, he agreed to Richelieu's request that Decazes and his young wife, pregnant at sixteen, should leave the country within a week for the embassy at Naples or St Petersburg: Pozzo, who was devoted to the Russophile Richelieu, kindly offered the Comtesse Decazes a fur coat to keep her warm when she got to Russia. Louis was heart-broken, and wrote to Decazes that he wished he was dead.[18]

But Richelieu could not patch a ministry together. So great was the distrust of the Ultras that none of his old colleagues was prepared to stay in a new, more right-wing ministry. Even Roy, who had replaced Corvetto at the Ministry of Finance on 8 December, and was the classic non-party politician, '*ni à droite ni à gauche*' as Louis wrote approvingly, refused to serve Richelieu, and this seems to have been decisive in convincing him that his attempt to form a new Government was doomed to failure. Moreover, when Richelieu turned even further to the right he met with a similar failure: by 26 December, it was clear that Villèle was too demanding to serve in a Richelieu ministry, and Villèle was the most moderate of the Ultras. The right and the centre-right were still too far apart, and too distrustful of each other, to work together. On 26 December, Richelieu sent Louis his final resignation, urging him not to worry about Talleyrand and to send for Maréchal Macdonald or Maréchal Marmont instead.[19]

Another reason for Richelieu's resignation has been put forward by Molé and by political observers like the Comte de Castellane and the Neapolitan ambassador, namely Richelieu's conviction that Louis would never really support a Government without Decazes. But this is only based on their observation of Louis's behaviour at Court to Decazes's father-in-law, who was greeted very warmly. Even Richelieu was sensible enough to attach more importance to the firm promise of Decazes's removal from France than to a few kind words at Court.

Just as Richelieu had shown himself incapable, tactless and ill-prepared in this crisis, so Decazes had emerged as a much more weighty figure than before. He was not just the king's favourite, the slightly disturbing Minister of Police, who was trying desperately to cling to power, despite his professions of devotion to Richelieu. His known attachment to liberal causes made him, as Richelieu admitted, the most popular man in the Council: he is one of the few popular royal favourites in history. And once it became clear that Richelieu could not form a new ministry, Decazes automatically became the key figure in the political situation, not only because of Louis's favour, but also because he could succeed where Richelieu had failed, and form a united and capable ministry.

Instead of following Richelieu's suggestion to send for Macdonald or Marmont, Louis, on Decazes's prompting, sent for General Dessolles, a moderate, rather colourless figure, who had been a *Ministre d'État* in 1814–15, and was the first of the *illustres épées* who were so often to be a solution to future French ministerial crises. Louis despised him as '*un bien pauvre homme*' – there was some unknown incident in 1815 when Louis had had to buy his loyalty. But, to suit Decazes, on 29 December Dessolles became *Président du Conseil* and *Ministre des Affaires Etrangères*. Louis, as always, intervened in the choice of ministers more to exclude some people – Pozzo di Borgo, the Duc de Doudeauville and Camille Jordan – rather than to make any strong propositions of his own, except for de Serre, a leading liberal orator. In the end the ministry contained Decazes as Minister of the Interior with control of the police, as he had wanted all along; de Serre as Minister of Justice; Baron Louis, an ally of Talleyrand and a friend of Decazes, as Minister of Finance; Baron Portal, a friend of Decazes from Bordeaux who had been a *Sous-Secrétaire d'État*, as Minister of the Marine, where he was a great success; and Gouvion Saint-Cyr, who throughout the crisis had attached himself to Decazes's fortunes, still as Minister of War. Talleyrand, who had been living for the summons to the Tuileries, could not believe that he had been passed over. Artois and the Duchesse d'Angoulême, who had been supporting Richelieu and thought they were already *maîtres du champ de bataille*, were appalled. The man they were coming to regard as their worst enemy had triumphed again.[21]

The new ministry, dominated by Decazes, was clearly more liberal and left-wing than its predecessor. It represents the end of the Government's publicly proclaimed aim in, for example, Decazes's circular of September 1816, to live above parties. From now on Louis's Governments, which had previously been able to appeal to both centre-left and centre-right, tended to appeal to either the right or the left. The aim of Louis and his ministers to ignore party passions had produced a worthy and useful Government in 1816–1818, but one which, as party divisions grew stronger, had begun to appear weak and unrealistic. The moderate ministerial block in the chamber steadily evaporated after 1817 until, by late 1819, there were 80 to 90 right and centre-right deputies, 110 to 115 left and centre-left, and only 60 who could be called ministerial. Thus to get laws passed in the chamber, the Government now had to appeal to right or left, rather than being able, as in 1817, to rely on a large, obedient block of its own supporters. The Ultras, who had always said that it was hopeless to try to reign above party, and much more sensible to use party spirit and passions in the service of the Government, had been right all along. But in January 1819 the party which Louis's Government allied itself with was the left.

The electoral law, which in December 1818 Louis and Decazes had admitted to be dangerous, was maintained, probably largely because it appealed so much to the left. In order to please the left, the *Gardes du Corps*, which Louis wanted to keep distinct from the army as a sacred privileged band responsible to the *Capitaines des Gardes*, were by an *ordonnance* of 7 January, as Decazes had long wanted, drawn closer to the army. In future *Gardes du Corps* would have to have attended *Écoles Militaires* or to have at least four years' service as officers in the regular army; and, as in the army, two thirds of promotions were to go by seniority. Another measure calculated to appeal to the left was that the remaining Ultra Government officials, including nineteen prefects, were replaced by moderate or liberal officials. In addition, in March and November 1819, in order to secure the Government's majority in the Chamber of Peers, a huge batch of sixty-eight new liberal peers was created. Finally, in May the press was, for the first time in Louis's reign, freed of all restrictions other than the usual laws of libel.

This turn to the left was extremely daring for the Royal Government. Since so many liberals had compromised themselves during the Hundred Days, it meant relying on men who had been, and perhaps still were, sworn enemies of the Bourbons. Thirty-nine of the sixty-eight new peers, and six of the nineteen new prefects, had served during the Hundred Days, as had many of the liberal deputies who now voted for the Government.

The results of employing such officials could be strange, to say the least. For example, Stanislas de Girardin, a prefect of the Hundred Days who became Prefect of the Côte d'Or in 1819, was an obedient official who lavished praise on Louis in his speeches. But Louis would have been horrified if he had known that one of his prefects was waging war on religious schools and the *missionnaires*, and was encouraging art students to paint scenes from the Napoleonic wars. Although Girardin was an extreme case, and the effects of the massive *épuration* of 1815–16 were never wholly undone, so that the Government's services still remained basically Royalist in composition, one can see why even a moderate Royalist like Roger de Damas could now write of Louis's '*haine pour les Royalistes*'. Had Louis become that dispiriting phenomenon, a king who is the friend of his own worst enemies?[22]

Louis no more liked the new left-wing direction of his Government than did the Royalists. He was personally opposed to liberalization of the press laws. He had fought tooth and nail to defend the privileges of the *Gardes du Corps*, exploding with rage till he was red in the face when Decazes first mentioned the subject to him. He had already admitted that the electoral law of 1817 was a disaster. He was very worried by the creation of so many new peers. So, as the Ultras feared, Decazes was now decisively influential not only over specific Government measures such as the dissolution of the *Chambre Introuvable*, but also over the general direction of Government policy. And the basis of his influence, Louis's favour, was as concrete as ever. When Decazes had married the hideously ugly liberal heiress Mademoiselle de Sainte-Aulaire in 1818, Louis's letters about the event were quite incredible in their obsessive sentimentally, and at Court people smiled at how naively happy the king looked. On 18 November 1818, Louis called himself '*ton pauvre vieux père qui t'aime tant*' ('your poor old father who loves you so much'): on 13 February 1820, the very day that all their dreams would be shattered by the assassin's blade, he called him '*le fils que j'aime de tout mon coeur*' ('the son whom I love with all my heart').[23]

But it was not love alone which made Louis agree to Decazes's policies, so many of which he had originally disliked. He genuinely believed that Decazes had the answers for France's problems. He really admired his *Elie's* abilities; in the space of one letter he compared him to Scipio, Cicero and the Cardinal de Retz. And Louis thought that, given the relentless opposition of the Ultras, the new left turn was a political necessity. The creation of the new peers, for example, was only a reaction to the Ultras' and the centre-right's decision to *supplier* the king for a change in the electoral law and – the sort of blow which particularly appalled Louis – to reject a vital financial law regulating the budget. Moreover, the Decazes-Dessolles ministry was genuinely monarchical. It relied on Louis's authority and in no way tried to exclude him from the business of government, unlike the other left-wing ministry of Louis's reign, the Talleyrand ministry of the summer of 1815.

To a certain extent the leftward turn in 1819 did pay off, as Decazes, who was just as devoted to the interests of his king as he was to his own, hoped. While many of the new peers and prefects were more devoted to liberal principles than to the Bourbon dynasty, none of them was actively disloyal after 1819. And they included five marshals and many generals, who would have been regarded as an ornament to any second chamber in the nineteenth century. The Government was trying to return political life to the situation of 1814, when everyone had worked within the framework of the Restoration. Most of the remaining political exiles, for example Savary, Duc de Rovigo, Maréchal Soult, and General Exelmans, were now allowed to return to France, and Decazes himself went out of his way to make their return easy. Many more Napoleonic generals now began to go to Court.

Moreover, Louis's reputation benefited from this experiment of which he did not really approve. It was now that even the most sceptical liberals were finally convinced that Louis did genuinely support and desire a parliamentary, constitutional Government. Thus Louis's favouritism was, as he may have realized, actually useful. He was known to be so fond of Decazes that no one would believe he was not whole-heartedly behind the Government's policy. It was now that a moderate liberal like Viennet, a future leader of the July Revolution and pillar of the July Monarchy, wrote in his diary with delight that Louis was an admirable king who '*ne répudie aucun héritage honnête de la Révolution*' ('repudiates no honest legacy of the Revolution'). It was now that a Napoleonic general like Rapp, who had served in the Hundred Days, was received in audience by the king, was delighted by his flattering welcome, and became a loyal supporter of Louis's Government in the *Chambre des Pairs* and a personal admirer of Louis himself: if only '*tous les autres grands*' (i.e. the princes) imitated him, Rapp sighed. From the point of view of his *considération*, of the liberal elite's trust in the king – factors which Louis himself thought extremely important – the experiment of 1819 was not wasted. Henceforth doubts would arise not over Louis's adherence to the *Charte* but over the possibility of him ever backing a Government of Ultras.[24] Far from going backwards, as Wellington complained, Louis's Government was making considerable progress in its attempts to win over the non-Royalist half of France.

If Louis supported Decazes's policies, and believed that they were the best solution to France's problems, it was a conscious decision, rather than a sign that Decazes now dominated Louis's mind as well as his heart. Louis was too sensible, too intelligent and too selfish ever to become that pathetic phenomenon, against which he had been warned in his youth, and of which European history offers so many examples, a prince who '*ne voit plus que par son favori* . . . [and] *se livre à toutes ses idées*' ('only sees through his favourite's eyes . . . [and] adopts all his ideas'). Moreover, there were material as well as personal factors which made a favourite's domination, in early nineteenth-century France, almost impossible.

In a country which had a relatively and, after May 1819, an

entirely, free press, Decazes could not hope to dominate Louis's mind, since Louis could not be prevented from receiving impressions and information from sources outside Decazes's control. Louis read several newspapers every day and complained to Decazes in June 1819 that his mornings were '*cent fois plus tristes que jadis*' from what he read in them.

Moreover Louis had another means of information at his disposal, which he used, like his grandfather before him, to check up on his ministers, namely the letters intercepted by the post office. When he was *Directeur-Général des Postes* in 1815, Beugnot found that he was expected to send Louis every day a *tableau synoptique* of news based on the reports of the provincial *Directeurs des Postes*, as well as copies of the most intersting intercepted letters, and to go and work with Louis every Tuesday and Friday morning at nine o'clock. Louis was always extremely conscious of the force of public opinion, and he was unwilling to rely on the account of it presented to him by the police and the newspapers: there still survives Beugnot's account of the public's favourable reaction to the fall of the Talleyrand ministry in September 1815 with Louis's royal *Bon* underneath. Louis also received copies of letters to or from abroad from the Ministry of Foreign Affairs. His pencilled comments on one letter about himself – '*parfaitement vrai . . . à peu près vrai . . . faux d'un bout à l'autre*' ('perfectly true . . . almost true . . . false from beginning to end') – can still be seen in the Quai d'Orsay.

Beugnot was replaced by an Ultra, the Marquis d'Herbouville, but on 13 November 1816 Louis, furious that he had not been given exact copies of some of Fouché's letters, replaced d'Herbouville with a moderate ex-prefect and deputy, Dupleix de Mézy. De Mézy may originally have been Decazes's choice, but he rapidly became a favourite of Louis. On 25 December 1818, at the height of the ministerial crisis, Richelieu wrote to his sister '*ce pauvre M. de Mézy n'a que le Roi pour appui . . . il lui coûtera plus à sacrifier que tout le Ministère*' ('that poor M. de Mézy has only the King for support . . . he will be more regretted than all the Ministry'). More than Decazes? This is hardly likely, but de Mézy, whom even Molé, the most uncharitable of all the memorialists of Louis's reign, called '*un honnête homme*', did survive the fall of Decazes by twenty-two months. So he was not entirely dependent on Louis's favourite. Thus in addition to the letters intercepted by the police and the Ministry of Foreign Affairs, Louis could read those sent to him by de Mézy. And his letters to Decazes often begin with phrases like '*j'ai lu ce matin une lettre . . .*' (20 February 1817), '*La correspondance de ce*

matin m'avait donné de l'humeur . . .' (13 October 1818), or '*lu
ce matin dans une lettre de madame de Rémusat que . . .'* (4
October 1819).[25]

The survival of these independent intercepted sources of information is a sign that Louis kept his mental independence of
Decazes just as much as he had of d'Avaray and Blacas. He was
perfectly prepared to be critical of the proposals of his *cher Elie*.
On 27 December 1818, for example, Louis wrote that some of
Decazes's ministerial projects were '*pas bien sensés*'. He told
Decazes that he was foolish to try to stop a pamphlet by Chateaubriand from coming out because '*la vanité d'auteur*' would
ensure that copies circulated somehow, and he refused to send
Angoulême to prevent publication. Louis told Decazes he was
wrong about the political sympathies of a deputy, wrong about
the number of times he had mentioned the Saint Esprit ('*Vous
vous trompez, mon cher fils . . .*') and wrong or deceitful about
the religious and monarchical content of a speech by an *académicien*. This is not the language of a blindly doting slave, which
is what even someone who knew Louis as well as Villèle made
him out to be.

Moreover, this mental independence was not simply an empty
royal attitude: it was also translated into action, in particular over
the two institutions closest to Louis's heart, the Court and the
Church. As has already been stated, (see page 279), Louis always
wanted there to be, as he put it, '*entre le Ministère et la Maison
une ligne impassable . . . pour que le . . . roi ait au moins une
ombre de liberté*' ('between the Ministry and the Household an
impassable line . . . so that the King . . . should have at least a
shadow of independence'). Decazes, like most politicians, wanted
to use the Court and Court favour for his own immediate political
purposes. But Louis refused Decazes's request to make Feltre, an
ex-minister, *Capitaine des Gardes* instead of Gramont, his
favourite courtier, or at least to give Feltre the Saint Esprit. Louis
refused the *Ministère de la Maison* to Decazes in January 1818
and February 1820, and to Decazes's candidate Pasquier in January 1819, because he did not want this position to be used as a
pawn in the political game.[26]

However, in the crisis of December 1818, he had consented to
make Pasquier *Ministre de la Maison* when it seemed that such
an appointment might be able to paper over the rifts in the
ministry and to keep Richelieu and Decazes together. When he
was convinced that it was really necessary, it is probable that he
would have allowed even the most cherished Court traditions to
be modified, as had already happened with the *Gardes du Corps*.

Only his increasing ill-health prevented him from being crowned, contrary to all the traditions of French Royalty, in Paris in Notre Dame or Sainte-Geneviève (now the Panthéon) in 1819. No more impressive tribute to Decazes's immense influence could have been imagined. But in early 1819, Louis again lost the use of his legs. His world was closing in, and his physical activity, never enormously varied, was becoming increasingly restricted to the invalid's trinity of bed, wheelchair and armchair. In the summer of 1819, he had to use a wheelchair to get from room to room in the Tuileries, although he could still do his *tour d'Europe* (i.e. go round all the ambassadors in the *Salle du Trône*) on his legs. '*L'essentiel était de ne pas être trop ridicule*' ('The essential thing was not to be too ridiculous'), he wrote to Decazes, and if he felt that he had succeeded in his palace, he was obviously far less sure of the effect he would create throughout the long, tiring and very public ceremony of a coronation.[27]

The other institution over which Louis had a policy of his own was the Church. Nothing could be further from the truth than the contrast so often drawn between a bigoted, priest-ridden Charles X, and a sceptical, irreligious Louis XVIII. There is no reason to believe that Louis was not a believing Catholic; and one of the guiding lights of his political career was a desire to protect and strengthen the Roman Catholic Church. This was one aspect of his constant interest in public opinion and in the *considération* necessary to protect the monarchy. For he genuinely believed that the Roman Catholic Church, with its close contact with the masses, its tradition of submission to established authority, and, after 1814, its delight in praising the virtues and sanctity of the Bourbons, would strengthen his throne, and reinforce his subjects' obedience. As Molé wrote '*le chemin le plus sûr pour arriver au coeur de Louis XVIII* [was] *en considérant le religion comme moyen de gouvernement*' ('the surest way to Louis XVIII's heart [was] in considering religion as a means of government').

When he came to the throne, Louis thought that the state of the Church was even worse than in the 1790s. There were only 36,000 priests in 1814 compared to 72,000 in 1789 and, Louis wrote to the Pope, '*Toutes les doctrines antireligieuses autant qu'antisociales ont inondé mes provinces*' ('All anti-religious like all anti-social ideas have invaded my provinces'). Louis was determined to halt this tide of irreligion. In 1814–16, in order to reward the bishops who had remained faithful to the royal cause and to remove fourteen Bonapartist or ex-revolutionary bishops, Louis's Government had wanted the French Church to revert at once to the status quo of 1789. This was incredible behaviour for a Government which was trying to calm public fears of such a reversion in political life. But the Papacy refused to go back on its Concordat of 1801 with the French Republic. There followed some extremely confusing negotiations, which finally ended in both the French Government and the Papacy agreeing, in August 1819, to return to the Concordat of 1801.

It is significant that Louis, often advised by his *Grand Aumônier*, the Cardinal de Périgord, who not only selected candidates for bishoprics, but also, for a few months in early 1816, was actually put in charge of ecclesiastical affairs (he probably had more influence over Louis XVIII than any priest did over Charles X) was personally involved in these negotiations; he was partly responsible for their confusion and contradictions. Decazes, who never showed great interest in the Catholic Church, was not, at first, told about the abortive Concordat of 1817. Thus Louis, who was very proud of all his Government had done to increase the number of *bourses* in seminaries, to augment priests' salaries, and to encourage ecclesiastical missions to revive the faith, rather than Decazes, was probably the driving-force behind his Government's determination to revive Roman Catholicism. Louis was personally involved in this issue far more than in most policy issues of his reign. His desire to revive the Church even affected his attitude towards one of his favourite poets, who had been his *Secrétaire Ordinaire* before the Emigration, J. F. Ducis. When Louis gave Ducis an audience in 1816, he told him to '*composer des vers utiles aux moeurs chrétiennes et à la vertu*' ('compose verses helpful for Christian morals and virtue'). Thus before 1820, Louis's Government was one of the very few avowedly liberal nineteenth-century Governments which also did all it could to revive the power and the prestige of the Roman Catholic Church.[28]

Not only over the Court and the Church, but even in details of ordinary politics, Louis was never entirely dominated by his deep admiration for Decazes's abilities. To take only a few examples; in March 1819, although he found no difficulty in readmitting distinguished soldiers like Marshals Suchet and Mortier and General Dejean, he refused to reappoint all the peers of 1814 who had accepted peerages during the Hundred Days, on the grounds that to reappoint them all at the same time would imply that it had been wrong to expel them in the first place. In February 1820, he told Decazes to introduce a law in the Chamber of Deputies instead of the Chamber of Peers, which he always rather despised, and he was obeyed. On 14 February 1820, he wrote to Decazes, '*Souviens-toi qu'il faut que les lois d'exception soient draconiennes et promptement proposées* ('Remember that the Laws of exception must be very severe and quickly introduced'), which they were.

Thus one can say that Louis XVIII remained independent and authoritative enough for the new leftward policy of 1819, much as he had disapproved of it originally, to have been a policy he had willingly adopted, rather than one which was imposed on him by a domineering favourite. Louis knew where Decazes was leading him. However, it is probable that there were aspects of Decazes's activities which Louis did not know about. Did Louis know that it was at Decazes's instigation that articles were inserted in the English newspapers in the summer of 1818, suggesting that Angoulême, rather than Artois, might succeed the king? Did Louis know that Decazes had police agents so devoted to himself that they were still sending him reports and intercepted diplomatic despatches several months after he had left the ministry?

Such activities were an outward sign of Decazes's main fault, which Louis pointed out to him in 1817, namely that allied to his wonderful '*facilité pour le travail*' was a '*paresse d'esprit*' ('mental laziness') like that which had destroyed Calonne so many years ago: '*je l'ai vu de mes propres yeux*'. ('I saw it with my own eyes.') No minister was more effective in getting a law through the chambers, or managing an election, or using every means to support his policies. But he was so convinced of his own abilities and his own correctness that he – and Louis – did not stop to think that many of his new officials were ill-chosen, or that his new leftward policy was the sort of leap in the dark best taken by a Government which is already in a position of unassailable strength. And unfortunately, the new leftward turn not only failed to create an atmosphere of peace or stability in the country, but also floundered on the fact that there were now some liberals who were deeply hostile to the Bourbons, and would not be won over by the advances of their Government.

Decazes had always prided himself on the management of elections. He prepared for them months in advance and gave extremely elaborate instructions to prefects, sometimes verging on the ridiculous, such as the recommendation to woo voters with '*un dîner ou donné ou simplement proposé*': or, if they could not face it, with '*un bonjour dit avec obligeance*'. In 1817, it was largely due to Decazes's indefatigable activity that the Royal Government had avoided the worst among the liberal candidates. In 1819, however, the extreme liberals won seventy per cent of that year's batch of seats, and among the new deputies was Benjamin Constant. The most spectacular result was in the Isère round

Grenoble, the department which had been so hostile to Louis's Government in 1815 and 1816. There, not only because the Ultras, as usual, preferred the extreme liberals to the moderate centre, but also as a result of the strength and passions of the extreme liberals, the Abbé Grégoire, famous for a declaration that '*Les rois sont dans l'ordre moral ce que sont les monstres dans l'ordre physique*', and for his public adherence to the execution of Louis XVI, was elected. The Ultras, rather than Guizot, had been right all along. One section at least of the liberals was irreconcilably hostile even to the most liberal of Louis's ministries.[29]

So Louis and Decazes now finally decided to do what Richelieu had hoped to do in December 1818, and turn to the right. Indeed they tried without success to get Richelieu to rejoin the Government. At a long and crucial Council meeting on 18 November Louis decided, over the opposition of Gouvion Saint-Cyr, to adopt de Serre's suggestion of a new electoral law. As Louis had foreseen in January, the more left-wing members of the Council, Dessolles, Gouvion Saint-Cyr and Baron Louis, now resigned. The ministry was reinforced by Pasquier, rather a favourite of Louis (Pasquier too was known as *l'inévitable*, since he had a habit of ending up a minister whatever the administration), as Minister of Foreign Affairs, by Roy, whom Louis also favoured, as Minister of Finance, and by the Comte de Latour-Maubourg, a former soldier of the Empire now devoted to the Bourbons, as Minister of War. Decazes now reached the summit of his ambitions and became *Président du Conseil*.

In his entire reign, this was probably the ministry which most pleased Louis and which satisfied his deepest political instincts. It was moderate, capable, loyal and had Decazes as its head. Moreover it seemed that at last Louis's and Decazes's dream was coming true, and that the Ultras, wiser and more moderate than in the past, were rallying to the ministry – rather than, as Artois had proposed in 1818, treating with it as equals. Artois, the Duchesse d'Angoulême and the more moderate Ultras like Villèle supported the new electoral law and even, to Louis's amazement, began to be polite to Decazes. To the horror of *enragés* like Corbière and Chateaubriand (far more extreme than his memoirs would suggest) who, Villèle wrote, preferred to follow their passions rather than their reason, Villèle managed to persuade the *réunion Piet* to vote for the Government's electoral law and the budget. On 23 December Louis wrote to Decazes that '*L'éclaircissement de l'horizon me fait plaisir*' ('The brightening of the horizon gives me pleasure'). By 2 February, he began to think that

even the most extreme Ultras, Mathieu de Montmorency, Sosthènes de La Rochefoucald and Fitzjames might be converted,
and he was particularly amiable at Court to Sosthènes's wife. All
he wanted, he wrote, was for people to know his friend as he
really was.[30] The new electoral law, giving two votes to voters
who paid more than 1,000 francs in taxes, and allowing elections
to take place in each *arrondissement*, rather than solely in the
capital of each department, was to be presented in the Chamber
of Deputies on 14 February 1820.

However, the election of the Abbé Grégoire had only been a
foretaste of what Bonapartist, un-Royalist France had in store for
the Bourbons. Etienne Louvel was a classic enemy of the Bourbons; converted to Bonapartism by a sense of outraged nationalism at France's defeats in 1814, and at the presence of Bourbon
princes with the Allied armies, this morose, unsociable bachelor
had worn the green and gold livery of the emperor as a stable-
hand on Elba and during the Hundred Days. Since 1815 he had
been attached to the king's stables, but had not wavered in his
hatred for the Bourbons, which would not have been lessened by
the liberal and Bonapartist periodicals he read. On the night of
13 February he carried out a plan he had long been meditating
and stabbed the Duc de Berri – the only Bourbon thought likely
to produce heirs – outside the Opera.

The wound was fatal. Berri was carried dying into the director's
office, and the room quickly filled up with courtiers, doctors,
ministers, cousins, politicians, onlookers, his illegitimate children,
his shrieking wife, and finally, at five o'clock the following morning the king (see illustration 17); the quick march of the *Gardes
du Corps* escorting his carriage could be heard long before he
arrived. Berri, who despite his hot temper and terrible manners,
had an honourable, even noble side to his character, beseeched
Louis feverishly for his assassin's life (he was frightened it might
have been someone he had insulted or cuckolded). But Louis,
showing yet again that he had a heart of stone, replied '*Tout cela
demande reflexion. Parlons de vous, mon fils. Cela vaudra mieux*'
('It all demands reflection. Let us speak of you, my son. That will
be more worthwhile'). Then, after the doctors had done their
worst to increase his sufferings, Berri died, and at six o'clock
Louis closed his eyes.[31]

Berri's death unleashed a torrent of hate on Decazes. This was
what his liberal policy and abolition of the censorship had led to!
Ultra newspapers openly accused him of responsibility for the
murder, and some Ultras believed it to their dying day. Chateaubriand, in a treacherous phrase, wrote a few weeks later that '*le*

pied lui a glissé dans le sang' ('his foot slipped in blood'). This was, however, the dreadful truth. For Decazes now had the terrible experience of being abandoned by fortune and his colleagues at the height of his career. Artois and many others on the right told Louis that the new electoral law, and the other repressive measures Decazes proposed on Louis's prompting (see page 368), after Berri's death, would be passed only if Decazes, the great hate-figure of the Ultras, left the Government. And, in contrast to 1818, Decazes could not rely on the votes of the left. Even Royer-Collard and the moderate left had been suspicious of his ministry since November, and no one on the left, not even some of Decazes's closest allies and *protégés*, would support the new electoral law and the new repressive measures.

By 17 February, Louis, who had at first hoped that they could ride out the storm, realized that he could not keep Decazes. A factor possibly just as decisive in Louis's mind as the impossibility of getting the laws through with Decazes was that some *Gardes du Corps*, and some units of the *Garde Royale* staffed with Ultra officers, and enflamed by Ultra politicians, were extremely hostile to Decazes and had to be confined to barracks. Moreover, as in 1802, both Angoulêmes formed a united front with Artois against their uncle. On 18 February, the Duchesse d'Angoulême, incited by extreme Ultras like Vitrolles, went down on her knees in the presence of her father and husband to beg Louis to dismiss Decazes. She even stooped to threats (according to Decazes), saying '*Sire, c'est pour épargner une victime de plus*' ('Sire, it is to spare another victim') – a reference to the threats of some *Gardes du Corps* to kill the minister whom they thought of as a traitor. It is ironical that the reign of the king who, more than most monarchs, desired and valued a large, loyal guard, should be the only time in the history of Europe west of the Niemen and north of the Pyrenees that a guard acted as an independent political force in disobedience to its sovereign.[32]

Whether it was for political or military reasons, Louis knew that Decazes could no longer stay in office. As in December 1818, his one fear was that he would have to turn to Talleyrand, who was already busy planning a liberal-Ultra ministry with Molé and Villèle. But to Louis's intense relief Richelieu decided to accept the *Présidence du Conseil* on 20 February. This was due not so much to Louis's persuasion as to a promise from Artois, who actually condescended to visit Richelieu, to be Richelieu's '*premier soldat*'. Louis refused to allow Decazes to serve under Richelieu (which Richelieu would have refused anyway), saying that it was up to the *Président du Conseil* to choose his colleagues – although

Louis had been quite prepared to intervene in Dessolles's choice of his colleagues in 1819. If he had been as absolute as Louis XVI before 1789, Louis wrote, nothing in the world could have stopped him from keeping on Decazes. But no king knew better when to bow to circumstances. Louis and Decazes continued to see each other and to exchange letters. Louis installed Decazes's portrait in his *Cabinet* (he had not needed it before) and wept with the Duc de Gramont at the thought of Decazes's fall. But Richelieu was as determined that Decazes should leave in 1820 as Talleyrand had been that Blacas should leave in 1815. France was so monarchical that no minister was strong enough to cope with independent royal favourite. Finally, having been made a duke and ambassador to England, Decazes left Paris on 26 February, sped on his way by a tiny, shattered note from his king: '*Adieu cher fils; c'est du fond d'un coeur brisé que je te bénis; je t'embrasse mille fois.*' ('Farewell, dear son; I bless you from the bottom of my broken heart; I kiss you a thousand times.')[33]

CHAPTER XV

The Triumph of Monarchy February 1820 – September 1824

Despite Berri's death, the year 1820 deserves to be called the year of the Third Restoration. For it saw Louis's Government emerge stronger than ever from a series of terrifying crises. The apparatus of the state was strengthened by the three emergency laws introduced by Decazes in February, which were finally passed, with a few alterations, by June 1820. Until the end of 1821 all people suspected of plotting against the safety of the state could be held for three months without trial, if the order for their arrest was signed by three ministers. Newspaper censorship was reintroduced, against the opposition of both the liberals and the Ultras (the Ultras, including Artois, were opposed to press censorship because they felt they had the best writers). Most important of all, the new electoral law proposed to give two votes to about 23,000 of the richest voters, as well as changing the place of elections from the chief town of each department to the chief town of each *arrondissement*, so that conservative country-dwellers could vote more easily.

The reign of Louis XVIII was now quite clearly taking on an illiberal air, and this illiberalism was to prove more dangerous for the regime, in the short term, than the liberalism of Decazes which the Ultras had attacked so vehemently. But Louis and his ministers (who were the same as before the fall of Decazes, except that Richelieu had replaced Decazes as *Président du Conseil*, and two senior, moderate, experienced bureaucrats, Comte Siméon and Baron Mounier, had become Minister of the Interior and *Directeur-Général* dealing with the departments and the police, respectively) felt that they were faced with a declared enemy, the same forces which had briefly triumphed in 1815. In 1820, these forces had to be fought with almost any means available. The laws about individual liberty and censorship were only temporary measures which came to an end in 1821; the electoral law was

374

much more serious, since it was an open attempt to give more influence to the richest of the already very rich electors. But this was an age which worshipped property and the measure, despite all the controversy which it aroused in 1820, soon came to be accepted.[1]

However, the violent hostility it aroused in 1820 was not restricted to speeches in the chambers. The organization of extreme liberal deputies and *notables*, which included Louis's old enemy La Fayette, the banker Laffitte, the Ultra-liberal Marquis d'Argenson, Manuel and a few others, and had begun the reaction by choosing Grégoire as a candidate in the Isère, thought it had a favourable opportunity to bid for power in 1820; and as so often with Restoration politicians, they were inspired by Spain. Just as the reaction of 1814 in Spain had increased French liberals' fears, so the rapid success of a liberal military coup in Spain in early 1820 increased their hopes: it could happen here. The new repressive laws fuelled their fervour and excitement, and soon the tribune of the Chamber of Deputies reverberated with violent attacks on the Government, which could be reported without any restrictions in the newspapers. On 18 May, another liberal noble, the Comte de Corcelles, said that France was at the end of its constitutional existence: on 27 May, La Fayette said that France was relieved of its duty to observe the *Charte*.

In the first days of June there were violent demonstrations outside the Chamber of Deputies between liberals and Royalists (many of whom were *Gardes du Corps* in civilian dress), in the course of which a student called Lallemand was killed. He at once became a liberal martyr. As the new electoral law began to go through the chamber the situation became more tense. A report written for Louis by Siméon pointed out that June 1820 was like August 1792, and that revolutionaries, in league with left-wing deputies, were trying to put pressure on the chamber as well as the palace. That summer, for the first time since 1817, the Court did not move to Saint-Cloud: Louis knew he was facing a crucial testing time for his regime, and wanted to be on the spot. On 5 June, after Lallemand's funeral, student demonstrators tried to recruit workmen from the Faubourg Saint-Antoine with cries of 'Vive la Charte! A bas les Royalistes!' and even 'A bas le Roi!' Although they did not have great success, a large crowd now began to move west, shouting the Bourbons' dreaded cry 'Aux Tuileries!' Luckily the sky, which in 1789 had favoured the Revolution by staying clear all summer, in 1820 favoured the monarchy with a providential downpour. The crowd quickly scattered. But even if there had been no rain, the crowd could not have taken the Tuileries. For the *Garde Royale*, under Maréchal Macdonald, the *Major-Général de service*, was stationed all round the palace, a daunting, determined and devoted force. Demonstrations continued, but the new electoral law was passed on 12 June, and the demonstrations had stopped by 15 June. Evidently they were to a large extent controlled by liberal deputies like Laffitte and Lafayette, who realized that the riots had lost their point, and were, perhaps, frightened by the popular response.[2]

The *Garde Royale* had been tested under the most difficult of circumstances, and had proved its worth. Louis, who must have gone through some rather unnerving moments, was delighted, and congratulated guards officers at Court not only for the *dévouement* but also for the *sagesse* of their men. For by the curious law which makes rioters' blood disastrous for the regimes they riot against (particularly if those regimes are monarchies), bloodshed would have been almost as fatal for the Restoration as disloyalty.

However, the regime's ordeal was not over. A third element in the extreme liberals' onslaught on Louis XVIII, in addition to liberal deputies and Paris crowds, was groups of discontented half-pay officers and ex-officials. The most resourceful of them were General Fabvier, a former Napoleonic officer from Lorraine; Colonel Nantil, a former officer of the *Garde Impériale*, also from Lorraine; and Joseph Rey, a former Napoleonic official in the Rhineland who came from Grenoble, and was a cousin of the man who had guided Napoleon I's advance on Grenoble in March 1815. The Restoration's most dedicated enemies tended to come from the same backgrounds and the same provinces. They were a small band, but one whose contacts, in 1820–23, were dangerously extensive. Fabvier, Nantil and Rey were in touch with students and discontented soldiers and *sous-officiers* through a secret society called *L'Union* and a masonic lodge called the *Loge des Amis de la Vérité*. On 10 August 1820, the anniversary of the assault on the Tuileries in 1792, they hoped to launch a military coup in Paris. Whether their aims were to replace Louis XVIII or simply, as had proved successful with his cousins of Spain and, by August 1820, Naples as well, to frighten him into adopting a more liberal policy, is not clear. Certainly many of the soldiers involved were still fervent Bonapartists.

Another aspect of the plot which is still not entirely clear is the nature of the involvement of liberal grandees like La Fayette, d'Argenson and Manuel. They were committed to the plot, but were they leaders or figureheads? Probably they thought the former, and Nantil, Rey and Fabvier the latter. But whoever the leaders were, the driving force of the plot was, as in Spain and

Naples, to come from the army. And here Louis's regime turned out to be much stronger than his cousins'. The plot, which had been postponed until 19 August, was betrayed to the authorities by two *sous-officiers* in the *Garde Royale*. Maréchal Marmont, the *Major-Général de service* after Macdonald, doubled the guard round the Tuileries, and the whole affair was a fiasco.[3]

What makes the August conspiracy so odd is that the ring-leaders either escaped (Rey, Nantil and Fabvier), or avoided prosecution (La Fayette, Laffitte and d'Argenson). To a certain extent this was because the police, hard as they tried, could never find *preuves de conviction* which would stand up in a court of law. It was also due to the unwillingness of the peers, even of Ultras like Mathieu de Montmorency, to condemn men for political reasons. There had been enough of that in 1815–16. The Government, like the Whigs faced with the problem of the English Jacobites in 1745, may also have been reluctant to advertise their lack of support by the punishment of *hommes marquants*. This is what a letter from Richelieu to de Serre written on 18 August suggests.

But the lack of prosecutions may also have been due to Louis's fear of extremely embarrassing attacks from La Fayette. Did not the ageing revolutionary, perhaps referring to the Favras Affair and the invasion of 1792, later declare in the chamber, to the applause of the left, that he wanted *'la plus grande publicité'*, in which to face his accusers, *'dans quelque rang qu'ils soient placés?'*[4] Louis was a king haunted by the past, his own as well as that of the French monarchy.

Louis's Government had emerged from the first student riots of the modern type, and from the sort of military conspiracy which had defeated his cousins (and, in 1820 the Kings of Portugal and Sardinia also), unscathed and unsmeared with blood, which was almost as important. Indeed by not repressing the riots and conspiracies very severely, for whatever motives, Louis's Government behaved rather better than people like La Fayette, who encouraged plots and riots from the safety of their social and parliamentary positions, but refused to join in until they were sure of success. And in September 1820, after so many shocks and alarms, Louis finally received a blessing.

On 14 February, the drama of Berri's dying hours had been heightened by his revelation that his wife was expecting a baby. And on 29 September, at four in the morning, she suddenly gave birth to the longed-for Bourbon heir. There were amazing scenes as the Duchesse de Berri's servants rushed madly round the palaces trying to find witnesses to the birth who were not attached to the Court and so could not be accused of bias. Just in time some

Gardes Nationaux and Maréchal Suchet, one of the witnesses Louis had chosen, arrived to see with their own eyes the precious umbilical cord connecting the prince to his mother. A few minutes later Louis himself arrived, greeted by the *Gouvernante des Enfants de France*, Madame de Gontaut, '*dans le plus complet négligé*', ecstatically opening the baby's clothes '*pour montrer son sexe*'. Louis was at first speechless with joy, then taking the baby in his arms, touched his lips with garlic and wine, as had been done, over two hundred years before, for the Bourbons' great hero, one of the most popular kings there has ever been, the future Henri IV. God had not abandoned the House of France.

Later that day after Mass, again showing his concern for direct contact with his subjects, Louis appeared on the balcony of the Tuileries. After the cheers of the huge crowd – probably bigger than the crowds of demonstrators in June – had died down, he declared '*Mes enfants, votre joie centuple la mienne, il nous est né un enfant à tous* [cheers]. *Cet enfant sera un jour votre père, il vous aimera comme je vous aime, comme tous les miens vous aiment.*' ('My children, a child has been born to us all. Your joy increases mine a hundred times. One day this child will be your father, he will love you just as I love you, just as all my family loves you.') Brave words, which show yet again how Louis tried to found Bourbon power on the French family as well as on divine right, and to relate his dynasty to his subjects' personal, family lives.

France and the world seemed delighted. At last the Bourbons were shown to have a future. Like Louis XV before him, and the *Prince Impérial* after him, the baby was hailed as *l'enfant de l'Europe* by the *Corps Diplomatique*. Much of France went wild with joy, but nowhere as wild as the city to which Louis had accorded the privilege of giving the prince his title of Duc de Bordeaux. The Bordelais rushed to offer thanks in their churches, and the *Chambre de Commerce* celebrated with a magnificent illumination of the royal baby, surrounded by symbols of trade and prosperity, and the inscription, so revealing of the nature of Bordeaux's Royalism, '*Illo Duce, quo non commercium*' ('with him as leader [or duke] trade will know no limits').

But every feast has its ghost. Bordeaux's birth shattered Orléans's hope of eventually, in the natural course of events, succeeding to the throne. When the Orléans appeared, rather late, in the Duchesse de Berri's apartment, Louis, in his sly way, said '*Ah, vous me manquiez*' ('Ah, I was looking for you'). The Orléans so lacked self-control – unlike Louis in similar circumstances in 1781 – that the Duchesse d'Orléans, pretending to be mystified at the speed of the birth, overwhelmed her niece with sweetly anxious, probing questions, while Orléans actually asked Maréchal Suchet (when Louis, but not Artois, had left the room) if he had really seen the baby attached to the Duchesse de Berri. All this was soon known to the Parisian public.[5]

Blessed with an heir, a loyal army and a capable, moderate and experienced ministry, it might have seemed that Louis would at last be able to reign in peace. He was even recovering from his love for Decazes, now that its original cause and basis, shared political interests, had gone. He still missed Decazes and their evening talks enormously. In March 1820 he wrote that the loss had grown a little less acute, and that he was not going to pretend to be *'le héros d'amitié'*. Louis saw Decazes on his return to Paris before going to England almost every day between 22 June and 10 July 1820, and they still corresponded, to the dismay of Louis's ministers. Louis still defended Decazes in conversation as, almost alone of Decazes's friends, he always would. But politics was pushing them apart. Louis loyally stuck to his ministers and was annoyed at Decazes's continued flirtation with some liberals, the political hopes he continued to entertain and the political advice he continued to lavish. Already, by the end of 1820, their correspondence was colder and less frequent.[6]

At the same time the Government was drawing nearer to the right. The elections in November 1820 for the 172 new seats elected by people with two votes, and for the annual fifth, gave an overwhelming majority to the right, not only in the departments, but also in the *arrondissements*: scared by the summer riots and conspiracies, the rich were moving in the same rightward political direction as the very rich. There were now 160 deputies on the right, 190 deputies supporting the Government, and only 80 on the left. Louis commented that he and his ministers were like someone who had prayed to St. George to be able to jump on his horse, and had been so successful that he had jumped right over it. His ministry had a firmer parliamentary base than that of Decazes, but the right had grown dangerously powerful.

So the ministry tried to make a deal with it. On 22 December, after some complicated negotiations managed by Chateaubriand, who had retained his access to the salon of Richelieu's sister Madame de Montcalm, Villèle, Corbière and Lainé joined the Council as ministers without portfolio. For the first time since the replacement of Feltre in 1817, there were Ultras in the Government. Was Louis, who had at one time considered them as little better than mad dogs, now eating his words?

He remained extremely distrustful of the Ultras. Artois, who often saw both the ministers and the Ultra deputies, and was constantly trying to push the Government to the right, called him a *cruel obstacle*. According to Richelieu, Louis was still more hostile to the Ultras than Richelieu himself in March 1821. But he realized that to include some Ultras in the ministry, given the change in the composition of the chamber, was a political necessity. Moreover, the Ultras had changed from the frenzied madmen of 1816. Louis has been called *'le royal souffleur'* ('the royal prompter'), and the aptness of the epithet becomes apparent when one considers the evolution of Villèle. This very capable Ultra leader had changed from the extreme reactionary of 1814–16 to a much more moderate politician, who was not only prepared to accept the *Charte* but also, by 1819, to work with the Decazes ministry. By late 1820, events, Louis's persistent moderation and their desire to join the Government, had forced most of Villèle's followers to adopt more moderate policies also. A convinced liberal like the Duchesse de Broglie was amused to find that, in the most important Ultra salons, *'on n'entend plus que cette phrase: Nous serons modérés. Ils seront modérés'* ('one no longer hears anything but the phrase: We will be moderate. They will be moderate'). This is exactly what Louis had always wanted them to say.

The moderation of people like Villèle is also shown by the fact that they now had enemies on the right, *exaltés* like La Bourdonnaye, Delalot and Agier, who were still quite powerful in the *réunion Piet*, and in the deputies' branch of the *Chevaliers de la Foi*. Their most powerful spokesman was Chateaubriand, whom Louis detested and distrusted for his attacks on Louis's and Decazes's sincerity. It was almost certainly Louis's influence which kept Chateaubriand from ministerial office in December 1820, and placed him in what he called the *exil* of the French Embassy in Berlin. In their accounts of the audience Louis gave Chateaubriand that month, Louis and Chateaubriand both allege that the other was very embarrassed. Neither, quite clearly, trusted the other.[7]

However, the new ministry fell apart on the question of office. Richelieu seriously seemed to expect that the Ultras should support his ministry solely for the sake of its many admirable qualities. The Ultras wanted at least a share of ministries: Villèle at the Marine, Corbière at *Instruction Publique* and *Cultes* and above all Maréchal Victor, Duc de Bellune, as Minister of War. At first Richelieu agreed, but the opposition of the three moderate ministers, Pasquier, Roy and Siméon, in 1821 as in December 1818, made any serious agreement with the Ultras impossible, and the offer of the three ministries was withdrawn. The next day, 27 July, Villèle and Corbière took their resignations to Louis. Louis held out his hands to them, and pleaded with them to stay. Villèle was almost persuaded but, as he wrote in his diary, '*Heureusement que Corbière a été inexorable*'. Ultras still thought it *fortunate* to be *inexorable* to the king.

That summer was the most peaceful of Louis's reign. The news of Napoleon I's lonely death on St. Helena (still in possession of four snuff-boxes he had taken from Louis's desk in the Tuileries on 20 March 1815) evoked little reaction among his former subjects. It is not an event, sighed Talleyrand, it is just a piece of news: the fate of the Richelieu ministry was far more interesting. Even Lyon, which had been so Bonapartist, but had given Angoulême quite a good reception in May 1820, was unaffected. All observers noticed that political passions in the country really were, finally, dying down.

But political passions among ministers and deputies were as strong as ever. And now Louis's personal life intervened again, as it had done so often in his political career in the past. Louis was so lonely, and so surrounded by etiquette, that he always felt the need for someone he could trust, who could become the friend of his heart and with whom he could talk. Madame de Balbi, d'Avaray, Blacas and then Decazes had successively occupied this difficult, envied and extremely rewarding position: Mlle. Lyzinska Rue had perhaps briefly approached it. In 1820, appeared the last of these favourites the Comtesse Zoë du Cayla. She was a plump, seductive, intelligent and rather fierce woman of thirty-five, who had been described in 1810, when she applied for presentation to the emperor, as '*spirituelle, aimable et joint à un exterieur fort agréable une fort bonne reputation*' ('witty, amiable, and combines a very agreeable appearance with a very good reputation'). She was married to a member of the old Court nobility, whose mother had in 1780 become a *dame pour accompagner* of Marie-Joséphine through the influence of Madame de Balbi, and whose father, a leading soldier of the Emigration, was *Premier Gentilhomme* of Louis's old cousin, the Prince de Condé. She was very much part of Louis's world and Louis's past.

Indeed so much so that her father, a member of an old *parlementaire* family called Talon, had been *Lieutenant Civil* of the Court which had juged Favras – whence a lot of stories, which Talon always denied, even to Bonaparte's police, that he possessed a document denouncing Louis, and which may have their origins in the fact that he had certainly possessed a document compromising the queen. Louis first got to know Madame du Cayla in

1817, when her mother-in-law wrote to him begging for his help in arranging her separation from Monsieur du Cayla. For Madame du Cayla was so charming and so forceful that even her husband's mother took her side rather than his. In the following years Decazes found time, to Madame du Cayla's delight, to help arrange the separation (Monsieur du Cayla retired to the provinces). Madame du Cayla became a friend of Louis and was granted the rarest and most envied of honours, a *correspondance*. A month after Decazes's fall, Louis wrote to her mournfully: '*Quand le malheur en veut à un homme, il l'attaque de tous côtés.*' ('When misfortune strikes a man, it strikes at him from all sides.')[8] But Madame du Cayla was there to console him.

This charming and fascinating woman soon began to fill the gap left by Decazes. She could understand Louis's jokes and allusions and assumptions, perhaps even better than Decazes himself. She had a son and a daughter in whom Louis could take an interest. By August 1820, she was writing with confident knowledge about the arrangements for Louis's *fauteuil mécanique* to go into his carriage. Soon they were seeing each other once a week, on Wednesday afternoons after the Council, when Louis's orders were that they should not be disturbed under any circumstance.

People began to talk about Madame du Cayla with all the venom traditionally reserved for the king's mistresses. '*Jamais les sens du Monarque n'ont été aussi vivement agité*' ('Never has the Monarch's temperament been more ardently agitated'), wrote one of his agents to Decazes. '*Madame Princeteau gagne beaucoup à la comparaison*' ('Madame Princeteau gains a lot by comparison'), commented the acid Duchesse d'Escars. On 8 July 1821 – anniversary of Louis's return in 1815 – a glaring sign of Madame du Cayla's favour was provided by the laying of the foundation stone of a new house, to be built for her by Louis just outside Paris at Saint-Ouen, where he had issued the Declaration of Saint-Ouen in 1814.[9] One of the people present was Sosthènes de La Rochefoucauld, Aide de Camp of the Comte d'Artois.

As the site and the company imply, the relationship between Louis and Madame du Cayla was already, like almost everything else in his life, beginning to take on a political aspect. Sosthènes de La Rochefoucauld had been an extreme Ultra, deeply involved in the Affair of Martin de Gallardon – as Madame du Cayla was well aware (she called Gallardon '*ce fameux pays . . . qu'habite ange ou diablerie, cher vicomte*'). He was a very good friend of Madame du Cayla and wrote or went to see her almost every day.

It appears that, sometime in 1821, Louis began to talk to

Madame du Cayla about politics. Her exact political views at this moment are not clear. She was by no means a die-hard Ultra, and had been opposed to aspects of the Ultras' policy in 1816–19. But it was Madame du Cayla, as well as the need to reassure the new ministers Villèle and Corbière, who was behind Louis's much less effusive reception of Decazes in March 1821, and his insistence that Decazes leave Paris as soon as possible. Louis could now address Decazes as his '*fils trop cher*'. After a last meeting in May 1822, they only saw each other at Court receptions and their correspondence, not very interesting in the last few months, dwindled away. Louis was indeed, as he had told Chateaubriand in December 1820, entering a new era.[10]

Whether Madame du Cayla was behind the fall of Richelieu's ministry in December 1821 – one of the most important events of Louis's reign – is hard to say. Ferdinand de Bertier, Sosthènes de La Rochefoucauld and, indirectly, Richelieu himself all said so after the event. But the changing circumstances of the political game also provide a perfectly adequate explanation. The annual elections held in the autumn of 1821 had returned fourteen deputies of the left, twenty of the ministerial centre, and fifty of the right – including twenty *exaltés* or *pointus*. The ministry's position was clearly growing weaker. And on 26 November what Villèle, continuing his moderate course, called '*la coalition monstreuse des pointus avec la gauche*' voted an outrageous address to the king which accused Louis of sacrificing national honour in foreign affairs, and Richelieu of favouring Russian grain imports at the expense of French agriculture. A chamber which could vote such an address was clearly incompatible with the ministry. Which of the two would go?

At first it seemed as if Louis, who was furious with the address, and gave the commission which came to present it on 30 November a terrifyingly cold reception, would continue to support his ministers. But he was opposed to Pasquier's suggestion (not mentioned in Pasquier's memoirs) to dissolve the chamber. The obvious alternative, favoured by Richelieu and de Serre, was a '*transition vers la droite*' in the ministry. By 8 December, Pasquier, Siméon, Portal, Mounier and Anglès (the Prefect of Police of Paris), the bug-bears of the right and of Artois, had resigned. But, as in December 1818 and July 1821, it proved impossible to fabricate a ministry uniting the right and the centre-right: they were too far apart in temperament and tastes, and there were too many politicians after too few ministries, for it to work.[11]

By 10 December, Richelieu, Roy and de Serre had also resigned and Louis decided, at Richelieu's suggestion and, it seems clear from a letter Richelieu wrote to his sister, to Richelieu's relief, *'de faire un Ministère avec son frère et de me laisser tranquille'* ('to make a Ministry with his brother and to leave me in peace'). This was the first time since September 1815 that all Louis's ministers had resigned at once, and people such as Villèle and Ferrand saw it as a blow to royal authority. The king was still so involved in the business of government that for him to change all his ministers at the same time as a result of the chamber's hostility seemed undignified and inconsequential.

But, as in September 1815, Louis probably thought the change inevitable. As has already been pointed out, he saw politics as a struggle, like that waged in England, between the ministry and the opposition. If his ministry could no longer continue to govern, it might as well go *en bloc* (although, as in 1818, he wanted to keep his *Directeur-Général des Postes*, Dupleix de Mézy). Richelieu says that the king insisted on the resignation of all the ministers *'avec force citations tirées de l'Angleterre'* ('with many examples quoted from England'). He was a truly constitutional monarch.

The new ministry, formed by Villèle and Corbière between 10 and 14 December, with the approval and advice of Artois, was however, based on a list provided by Richelieu – something he omits to mention in his bitter account of his fall from power. The Ultra leaders Villèle, Corbière and Bellune became Ministers of Finance, the Interior and War respectively. Villèle and Corbière rejected Richelieu's suggestions of Blacas, Chabrol-Crousol and Pastoret, for Foreign Affairs, the Marine and Justice, on the grounds that the first was too unpopular and the others not good enough speakers to appear in the chambers. Instead they substituted Clermont-Tonnerre, a moderate Royalist and *protégé* of Louis and Ferrand, and Peyronnet, another moderate, possibly protected by Madame du Cayla, as Ministers of the Marine and Justice. Louis insisted on keeping Lauriston as *Ministre de la Maison* rather than giving it to Mathieu de Montmorency, who received Foreign Affairs instead. When Clermont-Tonnerre saw Louis for the first time on 16 December, he noted that the king was *'paraît satisfait'*.[12]

The new ministry, whose leading figure was Villèle, was the strongest and most reliable of Louis's reign. It was united, it had a firm parliamentary majority and it had a capable leader as respected by his followers as he was trusted by the king. Villèle's law of March 1822, abolishing the emergency censorship of 1820 but tightening the penalties and extending the scope of the 1819 law, was just the sort of carefully-regulated freedom of the press which Louis appreciated. Villèle, a dry, business-like provincial noble from Toulouse, totally devoid of charm, could not have been more different from Decazes. But Louis was never dominated by his affections, and Villèle soon began to bask in the sun of royal favour. In the summer of 1822, Villèle and his wife were lent the apartment of the Duchesse d'Escars at Saint-Cloud – no minister had received such a favour before. On 5 September, to the dismay of all the other ministers, Louis even made Villèle *Président du Conseil*. Louis was extremely satisfied with the new ministry, and one day in November 1822, when Villèle said at a Council meeting that an affair was going well, Louis, having looked at each minister in turn, said *'mais qu'est-ce qui ne va pas bien aujourd'hui?'* ('but what is not going well these days?')

And he defended his wonderful new minister against two people with whom he had much more in common, Blacas and Mathieu de Montmorency. Blacas resigned his post as ambassador to Rome in the summer of 1822, ostensibly to perform his duties as *Premier Gentilhomme*, when his year came up in 1823. But many people feared that his return to Court had more to do with those dormant political ambitions which had nearly been realized in December 1821. Would Louis restore Blacas to the favour and influence he had enjoyed during the First Restoration? Louis put an end to people's doubts in a characteristically clear, but indirect fashion. When Blacas appeared at the Tuileries in the course of a reception, Louis greeted him with the words, *'Ah! vous voilà de retour de votre campagne, Monsieur de Durfort!'* ('Ah! There you are back from your estate, Monsieur de Durfort!') Duras hastened to correct the king: *'Mais, Sire, c'est Monsieur de Blacas!'* *'Allez!'* said Louis, and was pushed on in his wheelchair. Thereafter there was little speculation about Blacas's political future, and he was able to perform his duties as *Premier Gentilhomme* in 1823 as smoothly and unobtrusively as the others.

Another threat to Villèle's position came from Mathieu de Montmorency, the admired chief of the *Chevaliers de la Foi*. The situation in Spain had been growing steadily worse since the *coup* of 1820, and Montmorency returned to Paris in December 1822 from the Congress of Verona determined to push a policy of intervention in conjunction with Austria, Russia and Prussia. Although all the other ministers agreed with Montmorency, Villèle, who preferred peace, financial retrenchment and an independent foreign policy, did not. Louis disliked and distrusted Montmorency as a man of coteries and salons (one salon he frequented was that of his mother, Madame de Laval, whose failure to become a *dame pour accompagner* of Marie-Joséphine had led to the

Montmorencys' resignation from Louis's household in 1780). And at an extremely tense Council meeting on 25 December Louis supported Villèle rather than Montmorency against all the other ministers, the petty noble from Toulouse rather than the member of one of the oldest noble families in France. Louis kept his snobbery firmly out of politics.[13] Montmorency resigned the next day, and was replaced by Chateaubriand. The fall of their leader and the survival of the ministry shows that the *Chevaliers de la Foi*, although they were an important Ultra club, did not control political events, even under Villèle.

Villèle's control of the Government has been seen as a sign that Louis was a cypher, a king who was prepared to sacrifice his principles of moderation and the *route moyenne* for the sake of a quiet life and a parliamentary majority. It is significant that in December 1821 Louis had been forced to accept in the key position of *Directeur-Général des Postes* the Duc de Doudeauville, father of Sosthènes de La Rochefoucauld, and a man Louis rather despised. (When the position was announced someone said: 'Who will be the Duc de Doudeauville?' The idea of a service nobility, serving in both the bureaucracy and the army, still seemed rather strange.) But in fact Villèle's ministry was not wholly Ultra. It included moderates like Lauriston, Clermont-Tonnerre (whose correspondence is full of dislike for the Ultras) and Peyronnet, and the ministry was supported in the chamber by most of the moderate, ministerial deputies who had supported the Richelieu ministry. It was opposed by the more extreme Ultras like La Bourdonnaye, Agier and Delalot who felt that Villèle was betraying the purity of Ultra principles, particularly by not instituting a purge of *les administrations*. In April 1822, the Duchesse d'Escars was speaking for many Ultras when she complained that she was beginning to find '*que le changement est plus dans les noms que les choses*'. And this was due not only to the sobering effects of office, but also to the personal influence of Louis himself, who was always leaning, Corbière complained, to *le système du milieu*. The king is '*toujours en garde contre le parti ultra*', wrote Clermont-Tonnerre in September 1823. No wonder Villèle, who saw so much of Louis, and owed him the *Présidence du Conseil*, began to seem luke-warm to the Ultras.

Louis still saw his ministers regularly and most details of policy, for example over the Congress of Verona or the revival of the French navy, still passed through his hands. He still gave his own orders through Villèle, on some matters, for example to stop an enquiry into war supplies, or to direct Angoulême's movements. Louis's encouragement and favour still seemed extremely important to his ministers. But his role in government was sinking with his health. When Wellington came to Paris in late 1822 he found a broken man, who clearly did not have long to live: 'From his appearance I should suppose that he had had a paralytic attack. One of his Majesty's eyes was more closed than the other and his head, which was in a great degree sunk upon his chest, inclined to one side.' Louis took much less part in the conversation than before although when he did, he talked 'with his usual precision and intelligence'. By the autumn of 1823, Louis was beginning to doze off at dinner with his family and during the evening audiences with his ministers. He was now a complete invalid, unable to walk and visibly decaying on his throne.[14]

Louis's increasing ill-health, coupled with the presence of a right-wing Government composed of Artois's political allies, increased Artois's political influence enormously. Indeed the joke in Paris, when the new ministry had been announced, was that 'the king had virtually abdicated. He will see in his life what would have happened after.' And Richelieu sourly agreed. Certainly the relations of the brothers were now completely different to what they had been since 1816 or even 1814. They now had basically the same political ideas, and the same political favourite, Villèle, whom Artois trusted and respected just as much as Louis. A sign of the transformation in their relations was the publication in 1822 of Louis's *Relation d'un Voyage à Bruxelles et Coblentz*, modelled on the *Relation d'un Voyage de Dantzick à Marienwerder* (1734) of his great-grandfather Stanislas Leczynski. It needed all Louis's authorial vanity, as well as his desire to evoke a time when he and Artois had been the most united of brothers, to break his wise practice of leaving the Revolution and the Emigration in oblivion.

However, Artois was not the king in all but name after 1821. He probably saw people like Villèle and Corbière less now (until early 1824) than when they had all been opposed to Louis's Government before 1820. He only found out what happened in the Council if Louis decided to tell him, or by asking Villèle or the other ministers. On 2 August 1823, for example, he wrote to Villèle that '*Chateaubriand ... m'a dit qu'il avait été convenu hier au Conseil que ...*' ('Chateaubriand ... told me that it had been agreed at the Council yesterday that ...'). Although his authority and control over the ministers increased in the last year of Louis's reign – his candidate, the Baron de Damas, replaced Bellune at the Ministry of War in November 1823 – one gets the impression of a powerful and respected prince quite clearly soon about to mount the throne, who nevertheless remained in a tact-

fully subordinate position. As late as August 1824, Louis and the
Council adopted a measure, the reestablishment of censorship, of
which Artois disapproved.[15]

Indeed Artois was still so distinct from the ministry that La
Rochefoucauld's letters to Madame du Cayla are full of fears that
Artois might be swinging to the side of the *exagérés* – who
included many of Artois's Aides de Camp, for example the Comte
de Bruges. La Rochefoucauld wrote hundreds of letters to
Madame du Cayla in the last three years of Louis's reign. He was
an extraordinary character, a sort of joke Vicomte who fully
deserved a name like Sosthènes. Very fond of women and extremely fond of himself, he rushed round Paris in a whirl of
amorous, political, social, artistic and religious activities. He was
so fatuously self-admiring that he could write that he felt *'tellement supérieur à lui [Villèle] que je l'ai regardé avec une sorte
de pitié'* ('so superior to him that I regarded him with a sort of
pity') – and that is not the most arrogant of his remarks. He was
so fond of women, even of the formidable Madame de Villèle,
that Madame du Cayla called him *'cher Vicomte des Dames'*: for
his amazing memoirs he wrote a *Galerie de Femmes* of 175
women, from Léontine, Comtesse de Noailles to Marguerite,
Miss Trotter, many of whom he seems to have known very well.
What his wife thought we do not know. But both Villèle and
Artois, and probably Madame du Cayla and Louis, realized that
La Rochefoucauld was ridiculous.

But they used him as an intermediary. La Rochefoucauld was
in a strong position. He was an Aide de Camp of Artois. He had
the confidence of Villèle. He was a close friend of Madame du
Cayla. His father, the Duc de Doudeauville, was a leading moderate politician. His father-in-law, Mathieu de Montmorency, was
an important Ultra. He himself was silly but by no means stupid
(he was to be an original *Directeur-Général des Beaux-Arts* from
1824 to 1830). And from 1822 he began to go and see Villèle
every morning, after which, no doubt following the great man's
directions, he would write a letter to Madame du Cayla with the
intention that she should put at least some of what he had written
to her in her daily letter to Louis. Thus Louis was at the end of
a chain of letters which had a definite political purpose.[16] One
sees that letters were not only or even primarily means of communication, but were also instruments of policy.

The exact importance of this correspondence, which has been
printed (in full?) in La Rochefoucauld's memoirs, is hard to assess,
especially since we lack the most important documents of all, the
correspondence of Louis and Madame du Cayla. From the evi-

dence of the letters published it seems that Madame du Cayla was used primarily to strengthen and cement the situation already in existence, that is to say the dominant political position of Villèle, and the reconciliation of Louis and Artois. And it is probable that Doudeauville also chose letters to show Louis with this purpose in mind. La Rochefoucauld was always passing on to Madame du Cayla admiring, respectful, or invented remarks made by Artois about Louis. Clearly, the enmity between the two brothers had gone so deep that Louis still needed constant reassurance that Artois did not hate him, and was more moderate than in the past. It was not until October 1823 that the reconciliation, at least on the surface, was complete; and that, as a sign of his gratitude, Louis gave La Rochefoucauld a vase, and an olive-branch carved in whale-bone (see page 302). In return, Artois was extremely grateful to Madame du Cayla and wrote to Sosthènes (in one of those royal letters which were the political equivalents of post-dated cheques, to be cashed in when the time was right) that she should '*jouir sans crainte du noble emploi qu'elle a fait des bontés et de la confiance de mon excellent frère*' ('enjoy without fear the noble use which she has made of the kindness and confidence of my excellent brother'). Artois was already beginning to sound more than a little patronizing.[17]

For Villèle it is clear that La Rochefoucauld and Madame du Cayla were important because Villèle's relations with Louis were not very easy. There was confidence and respect, on both sides, but no familiarity. The king was surrounded by his intimidating formality and Villèle lacked the courtier's or *grand seigneur's* ability – which Talleyrand, Richelieu and Decazes had all had – to say what he wanted not only about policy, but also about personalities and minor everyday problems. Louis and Villèle found it difficult to be expansive with each other. Part of Madame du Cayla's task was to get Louis to say the polite and flattering remarks which came so well from his royal lips, and which meant so much to Villèle.

Whether the correspondence was more important and affected '*la haute direction politique*' is hard to say. Villèle denied it in his memoirs. But La Rochefoucauld did write to Madame du Cayla to say that Louis should give Villèle the *Présidence du Conseil*. Did Louis make Villèle *Président du Conseil* to please Madame du Cayla? There are so many obvious political reasons why he should want to do so (see page 385) that it seems unlikely, but one cannot be entirely sure.[18]

In other political matters it is clear that, as Clermont-Tonnerre wrote at the time, Madame du Cayla's influence was very limited.

She was opposed to Chateaubriand's nomination as Minister of Foreign Affairs in December 1822. She disliked and wanted to remove Corbière, the right-wing Minister of the Interior, who was still in office when Louis died – although Louis had complained about him to Villèle. She wanted Sosthènes de La Rochefoucauld and Doudeauville to be given ministerial office (Sosthènes was sure he would be a brilliant Minister of the Interior), but they did not get it until August 1824. Louis maintained Lauriston, whom he liked, as *Ministre de la Maison*, instead of giving the post to Doudeauville. In 1823 and 1824, La Rochefoucauld and Madame du Cayla were constantly complaining about Villèle's neglect, and his shameful unwillingness to reward his real friends, but this did not affect Louis's confidence in Villèle. And Louis was prepared to tell Madame du Cayla '*Il faut . . . marcher du même pied que le premier ministre*' ('we must move in the same direction as the prime minister').

The one area where Madame du Cayla might have been expected to be important was royal favours. And one of the most extraordinary documents in the Manuscripts Department of the *Bibliothèque Nationale* is the register, kept by her secretary, of her 687 outgoing letters from 13 July 1823 to 1 February 1824. It shows that there were few people, however grand, or however well-placed at Court, who did not stoop to ask her help to obtain a military governorship, the Order of the Saint Esprit, or even just a post of *Maître des Requêtes* for a relation. Among her supplicants were the Duc de Mouchy (head of a branch of the Noailles family), d'Avaray's father, the Duc de Castries, the Duc de Montmorency, and the Princesse de Poix. But even in this field Madame du Cayla's influence was limited, although after writing to her, d'Avaray's father, the ancient Duc d'Avaray, did become governor of a military division. She failed to get Sosthènes's cousin Anatole de Montesquiou made a *Gentilhomme de la Chambre*, or Blacas appointed *Grand Veneur* (a less intimate position than *Premier Gentilhomme*). She even failed to get herself named by Louis as one of the thirty women invited to a royal fête and commented, sadly and truly, '*mais je ne suis pas Decazes*'.[19] Indeed, her influence was less than that of Decazes; and she herself wrote that Louis only really opened his heart to her just before he died.

What then was the basis of their relationship? One has to remember that it was a relationship which was far from being secret or private. Louis was building Saint-Ouen for her at the gates of Paris. He saw her once a week on Wednesday afternoons and, just like anyone else having an audience, she had to go through the *Salle des Gardes* and be ushered into the king's

Cabinet Particulier by the *Premier Gentilhomme*. There was no nonsense about secret audiences such as those given to their confidants by Marie-Antoinette and Artois, nor was Madame du Cayla installed in private apartments in the palace like Madame de Pompadour or Madame du Barry. It was a relationship which in Louis's mind could be presented to public opinion without shame.

Its basis was probably neither physical pleasure (Louis was far past that) nor political discussion but emotional intimacy. To Louis, Madame du Cayla was a charming and amusing new friend, who was the only person he could talk to in a relaxed and intimate way. Conversation included politics – as did their correspondence – and she was someone Villèle had to keep on his side. But otherwise her influence was limited. She was certainly not, as Metternich liked to pretend, continuing the Austrian tradition of denigration of the Bourbons, more powerful than Madame de Pompadour or Madame de Maintenon, a mistress whom Villèle had to see 'three or four hours daily'.

She was a very agreeable companion for an ageing invalid. She could keep him amused. She had two children whom he saw once a month. And he could spend happy hours planning the lay-out and decoration of her new house at Saint-Ouen, whose basic plan and structure is entirely Louis's idea, not the architect's.

It is really a very strange building indeed. Forty years before, in the *pavillon* and the *hôtel* he had built for Madame de Balbi, Louis had preferred rounded rooms, and chairs and sofas with slightly curved backs: shapes suited to the voluptuous ease of the late eighteenth century. The Château de Saint-Ouen, however, is a square block of architecture, startlingly simple and sober in appearance, without a single decorative feature on the outside and very few inside. No doubt the bare classic walls only served to set off the luxury of the furniture and fittings, the panels by Gérard of the 'Four Seasons' in the *Salle de Billard* (one of the few features Saint-Ouen shared with the *pavillon* of Madame de Balbi was a billiard-room) and the sumptuous glow from Gérard's portrait of Louis in his *Cabinet* (see illustration 13). Gérard's portrait was a sign that Louis intended Saint-Ouen to be not only a present to Madame du Cayla but also a monument to himself. The foundation stone contained writings by himself and medals commemorating his reign. The *Petit Salon* was dominated by a marble plaque with the inscription, composed by Louis himself, '*Ici, le 2 mai 1814, a commencé une ère nouvelle*'. Louis enjoyed planning Madame du Cayla's parties, and perhaps he planned the biggest party of all, a party epitomizing his reign, a Catholic and Royalist celebration of a constitutional declaration, which inaugurated the château on 2 May 1823. After the chapel was blessed by the Archbishop of Paris, 450 guests, including the Papal Nuncio, listened to a short play by a Royalist playwright, Alissan de Chazet, and then sat down to lunch while the choir of the Opera sang cantatas in honour of the king.[20]

Louis became more and more dependent on his new friend, and when she went away on a journey to the Midi, he showed all the egotism of ageing affection, and was extremely cross. But he got over it, and his letters to her during this journey (the only ones which have been allowed to be published) are extremely loving. A letter he has received is like *'une pluie bienfaisante à la terre altérée par une longue sécheresse'* ('a shower of rain on parched ground'). *'Agréez l'hommage d'un sentiment bien tendre qui ne diffère de l'éternité que parce qu'il a eu un commencement'* ('Accept the homage of a most tender feeling which differs from eternity only because it has had a beginning.') *'Ma personne est aux Tuileries, mais ma pensée entière est avec vous.'* ('My person is in the Tuileries, but all my thoughts are with you.') He kissed her white hands, and every stage of her return to Paris was *'une petite suite d'idées agréables'*. Politics was never mentioned, no doubt for fear of the letters being read in the post.

Happy though this friendship with Madame du Cayla made Louis, to many of his subjects it appeared ridiculous: the grotesquely fat old king and the beautiful, ambitious, woman with a past (among her lovers had probably been Napoleon's Minister of Police, the Duc de Rovigo). Stories soon began to circulate: that Louis took snuff on Madame du Cayla's voluptuous white bosom; that Louis had fallen over when fondling Madame du Cayla, and none of his valets dared answer the bell because the orders not to disturb him when Madame du Cayla was there were so strict; that Louis had said *'C'est vous, Zoë?'* when the rustle of the *Garde des Sceaux's* legal robes had sounded like a dress, so that for ever after Peyronnet was known as Robinson Cru-zoë (*robin* is a slang word in French for lawyer; *cru-zoë* means 'believed to be Zoe').[21]

But such stories (the last two of which were probably true) seem to have been confined to a small Parisian circle, unlike the gossip about Marie-Antoinette before 1789. And the monarchy was now so strong that it could take such sneers. It had withstood so much, not only the plots and riots of 1820, but in 1822 an outburst of military conspiracies inspired by Spain and Piedmont, and organized by secret societies known as *Carbonari* which had contacts in as many as fifteen to twenty regiments. La Fayette was, inevitably, involved. His general's uniform (it must have been made especially for the occasion, unless it survived from 1792) actually arrived in Belfort, where the *coup* was to begin, ahead of him. But the *coup* was betrayed, and La Fayette turned back, bravely leaving his subordinates and devotees to suffer the consequences. Ten soldiers were executed between February and October 1822; as in 1815–16, Louis was inexorable in refusing pardons, even to the most touching pleas, for example those in favour of the *Quatre Sergeants de la Rochelle*. He stuck to his belief that *'le devoir marche avant la pitié'* ('duty comes before pity'). Only in 1823, when the threat had been eliminated, would he begin to exercise his right of pardon. No doubt he felt that only the severest repression would spare France the fate of Spain or Piedmont.[22]

After 1821, the growing strength and stability of Louis's throne allowed France, at last, to have an active foreign policy. Until late 1818, this had been dominated by the need to end the Allied occupation. Only when that aim was achieved could France act as an independent power again. And French foreign policy after 1818 was, like so much of Louis's reign, dominated by the two basic facts that his monarchy was both legitimate and constitutional. In an age of revolts against legitimate monarchies, usually in the search of some sort of constitution, in Italy, Spain, Portugal and Latin America, this combination was bound to be of extreme importance – particularly since France had the traditional Bourbon connection with Spain and Naples.

But for the first three years after the liberation of French territory in 1818 French foreign policy did not achieve much. Any intervention in Italy was hindered by geography, since Piedmont blocked France's path. Austria, whose territory stretched to the Po, was able to reinstate Louis's cousin Ferdinand I of the Two Sicilies, after the Neapolitan revolution of 1820, without interference from France. The hopes of Louis and his ministers to persuade Ferdinand I to grant a constitution like the *Charte*, which certainly existed, were doomed by the fact of Austrian power as well as by the old king's helplessly conservative and pro-Austrian character.

There was, however, no geographical obstacle to interference in Spain, where Ferdinand VII faced a steadily deteriorating situation after the success of the liberal officers' *coup* in 1820. The Villèle ministry was encouraged to intervene in Spain not only because it wanted to support monarchy, in particular Bourbon monarchy, but also in order to assert French influence and independence. One of the reasons Montmorency resigned as Foreign

Minister on 26 December 1822 was that he was proposing to intervene in Spain not independently but in agreement with the three 'Northern Powers', Austria, Prussia and Russia.

The new Foreign Minister, Chateaubriand, had been chosen by Villèle as a representative of the extreme Ultras who were beginning to cause Villèle a lot of trouble, and perhaps also as a result of the efforts of Chateaubriand's loving ally, the Duchesse de Duras. Louis disliked and distrusted Chateaubriand, who had so often behaved as his and Decazes's personal enemy. He was certainly very different from the ordinary run of Restoration ministers. Who else, in a flattering letter to Louis about going to Hartwell, would have compared it to a pilgrimage to the Holy Land? But Louis knew how to deal with authors. He kept Chateaubriand for more than an hour during the first audience, and later asked him to read out his Moorish romance, *'L'Abencérage'*, saying *'L'Abencérage, ce sont aussi les Affaires Etrangères'* (*'L'Abencérage*, that is also Foreign Affairs').

Although Chateaubriand had originally been appointed as someone who represented a peaceful policy, circumstances rapidly forced the Government to intervene in Spain. In April 1823, an army of 100,000 French soldiers, commanded by Angoulême, crossed the Pyrenees and, meeting with very little resistance, soon occupied Madrid. By October, Ferdinand VII was released and restored to the absolute authority of his fathers. Louis and his Government, and particularly Angoulême, had genuinely hoped to install a constitutional regime in Spain. But as with Ferdinand I of the Two Sicilies, the attempt fell down when it came to the monarch in question. But at least Ferdinand VII's Government after 1823 was not as reactionary as it had been before 1820, and for this Angoulême and successive French ambassadors and commanders (there was a French army of occupation until 1828) can perhaps take some credit.

Even more important than the restoration of Ferdinand VII was that the expedition demonstrated, as it was meant to, that Louis had a reliable army. It was this expedition which finally put an end to the rivalries between officers of the former Napoleonic army and officers who had never served *l'usurpateur*, which in some cases had persisted into the early 1820s. Now they had all faced enemy fire together. And another sign of the strength and Royalism of the new French army was that some of the enemy fired on, when the army crossed the Bidassoa into Spain, were liberal exiles like Fabvier, who were wearing the green uniform of the *Garde Impériale*, waving the tricolour and crying either *'Vive la Liberté'* or *'Vive Napoléon'*: the doubt arises because the liberals claimed the former, and French officers, probably more truthfully, the latter. Liberals were ashamed of the fact that only their dynastic connection gave them dedicated non-intellectual supporters.

But it did not do them much good in Spain in 1823. The royal troops, in the blue uniform of the French infantry, obeyed their commander's orders to open fire, and marched on regardless. Some Parisian liberals, who had hoped the royal army would turn round and invade France (again one sees how unpatriotic the *parti national* really was), were shattered. Even Stendhal now realized that the Bourbons were firmly established on the French throne. The Blue had beaten the Green.[23]

One of the soldiers who fought with the French army, and was given the epaulettes of a *Grenadier de la Garde Royale* as a reward for his bravery in action, was Charles-Albert, Prince de Carignan, the heir to Piedmont. Louis was particularly interested in Piedmont not only because the king was his brother-in-law but also because it was the last remaining power in Italy independent of *cette hydre* (as he had called it in 1778), the House of Habsburg. For this reason one of Talleyrand's aims at the Congress of Vienna had been to get Charles-Albert, rather than the king's Habsburg son-in-law, recognized as the heir to the throne. In this he was successful, but in 1820 Charles-Albert disgusted the King of Sardinia by dabbling in revolution, and had to go into exile. In very difficult circumstances, when it seemed that Charles-Albert might be barred from the succession and that the Habsburgs might manage to reinstate their candidate, his only support was Louis's ambassadors and Louis's letters to his brother-in-law urging forgiveness: Louis disliked Habsburg hegemony even more than a royal revolutionary.

In the end, a period in the French army was agreed on as a purifying course in Royalism before Charles-Albert could return to Turin. At the victory celebrations in Paris in December 1823, where the Duchesse d'Angoulême, overjoyed by her husband's victories, delighted the Parisians by, at last, looking happy and relaxed, Charles-Albert was treated as a hero. Louis was extremely friendly, called him *mon enfant*, and gave him the Saint Esprit. At a long private audience, Louis offered Charles-Albert *'les avis les plus sages et les plus paternels . . . rappelant sa position passée et présente, il entre dans de grands détails sur sa position future'* ('the wisest and the most paternal advice . . . recalling his position in the past and at the present, he went into great details about his position in the future'). Alas, we do not know what was actually said. While in Paris, Charles-Albert had sworn, in the presence of the Piedmontese ambassador, not to alter the internal state of Piedmont in the future. So perhaps Louis's *'avis ... paternels'* dealt with the prince's future policy to Austria – a power which, as many statesmen already realized, was unlikely to last for ever as the dominant country in the Italian peninsula.[24]

In contrast to the 1790s, when France had been the exporter and upholder of republics, the France of Louis XVIII, as befitted a monarchical age, was a guardian of European monarchy, restoring to Piedmont an heir, and to Spain its king. But France's monarchical ambitions were not restricted to Europe. Louis had been interested in the commercial possibilities of South America since he was a prince, and in its political future since 1808 (see page 157). He had been dismayed that the Spanish Bourbons had left their faithful colonies without a representative of the monarchy – unlike the Braganzas, who had sensibly escaped to Brazil when Portugal was overrun by the French in 1808. After 1810, it began to seem as if the colonies, abandoned by their sovereign, might follow the United States and become republics, rather than monarchies like every European state. After 1814, Ferdinand VII had little success in his attempts to reconquer them, and Louis and his ministers began to worry about the potential challenge to European monarchies presented by the taming and acclimatization of republican systems in South America. By 1818, Richelieu was hoping to install constitutional Bourbon princes in Mexico, Peru and Buenos Aires in order to strengthen *le système monarchique* – and favour French trade: there was a genuine ideological commitment to monarchy as such, as well as a desire to increase French and Bourbon influence. When the Tsar came to Paris in October 1818 Louis, on his own initiative, suggested a Franco-Russian demarche to Ferdinand VII to try to solve the problem of Spain's colonies. And up to Louis's death there were constant French proposals, in which Louis was extremely interested, to install constitutional Bourbon monarchies in South America, particularly in the year following Angoulême's restoration of Ferdinand VII. But they came up against two implacable obstacles.

First, England, even though it too favoured a monarchical solution, was opposed to any attempt by a foreign power, particularly France, to use force in South America. England was the greatest naval power in the world; and in December 1823 President Monroe's proclamation of his doctrine which, it is often forgotten, was partly directed against the menace of Bourbon power in the New World, showed that France would have two enemies to fight if it tried to intervene in the New World.

These obstacles were not, perhaps, of decisive importance, since neither country could object to Spain's efforts to reconquer its colonies – which had still not received legal recognition from any power – and there were always ways in which France could help Spain. The second, crucial factor was the physical absence of potential monarchs in South America. After 1814, Ferdinand VII always refused to allow any members of his family – or Charles, Duke of Lucca, of the Bourbon-Parma branch – to go to South America. Since few people wanted a restoration of the Spanish colonial empire, this effectively destroyed Bourbon prospects in America. By 1824, the republics under which South America was to become a bye-word for corruption, instability, and bloodshed were established in all the former Spanish colonies.

However, France was able to intervene to uphold *le système monarchique* in Brazil and Portugal. Here again, its role was made more difficult by the monarchs themselves. No legitimate monarch could approve of the fact that Pedro I had declared Brazil's independence in 1822 in revolt against his father Joao VI. But in 1823 Louis and his ministers did send Pedro I the Saint Esprit, and a naval squadron to help protect him against any possible *commotion populaire*. In Portugal, in April 1824, it was the French ambassador, a former Royalist conspirator called Hyde de Neuville, who strengthened Joao VI's will when he was threatened by a *coup* launched by his wife and his younger son, Dom Miguel. And, like Charles-Albert of Piedmont, Dom Miguel was despatched to Paris for a cleansing period of modern Royalism. In 1824 French influence in Portugal and Brazil was stronger than it would be for the rest of the nineteenth century.

Under Louis XVIII France not only emerged as the upholder of *le système monarchique*, but also began – although only very slowly – to reassert itself in more traditional areas of interest overseas. In 1814 it recovered all the colonies it had lost since 1789 except Tobago, Mauritius and Haiti (which it tried vainly to recover through diplomatic negotiations until 1825), and it began to penetrate the Pacific and Madagascar. From 1824, during the embassy of Comte Guilleminot, who had been Angoulême's Chief of Staff in Spain, France also began to reassert its interests and influence in the Ottoman Empire – having refused the Tsar's projects of dismemberment in 1821.

Thus in 1824 France's international position was relatively strong. It was true that it had few real friends among the great powers. Prussia was an enemy. The Tsar had now definitely turned to Metternich and renounced his liberal or pro-French tendencies. Metternich instinctively loathed and despised a monarchy like that of Louis XVIII, which was both Bourbon and constitutional.

England had been furious at French intervention in Spain: indeed after the invasion of Algeria in 1820, it was probably the single French action which most infuriated England between 1814 and 1914. But Louis and his ministers were perfectly prepared, indeed eager, as Louis told his Minister of Marine, to '*balancer la puissance anglaise*'. Indeed Louis's *système*, as he had written to Talleyrand in 1814, was: '*alliance générale, point de particulière, celles-cy sont une source de guerre, l'autre est un garant de paix*' ('general alliance not separate alliance, the latter are a cause of war, the former is a guarantee of peace').

France could, in fact, afford to do without Great Power alliances. It had restored its navy, colonies and traditional spheres of influence – all abandoned under Napoleon I. It had found a new role, full of promise, as the protector of monarchy, and as Austria's rival in Italy. And it had assured that it was surrounded by friendly neighbours in Piedmont and Spain. One of the most remarkable legacies of the Government of Louis XVIII in foreign affairs was that it left France with a stable, friendly regime in Madrid, free from non-French interference – something which neither the First nor Second Empires, nor the July Monarchy, nor the Third Republic managed to do.[25]

The internal situation in the last year of Louis's reign was also satisfactory. Under Villèle's expert management, French finances were in a flourishing state, and bore the burden of the Spanish expedition without difficulty. In 1824, which was much the same as the other years since the end of the occupation in 1818, the revenue of the French state was 919,276,468 francs. Out of a total expenditure of 901,472,000 million francs, 3.5 per cent went on the *Liste Civile*, 2 per cent on the Ministry of Justice, 1 per cent on Foreign Affairs, 12.5 per cent on the Interior, 21 per cent on War, 6.5 per cent on Marine and Colonies, 26 per cent on the Ministry of Finance and the Debt, and 28 per cent on the debt arising from the intervention in Spain. The differences in allocation of expenditure compared with 1815 are not enormous. The lower proportion of the budget spent on the army is balanced by the amount spent on the intervention in Spain.

The main difference is one of size. The revenue had gone up enormously, compared to the 542 million francs of 1815, let alone the 475 million livres of 1787. It is suggestive of the elitist nature of the Restoration, and of the growing prosperity of the country, that the rate at which *contributions directes* were levied had been constantly reduced, without lowering their yield, while the rate at which *contributions indirectes* were levied was not altered, but their yield increased enormously. The state was now so strong financially that it could afford both to favour, quite consciously, the richer tax-payers, and to mount an armed intervention in Spain, without any difficulty.

Indeed by May 1824, the state was so rich that the Government was able to raise the theoretical annual intake of conscripts into the army from 40,000 to 60,000, to lengthen their military service from six to eight years and so to raise the real size of the army from 140,000 to 250,000. The Restoration's military and financial base was stronger than ever.

In 1824, the Government was further strengthened by the introduction of a law abandoning the system of electing a fifth of all parliamentary seats each year for a chamber elected every seven years. And the elections of March 1824 returned a huge majority for the Government of 410 'Royalists' compared to only 19 liberals. By 1824 the most worrying phenomenon was precisely this continued division of Frenchmen into 'Royalist' and liberals, which was not simply a matter of parliamentary elections, but appeared to confirm Louis's fear that he was *roi de deux peuples*. All over France there were rival cafés and clubs and *quartiers* appealing to one side or the other. In Beaune, near Lyon, for example, there was the *Cercle des Amis du Roi*, frequented by aristocrats and officials, and the *Cercle du Commerce*, frequented by *négociants* and *propriétaires*. In Paris the Faubourg Saint-Germain was still Royalist and the Chaussée d'Antin liberal. There was a similar contrast in other towns, for example in Lyon between Bellecour and Les Terreaux; and in Angoulême, as Lucien de Rubempré knew so well, between the Ville Haute and L'Hommeau. All over France the *quartier* of the aristocracy and officialdom and the *quartier* of the *notables* engaged in commerce snubbed and sneered at each other.

In 1814–15, this opposition had not been of overwhelming significance, since the causes of Louis XVIII and Napoleon I had been able to appeal to both sides (see page 234). Before 1820, Louis's support for his liberal ministers, and the opposition of the Ultras, had prevented the magic names of king and Royalist being chained to one party or one social group. But by 1824, clubs with names like *Cercle des Amis du Roi*, and the adoption for the ministry's candidates of the name *Royaliste*, by which they were known even in the *Moniteur*, deliberately implied that those who did not join Royalist clubs or vote for ministerial candidates were not *Amis du Roi*. As they had hoped all along, as even someone as sensible and moderate as Richelieu had wanted, the right had succeeded in capturing Louis's name and the title of Royalist for themselves. Were they turning Royalism from the state of mind of half of France into a club of the right?

Such a possibility would have been very dangerous indeed if the regime had still not been really stable. But in fact, especially after the royal army's baptism of fire and Royalism in Spain, the regime did, finally, seem secure. Moreover, it was a security which was tested and proven: it was not a deceptive façade. Few Governments have suffered such a relentless series of hammer-blows as the Government of Louis XVIII – the return of Napoleon I, the rebellion of half of France, the invasion of all of Europe, a Regicide minister, a bread shortage, an assassination, liberal plots, Ultra conspiracies, student riots, a bitterly divided Royal Family, and a conspiratorial liberal prince – it had been spared nothing. But it had triumphed over all its rivals, its open and secret enemies as well as its so-called friends.

By 1824, all over France, there was the utmost calm. Even in Bonapartist Alsace, although there were still many people who disliked the regime, the prefect could report, in late 1823, that *'le département n'a jamais offert un aspect aussi paisible'* ('the department has never appeared more peaceful'). Beugnot commented on the same phenomenon when he went on a journey round the south of France. He repeated the elite's belief that *'le peuple a abdiqué'*, and observed that, in contrast to the squabbles and rows between rival authorities which had been so common under the *Ancien Régime*, *'en aucun temps le pouvoir ne glissa avec autant d'assurance sur un sol mieux nivelé'* ('at no time did authority operate with such assurance over such an unresisting surface').

Against this background the liberals were no longer a serious threat to the regime. Even the most extreme among them had given up hope of coming to power by means of riots, a *coup d'état*, or a change of dynasty. Once this hope had been abandoned, the liberals could work quite well within the framework of the Restoration. For there was no fundamental ideological incompatibility between them and the Restoration. The Restoration was still a relatively liberal regime, functioning according to the *Charte*. The emergency legislation of 1820 had come to an end, as promised, in 1821. The two chambers were operating freely (although one liberal deputy, Manuel, was expelled in 1821 for excusing the execution of Louis XVI). In December 1822 Louis was able to take Wellington to the window of his *Cabinet*, show him the Chamber of Deputies on the other side of the Seine, and boast that, in contrast to Bonaparte, he could allow the deputies freedom of speech, and do 'very well with it'. Only the two votes given to the 23,000 richest voters, and the mild press censorship, made the regime slightly less liberal than it had been in 1814 and 1819.

But the Restoration was now so strong, and the liberals were still so monarchical, that by 1824 they accepted the Bourbons almost as completely as they had done in 1814. The Restoration was the only nineteenth-century French regime to be accepted by almost the entire educated, property-owning political elite. United by their acceptance of the dynasty and its *Charte*, at the end of Louis's reign the *deux peuples*, although still distinct, were drawing gradually closer to each other. There was no alternative. So by 1824 the liberal deputies, more of whom were of higher social status, and fewer of whom had Revolutionary backgrounds, than in 1817–19, provided Louis's Government with that rare phenomenon in French history, a loyal opposition. Among their leaders were people like Royer-Collard, Guizot, and the Comte de Sainte-Aulaire (Decazes's father-in-law) who felt no hostility to, and some attachment for, the Bourbon dynasty. General Foy, the liberals' greatest orator, often proclaimed his loyalty to the dynasty.

The existence of this loyal opposition meant that the long-term prospects of the regime were fairly good. Louis saw politics as essentially a contest between his ministers and a (preferably united) opposition. Since, as no one knew better than Louis himself, no ministry can go on for ever, this meant that the opposition had the hope of becoming the king's Government – as happened in September 1815 and December 1821. There is nothing to suggest that, after 1823, the liberals would not have been able to provide a ministry just as effective and monarchical as that of Villèle and his colleagues. Even students who refused to drink the health of the king, or *Gardes Nationaux* who refused to arrest Manuel, wanted nothing more than observation of the *Charte*, which was as monarchical as it was liberal.

One of the threads running through the different periods of Louis's life was his conflict with La Fayette. They had been rivals over South American commerce in the 1770s and the Favras Affair in 1789. In 1792, Louis hoped to have La Fayette imprisoned; in July 1815 La Fayette hoped to prevent Louis's return to the throne. In 1820–23 La Fayette was the most dangerous and determined opponent of Louis's regime. But in July 1824 La Fayette, acknowledging that Louis had won, left France to revisit the United States. When he returned in 1825, he was a little more moderate, and even as late as 1830, after a series of catastrophically unpopular measures by the Government, La Fayette acknowledged that '*La presque totalité de la France se trouve assez bien dans le cercle, étroit à mon avis, où la Charte a mis les libertés publiques*' ('Almost all of France is quite happy with the, in my opinion, rather narrow definition of public liberties provided by the *Charte*'). If even La Fayette admitted this, then the *Charte* was indeed, as Louis had hoped and written, '*le rocher contre lequel doivent venir briser les idées révolutionnaires*' ('the rock against which revolutionary ideas will dash themselves in vain') – a rock in many ways stronger than the most powerful autocracy.[26]

Thus by 1824, the dynasty and the constitution were secure. The regime's emotional base was also hard to shake. Feelings of love and loyalty for the dynasty, although far less passionate than in 1815–16, were still there, as would be shown by the widespread sorrow at Louis's death (see page 410). The longing for peace and quiet, and family life, were even more firmly tied to a regime which was so well established than in 1814. Honour still rivetted people by their oaths to the king.

The Restoration's greatest emotional enemies were ambition, fear and nationalism, the three great spurs to rally to the side of Napoleon I in 1815. None of them was entirely eliminated by 1824. Thus there was still a fairly large pool of ex-officers and officials of the Empire, who had been dismissed in 1814 or 1816, and, given the opportunity, would be willing to fight the Bourbons. But otherwise the bureaucracy and the army offered relatively accessible careers for the ambitious. Not only the heroes of Balzac, who, suitably, come from the Royalist west and southwest, like Félix de Vandenesse, Lucien de Rubempré and Rastignac, but also Stendhal's hero, Julien Sorel, who comes from Bonapartist Dauphiné, want to get on *within* the framework of the regime. Sorel even wants to be a priest, and he is inspired by a real character, Monseigneur Feutrier, son of a civil servant, *Vicaire-Général de la Grande-Aumônerie* under Louis XVIII, and Bishop of Beauvais and Minister of Ecclesiastical Affairs under Charles X.

There was no noble reaction, giving all places to the old nobility, under Louis XVIII, as can be seen by a glance at the *Almanach Royal* for 1824. For example, four of the twenty-four ambassadors or ministers abroad – officials whose choice was likely to be affected by European as well as French snobbery – were non-nobles, including M. de Rayneval, son of a *Premier Commis*, at the very aristocratic court of Berlin. Twenty-six of the eighty-six prefects were non-nobles. In the army, the highest ranks in the *Garde Royale* were largely, although not exclusively, an aristocratic preserve. But of the 125 colonels of regiments of the line, sixty were non-noble, and sixty-five noble (these figures are only estimates since who was, or was not, noble during the Restoration is extremely hard to define). The French Monarchy was served by an effective and obedient bureaucracy, recruited from both the nobility and bourgeoisie, as well as by a loyal army. It had possessed neither in 1789. Thus non-noble as well as noble ambition could find an outlet within the Church, the army, or the bureaucracy during the Restoration – which is one reason why so many Royalist nobles complained of *l'ingratitude des Bourbons*.

Fear was much less than it had been in 1815. Ultras had finally come to power and were not doing anything to restore the *Ancien Régime*. Fear of the return of the tithe and feudal dues was much diminished – although as late as 1873 the Comte de Chambord (as the Duc de Bordeaux was known in exile) was still having to assure the French that he did not intend to restore them. Moreover, the Ultras, and even Artois, were genuinely much less terrifying now. Louis had, as he had told Pozzo di Borgo he hoped to do in 1817, lived long enough to destroy most of Artois's *erreurs*. In 1824, Artois declared to Louis's ministers that '*son opinion était qu'il fallait rapprocher l'ancien régime du nouveau, et non le nouveau de l'ancien, attendu que c'était le nouveau qui devait servir de base ... qu'il n'avait pas toujours pensé ainsi, mais qu'il avait changé au bout de quatre ans, par le fait de l'observation et de l'expérience*' ('his opinion was that the old regime must be drawn to the new, and not the new to the old, since it was the new which should act as the basis . . . he had not always held this opinion, but he had changed after four years, as a result of observation and experience'). It was bad enough that Artois was still even talking about the *Ancien Régime*, but at least he had accepted the *Charte* and the system of Louis XVIII – as his actions in the first five years of his reign would show. The Ultra, as well as the liberal, threat to Louis's regime was greatly diminished. His friends were wiser, and his enemies less hostile.

The fear that was beginning to grow at the end of Louis's reign – although it did not reach its full development until the reign of Charles X– was fear of the Church, for which Louis's own desire to increase its power and prestige was partly responsible. Louis encouraged the missions which so disturbed sections of public opinion – indeed one of the medals of his reign commemorates the planting of a cross. Louis insisted that Frayssinous, a celebrated preacher whom he had made his *Premier Aumônier* in 1821 – an extraordinary honour for a non-noble – become *Grand Maître de l'Université* in 1822 and so head of French secondary education. Louis was delighted to make nineteen bishops peers in 1822, and to make Frayssinous Minister of Ecclesiastical Affairs as well in August 1824. The increasing influence of the Church, particularly in education, was storing up trouble for the Restoration. But Louis's reputation was so much that of someone rational, sceptical and basically sensible that public feeling, fanned by the liberal press, would only be really aroused under his successor.

Nationalism was far the strongest emotion opposing Louis in 1815, and was still one of the strongest bonds uniting the liberals in the 1820s. In 1822, for example, General Foy, the great liberal orator, wrote to Villèle that his aim was *'avant tout et par-dessus tout l'indépendance nationale'* ('before everything and above everything national independence').[27] By 1824, Louis had to a certain extent hitched nationalism to his dynasty by the Spanish campaign. But it was not much compared to other, infinitely more glorious campaigns. Who cared about the restoration of Ferdinand VII compared to the Rhine frontier? What was the Trocadéro beside Austerlitz? This was the most serious weakness of the regime, which only a much more aggressive foreign policy in Europe – or perhaps South America – could have eliminated. But at least the army was now loyal.

In the last year of his reign Louis's health took a turn for the worse. He had both wet and dry gangrene at the base of his spine and in his right foot, and he had a tumour in his stomach. The doctors' reports give no indication of what caused these diseases; perhaps it is enough to say that he was old and fat, ate too much, never took exercise, and was not likely to have benefited physically from his years of uncomfortable exile. Although less agonizingly painful, his gangrene must have been just as distressing as his gout. On 23 November 1823, at the Te Deum in Notre Dame for the liberation of Ferdinand VII, which was the last time Louis showed himself outside his palace or his carriage, he fell asleep several times; the wrapping round his bad leg came apart, as it often did now, and liquid oozed out on the cathedral floor. He was visibly dying, his clothes were now too large for him, and his spine was so weak that his head was usually slumped on his chest or his desk. When he opened the chambers on 24 March 1824 – a symbol of the new strength of the regime was that this impressive ceremony now took place in the royal palace of the Louvre rather than, as it had done before 1820, in the Chamber of Deputies – Louis fell asleep while reading out his speech. There may be some truth, now, in the stories of Chateaubriand, Villèle and Corbière that Louis spent all the Council meetings and ministers' audiences talking about forgotten operas of his youth, or the poets of Toulouse, or a parrot's embarrassing indiscretions – although neither Clermont-Tonnerre in his diary and letters, nor Damas in his memoirs, mention any such distractions.[28]

Madame du Cayla and La Rochefoucauld were becoming more and more influential, and were pressing for the inevitable rewards: in the summer of 1824 Louis bought Madame du Cayla an *hôtel* on the *quais*, and this was certainly not her only present. La Rochefoucauld wanted a ministry for his father; events soon made one available. One of Louis's favourite projects was to heal what was known as '*la dernière plaie de la révolution*' ('the last wound of the revolution') by compensating the former owners of the confiscated *biens nationaux*. So strong was the opprobrium of the *biens nationaux's* origins that this would benefit their purchasers as well, since they were still being sold far below the market price. In early 1824 the Government stocks, which had been at 60 in September 1816, reached 100 – a tribute to Villèle's excellent financial management and to increased confidence in the regime. With Louis's enthusiastic backing, Villèle now decided on a scheme whereby Government stock would be converted from 5 per cent to 3 per cent interest in order to release funds to compensate former owners of *biens nationaux*.

But this law was rejected in the Chamber of Peers by a coalition of the centre-right led by Pasquier (the centre-right was especially good at weakening ministries, as it had shown in 1818 and 1821), and Court peers such as Blacas, Duras and Gramont. Louis was particularly grieved and angered by this betrayal, and the person who suffered was Chateaubriand. Chateaubriand had never been liked by either Louis, Artois, or Madame du Cayla. He had been chosen and maintained as minister primarily by Villèle, who was well aware of his political importance outside as well as within the Royalist party. However, Chateaubriand had not only failed to speak for the *conversion des rentes* in the chambers, but had also, it was rumoured, spoken against it in the salons, particularly that of the Duchesse de Duras. It is also said that Louis read an intercepted letter from Chateaubriand to the Archbishop of Paris, urging the Archbishop to vote against the law: Doudeauville would certainly have been delighted to show it to him. Nothing revolted Louis more than opposition and disloyalty inside his Council, except, perhaps, the political influence of the salons. On Sunday 6 June, while he was listening to Mass in the gallery of the chapel of the Tuileries, Chateaubriand was brought a note to say that his secretary wanted to see him in the *Salle des Maré-*

chaux. He had just received an *ordonnance* curtly announcing Chateaubriand's dismissal from his ministry.[29]

In the next few weeks there was a ministerial reshuffle which gave Damas Foreign Affairs, Chabrol-Crousol the Marine, Clermont-Tonnerre War, and the *Ministère de la Maison* to Doudeauville. Louis's dismissal (probably on his own initiative) of Chateaubriand – as Chateaubriand said, like a servant who had been caught stealing – was the last manifestation of the haughty tactlessness which Louis had often shown in the past, for example in his attitude to the *Légion d'Honneur* or the Tsar. It meant that Chateaubriand and his following of *exaltés* immediately began to attack the Villèle ministry with unequalled venom, and they had the powerful *Journal des Débats* on their side. This was a disaster for the ministry and Villèle.

But it was not necessarily a bad thing for the throne. It meant that, as before 1821, there was a Royalist as well as a liberal opposition, so that Royalism could no longer be completely associated with one ministry. And there now began the interesting and important development by which the Court peers began to move to the political centre. Chateaubriand had always had exceptionally good contacts with the Court through the Duchesses de Duras and de Lévis, and it may have been partly due to his influence, as well as to the increasing moderation of Restoration policies, and the evolution of Artois, that this transformation took place.

The ministerial reshuffle of July and August was the last important political act of Louis's reign. He was now sinking fast. But, Parisian to the end, he insisted on returning to the Tuileries to receive the ritual homage of the *Corps* and *Cours* and of Society on the Fête de Saint-Louis; he often said that '*un roi pouvait mourir, mais il ne devait jamais être malade*' ('a king could die, but he should never be ill'). People were appalled at the receptions to see how thin and blind and bent he was, and to hear how faint his voice had become. Decazes, who was in Paris and went to Court throughout the last weeks of Louis's reign, wrote sadly that '*la tête est tout à fait penchée vers la terre*' ('his head is bent completely towards the ground'). Nevertheless the Duchesse d'Orléans noted that, by a superhuman effort, Louis managed to address a few words to each person in the *Grand Cabinet*, '*même à ceux auxquels il n'était pas habitué de parler, comme s'il voulait prendre congé de tout le monde*' ('even to those whom he was not accustomed to address, as if he wanted to take leave of everyone').

He still continued to see his ministers, but they only talked about trifles. His last drive was on 28 August – what a terrible sight the royal carriage must have been, surrounded by guards and equerries and footmen, and inside just a tiny bent form with his head on his knees. When she went to see Louis on 31 August, the Duchesse d'Orléans found him sitting with his head on his desk, speaking in a voice so quiet that she had to move right up to him to hear it. His hand was like that of a skeleton. But he was not so far gone that, a few days later, he could not prevent her eldest son from receiving the Saint Esprit before the traditional age (a typical attempt by the Orléans to try to advance their own status surreptitiously).[30] The time was drawing near when he must confess and take the last sacraments. But he was still so frightening that none of his family, and none of his Court officials except Frayssinous, dared tell him so. Eventually Madame du Cayla, on the urging of the family, brought the subject up at her last audience, on 11 September. Louis, very reluctantly, agreed, and thanked her for all the happiness she had given him. Then, going over the past, he opened his heart to her *'comme cela n'était jamais arrivé'* ('as never before'). He still thought he would not die quite yet. But between her tears she could see death *'couler dans ses veines'* ('flowing in his veins').[31]

On 12 September he was put to bed. The Bourse, the theatres and all *lieux de fêtes publiques* were closed. One of his last worries – a typical combination of Catholicism and capitalism, which Decazes found extremely moving – had been that the news that he had taken the last sacraments would send Government stocks down. But it was no longer relevant. On the morning of 13 September the Royal Family and the Court, with lighted candles in their hands, escorted the sacrament from the chapel to his bedroom. Louis received communion and the last rites, following and correcting the prayers with an unfaltering voice. At the end the Royal Family fell on their knees to ask for his blessing, and he said, *'Adieu, mes enfants, que Dieu soit avec vous'* ('Goodbye, my children, may God be with you'). He was now in considerable pain, his body was subject to hot and cold flushes, and he had increasing difficulty in breathing. His pulse and heart were getting weaker, and while he was still alive, his body was rotting away; three or four toes – they were such a mass of decaying flesh that it was hard to tell the exact number – came off his right foot.[32]

In contrast to the dying monarch, the Tuileries palace on 14 and 15 September 1824 offered a remarkable image of a living monarchy, connected, as it had been throughout Louis's reign, with the people, the political and social worlds, and the world of Catholic European royalty. Outside in the garden, all day long, there was a huge, silent crowd, drawn by the sheer magnetism of a royal death-bed, as well as by the fact that other public places were shut. The crowd was so silent that inside the palace you could not guess that there were people in the garden unless you looked out of the window. Up on the first floor, the *Galerie de Diane* was crowded with courtiers, marshals, ex-ministers, all the notables of the Restoration monarchy. They provided Louis with a more serious and important cortege, from a far greater variety of backgrounds, than the glittering, idle throng who fifty-three years before had attended another ceremony, in another palace, when Louis had first appeared on the stage of the world, to be married. Louis's departure from the world was attended by people like Villèle, Pasquier, Decazes, Maréchal Marmont, Maréchal Suchet, the Duc de Fitzjames, who, wearing the impressive uniforms of their rank in the king's service, were solid symbols of the strength of the French monarchy.

The private apartments preceding Louis's bedroom were filled with doctors, ministers, the Neapolitan ambassador, the Papal Nuncio, Dom Miguel, the Royal Family, and exhausted valets and Court officials, many of whom were not *de service*, and were there out of love, loyalty or desire not to be left out, rather than out of duty. Among them were some of Louis's oldest friends (Charles de Damas, Gramont, Havré and Blacas), and, inevitably, his old enemy, Talleyrand: did pity stir that frozen heart? Even the Princes du Sang, Orléans and the Duc de Bourbon, in contrast to their fathers in 1771, were in their rightful places in attendance on the king.

In Louis's bedroom were Frayssinous, the *Grand Aumônier*, the Archbishop of Paris and Louis's confessor Abbé Rocher. The night of 15–16 September Louis grew much weaker. People now crowded into his bedroom, where the stifling silence was interrupted only by Louis's short, gasping breaths, and the priests reading out the prayers for the dying. Louis died at four o'clock in the morning.[33] The throne had never been more secure.

Conclusion

Despite its startling element of inconsistency and insincerity Louis's career, at least after 1800, was dominated by two essential components, two things about which he was sincere, namely that he was a monarch and a moderate: or, as Chateaubriand wrote a few days after Louis's death, *'les deux traits dominans de son caractère étaient la modération et la noblesse'* ('the two dominant traits of his character were moderation and grandeur').

In exile, unlike his cousins of Parma and Spain, or the Prince of Orange, Louis remained true to his role as a legitimate monarch, and rejected some tempting bribes to give up. He showed that he was himself, and that he believed in himself: basic virtues which are far from common among monarchs in a time of revolution. On the throne he was a regal monarch who, as Talleyrand wrote to the Tsar, *'sait donner un caractère royal à tout ce qui émane de lui'* ('knows how to give a royal character to everything he does').

Louis's *caractère royal*, or style, was official, formal and unpartisan, with moments of simplicity, domesticity and accessibility. Despite the virulence of party passions during his reign he tried to rule above parties (except in 1815–1816), and to end the division of his subjects into two kinds of Frenchmen. He tried to rally the Napoleonic élite to his side, in many cases successfully, with flattery, offices and power. Above all, he relied on ritual and force, an elaborate Court and a splendid guard, which he maintained despite considerable pressure and mockery, to help surround his throne with that *considération* which he always felt to be necessary.

The behaviour of his subjects at the time of his death showed the degree to which he had succeeded in this aim. Not only were there silent respectful crowds outside the palace while he lay dying, but thousands of people – the *Moniteur* said 23,000 in the first few days – filed past his body as it lay in state in the *Salle du Trône*. A former Chamberlain of Napoleon I wrote *'Jamais pour*

aucun événement on n'a vu plus d'affluence' ('Never for any
occasion have there been bigger crowds'). Thiers, an extreme
liberal journalist, claimed that *'La population entière de Paris a
pris le deuil … pas par douleur … mais par mode et par une
vanité singulière … Toute la semaine on a assiégé les Tuileries
pour voir la Salle du Trône'* ('The entire population of Paris has
put on mourning … not out of sorrow … but out of fashion
and from a bizarre vanity … All week people have been besieging
the Tuileries to see the *Salle du Trône'*). Even in death vanity was
one of the pillars of Louis's monarchy.

Mourning was perhaps more genuine outside Paris. In Semur
Madame Champagne wrote that *'la ville est consternée'*, and that
'tous les Royalistes de toutes les classes' went to a service in
memory of the king. In Touraine the Duchesse d'Escars, still
passionately Ultra, and normally unwilling to believe any good of
the local peasants, noted that *'les paysans en sont fort attristés'*
('it has made the peasants very sad'). Louis XVIII, not Louis XIII,
as is often said, was the last King of France for whom his people
mourned (and Louis XVI had also been deeply mourned).

But Louis's monarchy was not just a matter of his style and his
considération. It also helped to provide and create a role for the
French nobility. This had been a lasting concern to Louis since
the late 1780s, when he had styled himself *le Premier des Gentilshommes*. During his reign, the re-emergence of the French nobility, which had started under Napoleon I, reached its peak. Sixty
per cent of his ministers were members of the old nobility, including men such as the Abbé de Montesquiou, the Duc de
Richelieu, the Comte de Villèle and the Vicomte de Chateaubriand. Just as competent as and certainly more liberal than their
European contemporaries or their Napoleonic predecessors, they
would never have reached their offices, nor even have entered
politics, but for Louis's return to France. The reign of Louis XVIII
also saw the French monarchy finally achieve what the Habsburg,
Hohenzollern and Romanov Monarchies had achieved in the
eighteenth century, and what eluded every other French regime in
the nineteenth century, namely a bureaucracy and an army able
to draw on and incorporate people from every section of the elite
with the ambition to serve the state.

Under Louis XVIII the old nobility also recovered much of its
social prominence. It occupied almost all the posts at his Court
and in 1814, due to Louis's return, people such as the Ducs de
Castries, de Noailles and d'Havré, recovered their *hôtels* in the
Faubourgs Saint-Germain and Saint-Honoré. Under Louis XVIII
the aristocratic salons which were to impress Balzac and dazzle

Proust emerged for the first time as centres of real social and political power.

But the monarchy of Louis XVIII was not merely a matter of a certain style, nor was it simply the benefactor of a certain class. It also left a degree of real power in the hands of the monarch. Louis exerted considerable influence over the drawing up of the *Charte* in May 1814; and Louis, not his ministers, made the final decisions about political questions as important as the dissolution of the *Chambre Introuvable* in August 1816, the new electoral law in October 1819, the position of Villèle and the nature of French intervention in Spain in September and December 1822. Louis also maintained a real influence over ministerial appointments. He was able to make some ministerial careers and break others – for example that of Talleyrand after 1815. Thus, although the monarchy of Louis XVIII was not as absolute as those of Louis XV and XVI, it was not a cypher in the hands of the politicians.

The second essential component of Louis's career and reign was that, after 1800, he was moderate, and in 1814 he granted France a liberal constitution. Whether Louis was a genuine liberal or a liberal by necessity is hard to tell, and perhaps not very important. Examples of his illiberalism abound after 1800 as well as before. He did not really want his Government to pay Protestant priests' salaries, and he was never very fond of unrestrained liberty of the press. In 1815-16 and in 1822 he showed himself inexorable in support of his law-courts' decisions to send Frenchmen to the guillotine or the firing-squad for political crimes. In 1820, he was eager to reintroduce repressive laws after his nephew's assassination.

Nevertheless in the really important matter, namely the application of the liberal *Charte*, Louis was, right from the beginning, steadfast. Such infringements of the *Charte* as took place during his reign – for example the mode of election in 1815 and 1816, or the revival of a form of conscription in 1814 and 1818 – were relatively minor, and the result of the policies of his liberal ministers (except for the *Loi du Double Vote* of 1820). Thanks to Louis's *Charte* France had its first real experience of parliamentary monarchy and, with the Netherlands, southern Germany and the United Kingdom, belonged to the liberal half of Europe, as opposed to the illiberal half epitomized by the Austria of Francis I.

Moreover, Louis was a genuinely constitutional monarch. During the First Restoration his ministers, responsible to the chambers, were counterbalanced by the princes and the *Ministres d'État*, who were not. But the responsible ministers retained actual executive power, and Government policy was always decided with the attitude of the chambers in mind. If the First Restoration had not been genuinely constitutional and liberal, such a large section of liberal opinion would not have continued to support Louis XVIII during the Hundred Days.

After the Hundred Days, Louis left almost all the business of government to his responsible ministers, provided they had a majority in the chambers, and he was perfectly prepared to be guided by the decision of the tiny elite of voters over whether a ministry could last. In September 1815, he changed all his ministers in order to fit in with the opinion of the newly elected Chamber of Deputies. In December 1821, he again changed all his ministers (except the *Ministre de la Maison*) after they had been shown not to have the confidence of the Chamber of Deputies. Louis's reign shows that hereditary monarchy can serve as well as any other system to create a liberal constitutional regime.

Louis's monarchy broke up, like so many others, on the fundamental irrationality of hereditary monarchy, a system which must inevitably produce unsuitable monarchs. Although Charles X (as Artois became) was far from stupid, and had his liberal moments, he was not the stuff of which nineteenth-century constitutional monarchs were made. By his appointment of the Ultra Polignac ministry in August 1829, and by the *ordonnances* of 26 July 1830 further restricting the franchise, and destroying the liberty of the press, Charles X declared war on the political nation and the people of Paris. Charles X had seriously thought that the liberals were a revolutionary threat to his throne. Now they became one. He was indeed, as Louis and his subjects had feared, the James II of the French Bourbons.

The *Garde Royale* fought bravely but, badly led by Maréchal Marmont, and faced with the fury of the people of Paris it began to desert *en masse* only three days after the start of the Revolution. On 16 August, unable to find any force willing to oppose the Revolution, Charles X, the Angoulêmes (Angoulême had lived up to Louis's fears that he would not be '*une garantie bien solide*' by becoming as Ultra as his father, the Duchesse de Berri and the Duc de Bordeaux sailed into exile. In Paris Orléans, having sworn to uphold the *Charte*, had been proclaimed Louis-Philippe I, *Roi des Français* on 9 August. The *ère nouvelle* of Louis's proud inscription at Saint-Ouen was already over.

As a result of Artois's folly in upsetting the status quo the final success and relative liberalism of Louis's reign have disappeared under the general scorn and obloquy attached to the later Bourbons since the July Revolution. There is no ensuing sequence of monarchs to give significance or point to the debates and issues and solutions of Louis's reign. It is a lost world, whose particular character and importance have been almost completely forgotten.

Artois's disastrously decisive role in weakening and destroying Louis XVIII's liberal monarchy, both during and after Louis's reign, as well as Louis's and Artois's role in destroying Louis XVI in 1791–92, confirms, if confirmation were needed, the supreme wisdom of the Ottoman system of immuring the Sultan's male relations in the palace, and choosing the most suitable, rather than the next in line of primogeniture, to succeed. For if a suitable prince, perhaps Angoulême freed of his father's influence, had succeeded Louis, the long-term prospects of his liberal and legitimate monarchy, with its well-tried power-base and well-functioning constitution (the only French constitution to be as popular after as before a revolution), were quite good. If any people believed the Marquis de La Mole in *Le Rouge et Le Noir* (1830), that '*dans cinquante ans il n'y aura plus en Europe que des présidents de republique et pas de rois*' ('In fifty years there will only be presidents of republics and no kings in Europe'), they were wrong. Monarchy is an irrational system. But with its unique ability to appeal to and satisfy the emotions, and (usually) to rely on the army, it could still be effective in nineteenth-century Europe. By 1880 there were more monarchies than ever before – even, as La Fayette had noted with dismay, in newly independent countries like Greece. France was the solitary republican exception.

Moreover, monarchy not only endured and spread in nineteenth-century Europe, it also showed itself capable of playing a constructive role, particularly once it had become constitutional. Just as the Bourbon Monarchy introduced France's first real parliamentary government after the adoption of the *Charte* in 1814, so the Hohenzollern and Savoy Monarchies, after they had in 1848 adopted constitutions strongly influenced by the *Charte* (the Prussian constitution was even *oktroyierte*), played indispensable parts in creating the German Empire and the Kingdom of Italy.[2]

That the Bourbon monarchy might also have had something to contribute is suggested by what happened to Louis's friends. If, as is commonly believed, a man can be judged by his friends, Louis's friends clearly do not entirely redound to his credit. D'Avaray was indiscreet and a bit of a fool. Blacas was arrogant and illiberal. Decazes was indiscreet and devious. Madame du Cayla was venal. But they all had some redeeming features. D'Avaray was more broad-minded than most *émigrés*. Blacas, an early western collector of Islamic art, and a patron of Ingres, was one of the most original art-patrons of his day. After 1830, until his death in 1839, he was the principal councillor of Charles X and Angoulême in exile. The money which Louis had left in London after 1815, and for which Blacas had been responsible, became the main resource of the exiled Bourbons, and paid for Frohsdorf, the Austrian Schloss which functioned as their headquarters. So Louis's foresight helped provide a firm financial basis for the Bourbons' continued role in nineteenth-century French politics.

Decazes consoled his absence from office by founding Decazeville, one of the earliest large iron-mills in France, in 1826. In 1829 Charles X and Polignac had appealed to him for help in forming a new ministry – a startling vindication of his role before 1820 which would have amused, but not surprised, Louis XVIII. But Decazes, who felt that Charles X and Polignac were the only people who threatened the stability of France under the Bourbons and the *Charte*, refused. He died, having been a pillar of the July Monarchy, although not of the Second Empire, in 1864.

One of Louis's least-known friends, Madame de Mirbel, was brave enough to hide Guizot for several days when he was fleeing from angry revolutionaries in February 1848. Madame du Cayla, who had tried to extract huge sums of money from Villèle for burning Louis's letters, received a pension of 50,000 francs from Charles X in addition to all she had received from Louis – his furniture (now in the possession of her descendants at the Chateau d'Haroué near Nancy) as well as his money. But she never felt it was enough to maintain Saint-Ouen and the sheep farm near La Rochelle where, probably at Louis' instigation (perhaps hoping to rival Louis XVI's efforts in the 1780s), she was making successful attempts to improve the stock of French sheep – an agricultural version of Decazeville. In 1832, with the minimum of fuss and publicity, she performed a remarkable service for Louis's family by finding a husband and, even more difficult, suggesting a story, for the imprisoned Duchesse de Berri, pregnant after ten months of plotting and intrigue in France. Madame du Cayla died in Louis's house at Saint-Ouen in 1852.[3]

Thus they all, like their king, had some useful qualities. Louis also had many weaknesses. He was too adaptable. He often did not think about the consequences of his words and actions and policies: his ministers were necessary to prevent him from making blunders as well as to relieve him of the burden of Government business. He also had many vices. He could be a liar, a forger and a cheat. His behaviour towards his brother Louis XVI in 1791–92 was villainous, and it went against the interests of his own monarchy, the institution which had given him everything except power, as well. He remained wedded to the extreme ideas of the Emigration, which also went against the interests of his own monarchy, until 1800. Despite his frequent assertions to the contrary, he did not really care about what he called *le bonheur des français*. Indeed that his monarchy would be just as callously industrial as other nineteenth-century French regimes is suggested by his remark to his ministers in August 1814 *'qu'il faudrait trouver moyen d'user dans nos grandes forges de procédés mécaniques qui diminuassent la main-d'oeuvre et qui nous mettront ainsi à même de donner le fer à bon prix'* ('a way must be found of using mechanical processes in our large iron forges so as to diminish the workforce and enable us to produce iron cheaply'). In the right hands the Bourbon Monarchy could have made as great a contribution to the industrial development of France as, under Louis XVIII, it did to the political, social and emotional life of the country.

But what really interested Louis was not *le bonheur des français* nor the rate of industrialization but the problems which directly affected *him*: the nature of royal power, the role of the chambers, the size of the franchise, the functions of the élite, the organization of the army, the direction of French foreign policy. In the light of the solutions he adopted or accepted, Louis appears as neither a Bourbon stuck in his royal world, nor as the representative of a particular class or party, but above all as a figure plunged in and reacting to his own time. Unlike other children of Versailles, the Revolutions, or the Emigration, he was able to *'prendre l'esprit du jour'*, to think of the future not of the past. Thus when advising his cousin the King of Naples to imitate the most important act of his life and grant Naples a constitution, he stressed neither its advantages nor its loopholes, but simply the fact that it was in accordance with *l'Esprit de notre Siècle*. Louis had become an authentic representative of the last layer of his life, the world of nineteenth-century constitutional monarchy. As Chateaubriand wrote, a few days after Louis's death, *'Le Prince comprenait son siècle et était l'homme de son temps'* ('The Prince understood his age and was the man of his time').[4]

REFERENCES

I

1. BM. Add.Mss.20708 Papillon de La Ferté (who, as Intendant des Menus-Plaisirs du Roi, was in charge of the technical arrangements for all entertainments at Court) 'Description et Relation . . . du Mariage de Louis Stanislas-Xavier de France, Comte de Provence, avec Marie-Joséphine-Louise, Princesse de Savoie' ff. 22–23, 39; idem, *Journal*, (considerably franker than the official *Relation*), 1887, pp. 298–299: 17.5.1771.

2. Duc de Croÿ, *Journal Inédit* (4 vols, 1905–1906), II, 486, 493: 1771; Paul d'Estrée et Albert Callet, *La Duchesse d'Aiguillon*, 1912, p. 15, letter from the Duchesse d'Aiguillon, 24.5.1771; Louis XV, *Lettres à son Petit-fils l'Infant Ferdinand de Parme*, ed. Philippe Amiguet, 1938, p. 79, letter of 8.6.1767; *Croÿ*, II, 483; Archivio di Stato, Torino, Lettere Ministri Francia (henceforward referred to as ATLMF) Mazzo 213 Comte de Viry to Comte d'Aigueblanche, 17.2.72; *Louis XV*, p. 178, letter of 20.5.1771; AN. K 138,8⁴ᴮ another official *Relation* of the marriage.

3. *Papillon de La Ferté*, p. 298: 17.5.1771; the Piedmontese Ambassador claimed that he had to give a *Bal masqué* rather than a *Bal paré*, in honour of the wedding, since no one would go to his ball unmasked ATLMF. AN. K 138,8⁴ᴮ op. cit; Abbé Terray to Louis XV, 1772, quoted in *Découverte* (Bulletin Trimestriel pour l'Etude de Louis XVI et de son Procès), VI, 31, A. Geffroy, *Gustav III et la Cour de France* (Deuxième Edition, 2 vols, 1867), I, 255, Comtesse de La Marck to Gustave III 13.6.1771; cf. ATLMF Mazzo 215 Comte de Viry to Comte d'Aigueblanche, 24.1.1774; cf. Madame de Chastenay, *Mémoires*, (2 vols. 1896–1897), I, 89, written between 1814 and 1818, '*on ne croyait pas qu'il tint à lui d'en* (children) *avoir*'.

4. Quoted in P. Girault de Coursac, *L'Education d'un Roi: Louis XVI*, 1972, p. 118; Letter of 10.6.1799 in 'Lettres Inédites de Louis XVIII', *Revue Hebdomadaire*, XVIII, 12.1905, p. 154; John Moore, *A View of Society and Manners in France, Switzerland and Germany*, (2 vols. 1780, but written earlier), pp. 39, 46, confirmed by L. S. Mercier, *Tableau de Paris*, Nouvelle Edition corrigée et augmentée, (8 vols. Amsterdam 1781), IV, 149; AAE. Sardaigne 251.62 Correspondance Interceptée Comtesse de Provence to her parents, the Duc and Duchesse de Savoie, 28.2.1772; *Mercier*, VIII, 260.

5. See Hugh Murray Baillie's excellent and perceptive article 'Etiquette and the Planning of State Apartments in Baroque Palaces', *Archaeologia*, (C.I.) 1967, pp. 169–201; AAE. 225 Sardaigne, Correspondance Interceptée f.3 Comtesse de Provence to her parents, 2.1.1773; AN. KK.540 Etat des Logements, 1787; quoted in *Girault de Coursac*, p. 170; cf. *Croÿ*, II, 426: 9.6.1770.

6. Louis XVIII, 'Réflexions Historiques sur Marie-Antoinette', *Revue des Deux Mondes*, 15.7.1904, p. 247; François Bluche, *Les Honneurs de la Cour* (2 vols. 1957); in his *Journal* (Genève 1977), p. 138: 13.8.1782, the Marquis de Bombelles claims that under Louis XV the *noblesse présentée* could pay their respects almost every day, a point which seems to be confirmed by the Duc de Lévis in *Souvenirs et Portraits*, 1882, p. 333; Saint-Simon, *Memoirs*, ed. Lucy Norton, (3 vols. 1970–1974), II, 483; quoted in Louis XVIII to Abbé de Montesquiou, 22.3.1801, *Revue de la Révolution*, XI, 1888, p. 220.

7. Quoted in *Découverte*, IV, 13; Samuel F. Scott. *The Response of the Royal*

416

Army to the French Revolution, Oxford 1978, pp. 5, 23; *Geffroy*, II, 371, Comtesse de Boufflers to Gustaves III, 25.10.1772; Abbé Proyart, *Vie du Dauphin, Père de Louis XVI*, 1788, p. 439, *Girault de Coursac*, p. 80.

8. A. de Boislisle, ed., *Choix de Lettres Adressées à Mgr. de Nicolay* (Nogent-le-Rotrou, 1875), pp. 15–16, letter from the Dauphin 21.4.1762; p. 16, letter of 6.1762; the Dauphine to the Abbé Soldini, quoted in *Girault de Coursac*, p. 96; Comte de Corbière 'Souvenirs d'un Ministre de Louis XVIII', *Revue des Deux Mondes*, 1.4.1966, p. 372.

9. Louis XVI, *Réflexions sur Mes Entretiens avec M. le Duc de La Vauguyon*, 1851, (copied by the Comte de Provence), pp. 124, 181, quoted in *Girault de Coursac*, p. 164; La Vauguyon to Père Berthier, 4.6.1766, quoted in *Girault de Coursac* p. 116.

10. AN. R⁵56 Création de la Maison; Comte de Saint-Chamans, *Mémoires* (Tulle 1899), p. 59; for the strength and persistence of the *parti Choiseul*, see Croÿ, II, 450: 9.6/14.12.1770, and M.–A. de Lescure, ed. *Correspondance Secrète Inédite sur Louis XVI, Marie-Antoinette, la Cour et la Ville*, (2 vols. 1866), I, 507: 30.9.1782, I, 557: 11.5.1785; BN. NAF. 14714.28 Abbé Soldini, 'Première Conversation avec Monseigneur le Duc de Berri le 1er avril'.

11. AAE. Sardaigne 251.62, 255.127,144 Correspondance Interceptée, the Comtesse de Provence to the Duc and Duchesse de Savoie, 28.2.1772, 12.6, 5.7.1773; Vicomte de Reiset, *Joséphine de Savoie, Comtesse de Provence*, 1913, p. 45; cf. ATLMF 213 despatch of 17.2.1772; AAE, 255.26 vo. Duc de Savoie to Comtesse de Provence, 26.2.1773; see, for example, the letter of 16.3.1772, AAE, 251.67, in which she says she is sure she cannot be pregnant, confirming despatches of the Piedmontese ambassador, ATLMF, 213, despatches of 6,26.1.1772.

12. F. Ribes 'Histoire de l'Ouverture et de l'Embaumement du Corps de Louis XVIII', *Mémoires et Observations d'Anatomie* (3 vols. 1841–1843), II, 442; Duc de La Force, *Dames d'Autrefois*, 1934, p. 197, Louis to Madame de Balbi, 20.4.1792; AN. R⁵56 Brevet of 18.7.1774 appointing the Marquise de Damas; C. Hippeau, *Le Gouvernement de Normandie au XVIIᵉ et au XVIIIᵉ Siècles*, (9 vols, Caen 1863–1869), Evènements Politiques, I, 191, Madame de Coislin to the Duc d'Harcourt, 15.11.1781, cf. pp. 188 and 196, letters of 15.11 and 27.12.1781; Croÿ II, 487: 16.5.1774; Sebastien Hardy, *Mes Loisirs*, 1912, p. 418: 8.9.1773; M. de Seguret, *Mémoires* (Lyon 1897), p. 18; Pierre Verlet, *Versailles*, 1961, p. 714.

13. Louis XVIII, 'Réflexions Historiques sur Marie-Antoinette', p. 252, and pp. 247, 253, 256; *Geoffroy*, II, 291, 293, Louis to Gustavus III, 12.6.1775, 29.3.1777; A. von Arneth et A. Geffroy, ed. *Correspondance Secrète entre Marie-Thérèse et le Comte de Mercy-Argenteau, avec les Lettres de Marie-Thérèse et de Marie-Antoinette*, (3 vols. 1874), II, 404, Marie-Antoinette to Maria-Theresa, 15.12.1775; cf. ibid, II, 410, Mercy-Argenteau to Maria-Theresa, 17.12.1775; this episode may have increased Louis XVI's dislike for his brother, see AN. C 145 f. 25 (papers of the *Liste Civile*) the Marquis de Montesquiou to Louis XVI, 25.7.1792.

14. *Girault de Coursac*, p. 52; the report of Père de Neuville, written between 1761 and 1765, in Abbé Proyart, *Louis XVI et Ses Vertus aux Prises avec la Perversité de son Siècle* (4 vols. 1808), I, 34; AN 60 AP (papers of Maison de Monsieur) 2, 1 Larchevin to? 22.11.1780; BN. NAF. 14714 f. 28 Abbé Soldini 'Première Conversation avec Monseigneur le Duc de Berri'; Louis XVIII 'Réflexions Historiques sur Marie-Antoinette', p. 253.

15. ATLMF, Mazzo 215, Comte de Viry, the Sardinian Ambassador, to Comte

d'Aigueblanche, the Sardinian Minister of Foreign Affairs, 16, 5., 3.6.1774; Louis XVIII, 'Notes de Lecture', (written during the Emigration), *Le Correspondant* (CCXXXVIII), 10.1.1910, pp. 40–44; cf. J – N Moreau (Louis's Premier Conseiller), *Mes Souvenirs* (2 vols. 1898–1901), II, 115–118; Conti's remark is quoted in a letter from Louis to the Comte d'Artois in February 1803: Ernest Daudet, *Histoire de l'Emigration* (3 vols. 1907–1908), III, 297; *Geffroy*, II, 293–294, Louis to Gustavus III, 29.3.1777.

16. *Girault de Coursac*, p. 277; *Arneth et Geffroy* III, 117, Maria-Theresa to Mercy-Argenteau, 1.10.1777; *Geffroy*, II, 395–396, Louis to Gustavus III, 25.6.1779; J. B. Regnault-Warin, *Les Prisonniers du Temple* (3 vols 1800) I, 62–68; cf. *Moniteur*, 10 Germinal, An VI, p. 302, quoting a letter to Durand-Maillane denouncing the Comte de Provence as the author of all France's woes, and for having tried to persuade the Duc de Fitzjames to denounce the Dauphin as a bastard. Both these sources seem to me totally unreliable, and have been well exposed in Eugène Welvert, *Lendemains Révolutionnaires*, n.d., pp. 316–337; A. von Arneth et J. Flammermont, *Correspondance Secrète du Comte de Mercy-Argenteau avec l'Empereur Joseph II et le Prince de Kaunitz*, (2 vols. 1889), I, 41n, Mercy-Argenteau to Kaunitz 31.5.1781. Louis was extremely unlikely to have had access to such a document.

17. Abbé de Véry, *Journal* (2 vols. 1933), I, 205: 15.11.1774; *Seguret*, p. 36; Oscar de Poli, *Louis XVIII* (Quatrième Edition, 1880), p. 152, Louis to Comte de Moreton–Chabrillant, 25.6.1783; Dussaulx, *De La Passion du Jeu*, 1778, XXV.

II

1. *Geffroy*, II, 295, Louis to Gustavus III, 5.10.1778; Gérard Walter, *Le Comte de Provence*, 1950, p. 439; AN. 37AP (papers of the Marquis de Bonnay) I III Madame Clotilde to Louis, 30.6.1801 (copy); *Walter*, pp. 53–78, 439; he also reviewed the Carabiniers, of whom he had been Colonel since 1758, in 1774, 1782, and 1786.

2. AN. R⁵33 Etat des Officiers de la Maison de Monseigneur le Comte de Provence ordonnée pour le servir, 1773; R⁵42 Sommier de la Maison 1778–1791; *Croÿ*, III, 51; Comte de Liederkerke–Beaufort, 'Souvenirs d'un Page du Comte de Provence', *Revue de Paris*, May 1952, p. 58; AN. R⁵56 Mémoire, n.d. *c.* 1771, cf. Cromot de Fougy to the Comte de Saint-Priest, 12.2.1790; 'Observations sur le Service des Gardes de M. le Comte de Provence relativement à celui des Gardes du Corps du Roi', n.d. (pre–1774).

3. AN. R⁵33 op.cit., AN. R⁵56 Règlement pour le service honorifique de Monseigneur le Comte de Provence, 1.4.1771; *Liederkerke-Beaufort*, pp. 65–55; A.V. Arnault, *Souvenirs d'un Sexagénaire* (4 vols. 1833), I, 166–167; *Moreau*, II, 286.

4. *Bombelles*, p. 138: 13.8.1782; Louis XVIII, 'Notes de Lecture', p. 27; Comte Alexandre de Tilly, *Mémoires*, 1965, p. 191: for the 'desertion' of Versailles, see, among others, *Croÿ*, III, 294; 14.6.1776/15.4.1777; *Lescure*, II, 86: 15.12.1786; *Arneth et Geffroy*, II, 355, Mercy-Argenteau to Maria-Theresa, 17.7.1775; 'Notes de Lecture', p. 39; *Moreau*, II, 286, 464.

5. AN. R⁵33 op. cit; Robert Dubois-Corneau, *Le Comte de Provence à Brunoy*, 1909, p. 109, AN. K. 138⁹⁻¹⁶ Appanage de Monsieur; Beatrice Hyslop, *L'Appanage de Philippe-Egalité*, 1964, p. 17; cf. AN. R⁵ 1.264 Décision de

Monsieur, 4.7.1772: '*j'écrirai dans toutes les villes de l'Appanage, au nom de Monseigneur, comme cela est d'usage dans la Maison d'Orléans.*'

6. See his extraordinary letter of 30.10.1774 to Turgot, complaining of the inadequacy of his income from his appanage and the meanness of the Royal Government, in *Oeuvres de Turgot* (5 vols. 1913–1921), ed. Gustave Schelle, IV, 116; AN. R⁵33 op. cit; *Moore*, p. 43; AN. R⁵1 Décision de Monsieur, 19.9.1771.

7. Letter of 5.3.1772, to the Duc de La Vrillière, Ministre de la Maison du Roi, Coll. Dr. Jean Gautier, Brunoy; AN. 60 AP. Papers of the Maison de Monsieur. 2, 1 Note lue au Prince dans son travail du 15 fevrier 1772; see for example, BN. NAF. 22411.14 Mémoire à Monsieur, 1.2.1777, cf. John McManners, *French Ecclesiastical Society under the Ancien Régime*, 1960, pp. 199, 194; René Petiet, *Contribution à l'Histoire de l'Ordre de Saint-Lazare de Jérusalem en France*, 1914, pp. 398–412; AN. R⁵48 Comptes 1787–1790. But a Report submitted to Assemblée Nationale on 31 July 1790 estimated the income from Louis's appanage at 1,518,834 livres: *Archives Parlementaries* (Série I), XVII 480.

8. Douglas Dakin, *Turgot and the Ancien Régime in France*, 1939, p. 126; cf. Baron Malouet (the Intendant at Cayenne), *Mémoires* (2 vols. 1866), I, 390; Régine de Plinaval de Guillebon, 'La Manufacture de Porcelaine de Clignancourt, dite du Comte de Provence', *Cahiers de la Céramique*, XXXI, 1963, p. 158; cf. BN. NAF. 22414. 181 Instruction to agents to search for coal and cobalt; *Turgot*, IV, 116, Louis to Turgot, 27.11.1774, in favour of M. Dumesjean; A. Bruel, 'Les Chartreux de Paris et le Comte de Provence', *Bulletin de la Société Historique du Sixième Arrondissement de Paris*, 1900, p. 71, Cromot to de Velye, 22.11.1778, pp. 72–76; A. Hustin, *Le Luxembourg. Son Histoire Domaniale, Architecturale, Décorative et Anecdotique* (2 vols. 1910), II, 93.

9. AN. R⁵459 Travail de Monsieur, Acquisitions; *Archives Parlementaires*, (Série I), XVII, 478, Rapport of 31.7.1790; 60 AP. 1 Mémoire of 2.5.1777 re debts; BN. NAF. 22408.169 Cromot to M. de Chalut n.d., and 19.5.1780; AN. 60 AP.2, 1 Cromot to M. de Maurepas, Ministre d'Etat, 29.4.1780; Copie d'une lettre de M. Cromot à M. le Marquis de Noailles du 22 avril 1780, cf. his letter of 4.10.1780; BN. NAF. 22414.172–173 Résultat des vérifications relatives à la Capitation des Enfants de France; ibid. 117 Cromot to the Contrôleur-Général, 25.12.1787.

10. AN. F⁴2680 Renseignements, Monsieur, Frère du Roi, Etat des Dettes au 1ᵉʳ janvier 1783; cf. d'Ormesson (Contrôleur-Général) to d'Amelot (Ministre de la Maison du Roi), 10.5.1783 (draft). Louis and his Premier Ecuyer, the Marquis de Montesquiou, had increased his ecuries by 91 horses and 219,031 livres p.a. since 1771: see BN. NAF. 22408.173; AN. R⁵523 Tableau de la recette générale des Biens acquis par le Roy et Monsieur de Monseigneur le Prince de Conti par contrat du 7.10.1783; cf. *Livre Rouge* (the accounts of the king's private funds), 1790, pp. 9–10, 30; in *Eclaircissements sur le Livre Rouge, en ce qui concerne Monsieur, Frère du Roi*, 1790, p. 5, Louis claimed that he was owed 7m. in all for his share of his relations' estates, and shows that he felt he deserved even more than this immense generosity: cf. AN. R⁵56 Mémoire concernant les droits successifs de Monsieur, frère du Roi, 1783.

11. Jean Gautier, 'Inventaire des Propriétés du Comte de Provence à Brunoy', *Bulletin de la Société Historique et Archéologique de Corbeil, d'Etampes et du Hurepoix*, Corbeil, 1976, p. 24; *Dubois-Corneau* p. 14; AN. R⁵523 Catalogue de mes Tableaux, 1781; Barbara Scott, 'Madame's *Pavillon de Musique*', *Apollo*, XCV, May 1972, p. 390; Hector Lefuel, *Georges Jacob*, 1923, pp. 130–

132; For examples of Louis's furniture, see *Lefuel*, planches XVII, XXI; Francis Watson, *Louis XVI Furniture*, 1960, illus. 46 and 61; *Connaissance des Arts*, July 1967, pp. 54–55; Dugourc, 'Autobiographie', *Nouvelles Archives de l'Art Français*, 1877, p. 369; Pierre Verlet, *Le Mobilier Français du XVIIIe Siècle*, (2 vols. 1956), II, 39.

12. Jacques Robiquet, 'La Propriété de la Comtesse de Balbi et du Comte de Provence à Versailles', *Revue de l'Histoire de Versailles*,1. 1921, pp. 1–15; Vicomte de Reiset, *Anne de Caumont La Force, Comtesse de Balbi* (Cinquième Edition, 1909), passim, and pp. 52–53; *Hippeau*, Evènements Politiques, I, 142, 159 letters of 21.12.1779, 2.10.1780; *Bombelles*, p. 32: 11.7.1780.

13. *La Force*, pp. 196, 203, Louis to Madame de Balbi, 20.4, 4.5.1792; *Hustin*, II, 50–51; AN. 86 AP, papers of the Marquis de Jaucourt 81.1.167 Portrait d'Hortense by Monsieur (copy). In my opinion, this copy is genuine. Jaucourt knew Louis well, and claims that the copy was given him by his sister, one of Marie-Joséphine's ladies-in-waiting, while she gave the original to her daughter-in-law, Louis's last favourite, Madame du Cayla

14. *La Force*, pp. 67–68; Reiset, *Comtesse de Balbi*, p. 138; Comte de Contades, *Coblentz et Quiberon, Souvenirs*, 1885, p. 17; *Seguret*, p. 35; See e.g. *La Force*, pp. 196, 203, letters of 20.4. and 4.5.1792; Reiset, *Comtesse de Balbi*, pp. 167–171;

15. *Dubois-Corneau*, p. 139; Reiset, *Joséphine de Savoie*, pp. 208–214, 216, Marie-Joséphine to Madame de Gourbillon, 24.10.1790; *Arneth et Geffroy*, II, 410, Mercy-Argenteau to Maria-Theresa, 17.12.1775; AN F⁷4730 Marie-Joséphine to Madame de Gourbillon, 12.4.1789.

16. *Arneth et Flammermont*, II, 224, Mercy-Argenteau to Kaunitz, 22.2.1789; ATLMF.212 Viry to Aigueblanche, 19.5.1771; AAE. 621.64, 89 vo, 112,159 vo, 190 vo, Marie-Joséphine to Madame de Gourbillon, 1799, 9.11.1808, 8.3., 26.11.1809; 621.60–67 Mémoire by Madame de Gourbillon, 19.7.1799; Comte Fleury, *Les Dernières Années de la Marquise de Bombelles*, 1906, p. 111, Journal du Marquis de Bombelles: 22/23. 1.1789; AN F⁷4730 Marie-Joséphine to Madame de Gourbillon, 12, 15, 20.4.1789.

17. *Dubois-Corneau*, pp. 156, 188, 226–227, 279 quoting Hardy's diary for 23.7.1781.

18. Guy Chaussinand-Nogaret, *La Noblesse au XVIIIe Siècle*, 1976, p. 96; *Mercier*, IV, 65, 70; *Chaussinand-Nogaret*, pp. 53–54; Colin Lucas 'Nobles, Bourgeois and the French Revolution', *Past and Present* (LX), August 1973, p. 119; *Dubois-Corneau*, pp. 84, 68, Voltaire to M. de Cromot, 20.9.1776.

19. *Statuts et Règlements du Premier Musée Autorisé par le Gouvernement, sous la Protection de Monsieur et de Madame, établi en 1781 par M. Pilatre de Rozier*, 1784; *de Poli*, p. 16; *Liste de Toutes les Personnes qui composent le premier Musée Autorisé par le Gouvernement sous la Protection de Monsieur et de Madame*, 1785; *Statuts et Règlements*, pp. 1, 5–6; *Dubois-Corneau*, p. 328; *Lévis*, p. 400; *Fleury*, p. 111, Journal du Marquis de Bombelles: 23.1.1789.

20. AAE. Sardaigne 251.121 Comtesse de Provence to the Duc and Duchesse de Savoie, 21.7.1772; André Rebsomen, 'Passages à Bordeaux des Comtes d'Artois et de Provence, 1777–1782', *Revue Historique de Bordeaux* (16e Année), Mars-Avril 1923, p. 101, Mme. Chazot-Dupplessy to Mme. de Cursol, 15.6.1777; *Geffroy*, I, 286, Comtesse de La Marck to Gustavus III, 7.8.1777; *Lescure*, I, 412: 12.7.1781; AN. 60 AP.1 a Mémoire by Montesquiou, Louis's Premier Ecuyer, continued in BN. NAF. 22408.179; AN. ABXIX Journal de la Cassette de Monsieur pour le Quartier de Juillet (1781–1790), by de Masgon-

thière, his Premier Valet de Chambre, records frequent payments caused by his *tirés*.

21. BN.NAF 21745.35–45 Catalogue des Livres du Cabinet de Monsieur; *Chaussinand-Nogaret*, p. 107; cf. Bibliothèque de l'Arsenal Mss. 5385 Catalogue des Livres provenant de chez Louis-Stanislav-Xavier Capet émigré; M. Nougaret *Anecdotes du Règne de Louis XVI 1777* (2 vols. 1778), II, 16; Louis XVIII 'Notes de Lecture', p. 39; Earl of Malmesbury, *Diaries and Correspondence* (4 vols. 1844), II, 68, Louis to Lady Malmesbury, 1790; his friendship with Lady Malmesbury probably dated from her visit to France to see her sister, Lady Eden, in 1786; Horace Walpole, *Règne de Richard III, ou Doutes Historiques sur les Crimes qui Lui sont Imputés*, 1800, p. 33: the manuscript of his translation was in his library at Versailles, see Arsenal Mss. 5385.

22. *Moreau*, II, 452; *Louis XV*, p. 192, letter to the Infant Ferdinand de Parme, 25.11.1771; *Geffroy* II, 386, 391, Louis to Gustavus III, 5.10.1778, BN, NAF. 14714. 9. Abbé Soldini 'Première Conversation avec Monseigneur le Duc de Berri'; Maréchale de Beauvau, *Souvenirs*, 1872, p. 118; *Dubois-Corneau*, p. 323; *Découverte*, XVIII, June 1977, p. 31, M. de Laporte to Louis XVI, 5.3.1791.

23. *Rebsomen*, p. 101, Mme. Chazot-Duplessy to Mme. de Cursol, 15.6.1777; Reiset, *Joséphine de Savoie*, diary of Charles-Felix, Duc de Genevois: 25.12.1793; James Greig, ed., *The Diaries of a Duchess*, 1926, p. 115: 6.5.1770; Gabriel de Broglie 'Le Sacre de Louis XVI', *Revue des Deux Mondes*, Juillet 1974, p. 50, Duc d'Orléans to Madame de Montesson, 12.6.1775; *Croÿ*, III, 193: 12.6./31.12.1775; Comte de Stedingk, *Mémoires ... rédigés sur des lettres, dépêches et autres pièces ...* (3 vols. 1844–1847), I, 59, Stedingk to Gustavus III, 22.10.1781.

24. *Rebsomen*, pp. 98–101, Mme. Chazot-Duplessy to Mme. de Cursol, 6.1777; *Liederkerke-Beaufort*, pp. 68, 83; AN. ABXIX 781 Journal de la Cassette de Monsieur; *Dubois-Corneau*, p. 113; *Geffroy*, I, 255, Comtesse de La Marck to Gustavus III, 17.6.1771, *Véry*, I, 241: 1.3.1775.

25. *Découverte*, XIV, December 1978, p. 48, quoting a letter by Thierry de Ville d'Avray, a Premier Valet de Chambre of Louis XVI; Robert Darnton, 'Reading, Writing, and Publishing in Eighteenth-Century France', *Daedalus*, C, 1971, p. 243; Arsenal Mss. 5385 Catalogue des Livres provenant de chez Louis-Stanislas-Xavier Capet, *émigré*.

III

1. PRO.PC 1/124 110.69 (Calonne Papers) Conférence tenue chez Monsieur le 2 mars 1787; Daudet, *Histoire de l'Emigration*, III, 297, Louis to Artois, 2.1803; Instituts, A et NF. 2190.48–54 Louis's Notes of 25.3.1787, cf. *Procès-Verbal et Observations Présentées au Roi par les Bureaux de l'Assemblée des Notables* (2 vols. 1787), I, 5, 53, 100, II, 112–116.

2. Comte de Brienne, *Journal de l'Assemblée des Notables de 1787*, ed. Pierre Chevalier, 1960, p. 24: 23.2.1787; *Procès-Verbal*, I, 112; cf. Institut A et NF 2190. 48–54 Louis's Notes of 25.3.1787, *Procès-Verbal*, I, 33; *Brienne*, p. 26: 28.2.1787; Pierre Renouvin, *L'Assemblée des Notables de 1787*, 1920, p. X, Calonne to Louis, 1.3.1787, pp. 6, 12, 13.

3. PRO.PC 1/124 110.22 Conférence tenue chez Monsieur le 2 mars 1787; Institut A et NF 2190.48 Louis's Note of 9.3.1787; *Procès-Verbal*, I, 4, II, 308,

Louis's Speech of 25.5.1787; PRO.PC.1/124 110.31 Conférence tenue chez Monsieur le 2 mars 1787.

4. Jean Egret, *La Pré-Révolution Française*, 1962, pp. 163, 167, 175; *Réflexions Patriotiques sur les Entreprises de Quelques Ministres de France, Adressées à Monsieur, Frère du Roi*, 1788; cf. *Lescure*, II, 257, 266: 16.5, 17.6.1788; Abbé de Lubersac, *Le Citoyen Conciliateur . . . Idées Sommaires, Politiques et Morales sur le Gouvernement Monarchique de la France* (3 vols. 1788), I, 11, 25, 26, III, 4, 78, 81.

5. *Procès-Verbal de l'Assemblée des Notables tenue à Versailles en 1788*, 1789, p. 101; Antonin Proust, *Archives de l'Ouest* (5 vols. Angers 1867–1869), IV, 45, speech by the Comte de Cossé, 19.3.1789; AN. F^{7}4730 Marie-Joséphine to Madame de Gourbillon, 16, 19.8.1789, 26.8, 10.10.1790; Georges Lefebvre, ed., *Recueil de Documents relatifs aux . . . Etats-Généraux* (2 vols. 1955–1962), II, 197, Comte de Saint-Priest to Louis XVI, 22.6.1789; cf. Baron de Staël Holstein, *Correspondance Diplomatique* (1783–1799), 1881, p. 103, Staël to Gustavus III, 25.6.1789.

6. The Gardes du Corps' declaration in *Journal des Amis de la Constitution*, 1.7.1789, is quoted in *Découverte* (XVIII), p. 42; Verlet, *Versailles*, p. 762; *Malouet*, I, 390; Général de La Fayette, *Mémoires, Correspondance et Manuscrits* (6 vols. 1837–38), I, 8.

7. *La Force*, p. 188, Louis to Madame de Balbi, 22.10.1789; Louis XVI, 'Declaration du Roi à sa Sortie du Royaume', *Archives Parlementaires* (Première Série), XXVII, 378; A. Bacourt, ed., *Correspondance entre le Comte de Mirabeau et le Comte de La Marck* (3 vols. 1851), I, 361, La Marck to Mirabeau, 13.10.1789; compare the contracts in Gustave Bord, *Autour du Temple* (3 vols. 1912), I, 359, and *La Fayette*, II, 496.

8. Gouverneur Morris, *A Diary of the French Revolution* (2 vols. 1939), I, 359: 5.1.1790; cf. *Monsieur au Conseil*, 1790 (a pamphlet), and Adrien Duquesnoy, *Journal sur l'Assemblée Constituante* (3 vols. 1894), III, 370: 10.2.1790; Alexis de Valon, 'Le Marquis de Favras d'après de nouveaux Documents', *Revue des Deux Mondes*, 6.1851, pp. 1112–1113, quoting the depositions of La Chatre and Papillon.

9. *Discours de Monsieur à la Commune*, 1789; *Morris*, I, 346; 27.12.1789; Comte d'Hérisson, *Autour d'une Révolution*, 1888, p. 76, quoting an account apparently by Sémonville; AN. BB^{30}82, doss. Favras, depositions of More 1, 29.12.1789, Chomel, 12.1.1790, Tourcaty, n.d, Favras, 18.1.1790; cf. Cromot de Fougy, *Etat des Fonds à Faire au Trésor de Monsieur pour les Paiements échus au mois de Janvier 1790*, trying to substantiate Louis's claim; AN. R^{5}48 Comptes 1787–1790.

10. *Bacourt*, I, 460, 447, Mirabeau to La Marck, 27.1.1790, 4.1.1790; Edmond Cleray, *L'Affaire Favras*, 1932, pp. 52, 63; cf. AN. BB^{30}82 deposition of Joffroy, in which he states that he had been following Favras for two months, presumably on someone's orders.

11. Louis XVIII, 'Notes de Lecture', p. 45n; N. Ruault, *Lettres à son Frère*, 1976, p. 174, letter of 28.12.1789; cf. BN. NAF. 4125. 358vo-359, the diary for 16.12.1789 of a left-wing deputy; *Bacourt*, I, 139, Souvenirs of La Marck.

12. *La Fayette*, II, 496, Louis XVI to La Fayette, 29.6.1790; *Archives Parlementaires* (LIII), 227, Marquise de Favras to M. de Septeuil, 15.11.1791; *Bacourt*, II, 96, Mirabeau to 'the Court', 9.6.1790; ibid, II, 287, La Marck to Mercy-Argenteau, 28.10.1790, for Marie-Antoinette's lack of influence over Louis XVI; Reiset, *Josephine de Savoie*, p. 214, Marie-Joséphine to Madame de Gourbillon 5.9.1790.

13. *Bacourt*, I, 460, Mirabeau to La Marck, 27.1.1790; cf. *Duquesnoy*, II, 370: 10.2.1790; BN. NAF. 22901.91 Montbarey to Cromot n.d. (copy); Comte de Vaudreuil, *Correspondance avec le Comte d'Artois* (2 vols. 1889), I, 300, 320, Vaudreuil to Artois, 18.9, 1.10, 1790.

14. (Louis XVIII), *Relation d'un Voyage à Bruxelles et à Coblentz (1791)*, 1822, p. 72; Louis XVI 'Declaration du Roi à sa sortie du Royaume', p. 378; Conseil-Général de la Commune, *Exposé des Faits qui se sont Passés dans la Séance du 22 fevrier 1791*, p. 30, quoting an eyewitness's letter; cf. *Départ Manqué de Monsieur par la Surveillance du Peuple*.

15. *Relation*, pp. 7, 17, 51; AN. F⁷4730 Marie-Joséphine to Madame de Gourbillon, 24.10.1790.

16. *Relation*, pp. 49, 52; Ernest Daudet, 'L'Ami du Roi', *Revue des Deux Mondes*, 15.11.1904, p. 253.

17. BN.NAF. 22408.179; *Relation*, p. 103.

IV

1. Prince de Condé, *Journal d'Emigration*, ed. Comte de Ribes, 1923, p. 209; 24.6.1791; *Relation*, pp. 108, 117; PRO. FO. 26 17. Wilson to Duke of Portland, 5.7.1791.

2. G. Lenôtre, *Le Marquis de la Rouerie et la Conjuration Bretonne, 1790–1793*, 1899, p. 96, Louis, Artois to La Rouerie, 12.3.1792; Comte d'Espinchal, *Journal d'Emigration*, 1912, p. 257: 14/19.8.1791; AN. ABXIX 196 Papiers du Comte de La Chapelle, *Major-Général de l'Infanterie*, Armée des Princes, Tableau Général et Nominatif.

3. Comte de Saint-Ange, *Code des Ordres de Chevalerie du Royaume*, 1819, p. 433; *Espinchal*, p. 250: 5/10.8.1791; P. de Vaissière, *Lettres d'Aristocrates*, 1923, p. 366, M. Bengy de Puyvallée to M. d'Alzac, 23.11.1791; Baron de Klinkowström, ed., *Le Comte de Fersen et la Cour de France* (2 vols. 1878), I, 7, diary for 25.7.1791; AN. F⁷ 6255 (papers of the Marquis de Lambert, Observations sur la position des Princes, 15.12. 1791.

4. *Espinchal*, p. 256: 14/19.8.1791; *Relation*, p. 132; *Klinkowström*, I, 7: 25.7.1791: *Malmesbury*, II, 447, diary of Lord Malmesbury, 26.5.1792; *Klinkowström*, I, 33: 29.10.1791; cf. L-J-A de Bouillé, *Souvenirs* (3 vols. 1908–11), II, 36, Marquis de Jaucourt to the Marquis de Bouillé, 18.7.1792.

5. PRO. FO. 95 630.150 Elector of Trier to Artois, 16.3.1792; PRO. FO. 95 632.369 Inventaire des piéces envoyées à Madrid le 16 juin 1792; PC1/131.371 Artois to Charles IV, 9.3.1792 (copy); *Condé*, 280: 28.4.1792; *Relation*, p. 130.

6. *Espinchal*, p. 285: 12.11.1791; *Relation*, p. 37; AN. F⁷6255 Observations sur la position des Princes, 15.12.1791. PRO. PC 1/4517 Calonne to Louis, 31.3.1792; *Espinchal*, p. 341: 6.1792; *Archives Parlementaires*, L11, 617, Instruction pour M. le Comte de Moustier, 3.9.1792.

7. PRO. PC/1/128.192 Minute de ce qui fut résolu le 20 novembre 1791 lorsqu'on crut le Roi sorti du Royaume; Baron F. S., Feuillet de Conches, *Louis XVI, Marie-Antoinette, et Madame Elizabeth* (6 vols. 1864–73), II, 138–139, Louis to the Baron de Breteuil, 2.7.1791; *Klinkowström*, I, 207, Marie-Antoinette to Fersen, 31.10.1791, Daudet; *Coblentz*, n.d., 317–318, Louis to the Queen, 20.2.1792.

8. AN. F⁷6255 Papers of the Marquis de Lambert 'Observations sur la position des Princes le 15.12.1791', by Lambert; *Feuillet de Conches*, II, 156; cf. *Klin-*

kowström, I, 212, Marie-Antoinette to Fersen, 7.11.1791; PRO. PC1/127 Exposé by Louis and Artois, n.d.; *Feuillet de Conches*, III, 379, Mémoire of Gustavus III, 5.7.1791.

9. AAE. France (Fonds Bourbon – Louis XVIII's papers. deposited at the Quai d'Orsay in 1814) 588. 42, 47 Louis XVI to Louis, 16.10.1791, 11.11.1791; AAE. 588.12 Louis and Artois to Louis XVI, 10.9.1791; *Feuillet de Conches*, IV, 261, Louis to Louis XVI, 3.12.1791. Musée des Archives Nationales, *Documents Originaux de l'Histoire de France*, 1872, p. 123, Louis and Artois to Louis XVI, 9. 1791.

10. AN. F⁷ 6255 Lambert, 'Réflexions sur l'opposition qui existe entre M. de Calonne et M. le baron de Breteuil', 18.3.1792; Victor de Saint-Génis, 'Une Conspiration Royaliste à Strasbourg en 1791', *Revue des Deux Mondes*, 15.3.1880, p. 422, Louis and Artois to Condé, 5.2.1792; this letter was then copied to be shown to officers of the Strasbourg garrison; *Girault de Coursac*, p. 165; *Geffroy*, II, 179, Gustavus III to the Comte de Stedingk, 6.7.1791.

11. Alfred Ritter von Vivenot, *Quellen zur Geschichte der Deutschen Kaiserpolitik Osterreichs Während der Französischen Revolutionskriege* (5 vols. Vienna 1873–1890), Note of 8.1791 by Louis; cf. *Klinkowström*, I, 6: 25.7.1791; *Protestation des Princes de la Maison de Bourbon contre l'Acceptation de la Constitution Française*, 1791; Daudet, *Coblentz*, 319, Louis to Marie-Antoinette, 20.12.1791; *Feuillet de Conches*, IV, 83, Louis and Artois to Catherine II, 12.1.1792.

12. PRO. FO. 632.224 Condé to Calonne, 9.8.1792; Daudet, *Coblentz*, 319, Louis to Marie-Antoinette, 20.2.1792; PRO. PC1/128.192 Minute de ce qui fut résolu le 20 novembre 1791 lorsqu'on crut le Roi sorti du Royaume; J. Crétineau-Joly, *Histoire des Trois Derniers Princes de la Maison de Condé* (2 vols. 1867), II, 54, Condé to the Duc de Bourbon, 4.7.1792.

13. PRO. PC1/126.145 Bordereau des differentes sommes reçues … pour le compte de Leurs Altesses Royales les Princes, Frères du Roy, 1791; P. Girault de Coursac, 'L'Argent des Princes', *Découverte* (XIII), 3. 1976, p. 20; AAE. 588.86 Louis and Artois to Catherine II, 25.10.1792; cf. for a figure larger by nearly 5m. livres, AN. O³2680, 2 Exercices 1791 et 1792 Apperçu des Depenses; ibid and P. Girault de Coursac, 'Les Princes Faux-Monnayeurs', *Découverte* (XV), September 1976, pp. 21–39.

14. PRO. PC1/4517 Calonne to La Queille, 16.4.1792; PC1/229.231 Condé to Calonne, 2.6.1792; PRO. PC1/4517 Calonne to Artois 27.3.1792; AN. ABXIX 196 Papers of Comte de La Chapelle, Ordres et Décisions des Princes, 19.8.1791, 21.9.1791; Georges Livet, *Recueil des Instructions données aux Ambassadeurs et Ministres de France*, XXVIII (Electorat de Trèves), 1966, p. 325; *Espinchal*, p. 289: 12.1791.

15. *Vivenot*, I, 396, Elector of Trier to Leopold II, 20.2.1792; *Condé* p. 270: 23.3.1792; *La Force*, p. 199, Louis to Madame de Balbi, 24.4.1792; PRO. PC1/128.196 Etat des forces effectives de l'armée des princes au 25 mai 1792; AN. ABXIX 196 Armée Royale, Tableau General et Nominatif.

16. *Espinchal*, p. 302: 1. 1791; p. 342: 6.1792; BN. NAF. 22738. 138 notes of Louis, 7 or 8.1792.

17. *Malmesbury*, II, 442, Malmesbury to Duke of Portland, 28.10.1791; Edmund Burke, *Correspondence* (10 vols. Cambridge-Chicago 1958–1978), VI, 373, Louis to Burke, 26.8.1791; AN. ABXIX 196 Armée Royale, Tableau Général et Nominatif; PRO. FO. 632.17 Calonne to Metzlar, 25.6.1792; *Vivenot*, I, 313, Elector of Trier to Leopold II, 6.1.1792.

18. Letter of 28.7.1792, *Nouvelle Revue Retrospective*, 1.1902, p. 3: PRO. FO.

632.56 Artois to Las Cases, 11.7.1792; AN. AE V, 5 Louis to the Marquis de Lambert, 23.8.1792; P. J. B. Buchez, et P.C.L. Roux, *Histoire Parlementaire de la Révolution Française* (40 vols. 1834–38), XII, 231–232, Message from Monsieur; 'Réflexions Historiques sur Marie-Antoinette', p. 245; *La Force*, p. 204, Louis to Madame de Balbi, 4.5.1792; PRO. PC1/128.254 Sur la Conduite à tenir en France – Déterminations proposées par les Princes.
19. PRO. PC1/128.220 Louis's speech to Longwy, n.d.; E. W. Harcourt, *The Harcourt Papers* (14 vols. Oxford 1880–1905), V, 335 General to Mrs. Harcourt, Longwy, 26.8.1792; A. Lapierre, *Campagne des Emigrés dans l'Argonne* (Sedan 1911), pp. 58–59, 69., cf. *Espinchal*, pp. 414–418; 11/14.9.1792; PRO. PC1/128.275 Résolutions du 2.9.1792.
20. Arthur Chuquet, *Les Guerres de la Révolution* (11 vols. 1886–96), I, 287; AN. AEV, 5 Louis to Lambert 5,17.9.1792; AN. F⁷6255 Baron de Roll to Lambert, 21.8.1792; cf. Sommation to Thionville, 4.9.1792; *Feuillet de Conches*, VI, 330, Prince of Nassau-Siegen to Catherine II, 22.8.1792; PC. 128/178 Conférence tenue chez le Baron de Breteuil, 7.9.1792; PRO PC1/128.259; *Klinkowström*, II, 379, Breteuil to Fersen, 2.10.1792.
21. *Klinkowström*, II, 41, Lévis to Fersen, 3.9.1792; *Harcourt*, XI, 394, Colonel W. Harcourt to Earl Harcourt, Verdun 8.9.1792; *Chuquet*, III, 223–225; *Vaudreuil*, II, 105, Vaudreuil to the Comte d'Antraigues, 9.7.1792; PRO. PC1/128. 244 Calonne to Artois, 13.9.1792; *Espinchal*, p. 444: 8.10.1792.
22. ibid, p. 423, 19.9.1792; cf. p. 440: 5.10.1792; p. 450:12.10.1792; pp. 499–501:25/30.11.1792; cf. *Klinkowström*, II, 48: 26.11.1792.
23. Daudet, *Histoire de l'Emigration* (henceforward referred to as *Daudet*'), I, 216, *Espinchal*, p. 451: 12.10.1792; *Vaudreuil*, II, 116, Artois to Vaudreuil, 28.12.1792; Jean Dutourd, *Rivarol*, 1963, p. 34; *La Force*, p. 263, Louis to Madame de Balbi, 26.1.1793; Pierre Verlet, *French Royal Furniture* 1962, p. 117.
24. Hans Glagau, *Die Französische Legislative und der Ursprung der Revolutionskriege* (Berlin 1896), p. 361, Mercy-Argenteau to Kaunitz, 31.7.1792, p. 363 Lambinet to Feletz, n.d.; *La Force*, p. 204, Louis to Madame de Balbi, 4.5.1792.

V

1. *Daudet*, III, 4, Louis to Lady Malmesbury, 15.11.1800; *Daudet*, I, 255; Paul Cottin, *Toulon et les Anglais*, 1898, p. 245; the invitation has not been seen and application to the Archives at Toulon has been fruitless. But it is referred to both by the English and Republican Governments neither of which were likely to invent a document so displeasing to themselves: *Moniteur*, 1.2.1794, p. 533. *Cottin*, pp. 246–247, 260; PRO. FO 28 Genoa 6 Francis Drake to Lord Grenville, Genoa, 17.11.1793; Reiset, *Madame de Balbi*, p. 248 Malmesbury to Madame de Balbi, 7.12.1793; Z. Pons *Mémoires pour servir à l'histoire de la Ville de Toulon en 1793*, 1825, p. 340, Hood, Elliot, to Comité Général des Sections, 23.11.1793; cf. *Extrait de Quelques Actes des Rebelles de Toulon*, 1795, pp. 12–13, quoting a speech of 12.11.1793 by M. Villecrose referring to the sections' invitation; AN. 326 Mi 26 (Chartrier de Castries) Maréchal de Castries to Artois 3/7.12.1793.
2. AN. 326 Mi 26 Castries to Artois, 24.11.1793; Reiset, *Joséphine de Savoie*, p. 294, diary of the Comte de Maurienne, 25.12.1794, PRO. FO 28. Genoa 6 Francis Drake to Lord Grenville, Livorno 16.12.1793; FO. 67 Piedmont 14 Trevor to Grenville, 1.2.1794; Marquis Dugon, *Au Service du Roi en Exil*, 1968,

p. 37; PRO. FO 27/45 Lord Macartney to Lord Grenville, 12, 15.8.1795. G. Caudrillier *La Trahison de Pichegru*, 1908, p. 256 n.

3. 'Un Voyage de Vérone à Riegel en 1796', *Feuilles d'Histoire*, 1.5.1909, p. 382; *Dugon*, p. 88, note of President de Vezet; cf. Comte de Pimodan, *Les Fiançailles de Madame Royale*, 1912, p. 61 Louis to Madame Royale, 5.5.1796; Ernest Daudet, 'Fiançailles d'Exil', *Revue des Deux Mondes*, 15.12.1904, p. 835, Report of d'Avaray, 4.5.1796.

4. André Lebon, *L'Angleterre et l'Emigration Française*, 1881, p. 192, William Wickham to Lord Grenville, 29.5.1796; cf. *Dugon* p. 88; *Caudrillier*, p. 271; BM. Add. Mss. (Puisaye Papers) 8041.82 La Thuillerie to the Comte de Puisaye, 26.4.1797; *Dugon*, p. 170; Rev. T. R. England, *Letters from the Abbé Edgeworth to His Friends*, 1818, p. 126, Abbé Edgeworth to Dr Moylan, 24.5.1798.

5. *Daudet*, III, 216 Louis to Marie-Joséphine, 2.01; Reiset, *Joséphine de Savoie*, pp. 366–367; Baron Hue, *Souvenirs*, 1903, p. 24.

6. *Daudet*, III, 363, 366; AN. 306 AP.28 (Chartrier de Castries) Louis to Castries, 19.2.1794; *Daudet*, II, 217, Louis to Duchesse d'Angoulême, 30.7.1798; ibid, III, 216, Louis to Marie-Joséphine, 25.2.1806.

7. J. Lucas-Dubreton, *Louis XVIII*, 1925, pp. 80–82; *Burke*, IX, 69–70, 25.8.1796; *Dugon*, p. 89; AN. 34 AP (Condé Correspondance) 4, letter of 7.9.1796 (copy); *Ribes* p. 431; Paul Bailleu, *Preussen und Frankreich von 1795 bis 1807* (2 vols. Leipzig 1881–1887), I, 464, Caillard to Talleyrand, 2.12.1797; Vicomte de Reiset, *Autour des Bourbons*, 1927, pp. 161–162; cf. AN. 198 AP (Papiers La Fare) Marquis de Bonnay to Mgr. de La Fare, 1.8.1804; AAE. Pologne 323.612 Galon-Boyer to the French Government, 2 fructidor an XII; Comte Boulay de La Meurthe, *Correspondance du Duc d'Enghien* (4 vols. 1904–1913), II, 55.

8. *Bailleu*, I, 464, Caillard to Talleyrand, 2.12.1797, II, 279, Frederick William III to Marchese Lucchesini, 20.7.1804, cf. p. 293; AN. 306 AP. 28 Castries to Artois, 27.4.1794; *La Force*, p. 230, Louis to Madame de Balbi, 30.5.1794; *Daudet*, III, 213; PRO. FO 27/45 Macartney to Grenville 22.4.1796; *Daudet*, III, 211, letter of 28.1.1801; *Boulay de La Meurthe*, II, 53, Goldsmith to Desmarest 1.9.1803.

9. AN. 197 AP. Louis to La Chatre 10.7.1796 (copy); BM. Add. Mss. 37876.100 State of the Sums Advanced by the British Government for the Service of His Most Christian Majesty; *Dugon*, pp. 263–265; AAE.615.314 Précis d'un Exposé sur la Situation du Roi envoyé à Petersbourg pour être mis sous les yeux de l'Empereur, 4/16.7.1807; *Daudet*, III, 247; AN. O³2667; AAE.615.14 d'Avaray to La Chatre, 13.4.1807; André Fugier, *Napoléon et l'Espagne* (2 vols. 1930), I, 44; Ernest Daudet, 'Le Budget des Pensions de Louis XVIII dans l' Emigration en 1807', *Revue Hebdomadaire* (IX), 9.1906, pp. 531–545. AAE.630.122 d'Avaray to d'Antraigues, 22.8.1794; *Daudet*, II, 368, Louis to Artois, 12.1804; *Boulay de La Meurthe*, I, 234–235, Markoff (Russian Ambassador in Paris) to Kotchubey, 4.7.1802; AAE. Mémoires et Documents Prusse 9.89,93,95 Instructions of Frederick William III to President de Meyer, n.d., Meyer to Frederick William III 3.1803, Haugwitz to Lucchesini 26.3.1803; *Walter*, p. 367; Daudet, 'Louis XVIII et Bonaparte', *Le Correspondant*, 10.3.1905, p. 873, Note of 1.1801; Cardinal Maury, *Correspondance Diplomatique et Mémoires Inédits* (2 vols. Lille 1891), II, 270 Louis to Maury 10.8.1803.

10. *Daudet*, III, 251, Louis to Duc de Serra-Capriola, 1801; AAE. 613.35 Précis d'un Exposé sur la Situation du Roi . . . 4/16.7. 1807; AN. AE I 5, 15 Louis to

Gustavus Adolphus IV, 10.10.1805; *Daudet*, III, 393, Louis to Prince of Wales n.d.; AN. 197 AP Louis to La Chatre, 27.9.1804.

11. *England*, p. 150, Abbé Edgeworth to Dr. Moylan, 13.3.1804; cf. AN. F⁷4730 Marie-Joséphine to Madame de Gourbillon, 11.4.1789; AN. 197 AP. Louis to La Chatre, 18.9.1791; *Maury*, I, 207, Louis to Cardinal Maury 20.10.1798; Daudet, 'Souvenirs de l'Emigration', *Revue Hebdomadaire*, VIII, 1906, p. 160, Louis to Madame de Marsan, 3.1801.

12. PRO. FO. 27/45 Macartney to Grenville 12.8.1795; Daudet, 'Fiançailles d'Exil', p. 858; AN. 198 AP. 2, 3 Bonnay to La Fare 19.9.1803; Louis XVIII, 'Lettres Inédites', *Revue Hebdomadaire* (XIII), 9. 12.1905, p. 287, Louis to Queen of Sardinia, 21.4.1799; Marquis Costa de Beauregard, ed., *Souvenirs . . . du Cte. A. de La Ferronays*, 1900, p. 303.

13. AAE. 630.106 Note by d'Avaray, 1795; AN. O³2680, 1 Recettes et Dépenses 1800 Coutent to d'Avaray cf. AAE. 603.293–4 Peronnet to Louis, 1808; AN. O³2681 Etats de la Maison du Roi et de la Reine, 1801–03, Personnel de la Maison du Roi, Decembre 1809; *Hue*, pp. 251–53. *Daudet*, III, 368, Louis to Artois, 1805.

14. ibid, I, 359; cf. Duc de Castries, *Le Maréchal de Castries*, 1956, p. 235; *Dugon*, p. 259, Courvoisier to the Président de Vezet, n.d.; *Hue*, pp. 257–258; AN. 198 AP. 7, Edgeworth to La Fare, 10.10.1804; *Hue*, p. 242, Règlement of 28.9.1801; *Dugon*, p. 265, d'Avaray to Vezet, 1.6.1801; *Daudet*, III, 372n.

15. Daudet, 'Le Budget des Pensions de Louis XVIII', p. 536; cf. Marie-Joséphine's judgement of the Duc d'Havré and the Archbishop of Reims as *bien honnêtes mais fort bêtes*; AAE. 621.190 Marie-Joséphine to Madame de Gourbillon, 7.2.1810; *Daudet*, III, 342; Duc de Gramont 'Journal', *Assemblée Générale de la Société d'Histoire Contemporaine*, 1908, p. 21: 10.1807, *Dugon*, p. 38, diary of Président de Vezet; 25.4.1794; Daudet, *Madame Royale* 1908, p. 241, Louis to his niece, 1798.

16. Constantin de Grunwald, *Stein*, 1940, p. 48, Stein to Frau von Berg, 3.10.1793; PRO. FO. 27/45 Macartney to Grenoble, 27.9 1795 (private); BM. 7972.86 La Thuillerie to Puisaye, 29.4.1797.

17. *England*, p. 151, Edgeworth to Dr. Moylan, 13.3.1804; Louis XVIII, 'Un Voyage de Vérone à Riegel en 1796', p. 382; Baron de Guilhermy, *Papiers d'un Emigré*, 1886, p. 145, Louis to Guilhermy, 27.11.1804; *Dugon* pp. 92, 293; PRO. PC 27/45 Macartney to Grenville, 8.2.1796; Mlle. Despréaux, 'La Cour de Mitau', *Intermédiaire des Chercheurs et des Curieux*, 1914, I, 476–479.

18. AN. 37 AP. 1 Louis to Bonnay, 28.9.1803; AE I 5, 16 Louis to Gustavus Adolphus IV, 20.6.1805; *Daudet*, II, 252–253; Léonce Pingaud, 'J-B Courvoisier', *Mémoires de la Société d'Emulation du Doubs* (Besançon 1883), pp. 334–335, Courvoisier to Vezet, 8.11.1796; cf. *Guilhermy*, p. 74, Guilhermy to d'Avaray, 7.1804; *Dugon*, p. 205.

19. *Castries* p. 232; AN. O³2565; Daudet 'Les Derniéres Années de l'Emigration', *Revue des Deux Mondes*, 15.7.1904, p. 280, Louis to d'Avaray, 24.3.1809; Daudet, 'Budget des Pensions de Louis XVIII', pp. 534–539.

20. BM. Add. Mss. 7972.2 Certificate of gratitude by Louis to Brotier, Des Pomelles and Lemaître, 9.7.1794; cf. BM. Add. Mss. 8055.33 Instruction Particulière pour les Agents de Paris, from the Cabinet du Roi; *La Force* p. 229, Louis to Madame de Balbi, 30.5.1794; Artois's agent Dutheil, was particularly convinced of the worthlessness of the Agence de Paris; see *Dugon*, p. 70, Dutheil to d'Avaray, 16.10.1795, p. 96 and p. 108, Dutheil to Hebert, 14.7.1795; BM. Add. Mss. 7972.5 Louis to Charette, 28.5.1795; Roger Langeron, *Madame Royale*, 1959, pp. 71, 104; cf. Jacques Godechot, *The Counter-Revolution*,

1972, pp. 184, 195; M. L. de Santi 'Notes et Documents sur les intrigues Royalistes dans le Midi', *Mémoires de l'Académie des Sciences ... de Toulouse*, 1916, pp. 63–65, 95–97.

21. *Dugon*, pp. 174, 266, and passim; *Papiers Saisis à Bareuth et à Mende, Département de la Lozère*, An X, passim; Daudet 'Louis XVIII et Bonaparte', *Le Correspondant*, 10.3.1905, p. 849; Comte Remacle, ed., *Relations Secrétes des Agents de Louis XVIII à Paris sous le Consulat* (1802–1803), 1899, pp. 21, 57, 263, reports of 6.6., 4.7, 1802 and 7.3.1803; AAE. Pologne 323, 578vo, despatch from Galon-Boyer, 21 fructidor An XI.

22. AN. 37 AP. 1 note of 9.4.1803; AAE. 630. 130 d'Avaray to d'Antraigues, n.d.; PRO. FO. 27/45 Macartney to Grenville, 12.8.1795; Daudet, 'Louis XVIII et bonaparte', *Le Correspondant*, 25.2.1905, pp. 691, 693; AN. 326 Mss. 21 Exposé de ce qui s'est passé chez le Roi le mercredi des Cendes; *Dugon*, p. 95; *Daudet*, II, pp. 76–77; AN. 198 AP. 4 Saint-Priest to La Fare, 16.11.1798.

23. AAE. 621. 38 drafts to La Fare, Bonnay, and the Duc de Coigny, 10.1.1801, by Louis; Daudet, *Joseph de Maistre et Blacas*, 1908, p. 235, Maistre to Blacas, 2/14.4.1813; Ambassador in Berlin 2 frimaire An 12; AN F⁷6371 doss. Delamarre, 1, Regnier, Grand Juge, to La Forest, Daudet, *Récits des Temps Révolutionaires*, 1908, p. 280, based on d'Avaray's extremely amusing account of the scene; *Nouvelle Revue Retrospective*, 1.1902, pp. 17–18, Louis to d'Hautefort, 18.11.1794; *Daudet*, II, 135, Louis to Madame de Tourzel, 19.9.1795.

24. cf. BN. Mss. Périgord 105.78 d'Avaray to Hautefort, 30.8.1795; Daudet, *Nouveaux Récits Révolutionnaires*, 1913, p. 140; *Daudet*, III, 353; *Sotheby's Catalogue*, 8.11.1977, p. 42, d'Avaray to Mallet du Pan, 8.7.1797; BN. Mss. Périgord 105.85 vo. d'Avaray to Hautefort, 1.10.1796; Paul Filleul, *Le Duc de Montmorecy-Luxembourg*, 1939, p. 222, d'Avaray to Luxembourg, 21.5.1797; *Dugon*, p. 35, diary of de Vezet: 1.11.1795.

25. AN. F⁷2655 note by Louis enclosed in a letter from Thauvenay to Lambert, 3.7.1802; cf. *Revue de la Révolution*, V, 1885, Documents, p. 161, Louis to Comte N. Roumiantsoff, 1/13.2.1805; *Castries*, p. 237, Castries to d'Avaray, 16.1.1796; *Dugon*, p. 98, Courvoisier to de Vezet, 8.11.1796, p. 244 d'Avaray to de Vezet, 1800; *Daudet*, II, 167, Louis to d'Avaray, 1797, III, 346–348.

26. *Dugon*, p. 271 Courvoisier to de Vezet, n.d.; AN. 198 AP. 2, 3 Louis to La Fare, 13.9.1804, d'Avaray to La Fare, 1.12.1805 (i.e. 1804); Daudet, 'Souvenirs de l'Emigration', *Revue Hebdomadaire*, 8.1906, pp. 154–157; *Daudet*, III, 496n, Louis to Comte de Blacas, post 1811, AN. 37 AP. 1 Bonnay to Countess Zichy, 1.1.1811; AE. 621.38 Louis's drafts to La Fare, Bonnay and the Duc de Coigny, 10.1.1801; *Dugon*, p. 44, Courvoisier to de Vezet, 1794. Daudet, *Joseph de Maistre et Blacas*, 1908, p. 115, Blacas to Maistre, 4.9.1810.

27. AN. 37 AP. 1 note of 19.10.1803, by Louis, AN. 197. 2, 3 d'Avaray to La Fare, 27.2.1805; Daudet, 'Fiançailles d'Exil', p. 858; idem, 'Le Budget des Pensions de Louis XVIII', p. 537.

28. *Daudet*, I, 230; *Castries*, p. 220; *Guilhermy*, pp. 50–52; *Dugon* p. 34; *Caudrillier*, p. 282n; AN. 34 AP. 3 Enghien to the Duc de Bourbon, 9.6.1796; *Dugon*, p. 91; cf. *Lebon*, pp. 27–28, Trevor to Wickham, 26.5.1795; *Guilhermy*, p. 51 Louis to Duc d'Harcourt, 28.9.1795.

29. Léonce Pingaud, *Un Agent Secret sous la Révolution et l'Empire*, 1893, pp. 129, 157, 175; AN. 198 AP. 2, 3 Louis to La Fare, 25.1.1805; *Boulay de La Meurthe*, III, 387n; Comte d'Angivillier, *Mémoires* (Copenhagen 1933), p. XXIII; AN. O³2680, 4, Bonnay to d'Avaray 4.9.1804; *Guilhermy*, p. 157.

30. *Dugon*, p. 271; *Daudet*, II, 120 Louis to Imbert–Colomès, 10.10.1797;

Paul R. Sweet, *Friedrich von Gentz* (Madison 1941), p. 108, Gentz to Adam Müller, 7.10.1805; cf. *Bouillé*, II, 464.

31. *Guilhermy*, p. 159; AN. 306 AP. 28 Rapport au Régent, 27.4.1794; AAE. 589, pp. 464-7 Mémoire sur la Discussion entre le Roi Louis XVIII et son frère; Gustave Gautherot, *Un Gentilhomme de Grand Chemin. Le Marèchal de Bourmont*, 1926, pp. 37, 42; 161 AP. Papiers Serent Observations relatives à quelques articles de la Note composant l'Instruction Particulière du Baron Roll pendant sa mission à Verone, 10.3.1796.

32. Daudet, 'Louis XVIII et le Comte d'Artois', *Revue des Deux Mondes*, 1.2.1906, p. 574, Louis to Artois, 30.10.1797; *Daudet*, III, 86-88; *Dugon* p. 238-239; Caudrillier, *L'Association Royaliste de l'Institut Philanthropique*, 1908, pp. 38, 41, Wickham to Grenville, 16.8.1800; AN. 198 AP. 2, 3 Bonnay to La Fare, 21.5.1804; *Guilhermy*, pp. 109, 127-137, 157, 165.

33. Daudet, 'Louis XVIII et le Comte d'Artois', *Revue des Deux Mondes*, 12.1906, pp. 567-568, Louis to Artois, 22.12.1796, early 1797, Artois to Louis, 1797, p. 580, note by Louis, 7.1798; Mallet du Pan, *Mémoires et Correspondance*, ed. A. Sayous (2 vols. 1851), II, 203, Mallet du Pan to Comte F. de Saint-Aldegonde, 7.2.1796, cf. II, 271, AAE. 589. 464-467 Mémoire sur la Discussion entre le Roi Louis XVIII et son frère; *Geffroy*, I, 396, Louis to Gustavus III, 25.6.1779.

34. *Daudet*, I, 94; Daudet, 'Louis XVIII et le Comte d'Artois', *Revue des Deux Mondes*, 1.2.1906, p. 594, Louis to Artois, 6.6.1800. AN 0^3605 Ordres et Discours de SAR. Monsieur, powers dated 25.1. and 8.11.1793, and 30.1.1814; *Vaudreuil* II, 161, Louis to Duc de Polignac, 19.11.1793; *Dugon*, p. 183, Louis to Agence de Souabe, 29.4.1798

35. ibid, pp. 239-240; *Daudet*, II, 417-420; Roger Langeron, *Un Conseiller Secret de Louis XVIII. Royer-Collard*, 1956, p. 55, Louis to Agence, 19.6.1800, *Daudet*, III, 330, Louis to Artois, 25.6.1804.

36. idem, 'Un Mariage Manqué, *Le Correspondant*, 10.11.1905, pp. 446-475; *Daudet*, II, 152, Louis to Comte d'Azara, early 1796; *Lebon* p. 151, Abbé Aimé to Condé, 13.12.1795; *Caudrillier*, p. 257, Ferrand to Condé, 13.2.1796; *Mallet du Pan*, II, 317, Mallet du Pan to Sainte-Aldegonde, 2.9.1797; BN. NAF. (Montesquiou papers) 15036.10 Montesquiou to Mme. de Laage, 1796, (copy).

37. *Daudet*, II, 145, Madame Royale to Louis, 1.1796; BM. Add. Mss. 27548.35 Mme. de Tourzel to Louis, 6.9.1795; Daudet, *Madame Royale*, p. 74, La Fare to Louis, 26.1.1796. BN. NAF. 23129.182 Cossé to Comte de Cély, 27.7.1799; *Daudet*, II, 363 Louis to Artois, n.d.; Daudet, *Madame Royale*, p. 179, Bonnay to d'Avaray, 24.12.1797; Pimodan, *Les Fiançailles de Madame Royale*, p. 53, Madame Royale to Madame Victoire, 8.2.1796.

38. Daudet, *Madame Royale*, pp. 168, 211, Madame to Louis 27.7.1797, La Fare to Louis, 28.8.1798, p. 257, Louis to Madame Royale 17.4.1799; Daudet, 'Louis XVIII et le Comte d'Artois', *Revue des Deux Mondes*, 15.2.1906, p. 847, Artois to Louis, 15.2.1802.

39. *Daudet*, II, 359-361, III, 91, 230-232, *Crétineau-Joly*, II, 413, Princesse Louise de Condé to Condé, 13.12.1803; AE 621 Marie-Joséphine to Madame de Gourbillon passim cf. AN. 37 AP. 1 Louis to Bonnay, 9.2.1804.

40. *La Force*, pp. 224, 230, letters of 22.10.1793, 30.5.1794; Ad. Lanne, in *Une Officine Royale de Falsification* (1912), claims that Louis could not have received these two precious tokens. But his evidence, from an analysis of the different editions of the Duchesse d'Angoulême's *Mémoire sur la captivité des Princes et Princesses ses Parents*, rests primarily on the fact, admittedly strange, that the Duchesse d'Angoulême shows no sign of knowing that her mother had

sent these objects, which is inconclusive since such secret messages might well have been hidden from a girl of fifteen. He fails to take into account some of the editions, such as that published in 1823 by the Imprimeur du Roi. The queen seems to have been in touch with Jarjayes later than Lanne alleges. Moreover, Louis's letter to Jarjayes can only mean that he had received something from the Temple. The variations in the editions are primarily questions of style and of the degree of degradation suffered by Louis XVI and Louis XVII. See Paul Gaulot, *Un Complot sous la Terreur*, 1889, pp. 172–173, Louis to Jarjayes, 14.5.1793, *Klinkowström*, II, 408, Marie-Antoinette to Jarjayes, 3 or 4. 1793.

41. Duchesse d'Angoulême, *Journal . . . 1789–92*, 1894, p. 75; cf. *Découverte* (XI), 9.1975, p. 38; *Daudet*, II, 165, Louis to Edgeworth, 19.9.1796; 306 AP. 28 Note défendant les Princes d'avoir compromis la vie du roi; *Papiers Saisis à Bareuth*, p. 340n.; Pingaud, *d'Antraigues*, p. 337.

42. *La Force*, p. 234, Louis to Madame de Balbi, 30.6.1794; *Vivenot*, V, 299, Thugut to Starhemberg, 11.7.1795; e.g. *Daudet*, II, 163, Madame Royale to Louis, 1797. About an early false Louis XVII, whom they both agreed to be a *chimère*, Louis wrote to his niece on 24.1.1799, 'All I can say is that if, contrary to all probability, it turned out to be true . . . the person most interested would feel sincere joy and would think that he had recovered a son' (*Le Figaro* 7.8.1904, p. 1); this careful, over-insuring attitude is in contrast, for example, to his description of Louis XVII to Cardinal Maury as 'a much-loved nephew whose death has been only too well proven' (*Maury*, I, 319, letter of 10.2.1800).

43. *La Force*, p. 218, Louis to Madame de Balbi, 12.4.1793; *Daudet*, III, 45, Orléans to Louis, 13.2.1800; AN. 198 AP. 2, 3 Bonnay to La Fare, 21.3.1804; *Guilhermy* pp. 145, 151; AN. 34 AP. 6 bis 19 Louis to Condé, 18.3.1796, Bourbon to Louis, 15.5.1796; *Daudet*, II, 52, note by d'Avaray, 3.2.1797.

VI

1. 'Les Devoirs d'un Roi', 1797, *Feuilles d'Histoire*, 1.9.1909, p. 233.

2. Copies of the Déclaration de Vérone are in AAE 588. 268–285, with projects in 236–268.

3. AAE.588.235 vo. Esquisse, 1795, cf. 391–397, Projet by Lally-Tollendal; AN. 326 Mi 18 Castries to Louis 1.6.1795 (draft); AAE.588. 218–19 Note remise à Mr. le Duc d'Harcourt par Milord Grenville.

4. AN. 326 Mi 18 Castries to Comte N. Roumiantsov, 21.11.1795 (draft).

5. Daudet, 'L'Ami du Roi', *Revue des Deux Mondes*, 15.11.1904, p. 245; BM. Add Mss. 8055 (Puisaye Papers, with contributions from d'Antraigues). 26 vo. Flachslanden to d'Antraigues, 8.7.1795; cf. *Wickham*, I, 181, Macartney to Wickham, 15.10.1795.

6. AN. 306 AP. 28 Réflexions sur le parti à prendre par M. le Regent, 1794.

7. ibid Louis to Castries 30.2.1794; cf., for the same fear that Louis's successors would disavow a Constitution, AAE., 617.259 Observations, 1805.

8. PRO. FO 27/45 Macartney to Grenville (private), 27.9.1795; cf. *Lebon* p. 150, Wickham to Grenville, 5.5.1796; *Dugon*, p. 101; ibid pp. 125, 213, d'Avaray to Vezet, 11.10.1797, 1799.

9. *Wickham*, I, 181, Macartney to Wickham, 15.10.1795.

10. A. Michel, *Correspondance de Mallet du Pan avec la Cour de Vienne*. (2 vols. 1884), I, 309, letter of 13.9.1795.

11. *Revue d'Histoire Diplomatique*, 1890, I, 89, Talleyrand to Madame de Staël 8.11.1793; D. Berthoud, *Le Général et La Romanciére*, 1959, p. 266.

Montesquiou to Madame de Montolieu, 4.8.1795; *Mallet du Pan*, II, 197, Chevalier de Panat to Mallet du Pan, 1.1796.

12. BM. Add. Mss. 8055.26 vo. Flachslanden to Antraigues, 8.7.1795; *Lebon*, pp. 78–79, Louis to Précy, 15.11.1795.

13. AAE. 588.381 Note sur l'état actuel de la France, late 1795;

14. *Dugon* pp. 298–303, Instructions aux Agens Principaux de Sa Majesté, 25.2.1796; pp. 307–312, Instructions of 16.3.1796.

15. Marcel Marion, *La Vente des Biens Nationaux pendant la Révolution*, 1908, pp. 326–327; *Lebon*, pp. 198–199, Louis to Brotier, 11.7.1796; *Wickham*, I, 416, 432, Wickham to Grenville, 16.7.1796, to F. Drake 21.7. 1796 (drafts).

16. *Daudet*, II, 24–25; Philippe Buchez et P. Roux, *Histoire Parlementaire de la Révolution Française* (40 vols. 1834–1838), XXXVII, 188, Instructions of 24.11.1796.

17. 'Les Devoirs d'un Roi', *Feuilles d'Histoire*, 1.9.1909, pp. 221–234.

18. *Saint-Priest*, pp. 22–25, Projet d'Instruction pour les Agents du Roi à Paris, 12.4.1797; AAE 617.25 De la Charte Constitutionelle, 31.3.1797.

19. P. Le Menuet de La Juganière, *Le Chouan Carlos Sourdat et son père l'Agent Royal*, 1932, p. 63.

20. *Buchez et Roux*, XXXVII, 243–244, Proclamation of 10.3.1797; *Dugon*, pp. 324–337, Instructions pour le Conseil Royal, 5.4.1797.

21. BM. Add. Mss. 8042 Marquis de La Jaille to Puisaye, 16.4.1797.

22. *Saint-Priest*, p. 81, Observations du Roi sur le precédent Mémoire de M. de Saint-Priest, 6.1799.

23. AAE. 607.66 Instructions pour mes Agens, 19.4.1799; *Dugon* pp. 340–346, Instructions of 25.6.1799; AAE. 607.84 Instructions Secrètes pour mon Conseil Royal, 23.2.1800; cf. *Dugon*, pp. 350–354, p. 224, d'Avaray to Vezet, 11.1799.

24. AN. 198 AP. 2, 3, d'Avaray to La Fare 1.12.1804; cf. *Archivio Storico per le Provincie Napoletane*, VIII, 1922, p. 341, Louis to the Duca di Serra-Capriola, 22.12.1804.

25. *Moniteur*, 12.4.1797, p. 811.

26. Hubert Cole, *Fouché. The Unprincipled Patriot*, 1971, pp. 48–52; Donald Greer, *The Incidence of the Terror during the French Revolution* (Harvard 1935), pp. 35, 97.

27. Marvin Lyons, *France under the Directory*, 1972, p. 18.

28. *Greer*, p. 97; idem, *The Incidence of Emigration in the French Revolution* (Harvard 1951), p. 64.

29. Robert Forster, 'The Survival of the Nobility During the French Revolution', *Past and Present*, XXXVII, 7.1967, p. 82; Norman Hampson, *A Social History of the French Revolution*, 1964, p. 253, citing Georges Lefebvre; Daudet, 'Le Budget des Pensions de Louis XVIII ... en 1807', *Revue Hebdomadaire*, IX, 9.1906, p. 532.

30. AN. 198 AP. 4 Rapport of 27.1.1804, anon.

31. Harvey Mitchell, 'Resistance to the Revolution in Western France', *Past and Present*, LXIII, 5.1974, p. 114.

32. Sir Gilbert Eliot to Henry Dundas, 23.11.1793; *Cottin*, p. 255; *Pons* pp. 310–311.

33. Gwynne Lewis, *The Second Vendee* (Oxford 1978), p. 89.

34. Harvey Mitchell, *The Underground War Against Revolutionary France*, Oxford 1965, p. 159.

35. *Mallet du Pan*, II, 393, Portalis to Mallet, 16.8.1799; Stendhal, *Oeuvres Intimes*, 1955, p. 598, Journal: 17.1.1805; *Remacle*, p. 45, report of 19.6.1802;

Henri Carré, *La Noblesse de France et l'Opinion Publique au XVIIIe Siècle*, 1920, p. 547 Bernadotte to Ministre de la Guerre, Rouen, 4.8.1799; *Godechot*, p. 325.

36. *Saint-Priest,* pp. 67–69, Mémoire of 5.6.1799; Louis XVIII, 'Notes de Lecture', p. 33.

37. Liliane Wellens de Douder, 'La Restauration de l'Ancien Régime dans le Nord de la France sous l'Occupation Autrichienne de 1793–1794', *Annales de la Société Royale d'Archaéologie de Bruxelles*, (L), 1961, pp. 251–255; Piers Mackesy, *The Strategy of Overthrow*, 1974, p. 87; *Fugier*, I, 46.

38. AN. 326 Mi 16 Note pour Mrs. d'Hervilly et de Kergorlay, 26.6.1793.

39. *Dugon*, p. 64, Louis to Vezet, 7.2.1796; cf. Georges de Cadudal, *Georges Cadudal et la Chonannerie*, 1887, pp. 419–420, Louis to Georges Cadudal, 15.7.1798; cf. Daudet 'Louis XVIII et le Comte d'Artois', *Revue des Deux Mondes*, 15.2.1906, p. 583, Louis to Artois, 1798 or 1799.

40. ibid, p. 565, Louis to Artois, 18.9.1795; Duc de La Trémoïlle, *Mes Parents*, 1901, pp. 61–62, 55–56, Prince to Duc de La Trémoïlle, 1798.

41. *Dugon*, p. 217; *Godechot*, p. 345; *Santi*, pp. 71, 98 (Brevet to Dupont Constant, 1.12.1798).

42. *Dugon*, p. 41, Courvoisier to Vezet, 6.12.1794; cf. AAE. 621.24 Mémoire n.d.; Mitchell, *Underground*, p. 155; *Dugon*, pp. 126–128.

43. AAE, 589.203–05 Mémoire sur les motifs qui ont déterminé le Roi à quitter l'armée le 14.7.1796; *Dugon*, pp. 329–330, Instructions pour le Conseil Royal, 5.4.1797.

44. BM. Add. Mss. 8041.82 La Thuillerie to Puisaye, 26.4.1797; Caudrillier *L'Association Royaliste de l'Institut Philanthropique*, pp. XII-XIV, XXIV; Mitchell, *Underground*, p. 144.

45. *Lebon*, p. 242, Saint-Priest to Wickham, 15.7.1797; *Saint-Priest* p. 27, Louis to Saint-Priest, 31.8.1797.

46. Mitchell, *Underground*, pp. 206–210; W. R. Fryer, *Republic or Restoration in France?* (Manchester 1965), pp. 270, 307–310; PRO. FO. 27/45 Macartney to Grenville, 31.1.1796.

47. *Saint-Priest*, p. 79 'Projet d'Instruction' for Artois, by Louis, 5.6.1799, AAE. 621.18 Louis to Marie-Joséphine, 20.5.1796.

48. *Daudet*, II, 253; *Nouvelle Revue Retrospective*, 1902, p. 122, Louis to Comte d'Hautefort 9.2.1798; Daudet 'Louis XVIII et Bonaparte', *Le Correspondant*, 25.2.1905, pp. 680, 692.

49. Marquis de Clermont–Gallerande, *Mémoires* (3 vols, 1826), I, XXI–XXII; Gustave Bord, 'Bonaparte, Louis XVIII, Leurs Relations', *Revue de la Révolution*, XI, 1888, pp. 210–220; cf. Daudet, 'Louis XVIII et Bonaparte', *Le Correspondant*, 25.2.1905, pp. 666–694, 10.3.1905, pp. 849–881; AN. 161 AP, anon to Duc de Sérent, 17.3, 3.4.1801.

50. Comte d'Hauterive, *La Police Secrète du Premier Empire* (5 vols. 1908–1965), II, 228, 236 reports of 16, 23.1.1806; cf. *Guilhermy*, pp. 165, 172.

51. AAE. 615.14, 28 d'Avaray to La Chapelle, 13.4, 18.5.1807.

52. For damning views of Louis's role, see AN. 306 AP. 28 'Observations', read to Castries and Artois, 29.5.1794, '*on les compte pour rien*; *Berthoud*' p. 256, Montesquiou to Madame de Montolieu, 1795, '*sa maladresse mettra dans l'embarras ses amis, qu'il est probable qu'il prendra pour ses ennemis*'. *Papiers Saisis à Bareuth et à Mende p. 341.

53. AAE. 589. 160 Louis to Pichegru, 25.4.1796 (copy); *Daudet*, III, 405, Louis to Alexander I, 2.1807.

References 433

References 433

References 433

54. *Daudet*, III, 481 Louis to the English Cabinet, 18.5.1808, Louis XVIII 'Notes de Lecture', p. 546.

55. *Guilhermy*, p. 53, Louis to Duc d'Harcourt, 28.9.1795; cf. PRO. FO. 27/45 Macartney to Grenville 7.10.1795; Louis XVIII 'Réflexions Historiques sur Marie-Antoinette', p. 255.

56. AAE. 621, 34 Louis to Marie-Joséphine, ?1798; cf. AN. 37 AP. 1 Louis to Bonnay, 23.1., 8.3.1804; *Revue des Deux Mondes*, 2, 1906, p. 568, Louis to Artois, early 1797; AN. 37 AP.1 Louis to Bonnay, 24.10.1803.

57. *Intermédiaire des Chercheurs et des Curieux*, 1913, II, 435, Notes de Madame de Königfelds; cf. Louis XVIII, *Correspondance Privée* (London 1836) p. 54, Louis to d'Avaray, 17.1.1811.

58. *Cadoudal*, p. 419, Louis to Cadudal, 15.7.1798; AN. 37 AP. 1 Louis to Bonnay, 10.10.1803; *Revue de la Révolution*, VI, 1885, (Documents), p. 161, Louis to Comte N. Roumiantsoff, 1/13.2.1805; AAE 621.140 Marie-Joséphine to Madame de Gourbillon 4.9.1809.

59. *Dugon*, pp. 38, 105 Journal of Vezet 25.4.1794, early 1797 recording remarks by the Abbé André; AN. 306 AP. 31.9. Castries to Artois, 1794; BM. Add. Mss. 8041.86 La Thuillerie to Puisaye, 29.4.1797; cf. *Intermédiaire des Chercheurs et des Curieux*, 1913, II, 434 Notes de Madame de Königfelds, Daudet, 'L'Ami du Roi', *Revue des Deux Mondes*, 15.11.1904, p. 277; AN. 37 AP. 1 Louis to Bonnay, 12.12.1803, 19.10.1803; F⁷2655 Thauvenay to Lambert, 3.7.1802. Another example of Louis's love for Horace can be found in *Dugon*, p. 324, Instructions pour le Conseil Royal.

60. PRO. FO. 27/45 Macartney to Wickham, 7.10.1795; BM. Add. Mss. 8041.85 La Thuillerie to Puisaye, 29.4.1797; AAE. 621.89 Marie-Joséphine to Madame de Gourbillon, 9.11.1808.

61. *Intermédiaire des Chercheurs et des Curieux*, 1913, II, 434, Notes de Madame de Königfeld, *Mallet du Pan*, II, 485, Malouet to *Mercure Britannique*, 1799; Louis XVIII, 'Notes de Lecture' p. 465 *Daudet*, II, 168, Louis to Madame Royale, 1797.

VII

1. See e.g. PRO. FO. 27/26 La Chapelle to Lord Howick, 15.1.1807.

2. Historical Manuscripts Commission, *The Mss. of J. B. Fortescue esq, preserved at Dropmore*, IX, 444–445, Louis to La Chapelle, 22.2.1806; Daudet, *Les Bourbons et la Russie*, p. 387, Louis to Grenville 18.10.1806.

3. AN. 198 AP.2, 3 Louis to La Fare, 11.2.1807, d'Avaray to La Fare, 22.6.1807.

4. *Daudet*, III, 411–412.

5. AN. 300 AP. III 16 Orléans to Comte de Beaujolais, 7.11.1807; *Stedingk*, II, 396, Stedingk to Gustavus IV Adolphus, Saint Petersburg, 5/17.10.1807.

6. AN. 198 AP. 2, 3 d'Avaray to Havré, 12.9.1807; *Daudet*, III, 418–427.

7. A. Aspinall, ed., *The Later Correspondence of George III* (5 vols. 1962–1970), IV, 641, Canning to George III, 26.10.1807; *Morning Post*, 9, 10, 19, 21, 26, 10.1807.

8. Lord Malmesbury, *Letters* (2 vols. 1870), II, 57, Charles Ross, Under Secretary of State to Malmesbury, 26.10.1807; PRO. FO 27/76 George III to Louis, 30.10.1807 (draft), Canning to George III 31.10.1807; AN. 300 AP. III 16 Orléans to Beaujolais, 4.11.1807.

9. Josceline Bagot, *George Canning and his Friends* (2 vols. 1909) I, 250, Canning to Bagot, 1.11.1807; Malmesbury, *Letters*, II, 59–60, Ross to Malmesbury, 2, 4.11.1807.

10. AN. 300 AP. III 16 Orléans to Beaujolais, 4.11.1807; *Daudet*, III, 434–437, Louis to d'Avaray, 4.11.1807.

11. AN. 198 AP. 2 d'Avaray to La Fare, 1.11.1807; *Daudet*, III, 382; I am greatly indebted to Dr. W. B. Taylor of Louisiana State University for information on English politics in this period.

12. AN. 300 AP. III 16 Orléans to Beaujolais, 26.12.1807; *Daudet*, III, 442, d'Avaray to Louis, 25.12.1807; AAE. 621.39 bis Louis to La Chatre, 22.3.1808.

13. AN. 37 AP. 1 Louis to Bonnay, 12.11, 8.12.1803; Rachel Leighton, ed. *Correspondence of Charlotte Grenville, Lady Williams Wynn*, 1920, p. 121, Henry Watkins Williams Wynn to Lady Williams Wynn, 14.1., 12,1.1808.

14. AN. 300 AP. III 16 Orléans to Beaujolais, 19.1.1808.

15. BM. Add. Mss. 33793.

16. Louis XVIII, *Correspondance Privée*, 1836, pp. 107–112, Louis to d'Avaray, 9.6.1811; AAE. 605.317 Blacas to Comte de Briou, 24.5.1812; Egerton Castle, ed., *The Jerningham Letters* (2 vols. 1896), I, 335, Edward Jerningham to Lady Jerningham, 14.3.1809; ibid II, 11, Lady Jerningham to Lady Bedingfield, 4.7.1811; Charles Greville, *Memoirs* (8 vols. 1938), I, 8–10: 14.4.1814; BM. Add. Mss. 41648, Thomas Clifford, 'Memoirs relating to the intercourse of the writer with His Most Christian Majesty Louis XVIII', 4–9.

17. Earl of Bessborough, *Lady Bessborough and Her Family Circle*, 1940, p. 173, Lord Bessborough to Lady Bessborough, 28.10.1808.

18. AN. 34 AP. 6 bis Louis to Condé, 26.12.1808; Gosfield, Buckingham to Sir George Lee, 10.3.1808 AN 0³20 Actes de Mgr. le Grand Aumônier pendant son séjour en Angleterre; W. H. Smyth, *Aedes Hartwellianae* (2 vols. 1851), I, 385.

19. AAE. 621.133, 205 vo. Marie-Joséphine to Madame de Gourbillon, 4.8.1809, 27.4.1810; *Correspondance Privée*, p. 39, Louis to d'Avaray, 7.1.1811.

20. AN F⁷4336B 5 Etat des Français qui ont assisté au Convoi de la Comtesse de Lille et dont les noms ne sont pas inscrits sur la Liste des Maintenus; *Correspondance Privée*, pp. 30–41, Louis to d'Avaray, 2.12.1810; cf. *Daudet*, III, 489–491, Blacas to d'Avaray, 18.11.1810.

21. BM. Add. Mss. 41648.5 Thomas Clifford, op. cit; AAE. 621.177 vo. Marie-Joséphine to Madame de Gourbillon, 2.2.1810; *Morning Post*, 23.6.1811.

22. AAE. 615. 254 Position annuelle de Mr. le Comte de Lille, 10.7.1811; PRO. FO 27/80 La Chatre to Marquess Wellesley, 1.5.1810; AN. 37 AP. 1 Blacas to Bonnay, 10.8.1809; AAE. 621.133 Marie-Joséphine to Madame de Gourbillon, 4.8.1809; PRO. FO 27/90 Note by La Chatre, 10.7.1811.

23. *Greville*, I, 10: 14.4.1814; Marquis Costa de Beauregard, ed., *Souvenirs … du Cte. A de La Ferronays*, 1900, p. 238, Comte to Comtesse de La Ferronays, 5.1808; Thomas Raffles, *Letters during a Tour through some parts of France, Savoy … in the Summer of 1817* (Third Edition, Liverpool 1820), p. 88.

24. *Correspondance Privée*, p. 86, Louis to d'Avaray, 5.5.1811; AAE. 621.179 vo. Marie-Joséphine to Madame de Gourbillon; 606.6 Blacas to Briou, 16.1.1813; AN. 198 AP. 3 Blacas to La Fare, 26.10.1813; 198 AP. 4,4 to La Fare 18.12.1813.

25. AN. 37 AP. 1 Blacas to Bonnay, 23.4.1812, 10.8.1809; *Hue* p. 267; Joyce Hemlow, ed., *Journal and Letters of Fanny Burney* VII (1978), 311, account of a reception written in 1825; Daudet, *L'Ambassadeur du Duc Decazes en Angleterre*, 1910, p. 156, Louis to Decazes, 1820; BM. Add. Mss. 41648.4; *Smyth*, I, 387; AAE.621.111 Marie-Joséphine to Madame de Gourbillon, 5.3.1809.

26. AN. 40 AP. Beugnot papers 15 Notes for Beugnot, Directeur-Général de Police, mai 1814 (?).

27. AAE.615.50–51 Observations sur l'instruction du 22 mars 1806 donnée par S. M. Louis XVIII; PRO. FO 27/80 letter of Fauche-Borel, 22.5.1810; Comte d'Hauterive, *La Police Secrète du Premier Empire*, (5 vols. 1908–1964), IV 297, 325, bulletins of 27.7, 1.8.1808.

28. PRO. FO 27/80 La Chatre to Culling Charles Smith, 11.5.1810; AAE 615.180 Jenkinson to La Chatre, 17.11.1809; *Sotheby's Catalogue*, 8.11.1977, de Stévenot to Franval, 5.12.1809.

29. *Pingaud*, p. 334; AAE. 616.56; *Hauterive*, IV, p. 263 bulletin of 25.6.1808.

30. AAE. 615.127 Puisaye to La Chatre, 25.2.1809, 129 La Chatre to Puisaye, 27.2.1809.

31. Duc d'Avaray, *Exposé des Faits relatifs aux Libelles publiés par M. de Puisaye dans les mois de janvier et fevrier 1809*, 1809, pp. 49–51; cf. AAE. 615.136–166 'Examen Raisonné et Rapport', 15.4.1809, by Lorges, La Bour-donnaye and du Bourblanc; Comte de Puisaye, *Réfutation d'un Libelle Diffa-matoire publié par M. Béziade d'Avaray*, 1809 passim.

32. AN. 224 AP. Journal du Comte de Broval 49, 29.7.1812; Lord Granville, *Private Correspondence* (2 vols. 1916), II, 445, Canning to Granville, 18.8.1812; Comte G. de Contades, *Emigrés et Chonans*, 1895, p. 322, Bertrand de Molle-ville to Puisaye, 6.8.1812.

33. *Daudet*, III, 478; AN. 37 AP. I Blacas to Bonnay, 10.8.1809; *Correspond-ance Privée*, passim; *Daudet*, III, 486–489, 495.

34. AAE. 621.181 Marie-Joséphine to Madame de Gourbillon, 12;1.1810; cf. AN. 224 AP. Journal du Comte de Broval 89: 13.7.1811; *Daudet*, III, 459, Louis to Blacas, n.d.

35. *Daudet*, III, 502, Louis to Blacas, 20.12.1812.

36. Gosfield Buckingham to Sir George Lee, 18.3.1808; AAE.621.182, 209 vo, 207 vo, Marie-Joséphine to Madame de Gourbillon, 4.8.1810. 12.1, 5.5, 27.4.1810.

37. AAE. 621.133, 213 Marie-Joséphine to Madame de Gourbillon, 4.8.1809, 24.5.1810; 615.241 Louis to Prince Regent, 8.2.1811 (copy).

38. *Correspondance Privée*, p. 105, Louis to d'Avaray, 9.6.1811; Lady Jackson, ed., *The Bath Archives* (2 vols. 1873), I, 271, George Jackson to Mrs. Jackson, 22.6.1811; Lord Colchester, *Diary and Correspondence* (3 vols. 1861), II, 336–337; 19.6.1811; *Morning Post* , 20–23.6.1811.

39. AN. 37 AP. 1 Angoulême to Bonnay, 8.8.1812; Hon. Amelia Murray, *Recollections*, 1868, p. 33, Queen Charlotte to Lady George Murray, 8.1812; D. M. Stuart, *The Daughters of George III*, 1939, Princess Augusta to Lady Harcourt, n.d.; AN. 37 AP. 1 Blacas to Bonnay, 10.9.1812.

40. AN. 34 AP. 6.20 Louis to Condé, 17.10.1808; PRO. FO 27/77 Louis to Canning, 6.6, 17.7.1808; AAE. 615.195 Reeve to La Chatre, 16.5.1810.

41. AAE. 605.324 Blacas to Comte de Briou, 23.7.1812; Chateaubriand, *Mémoires d'Outre-Tombe* (Librairie Générale Française, 3 vols. 1951), II, 215; AN. 198 AP. 2, 3, Havré to La Fare, 13.4.1807; 359 AP. Archives Clermont-Tonnerre 82 Mémoires du Marquis de Clermont-Tonnerre. 88.

42. Emile Dard, *Le Comte de Narbonne*, 1943, pp. 267–268; Emile de Perceval, *Le Vicomte Lainé* (2 vols. 1926–27), I, 216–218, 'Note sur les événements de décembre 1813', 14.1.1814; Duke of Wellington, *Supplementary Despatches* (15 vols. 1858–72), XIV, 381, Maréchal Soult to Maréchal Suchet, 9.2.1814; Maréchal de Castellane, *Journal* (5 vols. 1896–97), I, 248: 16.2.1814; AN. F⁷4290 31 Commissaire–Général de Police to Rovigo, Boulogne, 23.1.1814;

Pierre Vialles, *L'Archichancelier Cambacérès*, p. 418, Cambacérès to Napoleon I, 19.2.1814; AAE.606.344 La Chatre to Blacas, 25.3.1814.

43. AN. 124 AP. 2, 1, 17, Statistique personelle des individus qui ont figuré dans l'affaire de Marseille et de Toulon; *Daudet*, III, 520; Paul Fauchille, *Une Chouannerie Flamande au temps de l'Empire 1813–1814*, 1905, p. 295, Devilliers du Terraye to Comte Réal, 18.2.1814, 'très confidentiel'.

44. General Bernard de La Frégeolière, *Mémoires*, 1881, pp. 204–220; Docteur Lormier, *Histoire des Régiments des Gardes d'Honneur*, 1924, pp. 284–290; *Fauchile*, pp. 45–51; Comte Lefebvre de Behaine, *Le Comte d'Artois sur la Route de Paris*, 1921, pp. 51–52; P. Gaffarel, *Dijon en 1814 et en 1815* (Dijon 1897), p. 37 quoting a diary of 1.2.1814; idem, 'Les Complots de Marseille et de Toulon (1812–13)', *Annales de la Société d'Etudes Provençales* (Aix-en-Provence, 4ᵉ Année, VI, 11/12, 1907), p. 339; G. de Bertier de Sauvigny, *Le Comte Ferdinand de Bertier et l'Enigme de La Congregation*, 1948, p. 95.

45. G. de Bertier de Sauvigny, *Le Comte Ferdinand de Bertier*, pp. 53–58, 112–114; idem *La Restauration*, 1955, p. 13; J. S. Rollac, *Exposé Fidèle des Faits Authentiquement Prouvés qui ont précédé la Journée de Bordeaux du 12 mars 1814*, 1816, p. 52; AAE. 615.201 Note by La Chatre, 24.9.1810.

46. *Rollac*, pp. 62n., 76, 96; Bertier de Sauvigny, *Le Comte Ferdinand de Bertier* pp. 106–108, Montalivet to Napoleon I, 14.12.1813, Prefet de Tarn et Garonne to Montalivet, 18.1.1814.

47. AAE. 606.8 Louis XVIII aux Français, 1.2.1813; AN. 37 AP. 1 Blacas to Bonnay, 17.3.1813; PRO. FO 27/91 Note of 19.12.1812.

48. AN. 37 AP 1 Blacas to Bonnay, 17.3.1813; BM. Add. Mss. 26669.1. Blacas to Bruges, 7.4.1813; 37 AP. 1 Blacas to Bonnay, 24.10.1813; AAE. 606.79 Blacas to Briou, 15.8.1813; Sir Charles Webster, *Documents on British Foreign Policy*, 1924, p. 149, Castlereagh to Liverpool, 16.2.1814.

49. BM. Add. Mss. 43073.279 vo. Wellington to Bathurst, 8.8.1813 (copy); Elizabeth Longford, *Wellington. The Years of the Sword*, 1969, p. 21.

50. *Rollac*, pp. 72, 106, La Chatre to Rollac, 12.3.1813; BM. Add. Mss. 38364 Wellington to Liverpool 20.12.1813; Duke of Wellington, *Despatches* (13 vols. 1834–39), XI, 381 Wellington to Comte de Gramont, 20.12.1813.

51. PRO. FO 27/105 Note by Louis XVIII, 2.1.1814; note by Brooklands, Liverpool's Secretary, of a conversation with Artois, 4.1.1814; BM. Add. Mss. 47245.104 (Lieven papers) Lieven to Nesselrode, 26.1.1814 (draft); PRO. FO 27/105 Liverpool to Artois, 5.1.1814 (copy); Sir Charles Webster *The Foreign Policy of Castlereagh* (2 vols. 1950, 1935), I, 510–513, 516 Liverpool to Castlereagh 29, 30, 12.1813, 6, 20.1.1814.

52. BM. Add. Mss. 38256.281 Artois to Duchesse d'Angoulême, 23.2.1814 (copy); *Wellington*, XI, 533, 543, Wellington to Angoulême, 28.2, 3.3.1814.

53. Ludovic de Contenson, 'Un Agent Royaliste en 1814', *Revue de Paris*, 15.7.1910, p. 322, Blacas to Baron de La Barthe, 8.3.1814; *Wellington* XI, 547, Wellington to Liverpool, Saint-Sever, 4.3.1814; *Grunwald*, p. 264, Stein to Alexander I, 10.2.1814, cf. p. 265, Alopeus to Stein; AN F⁷4290.31 Commissaire – Général de Police to Minister of Police, Boulogne, 23.1.1814. AAE. 606.311 vo, Rapport by Wildermeth to Artois, 3.1814; .268 Chabannes to Blacas, 6.3.1814.

54. *Wellington*, XI, 577, Beresford to Wellington, 12.3.1814; cf. Bertier de Sauvigny, *Le Comte Ferdinand de Bertier*, pp. 129–130; *Wellington* XI, 585, 609, Wellington to Angoulême, 16.3, 29.3,1814.

55. *Webster*, I, 243; *Contenson*, p. 325, La Barthe to Angoulême, late 3.1814;

PRO. FO 27/104 La Chatre to Hamilton, 30.3.1814; cf. *Morning Post*, 12, 18.4.1814.
56. *The Times*, 21.4.1814.
57. *London Gazette*, 30.4.1814; Frances Lady Shelley, *Diary* (2 vols. 1912–13), p. 54; 22.4.1814; *Morning Post*, 22, 23,4.1814.
58. Viscount Castlereagh, *Memoirs and Correspondence* (12 vols. 1848–53), XI, 397, Sir Charles Stuart to Castlereagh, 8.12.1817; *Morning Post*, 25.4.1814.

VIII

1. Louis Bergeron, *L'Episode Napoléonien*, 1969, pp. 124–129, 211.
2. Madame Soutade-Roger, 'Les Notables en France sous la Restauration', *Revue d'Histoire Economique et Sociale*, 1960, pp. 99–109.
3. *La Fayette*, V, 489, La Fayette to Jefferson, 14.8.1814; G. Pallain, ed., *Correspondance Inédite du Prince de Talleyrand et du Roi Louis XVIII pendant le Congrès de Vienne*, 1881, p. 339, Talleyrand to Louis XVIII, 23.4.1815.
4. Maréchal Macdonald, *Souvenirs*, 1892, p. 415.
5. BN. NAF. 24062 (Procès-Verbaux du Conseil des Ministres 1814–15), 225: 15.6.1814; see e.g. Archives X Duchesse d'Escars to Madame de Podenas, 27.11.1827.
6. BN.NAF. 15036.193 Montesquiou to Madame de Laage, 9.8.1806 (copy); Vicomtesse de Noailles, *Vie de la Princesse de Poix*, 1855, p. 69; Madame de Chastenay, *Mémoires* (2 vols. 1896–97), II, 111.
7. *Moniteur*, 8.4.1814; A. Polovtsov, ed., *Correspondance Diplomatique des Ambassadeurs et Ministres de Russie en France et de France en Russie, avec Leurs Gouvernements de 1814 à 1830* (3 vols. 1902–07), I, 3, Pozzo di Borgo (Russian Ambassador in France) to Nesselrode (Russian Foreign Minister), Compiegne, 30.4.1814; AAE. 646.27 Talleyrand to Louis XVIII, 21.4.1814 (copy); *Morning Post*, 13.4.1814.
8. AAE. 646.41 Observations du Roi, n.d.
9. BM. Add. Mss 58899 Marquess of Buckingham to Lord Grenville, Bordeaux, 24.4.1814; Georges Ribe, *L'Opinion Publique et la Vie Politique à Lyon, 1815–1822*, 1957, p. 35; G. Lacour-Gayet, *Talleyrand* (4 vols. 1928–34), IV, 119, letter to the Editor of the *Moniteur*, 8.4.1814; *Moniteur*, 16, 20.4.1814; AN.AF V (papers of the Secrétairerie d'Etat), 2f Duc de Feltre to Talleyrand, n.d.; AF V 1 Administration de la Légion d'Honneur to the Provisional Government, 9.4.1814.
10. BM. Add. Mss 41648. 17–20 account by Sir Thomas Clifford Constable, n.d.; Royal Archives Windsor (henceforward known as RA.) 45072–3 Duchesse d'Angoulême to Duke of Clarence, 25.4.1814; *Moniteur*, 30.4.1814, p. 474.
11. RA.21439–40 account of the journey sent to the regent, perhaps by Père Elysée; AN. AF V 4, 2 Directeur des Postes at Amiens to Bourienne, n.d.; *Moniteur*, 4.5.1814, p. 490; A. Bardoux, *La Duchesse de Duras*, 1898, p. 162, Duchesse to Claire de Duras, 29 or 30.4.1814.
12. AN. O³605 Réception du Roi, Beugnot to Artois, 25.4.1814.
13. AAE. 606.311 vo. Note sur la conduite … des Puissances Alliées, avril 1814, by M. de Wildermeth; Maréchal Marmont, *Mémoires* (9 vols. 1857), VII, 33; General de Caulaincourt, *Mémoires* (3 vols. 1933), III, 197.
14. *Gaffarel*, p. 74; Comte Ferrand, *Mémoires*, 1896, p. 73; Baron de Vitrolles, *Mémoires* (2 vols. 1950–52), II, 51–53n.
15. Cdt. M-H Weil, *Joachim Murat, Roi de Naples. La Dernière Année de*

Règne (5 vols. 1909), I, 144, Orléans to Ferdinand IV, 10.7.1814; Roger Langeron, *Decazes, Ministre du Roi*, 1960, pp. 89, 273, Louis to Decazes, 1816, 1820; P. Duvergier de Hauranne, *Histoire du Gouvernement Parlementaire en France* (10 vols. 1857–71), V, 276, Louis to Decazes, 31.10.1819; Daudet, *Louis XVIII et le Duc Decazes* (henceforward referred to as *Decazes*), 1899, p. 127, Louis to Decazes, 1816.

16. *Moniteur*, 3.5.1814, p. 487; *Ferrand*, p. 65; P. Simon, *L'Elaboration de la Charte Constitutionelle de 1814*, 1906, p. 67.

17. *Moniteur*, passim, esp. 24.5, 10.7.1814.

18. Comte Beugnot, *Mémoires* (2 vols. 1868), II, 169; *Ferrand*, pp. 73–77, 84.

19. AN. BB[30] 191[(1)] Louis's comments on Montesquiou's suggestions; *Ferrand*, p. 75.

20. *Ferrand*, p. 81; AN. 41 AP.7.144 Montesquiou to Beugnot, 22.5.1814; 40 AP. 18 Dambray to Beugnot, 3.6.1814.

21. *Simon*, pp. 88, 135.

22. BN. NAF. 24062.437 (Procès-Verbaux du Conseil des Ministres): 12.9.1814 for Louis speaking about the *Charte*; *Moniteur*, 7.6.1814, p. 628; *Ferrand*, p. 79.

23. *Moniteur*, 24.5, 4.6, 18.5, 20.5.1814, pp. 615, 447, 553, 582.

24. Joseph de Maistre, *Lettres et Opuscules Inédites* (2 vols. 1851), II, 62, Bonald to Maistre, 7.10.1814; *Crétineau-Joly*, II, 492, Bourbon to Condé, 1.5.1815.

25. AN. AF V5, 1 (papers of the Conseil des Ministres), report by Comte Anglès to Artois, 10.5.1814; Irene Collins, *The Government and the Newspaper Press in France* (Oxford 1959), pp. 4–5; AN. AF V5, 2 Vitrolles to Angoulême, 6.5.1814 (draft).

26. *Dugon*, pp. 287–288: 1.12.1814.

27. *Girault de Coursac*, p. 165; BM. Add. Mss 38357.262 anon to Guilhermy, 18.4.1803.

IX

1. *Martin-Doisy*, p. 347.

2. Eugène Titeux, *Le Général Dupont* (3 vols. Puteaux-sur-Seine 1903), III, 583; *Beugnot*, II, 158–162.

3. See AN. F[1a] 262 for the travail of the Minister of the Interior with Louis XVIII; and 40 AP.14 for that of the Minister of the Marine; 40 AP.14 Feuille de travail, 27.11.14, and 40 AP.18 Dambray to Beugnot, 12, 20.10.1814, for some examples of Louis's intervention; *Castellane*, I, 264, 16.10.1814.

4. AN. 40 AP.18 Dambray to Beugnot, 13.10, 6.11.1814.

5. AN. 40 AP.14 Extraits du Registre du Procès-Verbal des Séances du Conseil des Ministres, 30.1.1815, 15.6.1814.

6. Michel Bruguière, *La Première Restauration et son Budget*, (Genève 1969), p. 80; BN.NAF. 24062.254; AN. AF V5, 2 (drafts of the Procès-Verbal by the Sécretaire d'Etat Provisoire) 20, 24.6.1814; 0³544.56 vo., Papers of the Maison du Roi 1814–30, Rapport au Roi, 12.2.1823.

7. *Bruguière*, p. 18; AN. AF V5, 1 & 2: (drafts of the Procès-Verbal) 10.5.1814; 8.5.1814, 15.7, 22.8, 2.9.1814 and passim.

8. AN. 40 AP. 16, Rapport au Roi by Beugnot, 1.7.1815; cf. Rapport au Roi, 1.7.1814; 40 AP.18 Dambray to Beugnot, 3.6.1814.

9. AN. AF V5, 1 Vitrolles circular, 25.4.1814; Marquis Terrier de Monciel,

'Note Historique sur les Evènements de l'Année 1814', *Annales Franc-Comtoises* (X), 4.1869, pp. 297–298.

10. *Perceval*, I, 300–302; AN. AF V5, 2, passim, and 12.9., 26.12.1814.

11. AN. O³1222 Dufour to Baron Mounier, 27.11.1814; Comte de Jaucourt, *Correspondance . . . avec le Prince de Talleyrand pendant le Congrès de Vienne*, 1905, pp. 54, 132, Jaucourt to Talleyrand, 24.10, 28.12.1814; for the nomination of Soult, see *Ferrand*, p. 111, *Jaucourt*, pp. 102, 117, Jaucourt to Talleyrand, 7, 14.12.1814.

12. *Moniteur*, 24.5.1814, AN. AF V5, 1: 13.5.1814; Prince Münster, *Political Sketches of the State of Europe*, 1868, pp. 173–174, Münster to the Regent, 15.5.1814; Marquis de Roux, *La Restauration*, 1930, p. 107; *Jaucourt*, pp. 53, 84, 157, Jaucourt to Talleyrand, 25.10, 16.12.1814, 20.1.1815; cf. *Wellington*, XII, 280, 598, Wellington to Castlereagh, 26.3, 11.8.1815.

13. *Geffroy*, II, 388, Louis to Gustavus III, 5.10.1778; *Saint-Priest*, p. 148, Note by Louis, 26.5.1800; Prince de Talleyrand, *Mémoires* (5 vols. 1891–1892), II, 214–256, Instructions du Roi, 8.1814.

14. *Weil*, II, 146, 432, 451–454, III, 13–15, IV, 402–403; G. de Bertier de Sauvigny, *Metternich et la France après le Congrès de Vienne* (3 vols. 1968–72), I, 130, 135; *Jaucourt*, p. 169, Jaucourt to Talleyrand, 25.1.1815.

15. *Wellington*, SD, X, 459, Orléans to Wellington, 12.6.1815; 1 AP.696 Blacas to Prince Louis de La Trémoïlle, 14.1.1815; *Ferrand*, pp. 65–67; *Moniteur*, 19, 23, 27.10.1814, pp. 1175, 1195, 1207; AN. AF V5, 2: 12.9.1814; *Jaucourt*, pp. 60–62, Jaucourt to Talleyrand, 12.9.1814.

16. AAE.681.54 Beugnot to Talleyrand, 1.11.1814; AN. 40 AP.6.113, Rapport au Roi, 11.5.1814; ibid. 4–6 Coup d'oeil sur le Ministère, 2.1815; *Jaucourt*, pp. 20, 176, Jaucourt to Talleyrand, 4.10.1814, 1.2.1815; *Ferrand*, p. 107; *Jaucourt*, pp. 36, 178, 156, Jaucourt to Talleyrand, 15.10.1814, 4.2.1815; 20.1.1815, AAE. 679. 49 vo. Blacas to Talleyrand, 4.12.1814.

17. Baron de Barante, *Souvenirs* (8 vols. 1890–1907), II, 59, Barante to Comte de Montlosier, 4.1814; Baronne de Staël, *Considérations sur . . . la Révolution Française* (3 vols. London 1818), III, 101; PRO. FO. 27/100 Wellington to Castlereagh, 4.10.1814; cf. *Chastenay*, II, 205; Benjamin Constant, *Journal Intime*, ed. Jean Mistler (Monaco 1946), p. 312: 6.8.1814.

18. *Bruguière*, p. 30; AN. AF V5, 2 Vitrolles to Angoulême, 5.5.1814 (draft); cf. AAE. 606.375 vo. Blacas to Briou, 19.6.1814.

19. Nicholas Richardson, *The French Prefectoral Corps 1814–1830* (Cambridge 1966), p. 54; *Titeux* III, 555, 573, 585; BN. NAF. 24062.11 (Council meeting) 9.1.1815; AN. AF V5, 1: 5.8.1814; O³2565.

20. AN. AF V5, 5: 5.5.1814; RA. 21533–4 Père Elysée to Regent, 12.11.1814; 21. Titeux, *La Maison Militaire du Roi* (2 vols. 1890), II, 119; AHMG. XAD10 Contrôles-Généraux of the two companies of Mousquetaires.

22. M. N. Balisson de Rougemont, *Le Rodeur Français ou les Moeurs du Jour* (6 vols. 1816–21), I, 20: 20.8.1814; *Moniteur*, 6.5.1814, p. 449, gives details of the new arrangements for going to Court.

23. Edmond Michelet, *Rome*, 1896, p. 56; cf. AN. O³487 doss. Longeuil, Marquise de Sémonville to Lauriston, 9.1.1821, stating that the '*habit habillé dans nos moeurs actuels rend tout de suite ridicule.*'

24. Etienne de Jouy, *Guillaume le Franc-Parleur* (2 vols. 1815–16), I, 65: 18.6.1814; Baron Thiébault, *Mémoires* (5 vols. 1893–95), V, 231; AN. 198 AP. 12, 8 La Fare to Mlle. de Choisy, 20.12.1814.

25. AN. 40 AP.8.27 Beugnot to Louis, 22/24.5.1814; ibid 10 idem to idem,

26.11.1814, cf. reports of 9, 29.11.1814; 40 AP.6.112 Rapport au Roi, 18.5.1814; 40 AP. 8 176–180, 211 Beugnot to Louis 25, 30.6.1814.

26. *Bruguière*, p. 83; *Gaffarel*, p. 133. Maire of Dijon to the Directeur des Impôts Indirects, 2.8.1814; Jean Vidalenc, *Le Département de l'Eure sous la Monarchie Constitutionelle*, 1952, p. 38; PRO. FO 27/97 Wellington to Castlereagh 4, 20.10.1814; ATLMF. 240 Marchese Alfieri di Sostegno to Comte de Vallaise, 25.10.1814; AN. 40 AP. 10 Beugnot to Louis 27/28.11.1814; 0³606 Reports by Moncey, Inspecteur-Général de la Gendarmerie, 10, 17.2.1815.

27. *Gaffarel*, p. 128; Henri Contamine, *Metz et la Moselle de 1814 à 1870* (2 vols. Nancy, 1932), I, 297; de Latouche, 'Souvenirs de 1814: Journal', *Revue d'Alsace* (LIV), 1903, p. 592: 30.6.1814; *Castellane*, I, 256: 3.5.1814; *Wellington*, XII, 248, Wellington to Bathurst, 18.1.1815.

28. *Vidalenc*, pp. 41, 50; BM. Add. Mss. 58899 Buckingham to Grenville, 24.4.1814; Howard C. Payne, 'The Bourbon Restoration's Commissaires Extraordinaires du Roi in 1814', *French Historial Studies* (IX), Spring 1975, pp. 58–59; *Lewis*, p. 169; *Contamine* I, 296, 300; *Jaucourt*, p. 189, Jaucourt to Talleyrand, 11.2.1815; BN. NAF. 24062.152: report from the Vendée read at the Council meeting of 20.5.1814.

29. *Jaucourt*, p. 20, Jaucourt to Talleyrand, 4.10.1814; des Rioux de Messimy, *Justification des Griefs imputés au Roi et à la Famille Royale*, juillet 1815, p. 160; AAE. 681.52 Beugnot to Talleyrand, 1.11.1814; 40 AP. 10 Beugnot to Louis, 26.10.1814; ibid 17.355 Lecoz, Archbishop of Besançon, to Beugnot, 8.11.1814; BN. NAF. 11771.19 Journal of Madame de Chastenay, 6.3.1815.

30. AN. 40 AP. 8.174 vo. Beugnot to Louis XVIII, 25.6.1814; 40 AP. 10, 5.10.1814; Baron Despatys, *Un Ami de Fouché*, 1911, p. 289; *Jaucourt*, p. 207, Jaucourt to Talleyrand, 18.2.1815.

31. AN. AF V4, 2 Directeur des Postes d'Amiens to Bourrienne, 28.4.1814; Prince Eugène, *Mémoires et Correspondance Politique et Militaire* (10 vols. 1858–60), X, 288, 300 Prince Eugène to Princesse Auguste, 9.5., 17.6.1814; Frédéric Masson, *Napoléon et sa Famille* (15 vols. 1908–19), X, 179–180, the Duchesse de Saint-Leu to Alexander I, 4.10.1814; *Journal des Débats*, 3.8.1814; *Moniteur*, 13.9.1814, p. 1028.

32. *Moniteur*, 31.12.1814, p. 1469; M.F.P.G. Maine de Biran, *Journal* (3 vols. Neuchâtel 1954–57), I, 35: 31.12.1814.

33. Anon, *Journal of a Tour in France, Switzerland, and Lombardy . . . during the Autumn of 1818* (2 vols. 1821), I, 29; Edward Stanley, *Before and After Waterloo*, 1909, p. 121 Edward Stanley to Mrs. Stanley, 8.7.1814; AN. 300 AP. III 16 Orléans to Madame de Saint-Laurent, 1.6.1814.

34. Chateaubriand, *Correspondance Générale*, ed. Louis Thomas (5 vols. 1912–24), II, 378, Chateaubriand to Duchesse de Duras, 6.10. 1814; *Jaucourt*, p. 103, Jaucourt to Talleyrand, 30.11.1814; *Journal des Débats*, 23.11.1814; AAE.681.84, ? to Talleyrand, 10.12.1814; AN. 279 AP. (Correspondance du Maréchal Macdonald) 9 Duchesse d'Istrie to Maréchal Macdonald, 8.12.1814; 40 AP.9.67 Beugnot to Louis, 9.7.1814; PRO. FO 27/97 Sir Charles Stuart to Castlereagh, 11.7.1814; *Macdonald*, pp. 322–324; AN. AF V5, 2: 17.6.1814.

35. *Moniteur*, 31.8.1814, p. 976, 11.11.1815, déposition du Maréchal Ney, p. 1246; BM. Add. Mss. 38257.237–8 Louis to the Regent, 12.5.1814; William Roots, *Journal or Paris in 1814* (Newcastle 1900), p. 47: 5.9.1814; AAE. 681.45 Beugnot to Talleyrand, 23.10.1814; *Jaucourt*, pp. 20, 90, Jaucourt to Talleyrand, 4.10, 19.11.1814; AN. 40 AP. 10 Beugnot to Louis, 23.9.1814; cf. BN. NAF. 11771.9 vo. Journal de Madame de Chastenay: 27.1.1815.

36. Philip Mansel, *The Court of France*, 1814–1830 (unpublished Ph. D.

Thesis, University of London 1978), pp. 135, 144; AN. O³1222 Dufour to Mounier, 2.7., 17.10., 20.11.1814; 40 AP. 9.104: 14.7.1814; *La Force*, p. 230, Louis to Madame de Balbi, 30.5.1794.

37. *Jaucourt*, pp. 91, 103, Jaucourt to Talleyrand, 19, 30.11.1814; *Barante* II, 85, Baron to Baronne de Barante, 8.10.1814; ATLMF. 240 Alfieri di Sostegno to Vallaise, 1.12.1814; AAE. 681.43 vo. Beugnot to Talleyrand, 23.09.1814.

38. *Polovtsov*, I, 210–213, despatch of 17.1.1815; *Jaucourt*, p. 158, Jaucourt to Talleyrand, 20.1.1815.

39. L. Pellissier, ed., *Le Portefeuille de la Comtesse d'Albany*, 1902, p. 255 Madame de Souza to Comtesse d'Albany, 9.9.1815; *Pallain*, p. 412, Talleyrand to Louis, 23.4.1815; *Jaucourt*, p. 106, Jaucourt to Talleyrand, 3.12.1814; AN. 40 AP. 10, Beugnot to Louis, 2.12.1814; anon, *Des Bourbons et des Puissances Etrangères au 20 mars 1815*, 1815, pp. 45–46.

40. AN. 40 AP.8 Beugnot to Louis, 1.8.1814; BN. NAF. 24062.280: 24.6.1814; RA. 21533–4, Elysée to the regent, 12.11.1814; AAE. 679.23, 46 Louis to Talleyrand, 27.10., 4.12.1814.

41. *Jaucourt*, p. 178. Jaucourt to Talleyrand, 4.2.1815; AN. 279 AP. 15 Duchesse de Massa to Maréchal Macdonald, 14, 27.11., 8.12.1814; 16 idem to idem, 24.1.1815; 3.2., 4.3.1815.

X

1. Webster, *The Foreign Policy of Castlereagh*, I, 439; Eugène Welvert, *Napoléon et la Police*, 1912, p. 188n; AAE.679.21, 55 Louis to Talleyrand, 21. 10.18., 12, 1814; *Weill*, IV, 451; AAE. 681.138 Comte d'Hauterive to Talleyrand, 14.2.1815; Baron Gourgaud, *Journal Inédit* (2 vols. 1899), I, 492.

2. Arthur Chuquet, 'De l'Ile d'Elbe au Golfe Juan', *Revue de Paris*, 1.1923, p. 246; idem, 'Napoléon à Grenoble', *Revue de Paris*, 1.11.1917, pp. 7, 37.

3. AAE.646.111 Blacas to Artois, 8.3.1815; *Polovtsov*, I, 155, Boutiaguine to Nesselrode, 7.3.1815.

4. *Macdonald*, p. 295; *Ribe*, p. 37; Emile Le Gallo, *Les Cent-Jours*, 1924, pp. 98, 101; Chuquet, *Lettres de 1815*, 1911, I, 272, 251, 263, accounts by Baron Capelle, Maréchal Ney, Marquis de Vaulchier.

5. *Moniteur*, 14, 16, 18.3.1815, pp. 295, 297, 312; AAE. 646.141, 145 Blacas to Feltre, 12.3.1815 (brouillon), 13.3.1815.

6. *Despatys*, pp. 312–314; AAE.646.157 Blacas to Feltre, 14.3.1815 (brouillon); A. Bardoux, *Madame de Custine*, 1888, p. 224; Louis Madelin, *Fouché* (2 vols. 1900), II, 330–335.

7. Charles H. Pouthas, *Guizot pendant la Resturation*, 1923, p. 74, circular by Montesquiou, 16.3.1815; *Jaucourt*, p. 225, Jaucourt to Talleyrand, 11.3.1815; *Moniteur*, 17.3.1815, p. 301.

8. *Greville*, I, 33: 30.3.1815; *Polovtsov*, I, 161, Boutiaguine to Nesselrode, 12.3.1815; ATLMF. 240 Alfieri di Sostegno to Vallais, 15.3.1815; BHVP.1013.98 ? to Mme. Girard, 13.3.1815; Alexandre de Laborde, *Quarante-huit Heures de Garde au Château des Tuileries*, 1816, p. 17, for the attitude of *le peuple; Jaucourt*, p. 237, Jaucourt to Talleyrand, 14.3.1815; G. Firmin-Didot, *Royauté ou Empire*, 1898, pp. 291–292, police reports of 13, 14.3.1815.

9. BHVP 1013.98? to Mme. Girard, 13.3.1815; Chuquet, *Lettres de 1815*, I, 289; idem, 'Napoléon à Grenoble', p. 37; Maréchal Marmont, *Mémoires* (9 vols. 1857), VII, 87; Chateaubriand, *Mémoires d'Outre-Tombe*, II, 270–271.

10. AAE. 646.165 Blacas to the Capitaines des Gardes, 14.3.1815 (brouillon); *Wellington*, SD, X, 39, Memorandum by Lord Harrowby of his Interview with

Louis XVIII (6.4.1815); *Macdonald*, pp. 360–364; *Perceval*, I, 366; *Maine de Biran*, I, 45–47: 19, 20.3.1815.

11. AN. O³627 Budget, 1815; *Hue*, pp. 279–283; Edouard Romberg et Albert Malet, *Louis XVIII et les Cent-Jours à Gand* (2 vols. 1898–1902), II, 15, Sir Charles Stuart to Castlereagh, 2.4.1815; *Marmont*, VII, 95–99; *Maine de Biran*, I, 45: 19.3.1815; *Laborde*, pp. 12–15; *Moniteur*, 21.3.1815, p. 323.

12. AN. 40 AP. 20 Louis to Dambray, 19.3.1815 (copy); AAE. 648.87 Blacas to Feltre, 17.3.1815 (brouillon); *Journal de Gand*, 14.4.1815, p. 2; *Macdonald*, p. 370; *Romberg et Malet*, I, 112, Artois to Louis, 21.3.1815.

13. Louis-Philippe d'Orléans, *Extrait de Mon Journal du Mois de Mars 1815* (Twickenham 1816), pp. 58, 105–107; *Talleyrand*, III, 129, Blacas to Talleyrand, Bruges 24.3.1815; *Macdonald*, p. 380.

14. *Hue*, p. 279; *Romberg et Malet*, I, 99–100, Blacas to Castlereagh, 25.3.1815, 114, Artois to Louis, 27.3.1815; *Jaucourt*, p. 247, Jaucourt to Talleyrand, 26.3.1815.

15. *Hue*, p. 285; Comte de Sémallé, *Souvenirs*, 1898, p. 225; *Romberg et Malet*, I, XXXV.

16. *Le Nain Jaune*, II, 44, 15.4.1815; AN. 40 AP. 20 Louis to Dambray, 19.3.1815 (copy); *Talleyrand*, III, 37, 168–173 Talleyrand to Louis, 25.1.1815, 23.4.1815; AAE. 679. 15, 27, 55 Louis to Talleyrand 3, 31.10., 18.12.1814 (drafts); *Polovtsov*, I, 31, Pozzo to Nesselrode, 6.7.1814; *Wellington*, SD, X, 61, 169, Wellington to Castlereagh, 11.4.1815, to Sir Henry Wellesley, 28.4.1815; *Lacour-Gayet*, IV, 130–131, Louis to Talleyrand, 26.3.1815.

17. *Wellington*, SD, X, 37 Memorandum by Lord Harrowby (6.4.1815); *Wellington*, X, 7–9, Comte Dejean to Napoleon I, 11.6.1815, 14–15 Rapport à l'Empereur, 12.6.1815, *Le Gallo*, p. 340; *Vidalenc*, p. 77; Vere Foster, *The Two Duchesses*, Frederick to Augustus Foster, 4.3.1815; *Le Gallo*, p. 371; BN. NAF. 24062. 437,465: 12.9., 3.10.1814. Louis insisted on the *franchise*, saying that 'Marseille a été la reine de la Mediterrannée.'

18. AN.O³627 Observations sur l'Esprit . . . de Paris, by Letuelle, Chasseur de la Garde Nationale de Paris; Frédéric Bluche, *Le Plébiscite des Cent-Jours* (Geneva 1974), pp. 37–38, 48, 100, and passim.

19. *Le Gallo*, p. 133, Le Coz to Napoleon I, 25.3.1815; *Moniteur*, 16.3.1815; Chuquet, *Lettres de 1815*, I, 341; *Maine de Biran*, I, 91: 21.6.1815.

20. For prints see the historical collections in the Musée Carnavalet, especially vol. 36B; F. S. Larpent, *Journal* (3 vols. 1852), II, 290: 26.4.1814; Reine Hortense, *Mémoires* (ed. Jean Hanoteau. 3 vols. 1927), III, 7; BN.NAF. 24062.606: 16.12.1814.

21. H. Clouzot et Ch. Follot, *Histoire du Papier Peint en France*, 1935, p. 174; AN. 279 AP. 16 Duchesse de Massa to Maréchal Macdonald, 3.2.1815; Robert Chantemesse, *Le Roman Inconnu de la Duchesse d'Abrantès*, 1927, pp. 222, 240; Archives Départmentales de la Côte d'Or (ADCO) IF555 Journal de Madame Champagne, passim; Edouard Herriot, *Madame Recamier et ses Amis* (2 vols, 1905), I, 346; Fantin des Odoards, *Journal*, 1895, p. 422: 16.3.1815.

22. *Constant*, p. 348: 14.4.1815; *Gaffarel*, p. 189.

23. *Mayne*, p. 29; *Le Nain Jaune*, II, 296: 10.6.1815; *Moniteur*, 21, 26.3.1815, Proclamations of 1, 10.3.1815; *Contamine* I, 304–312; *Wellington*, SD, X, 37, Memorandum by Lord Harrowby (6.4.1815).

XI

1. *Constant*, p. 350; *Castellane*, I, 287; Thomas D. Beck, *French Legislators, 1800–1834*, 1974, p. 39.

2. Titeux, *La Maison Militaire du Roi*, II, 188–190; AAE. 646.276 Rapport of 22.4.1815; *Romberg et Malet*, I, 31, II, 144, Stuart to Castlereagh, 5.4, 2.6.1815.

3. *Beugnot*, II, 487, 241; *Pouthas*, pp. 88–89, note by Guizot after an audience of 1.6.1815; X. de Montépin, ed., *Souvenirs Intimes et Anecdotiques d'un Garde du Corps des Rois Louis XVIII et Charles X* (5 vols. 1857), II, 114; Comte d'Hérisson, *Un Secrétaire du Cabinet de Napoléon 1er*, (Dèuxieme Edition 1894), p. 387, Monsieur to Madame Mounier, 29.5.1815; Chateaubriand, *Mémoires d'Outre-Tombe*, II, 290–291; V. Stuart Wortley, *Highcliffe and the Stuarts*, 1927, p. 226, Charles Stuart to Lady Elizabeth Yorke, 4.1815.

4. *Hérisson*, p. 383, Mounier to Madame Mounier, 29.5.1815; *Ferrand*, pp. 133, 138; *Perceval* I, 354; *Romberg et Malet*, I, 138, Dandré to Blacas, 31.3.1815; *Castlereagh*, X, 32 Pozzo to Castlereagh, 21.4.1815; AN.O³627 Observations sur l'Esprit . . . de Paris.

5. AAE. 647.263 Declaration of 15.4.1815; *Romberg et Malet*, II, 18, Stuart to Castlereagh, 2.4.1815; 93–94, Blacas to Stuart, 23.4.1815; *Jaucourt*, p. 288, Jaucourt to Talleyrand, 24.4.1815; AAE. 646.307–309 note by Lally; *Moniteur de Gand*, 21.6.1815, p. 83.

6. *Romberg et Malet*, I, 121–134, Artois to Louis, 3–6.1815; II, 61, Stuart to Castlereagh, 21.4.1815; *Jaucourt*, p. 343–344 Jaucourt to Talleyrand, 11.5.1815; *Romberg et Malet*, II, 83, Stuart to Castlereagh, 2.5.1815; *Moniteur de Gand*, 5.5.1815, p. 27.

7. AN.O³627 Affaires Etrangères Declaration by Louis; *Romberg et Malet*, I, 70, Pouvoirs au Duc de Tarente, 1.6.1815; *Moniteur de Gand*, 17.6.1815; *Romberg et Malet*, II, 150, Stuart to Castlereagh 2.6.1815.

8. *Romberg et Malet*, II, 99, Stuart to Castlereagh, 12.5.1815; *Orléans*, pp. 110–111; Marie-Amélie, Duchesse d'Orléans, *Journal*, ed. Duchesse de Vendôme, 3 vols., 1935–43, II, 117: 21.5.1815; AN. 300 AP. III, 20 2.53 Lally-Tollendal to Orléans, 16.5.1815; AAE. 681.271 Chateaubriand to Talleyrand, 6.5.1815; *Talleyrand*, III, 184, Louis to Talleyrand, 5.5.1815.

9. AAE. 679.67 vo. Louis to Talleyrand, 7.1.1815, and passim; BM. Add. Mss. 38261.197 vo. Frisell to Liverpool, 7.4.1815; *Jaucourt*, pp. 291, 323, 329, Jaucourt to Talleyrand, 24.4., 2.5., 6.5.1815; Alfred Nettement, *Histoire de la Restauration* (8 vols. 1860–72), III, 388, Castel-Cicala to Blacas, 9.5.1815.

10. *Wellington*, SD, 37, Memorandum by Lord Harrowby (6.4.1815); *Romberg et Malet*, I, 67, Instructions au Duc d'Angoulême, 5.1815, 70, Pouvoirs au Duc de Tarente, 1.6.1815.

11. *Hérisson*, p. 424, Monsieur to Madame Mounier, 20.6.1815; PRO. FO 27/113 Stuart to Castlereagh 21.6.1815; *Romberg et Malet*, I, 220, Pozzo to Louis, 19.6.1815; II, 178, note by Stuart 19.6.1815; *Wellington*, XII, 393, Wellington to Talleyrand, 24.6.1815; 527, Wellington to Blücher 2.7.1815; 596, Wellington to Castlereagh 11.8.1815; 492, Wellington to Feltre, Berri, 20.6.1815.

12. *Wellington*, SD, X, 77, 447 Feltre to Wellington, 14.4. 10.6.1815; ibid, XIV, 560 Louis to Wellington, 19.6.1815; *Wellington*, XII, 493, General Order of 20.6.1815; *Moniteur de Gand*, 21.6.1815.

13. *Wellington*, SD, X, 553, Feltre to Wellington, 20.6.1815; 411, Lord Stewart to Wellington, 2.6.1815; *Jaucourt*, p. 303, Jaucourt to Talleyrand, 26.4.1815; *Talleyrand*, III, 228, Metternich to Talleyrand, 24.6.1815.

14. *Wellington*, SD, X, 566–567, Feltre to Wellington, 23.6.1815; *Revue d'Histoire Diplomatique*, 1896, p. 31, Comte de Fagel to William I, 24.6.1815; Daudet, *Joseph de Maistre et Blacas*, p. 296n, Louis to Blacas, 22.6.1815; Chateaubriand, *Mémoires d'Outre-Tombe*, II, 327. There is an account of the intrigues at Mons as seen by Blacas in Orléans's diary for 9 July (AN. 300 AP. III 20 2.135–145). But it is unlikely to be especially reliable since it recounts events from the point of view of two extremely prejudiced politicians.

15. C. P. Snow, *Variety of Men*, 1967, p. 192; General C. Mercer, *Journal of the Waterloo Campaign* (2 vols. 1870), II, 18: 24.6.1815; Thomas Creevey, *The Creevey Papers*, (2 vols. 1903), I, 239, Lord Arthur Hill to Creevey, 25.6.1815; *Beugnot*, II, 308; *Wellington*, SD, X, 583, Stuart to Wellington, 25.6.1815; *Romberg et Malet*, II, 267–9, Goltz to Hardenberg, 25.6.1815; *Polovtsov*, I, 269, Pozzo to Nesselrode, 26.6.1815.

16. *Wellington*, SD, X, 564, Stuart to Wellington, 23.6.1815; AN. 40 AP. 16 drafts of the Proclamation of Cambrai; *Moniteur*, 7.7.1815; p. 773; *Wellington*, SD, X, 611, 614, 625 Stuart to Wellington, 27, 28., 29.6.1815.

17. *Wellington*, XII, 536, Wellington to Bathurst, 2.7.1815; cf. BM. Add. Mss. 60399.15 vo. Fouché to Wellington, 1816; Chancelier Comte de Nesselrode, *Lettres et Papiers* (11 vols. 1904–11), V, 222, Hortense to Alexander I, 15.7.1815; *Wellington*, SD, XIV, 564, Wellington to Talleyrand, 29.6.1815; *Polovtsov*, I, 276, Pozzo to Nesselrode, 1.7.1815; *Frances, Lady Shelley*, I, 120: 7.1815.

18. *Vitrolles*, II, 225; *Mercer*, II, 90: 7.7.1815; *Jaucourt*, p. 332, Jaucourt to Talleyrand, 6.5.1815; *Beugnot*, II, 328–331; Marquise de Montcalm, *Mon Journal pendant le Premier Ministère de mon Frère*, 1935, p. 87n: 8.7.1815; *Wellington*, XII, 550 Wellington to Bathurst, 8.7.1815.

19. Chateaubriand, *Mémoires d'Outre-Tombe*, II, 331, 335; *Mercer*, II, 93: 7.7.1815; M. de Bourrienne, *Mémoires* (10 vols. 1829), X, 41.

20. *Wellington*, SD, X, 611, Davout to Fouché, 27.6.1815; Edmond Géraud, *Un Témoin des Deux Restaurations*, n.d., pp. 251–252, Gergères to Geraud, 6 (?).7.1815; AN. 359. AP. 99 Marquis to Marquise de Clermont-Tonnerre, 9.7.1815; (John Cam Hobhouse), *The Substance of Some Letters written from Paris* (2 vols. 1816), II, 172; AN. 197 AP. Louis to La Chatre, 20.7.1815.

21. *Castlereagh*, X, 420, Castlereagh to Liverpool, 8.7.1815; AN. 359 AP. 99 Marquis to Marquise de Clermont-Tonnerre, 9.7.1815; *Shelley*, I, 104: 7.1815; Bernard Pool, ed., *The Croker Papers*, 1967, p. 23, Croker to Mrs. Croker, 12.7.1815; Jane Vansittart ed., *Surgeon James's Journal*, 1964, p. 101; James Simpson, *Paris after Waterloo*, 1853, pp. 255–257.

22. Louis Girard, *La Garde Nationale*, 1964, p. 52; *Scott*, p. 294; Malmesbury, *Letters*, II, 456, Captain G. Bowles to Lord Fitzharris, 9.8.1815; *Fellowes*, p. 108: 20.7.1815; *Géraud*, p. 274.

23. *Stanley*, p. 290, Edward to Mrs. Stanley, 9.7.1816; Vidalenc, *Département de l'Eure*, pp. 97–99; *Lewis*, pp. 199, 211; Prince de Metternich, *Mémoires, Documents, et écrits divers* (8 vols. 1880–1884) II, 524, Metternich to Marie de Metternich, 13.7.1815; AAE. 691.216–218 vo. Talleyrand to the allied ambassadors, n.d.

24. AAE. 690–691 passim; *Molé*, II, 282, III, 223; *Langeron*, p. 96, Louis to Decazes, 18.4.1816; *Talleyrand*, III, 253; *Castellane*, I, 302: 2.9.1815; *Pouthas*, p. 113; *Richardson*, p. 65; *Vitrolles*, II, 257, 282.

25. Baron Portal, *Mémoires*, 1844, pp. 33–39; AN. 359 AP. 84.712 Souvenirs of Clermont-Tonnerre; *Langeron*, p. 130, Louis to Decazes 9 and 26.9.1817; Comte L. M. Molé, *Le Comte Molé . . . sa Vie, ses Mémoires*, (6 vols. 1922–

30), III, 184, Louis to Molé, 18.3.1818; Daudet, 'Le Duc de Richelieu au Congrès d'Aix-la-Chapelle', *Nouvelle Revue*, CXIV, 1898, passim and pp. 403, 605, Richelieu to Decazes, 12.10., 2.11.1818; cf. for Louis's involvement in government, Comte de Villèle, *Mémoires et Correspondance* (5 vols. 1898–1901), III, 367, 417, IV, 37, 272, 371, Villèle to Angoulême, 24.4., 4.5.1823, to Martignac, 8.6.1823, to Angoulême, 31.7., 6.9.1823.

26. E. D. Pasquier, *Histoire de Mon Temps* (6 vols. 1893–95), III, 208–209, 362, 375, 382; *Collins*, p. 9; Baron Gay de Vernon, *Vie du Maréchal Gouvion Saint-Cyr*, 1856, pp. 397–401; Vidalenc, *Les Demi-Solde*, 1955, pp. 20–25; AHMG (Archives Historiques du Ministère de la Guerre) XAE 6 (papers of the Garde Royale), the Minister of War to the Prefects, 10.1815.

27. *Portal*, p. 44; *Villèle*, IV, 232, 236, 272, 306, 371, Villèle to Angoulême, 16., 31.7., 11.8., 16.9.1823; BVC.FR. 72.17, 83.163 Louis to Lainé, 7.5.1816, Richelieu to Lainé, n.d.; *Molé*, II, 379; *Portal*, p. 30; BVC. FR. 80.20, Louis to Richelieu 2.1820; Chateaubriand, *Correspondance Generale*, III, 313, Chateaubriand to Madame Recamier, 28.12.1822; Comte de Corbière, 'Souvenirs d'un Ministre de Louis XVIII', *Revue des Deux Mondes*, 4.1966, p. 366.

28. *Pasquier*, IV, 206; *Molé*, III, 282, IV, 161; BN. NAF. 20280, 240 Richelieu to Decazes, n.d.; BVC. FR. 78.18, 87 Decazes to Richelieu, 4., 15.11.18; *Decazes*, p. 468n., Pasquier to Decazes, 11.1818; *Moniteur*, 11.12.1818, p. 1441; Comte de Serre, *Correspondance* (6 vols. 1876–77), II, 491, Serre to Decazes, 18.12.1819.

29. Abbé Moulard, *Le Comte Camille de Tournon* (3 vols. 1927–32), II, 64n., Tournon to Barante, 21.8.1815; Louis's famous letter to Talleyrand, '*Quant à moi, s'il le faut, je me porterai sur le pont; on me fera sauter si l'on veut*' (the 'original' is in AN. 300 AP. III) is dated 15 July; but the King of Prussia had stopped the explosion on 10 July, in response to pressure from Vitrolles, Talleyrand, Wellington, Duras (almost certainly on Louis's instructions) and Castlereagh (AAE. 691.10 Goltz to Talleyrand, 10.7.1815; 346.13 Vitrolles to Goltz, [brouillon]; *Wellington*, SD. XI, 20, M. Chambine to Wellington, 9.7.1815; *Wellington*, XII, 553, Wellington to Blücher, 9.7.1815; *Castlereagh*, X, 420, Castlereagh to Liverpool, 8.7.1815). Moreover, the bridge's name had been changed, in order to spare Prussian susceptibilities, on 9 July (*Moniteur*, 10.7.1815, p. 795). Therefore Louis's letter cannot have had much effect, unless Blücher tried a second time; AN. 86 AP. (Jaucourt Papers) 8 1.78 Louis to Talleyrand, 22.7.1815 (copy); C. M. Wodehouse, *Capodistria*, 1977, p. 134; *Talleyrand*, III, 277–285, allied note of 20.9.1815.

30. Fouché, *Rapport au Roi*, 8.1815; *Decazes*, pp. 57–58; Eugène Forgues, *Le Dossier Secret de Fouché*, 1908, p. 53, Foudras to Vitrolles, 12.8.1815; Simone Fizaine, *La Vie Politique dans la Côte d'Or sous Louis XVIII*, 1931, p. 53, Circular by Pasquier, 21.7.1815; cf. *Castellane*, I, 229: 10.8.1815; *Wellington*, SD, X, 166–7, Castlereagh to Liverpool, 21.9.1815; Francis Ley, *Madame de Krüdener et son Temps*, 1961, pp. 487, 499, diary of Juliette de Krüdener: 15., 22.9.1815; *Montcalm*, p. 92–93: 28.9.1815; *Langeron*, p. 55, Souvenirs of Decazes; *Wellington*, XII, 643, Wellington to Castlereagh, 23.9.1815; *Scott*, pp. 335, 348; Musée Carnavalet, Estampes, Vol. 36D; *Romberg et Malet*, II, 268, Goltz to Hardenberg, 26.6.1815; *Polovstsov*, I, 211, Mémoire of 3.5.1815 by Alexander I.

XII

1. *Langeron*, pp. 195, 232, Louis to Decazes 24.4.1818, 1.1819; *Nettement*, IV, 643, Blacas, 'Rapport au Roi', 20.12.1823; ABR. (Archives of Comte Lodovico Luichese-Palli, Schloss Brünnsee, Austria) Album Verde, Louis to Duchesse de Berri, 25.5.1816; AN. O³2886 Compte de Recettes et Dépenses Secrètes; O³529 Rapport au Ministre, 12.1820; BN.NAF. 24062.168: 27.5.1814; *Smyth*, I, 395; *Metternich*, I, 197; anon, *Mementoes, Historical and Classical, of a Tour in France* (2 vols. 1824), I, 21, 35; (Countess of Blessington), *Journal of a Tour through the Netherlands to Paris in 1821, 1822*, pp. 113–114; *Duchesse d'Orléans*, II, 51; 9.1814; AN. 300 AP. III 16 Orléans to Madame de Saint-Laurent, 1.6.1814.

2. Hemlow, *The Journal and Letters of Fanny Burney*, VII, 450, Monsieur to Madame d'Arblay, 28.8.1814; AN. O³1984 Thierry de Ville d'Avray to Duras, 9.9., 30.10.1815; O³1878, 5 Soumission of Bellanger, 16.10.1815, Soumission Supplémentaire, 17.11.1815; Thierry de Ville d'Avray to Pradel, 24.11.1815.

3. Alphonse de Lamartine, *Histoire de la Restauration* (8 vols. 1851–52), VII, 304; S. de La Rochefoucauld, *Mémoires* (15 vols. 1861–64), VII, 580; *Vitrolles*, II, 91; cf. AN. O³1985 Thierry de Ville d'Avray to Pradel, 16.9.1817, 14.8.1817.

4. *Mansel*, p. 92; AN. O³414 Ordres by the Marquis de Vernon, 2.4.1817, 23.9.1820; *Decazes*, p. 58; AN. 359 AP. 82.358 Souvenirs of the Marquis de Clermont-Tonnerre.

5. *Castellane*, I, 368: 2.1819, *Montépin*, II, 58–60; *Mansel*, p. 292.

6. *Mansel*, p. 54; *Duchesse d'Orléans*, II, 75: 4.12.1814; AN. O³73 Etat des Fruits et Légumes fournis pour le Service de la Bouche de Sa Majesté; ATLMF. 240, Alfieri di Sostegno to Pralormo, 23.12.1814; R. Perrin du Lac, 'Journal', *Revue de l'Histoire de Versailles*, 1913, pp. 330–331: 27.7.1818; A. Aspinall, ed., *The Letters of King George IV, 1812–1830* (3 vols. 1938), II, 175, Cambridge to the Regent, 4.11.1816.

7. AN.O³388 Blacas to Vernon, 28.2.1815; O³537.449 Rapport au Roi, 16.8.1817; O³234 Inventaire du 12.7.1815; *Montépin*, V, 183; *Langeron*, p. 179, Louis to Decazes, 7.9.1818; AHMG. XAD 12 Ordres by the Capitaine des Gardes de service, 5.11, 25.12.1815, Feltre to Macdonald, 7.5, 11.6.1816; AN. 359 AP.99 Marquis to Marquise de Clermont-Tonnerre, 11.9.1815; Comte de Chabannes, *Histoire de la Maison de Chabannes* (6 vols. 1893–95), III, 682, 685, Madame de Chabannes to J. van Lennep, 26.8.1822, 8.12.1823; AHMG. XAD 14 Rapport Général des Différents Postes formés par les Gardes Nationale et Royale, 3/4.5.1823.

8. AN. O³628 La Chatre to Lauriston, 13.12.1820; O³195.13 vo. Décision du Premier Gentilhomme, 21.8.1816; O³211 Placets, Analyse des Demandes et Réponses; O³194 Aumont to Héron de Villefosse, 14.1.1821; Duchesse de Gontaut, *Mémoires*, 1893, p. 194; *Langeron*, p. 140, Louis to Decazes, 11.8.1817; AN. 197 AP. Louis to La Chatre, 10.3.1816.

9. AN. O³205.109 vo. Décision du Premier Gentilhomme, 23.8.1816; AN. 197 AP. Louis to La Chatre, 10.3.1816; ADCO. Fonds Commarin (henceforward known as ADCOFC) Louis to Charles de Damas, 27.6.1816, cf. *Langeron*, p. 94, Louis to Decazes, 15.6.1816; *Mansel*, p. 413.

10. Abbé G. Pailhès, *La Duchesse de Duras et Chateaubriand*, 1911, p. 246, Chateaubriand to Duchesse de Duras, 24.9.1823; BVC FR.73.66 Bonnay to Richelieu, 23.10.1816; *Decazes*, p. 454, Louis to Decazes, 1817; *Perrin du Lac*, p. 331: 27.7.1818; *Villèle*, II, Villèle to Madame de Villèle, 31.1.1817, cf. Jean de Boislisle, 'L'Abbé de Montesquiou, Ministre de la Restauration', *Annuaire-*

Bulletin de la Société de l'Histoire de France, 1927, p. 253, Louis to Abbé de Montesquiou, 28.1.1817; *Perrin du Lac*, 1913, p. 330: 27.7.1818; Comte de Saint-Chamans, *Mémoires*, 1896, p. 389: 16.1.1821; Daudet, *L'Ambassade du Duc Decazes*, p. 10, Louis to Decazes, 27.2.1820; ADCOFC. Roger to Charles de Damas, 15.8.1819; Archives X, Duchesse d'Escars to Madame de Podenas, 15.4.1821.

11. Archives X Duc to Duchesse d'Escars n.d.; *Saint-Chamans*, pp. 391–392: 17., 20.1.1822, cf. *Molé*, II, 49; *Lacour-Gayet*, III, 59, Talleyrand to Duchesse de Courlande, 15.6.1816; A. Lhôte de Selancey, *Des Charges de la Maison Civile des Rois de France*, 1847, pp. 99–103; AN. 359 AP. 84.62 Notes Sténographiées du Marquis de Clermont-Tonnerre: 18.10.1823; *Lacour-Gayet*, III, 142; J. F. Bernard, *Talleyrand*, 1974, p. 462.

12. Hugh Murray Baillie, 'Etiquette and the Planning of State Apartments in Baroque Palaces', *Archaeologia* (CI), 1967, pp. 169, 201; AN. 0^3628 La Chatre to Lauriston, 13.12.1820, *'Jamais dans les appartements du roi une porte ne reste ouverte'*; *The Letters of Queen Victoria . . . Between The Years 1837 and 1861* (3 vols. 1907), II, 173, 177, Queen Victoria to Leopold I, 23.8.1855, to Baron Stockmar, 1.9.1855; 0^374 Condé to Blacas, 11.12.1814; 0^31986 Thierry de Ville d'Avray to Lauriston, 26.10.1821; 'Les Devoirs d'un Roi', *Feuilles d'Histoire*, 1.9.1909, p. 277; cf. B.N.NAF. 24062: 276 24.6.1814 where Louis speaks of the need of *'du faste et de la réprésentation à la Cour'*; cf. *Molé*, III, 154; ADCOFC. Comtesse to Comte Charles de Damas, 23.6.1817; AN. 279 AP. 9, Maréchal Macdonald to Duchesse d'Istrie, 26.6.1817; ATLMF. 247, Comte de Vignet to Comte de Laval, 14.8.1821; Archives X, Duchesse d'Escars to Madame de Podenas, 22.7.1822; Stendhal, 'Souvenirs d'Egotisme', *Oeuvres Intimes* (Gallimard Angers 1955), p. 1465; *Langeron*, p. 93, Louis to Decazes, 16.5.1816; $0^3228.32$ Thierry de Ville d'Avray to Duras, 5.8.1815.

13. AN 0^3519 Consigne Générale des Gardes du Corps, cf. AHMG XAE 6 Compagnies Sédentaires, Vicomte de Fezensac to Comte de Bourmont, 20.3.1821; 0^3529 Décision de Sa Majesté sur l'Ordre et la Composition de Son Cortège dans l'intérieur de ses Appartements, 31.12.1820; Henry Wansey, *A Visit to Paris in June 1814*, 1814, p. 92: 18.6.1814; Seth William Stevenson, *Journal of a Tour through Part of France, Flanders and Holland . . .* (Norwich 1817), pp. 132–133: 27.5.1816; the quotations are from: James Simpson, *Paris after Waterloo*, 1853, pp. 130–131: 8.1815; Surgeon James, *Journal*, ed. Jane Vansittart, 1964, pp. 52–53; Thomas Raffles, *Letters during a tour through some parts of France, Savoy . . . in the Summer of 1817* (Third Edition, Liverpool 1820), pp. 86–88.

14. Edward Bellasis, *Memorials of Cherubini*, 1874, pp. 211–237; Duc de Broglie, *Souvenirs* (4 vols. 1886), II, 215, Journal of the Duchesse de Broglie: 27.9.1821; Institut, Fonds Royer-Collard 3.990 Talleyrand to Royer-Collard, 3.10.1822; BN. NAF. 14098 (papers of Madame Recamier). 61 Mathieu de Montmorency to his wife, Vienna, 7.9.1822; 0^31892 Rapport to Lauriston, 22.10.1821; 0^32008 Inventaire du Mobilier: 29.1.1822; J. G. Legrand et C. P. Landon, *Description de Paris et de ses Edifices* (Second Edition, 2 vols. 1818), I, 250; *Robiquet*, p. 25.

15. Louis Trénard, *Salvandy en son Temps*, 1968, p. 62, Journal: 27.4., 3.5.1817; *Maine de Biran*, II, 213: 8.3.1819; ADCOFC. Roger to Charles de Damas, 22.11.1818; *Sémallé*, p. 292; *Molé*, III, 107, IV, 243, 248; *Villèle*, III, 112, Mathieu de Montmorency to Villèle, 9.10.1822.

16. Daudet, *L'Ambassade du Duc Decazes*, p. 37, Louis to Decazes, 1820;

448 *Louis XVIII*

Langeron, p. 191, 'Souvenirs' of the Duchesse Decazes; AN. O³199 Registre des Présentations; *Mansel*, p. 247.

17. *Moulard*, III, 88, 105, 543; Bertier de Sauvigny, *Le Comte Ferdinand de Bertier*, p. 228; Balzac, *Le Cabinet des Antiques* (2 vols. 1839), II, 73; Archives X, Duchesse d'Escars to Marquis de Nadaillac, 28.6.1821.
18. *Villèle*, III, 4, cf. Baron de Damas, *Mémoires* (2 vols. 1923), II, 33; AN. O³90 Distributions, Soirées de la Duchesse d'Escars; Archives X, Duc to Duchesse d'Escars, n.d. and passim; Daudet, *L'Ambassade du Duc Decazes*, p. 37, Louis to Decazes, 1820, cf. p. 162; AAE. 646.111 Blacas to Artois, 8.3.1815.
19. AN. O³195 Décisions du Premier Gentilhomme, on Court mourning, passim; Egon Conte Corti, *Ludwig I of Bavaria*, 1938, p. 146, Crown Prince to Crown Princess of Bavaria, 23.7.1815; Daudet, 'Le Duc de Richelieu au Congrès d'Aix-la-Chapelle', *Nouvelle Revue* (XIV), 1898, p. 405, Richelieu to Decazes, 16.10.1818; ABR Album Verde, Louis to Duchesse de Berri, 25.5.1816; Chateaubriand, *Mémoires d'Outre-Tombe*, II, 248; ABR. Journal de la Duchesse de Berri: 16., 17., 21.1.1820, 21.1.1821; *Decazes*, p. 259, Louis to Artois, 21.1.1818.
20. *Duchesse d'Orléans*, II, 35: 5.1.1824; AN. 300 AP. III 20, 1.39 Orléans to Louis, 17.5.1815; III, 21 Orléans and Bourbon to Louis, 28.4.1821; O³526 'Relation' of the annual memorial service by the Marquis de Rochemore, 16.10.1819, records that Orléans talked to him for half an hour about the right of the Princes du Sang to kneel on two hassocks; ATLMF 246 de Vignet to Laval, 1.1.1820; *Duvergier de Hauranne*, V, 401, Louis to Decazes, 7.1.1819.
21. *Decazes*, p. 433, Louis to Decazes, 18.2.1820; *Perrin du Lac*, p. 331: 27.7.1818; *Nettement*, III, 533; *Langeron*, p. 213, Louis to Decazes, 1818; *Damas*, I, 336, Angoulême to Damas, 9.1.1819.
22. Balzac, *Splendeurs et Misères des Courtisanes*, Garnier-Flammarion, ed. A. Adam, 1958, p. 43; *Langeron*, p. 78, Louis to Decazes, 16.1.1816; *Molé*, IV, 13; *Decazes*, p. 391, Louis to Decazes, 3.1.1820; *Langeron*, p. 150, Artois to Louis, 31.1.1818; *Decazes*, pp. 447, 464, Louis to Decazes, 25.8.1819, 9.1816; *Langeron*, p. 56, Louis to Decazes, 18.11.1818.
23. Daudet, *L'Ambassade du Duc Decazes*, p. 22, Louis to Decazes, 14.3.1820; *Decazes*, Louis to Decazes, 15.10.1816; AN. 359 AP. 84.62 Notes by Clermont-Tonnerre: 25.12.1822; AN. F⁷4347, 3 Inventaire, 3.1824, of papers sent to the Minister of the Interior to be shown to the king.
24. BVC. FR. 79.102 vo. Richelieu to Decazes, 22.6.1819; Z. Frappaz, *Vie de l'Abbé Nicolle*, 1857, pp. 109, 112, Richelieu to Abbé Nicolle, 1.1816 (by post), 12.1.1816 (by courier); *Hue*, p. 317, Madame Hue to Pradel, 1818; *Moniteur*, 31.12.1821, p. 1753, 2., 3.1.1824, pp. 7, 11; J. Lucas-Dubreton, *Louis XVIII*, p. 279, Louis to Madame du Cayla, n.d.; Comte de Montbel, 'Les Derniers Moments de Louis XVIII', *Le Correspondant* (CCXCVI), 10.9.1924, pp. 763–768; *Pasquier*, IV, 69; *La Rochefoucauld*, II, 83; Baron Henrion, *Vie de M. Frayssinous, Evêque d'Hermopolis* (2 vols. 1844), II, 374; G. A. Geffroy de Grandmaison, *L'Expédition Française d'Espagne en 1823*, 1928, p. 36.
25. Daudet, *L'Ambassade du Duc Decazes*, p. 159, Louis to Decazes, 9.8.1820; *Langeron*, pp. 66, 192, Souvenirs de la Duchesse Decazes, 193, Louis to Decazes, 19.3.1818; *Beugnot*, II, 287, cf. *Molé*, III, 47, for the Comtesse de Narbonne; René Jean, 'Madame de Mirbel', *Gazette des Beaux-Arts*, 1.2.1906, pp. 131–147; cf. AN. O³222.17 Concierge of Saint-Cloud to Pradel, 4.9.1819; Bardoux, *La Duchesse de Duras*, p. 347, Duchesse de Duras to Chateaubriand, 28/29.6.1822; *La Rochefoucauld*, VII, 490, Madame du Cayla to La Rochefoucauld, 1824; for figures of money, see *Mansel*, pp. 413–414, and, for Madame

du Cayla, AN. O³543.326 Rapport au Roi, 24.5.1822, 546.221 Rapport au Roi, 30.4.1824, 547.10 Rapport au Roi, 3.7.1824; O³2888 Etat des Fonds Secrets du Roi, 1824.

26. Comte de Corbière, 'Souvenirs d'un Ministre de Louis XVIII', *Revue des Deux Mondes*, 1.4.1966, p. 369; AN. O³239 Comptabilité, Exercice 1820; Owen Chadwick, *Catholicism and History* (Cambridge 1978), pp. 20–21; AN. O³538.406 Rapport au Roi, 30.10.1818; Chateaubriand, *Mémoires, Lettres et Pièces Authentiques touchant la Vie et la Mort de S. A. R. Monseigneur Charles-Ferdinand d'Artois, Fils de France, Duc de Berry*, 1820, p. 7; Edmond Biré, *Victor Hugo et la Restauration*, 1869, pp. 421–422; Archives X Lettres à la Duchesse d'Escars 133, Lamartine to Duchesse d'Escars, n.d.; O³543.484 Rapport au Roi, 31.8.1822.

27. M. Campenon, *Essai de Mémoires, ou Lettres sur la Vie, le Caractère et les Ecrits de J.–F. Ducis*, 1824, p. 155: 10.1.1816; *Decazes*, pp. 127, 168, Louis to Decazes, 1816, 24.2.1817; AN. O³821 Duc de Richelieu to Pradel, 11.2.1817; M. Alibert, *Physiologie des Passions* (Deuxième Edition, 2 vols. 1827), I, 48–50, 62, 345, II, 13, 16, 64, 301–320.

28. Ruth Kaufmann, 'François Gérard's Entry of Henri IV into Paris', *The Burlington Magazine* (CXVII), 12.1975, pp. 796–802; Pierre Angrand, *Le Comte de Forbin et le Louvre en 1819*, 1975, p. 103; Cecil Gould, *Trophy of Conquest*, 1962, p. 119; *Moniteur*, 3.8.1817, p. 851; Dimitri Sorokine, *Champollion et les Secrets de l'Egypte*, 1967, p. 122; Archives Sèvres (henceforward referred to as AS.) V665, 6 Objets Livrés à Crédit, 9.8., 12.1815, 26.6.1816, 1.1817, 1.1., 1.11.1820, 7.1.1822, 7.1., 19.6.1824, passim; U21 Liasse 2 Brogniart to Blacas, 1.7.1814, Pradel to Brogniart, 1.3.1817.

29. AN. 1 AP. 488 Rapport au Roi, 22.1.1816, 1 AP.696 Blacas to Prince Louis de La Trémoïlle, 14.1.1815. BN. NAF.24062.13: 9.1.1815; O³539.437–431 Rapport au Roi, 26.12.1819; O³2929 Fonds Particuliers du Roi 1815; Emile Gabory, *Les Bourbons et La Vendée*, 1908, passim, gives details of the official positions given to Vendéen families; O³531.145; O³2888 Etats des Fonds Particuliers du Roi, 1814; *Despréaux*, p. 435; BM. Add. Mss. 3825.359 Blacas to Sir Charles Stuart, 8.10.1814 (Clifford); *Jerningham*, II, 54; *Castellane*, I, 389: 15.1.1820 (Balbi).

30. *Guilhermy*, pp. 486–487; Comte de Puymaigre, *Souvenirs*, 1884, p. 179; BVC. FR. 74.117 Bonnay to Richelieu, 4.3.1817; O³2929.24–25 Fonds Particuliers du Roi; AN. O³539.427–431 Rapport au Roi, 26.12.1819; O³2886 Fonds Particuliers du Roi, 1815; O³2888 Dépenses Secrètes, 1824.

31. AN.O³2862 Dépenses Extraordinaires 1817–1820; *Moniteur*, 4.6.1814, p. 615; O³546.312–328 Rapport au Roi, 1820; A Gautier, *Etude sur la Liste Civile en France*, 1884; passim; *Moulard*, III, 568.

32. *Mansel*, p. 413; *Decazes*, p. 53n. Louis to Decazes, 7.9.1818; Joan Wilson, 'Little Gifts Keep Friendship Alive', *Apollo*, CII, no. 161, 7.1965, p. 57; *Langeron*, p. 136, Louis to Decazes, 9.1818; Daudet, 'Le Duc de Richelieu au Congrès d'Aix-la-Chapelle', *Nouvelle Revue*, 1898, p. 405n., Decazes to Richelieu, 17.11.1818; G. Bapst, *Histoire des Joyaux de la Couronne de France*, 1889, p. 620; *Langeron*, p. 246, Decazes to Wellington, 17.9.1819; R. J. Charleston, 'French Porcelain for the Duke', *Apollo*, XCVIII, no. 139, 9.1973, p. 27; AS. V666: 28.3.1823.

33. AN. O³2886 Fonds Particuliers du Roi; O³543.326 Rapport au Roi, 24.5.1822; 546.221 Rapport au Roi, 30.4.1824; 547.10 Rapport au Roi, 3.7.1824; O³2888 Etat des Fonds Secrets du Roi; I am most grateful to P. Girault

de Coursac for information about Louis XVI's debts; *Gautier*, p. 78; 0³533.250 Rapport au Roi, 3.11.1815.

34. AN.O³2862 Dépenses Extraordinaires 1817; *Webster*, I, 251; Paul Mallez, *La Restauration des Finances Françaises après 1814*, 1927, p. 263, cf. *Richelieu*, pp. 27–28, Richelieu to Osmond, 22.4.1816.

35. Alfred de Vigny, *Servitude et Grandeur Militaires* (Nelson, n.d.), p. 160; BN. NAF. 24062.91: 5.5.1814; AAE. 646.145 Blacas to Feltre, 12.3.1815; *Hue*, p. 282; G. Lenôtre, *Martin le Visionnaire*, 1924, p. 89; AN. 0³542.107 Rapport au Roi, 5.9.1821; cf. 0³547.194 Etat des Sommes, 26.9.1824.

37. AN. 0³204, 206, 207, 208, Affaires de la Chambre, passim; 0³205.99 vo., 0³206.63 vo., Demandes d'Audiences, 20.2., 31.7.1816; 0³224 Feltre to Aumont, 27.3.1816; AN. 234 AP. (Papiers du Baron Mounier) 1 police report of 5.5.1820; AAE. 348 (intercepted letters). 242 Peltier to Nettement, 16.11.1820, cf. *Serre*, III, 238, La Boulaye to Serre, 22.3.1820.

38. G. Lenôtre, *Martin le Visionnaire*, p. 77; Chateaubriand, *Mémoires d'Outre-Tombe*, II, 334; *Pouthas*, pp. 87–88, account of 1.6.1815; *Maine de Biran*, I, 223:21.10.1816; *Duchesse d'Orléans*, II, 240: 20.8.1820; Duchesse de Gontaut, *Mémoires*, 1893, p. 193; *Macdonald*, p. 319; *La Rochefoucauld*, X, 272; Lamartine, *Mémoires Inédits*, 1870, p. 243.

39. AN. 107 AP. 14 Journal du Marquis de Galliffet: 2.1821; 0³147, 143 Comte de Nantouillet to Pradel, 8.7.1819; BM. Add. Mss. 47381.62 Lieven Papers, diary of Princess Lieven: 10.1817; *Ferrand*, p. 302.

40. *Broglie*, III, 215, Journal de la Duchesse de Broglie: 27.9.1821; *Raffles*, p. 89; *Langeron*, p. 68, Louis to Decazes, 2.1816.

41. *Corbière*, pp. 369–370; *Decazes*, p. 458, Louis to Decazes, n.d.; *Langeron*, pp. 195, 217, Louis to Decazes, 10.5., 26.10.1818; Jean Fourcassié, *Villèle*, 1954, p. 211, Louis to Villèle, 9.11.1822; the remark about the Marshal's baton is commemorated on a Sèvres vase now at Saint-Cyr.

42. AN. AF V 5, 2: Procès-Verbal of Council, 17.6.1814; Abbé Liautard, *Mémoires* (2 vols. 1844), II, 202; Lamartine, *Histoire de la Restauration*, VI, 187, Louis's account of a ministerial crisis in December 1818.

43. *Saint-Chamans*, 1898, pp. 382–384; AN. 0³414 Ordre of Marquis de Vernon, 2.4.1817; *Langeron*, p. 91, Louis to Decazes, 10.2., 21.5., 11.8.1816; *Decazes*, pp. 460–461, Louis to Decazes, 13, 14.8.1816, 5.6.1817.

44. AN. 359 AP. 82.711-712, 436 Memoirs of Clermont-Tonnerre; cf. *Corbière*, p. 369; AAE. 346.38 Mémoire by Soult, 15.10.1815; Comte de Vaublanc, *Mémoires sur la Révolution de France* (4 vols. 1833), III, 291; *Mansel*, p. 413; AN. 0³2862 Dépenses Extraordinaires, 1819; *Fourcassié*, p. 288; *Perceval*, II, 507.

45. *Mansel*, p. 174, and Chapter V; *Villèle*, II, 437: carnet of 23.2.1821; *Beugnot*, II, 377; Comte Artaud de Montor, *La Vie et les Travaux du Comte d'Hauterive*, 1844, p. 435.

XIII

1. Jean Loubet, 'Le Gouvernement Toulousain du Duc d'Angoulême après les Cent-Jours', *La Révolution Française*, LXIV, 2.1913, pp. 162–163; AAE. 346.22 vo. Marquis de Rivière to Talleyrand, 22.7.1815; III, 61, 85, Comte de Tournon to Barante, Bordeaux 21.8., 30.7.1815; Moulard, Madame de Rémusat, 'Lettres de Province', *Revue de Paris*, 1.8.1902, p. 498, letter of 6.9.15, from Toulouse; AN. AFV5 Berri to Louis XVIII, 8.1815 (telegram); Archives du

Comte Charles de Nicolay, Duc to Duchesse de Lévis, Arras 23.8.1815; A. Bardoux, *La Duchesse de Duras,* p. 184, Chateaubriand to the Duchesse de Duras, 16.8.1815.

2. ADCO. IF 555 Journal de Madame Champagne: 14.1.1816; cf. *Maine de Biran,* I, 155: 29.6.1816.

3. *Beck,* pp. 45–53; Bertier de Sauvigny, *Le Comte de Ferdinand de Bertier,* p. 184; *Fizaine,* pp. 45–46; Daniel P. Resnick, *The White Terror and the Political Reaction after Waterloo,* (Cambridge Mass. 1966), pp. 17, 46–58.

4. ibid, pp. 111–114; *Ribe,* p. 207;

5. *Decazes,* p. 69; Baron de Maricourt, *Idylle et Drame. Georgine de Chastellux et Charles de La Bédoyère,* 1924, p. 188, Journal d'Henri de Chastellux: 25.8.1815; BM. Add. Mss. 51638.120 Madame de Coigny to Lady Holland, 17.1.1816; AN. 197 AP. La Chatre to Louis, early 1816; *Moniteur,* 28.10.1815, p. 1186, 30.10.1815, p. 1194.

6. *Moniteur,* 12.1.1816, p. 49; BVC. FR. 77.33 vo. Richelieu to the Tsar, 1.1816; *Moniteur,* 4., 6.1.1816, pp. 1, 23.

7. Bertier de Sauvigny, *Le Comte Ferdinand de Bertier,* p. 221; idem, *La Restauration,* p. 182; *Fourcassié,* p. 89, Villèle to his father, 4.10.1815; *Moniteur,* 31.10.1816, p. 1199, 4.1.1816, p. 11, 8.4.1816, p. 414, 28.10.1816, p. 1188, 19.1.1816, p. 71, 20.3.1816, p. 325.

8. *Langeron,* pp. 88, 90, Louis to Decazes, 25.1.1816; *Polovtsov,* I, 364, Pozzo to Nesselrode, 18/30.12.1815; *Richelieu,* pp. 5, 9, Richelieu to Osmond, 30.1., 12.2.1816; *Webster,* I, 475; AAE. 647 256 vo. Rapport au Roi, 11.15; Historical Manuscripts Commission, *Report on the Mss. of Earl Bathurst,* 1923, pp. 403–404, Wellington to Bathurst, 4.12.1815; Malmesbury, *Letters,* II, 477, Lady to Lord Malmesbury, 14.7.1816; AN. 37AP. I Louis to Bonnay, 13.1.1804.

9. *Langeron,* p. 58, 66, 99; *Moulard,* III, 114–115.

10. *Richelieu,* pp. 22, Richelieu to Osmond, 25.3.1815; BVC. FR. 96.172 Mémoire par le Duc de Richelieu à sa sortie du Ministère., 7.1.1822; *Vaublanc,* III, 284; Malmesbury, *Letters,* II, 475, Lady to Lord Malmesbury, 11.7.1816; *Castlereagh,* XI, Stuart to Castlereagh, 1.1.1816; *Wellington,* SD, XI, 376, William A'Court to Stuart, 8.4.1814.

11. The account of Martin de Gallardon is based on his dossier in the Police Archives (AN.F.⁷6809, 1615), especially Prefet d'Eure et Loir to Decazes, 16.9.1816, and 'Relation détaillée de l'Entrevue de Thomas Ignace Martin, Laboureur à Gallardon, avec S. M. Louis XVIII', 7.1816; Directeur de Charenton to Decazes, 3.4.1816, Curé de Gallardon to Evêque de Versailles, 23.3.1816 (many pieces of the dossier are missing); and on Lenôtre, *Martin le Visionnaire; La Rochefoucauld,* XII, 520–544, Memoir of 26.3.1834; and Georges de Manteyer, 'Martin de Gallardon, les Montmorency et Louis XVIII', *Journal des Débats,* 11.5.1912, pp. 2–3; cf. ADCOFC. Comtesse to Comte Charles de Damas, 5.5.1816; AN. 300 AP. III 83 ? to Duchesse d'Orléans, 4.4.1816.

12. *Montcalm,* p. 122: 10.1.1816, p. 125: 7.2.1816, p. 131n: 28.2.1816; AD COFC. Comtesse to Comte Charles de Damas, 2.5.1816.

13. *Montcalm,* p. 151: 2.5.1816; cf. BN. NAF. 20280. 49 Richelieu to Decazes, n.d.; Louis Girard, *La Garde Nationale 1814–1871,* 1964, pp. 61–65, 69, 77, 81; AN. O³226 Lettre du Premier Gentilhomme, 1.6.1816; *Decazes,* p. 137, Comte von der Goltz, Prussian Ambassador, to Prince von Hardenberg, Prussian Chancellor, 6.7.1816 (intercepted).

14. *Pallain,* p. 247, Talleyrand to Louis, 25.1.1815; AN. O¹231 Historique du Service de la Chambre, 1816; *Langeron,* p. 94, Louis to Decazes, 15.6.1816.

15. *Richelieu*, p. 39, Richelieu to Osmond, 13.6.1816; BVC. FR.72.9. Alexander I to Richelieu, 29.4.1816; *Decazes*, pp. 138–141, Louis to Decazes 18.8.1816, pp. 142–145; *Langeron*, pp. 102–104; François Guizot, *Mémoires pour servir à l'Histoire de mon Temps* (8 vols. 1858–67), I, 431–436, Note by Lainé; *Decazes*, p. 133, Maine de Biran to Decazes, 20.7.1816.
16. *Barante*, II, 251, Molé to Barante, 20.7.1816; *Guizot*, I, 407, Montesquiou to Guizot, 8.6.1816; *Ferrand*, p. 174; AN.359 AP.82.333 Souvenirs of Clermont-Tonnerre; Baron d'Haussez, *Mémoires* (2 vols. 1896), II, 48; *Maine de Biran*, I, 190; 2.8.1816; *Pouthas*, pp. 136–137, note by Guizot; *Serre*, II, 491, Serre to Decazes, 18.12.1819.
17. *Decazes*, pp. 142–145; *Langeron*, pp. 103–105; BN.NAF.20280.62, Richelieu to Decazes, n.d.; *Montcalm*, p. 187: 10.9.1816.

XIV

1. *Polovtsov*, I, 610, Pozzo to Nesselrode, 8.9.1816; *Langeron*, p. 110; *Beck*, p. 59; ADCOFC. Louis to Charles de Damas, 25.9.1816; Daudet, *La Police Politique*, 1912, p. 167, Louis to Decazes, n.d.; *Montcalm*, p. 265: 15.5.1817; cf. Chateaubriand, *Correspondance Générale*, I, 313, Chateaubriand to Duchesse de Duras, 5.1817.
2. *Decazes*, pp. 455, 499, Louis to Decazes, 1817, 1818; *Molé*, III, 184, Louis to Molé, 18.3.1818; *Maine de Biran*, I, 223: 21.10.1816; H. Baumont, 'Stanislas de Girardin, Prefet de la Côte d'Or', *La Révolution Française*, LV, 9.1908, p. 196n; *Ribe*, p. 275; *Decazes*, pp. 259–260, Louis to Artois, 29.1.1818, p. 445, Louis to Decazes, 9.3.1817; Daudet, *Joseph de Maistre et Blacas*, pp. 329, 350, Maistre to Blacas, 26.11.1817, 23.8.1818.
3. AAE. 347.45 Observations by Ferrand, 17.7.1817; *Molé*, IV, 185; *Decazes*, p. 453, Louis to Decazes, 17.1.1817.
4. *Decazes*, p. 475, Louis to Decazes, 16.3.1819; p. 446, Louis to Decazes, 9.3.1817; p. 464, Louis to Decazes, 9.1816.
5. *Vitrolles*, II, 451–458; Dr. Cabanès, *Les Morts Mystérieuses de l'Histoire* (2 vols. 1901), II, 271, 286–288, police reports of 16.11.1816, 2.8.1817; *Moulard*, III, 175–178, Tournon to Decazes, 6.8., 8.11.1817; *Ribe*, p. 278.
6. *Decazes*, pp. 181–196; BN.NAF. 20280.110, 120 vo. Richelieu to Decazes, n.d; *Pasquier*, IV, 244–248; *Wellington*, SD, XII, 600, Wellington to Castlereagh, 17.7.1818; James K. Kieswetter, in 'Etienne-Denis Pasquier, The Last Chancellor of France', *Transactions of the American Philosophical Society*, LXVII, pt. 1, 1977, p. 86, who has gone through the papers of Pasquier, Minister of Justice in 1818, believes there was a plot.
7. *Richelieu*, p. 107, Richelieu to Osmond, 17.4.1817; *Beck*, pp. 64–65; *Collins*, pp. 21–28.
8. *Duvergier de Hauranne*, IV, 16; Henri Contamine, *Diplomatie et Diplomates à l'Epoque de la Restauration*, 1970, p. 64; 'Lettres de l'Empereur Alexandre 1er et de Madame de Staël', *Revue de Paris*, 1.1.1897, p. 21, Madame de Staël to Alexander I, 14.12.1816; Michel Denis, *Les Royalistes de la Mayenne et le Monde Moderne*, 1977, pp. 130–132; AN.40 AP.18 Decazes to Beugnot, 24.10.1817; *Leulliot*, III, 203.
9. *Ribe*, pp. 297–298, Procureur-Général of Lyon to Minister of Justice, 7.3.1820; *Leulliot*, III, 147; *Moulard*, III, 176; *Fizaine*, p. 130; Comte A. de Rougé, *Le Marquis de Vérac et ses Amis*, 1890, 208, Richelieu to Vérac, 21.3.1819; Jean Tulard, 'Du Paris Impérial au Paris de 1830 d'après les Bul-

letins de Police' *Bulletin de la Société de l'Histoire de Paris et de l'Ile-de-France*, 1969, p. 171, police report of 10.1.1819; Paul Fauchille, 'Comment se préparaient les Elections en 1818', *Revue de Paris*, 1.7.1902, pp. 160–162; *Le Constitutionnel*, 5.7.1818.

10. *Langeron*, pp. 93, 125, Louis to Decazes, 17.4., 16.5.1816; Robert Marjolin, 'Troubles provoqués en France par la Disette de 1816–1817', *Revue d'Histoire Moderne*, VIII, 1933, pp. 424, 438.

11. Vidalenc, *Les Demi-Solde*, 1955, p. 26; J. Monteilhet, *Les Institutions Militaires de la France. 1814–1924*, 1926, pp. 7–9; *Langeron*, p. 174, Louis to Decazes, 9.1.1818; *Almanach Royal*, 1817, 1819; *Rougé*, p. 188, Richelieu to Vérac, 9.2.1819.

12. André Nicolle, *Comment la France a payé après Waterloo*, 1929, p. 189; *Wellington*, SD, XII, 486, Louis to Wellington, 19.4.1818; Daudet, 'Le Duc de Richelieu au Congrès d'Aix-la-Chapelle', *Nouvelle Revue*, 1898, pp. 606, 204, Louis to Decazes, 1.11.1818, Louis to Richelieu, 11.11.1818.

13. *Decazes*, pp. 458, 478, Louis to Decazes, 8.18, Decazes to Louis, 16.8.1817; BN.NAF.20280.122 vo. Richelieu to Decazes, 1817; Bertier de Sauvigny, *Metternich*, I, 183.

14. Daudet, op. cit., *Nouvelle Revue*, 1898, pp. 411, 413, Richelieu to Decazes, 27.10.1818; *Montcalm*, p. 320; 14.1.1818; Lamartine, *Histoire de la Restauration*, VI, 166–167: throughout this chapter all quotations from Lamartine's *Histoire de la Restauration* quote Louis's account of the ministerial crisis of December 1818.

15. *Lamartine*, VI, 164, 169–170; BVC. FR.78.12, 66, Molé to Richelieu, 2.11.1818, Richelieu to Madame de Montcalm, 13.11.1818.

16. *Langeron*, p. 216, Louis to Decazes, 22., 24.10.1818; BVC.FR.78.78. Louis to Richelieu, 15.11.1818; *Decazes*, p. 297; Jean de Boislisle, 'L'Abbé de Montesquiou', *Annuaire-Bulletin de la Société de l'Histoire de France*, 1927, p. 249, Louis to Montesquiou, 12.1.1817; *Decazes*, pp. 373, 380, Louis to Decazes, 11., 10.12.1819.

17. ibid, pp. 174, 178; Daudet, *La Police Politique*, p. 255; BM. Add. Mss. 51638.168, 170, Madame de Coigny to Lady Holland, 30.10.1817, 23.3.1818; *Langeron*, p. 225, Louis to Decazes, 5.12.1818.

18. *Lamartine*, VI, 184–186; BVC. FR.78.135–136, Richelieu to Louis, 23.12.1818 (copy); *Langeron*, p. 226, Louis to Decazes, 23.12.1818; *Decazes*, p. 304, Louis to Comtesse Decazes, 23.12.1818.

19. *Molé*, IV, 175; *Montcalm*, p. 346: 10.2.1819; *Lamartine*, VI, 187–189; *Fourcassié*, p. 156; *Decazes*, p. 300, Louis to Decazes, 22.12.1818.

20. *Wellington*, SD (New Series, 8 vols. 1857–1880, henceforward referred to as SDNS), I, 5–6, Castel-Cicala to Wellington, 6.1.1819; *Castellane*, I, 362–363: 25–27.12.1818; *Polovtsov*, III, 1–10, Pozzo to Nesselrode, 29.12./1.1.1819; *Montcalm*, p. 342; 10.2.1819; *Molé*, IV, 166; BVC. FR.78.93 vo., Decazes to Richelieu, 17.12.1818; ibid 79.4 Richelieu to Decazes, 12.1.1819.

21. *Lamartine*, VI, 189; *Decazes*, pp. 308, 475–476, Louis to Decazes, 27.12.1818; *Wellington*, SDNS, I, 6, Castel-Cicala to Wellington, 1.1819.

22. *Duvergier de Hauranne*, V, 307; BN.NAF.20280.235 Decazes to Richelieu, 1818; *Langeron*, pp. 179–180, Louis to Decazes, 7.9., 6.10.1818; *Gay de Vernon*, p. 461; *Moniteur*, 7.1.1819; p. 25; *Richardson*, pp. 72, 75; *Collins*, p. 24; ADCOFC Roger to Charles de Damas, 15.9.1819; *Baumont*, pp. 209–210, 219.

23. *Decazes*, p. 478, Louis to Decazes, 27.12.1818; *Langeron*, p. 216, Louis to Decazes, 24.10.1818, pp. 193–201, 156, Louis to Decazes, 18.11.1818; *Decazes*, p. 400, Louis to Decazes, 13.2.1820.

24. *Langeron*, p. 253, letter of late 1819; *Decazes*, p. 352; *Ferrand*, pp. 208–209; J. P. G. Viennet, *Journal*, 1955, p. 42: 7.3.1819; L. Spach, *Oeuvres Choisies* (5 vols. 1866–71), I, 502; André Brandt, 'Rapp et les Libéraux de Mulhouse', *Revue d'Alsace*, XCIV, 1955, pp. 145–157.

25. BN.NAF.14714.15 Abbé Soldini, 'Entretien avec Monseigneur le Dauphin'; *Langeron*, p. 244, Louis to Decazes, 6.6.1819; *Beugnot*, II, 330; AN.40 AP.17.366; AAE.348 passim and to 28 ? J. H. Ward, M. P., 16.3.1820; *Duvergier* de Haurane, IV, 17; BVC.FR.78.143, Richelieu to Madame de Montcalm, 25.12.1818; *Molé*, III, 392n; *Decazes*, pp. 467, 473, 370, Louis to Decazes, 20.2.1817, 13.10.1818, 4.10.1819.

26. *Decazes*, pp. 476, 156, 471, Louis to Decazes, 27.12.1818, 18.9.1816, 1818; *Langeron*, p. 132, Louis to Decazes, 13.10.1817; *Decazes*, p. 324, Louis to Decazes, 27.6.1819; pp. 469–471, p. 316, Louis to Decazes, 18.1.1818, 20.1.1819.

27. *Lamartine*, VI, 187; Bertier de Sauvigny, *Metternich et Decazes d'après leur Correspondance, 1816–1820*, 1953, p. 86, Decazes to Metternich, 19.5.1819; *Nesselrode*, VI, 61, Comtesse to Comte de Nesselrode, 18.4.1819; *Decazes*, p. 327.

28. *Molé*, III, 83; Bertier de Sauvigny, *La Restauration*, p. 304; Abbé Feret, *La France et le Saint Siège* (2 vols. 1911), II, 69, letter of 25.4.1816; Philippe Sagnac, 'Le Concordat de 1817. Les Rapports de l'Eglise et de l'Etat sous la Restauration', *Revue d'Histoire Moderne*, VII, 1905–6, pp. 191, 447, 444–445.

29. *Decazes*, pp. 350, 399, 411, Louis to Decazes, 26.2.1819, 10.2., 14.2.1820; Daudet, *La Police Politique*, based on the Archives Decazes, contains copies of the Prussian Ambassador's despatches to Berlin until May 1820, three months after Decazes's fall from power; A. Marquiset, *Une Merveilleuse (Mme. Hamelin)*, 1909, pp. 209ff; J. B. Salgues, *Les Mille et Une Calomnies* (2 vols. 1822), I, 65, Morning Chronicle, 18.8.1818, cf. *Langeron*, p. 168, Louis to Decazes, 6.1818; p. 142, Louis to Decazes, 6.12.1817; Fauchille, 'Les Elections en 1818', pp. 166–167; Adeline Daumard, *La Bourgeoisie Parisienne de 1815 à 1848*, 1964, pp. 560–561; *Nettement*, V, 164.

30. *Portal*, p. 72; *Gay de Vernon*, p. 476; *Decazes*, p. 373; *Fourcassié*, pp. 166–167, Carnet of Villèle: 20, 23/24.12.1819; *Nettement*, V, 217; *Langeron*, pp. 248, 253, Louis to Decazes, 23.12.1819; *Decazes*, pp. 391, 398, Louis to Decazes, 2.1., 10.2.1820.

31. J. Lucas-Dubreton, *Louvel le Régicide*, 1925, pp. 15, 40, 50, and passim.

32. *Decazes*, pp. 429, 432, Louis to Decazes, 17., 18.2.1820, p. 414, Prefet de Police to Decazes, 15.2.1820; *Duvergier de Hauranne*, V, 379–388, 393; BM. Add. Mss. 41533.14, Stuart to Castlereagh, 21.2.1820 (copy); *Decazes*, p. 426.

33. *Nettement*, V, 278; *Decazes*, p. 435, Louis to Decazes, 19.2., 16.2.1820, p. 439; *Duvergier de Hauranne*, V, 393; *Langeron*, p. 265, Louis to Decazes, 21.2.1820.

XV

1. *Beck*, p. 73; *Collins*, p. 3; Daudet, *L'Ambassade du Duc Decazes*, p. 44, Decazes to Louis, n.d.

2. Alan B. Spitzer, *Old Hatreds and Young Hopes. The French Carbonari against the Bourbon Restoration* (Cambridge Mass. 1971), p. 37; Edgar Leon Newman, 'The Blouse and the Frock Coat: the Alliance of the Common People of Paris with the Liberal Leadership and the Middle Class during the Last Years

of the Bourbon Restoration', *Journal of Modern History* (XLVI), 3.1974, pp. 38–39; Comte d'Hérisson, *Un Pair de France Policier*, 1894, pp. 209, 218–220, Anglès to Mounier, 5.6.1820, Siméon to Louis, 6.6.1820.

3. *Moniteur*, 20.6.1820; *Spitzer*, pp. 212–225, Antonin Debidour, *Le Général Fabvier*, 1904, p. 162.

4. Hérisson, *Pair de France*, p. 187, Anglès to Mounier, 10.4.1820; BVC. FR. 95.21–35 Partie du Réquisitoire du Procureur-Général dans l'affaire du 19 aôut 1820 dont la Cour n'a pas autorisé l'impression; *Serre*, IV, 88, Richelieu to Serre, 18.8.1820; *Moniteur*, 3.8.1822, p. 1144.

5. *Duchesse d'Orléans*, II, 249–250: 29.9.1820; *Moniteur*, 30.9.1820, p. 1327; Duc de Broglie, *Souvenirs*, II, 182, Journal de la Duchesse de Broglie, 4.10.1820; *Moulard*, III, 216; AN. 234 AP. 2 police reports of 19., 21.10., 4.11.1820.

6. AN. 359 AP. 99 Marquis to Marquise de Clermont-Tonnerre, 13.12.1820; Daudet, *L'Ambassade du Duc Decazes*, pp. 29, 34–35, 54, 173, 179, 195; *Corbière*, p. 378.

7. Chateaubriand, *Mémoires d'Outre-Tombe*, II, 418, Richelieu, Mathieu de Montmorency to Chateaubriand, 20.12.1820; *Fourcassié*, p. 455, Artois to Villèle, 18.8.1820; Hérisson, *Pair de France*, p. 399, Richelieu to Mounier, 18.3.1821; Charles Brifaut, *Souvenirs d'un Académicien* (2 vols. 1921), I, 362; Duchesse de Broglie, *Lettres*, 1896, p. 74, letter to Comtesse de Castellane, 25.11.1820; Daudet, *L'Ambassade du Duc Decazes*, p. 184, Louis to Decazes, 1.1821; *Pailhes*, p. 188, Chateaubriand to Duchesse de Duras, 12.1820.

8. *Nettement* V, 623, Carinet of Vilèle, ?1821; Bertier de Sauvigny, *Le Comte Ferdinand de Bertier*, p. 312; *Viennet*, pp. 58: 5.7.1821; *Ribe*, p. 303; *Moulard*, III, 225, Tournon to Mounier, 20., 21, 7.1821; AN. 349 AP. (Montesquiou papers) I Liste des Personnes Présentées à S. M. l'Empereur et Roi; Edouard Perret, *La Dernière Favorite des Rois de France. La Comtesse du Cayla*, 1937, p. 18; Daudet, *L'Ambassade du Duc Decazes*, p. 232; Lucas-Dubreton, *Louis XVIII*, 1952, p. 214n; Chateaubriand secretly longed for a Correspondance with Louis: see *Correspondance Générale*, III, 94, Chateaubriand to Duchesse de Duras, 24.5.1822.

9. *La Rochefoucauld*, VII, 406, Madame du Cayla to La Rochefoucauld, 25.8.1820; *Marquiset*, p. 234; Archives X Duchesse d'Escars to Madame de Podenas, 19.5.1821; *Perret*, p. 78.

10. *La Rochefoucauld*, VII, 450, 382 Madame du Cayla to La Rochefoucauld, n.d.; Daudet, *L'Ambassade du Duc Decazes*, pp. 195, 219, Louis to Decazes, 14., 22.3.1821; BVC. FR. 96.218 vo.; Bertier de Sauvigny, *Le Comte Ferdinand de Bertier*, pp. 316–317; *Villèle*, II, 495; *La Rochefoucauld*, VI, 360, 567, La Rochefoucauld to Madame du Cayla.

11. *Nettement*, III, 533; *Villèle*, II, 474, Villèle to Madame de Villèle, 3.12.1821; AN. 234 AP. 2 police report of 26.11.1821; BVC. FR. 96.216 'Mémoire' by Richelieu on the dissolution of his ministry, 2.1.1822; ibid 83.147 diary of Baron Mounier, 28.11.1821; *Villèle*, II, 477, Carnet: 8.12.1821.

12. BVC. FR. 83.203 Richelieu to Madame de Jumilhac, n.d.; *Nettement*, III, 664, Carnet of Villèle, 10.12.1821; *Villèle*, II, 477, 483, 493, Villèle to Madame de Villèle, 9, 13.12.1821; BVC. FR. 96.149 diary of Mounier, 13.12.1821; AN. 359 AP. 99 Marquis to Marquise de Clermont-Tonnerre, 16.12.1821.

13. *Beck*, p. 37; AN. 359 AP. 84.61 Notes Sténographiées of Clermont-Tonnerre. 2.9., 1.12.1822; ibid, 100 Marquis to Marquise de Clermont-Tonnerre, 24.9.1822; Bertier de Sauvigny, *Metternich et la France*, II, 586–588; BN. NAF.

14098.167 vo. Duchesse Mathieu de Montmorency, 'Mes pensées'; *Grand-maison*, pp. 36, 38.

14. AN. 359 AP. 100 Marquis to Marquise de Clermont-Tonnerre, 24.9.1822; ibid 84. 62 Notes, 10.1., 19.9.1823; *Villèle*, V, 177, 232, 236, 257, 306, Villèle to Angoulême, 1., 16., 17., 24.7., 11.8.1823; *Wellington*, SDNS, I, 646, Wellington to Canning, 12.12.1822; AN. 359 AP. 84.62 Notes, 19.9.1823; *Duchesse d'Orléans*, II, 15–16: 12.10., 17.11.1823.

15. Philipp von Neumann, *Diary*, ed. E. Beresford Chancellor (2 vols. 1928), I, 89: 11.1.1822; *Fourcassié*, p. 252, Artois to Villèle, 2.8.1823; *Villèle*, III, 288, 308, IV, 467 Artois to Villèle, 6.3., 4.4.1823, 20.3.1824, *La Rochefoucauld*, VI, 360.

16. *La Rochefoucauld*, VIII, 94, 130, 180, La Rochefoucauld to Madame du Cayla, cf. VII, 420, *Villèle*, V, 59, Artois to Villèle, 30.3.1824, ibid, 124.

17. *La Rochefoucauld*, VIII, 161, 244, VI, 371, 495, VII, 461, La Rochefoucauld to Madame du Cayla; VI, 488 Artois to La Rochefoucauld, 24.2.1823.

18. *La Rochefoucauld*, VIII, 93, 150, 173, 181, 142, 240, 213, 158, La Rochefoucauld to Madame du Cayla; *Villèle*, V, 123: IV, 467, Artois to Villèle, 18.10.1823.

19. AN. 359 AP. 84.63, Notes of Clermont-Tonnerre: 29.12.1823, 22.1.1824; *Villèle*, IV, 594n, Carnet of 12.12.1823; *La Rochefoucauld*, VIII, 112; 169, 179–180, VII, 571–572 La Rochefoucauld to Madame du Cayla; VI, 503, La Rochefoucauld to Villèle, 21.10.1823; BN. NAF. 4760; *La Rochefoucauld*, VII, 473, 469, Madame du Cayla to La Rochefoucauld.

20. *La Rochefoucauld*, VI, 428, La Rochefoucauld to Madame Bourdon; *Fourcassié*, p. 477, Artois to Villèle, 4.1.1824; Henry Wellesley, first Lord Cowley, *Diary and Correspondence*, 1930, Cowley to Canning, Vienna 6.7.1823; *La Rochefoucauld*, VI, 251; *Corbière*, pp. 372–373; *Castellane*, I, 459: 2.5.1823.

21. *La Rochefoucauld*, VII, 449, Madame du Cayla to La Rochefoucauld; Lucas-Dubreton, *Louis XVIII*, 1952, pp. 221–223; *Castellane*, II, 11: 22.12.1823; AN. 359 AP. 100 Marquis to Marquise de Clermont-Tonnerre, 15.5.1825.

22. *Spitzer*, p. 232, 249, 259; *Fourcassié*, p. 213.

23. *Fourcassié*, p. 241, Duchesse de Duras to Villèle, 27.12.1822; Chateaubriand, *Correspondance Générale*, III, 365, 312, 315, Chateaubriand to Louis XVIII, 1.9.1822, to Villèle, 28.12.1822 to Duchesse de Duras, 31.12.1822; *Debidour*, pp. 238–240; *Villèle*, III, 318, Bellune to Villèle, 7.4.1823; Stendhal, *Courrier Anglais*, IV, 51: 1.2.1825.

24. Niccolo Rodolico, *Carlo Alberto, Principe di Carignano* (Firenze 1931), p. 393, Alfieri di Sostegno to Pralormo, 11.2.1824.

25. *Richelieu*, p. 154, Richelieu to Osmond, 19.2.1818; Daudet 'Le Duc de Richelieu au Congrès d'Aix-la-Chapelle', *Nouvelle Revue*, p. 207, Louis to Decazes, 28.10.1818; William Spence Robertson, *France and Latin American Independence* (Baltimore 1939), pp. 154, 251, 167, 267, 209; Harold Temperley, 'French Designs in Spanish America in 1820–5', *English Historical Review*, CLVII, January 1925, pp. 35, 40, 42; Edward Howland Tatum jr., *The United States and Europe. 1815–1823*, (Berkeley Cal. 1936), pp. 257, 260; AN. 359 AP. 88 Instructions Secrètes of Clermont-Tonnerre to Capitaine de Grivel, 11.1823; AAE. Brésil 2 Chateaubriand to Comte de Gestas, 27.11.1823, Pedro I to Louis XVIII, 12.8.1822, Louis to Pedro I, 15.7.1823; Denyse Dalbian, *Dom Pedro*, 1956, p. 144; E. Driault et M. L'Heritier, *Histoire Diplomatique de la Grèce* (5 vols. 1925–26), I, 156, 241–242; AN. 359 AP. 100 Marquis to

Marquise de Clermont-Tonnerre, 25.9.1822; AAE. 679.43 Louis to Talleyrand 26.11.1814.
26. *Mallez*, pp. 264–265, 274–275, 229; *Monteilhet*, p. 11; David Porch, *Army and Revolution. France 1815–1848*, 1974, pp. 11–13; *Fizaine*, p. 193; *Moulard*, III, 542; AN. 40 AP. 19 Richelieu to Beugnot, 3.9.1820; *Leulliot*, III, 261, 415; AN. 40 AP. 21. 334–335 'Voyage dans le Midi de la France'; BM. Add. Mss. Holland House Papers 51635.190 vo. La Fayette to Lord Holland, 14.4.1830; Daudet, 'Quelques Lettres de Louis XVIII', *Nouvelle Revue*, CXVI, 1.1899, p. 33, Louis to Decazes, 3.9.1819.
27. *Henrion*, II, 353, 473; *Polovtsov*, II, 120–121, Pozzo to Nesselrode, 31.3/ 12.4.1817; AN. 359 AP. 84.63 Notes of Clermont-Tonnerre, 17.9.1824; *Fourcassié*, p. 218, Foy to Villèle, 29.9.1822.
28. *Castellane*, I, 16: 16.1.1824; *Cabanès*, II, 357–361, Procès-Verbaux de l'Ouverture et de l'Embaumement du Corps du Feu Roi Louis XVIII, 17.9.1824; *Ribes*, II. 431–440: AN. 107 AP. 41 Journal du Marquis de Galliffet 1821–24; *Villèle*, V, 122; Chateaubriand, *Congrès de Vérone. Guerre d'Espagne* (2 vols. 1838), I, 243, 376; *Damas*, II, 53.
29. AN. 359 AP. 84.61 Notes of Clermont-Tonnerre, 21.12.1822; *Villèle*, V, 15, 123; AN. 359 AP 84.63 Notes of Clermont-Tonnerre, 7.6.1824; Archives X Duchesse d'Escars to Madame de Podenas, 5., 7., 19.6.1824; Madame Charles Lenormant, ed., *Souvenirs et Correspondance tirés des Papiers de Madame Recamier* (2e Edition, 2 vols. 1860), II, 112, 116, Doudeauville to Madame Recamier, 9.6., 4.7.1824; *Fourcassié*, p. 477, Artois to Villèle, 4.1.1824; Bertier de Sauvigny, *Metternich et la France*, II, 901.
30. AN. 107 AP. 41 Journal du Marquis de Galliffet, 1.9.1824; *Lenormant*, II, 130, Doudeauville to Madame Recamier, 1.9.1824; Marquis d'Aragon, 'Le Duc Decazes et les Dix Dernières Années de la Restauration', *Revue des Questions Historiques*, 1.1934, p. 585, Decazes to Aragon, n.d.; *Duchesse d'Orléans*, II, 52–53: 25., 31.8.1824; *Villèle*, III, 4, Orléans to Villèle, 2.9.1824.
31. *La Rochefoucauld*, VII, 489 Madame du Cayla to La Rochefoucauld; *Henrion*, II, 479–480; *Damas*, II, 54n.
32. 'Bulletins de la Dernière Maladie et de la Mort du Roi Louis XVIII', *Revue de l'Histoire de Versailles* (Versailles 11.1903), pp. 315–320; *Aragon*, p. 587, Decazes to Aragon, 17.9.1824; AN. O³527 Dreuz-Brézé, 'Relation de la Pompe Funèbre du Roi Louis XVIII'; *Cabanès*, II, 357–361, 'Proces-Verbaux de l'Ouverture et de l'Embaumement du Corps du Feu Roi Louis XVIII'.
33. *Moniteur*, 15.9.1824, pp. 1252–3; Archives X letter from an officer of the Gardes du Corps, 19.9.1824; Comte de Rumigny, *Souvenirs*, 1921, p. 165, diary for 16.9.1824; *Duchesse d'Orléans*, II, 62: 16.9.1824.

Conclusion

1. *Nesselrode*, V, 192–193, Talleyrand to Alexander I, 13.6.1814; AN. 107 AP. 14 Journal du Marquis de Galliffet, 16.9.1824, cf. *Moniteur*, 23.9.1824, p. 1285; AN. 349 AP. 13 Correspondance du Comte Anatole de Montesquiou, Comte to Comtesse Anatole de Montesquiou, 22.9.1824; Robert Marquant, *Thiers et le Baron Cotta*, 1959, p. 177, Thiers to Cotta 24.9.1824; ADCO. 1F 563 Journal de Madame Champagne, 17., 19.9.1824; Archives X Duchesse d'Escars to Marquise de Podenas 19.9.1824.
2. Stendhal *Le Rouge et le Noir*, ed. Michel Crouzet (Garnier-Flammarion 1964), p. 384; Agatha Ramm, *Germany 1789–1919*, 1967, p. 204; Emilio

Crosa, 'La Concessione dello Statuto', *Memoire dell'Istituto Giuridicio della R. Universita di Torino*, Serie II, XXX, pp 68, 72 Chateaubriand, *Le Roi est Mort: Vive le Roi*, 1824, p. 14.

3. ABR. 'Rectifications de quelques Passages des Mémoires de Madame la Duchesse de Gontaut concernant Mr. de Blacas' written in a copy of the 1855 edition of her Mémoires; Luigi Bader, *Les Bourbons de France en exil à Gorizia*, 1977, p. 369, Blacas's will, 15.11.1839; Marquis d'*Aragon*, pp. 587, Decazes to d'Aragon 8.10.1824, 1.1829; Daudet, *L'Ambassade du Duc Decazes*, p. 267; *Fourcassié*, p. 293, J. Lucas-Dubreton, *La Princesse Captive*, 1924, p. 200.

4. BN. NAF. 24062. 91, 387. 5.5.1814; 13, 19.8.1814; Chateaubriand, *Le Roi est mort: Vive le Roi*, 1824, p. 13.

Sources

Louis XVIII wrote to Talleyrand in 1814 that '*Verba volant, scripta manent*'. But in his case, ironically for someone who was so aware of the power of the written word, this is not wholly true. I have discovered that it is impossible to gain access to the private archives which contain an enormous proportion of Louis XVIII's papers and correspondence. However, I have been assured that Ernest Daudet, who did gain access, was perfectly accurate in his quotations from them. Since he wrote and quoted at enormous length, I hope that my failure to gain access to the original material will not prove too serious. I am profoundly grateful to the following people who allowed me to consult their archives: Dr. Jean Gautier, Comte François de Nadaillac, Comte Charles de Nicolay, Monseigneur le Comte de Paris and Conte Ludovico Lucchese-Palli. Furthermore, I gratefully acknowledge the gracious permission of Her Majesty the Queen for permission to consult the Royal Archives at Windsor.

I would also like to express my gratitude to all who helped me to write this book; particularly to the Marquis de Brantes, to Père de Bertier de Sauvigny, who kindly allowed me to consult his filing-cabinet on the Restoration, to Dr. Hugh Collingham, to Dr. W. B. Taylor, to Veronica Bowring, who typed the manuscript with great understanding, and to Michael Weinstein, who gave invaluable assistance with the maps. I am deeply indebted to all those, too numerous to name, whose kindness and hospitality made it possible for me to do research in Paris. Above all I am grateful to M. and Mme. Girault de Coursac, who have been as stimulating, original and helpful in conversation as they are in their writings.

Manuscript Sources

1. Archives Départementales de la Côte d'Or (ADCO), Dijon.
IF 555–563 Journal de Madame Champagne, 1814–1824
Fonds Commarin (FC) Papers of Comte Charles de Damas.

2. Archives du Ministère des Affaires Etrangères (AAE)

afПоказ

France, Fonds Bourbon: Papers of the Royalist Government in exile
588, 589, 590, 605, 606, 607, 613–617, 621, 630
Political papers from the Restoration 674, 346, 347, 646, 647, 679, 681, 690, 691, 699, 721
Brésil 2 Diplomatic Correspondence 1821–1824
Pologne 323 Despatches from Warsaw 1801–1804
Prusse Mémoires et Documents 9 Negotiations for Louis XVII's renunciation 1803
Sardaigne 251, 255 Correspondance Interceptée 1771–1774.

3. Archives Historiques du Ministère de la Guerre (AHMG.), Vincennes
XAD 10–12 Papers of the Maison Militaire 1814–1824
XAE 6, 14 Papers of the Garde Royale 1814–1824

4. Archives Nationales (AN)
ABXIX 196 Papers of the Comte de La Chapelle
AB XIX 781 Journal de la Cassette de Monsieur pour le Quartier de Juillet
AE I 5 Letters of Louis XVIII to Gustavus IV Adolphus
AE V 5 Letters of the Comte de Provence to the Marquis de Lambert
AF V 1–5 Papers of the Secrétairerie d'État 1814–1815
BB³⁰82 Doss. Favras
BB³⁰191 Papers of the Abbé de Montesquiou 1814
C 145 Papers of the Liste Civile of Louis XVI 1790–1792
F⁴2680 Finances of Monsieur 1783

F⁷Papers of the Ministry of Police
4290 Police reports of Royalist activity
4336–7 Police reports of Royalist activity
4347, 3 Papers of Louis XVI shown to Louis XVIII
4730 Letters of Marie-Joséphine to Madame de Gourbillon 1789–1791
6255 Papers of the Marquis de Lambert
6371 Doss. Delamarre
6809, 1615 Doss. Martin de Gallardon

O³ Papers of the Maison Civile and the Liste Civile, 1814–1824 20, 73, 74, 90, 194, 204–208, 211, 228, 231, 234, 388, 414, 489, 519, 526–529, 530, 531, 533–546, 628, 821, 1875, 1892, 1222, 1984–1986, 2008, 2888, 2862, 2929
605, 606, 627 Political Papers, 1814–1815
2565, 2601, 2667, 2680, 2681 Papers of the Emigration.
R⁵ Papers of the Household and Appanage of the Comte de Provence 1, 19, 26–28, 33, 42, 44, 47, 48, 56, 144, 147, 459, 478, 523.
Archives Privées (AP)
1 AP. 487, 488, 696, Papers of the Prince de La Trémoïlle
34 AP. 3, 4, 6, 6 bis, 7, 11, 11 bis Correspondence of the Prince de Condé and the Duc de Bourbon

37 AP. 1, 2 Papers of the Marquis de Bonnay
40 AP. 7–20 Papers of Comte Beugnot
60 AP. 1, 2 Papers of the Maison de Monsieur
86 AP. 8 1, 2 Papers of the Marquis de Jaucourt
107 AP. 14 Journal of the Marquis de Galliffet 1821–1824
161 AP. Papers of the Comte de Serent
197 AP. Letters to the Duc de La Chatre
198 AP. 2–7 Papers of Cardinal de La Fare
224 AP. 1 Journal of the Comte de Broval
234 AP. 1, 2 Papers of Baron Mounier
279 AP. 9–18 Correspondence of Maréchal Macdonald with his daughter
300 AP. III 1, 8, 16, 20, 21, 22, 83, 123 Papers of the Duc and Duchesse d'Orléans
306 AP. 22–31 (mi. 14–21) Papers of the Maréchal de Castries
349 AP. 1, 13 Papers of the Montesquiou family
359 AP. 58, 61, 62, 63, 82, 84, 88, 99, 100 Papers of the Marquis de Clermont-Tonnerre

5. Archives of Schloss Brünnsee, Austria (ABR. prop. Conte Ludovico Lucchese Palli)
Album Verde. Letters to the Duchesse de Berri
Journal de la Duchesse de Berri 1820–1821

6. Archives of the Manufacture de Sévrès (AS)
V665–666 Objets Livrés à Crédit 1815–1824
U 21 Correspondence 1814–1820

7. Archives X (name withheld at request)
Papers of the Duc and Duchesse d'Escars 1814–1824

8. Archivio di Stato Torino, Lettere Ministri Francia (ATLMF.)
212–215 1771–1774
240–242 1814–1815
246–248 1820–1821

9. Bibliothèque Historique de la Ville de Paris
Mss. 1013 Letters from Paris to Madame Girard 1815

10. Bibliothèque de l'Arsenal
Mss. 5385 Catalogue des Livres provenant de chez Louis Stanislas Xavier Capet, *émigré*.

11. Bibliothèque Nationale. Nouvelles Acquisitions Françaises (BN. NAF)
4125 Diary of an anonymous left-wing Deputy, 1789–1790
4760 Registre de Correspondance de Madame du Cayla, 1823–1824
5215 Notes by the Comte de Provence, 1787

11771 Journal de Madame de Chastenay, 1815
14098 Papers of Mathieu de Montmorency
14714–5 Abbé Soldini, Conversations avec Monseigneur le Dauphin
15022, 15035–6 Papers of the Comte and Abbé de Montesquiou
20280 Lettres et Correspondance du Duc de Richelieu, 1815–1820
21475 Catalogue des Livres du Cabinet de Monsieur
22408–22414, 22419–22420 Papers of the Maison de Monsieur
22738 Notes by the Comte de Provence, 1792
23129 Papers of the Comte de Cély
24062 Procès-Verbaux des Séances du Conseil du Roi du 17 avril 1814 au 10 fevrier 1815.
Mss. Périgord 105 Papers of the Comte d'Hautefort

12. Bibliothèque Victor Cousin. Fonds Richelieu (BVC. FR)
70–88, 93–97, 100–106 Papers of the Duc de Richelieu

13. British Museum (BM.) Add. Mss.
7972, 8041, 8042, 8055 Puisaye Papers (with contributions from the papers of the Comte d'Antraigues)
20708 Papillon de La Ferté 'Description et Relation . . . du Mariage de Louis Stanislas Xavier de France avec Marie-Joséphine-Louise Princesse de Savoie'
26669 Papers of the Comte de Bruges, 1813
27548 Madame de Tourzel to Louis XVIII, 1795
33793 Portraits du Roi et de la Famille Royale, 1813
37876 Finances of the Emigration
38256, 38261, 38364 Liverpool Papers
41648 Thomas Clifford 'Memoirs relating to the Intercourse of the Writer with His Most Christian Majesty Louis XVIII'
47245, 47381 Lieven Papers
51635, 51638 Holland House Papers
58899 Letters of Lord Buckingham to Lord Grenville
60399 Fouché to Wellington

14. Institut, Ancien et Nouveau Fonds 2190. 48–54 Notes of Monsieur at the Assemblée des Notables, 1787

15. Musée Carnavalet, Réserve des Estampes, Série Historique, 1814–1824

16. Public Record Office (PRO)
FO 26/17 despatches from Brussels 1791
27/45 despatches from Verona 1796–96
27/76–105 Correspondence between the English Government and Louis's Government in exile 1800–1814
28/6 despatches from Genoa 1793–1794
67/14–15 despatches from Turin 1793–1794
95/630–632 Calonne Papers 1787–1795

PC 1/124–131 Calonne Papers
            5417 Calonne Papers

17. Royal Archives, Windsor (RA.)
18795–21596 Papers of the Prince Regent, 1811–1814
45072 Duchesse d'Angoulême to Duke of Clarence, 1814.

Bibliography

Unless otherwise stated, all works in French are published in Paris and
all works in English are published in London. Items with an asterisk
contain material by Louis XVIII.

Aillaud, L, 'Passage à Nîmes de Monsieur, Frère de Louis XVI, en
1777' *Nouvelle Revue du Midi*, pp. 77–85, 1925.

Alibert, M, *Physiologie des Passions*, 2 vols, Seconde Edition, 1827

Angivillier, Comte d', *Mémories*, Copenhagen, 1933

Angrand, Pierre, *Le Comte de Forbin et le Louvre en 1819*, 1975

Anon. 'Bulletins de la Dernière Maladie et de la Mort du Roi Louis
XVIII' *Revue de L'Histoire de Versailles* Versailles, 11.1903
pp. 315–320

Départ Manqué de Monsieur par la Surveillance du Peuple,
1791

*Des Bourbons et des Puissances Etrangères au Mois de Mars
1815*, 1815

*Eclaircissements sur le Livre Rouge en ce qui concerne
Monsieur, Frère du Roi*, Imprimerie du Monsieur, 1790

*Journal of a Tour in France, Switzerland and Lombardy . . .
during the Autumn of 1818*, 2 vols, 1821

*Liste de Toutes les Personnes qui composent le Premier Musée
Autorisé par le Gouvernment sous la Protection de Monsieur
et de Madame*, 1785

Livre Rouge, 1790

Troisième Registre des Dépenses Secrètes de la Cour, 1793

Mementoes, Historical and Classical of a Tour in France,
1824

*Memorandums of a Residence in France in the Winter of
1815–16*, 1816

*Papiers Saisis à Bareuth et à Mende, Département de la
Lozère*, An X

*Procés-Verbal et Observations Présentes au Roi par les
Bureaux de l'Assemblée des Notables*, 2 vols, 1787

*Réflexions Patriotiques sur les Entreprises de Quelques
Ministres de France adressées à Monsieur Frère du Roi*, 1788.

*Relation Concernant les Evénemens qui sont arrivés à un
Laboureur de la Beauce dans les Premiers Mois de 1816*, 1817

Statuts et Règlements du Premier Musée autorisé par le

Gouvernement sous la Protection de Monsieur et de Madame, établi en 1781 par M. Pilatre de Rozier, 1784

Antonetti, Guy *Louis-Philippe* 1994

Aragon, Marquis d', 'Le Duc Decazes et les Dix Dernières Années de la Restauration' *Revue des Questions Historiques*, 1934, pp. 582–600 *Archives Parlementaires*, Première Série (Reprint Leichtenstein 1969)

Arnault, A.V., *Souvenirs d'un Sexagénaire*, 4 vols, 1833

Arneth, A von, et Flammermont, J, *Correspondance Secrète du Comte de Mercy–Argenteau avec L'Empereur Joseph II et le Prince de Kaunitz*, 2 vols, 1889

Arneth, A von, et Geffroy, A, ed., *Correspondance Secrète entre Marie-Thérèse et le Comte de Mercy-Argenteau avec les Lettres de Marie-Thérèse et de Marie-Antoinette*, 3 vols, 1874

Artaud de Montor, Comte, *La Vie et les Travaux du Comte d'Hauterive*, 1844

A(uguis), P. R., *Correspondance de Louis XVIII*, avril 1815

Aspinall, A, ed., *The Letters of King George IV 1812–1830*, 3 vols 1939
    The later Correspondance of George III, 5 vols, 1962–1970

Avaray, Comte d', 'Louis XVIII expulsé de Russie en 1801' *Feuilles d'Histoire*, 1.11.1909 pp 400–409, 516–525
    Exposé des faits relatifs aux Libelles publiés par M. de Puisaye dans les mois de Janvier et Fevrier 1809, 1809

Bacourt, A. ed., *Correspondance entre le Comte de Mirabeau et le Comte de La Marck pendant les Années 1789, 1790 et 1791*, 3 vols, 1851

Bader, Luigi, *Les Bourbons de France en exil à Gorizia*, 1977

Bagot, Josceline, *George Canning and His Friends*, 2 vols, 1909

Bailleu, Paul, *Preussen and Frankreich von 1795 bis 1807*, 2 vols, Leipzig, 1881–1887

Baillie, Hugh Maurray, 'Etiquette and the Planning of State Apartments in Baroque Palaces' *Archaeologia*, CI, 1967, pp. 169–201

Balisson de Rougemont, M. N., *Le Rodeur Français ou les Moeurs du Jour*, 6 vols, 1816–21

Balzac, *Le Cabinet des Antiques*. 2 vols, 1839
    Splendeurs et Misères des Courtisanes, ed. A. Adam, 1958

Bapst, Germain, *Histoire des Joyaux de la Couronne de France*, 1889
    ed., 'Lettres d'un Attaché de la Légation de Saxe à Paris 1788–90' *Revue de la Révolution*, 1884, pp. 161–171, 'Documents' pp. 24–31, 65–74, 33–40

Barbey, Jean, *Le Conseil des Ministres sous la Restauration*, 1937

Bardoux, A., *La Duchesse de Duras*, 1898
    Madame de Custine, 1888

Barentin, M. de, *Mémoire Autographe . . . sur les Derniers Conseils du Roi Louis XVI*, 1844

Barrère, M., *Conduite des Princes de la Maison de Bourbon durant la Révolution, l'Emigration et le Consulat*, 1835

Baumont, H., 'Stanislas de Girardin, Prefet de la Côte d'Or' *La Révolution Française*, LV, 9.1908, pp. 193–235

Beauvau, Maréchale de, *Souvenirs*, 1872

Beck, Thomas D., *French Legislators 1800–1834*, 1974

Bergeron, Louis, *L'Episode Napoléonien*, 1969

Bernard de La Frégeoliere, Général de, *Mémoires*, 1881

Berthoud, D., *Le Général et la Romancière*, Neuchâtel, 1959

Bertier, Ferdinand de, *Souvenirs Inedits d'un Conspirateur* 1990

Bertier de Sauvigny, G. de., *Le Comte Ferdinand de Bertier et l'Enigme de la Congragation*, 1948
    Metternich et Decazes d'aprés leur Correspondance, 1816–1820, 1953
    Metternich et la France après le Congrès de Vienne, 3 vols, 1968–72

Bessborough, Earl of, *Lady Bessborough and her Family Circle*, 1940

Beugnot, Comte, *Mémoires*, 2 vols, 1868

Biré, Edmond, *Victor Hugo et la Restauration*, 1869

(Blessington, Countess of) *Journal of a Tour through the Netherlands to Paris in 1821*, 1822

Bluche, François, *Les Honneurs de la Cour*, 2 vols, 1957

Bluche, Frédéric, *Le Plébiscite des Cent-Jours*, Genève, 1974

Boislisle, A. de, ed., *Choix de Lettres adressées à Mgr. de Nicolay*, Nogent-le-Rotrou, 1875

*Boislisle, Jean de, 'L'Abbé de Montesquiou, Ministre de la Restauration' *Annuaire-Bulletin de la Société de l'Histoire de France*, 1927, pp. 224–261

Bombelles, Marquis de, *Journal*, vol I, Génève, 1977

*Bord, Gustave, *Autour du Temple*, 3 vols, 1912
    *Bonaparte, Louis XVIII. Leurs Relations' *Revue de la Révolution*, XI, 1888, pp. 189–221

*Bouillé, L. J. A. de, *Souvenirs*, 3 vols, 1908–11

*Boulay de La Meurthe, Comte, *Correspondance du Duc d'Enghien*, 4 vols, 1904-13

Bourrienne, M. de, *Mémoires*, 10 vols, 1829

Boyer, Ferdinand, 'Louis XVIII et la Restitution des Oeuvres d'Art Confisquées sous la Révolution et l'Empire' *Bulletin de la Société de l'Histoire de l'Art Français, 1965*, pp. 200–207

Brandt, André, 'Rapp et les Libéraux de Mulhouse' *Revue d'Alsace*, XCIV, 1955, pp. 145–157

*Brette, A., *Recueil de Documents Relatifs à la Convocation des États-Généraux de 1789*, 4 vols, 1890–1915

Brienne, Comte de, and Mgr. de Briennes, *Journal de l'Assemblée des Notables de 1787*, ed. Pierre Chevalier, 1960

Brifaut, Charles, *Souvenirs d'un Académicien*, 2 vols, 1921

Bringmann, Wilhelm, *Louis XVIII. von Frankreich im Exil. Blankenburg 1796–1798* Frankfurt am Main 1995

Broglie, Duc de, *Souvenirs*, 4 vols, 1886

Broglie, Duchesse de, *Lettres*, 1896

Broglie, Gabriel de, 'Le Sacre de Louis XVI' *Revue des Deux Mondes*, 1974, pp. 41–57

Browning, Oscar, ed., *Despatches from Paris 1784–1790*, 2 vols, Camden Third Series, XVI, XIX, 1909–1910

*Bruel, A, 'Les Chartreux de Paris et le Comte de Provence' *Bulletin de la Société Historique de Sixième Arrondissement de Paris*, 1900, pp. 70–77

Bruguière, Michel, *La Première Restauration et son Budget*, Genève, 1969

*Buchez, Philippe et P. Roux, *Histoire Parlementaire de la Révolution Française*, 40 vols, 1834–38

*Burke, Edmund, *Correspondence*, 10 vols, Chicago and Cambridge, 1958–70

Cabanès, Dr. *Les Morts Mystérieuses de l'Histoire*, 2 vols, 1901

*Cadoudal, Georges de, *Georges Cadoudal et la Chouannerie*, 1887

Campenon, M., *Essai de Mémoires ou Lettres sur la Vie, le Caractère et les Ecrits de J. F. Ducis*, 1824

Carré, Henri, *La Noblesse de France et l'Opinion Publique au XVIIIe. Siècle*, 1920

Castellane, Maréchal de, *Journal*, 5 vols, 1896–97

Castle, Egerton, ed., *The Jerningham Letters*, 2 vols, 1896

Castlereagh, Viscount, *Memoirs and Correspondence*, 12 vols, 1848–53

*Castries, Duc de, *Le Maréchal de Castries*, 1956 *
        Louis XVIII, 1969

Caudrillier, G., *L'Association Royaliste de l'Institut Philanthropique*, 1908
        La Trahison de Pichegru, 1908

Caulaincourt, Général de *Mémoires*, 3 vols, 1933

*Chabannes, Comte de, *Histoire de la Maison de Chabannes*, 6 vols, 1893-95

Chadwick, Owen, *Catholicism and History*, Cambridge, 1978

Chantemesse, Robert, *Le Roman Inconnu de la Duchesse d'Abrantès*, 1927

Charleston, R. J., 'French Porcelain for the Duke *Apollo*, XCVIII, 9. 1973, pp. 27–33

Chastenay, Madame de, *Mémoires*, 2 vols, 1896–97

Chateaubriand, *Correspondance Générale*, ed. Louis Thomas, 5 vols, 1912–24
        Congrès de Verone: Guerre d'Espagne, 2 vols, 1838
        Le Roi est Mort: Vive le Roi! 1824
        Mémoires d'Outre-Tombe, 3 vols, 1951
        Mémoires, Lettres et Pièces Authentiques touchant la Vie et la Mort de S.A.R. Monseigneur Charles-Ferdinand d'Artois, Fils

        de France, Duc de Berry, 1820

        Réflexions Patriotiques sur Quelques Écrits du Jour et sur les Intérêts de Tous les Français, 1814

Chaussinand-Nogaret, Guy, _La Noblesse au XVIIIe Siècle_, 1975

Chuqet Arthur, 'De L'Ile d'Elbe au Golfe Juan' _Revue de Paris_, 1. 1923, pp. 225–253

        Napoléon à Grenoble' _Revue de Paris_, 1., 15. 11. 1917, pp. 356–386

        Les Guerres de la Révolution, 11 vols, 1886–1896

        Lettres de 1815, 1911

*Cleray, Edmond, _L'Affaire Favras_, 1932

*Clermont-Gallerande, Marquis de, _Mémoires_, 3 vols, 1826

Clouzot, H., et Follot, Ch., _Histoire du Papier Peint en France_, 1935

Colchester, Lord, _Diary and Correspondence_, 3 vols, 1861

Cole, Hubert, _Fouché, The Unprincipled Patriot_, 1971

Collins, Irene, 'Liberalism and the Newspaper Press during the French Restoration 1814–1830' _History_, XLVI, 1961, pp. 17–32

        The Government and the Newspaper Press in France, 1814–1881, Oxford, 1959

*Commune, Conseil-Général de la, _Exposé des Faits qui se sont passés dans la Séance du 22 Fevrier 1791_, 1791

Condé, Prince de, _Journal d'Emigration_, ed. Comte de Ribes, 1923

*Condé, Maison de, _Mémoires_, 2 vols, 1820

Constant, Benjamin, _Journal Intime_,. ed., Jean Mistler Monaco, 1946

*Contades, Comte de, _Coblentz et Quiberon. Souvenirs, 1885 Émigrés et Chouans_, 1895

*Contamine, Henri, _Diplomatie et Diplomates à l'Epoque de la Restauration_, 1970

        Metz et la Moselle de 1814 à 1870, 2 vols, Nancy, 1932

Contenson, Ludovic, 'Un Agent Royaliste en 1814' _Revue de Paris_, 1. 7. 1910, pp. 145–162, 15. 7. 1910, pp. 315–332

Corbière, Comte de, 'Souvenirs d'un Ministre de Louis XVIII' _Revue des Deux Mondes_, 1. 4. 1966, pp. 364–379

Corti, Egon Conte, _Ludwig I of Bavaria_, 1938

*Costa de Beauregard, Marquis de, ed., _Souvenirs . . . du Cte. A. de La Ferronays_, 1900

Cottin, Paul, _Toulon et les Anglais en 1793_, 1898

Creevey, Thomas, _The Creevey Papers_, 2 vols, 1903

*Crétineau-Joly, J., _Histoire des Trois Derniers Princes de la Maison de Condé_, 2 vols, 1867

*Croce, Benedetto, 'Il Duca di Serra-Capriola et Giuseppe de Maistre' _Archivio Storico per le Provincie Napoletane_, XLVII, 1922, pp. 313–365

Crosa, Emilio, 'La Concessione dello Statuto' _Memorie dell' Istituto Giuridicio della R. Universita di Torino_, Serie II, XXX, 1936, pp. 10–94

Croÿ, Duc de, _Journal Inédit_, 4 vols, 1905–1906

Dakin, Douglas, *Turgot and the Ancien Régime*, 1939

Dalbian, Denyse, *Dom Pedro*, 1956

Dallas, Gregor, *1815: The Roads to Waterloo*, 1995

Damas, Baron de, *Mémoires*, 2 vols, 1923

Dard, Emile, *Le Comte de Narbonne*, 1943

Darnton, Robert, 'Reading, Writing and Publishing in Eighteenth-Century France: a Case Study in the Sociology of Literature' *Daedalus*, C. 1971, pp. 214–256

Daudet, Ernest, *Coblentz*, n.d.

      'Fiançailles d'Exil' Revue des Deux Mondes, 15, 12, 1904, pp. 834–870

      Histoire de l'Emigration, 3 vols, 1904–1907

      Joseph de Maistre et Blacas, 1908

      L'Ambassade du Duc Decazes en Angleterre, 1910

      L'Ami du Roi' *Revue des Deux Mondes*, 15. 11. 1904, pp. 241–276

      La Police Politique, 1912

      'Le Duc de Richelieu au Congrès d'Aix-la-Chapelle' Nouvelle Revue, CXIV, 1898, pp. 193–213, 400–415, 603–620

      Les Bourbons et la Russie pendant la Révolution Francaise, n.d.

      'Les Dernières Années de l'Emigration' Revue des Deux Mondes, 15. 7. 194, pp. 273–308, 1. 8. 1904, pp. 631–666

      'Louis XVIII et Bonaparte' Le Correspondant, 25. 2. 1905, pp. 666–694, 10. 3. 1905, pp. 849–881

      'Louis XVIII et le Comte d'Artois' Revue des Deux Mondes, 1. 2. 1906, pp. 559–595, 15. 2. 1906, pp. 824–860

      'Louis XVIII et Madame Atkyns' Le Temps, 21. 5. 1905, p. 3

      Madame Royale, 1912

      Nouveaux Recits des Temp Révolutionnaires, 1910

      'Quelques Lettres de Louis XVIII' Nouvelle Revue, CXVI, 1. 1899, pp. 26–45

      Récits des Temps Révolutionnaires, 1908

      'Souvenirs de l'Emigration' Revue Hebdomadaire, 7. 1906, pp. 385–410, 8. 1906, pp. 137–162, 392–415

      'Un Mariage Manque' Le Correspondant, 10. 11. 1905, pp. 446–475

Daumard, Adeline, *La Bourgeoisie Parisienne de 1815 à 1848*, 1964

Debidour, Antonin, *Le Général Fabvier*, 1904

Decours, Catherine, *La Dernière Favorite. Zoe du Cayla le grand amour de Louis XVIII* 1993

Demombrynes, Gabriel, *Le Départ du Comte de Provence pour Coblentz*, 1905

Denis, Michel, *Les Royalistes de la Mayenne et le Monde Moderne*, 1977

Denys, Abbé A., *Mémoires de l'Abbé Liautard*, 2 vols, 1844

Despatys, Baron, *Un Ami de Fouché*, 1911

Déspreaux, Mlle. E., 'Louis XVIII en Courlande' *Le Monde Slave*, IX, 9. 1928, pp. 403–422

Des Rioux de Messimy, M., *Justification des Griefs imputés ou Roi et à la Famille Royale*, juillet 1815

*Doisy-Martin, M., *Manuscrit Inédit de Louis XVIII*, 1839

Driault, E. et L'Heritier, M., *Histoire Diplomatique de la Grèce*, 5 vols, 1925–26

*Droz, E., ed., *Le Comte de Modène et ses Correspondants*, 2 vols, 1942

*Dubois-Corneau, Robert, *Le Comte de Provence à Brunoy*, 1909

Duckworth, Colin, *The D'Antraigues Phenomenon. The Making and Breaking of a Revolutionary Royalist Espionage Agent* Newcastle upon Tyne 1986

*Dugon, Marquis, *Au Service du Roi en Exil*, 1968

Dugourc, M., 'Autobiographie' *Nouvelles Archives de l'Art Français*, 1877, pp. 367–371

*Du Lac, R., *Le Général Comte de Précy*, 1908

Durand, Yves, *Les Fermiers-Généraux au XVIIIe Siècle*, 1971

Dusquenoy, Adrien, *Journal sur l'Assemblée Constituante*, 3 vols, 1894

Dutourd, Jean, *Rivarol*, 1963

Duvergier de Hauranne, P., *Histoire du Gouvernement Parlementaire en France*, 10 vols, 1857–1871

Egret, Jean, *La Prérévolution Française*, 1962
        'La Seconde Assemblée des Notables' *Annales Historiques de la Révolution Française*, XXI, 1949, pp. 193–228

Ellis, George, *History of the late Revolution in the Dutch Republic*, 1789

*England, Rev. Thomas R., *Letters from the Abbé Edgeworth to His Friends*, 1818

*Espinchal, Comte d', *Journal*, 1912

Estrée, Paul d'et Callet, Albert, *La Duchesse d'Aigullon*, 1912

Eugène, Prince, *Mémoires et Correspondance Politique et Militaire*, 10 vols, 1858–60

Fauchille, Paul, 'Comment se préparaient les Elections en 1818' *Revue de Paris*, 1. 7. 1902, pp. 155–174

Une Chouannerie Flamande au temps de l'Empire (1813–1814), 1905

Favras, Thomas de Mahy de, *Testament de Mort*, 1790

*Feret, Abbé, *La France et le Saint Siège*, 2 vols, 1911

Ferrand, Comte, *Mémoires*, 1896

Feuillet de Conches, Baron F.S., *Louis XVI, Marie-Antoinette et Madame Elizabeth*, 6 vols, 1864–73

Filleul, Paul, *Le Duc de Montmorency-Luxembourg*, 1939

Firmin-Didot, G., *Royauté ou Empire*, 1898

Fizaine, Simone, *La Vie Politique dans la Côte d'Or sous Louis XVIII*, 1931

Fleury, Comte, *Les Dernières Années de la Marquise de Bombelles*, 1906

Fontaine, Pierre Francois Léonard, *Journal 1799–1853*, 2 vols. 1987

Forgues, Eugène, *Le Dossier Secret de Fouché*, 1908

Forster, Robert, 'The Survival of the French nobility during the French Revolution' *Past and Present*, 7. 1967, pp. 71–86

Foster, Vere, *The Two Duchesses*, 1898

*Fourcassié, Jean, *Villèle*, 1954

Franklin, Robert, *Lord Stuart de Rothesay*, 1993

Frappaz, Z., *Vie de l'Abbé Nicolle*, 1857

*Fryer, W.R., *Republic or Restoration in France?*, Manchester, 1965

Fugier, André, *Napoléon et l'Espagne*, 2 vols, 1930

Gabory, Emile, *Les Bourbons et la Vendée*, 1923

Gaffarel, Paul, *Dijon en 1814 et en 1815*, Dijon, 1897

    'Les Complots de Marseille et de Toulon (1813-1814)' *Annales de la Société d'Études Provençales*, Aix-en-Provence, 4 ev, Année, 9. 1907, pp. 273–306, 11. 1907, pp. 337–378

*Gaulot, Paul, *Un Complot sous la Terreur*, 1889

*Gautherot, Gustave, *Un Gentilhomme de Grand Chemin. Le Maréchal de Bourmont*, 1926

Gautier, A., *Étude sur la Liste Civile en France*, 1884

Gautier, Jean, 'Inventaire de Propriétés du Comte de Provence à Brunoy' *Bulletin de la Société Historique et Archaéologique de Corbeil, d'Etampes et du Hurepoix*, Corbeil, 82e Année, 1976, pp. 21–49

Gay de Vernon, Baron, *Vie du Maréchal Gouvion Saint-Cyr*, 1856

*Geffroy, A., *Gustave III et la Cour de France*, Deuxième Edition, 2 vols, 1867

Geffroy de Grandmaison, G.A., *L'Expédition Française d'Espagne en 1823*, 1928

Géraud, Edmond, *Un Témoin des Deux Restaurations*, 1893

Girard, Louis, *La Garde Nationale. 1814–1871*, 1964

Girault de Coursac, P., *L'Education d'Un Roi: Louis XVI*, 1972

Girault de Coursac, Paul et Pierrette, *Enquête sur le Procès du Roi Louis XVI*, 1982

    Louis XVI et Marie Antoinette: vie conjugale – vie politique, 1990

Glagau, Hans, *Die Französische Legislative und der Ursprung der Revolutions kriege*, Berlin, 1896

Godechot, Jacques, *The Counter Revolution*, 1972

Gontaut, Duchesse de, *Mémoires*, 1893

Gould, Cecil, *Trophy of Conquest*, 1964

Gourgaud, Baron, *Journal Inédit*, 2 vols, 1899

Gramont, Duc de, Journal '*Assemblée Génerale de la Sociéte d'Histoire Contemporaine*', 1908, pp. 15–30

Granville, Lord, *Private Correspondence*, 2 vols, 1916
Greer, Donald, *The Incidence of the Terror during the French Revolution*, Harvard, 1935
    The Incidence of Emigration in the French Revolution, Harvard, 1951
Greig, James, ed., *The Diaries of a Duchess*, 1926
Greville, Charles, *Memoirs*, 8 vols, 1938
Grunwald, Constantin de, *Stein*, 1940
*Guibaud, Louis, *Auget de Montyon*, 1909
*Guilhermy, Baron de, *Papiers d'Un Émigré*, 1886
Guizot, François, *Mémories pour Servir à l'Histoire de mon Temps*, 8 vols, 1858–67

Hampson, Norman, *A Social History of the French Revolution*, 1964
Harcourt, Edward William, *The Harcourt Papers*, 14 vols, Oxford, 1880–1905
Hardman, John, *French Politics 1774–1789*, 1995
Hardy, S. B., *Mes Loisirs*, 1912
Haussez, Baron d', *Mémoires*, 2 vols, 1896
Hauterive, Comte, d', *La Police Secrète du Premier Empire*, 5 vols, 1908–65
Henrion, Baron, *Vie de M. Frayssinous Evêque d'Hermopolis*, 2 vols, 1844
Herisson, Comte d', *Autour d'une Révolution*, 1888
    Un Secrétaire du Cabinet de Napoléon Ier, Seconde Edition, 1894
    Un Pair de France Policier, 1894
Herriot, Edouard, *Madame Recamier et ses Amis*, 2 vols, 1905
Higgs, David, *Ultraroyalism in Toulouse*, Baltimore, 1973
Hippeau, C., *Le Gouvernement de Normandie au XVIIe et au XVIIIe Siècle*, 9 vols, Caen, 1863-69
Historical Manuscripts Commission, *Report on the Manuscripts of Earl Bathurst*, 1923; *The MSS of J.B. Fortescue esq. preserved at Dropmore*, 10 vols, 1892–1927;
(Hobhouse, John Cam) *The Substance of Some Letters written from Paris*, 2 vols, 1816
Hortense, Reine, *Mémoires*, ed. Jean Hanoteau, 3 vols, 1927
*Hue, Baron, *Souvenirs*, 1903
Hustin, A, 'Madame de Balbi' *Nouvelle Revue*, 1. 7. 1905, pp. 39–52, 1. 8. 1905, pp. 323–336, 1. 9. 1905, pp. 43–54, 1. 10. 1905, pp. 313–327
    Le Luxembourg. Son Histoire Domaniale, Architecturale, Décorative, et Anecdotique, 2 vols, 1910
Hyde de Neuville, Baron, *Mémoires et Souvenirs*, 3 vols, 1892
Hyslop, Béatrice, *L'Appanage de Philippe Egalité*, 1964

Jackson, Lady, ed., *The Bath Archives*, 2 vols, 1873
Jaucourt, Comte de, *Correspondance avec le Prince de Talleyrand pendant le Congrès de Vienne*, 1905

Jean, Réne, 'Madame de Mirbel' *Gazette des Beaux-Arts*, 1. 2. 1906, pp. 131–147

Jouanne, René, *Cahiers de Doléances . . . de la Ville d'Alençon*, Alençon, 1929

Jouy, Etienne de, *Guillaume le Franc-Parleur*, 2 vols, 1815–16

Kaufman, Ruth, 'François Gérard's Entry of Henri IV into Paris' *The Burlington Magazine*, CXVIII, 12. 1975, pp. 796–802

Kieswetter, James K., 'Metternich and the Bourbon Succession' *East European Quarterly*, VI, 9. 1972, pp. 363–375
        'Etienne-Denis Pasquier, the Last Chancellor of France' *Transactions of the American Philosophical Society*, LXVII, 1977, part 1, pp. 1–190

Kowström, Baron de, *Le Comte de Fersen et la Cour de France*, 2 vols, 1878

*(Konigfeld, Madame de) 'Louis XVIII à Blankenfeld d'apres les Documents Inédits' *Intermediare des Chercheurs et des Curieux*, II 1913, pp. 418–423, 434–441, 481–484

Laborde, Alexandre de, *Quarante-huit heures de Garde au Château des Tuileries*, 1816

Lacour-Gayet, G., *Talleyrand*, 4 vols, 1928–34
        Autour de Louis XVIII, 1926

La Fayette, Général de, *Mémoires, Correspondance et Manuscrits*, 6 vols, 1837–38

*La Force, Duc de, *Dames d'Autrefois*, 1933

La Maisonfort, Marquis de, *Mémoires d'un Agent Royaliste*, 1998

*Lamartine, Alphonse de, *Histoire de la Restauration*, 8 vols, 1851–52
        Mémoires Inédits, 1870

Langeron, Roger, *Decazes Ministre du Roi*, 1960
        Madame Royale, 1959
        Un Conseiller Secret de Louis XVIII, Royer-Collard, 1956

*Lanne, A. D., *Une Officine Royale de Falsification*, Troisième Edition, 1912

Lapierre, A., *Campagne des Émigres dans l'Argonne*, Sedan, 1911

Larpent, F. S., *Private Journal*, Second Edition, 2 vols, 1853

La Rochefoucauld, S. de, Duc de Doudeauville, *Mémoires*, 15 vols, 1861-64

Latouche M. de, 'Souvenirs de 1815' *Revue d'Alsace*, LV, 1904, pp. 212–221, 314–321, 650–6, 655

La Trémoïlle, Duc de, *Mes Parents*, 1901

*Lebon, André, *L'Angleterre et l'Emigration Française*, 1882

*Lecoq, Marcel, *La Conspiration du Marquis de Favras*, 1955

Lefebvre, Georges, ed., *Recuiel de Documents relatifs aux . . . États Généraux*, 2 vols, 1955–62

Lefebvre de Behaine, Comte, *Le Comte d'Artois sur la Route de Paris*, 1921

474 *Louis XVIII*

Lefuel, Hector, *Georges Jacob*, 1923

Le Gallo, Emile, *Les Cent-Jours*, 1924

Legrand, J. G. et Landon, C. P., *Description de Paris et de ses Édifices*, 2 vols, 1818

Leighton, Rachel, ed., *Correspondence of Charlotte Grevlle, Lady Williams Wynn*, 1920

*Le Menuet de la Juganière, Baron, *Le Chouan Carlos Soudat*, 1932

Lenôtre, G., *Le Marquis de La Rouerie et la Conjuration Bretonne*, 1899
    Martin le Visonnaire, 1924
    Monsieur de Charette, 1924
    Two Royalist Spies of the French Revolution, 1924

Lenormant, Madame Charles, *Souvenirs et Correspondance tirés des papiers de Madame Recamier*, Seconde Édition, 2 vols, 1860

Lescure, M–A de, *Correspondance Secrète Inédite sur Louis XVI, Marie Antoinette, La Cour et la Ville*, 2 vols, 1866

Lévis, Duc de, *Souvenirs-Portraits suivis de Lettres Intimes de Monsieur Comte de Provence au Duc de Lévis*, 1993

Lévis, Duc de, *Souvenirs et Portraits*, 1872

Lewis, Gwynne, *The Second Vendée*, 1978

Ley, Francis, *Madame de Krüdener et son Temps*, 1961

*Lhomel, Georges de, *Jean Pierre Antoine Comte de Béhague*, Abbeville, 1907

Lhôte de Selancey, A., *Des charges de la Maison Civile des Rois de France*, 1847

Liederkerke-Beaufort, Comte de, 'Souvenirs d'un Page du Comte de Provence' *Revue de Paris*, 5, 1952, pp. 56–84

Livet, Georges, *Recueil des Instructions Données aux Ambassadeur et Ministres de France XXVIII (Electorat de Trèves)*, 1966

Longford, Elizabeth, *Wellington. The Years of the Sword*, 1969

Lormier, Docteur, *Histoire des Régiments des Gardes D'Honneur*, 1924

Loubet, Jean, 'Le Gouvernement Toulousain du Duc d'Angoulême après les Cent Jours' *La Révolution Française*, LXIV, 2. 1913, pp. 149–165, 4. 1913, pp. 337–366

Louis XV, *Lettres à son Petit fils l'Infant Ferdinand de Parme*, ed. Philippe Amiguet, 1938

Louis XVI, *Réflexions sur Mes Entretiens avec M. le Duc de La Vauguyon*, 1851

Louis XVIII, *Correspondance Privée*, 1836
    *'Deux Lettres inédites' *Revue de l'Histoire de Versailles*, 4e Année, 11. 5. 1902, pp. 158–160
    Discours de Monsieur à la Commune, 1790
    *'Les Devoirs d'un Roi' *Feuilles d'Histoire*, 1. 9. 1909, pp. 221–234
    'Lettres 'Nouvelle Revue Retrospective, XVI, 1. 1902, pp. 1–24, 121–141

*Lettres et Instructions au Comte de Saint-Priest, 1845
*'Lettres Inédites' *Revue Hebdomadaire*, XIII, 12. 1905, pp. 138–158, 275–293, 385–407
'Notes de Lecture' *Le Correspondant*, CCXXXVIII, 10. 1. 1910, pp. 24–47
'Réflexions Historiques sur Marie-Antoinette' *Revue des Deux Mondes*, 15. 7. 1904, pp. 241–263
Relation d'un Voyage à Bruxelles et à Coblentz (1791), 1822
'Un Voyage de Vérone à Riegel en 1796' *Feuilles d'Histoire*, 1. 5. 1809, pp. 373–383

Lubersac, Abbé de, *Le Citoyen Conciliateur . . . Idées Sommaires, Politiques et Morales sur le Gouvernement Monarchique de la France*, 1788
Vues Politiques et Patriotiques sur l'Administration des Finances de la France . . . Dédiées à Monsieur, Frère du Roi, 1787

Lucas, Colin, 'Nobles, Bourgeois and the French Revolution' *Past and Present*, LX, 8. 1973, pp. 84–126

Lucas-Dubreton, J., *Louvel le Régicide*, 1925
*Louis XVIII, 1925

Lyons, Marvin, *France under the Directory*, 1972

Macdonald, Maréchal, *Souvenirs*, 1892
Mackesy, Piers, *The Strategy of Overthrow*, 1974
Madelin, Louis, *Fouché*, 2 vols, 1900
Maine de Biran, M. F. P. G., *Journal*, 3 vols, Neuchâtel, 1954–57
Maistre, Joseph de, *Lettres et Opuscules Inédites*, 2 vols, 1851
Mallet du Pan, *Mémoires et Correspondance*, ed. A. Sayous, 2 vols, 1851
Mallez, Paul, *La Restauration des Finances Françaises après 1814*, 1927
*Malmesbury, Earl of, *Diaries and Correspondence*, 4 vols, 1844
Letters, 2 vols, 1870
Mansel, Philip, *The Court of France 1814–1830*, unpublished Ph.D Thesis, University of London 1978
Manteyer, Georges de, 'Martin de Gallardon, Les Montmorency et Louis XVIII' *Journal des Débats*, 11. 5. 1912
Maricourt, Baron de, *Idylle et Drame. Georgine de Chastellux et Charles de la Bédoyère*, 1924
Marion, Marcel, *La Vente des Biens Nationaux pendant la Révolution avec Étude Spéciale des Ventes dans les Départements de la Gironde et du Cher*, 1908
Marjolin, Robert, 'Troubles provoqués en France pendant la Disette de 1816–1817' *Revue d'Histoire Moderne*, VII, 1. 1933, pp. 423–440
Marmont, Maréchal, *Mémoires*, 9 vols, 1857
Marquant, Robert, *Thiers et le Baron Cotta*, 1959

Marquiset, A., *Une Merveilleuse (Mme. Hamelin)*, 1909

Masson, Frédéric, *Napoléon et sa Famille*, 15 vols, 1908–19

*Maury, Cardinal, *Correspondance Diplomatique et Mémoires Inédits*, 2 vols, Lille, 1891

McManners, John, *French Ecclesiastical Society under the Ancien Régime*, 1960

Mercer, General C., *Journal of the Waterloo Campaign*, 2 vols, 1870

Mercier, L. S., *Tableau de Paris. Nouvelle Édition Corrigée d'Augmentée*, 8 vols, Amsterdam, 1782

Metternich, Prince de, *Mémoires, Documents et Écrits Divers*, 8 vols, 1880–84

Michel A., ed., *Correspondance de Mallet du Pan avec la Cour de Vienne*, 2 vols, 1884

Michelet, Edmond, *Rome*, 1896

*Mitchell, Harvey, *The Underground War against Revolutionary France*, Oxford, 1965

  'Resistance to the Revolution in Western France' *Past and Present*, LXIII, 5. 1974, pp. 94–131

*Molé, Comte L. M., *Le Comte Molé . . . Sa Vie Ses Mémoires*, 6 vols, 1922–30

Monciel, Marquis Terrier de, 'Note Historique sur les Evénements de l'Année 1814' *Annales Franc-Comtoises*, X, 4. 1869, pp. 274–298

Montbel, Comte de, 'Les Derniers Moments de Louis XVIII' *Le Correspondant*, CCXCVI, 10. 9. 1924, pp. 763–768

Montcalm, Marquise de, *Mon Journal Pendant le Premier Ministère de mon Frère*, 1935

Monteilhet, J., *Les Institutions Militaires de la France 1814–1924*, 1926

Montépin, X. de, ed., *Souvenirs Intimes et Anecdotiques d'un Garde du Corps des Rois Louis XVIII et Charles X*, 5 vols, 1857

Moore, John, *A View of Society and Manners in France, Switzerland and Germany*, 2 vols, 1780

Moreau, J. N., *Mes Souvenirs*, 2 vols, 1898–1901

  Exposition et Défense de Notre Constitution Monarchique Française, 2 vols, 1789

Morris, Gouverneur, *A Diary of the French Revolution*, 2 vols, 1939

Münster, Prince, *Political Sketches of the State of Europe*, 1868

Moulard, Abbé, *Le Comte Camille de Tournon*, 3 vols, 1927–32

Murray, Hon. Amelia, *Recollections*, 1868

Nervo, Baron, de, *Le Comte Corvetto*, 1869

Nesselrode, Chancelier Comte de, *Lettres et Papiers*, 11 vols, 1904–1911

Nettement, Alfred, *Histoire de la Restauration*, 8 vols, 1860–72

Newman, Edgar Leon, 'The Blouse and the Frock Coat: the Alliance of the Common People of Paris with the Liberal Leadership and the Middle Class during the Last Years of the Bourbon Restoration' *Journal of Modern History*, XLVI, 3, 1974, pp. 26–59

Nicolle, André, *Comment la France a payé après Waterloo*, 1929
Noailles, Vicomtesse de, *Vie de la Princesse de Poix*, 1855
Nougaret, M., *Anecdotes du Règne de Louis XVI. 1777*, 2 vols, 1778

Orléans, Louis-Philippe d', *Extrait de Mon Journal du Mois de Mars 1815*, Twickenham, 1816
Orléans, Marie-Amélie, Duchesse d', *Journal*, ed. Duchesse de Vendôme, 3 vols, 1935-43

Pailhès, Abbé G., *La Duchesse de Duras et Chateaubriand*, 1911
*Pallain, G., *Correspondance Inédite du Prince de Talleyrand et du Roi Louis XVIII pendant le Congrès de Vienne*, 1881
Papillon de la Ferté, M., *Journal*, 1887
Pasquier, E. D., *Histoire de Mon Temps*, 6 vols, 1893–95
Payne, Howard C., 'The Bourbon Restoration's Commissaires Extraordinaires du Roi in 1814' *French Historical Studies*, IX, Spring 1975, pp. 33–62
Pellissier, L., ed., *Le Portefeuille de la Comtesse d'Albany*, 1902
Perceval, Emile de, *Le Vte. Lainé*, 2 vols, 1926–28
Perret, Edouard, *La Dernière Favorite des Rois de France. La Comtesse du Cayla*, 1937
      Le Château de Saint-Ouen, 1940
Perrin, René, *L'Esprit Public dans le Département de la Meurthe de 1814 à 1816*, 1913
Perrin du Lac, R., 'Journal' *Revue de l'Histoire de Versailles*, XV, 1914, pp. 68–96, 150–169, 239–263, 307–334, 1913. XVI, pp. 56–82, 181–208, 268–281, 404–423
*Petiet, René, *Contribution à l'Histoire de l'Ordre de Saint Lazare de Jérusalem en France*, 1914
*Pimodan, Comte de, *Les Fiançailles de Madame Royale*, 1912
Pingud, Léonce, 'J.B. Courvoisier' *Mémoires de la Société d'Emulation du Doubs*, Besançon, 1883, pp. 323–346
      Un Agent Secret sous la Révolution et l'Empire, 1893
Pionnier, Edmond, *Essai sur l'Histoire de la Révolution à Verdun*, Nancy, 1905
Plinval de Guillebon, Régine de, 'La Manufacture de Porcelaine de Clignancourt dite du Comte de Provence' *Cahiers de la Céramique*, XXXI, 1963, pp. 146–171
*Poli, Oscar de, *Louis XVIII*, Quatrième Edition, 1880
Polovstov, A., ed., *Correspondance Diplomatique des Ambassadeurs et Ministres de Russie en France et de France en Russie avec Leurs Gouvernements de 1814 à 1830*, 3 vols, 1903–7
Poniatowski, Michel, *Louis-Philippe et Louis XVIII*, 1981
Ponz, Z., *Mémoires pour servir à l'Histoire de la Ville de Toulon en 1793*, 1825
Pool, Bernard, ed., *The Croker Papers*, 1967
Porch, David, *Army and Revolution in France 1815–1848*, 1974
Portal, Baron, *Mémoires*, 1846

Pouthas, Charles, *Histoire Politique de la Restauration,* Les Cours de Sorbonne, n.d.
  Guizot pendant la Restauration, 1923
Prince, Munro, *Preserving the Monarchy. The Comte de Vergennes 1774–1787,* 1995
  Un age d'or des arts décoratifs. Grand Palais, 1991
Proust, Antonin, *Archives de l'Ouest. Recueil de Documents concernant l'Histoire de la Révolution,* 5 vols, Angers 1867–69
Proyart, Abbé, *Louis XVI et ses Virtus aux prises avec la Perversité de son Siècle,* 4 vols, 1808
  Vie du Dauphin Père de Louis XVI, 1788
Puisaye, Comte de, *Réfuation d'un Libelle Diffamatoire publie par M. Béziade d'Avaray,* 1809

Raffles, Thomas, *Letters during a Tour through some parts of France, Savoy . . . in the Summer of 1817,* Third Edition, Liverpool, 1820
Ramm, Agatha, *Germany 1789–1919,* 1967
Rebsomen, André, Passages à Bordeaux des Comtes d'Artois et de Provence, 1777–1782' *Revue Historique de Bordeaux,* 3–4, 1923, pp. 86–101
Regnault-Warin, J. B., *Les Prisonniers du Temple,* 3 vols, 1800
Reiset, Vicomte de, *Anne de Caumont La Force, Comtesse de Balbi,* Cinquième Edition, 1909
  Joséphine de Savoie, Comtesse de Provence, 1913
  'Les Bourbons à Turin pendant la Révolution et le diario inédit de Charles-Felix, Duc de Genevois' *Revue des Deux Mondes,* 1. 11. 1911, pp. 143–174
Remacle, Comte, *Relations Secrètes des Agents de Louis XVIII à Paris sous le Consulat (1802–1803),* 1899
Renouvin, Pierre, 'L'Assemblée des Notables de 1787. La Conférence du 2 Mars, 1920
Resnick, Daniel, P., *The White Terror and the Political Reaction after Waterloo,* Cambridge Mass., 1966
Ribe, Georges, *L'Opinion Publique et la Vie Politique à Lyon 1815–1822,* 1957
Ribes, Dr. F., 'Histoire de l'Ouverture et de l'Embaumement du Corps de Louis XVIII' *Mémoires et Observations d'Anatomie,* 3 vols, 1841–43, II, pp. 429–453
Richardson, Nicholas, *The French Prefectoral Corps, 1814–1830,* Cambridge, 1966
Richelieu, Duc de, *Lettres . . . au Marquis d'Osmond,* 1939
Rickwood, Gerald O., 'King Louis XVIII at Gosfield Hall' *Essex Review,* XLIX, 1940, pp. 190–197
Righi, Allessandro, *Il Conte di Lilla e l'Emigrazione Francese a Verona,* Perugia, 1909
Robertson, William Spence, *France and Latin American Independence,* Baltimore, 1939

Robiquet, Jaques, L'Art et le Goût sous la Resturation, 1928 'La Propriété de la Comtesse de Balbi à Versailles' *Revue de l'Histoire de Versailles*, 1921, pp. 1–15

Rodolico, Nicolo, *Carlo Alberto Principe di Carignano*, Firenze, 1931

Rollac, J. S., *Exposé Fidèle des Faits Authentiquement Prouvés qui ont Précédé et Amené la Journée de Bordeaux du 12 Mars 1814*, 1816

*Romberg, Edouard, et Malet, Albert, *Louis XVIII et les Cents Jours à Gand*, 2 vols, 1898

Roots, William, *Journal of Paris in 1814*, Newcastle, 1900

Rougé, Comte A. de, *Le Marquis de Vérac et ses Amis*, 1890

Roussier, Michel, 'Le Conseil Municipal de Paris et le Retour des Bourbons' *Bulletin de la Société de l'Histoire de Paris*, 1962, pp. 91–109

Ruault, N., *Lettres à son Frère*, 1976

Sagnac, Philippe, 'Le Concordat de 1817. Etudes des Rapports de l'Eglise et de l'Etat sous la Restauration' *Revue d'Histoire Moderne*, VII, 1905–6, pp. 189–210, 269–288, 433–453

*Saint-Ange, Comte Garden de, *Code des Ordres de Chevalerie du Royaume*, 1819

Saint-Chamans, Comte de, *Mémoires*, 1896

Saint-Chamans, Comte de, *Mémoires*, Tulle, 1899

*Saint-Génis, Victor de, 'Une Conspiration Royaliste à Strasbourg en 1792' *Revue des Deux Mondes*, 15. 3. 1880, pp. 392–429

Salgues, J. B., *Les Mille et Une Calomnies*, 2 vols, 1822

Santi, M. L. de, 'Notes et Documents sur les Intrigues Royalistes dans le Midi' *Mémoires de l'Académie des Sciences . . . de Toulouse*, 1916, pp. 37–114

Scott, Barbara, 'Madame's Pavillon de Musique' *Apollo*, XCV, 5. 1972, pp. 390–399

Scott, John, *Paris Revisited in 1815*, Third Edition, 1816

Scott, Samuel F., *The Response of the Royal Army to the French Revolution*, 1978

*Ségur, Pierre de, *La Dernière des Condé*, 1899

Seguret, M. de, *Mémoires*, 1897

Sémallé, Comte de, *Souvenirs*, 1898

Serre, Comte de, *Correspondance*, 6 vols, 1876–77

Sévin, André, *Le Défenseur du Roi. Raymond de Sèze*, 1936

Shelley, Lady Frances, *Diary*, 2 vols, 1912–13

*Simon, Pierre, *L'Elaboration de la Charte Constitutionelle de 1814*, 1906

Simpson, James, *Paris after Waterloo*, 1853

Smyth, W. H., *Aedes Hartwellianae*, 2 vols, 1851

Snow, C. P., *Variety of Men*, 1967

Söderhjelm, A., ed, *Marie-Antoinette et Barnave. Correspondance Secrète*, 1934

Sorokine, Dimitri, *Champollion et les Secrets de l'Egypte*, 1967

480 *Louis XVIII*

4
Soutade-Roger, Madame, 'Les Notables en France sous la Restauration' *Revue de l'Histoire Economique et Sociale*, XXXVIII, 1960, pp. 98–110

Spitzer, Alan B., *Old Hatreds and Young Hopes. The French Carbonari against the Bourbon Restoration*, Cambridge Mass., 1971

Staël-Holstein, Baron de, *Correspondance Diplomatique (1783–1799)*, ed. L. Léouzon Leduc, 1881

Staël-Holstein, Baronne de, *Considérations sur . . . la Révolution Française*, 3 vols, London, 1818

Stanley, Edward, *Before and After Waterloo*, 1909

Stedingk, Comte de, *Mémoires . . . rédigés sur des Lettres, Dépêches et Autres Pièces Authentiques*, 3 vols, 1844–47

Stendhal, *Le Rouge et Le Noir*, ed. Michel Crouzet, Garnier-Flammarion, 1964

Oeuvres Intimes, Gallimard, Angers, 1955

Stevenson, Seth William, *Journal of a Tour Through Part of France, Flanders and Holland*, Norwich, 1817

Stuart, D. M., *The Daughters of George III*, 1939

Stuart Wortley, V., *Highcliffe and the Stuarts*, 1927

Sweet, Paul R., *Friedrich von Gentz*, Madison, 1941

*Talleyrand, Prince de, *Mémoires*, 5 vols, 1891–92

Tatum jr., Edward Howland, *The United States and Europe 1815–1820*, Berkeley Cal., 1936

Taylor, George V., 'Non Capitalist Wealth and the Origins of the French Revolution' *American Historical Review*, LXXII, 2. 1. 1967, pp. 469–496
    'The Paris Bourse on the Eve of the Revolution 1781–1789' *American Historical Review*, LXVII, 4. 7. 1962, pp. 951–977

Temperley, Harold, 'French Designs on Spanish America in 1820–25' *English Historical Review*, CLVII, 1. 1925, pp. 34–53

Thierry, Marc Antoine, Baron de Ville d'Avray, 'Mémoires' *Revue de l'Histoire de Versailles*, 5. 1908, pp. 81–107, 8. 1908, pp. 209–226, 2. 1909, pp. 81–96

Tilly, Comte Alexandre de, *Mémoires*, 1965

Titeux, Eugene, *La Maison Militaire du Roi*, 2 vols, 1890
    Le Général Dupont, 3 vols, Puteaux sur Siene, 1903

Trénard, Louis, *Salvandy en son Temps*, 1968

Trucco, A. F., 'Il Marchese di Cordon à Vittorio Amadeo III' *Rivista di Storia di Alessandria*, XXV, 1. 1907, pp. 400–439, XXVIII, 10. 1907, pp. 473–512, XXIX, 1. 1908, pp. 183–231; XXXI, 10. 1908, pp. 466–488, XXXI, 7. 1908, pp. 304–340

Tulard, Jean, 'Du Paris Impérial au Paris de 1830 d'après les Bulletins de Police' *Bulletin de la Société de l'Histoire de Paris et de l'Ile-de-France*, 1969, pp. 157–175

*Turgot, *Oeuvres*, ed. Gustave Schelle, 5 vols, 1913–1921

Un age d'or des arts décoratifs 1814–1848. Grand Palais, 1991

Vaissière, P. de, *Lettres d'Aristocrates*, 1923
Valon, Alexis de, 'Le Marquis de Favras d'après de Nouveaux Documents' *Revue des Deux Mondes*, 6, 1851, pp. 1091–1135
Vansittart, Jane, ed., *Surgeon James' Journal*, 1964
Vaublanc, Comte de, *Correspondance avec le Comte d'Artois*, 2 vols, 1889
Veddeler, Peter, *Franzosische Emigranten in Westfalen 1792–1802*, Munster 1989
Verlet, Pierre, *French Royal Furniture*, 1963
    Versailles, 1961
Véry, Abbé de, *Journal*, 2 vols, ed. Baron de Witte, 1933
Vialles, Pierre, *L'Archichancelier Cambacérès*, 1908
Vidalenc, Jean, *Le Département de l'Eure sous la Monarchie Constitutionnelle*, 1952
    Les Demi-Solde, 1955
Viennet J. P. G., *Journal*, 1955
Vigny, Alfred de, *Servitude et Grandeur Militaires*, Nelson, n.d.
*Villèle, Comte de, *Mémoires et Correspondance*, 5 vols, 1898–1901
Vitrolles, Baron de, *Mémoires*, 2 vols, 1950–52
*Vivenot, Alfred Ritter von, *Quellen zur Geschichte der Deutschen Kaiserpolitik Osterreichs Während der Französischen Revolutionskriege*, 5 vols, Vienna, 1873–90

*Walpole, Horace, *Règne de Richard III ou Doutes Historiques sur les Crimes qui lui sont Imputés* (tr Louis XVIII), 1800
*Walter, Gérard, *Le Comte de Provence*, 1950
Wansey, Henry, *A Visit to Paris in June 1814*, 1814
Waquet, Françoise, *Les Fêtes Royales sous la Restauration*, Genève 1981
Waresquiel, Emmanuel de, *Le duc de Richelieu 1766–1822*, 1990
    Talleyrand, le prince immobile, 2003
Waresquiel, Emmanuel de and Yvert, Benoit, *Histoire de la Restauration 1814–1830. Naissance de la France Moderne*, 1996
Watson, Francis, *Louis XVI Furniture*, 1960
Webster, Sir Charles, *Documents on British Foreign Policy*, 1924
    The Foreign Policy of Castlereagh, 2 vols, 1950, 1935
Weil, Cdt. M-H, *Joachim Murat, Roi de Naples. La Dernière Année de Règne*, 5 vols, 1909
Wellens de Dowder, Liliane, 'La Restauration de l'Ancien Régime dans le Nord de la France sous l'Occupation Autrichienne de 1793–94' *Annales de la Société Royale d'Archæologie de Bruxelles*, L, 1961, pp. 249–274
Wellington, Duke of, *Despatches*, 13 vols, 1834–39
    Supplementary Despatches, 15 vols, 1858–72
    Supplementary Despatches (New Series) 8 vols, 1867–80

Welvert, Eugène, *Lendemains Révolutionnaires*, n.d.
        Napoléon et la Police, 1912
*Wickham, William, *Correspondance*, 2 vols, 1870
*Wilson, Joan, 'Little Gifts Keep Friendship Alive' *Apollo*, 7, 1965, pp. 50–61
Wodehouse, C.M., *Capodistria*, 1977
Wodzinski, Comte A., 'Les Bourbons en Pologne', *Nouvelle Revue*, CXVIII, 1899, pp. 385–407

Newspapers and Journals

Découverte (Bulletin Trimestriel pour l'Étude de Louis XVI et de son Procès), 1973–
Journal des Débats, 1814–15
Mémorial Bordelais, 1814–15
Moniteur, 1789–91, 1814–24
Morning Post, 1807, 1811, 1814
Le Nain Jaune, 1814–15
The Times, 1807, 1811, 1814

Index

Abbeville, 177, 227–9, 267

Abrantès, Duchesse d', 237

Adélaïde, Madame, 6, 20, 304

Agier, M., 380

Agoult, Vicomte d', 79, 349

Aire, 233

Aix-en-Provence, 220

Aix-la-Chapelle, 56, 64, 75, 355

Albignac, M. d', 243

Alexander I 80, 83, 98, 129, 135, 150, 159, 163, 168, 175, 195, 197, 211, 220, 231, 243, 247, 254, 262, 264–6, 268–9, 321, 329, 331, 339–40, 355, 358, 396, 406, 409

Alibert, Baron, 294, 299–300

Alissan de Chazet, 298, 392

Allent, M., 337

Alost, 242, 250

Amiens, 177, 211, 252

André, Abbé, 94–5, 100, 116, 304

Angers 176

Angivillier, Comte d', 100

Anglès, Baron, 251, 383

Angoulême, Duc d', 101, 104–6, 111, 116, 138, 140, 143, 157, 163, 165–8, 191–2, 194–5, 210, 246, 248, 259, 263–4, 271, 275, 290,

321, 323, 335, 347, 351–2, 369, 372, 381, 386, 394, 412–4

Angoulême, Duchesse d' (Madame Royale before 1799), 6, 81, 82–3, 89, 105–6, 108, 143, 145, 166, 168, 176, 192, 194–5, 219, 230, 232, 264, 266, 280, 290–3, 297, 300, 321, 326, 330, 332, 347–9, 361, 366, 370, 372, 395, 412

Anne, Grand Duchess 231, 321

Antraigues, Comte d', 78, 84, 93, 95, 100, 108, 116, 135, 149, 150–2, 209

Antwerp, 249

Aragon, 228

Argenson, Marquis d', 375–7

Arlincourt, Vicomte d', 298

Arlon, 74–5

Armentières, 233, 249

Arnouville, 255, 257

Arras, 322

Artois, Comte d', later Charles X, 5, 11, 14, 18, 20, 27, 39, 40–1, 43, 51–2, 56, 58–60, 63–71, 73, 75–6, 83–4, 92, 99, 101–4, 106–110, 112–3, 116, 124–6, 128–130, 132–5, 137–140, 142, 146, 148–151, 153, 154,

163–6, 168, 172, 176, 180, 185–6, 190–5, 200, 205, 209–11, 222–3, 227–9, 235, 244–7, 251, 253–4, 256, 266–7, 271, 288, 290–3, 302, 306, 308, 312, 322–3, 326, 330, 332–3, 337, 341, 343, 345, 347–9, 351–3, 357, 361, 367, 369–70, 372, 374, 387–9, 391, 403, 406, 412–4

Aubusson, 7, 270

Aumont, Duc d', (Duc de Piennes until 1814) 88, 91, 277–8

Austria, Francis I, Emperor of, 67, 76, 105, 285, 340, 357, 411

Avaray, Comte, later Duc d' 53–4, 57, 60, 79–81, 87–9, 91, 96–101, 106, 109, 113–4, 119, 129, 133–5, 138, 140, 145, 151–3, 155, 251, 273, 318, 330, 366, 381, 413

Avaray, Marquis d', later Duc d' 45, 276, 390

Avignon, 20, 63

Ayen, Duc d', 114, 160

Aylesbury, 144

Bailleul, 233, 249

Balbi, Madame de, 29, 32, 34, 38, 47, 53–4, 57, 59–60, 68, 71, 75, 78, 96, 107, 216, 251, 304, 330, 381, 391

Balzac, Honoré de, 174, 188, 292, 350, 402, 410

Barante, Baron de, 157

Barbe-Marbois, Marquis de, 267, 337

Barentin, M. de, 243

Barnave, M., 63

Barras, Comte de, 92, 127, 159

Barthélemy, Marquis de, 248

Bayreuth, 94

Beaune, 399

Beauvais, 219, 228, 270, 301

Béhague, Comte de, 125

Belfort, 235, 393

Belliard, General, 223

Beresford, Marshal, 166

Berlin, 81–2, 93, 331, 380, 402

Bernadotte, 163, 195

Berri, Duc de, 101, 104, 141, 145, 148, 165, 192, 194, 209–10, 219, 227, 231, 237, 242, 249–51, 253, 271, 278, 290, 293, 321–2, 326, 338–9, 347, 371, 377

Berri, Duchesse de, 270, 278, 292, 338–9, 348, 377–8, 412, 414

Berthier, Maréchal, later Prince de Wagram, 121, 127–8, 150, 177–8, 204, 219, 230, 238, 329

Bertier, Comte Ferdinand de, 161, 327, 348, 383

Bertin brothers, 126, 186, 243

Bertrand, General, 221

Besançon, Mgr. Lecoz, Archbishop of, 211, 235

Béthisy, Comte de, 326

Béthune, 228

Beugnot, Comte, 181–3, 189–90, 193, 200, 203, 217, 234, 242, 246, 252, 365

Beurnonville, Général de, 187, 200, 242, 252, 262

Blacas, Comte de, 68, 99, 146, 153–4, 156, 159, 162–5, 180, 186–7, 190, 197, 198, 200–1, 213–4, 220, 223, 226–7, 229–30, 243, 246–

9, 251–2, 260, 263, 270, 276, 286, 288, 295, 301–3, 308, 318, 330, 333, 346, 348, 349, 366, 373, 381, 384–5, 390, 405, 408, 413, 414

Blankenburg, 87–8, 92–3, 116–7, 119, 123, 141, 272

Blankenfeld, 90, 119, 304

Blondel d'Aubers, M., 326

Blücher, Marshal, 250, 252, 264

Boisgelin, Marquis de, 276

Boissy d'Anglas, 33, 116, 120, 127

Bonald, Vicomte de, 185

Bonaparte, General, *see* Napoleon I,

Bonnay, Marquis de, 87, 93, 95–6, 98–100, 102, 105, 108, 134, 141, 305, 325, 341

Bonté, Baronne de, 310

Bontemps-Dubarry, 166

Bordeaux, 20, 38, 94, 125, 159, 161–4, 166–7, 170, 176–7, 191, 194, 195, 208, 210, 217, 226, 228, 233–6, 258–9, 265, 287, 304, 321, 342, 347, 378

Bordeaux, Duc de, 295, 378, 403, 412

Bouillé, Comte de, 163

Boulogne, 159, 166, 177

Bourbon, Duc de, 81, 231

Bourdon, Comte de, 301

Brazil, Pedro I, Emperor of, 397

Brenet, M., 344

Breteuil, Baron de, 57, 62, 72–3, 201

Briey, 71

Broglie, Duc de, 313–4

Broglie, Duchesse de, 313, 380

Brotier, Abbé, 93, 95, 116

Bruges, 229

Bruges, Comte de, 163, 192, 194, 337, 349, 388

Brune, Maréchal, 323

Bruneau, Mathurin, 348

Brunoy, 24, 27, 30–1, 33, 36, 38, 87, 216, 275

Brunswick, Duke of 70, 73, 79

Brussels, 56, 62

Buckingham, Marquess of, 140–1, 144, 155

Burke, Edmund, 69, 81

Burney, Fanny, 148, 228

Byron, Lord, 269, 298

Cadoudal, Georges, 102

Calais, 176–7

Calmar, 119

Calonne, 40–1, 59–60, 65–7, 72–3, 93, 173–4, 201, 308

Cambacérès, 159

Cambon, 172

Cambrai, 253, 333, 355

Cambridge, Duke of, 274, 302

Campenon, M. de, 299, 351

Cannes, 221

Canning, George, 139, 146, 152, 185, 288, 310

Canuel, Colonel, 349

Capodistria, Count, 266, 310

Carignan, Charles-Albert, Prince de, 395, 397

Carlscrona, 138

Carnot, Comte, 171, 213

Castelbajac, Marquis de, 341

Castelcicala, Prince, 289, 360

Castellane, Colonel, later Maréchal de, 159, 242, 275, 360

Castlereagh, Viscount, 167, 185, 221, 247, 251, 258, 266, 355

Castries, Maréchal de, 80, 92, 95, 97, 100–1, 112–3

Catherine II, 9, 65–6, 75–6, 83

Caulaincourt, Comte de, 159, 231, 254

Chabannes, Comte de, 275

Chabannes, Marquis de, 166

Chabrol, Comte de, 188

Chabrol-Crousol, Comte de, 248, 384, 406

Chalgrin, M., 27–8, 30, 216

Chalus, Comte de, 124

Chambéry, 221

Champagne, Madame, 237, 322, 410

Champollion, M., 301

Charenton, 334

Charette, M. de, 93, 112, 114, 125

Charles X, *see* Artois, Comte d'

Charles, Madame, 243

Charlotte, Queen, 143, 156

Chastenay, Madame de, 207

Chateaubriand, Vicomte de, 68, 157–8, 160, 178, 202, 205, 213, 242–3, 245–7, 251–2, 256, 263, 290, 297–9, 314, 322, 335, 344–5, 366, 370, 372, 379–80, 386–7, 389, 394, 404–6, 410, 415

Châtillon, 165

Cherbourg, 168, 296

Cherubini, 284

Choiseul, Duc de, 9, 12, 29

Choiseul, Duchesse de, 310

Choisy, Mademoiselle de, later Vicomtesse d'Agoult 89

Clermont-Gallerande, Marquis de, 94, 128

Clermont-Tonnerre, Marquis de, 261, 275, 341, 384,

386, 389, 405–6

Cléry, 107, 140

Clifford, Sir Thomas, 143, 304

Clotilde, Madame, 5, 20, 87, 147

Coblentz, 56–70, 74, 76–7, 81–2, 84, 87, 91, 95, 100, 102, 112, 132, 135, 141, 194, 215, 243, 257, 308, 345

Coburg, 94

Coigny, Chevalier de, 104

Colchester, 139–40

Compiègne, 27, 31, 148, 173, 177–9, 254, 270

Condé, Prince de, 59, 60, 65–8, 75, 78, 81, 100, 103, 105, 139–40, 142–43, 148, 156, 158, 168, 185, 231, 308, 381

Constant Benjamin, 172, 174, 202, 238–9, 242, 320–1, 350, 370

Conti, Prince de, 17, 27, 40

Corbière, Comte de, 357, 370, 379–81, 383–4, 386–7, 389, 404

Corcelles, Comte de, 375

Corvetto, Comte, 195, 276, 360

Cossé, Comte de, 44–5, 87–8, 102

Costume, 33, 58, 79, 142, 155, 173, 206–7, 214, 284, 349

Courvoisier, M., 91–2, 97–8

Coutard, Colonel, 317

Coutent, 88, 273

Cromot du Bourg, M., 17, 23, 25–26, 33, 36, 51

Cromot de Fougy, M., 23, 305

Croÿ, Duc de, 3–4, 14, 16, 37, 69

Crussol, Baillie de, 248

Curial, General, 178
Custine, Astolphe de, 160

Dalberg, Duc de, 187, 195, 200
Damas, Baron de, 387, 405–6
Damas, Charles de, 57, 133, 205, 278, 280, 336, 344, 408
Damas, Roger de, 286, 362
Dambray, Chancellor, 181–3, 185–7, 190, 193, 200–1, 223, 242, 246, 252–3, 259, 318, 337, 356, 358
D'André, M., 94–5, 102, 116, 124, 126, 135, 190, 305
Daru, Comte, 221
Dauphin, 11
Davout, Maréchal, 121, 207, 257
Decaen, General, 235
Decazes, Elie, later Duc, 173–4, 265–7, 273, 277, 289, 291, 293–4, 296, 302, 313, 317, 326, 328–32, 334–6, 339–374, 379, 380–83, 389, 394, 406–8, 413–4
Decazes, Comtesse, later Duchesse, 296, 314, 360, 363
Dejean, General, 368
Delaborde, General, 178, 215
Delalot, M., 380
Delessert, Benjamin, 255
Dennilée, Baron, 188
Descoeurs, 273
Des Pommelles, M., 93–4, 126, 149
Dessolles, General, 187, 199, 200, 361, 370, 373
Develly, 302
Devonshire, Duchess of, 310
Didier, J. P., 239
Dieppe, 229

Dijon, 161, 167, 233, 239, 344
Donnissan, Marquis de, 122
Doudeauville, Duc de, 381, 386, 388, 390, 405–6
Douglas, Admiral, 139–40
Dover, 168, 170, 229
Dreux-Brézé, Marquis de, 88
Druault, Colonel, 317
Du Barry, Madame, 9, 12–3, 391
Du Bouchage, Vicomte, 248, 267, 356
Dubourg de Pourquery, M., 126
Dubreuil, 88
Du Cayla, Madame, 297, 302, 307, 381–2, 388–9, 405, 407, 413–4
Ducis, J. F., 33, 299, 301, 368
Dugourc, 27, 285
Dumouriez, 152
Dun, 71
Dunkirk, 167–8, 176, 228–9, 252, 267
Dupleix de Mézy, M., 365, 384
Dupont, General, 186, 189–90, 200
Duras, Duc de, 88, 226, 230, 252, 276, 278–80, 336, 385, 405
Duras, Duchesse de, 177, 243, 297, 394, 405–6
Duverne de Presle, 90, 93

Edgeworth, Abbé, 86, 89, 98, 107, 134
Elisée, Père, 156, 204, 209, 219, 294
Elite, French, relations with the Crown, 4, 5, 9–10, 31, 37, 41–3, 61, 68, 74, 99,

147, 172, 177, 201–2, 402–
   3, 408, 410, 411
Elizabeth, Madame, 5, 53, 86,
   107, 111, 145, 216
Enghien, Duc d', 81, 231
Escars, Duc d', 274, 276–7,
   280, 288, 298
Escars, Duchesse d', 280, 336,
   382, 385, 410
Esclimont, Château d', 334
Espinchal, Comte d', 60–1,
   74–5
Etain, 71
Eugène, Prince, 211, 321
Exelmans, General, 192, 194,
   364

Fabvier, General, 376–7, 394
Fantin des Odoards, Colonel,
   238
Fauche-Borel, 128, 149–50
Favras, Marquis de, 48–50,
   129, 210, 377, 381
Favras, Marquise de, 50–1,
   83, 304
Feletz, Abbé de, 298
Feltre, Clarke, Duc de, 222,
   229, 242, 245, 250–3, 267,
   337, 353–6, 379
Ferdinand IV, *see* Naples
Ferdinand VII, *see* Spain
Ferrand, Comte, 100, 179,
   181, 183, 187, 190, 200,
   244, 247, 260, 312, 318,
   341, 347, 384
Fersen, Count, 59
Feutrier, Mgr., 402
Fitzjames, Duc de, 161, 192,
   350–1, 371, 408
Flachslanden, Baron de, 92,
   95, 114
Flahault, General de, 221
Flahault, Madame de, 217
Fleuriel, Abbé, 91, 198, 226

Fleury, Duc de, 91, 276
Fontainebleau, 27, 31, 173,
   178, 220, 228, 238, 293,
   305, 329, 338
Fouché, Joseph, later Duc
   d'Otrante, 119, 149, 171,
   211, 221, 223, 233, 252,
   254–9, 261, 264–6, 268,
   323–4, 365
Foy, General, 320, 401, 404
Frayssinous, Mgr., 403–4,
   407–8
Froment, M., 210
Fruchart, Louis, 160, 305

Gap, 238
Garat, M., 172
Garde Royale, *see* Guards,
   French Royal,
Gardes du Corps, *see* Guards,
   French Royal,
Gardes Nationales, 47, 49–50,
   54, 61, 71, 126, 180, 193,
   199, 208, 212, 218, 223–5,
   229, 232–3, 251, 255, 337,
   353, 357
Gentz, Friedrich von, 82, 101
George III, 17, 23, 65, 78,
   124, 139, 143, 332, 342
George IV, (previously Prince
   of Wales and Prince
   Regent), 25, 144, 155, 163,
   165, 168, 188, 195, 204,
   240, 247, 260, 274, 279,
   285, 287, 302
Gérard, Baron, 174, 300,
   302, 337, 391
Géricault, Théodore, 205
Ghent, 229–30, 233, 243–4,
   247–50, 255, 261, 281,
   313–4, 333
Girardin, Stanislas de, 362
Girodet, 300
Gobelins, 7, 270, 301

Gonet, 144, 226, 230, 273
Gontaut, Madame de, 277, 311, 378
Gosfield, 140, 143, 146, 150, 302
Gourbillon, Madame de, 30–1, 46, 51, 53, 60, 106, 134, 144, 304
Gouvion Saint-Cyr, Maréchal, 233, 238, 259, 261, 317, 353–4, 356–8, 361
Gramont, Comte de, 164
Gramont, Duc de, 88, 90, 138, 140, 148, 205, 226, 276–7, 280, 287, 297, 304, 336, 366, 373, 405, 408
Grasse, 221, 236
Greffuhle, Comte, 243, 338
Grégoire, Abbé, 350, 370–1, 375
Grenoble, 180, 221–2, 234, 301, 336, 370, 376
Grenville, Lady Mary, 141–2
Grenville, Lord, 131
Grimm, Baron, 82
Gros, Baron, 227, 300, 349
Grosbois, 26–7, 329
Grosbois, Président de, 248
Guards, French Royal, 8, 23, 43, 46, 49, 63–4, 67, 79, 88, 126, 193, 204–5, 208, 218, 224–5, 227–9, 232, 237–8, 240, 242, 247, 249–50, 255, 259, 261–2, 275–6, 284, 289, 304, 306, 317, 339, 349, 353, 362, 372, 376
Guignet, 79, 88, 226, 230
Guilhermy, M. de, 57, 91–2, 100–1, 128, 152, 305
Guilleminot, Comte, 397
Guizot, François, 185, 233, 242, 250–1, 311–2, 343, 350–1, 401, 414

Gustavus III, 7, 16, 29, 38, 44, 56, 64, 103, 131, 138, 156, 196
Gustavus IV Adolphus, 87, 131, 138, 141, 144, 156

Habsburg, House of, 5, 10, 14, 53, 82, 195, 197, 395–6
Hamburg, 83, 97, 101, 154
Hamm, 75, 77, 83, 96, 110–1, 123–4, 141
Harcourt, Duc d', 78
Harrowby, Lord, 248
Hartwell, 143–4, 146–8, 153–4, 162, 167–8, 192, 220, 229, 248, 269, 271, 273, 273–6, 282, 302, 304, 394
Haussez, Baron d', 341
Hautefort, Comte d', 96, 133
Hauterive, Comte d', 318
Havré, Duc d', 148, 150, 157, 176, 205, 230, 276, 292, 408, 410
Hazebrouck, 233
Henri IV, 7, 32, 111–2, 156–7, 179–80, 207, 217, 285, 300, 378
Herbouville, Marquis d', 248, 365
Herrmann, M., 91, 102
Hervilly, Comte d', 124
Hobhouse, John Cam, 257
Hohenzollern, House of, 5, 53, 197
Hortense, Queen, 211, 236, 254
Hue, Baron, 89, 107, 140, 148, 227, 229, 273, 295, 309
Hugo, Victor, 160, 298
Hume, David, 86–7, 351

Jacotot, Madame, 301–2
James II, 351, 412

Jaucourt, Marquis de, 187, 196–7, 200–1, 217, 219, 223–4, 229–30, 245–8, 251, 259

Jefferson, Thomas, 171

Jerningham, Edward, 143, 304

Jordan, Camille, 310, 351, 361

Josephine, Empress, 326

Jourdan, Maréchal, 178, 199, 286

Jouy, Etienne de, 321

Kent, Duke of, 146, 152, 212, 302

Königfeld, Count and Countess, 80, 135, 304

Königsberg, 88

Kourakine, Princess, 310

Krüdener, Madame de, 266

La Bédoyère, Comte de, 221–2, 325–6

La Bédoyère, Comtesse de, 325

Laborie, M., 252

La Bourdonnaye, Comte de, 380, 386

La Chapelle, Comte de, 92, 103

La Chatre, Comte, later Duc de, 12, 29, 45, 48, 86, 133, 139, 148, 150, 159, 163, 165, 257, 260, 276, 278, 288, 325, 332

Lacretelle, M. de, 243

La Fare, Mgr. de, 96, 101, 207

La Fayette, 18, 45, 47–50, 63, 72, 76, 171, 320–1, 350, 357, 375, 377, 392, 401

La Ferronays, Comte de, 147, 163

Laffitte, Louis, 237

Laffitte, M., 350, 375–7

La Frégeolière, General de, 160

Lagarde, General de, 324

Lainé, Vicomte, 159, 211, 233, 244, 246, 263, 317, 328, 337, 357, 379

La Jaille, Marquis de, 118

Lallemand, M., 375

Lally-Tollendal, Comte de, 245, 247, 251

La Maisonfort, Marquis de, 180, 193

Lamarque, General, 320

Lamartine, 160, 205, 219, 228, 243, 272, 298

Lambert, Marquis de, 62

La Rochefoucauld, Sosthènes de, 295, 334, 371, 382–3, 386, 388, 390, 405

La Rochelle, 234

La Rochejaquelein, Marquis de, 157, 161, 166, 177, 305

La Rouerie, Marquis de, 57, 124

La Thuillerie, M. de, 90

La Tour du Pin, Baron de, 160

Latour-Maubourg, Comte de, 370

La Trémoïlle, Prince de, 199, 102, 125–6, 226

Lauriston, Marquis, later Maréchal de, 254, 318, 384, 386, 390

Laval, Madame de, 385

LaVallette, Comte de, 223, 325–6, 328, 334

LaVallette, Comtesse de, 325

La Vauguyon, Duc de, 11–2

La Vauguyon, Duc de, (son of above), 93, 95, 103, 116

Le Cateau, 252–3

Lecourbe, General, 150, 199
Leczynski, Stanislas, 10, 21, 82, 387
Leduc, Louis, 307
Lemaître, M., 93
Lenoncourt, Duc de, 277
Leopold II, Holy Roman Emperor, 11, 59, 63, 67
Le Quesnay, 253
Lévis, Comte, later Duc de, 12, 20, 45, 47, 51–3, 57, 73, 322
Lévis, Duchesse de, 177, 243, 406
Liebau, 138
Lieven, Princess, 310, 312, 331
Lille, 121, 160, 226–30, 234, 249, 261, 263, 322
L'Isle–Adam 27, 139
Liverpool, Lord, 164–5, 185, 232
London, 91, 93, 101–2, 137, 139, 168
Longwy, 54, 71, 73
Lons-le-Saulnier, 222
Lorimier de Chamilly, 273
Louis XV, 3–6, 13–4, 155, 172, 197, 258, 272, 307, 378, 410
Louis XVI, 3–5, 7, 9, 11, 15, 18, 25–7, 31–2, 39, 41, 43, 45–54, 56, 60, 62–5, 67, 70, 72, 75, 88, 90, 103, 107–8, 111, 113, 119, 129, 131, 145, 158, 166, 172, 175–6, 180–1, 201, 205, 209, 215–6, 256, 258, 271–2, 285, 291, 293–5, 306, 308, 315, 345, 400, 410–11, 414
Louis XVII (Duc de Normandie 1785–1789, Dauphin 1789–1793), 27, 64, 84–5, 91, 108, 294, 298, 335, 348
Louis, Baron, 186, 190–1, 199–200, 202, 223, 234, 246, 251, 259, 265, 267, 361, 370
Louvel, Etienne, 371
Louvre, 267, 272, 300–2, 329
Lucca, Charles Duke of, 397
Lure, 165
Luxembourg, 56
Luxembourg, Duc de, 276
Luxembourg, Palais du, 26, 29–31, 46, 51, 54
Luynes, Duc de, 121
Luynes, Duchesse de, 128, 334
Lynch, Comte, 166–7
Lyon, 20, 119–21, 167, 170–1, 176, 222, 233–5, 251, 287, 306, 324, 352, 381, 399

Macartney, Lord, 78, 87, 90–1, 113
Macdonald, Maréchal, 150, 172, 211, 222–3, 225–6, 228–9, 238, 248, 256, 262, 311, 360, 376–7
Mâcon 235
Mailhos, M., 164
Maine de Biran, 212, 225–6, 236, 286, 310–2, 341–2
Maison, General, 188
Maison Militaire, *see* Guards, French Royal,
Maistre, Joseph de, 96, 119, 346
Malet, General, 158, 179
Mallet du Pan, 105
Malmesbury, Lady, 77, 330
Malmesbury, Lord, 59, 69
Malouet, Baron, 135, 186, 193, 200
Manners at court, 8, 15, 21,

32, 37–8, 47, 69, 74, 90, 143, 153, 156, 168, 173, 211–2

Manuel, 172, 350, 357, 375–6, 400

Marche-en-Famenne, 56

Marceau, General, 127

Maret, later Duc de Bassano, 221

Marie, Abbé, 89

Marie-Antoinette, 3, 8, 12, 14–7, 26–7, 31, 33, 39, 45–46, 49–53, 61–2, 65, 67, 72, 83, 107–8, 111, 130, 145, 288, 291, 293–4, 391–2

Marie-Josèphe of Saxony, 5, 11

Marie-Joséphine, 3–4, 6–7, 12–4, 17, 27, 29–31, 33, 37, 45–6, 51, 53, 60, 80, 91, 106–7, 127, 134, 143–6, 148, 153, 216, 273, 304, 338, 381, 385

Marie-Louise, Empress of the French, Duchess of Parma, 154, 197–8, 218

Marmont, Maréchal, 121, 178, 204, 211, 225–6, 238, 262, 325, 360, 377, 408, 412

Marsan, Comtesse de, 11–2, 86

Marseille, 20, 127, 159, 161, 233–6, 252, 321, 323

Martin de Gallardon, 333–6, 832

Massa, Duchesse de, 219

Masséna, Maréchal, 235

Maury, Cardinal, 85, 100

Melling, 302

Melun, 223, 226

Menin, 229

Mercier, J. S., 6, 32

Merlin de Thionville, 160

Mermet, Colonel, 317

Metternich, Prince, 167, 178, 197, 221, 248, 251, 259, 271, 331, 355, 391, 397

Metz, 235

Michaud, M., 126, 186

Michelet, Edmond, 206

Miguel, Dom, 397, 408

Mirabeau, Comte de, 47–52, 88

Mirbel, Madame de, 296, 381, 414

Mittau, 79–80, 83, 88–9, 91, 93–4, 97, 102, 104–6, 123, 125, 129, 137–8, 143, 146, 149–50, 163, 272

Molé, Comte, 286, 314, 320, 341, 356–7, 360, 365, 367

Moncey, Maréchal, 177, 187, 193, 200, 209, 211, 221

Mons, 54, 234, 250, 252, 355

Montauban, 162

Montbarey, Prince de, 15, 51, 57

Montcalm, Madame de, 335, 337, 379

Mont-de-Marsan, 165

Montesquiou, Abbé de, 94–5, 102, 128, 167, 168, 172, 174, 180–1, 183, 186, 200–2, 223, 229, 235, 259, 279, 341, 358, 410

Montesquiou, Comte de, 235

Montesquiou, Marquis de, 32, 45, 114, 122

Montmédy, 54

Montmorency, Mathieu de, 159, 178, 192, 215, 285, 334, 371, 384–6, 388, 393

Montpellier, 252

Moreau, General, 128, 159, 202, 300

Moreau, J. N., 35, 37, 43, 110

Moreton-Chabrillant, Comte de, 20, 57
Morlaix, 150
Mortemart, Duc de, 276–7
Mortier, Maréchal, 178, 228, 368
Mouchy, Duc de, 276, 390
Mounier, Baron, 242–3, 251, 263, 374, 383
Mouton, General, 320
Murat, Joachim, King of Naples, 192, 194, 197–8

Nancy, 235
Nansouty, Comte de, 204
Nantes, 234
Nantil, Colonel, 376–7
Naples, Ferdinand IV, King of, (after 1816 Ferdinand I, King of the Two Sicilies), 11, 66, 80, 104, 106, 179–80, 185, 291, 338, 392, 415
Napoleon I, 66, 78, 81–2, 85, 94–5, 102, 104, 106, 115, 119, 122–3, 127–131, 133, 138, 144, 149, 154–5, 157, 159, 162, 167, 171, 175, 177–8, 183, 185–6, 190, 196–8, 201–2, 206, 213–6, 218, 220–2, 224–5, 228, 230–2, 234–6, 238–41, 243–4, 249, 254, 258, 271, 274–5, 284, 288, 290, 308, 312–3, 315, 318, 320, 381, 400, 409
Napoleon II, *see* Reichstadt, Duke of,
Narbonne, Comte de, 159
Narbonne, Madame de, 296
Necker, M., 10, 17, 26, 43, 46, 48–50, 123
Netherlands, William I King of, 229, 409

Ney, Maréchal, 178, 207, 214, 222, 232, 313, 325–6
Ney, Maréchale, 207, 213, 325
Nîmes, 323–4
Noailles family, 9, 45, 114, 160, 171, 174, 390
Noailles, Comte Alexis de, 157, 159, 160–1, 163, 248
Noailles, Marquis de, 20, 160
Noailles, Vicomtesse de, 174
Nodier, Charles, 298

Orange, Prince of, 229, 321
Orléans, 234, 322
Orléans, Duc d', later Louis-Philippe I, 28, 103, 108–9, 112, 116, 137–40, 142, 152, 157, 171, 175, 198–9, 212, 222, 228–9, 231, 244, 246, 249, 260, 262, 268–9, 291, 308, 313, 344, 351, 378, 408, 412
Orléans, Duchesse d', 272, 274, 281, 291, 311–2, 378, 406–7
Osmond, Marquis d', 339
Ostend, 229, 230–1, 243
Oudinot, Maréchal, 178, 187, 193, 200, 238, 254, 262, 288

Palermo 93
Paris 6, 13, 24, 32–3, 42, 44–8, 52, 63, 75, 77, 94–5, 107, 110, 116, 161, 167, 172–3, 176, 184–6, 192, 196, 209, 214, 217, 220, 224–6, 228, 234, 249–50, 252–4, 256, 258–9, 266–7, 270, 282, 329, 352–3, 367, 375–6, 399
Parma, Duke of, 11, 84

Pasquier, Baron, 157, 248, 256, 259–60, 265, 295, 356, 366, 370, 380, 383, 408

Pau, 165

Paul I, 79, 81, 83, 91, 97, 105, 131

Péfaut de la Tour, 162

Pérignon, Maréchal, 121, 203, 238, 288

Périgord, Archambaud de, 96

Périgord, Mgr., later Cardinal de, 88, 119, 148, 211, 252, 276, 278, 334, 337, 368

Perlet, M., 149, 158

Péronne, 49, 253

Peronnet, M., 87, 133, 273

Perrin, M., 162, 304

Pétion, M., 63

Peyronnet, Comte de, 317, 384, 386, 392

Pichegru, General, 127, 129, 132, 300

Piedmont, Prince of, later Charles Emmanuel IV King of Sardinia, 20, 34

Piennes, Duc de, *see* Aumont, Duc d' 325, 347, 380

Piet, M., 325, 347, 380

Pitt, William, the Younger, 66, 69

Poix, Prince de, 114, 160, 230, 336

Polignac, Jules, later Prince de, 192, 266, 337, 412, 414

Pontlabbé, Baron de, 124

Portal, Baron, 185, 251, 263, 361, 383

Portalis, M., 122

Portugal, João VI, King of, 397

Potin, 273

Pozzo di Borgo, Count, 231, 244–6, 249, 254, 264, 307, 328, 339, 357, 360–1, 403

Pradel, Comte de, 318

Précy, Comte de, 94, 116, 124, 305

Princeteau, Madame, 296, 338, 382

Pringent, M. de, 150–1

Prussia, Frederick William II, King of, 59, 63, 66, 72, 74–5

Prussia, Frederick William III, King of, 80, 82, 91, 163, 263, 308

Puisaye, Comte de, 92, 97, 102, 188, 124, 126, 149–52, 209

Quiberon, 97, 124, 151

Rambouillet, 27, 270

Ramel, General, 324

Rapp, General, 212, 364

Rastignac, Eugène de, 188, 330, 402

Raucourt, Mlle., 217

Ravez, M., 263

Récamier, Madame, 202, 238, 263

Regent Prince, *see* George IV

Reichstadt, Duke of, (Napoleon II), 197–8, 336

Reille, General, 212

Reims, 5

Rennes, 209

Rey, Edouard, 221

Rey, Joseph, 376–7

Richelieu, Duc de, 68, 266–7, 289, 294, 302, 306, 317–8, 328–9, 332–3, 335, 337, 339, 343, 349, 353–361, 365–6, 370, 372–3, 377, 380, 383–4, 387, 389, 396, 399, 410

Riegel, 79, 116, 127

Robespierre, 120

Rohan, Duc de, 276–8

Romanov, House of, 5, 231, 254, 338

Rome, 93, 154, 348, 385

Rothschild, James de, 306

Rougé, General, 125, 127

Rovigo, Savary, Duc de, 221, 364, 392

Roy, Comte, 360, 370, 380, 383

Roye, 254–6

Royer-Collard, 94–5, 104, 150, 285, 305, 351, 374, 401

Rubempré, Lucien de, 298, 330, 399, 402

Saint-Chamans, Comte de, 280

Saint-Cloud, 27, 173, 193, 270, 272, 282–3, 294, 297, 300, 302, 349, 375

Saint-Denis, 226, 256–7, 293

Saint-Germain, 27, 80, 275

Saint-Jean de Luz, 165–6

Saint-Laurent, Madame de, 212

Saint-Ouen, 180, 382, 383, 390–91, 414

Saint Petersburg, 82, 93, 360

Saint-Pol, 228

Saint-Priest, Comte de, 93, 95–6, 98, 107, 117–8, 123, 125, 151, 197, 305

Salvandy, Narcisse de, 205, 285, 298

Sardinia, King of, 10, 60, 78, 82

Savoy, House of, 5, 10, 17

Saxony, Frederick Augustus, Elector, later King of, 11, 84, 197–8

Scépeaux, Comte de, 122

Sébastiani, General, 221

Sémonville, Marquis de, 48, 248

Semur, 237, 322, 410

Serre, Comte de, 68, 317, 361, 370, 377, 383

Sèvres, 7, 270, 301–2, 307

Shelley, Lady, 255

Sieyès, Abbé, later Comte, 93, 171

Siméon, Comte, 374–5, 380, 383

Soissons, 54

Soult, Maréchal, 159, 190, 194, 200, 207, 211, 223, 256, 288, 293, 310, 364

Sourdat, 93

Spain, Charles IV, King of, 11, 59, 82–3, 131

Spain, Ferdinand VII, King of, 157, 185–6, 196, 210, 294, 342, 393–4, 396, 404, 409

Staël, Madame de, 114, 202–3, 288, 308, 310, 313, 349, 352

Stanmore, 168

Stein, Baron von, 90, 165

Stendhal, 202, 238, 283, 299, 336, 395, 402

Stowe, 141–2

Stralsund, 138

Strasbourg, 64, 170, 209, 233, 352

Stuart, Sir Charles, 244–6, 333

Suchet, Maréchal, 368, 378–9, 408

Taffard de Saint-Germain, 162–4, 166

Talleyrand, Prince de, 48–9, 81, 84, 88, 96, 114, 122, 128, 159, 161, 167–8, 171–2, 174–6, 178, 181, 186–7,

194, 197–8, 200, 202–3, 217, 219, 221, 229, 232, 234, 245, 247–9, 251–4, 256, 259–266, 268, 281, 286, 329, 331, 338, 359, 361, 363, 365, 372–3, 389, 395, 398, 408–9
Talon, Omer, 381
Talon, Vicomte, 275
Ternaux, Baron, 243, 351
Terrier de Montciel, Marquis, 193–4
Thauvenay, M. de, 93, 100, 305
Thierry de Ville d'Avray, 273
Thiers, Adolphe, 160, 410
Thionville, 71
Thugut, Baron von, 108
Toulon, 77–8, 100, 114, 119, 122, 124, 129, 133
Toulouse, 20, 42, 94, 121, 125, 127, 162, 167, 176, 226, 233, 236, 259, 321, 323, 385
Tournus, 235
Tours 160, 166
Trier, Elector of, 11, 57, 59, 69, 82, 308
Troyes, 165
Tuileries, Jardin des, 212, 217, 224, 233, 236, 257–8, 271, 283, 311, 323, 342
Tuileries, Palace of the, 47, 53, 62, 65, 73, 173, 180, 183–5, 190, 193–4, 201, 205–8, 210, 212, 214, 219, 224–6, 230, 234, 252, 257, 259, 261, 265, 270, 271–8, 282–91, 294–5, 300–2, 306, 311, 314–5, 325, 343, 349–50, 375–6, 378, 406–8, 410
Turin, 13, 31, 60, 78, 87, 106, 127, 155, 274, 395

Two Sicilies, Ferdinand I King of, see Naples,

Valence, 235
Vandenesse, Félix de, 402
Varennes, 107, 180
Vaublanc, Comte de, 252, 266, 332, 337
Vaudémont, Princesse de, 223
Vellecour, M. de, 305
Venice, 82, 267
Vennevelles, Madame de, 296
Verdun, 71–3
Verneuil, 233
Verona, 96–7, 111–4, 117–9, 210, 386
Versailles, 3, 7–10, 14, 16, 18, 20, 22–3, 27–8, 30–1, 35, 43, 45, 57–8, 75, 80–1, 89, 106, 121, 132, 138, 143, 147–8, 155, 170, 173, 194, 202, 205–7, 215–6, 257, 270, 274–5, 278, 283, 287–8, 338, 415
Vesoul, 165
Vezet, Président de, 94, 97–100, 187–8, 305
Victor Emmanuel I, King of Sardinia, 185
Victor, Maréchal, 178, 238, 250, 262, 380, 384
Vienna, 93, 96, 105, 207, 220, 231–3, 249, 263
Viennet, M., 364
Vigée-Lebrun, Madame, 173–4
Vigny, Alfred de, 160, 205, 228, 309
Villèle, Comte de, 162, 317, 327–8, 333, 340, 347–8, 352, 357, 360, 366, 370, 372, 379–80, 383–7, 389, 393, 398, 401, 404–5, 408, 410

Villemain, M., 298
Villequier, Duc de, 88
Vioménil, Baron de, 62
Vitrolles, Baron de, 179–80, 194, 226, 255–6, 260, 265, 310, 348, 374
Volney, 122
Voltaire, 7, 33–4, 69

Wagram, Prince de, *see* Berthier, Maréchal
Wales, Prince of, *see* George IV,
Wanstead, 140, 143, 148
Warsaw, 80–4, 88–9, 95, 101, 123, 141

Waterloo, 249–50
Wellington, Duke of, 157, 163–7, 202, 209, 214, 231, 245, 247, 249–56, 258, 266–7, 289, 307, 329, 331, 333, 354, 387, 400
Wickham, William, 90, 116, 126, 135
Wiesbaden, 249, 251
Willot, General, 127
Württemburg, Prince Royal of, 231

Yarmouth, 138–40
Ypres, 229

Zurich, 79, 90, 93

List of Illustrations

1 The meeting of Louis XV and Marie-Joséphine of Savoy in the Forest of Fontainebleau. Miniature by Van Blarenberghe. 1771. National Trust, Waddesdon.

2 Monsieur, Comte de Provence. J. S. Duplessis. Musée Condé, Chantilly. Photo Giraudon.

3 Madame, Comtesse de Provence, J. B. Gautier-Dagoty. Musée de Versailles. Cliché des Musées Nationaux.

4 Madame de Balbi. Le Français. 1785. Coll. Jeanvrot, Musée des Arts Décoratifs, Bordeaux.

5 The Comte d'Avaray. From *Relation des Derniers Moments de la Captivité de Monsieur*. 1823. Photo British Library.

6 View of Gosfield House. Melling. 1817. Musée du Louvre. Photo Giraudon.

7 Louis XVIII in England. Engraving, 1814. Coll. Viollet.

8 Arrival of Louis XVIII at Calais. Goubaud. Musée de Versailles. Cliché des Musées Nationaux.

9 Soirée at the Odéon, 1814. Buffet. Musée de Versailles. Photo N. D. Roger-Viollet.

10 Departure of Louis XVIII on the night of 19/20 March 1815. Gros. Musée de Versailles. Cliché des Musées Nationaux.

11 Return of Louis XVIII, 8 July 1815. Print, Musée Carnavalet. Photo Lauros-Giraudon.

12 The Fête de Saint Louis, 1815. Melling. 1816. Louvre, Cabinet des Dessins. Cliché des Musées Nationaux.

13 Louis XVIII in his Cabinet in the Tuileries. Gérard, 1823. Palais de Versailles. Photo Giraudon.

14 The reception of the Duchesse de Berri, 1816. H. Lecomte. Musée de Versailles. Cliché des Musées Nationaux.

15 The Duc de Richelieu. Lawrence. Musée des Beaux – Arts, Besançon. Photo Lauros-Giraudon.

16 The Duc Decazes. Print from the portrait by Gérard. Bibliothèque Nationale. Photo Harlingue-Viollet.

17 The last moments of the Duc de Berri. 1820. Menjaud. Musée de Versailles. Cliché des Musées Nationaux.

18 Madame du Cayla with her children. Gérard. Coll. Prince de Beauvau, Château d'Haroué. Photo Gil.

Table I   The Royal Family of France.
Table II   The House of Bourbon

Map I   Louis's travels in exile, 1791–1814.
Map II   The movements of Louis XVIII during the Hundred Days.